New Pattern

Data Analysis

& Interpretation

for

SBI / IBPS BANK PO / SO / CLERK / RRB / SSC EXAMS

- **Corporate Office :** 45, 2nd Floor, Maharishi Dayanand Marg, Corner Market,
  Malviya Nagar, New Delhi-110017
  Tel. : 011- 49404757/ 49404758/ 49404768

Typeset by Disha DTP Team

For further information about the books from DISHA,
Log on to **www.dishapublication.com** or email to **info@dishapublication.com**

CONTENTS

1   BAR GRAPH

Bar graph is a rectangular shape figure which shows the comparative study of category of data and values. Bar graph is a horizontal or vertical rectangular shape. There are some different types of bar graphs.

(1) VERTICAL BAR GRAPH: These are three types of Vertical Bar graphs.

   (i)   **Separate data graph:** In this type of bar graph, we can see the comparison of single or complete data.

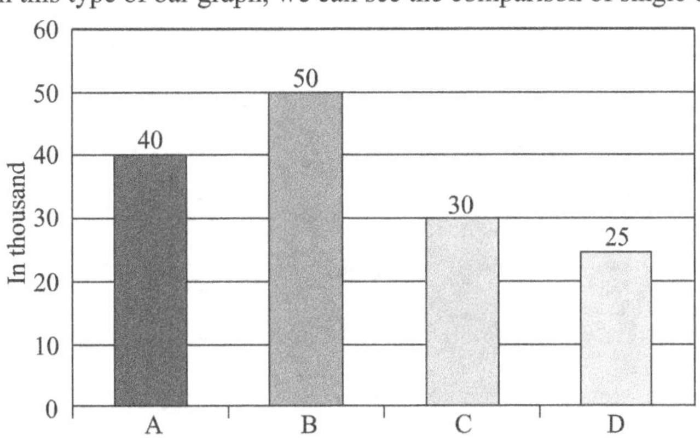

Example:

Q.   If salaries of different persons are given in Bar graph then what is average salary of all persons.

Average salary

$$= \frac{40+50+30+25}{4} \times 1000$$

$$= \frac{145000}{4} = 36250$$

   (ii)   Salary of A = 40000

        Salary of B = 50000

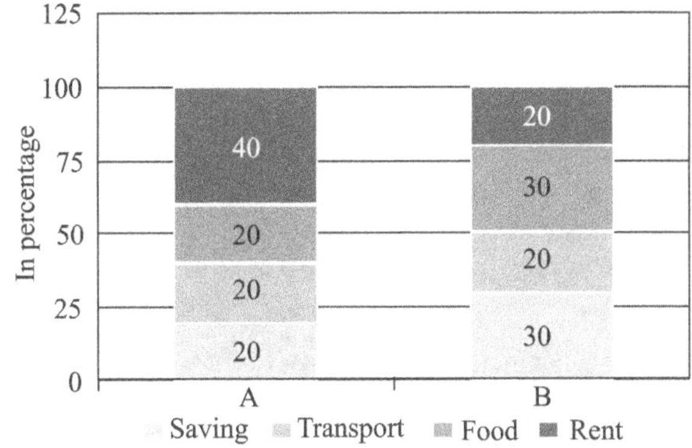

Example:

Q.   What is respective ratio of transport expenditure of A and B

Required ratio $= 40000 \times \dfrac{20}{100} : 50000 \times \dfrac{20}{100} = 4 : 5$

   (iii)   Combined data graph:

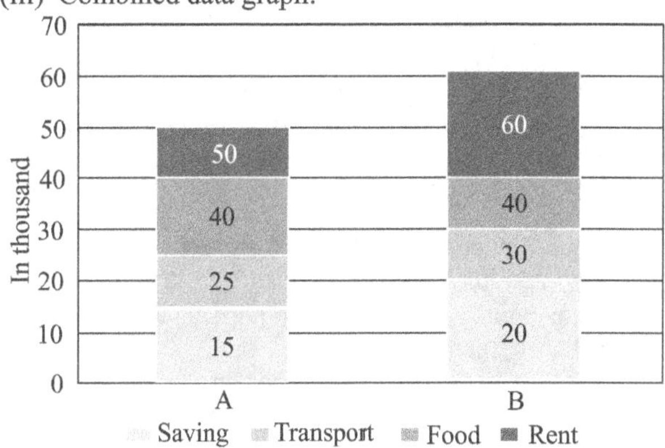

Example:

Transport expenditure of A is what percent of that of B ?

Required % $= \dfrac{25}{30} \times 100 = 83.3\%$

(2)   HORIZONTAL BAR-GRAPH : This is same graph as combined data graph

EXERCISE

DIRECTIONS (Qs. 1-5) : *Study the following graph and answer the questions given below :*

No. of students (in thousands) who opted for three different specializations during the given five years in a university

[IBPS-PO-2011]

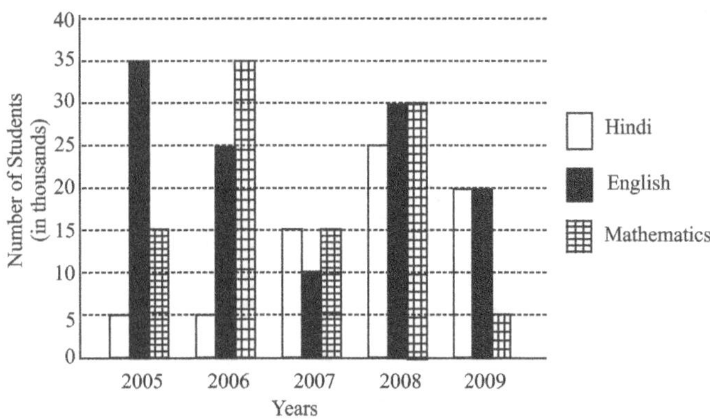

1. The total number of students who opted for Mathematics in the years 2005 and 2008 together are approximately what percent of the total number of students who opted for all three subjects in the same years ?
   (a) 38   (b) 28
   (c) 42   (d) 32
   (e) 48

2. Out of the total number of students who opted for the given three subjects, in the year 2009, 38% were girls. How many boys opted for Mathematics in the same year ?
   (a) 1322   (b) 1332
   (c) 1312   (d) Cannot be determined
   (e) None of these

3. What is the respective ratio between the number of students who opted for English in the years 2006 and 2008 together and the number of students who opted for Hindi in the year 2005 and 2009 together ?
   (a) 11 : 5   (b) 12 : 7
   (c) 11 : 7   (d) 12 : 5
   (e) None of these

4. If the total number of students in the university in the year 2007 was 455030, then , the total number of students who opted for the given three subjects were approximately what percent of the total students ?
   (a) 19   (b) 9   (c) 12   (d) 5
   (e) 23

5. What is the total number of students who opted for Hindi and who opted for Mathematics in the years 2006, 2007 and 2009 together ?
   (a) 97000   (b) 93000
   (c) 85000   (d) 96000
   (e) None of these

DIRECTIONS (Qs. 6-10) : *In the following bar diagram the number of engineers employed in various companies has been given. Study the bar diagram carefully to answer the questions.*

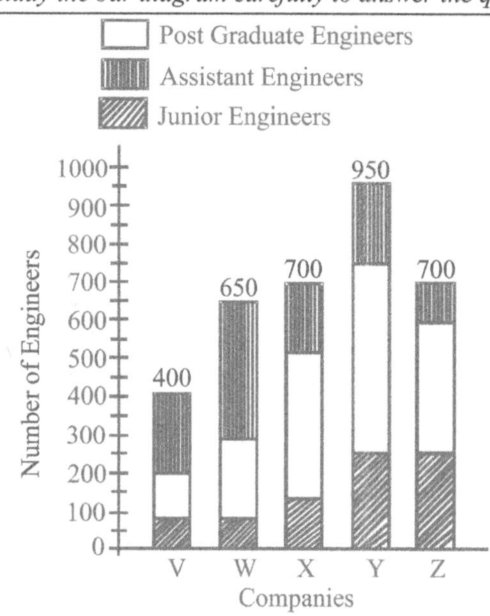

6. The number of post graduate engineers employed in the company W is what per cent of the total engineers employed in that company ?
   (a) $33\dfrac{1}{3}\%$ (b) $30\dfrac{10}{13}\%$
   (c) $25\dfrac{1}{3}\%$ (d) $36\dfrac{1}{3}\%$
   (e) None of these

7. What is the average number of junior engineers employed in all the companies?
   (a) 150   (b) 170
   (c) 160   (d) 180
   (e) 190

8. What is the difference between the average number of junior engineers and assistant engineers taking all the companies together?
   (a) 18   (b) 15
   (c) 40   (d) 22
   (e) 25

9. If the number of assistant engineers employed in all the companies be increased by 37% and the number of post graduate engineers employed in all the companies be decreased by 20%, by what percent will the number of assistant engineers be less than that of post graduate engineers?
   (a) 5.6%   (b) 7.8%
   (c) 8%   (d) 16.6%
   (e) None of these

10. If the numbers of all the engineers in the company V, company X and company Y be increased by 30%, 35% and 40% respectively, what will be the overall percentage increase in the number of all engineers of all the companies taken together?
    (a) 20%   (b) 22%   (c) 24%   (d) 25%
    (e) None of these

DIRECTIONS (Qs. 11-15) : *In the following bar diagram, the number of passengers carried to different cities in first quarter of a year by four airlines A, B, C and D has been given. Study the following diagram carefully and answer the questions.*

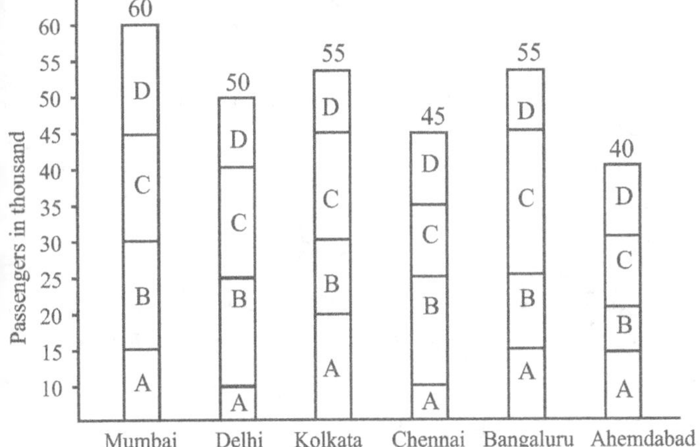

11. What is the difference between the number of passengers travelling to all cities by the airlines A and C ?
    (a) 0   (b) 6000
    (c) 5500   (d) 6500
    (e) 15000

12. The number of passengers travelling to Delhi and Kolkata by airline C is what per cent of the number of all passengers travelling by the same airline?
    (a) 32   (b) 35   (c) 38   (d) 42
    (e) 44

13. What is the respective ratio of the number of passengers who travelled to Chennai and Bangaluru by airline B and that to Mumbai and Ahmedabad by airline D ?
    (a) 6 : 7   (b) 3 : 4   (c) 1 : 1   (d) 7 : 6
    (e) None of these

14. The number of passengers travelling to Chennai by airline A in second quarter is 150% of that in first quarter by the same airline. The number of passengers in the second quarter by the same airline is 120% of that in the third quarter.
    What is the percentage increase in the number of passengers in third quarter from that in first quarter ?
    (a) 15%   (b) 18%   (c) 20%   (d) 25%
    (e) 30%

15. The number of passengers going to Bangaluru and Kolkata in first quarter by airline B is what per cent of the number of passengers going to the same cities in second quarter if there be an increase of 30% in the number of passengers going to Bangaluru from first quarter to second quarter and in that going to Kolkata shows a 40% increase from first to second quarter ?
    (a) 68   (b) 60   (c) 65   (d) 74
    (e) None of these

DIRECTIONS (Qs. 16-19): *Study the following graph and answer the questions that follow.*

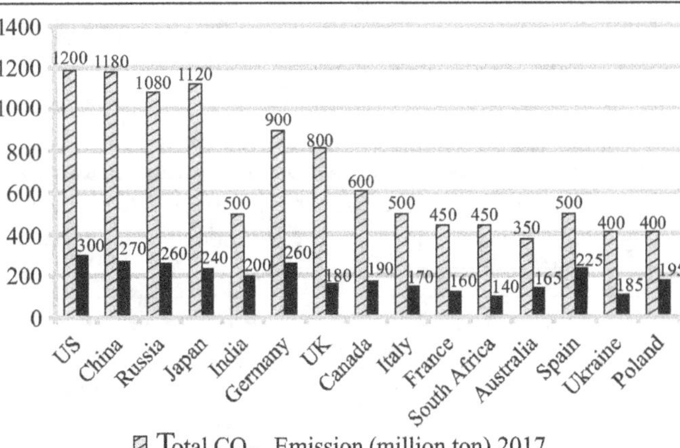

16. If the world energy council formulates a norm for high emission countries to reduce their emission each year by 12.5% for the next two years then what would be the ratio of CO_2 emission to per capita income of US, China and Japan after two years. The per capita income of China, Japan and US is expected to increase every year by 4%, 3% and 2% respectively.
    (a) 3.5, 3.8, 4.1   (b) 3.4, 3.5, 3.9
    (c) 2.9, 3.1, 3.4   (d) None of these

17. If US and China, decide to buy carbon credits, from Spain and Ukraine to make up for their high emissions, then in how many years US, and China would be able to bring down its ratio of CO_2 emission (million tonnes) to per capita income to world standard benchmark of 0.75. (per capita income of the given countries remain same, 0.5 CO_2 emissions (million tonnes) is compensated by purchase of 1.25 units of carbon credit, and a country can buy carbon credit units in three lots of 15, 20 and 30 units in a single year.
    (a) 3.8 years   (b) 38 years
    (c) 30 years   (d) None of these

18. France, South Africa, Australia, Ukraine and Poland form an energy consortium which declares CO_2 emission of 350 million ton per annum as standard benchmark. The energy consortium decides to sell their carbon emission savings against the standard benchmark to high carbon emission countries. It is expected that the per capita income of each country of the energy consortium increases by 2%, 2.5% and 3.5% p.a. for the next three years respectively. The ratio of CO_2 emission to per capita income of the each energy consortium country reduces by 50% and remains constant for the next three years. By selling 0.5 CO_2 emissions (million ton) the energy consortium earns 1.25 carbon credits, then determine the total carbon credits earned by energy consortium in three years.
    (a) 3560   (b) 4506
    (c) 5060   (d) None of these
    (e) 4605

19. Select the wrong statement in reference to the position of India vis-a-vis countries in the graph in terms of the ratio of CO_2 emission to per capita income (increasing order)

(a) India stands at 5th position if 50 is added to the given per capita income figures of each country.

(b) India stands at 5th position at the given CO_2 emission level and per capita income of each country

(c) India stands at 5th position if 200 million ton CO_2 emission is deducted from the given CO_2 emission figures of each country.

(d) India stands at 5th position if 200 million ton CO_2 emission is deducted from the given CO_2 emission figures of each country and 50 is added to the given per capita income of each country.

DIRECTIONS (Qs. 20-22): *The following graph shows population data (males and females), educated people data (males and females) and number of male in the population for a given period of 2002 to 2017. All data is in million. From the information given in the graph answer the questions that follow.*

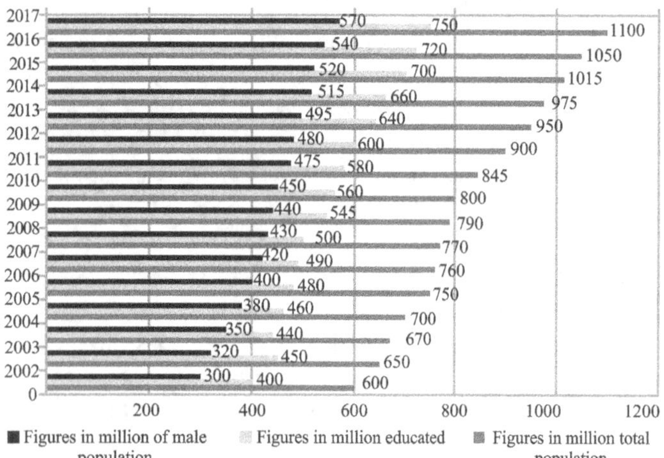

20. In which year the percentage increase in the number of females over the previous year is highest?
 (a) 2003　　(b) 2006　　(c) 2010　　(d) 2012
 (e) None of these

21. In 2009 if the ratio of number of educated male to professionally educated female was 5:4. If the number of educated males increased by 25% in 2010. What is the percentage change in number of uneducated females in 2010?
 (a) 25%　　(b) 35%　　(c) 34%　　(d) 56%
 (e) None of these

22. In year 2012 total population living in urban area is equal to sixty eight percent of educated population. The ratio of number of people living in urban area to people living in rural area is 43:12 in 2017. What is the ratio of the rural population in 2012 to that in 2017?
 (a) 0.8
 (b) 0.47
 (c) 2.05
 (d) None of these

DIRECTIONS (Qs. 23-27): *On the basis of the data given in two charts.*

Sodium carbonate, also called as soda ash is an important ingredient for glass, soaps and detergents, and many other products. There were two ways of producing soda ash. The first is producing soda ash from trona obtained naturally. The second method was producing soda ash from common salt through Solvay process. Soda ash produced thus was called synthetic soda ash. Tata Chemicals was one of largest producer of soda ash. Given below are two charts- first chart shows production of two varieties of soda ash at Tata Chemicals. The second chart shows production of two varieties of soda ash in the world.

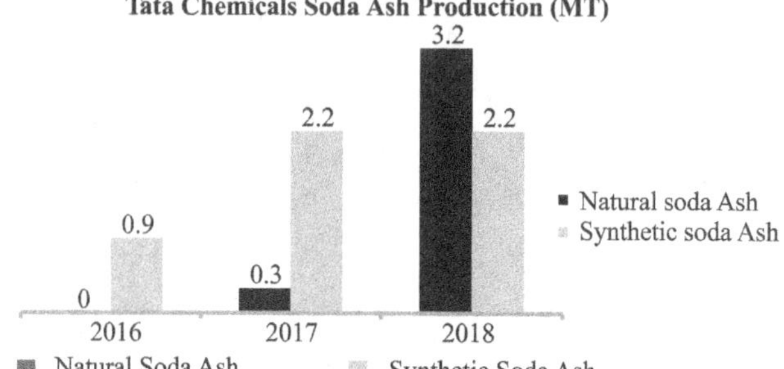

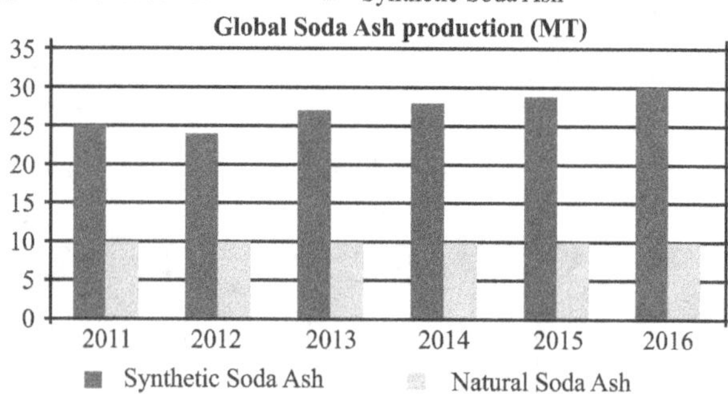

23. It was expected that global soda ash production would be same for 2016, 2017 and 2018 (only for this question). What could be a possible reason for different patterns of production in Tata Chemicals and the world?
 (a) Tata Chemicals built new plants of 2.2 MT natural soda ash capacity in 2017.
 (b) Tata Chemicals built 3.8 MT of natural soda ash capacity from 2015 to 2018.
 (c) Tata Chemicals produced 2.7% of total soda ash in the world.
 (d) None of the above conclusions could possibly be drawn.
 (e) Can't be determined

24. Suppose the total global production increased (year on year) from 2015 to 2018 by the amount Tata Chemicals' synthetic production (year on year) increased in the same period. By what percentage did the total global production increase from 2017 to 2018?
 (a) Cannot be calculated at all from the tables above.
 (b) Increased by 10.16%
 (c) Increased by 9.48%
 (d) Did not increase at all.

25. Which of the following statements are true?
 1. Proportion of natural soda ash to synthetic soda has decreased from 2011 to 2016 globally.
 2. Proportion of natural soda ash to synthetic soda ash has increased from 2011 to 2016 globally.
 3. Proportion of synthetic soda ash to total soda ash has decreased for Tata Chemicals from 2015 to 2017.
 4. Proportion of synthetic soda ash to total soda ash has increased for Tata Chemicals.
 (a) 1 and 3　　(b) 1 and 4　　(c) 2 and 4　　(d) 2 and 3

26. What is Tata Chemical's share of global production in 2018?

(a) 12.86%   (b) 17.42%

(c) 59.34%   (d) Incomplete data

27. Suppose total global production of soda ash in 2018 was 40 MT and Tata Chemicals was second highest producer of soda ash globally after another company called Solvay. FMC Wyoming was the third highest producer. Two Indian giants, Tata Chemicals and Nirma have a combined production capacity of 8.8 MT. Which of the following statements are right?

1. Solvay's market share was more than 20.66%
2. Solvay's market share was more than 13.5%
3. FMC's share was less than 10.33%
4. FMC share was less than 13.5%
5. Nirma, which was sixth largest producer, had a share of less than 8.5%

Choose the right option.

(a) 1 and 3   (b) 1 and 5   (c) 2 and 4   (d) 1, 3 and 5

DIRECTIONS (Qs 28–30) : *These questions are based on the information and graph given below.*

There are six companies, 1 to 6. All of these companies use six operations, A to F. The following graph shows the distribution of efforts put in by each company in these six operations.

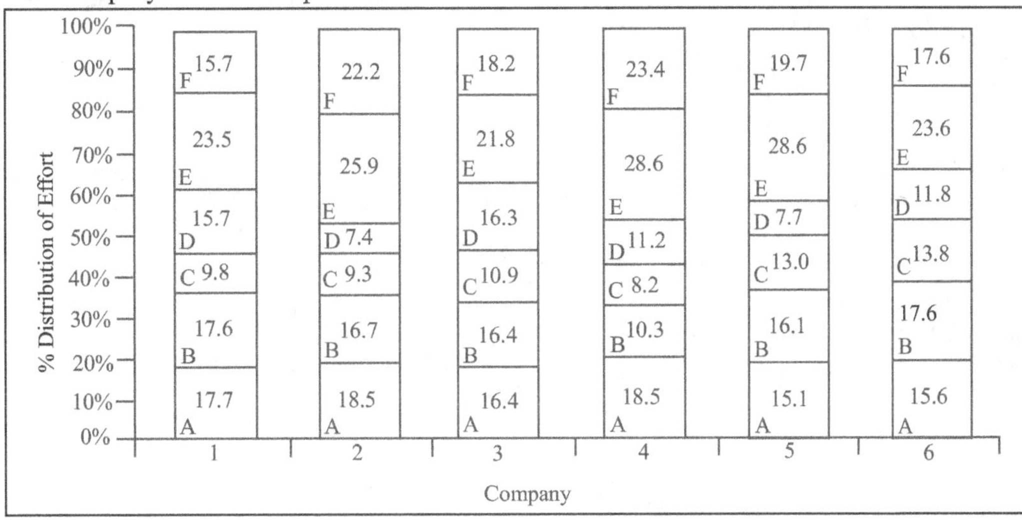

28. Suppose effort allocations is inter-changed between operations B and C, then C and D, and then D and E. If companies are then ranked in ascending order of effort in E, what will be the rank of company 3?

(a) 2   (b) 3

(c) 4   (d) 5

29. A new technology is introduced in company 4 such that the total effort for operations B to F get evenly distributed among these . What is the change in the percentage of effort in operation E?

(a) Reduction of 12.3   (b) Increase of 12.3

(c) Reduction of 5.6   (d) Increase of 5.6

30. Suppose the companies find that they can remove operations B,C and D re-distribute the effort released equally among the remaining operations. Then, which operation will show the maximum distribution of effort across all companies and all operations?

(a) Operation E in company 1

(b) Operation E in company 4

(c) Operation F in company 5

(d) Operation E in company 5

DIRECTIONS (Qs 31–36) : *These questions are based on the graph given below.*

Graph indicates the annual sales tax revenue collections (in Rupees in crores) of seven states from 2012 to 2017. The values given at the top of each bar represents the total collections in that year.

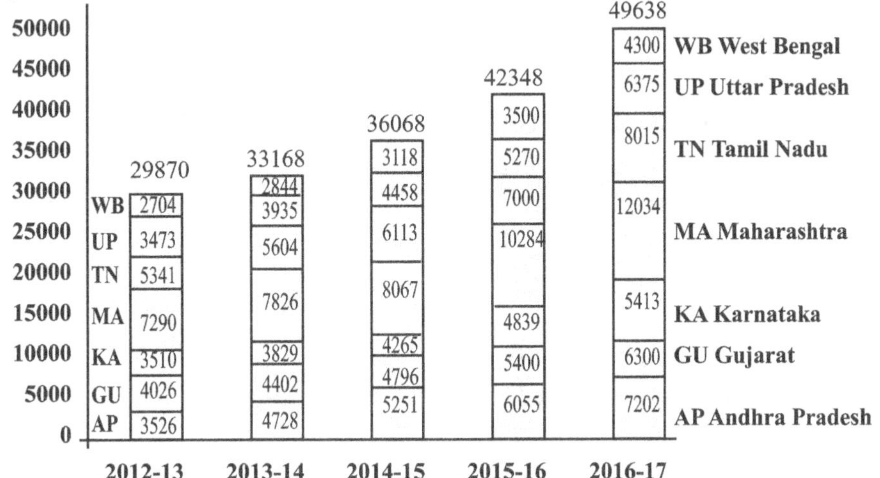

31. If for each year, the states are ranked in terms of the descending order of sales tax collections, how many states don't change the ranking more than once over the five years
    (a) 1   (b) 5
    (c) 3   (d) 4

32. Which of the following states has changed its relative ranking most number of times when you rank the states in terms of the descending volume of sales tax collections each year?
    (a) Andhra Pradesh   (b) Uttar Pradesh
    (c) Karnataka   (d) Tamil Nadu

33. The percentage share of sales tax revenue of which state has increased by maximum from 2013 to 2017?
    (a) Tamil Nadu   (b) Karnataka
    (c) Gujarat   (d) Andhra Pradesh

34. Which pair of successive years shows the maximum growth rate of tax revenue in Maharashtra?
    (a) 2013 to 2014   (b) 2014 to 2015
    (c) 2015 to 2016   (d) 2016 to 2017

35. Identify the state whose tax revenue increased exactly by the same amount in two successive pair of years?
    (a) Karnataka
    (b) West Bengal
    (c) Uttar Pradesh
    (d) Tamil Nadu

36. Which state below has been maintaining a constant rank over the years in terms of its contribution to total tax collections?
    (a) Andhra Pradesh
    (b) Karnataka
    (c) Tamil Nadu
    (d) Uttar Pradesh

DIRECTIONS (Qs. 37-40): *These questions are based on the information and charts given below.*

The profitability of a company is defined as the ratio of its operating profit to its operating income, typically expressed in percentage. The following two charts show the operating income as well as the profitability of six companies in the Financial Years (F. Y.s) 2016-17 and 2017-18.

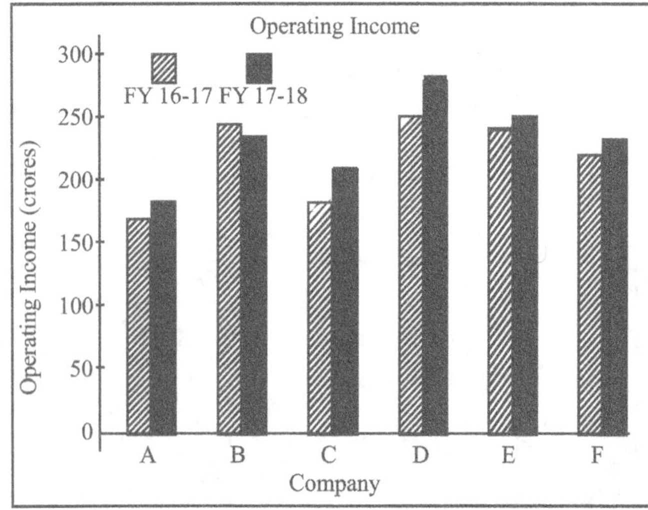

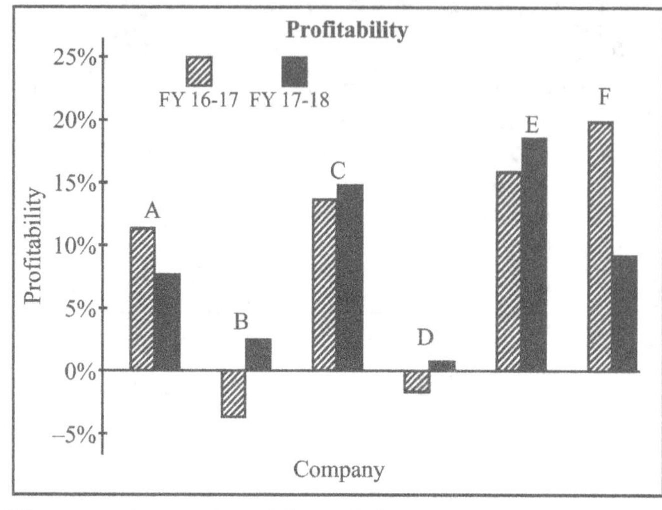

The operating profits of four of these companies are plotted against their respective operating income figures for the F. Y. 2017-18, in the third chart given below.

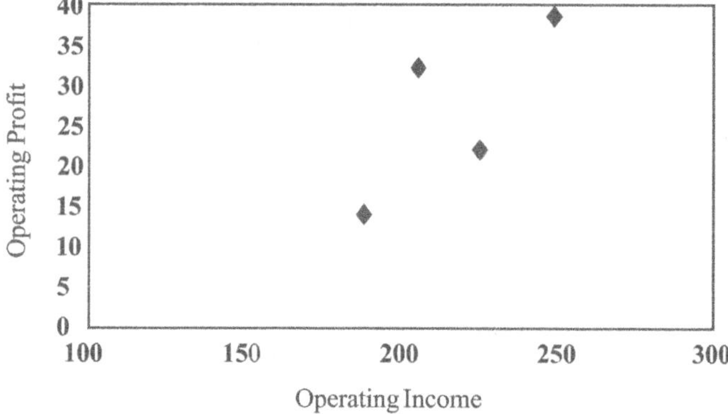

37. What is the approximate average operating profit, in F.Y. 2016 - 2017, of the two companies excluded from the third chart?
    (a) – 7.5 crore   (b) 3.5 crore
    (c) 25 crore   (d) Cannot be determined.

38. Which company recorded the highest operating profit in F. Y. 2017-18?
    (a) A   (b) C   (c) E   (d) F

39. Which of the following statements is NOT true?
    (a) The company with the third lowest profitability in F.Y. 2016-17 has the lowest operating income in F. Y 2017-18
    (b) The company with the highest operating income in the two financial years combined has the lowest operating profit in F. Y. 2017-18
    (c) Companies with a higher operating income in F. Y. 2016-17 than in F.Y. 2017-18 have higher profitability in F. Y. 2017-18 than in F. Y. 2016-17
    (d) Companies with profitability between 10% and 20% in F. Y. 2016-17 also have operating incomes between 150 crore and 250 crore in F. Y. 2017-18

40. The average operating profit in F. Y. 2017-18, of companies with profitability exceeding 10% in F. Y. 2017-18, is approximately
    (a) 17.5 crore   (b) 25 crore
    (c) 27.5 crore   (d) 35 crore

Birth Rates & Death Rates (per 1000 persons) in the year 2018

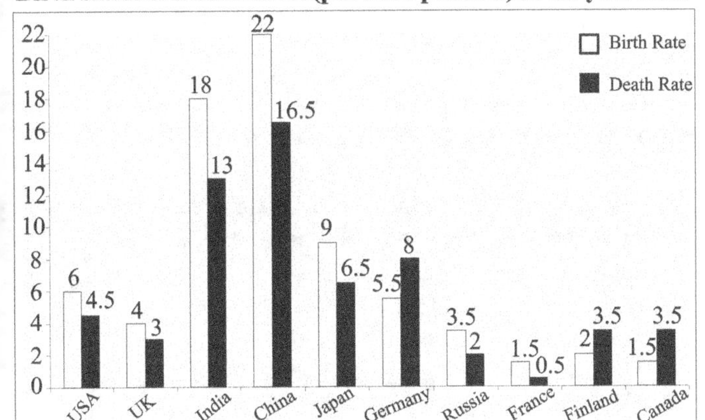

Note : Rate of growth of population = Birth rate – Death rate

41. If the rate of growth of population is expressed in percentage terms instead of number per 1000 persons, then among the countries with a positive growth rate, the rate of growth for the country whose population is growing by the fastest rate is how many percentage points more than that of the country whose population is growing by the slowest rate?
    - (a) 0.45
    - (b) 4.5
    - (c) 0.045
    - (d) None of these

42. If the total population of USA in the year 2018 was 250 million and that of Russia 150 million, then by what percent is the total births in USA more than total deaths in Russia?
    - (a) 200%
    - (b) 80%
    - (c) 300%
    - (d) 400%

43. The infant mortality rate is defined as number of deaths of new born babies for every 1000 births. If the total population of Japan in the year 2018 is 150 million and its infant mortality rate is 3, then what is the number of infants dying at birth expressed as a percentage of the total number of deaths in Japan?
    - (a) 4%
    - (b) 0.4%
    - (c) 40%
    - (d) 400%

44. If the given rates remain constant for the next ten years, then what will be the approximate percentage increase in the population of India after two years from the year 2018?
    - (a) 1%
    - (b) 0.5%
    - (c) 2.5%
    - (d) Cannot be determined

45. For how many of the given countries is the rate of growth of population, when expressed in percentage terms, greater than 0.25%?
    - (a) 3
    - (b) 4
    - (c) 2
    - (d) None of these

Cost per kg of orange and
Cost per dozen of banana

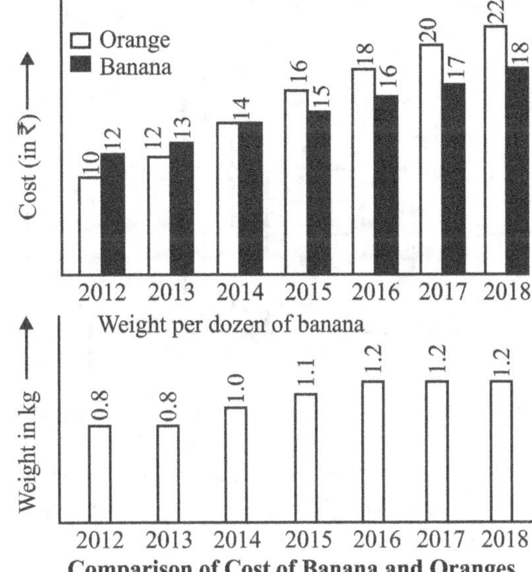

Comparison of Cost of Banana and Oranges

46. In 2012, how much less does 1 kg of orange cost as against 1 kg of banana?
    - (a) 50%
    - (b) 25%
    - (c) 20%
    - (d) $33\frac{1}{3}\%$
    - (e) None of these

47. Find the difference of average cost of 1 kg of orange and that of 1 kg of banana.
    - (a) ₹ 1
    - (b) Zero
    - (c) ₹ 1.53
    - (d) ₹ 2
    - (e) None of these

48. If a person pays equal amounts for 1 kg of orange and 1 kg of banana, then he bought these fruits in
    - (a) 2014
    - (b) 2017
    - (c) Never in the given period
    - (d) 2018
    - (e) None of these

49. If the costs were to rise at the same rate, how much would 1 kg of banana cost in the year 2014?
    - (a) ₹ 24
    - (b) ₹ 28
    - (c) ₹ 23
    - (d) Data insufficient
    - (e) None of these

50. Find the percentage increase in the cost of 1 kg of banana between 2012 and 2018.
    - (a) 50
    - (b) $33\frac{1}{3}$
    - (c) $66\frac{2}{3}$
    - (d) 0
    - (e) None of these

The bar chart below shows the revenue received, in million US Dollars (USD), from subscribers to a particular Internet service. The data covers the period 2003 to 2007 for the United States (US) and Europe. The bar chart also shows the estimated revenues from subscription to this service for the period 2008 to 2010.

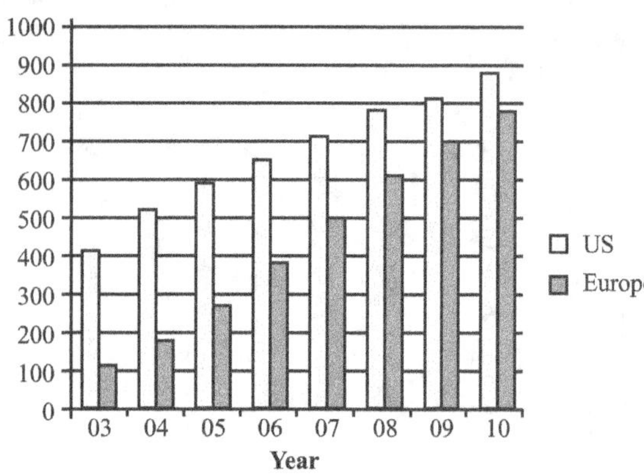

51. While the subscription in Europe has been growing steadily towards that of the US, the growth rate in Europe seems to be declining. Which of the following is closest to the percent change in growth rate of 2007 (over 2006) relative to the growth rate of 2005 (over 2004)?
 (a) 17 (b) 20
 (c) 35 (d) 60
 (e) 100

52. The difference between the estimated subscription in Europe in 2008 and what it would have been if it were computed using the percentage growth rate of 2007 (over 2006), is closest to :
 (a) 50 (b) 80 (c) 20 (d) 10
 (e) 0

53. In 2003, sixty percent of subscribers in Europe were men. Given that women subscribers increase at the rate of 10 percent per annum and men at the rate of 5 percent per annum, what is the approximate percentage growth of subscribers between 2003 and 2010 in Europe? The subscription prices are volatile and may change each year.
 (a) 62 (b) 15 (c) 78 (d) 84
 (e) 50

54. Consider the annual percent change in the gap between subscription revenues in the US and Europe. What is the year in which the absolute value of this change is the highest?
 (a) 03-04 (b) 05-06 (c) 06-07 (d) 08-09
 (e) 09-10

DIRECTIONS (Qs. 55-59): *Bar chart given below shows different discount rates are given for different products of different shops, for some products discount rate is missing which you have to find out according to data given in different questions if they are necessary. Answer the following questions with the help of given Bar chart. Selling price is same for a particular product (excluding cooking oil and sugar) for all shops. (MP = market price, CP = Cost price, SP = selling price)*

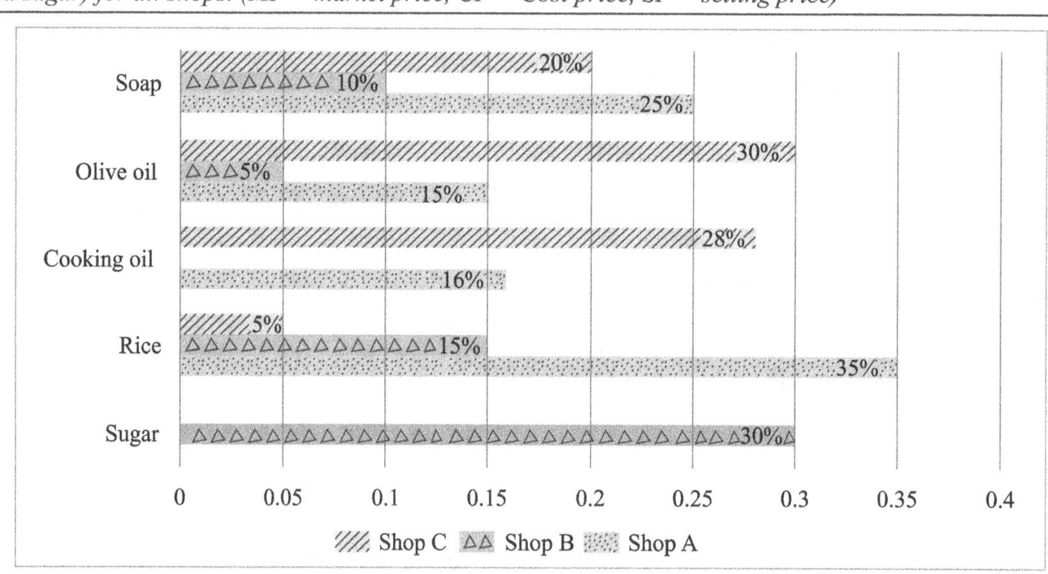

55. If the average MP of Soap for all three shops is 7980 then find MP of soap for shop B?
 (a) 6900 (b) 7200
 (c) 8540 (d) 6600
 (e) None of these

56. Difference between MP of Olive oil of Shop A and shop B is ₹1008 then find MP of Olive oil for Shop C?
 (a) 11628 (b) 11356
 (c) 9356 (d) 12468
 (e) None of these

57. If MP of cooking oil is same for all shops and Average SP of cooking oil for shop A and shop B is ₹7456 and average SP of cooking oil for shop B and shop C is 6736, then find SP of cooking oil by shop C?
 (a) 4512 (b) 5720
 (c) 3780 (d) 4900
 (e) 4320

58. If difference between MP and SP for rice in shop B is ₹1482 find average MP of rice of shop A and shop C?
 (a) 12840 (b) 10720
 (c) 10880 (d) 13280
 (e) None of these

59. If market price is equal for all shops for sugar. Ratio of discount for sugar of shop A and B is 1/3, difference between SP for sugar of shop A and C is ₹ 1560, if SP of shop A is 1360 more than shop B, then find SP of sugar by shop C?
 (a) 4856 (b) 4512 (c) 5572 (d) 4560
 (e) None of these

DIRECTIONS (Qs.60-64): *Study the following information carefully and answer the questions given below.*

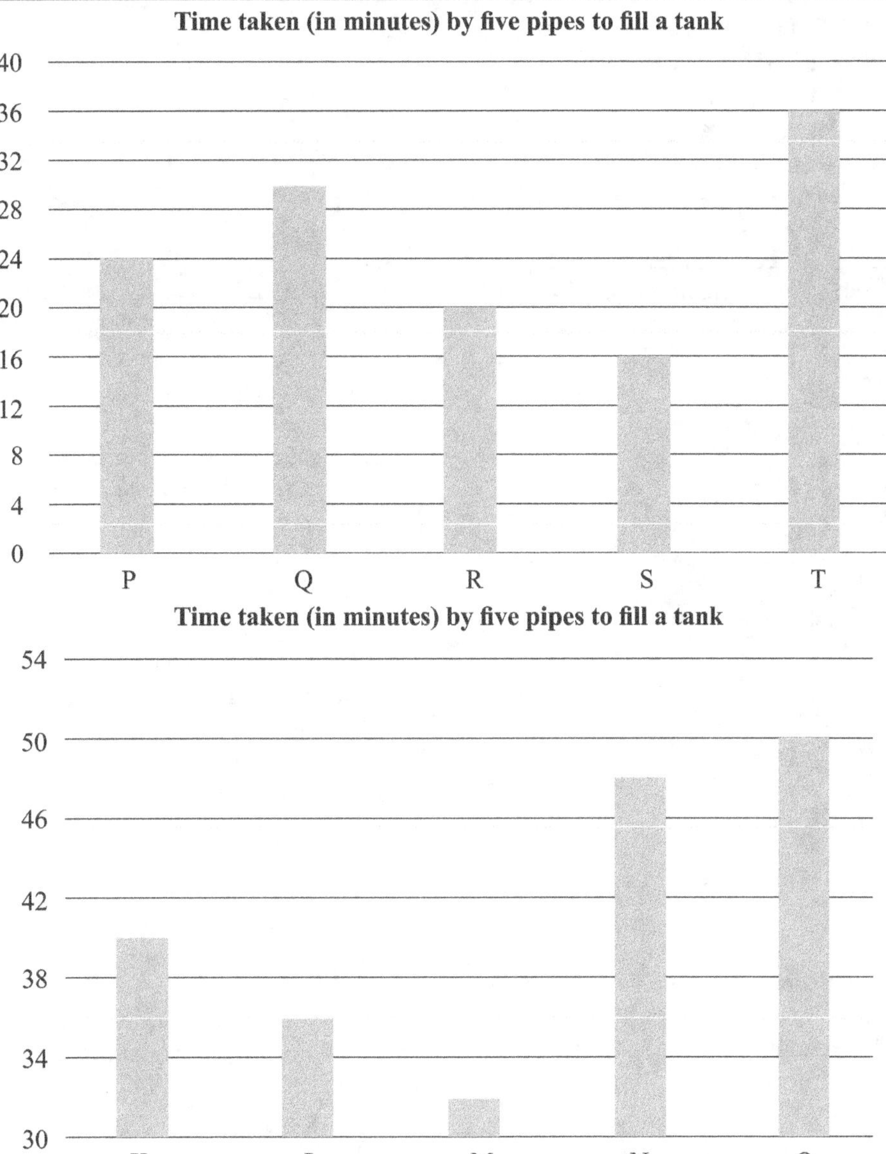

The following table shows the ratio of time taken by pipes to fill the tank.

Q : U	3 : 2
R : V	5 : 6
S : W	4 : 5
T : X	9 : 10

60. Pipe P and Pipe Q opened simultaneously for 4 minutes, then closed and then pipe T and pipe L are opened for 2 minutes, then closed. Find the time taken by pipe U to fill the remaining part of the tank.
(a) 14 minutes
(b) 529/36 minutes
(c) 15 minutes
(d) 178/39 minutes
(e) None of these

61. Efficiency of pipe Z is 75% of the efficiency of pipe P and efficiency of pipe Y is 1.5 times the efficiency of pipe N. Pipe R and pipe Z are opened simultaneously for 3 minutes and then closed. Find the time taken by pipe Y and pipe M together to empty the filled part of the tank.

(a) 4 minutes
(b) 47/12 minutes
(c) 39/10 minutes
(d) 5 minutes
(e) None of these

62. Time taken by pipe I to fill the tank is 20% more than the time taken by pipe W to fill the tank and efficiency of pipe G is twice the efficiency of pipe X. Time taken by pipe I and pipe G to fill the tank is what percent to the time taken by pipe S and pipe T together to fill the tank.
(a) 67.67%
(b) 74.44%
(c) 98.48%
(d) 81.14%
(e) 83.33%

63. Find the respective ratio of time taken by pipe Q, pipe V and pipe K together to fill the tank and time taken by pipe T, pipe V and pipe N together to fill the tank.
(a) 4 : 5
(b) 5 : 6
(c) 6 : 7
(d) 3 : 4
(e) None of these

64. Pipe P, pipe R and pipe T are opened simultaneously for 4 minutes then closed and pipe K and pipe N are opened for 2 minutes then closed. Find the time taken by pipe U and pipe X to fill the remaining part of the tank.

  (a) $\dfrac{277}{13}$ (b) $\dfrac{221}{27}$

  (c) $\dfrac{311}{11}$ (d) $\dfrac{511}{29}$

  (e) None of these

DIRECTIONS (Qs. 65-69): *Study the graph carefully to answer the questions that follow.*

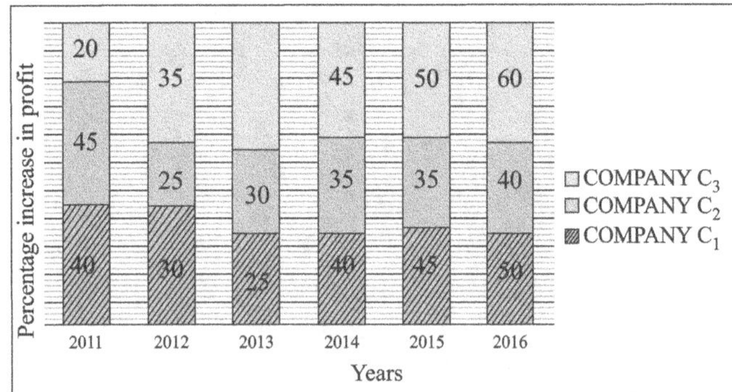

65. If profit for company C2 in 2012 is 2000 and expenditure in 2013 for company C2 is 50,000, then what is the total revenue in 2013 for C2? Given that total revenue = expenditure + profit.
  (a) 52600 (b) 54200
  (c) 53280 (d) 55800
  (e) None of these

66. If profit in year 2015 for company C_3 is 3000 and profit of company C_1 in 2013 is equal to profit of company C_3 in 2014 then what is the profit of company C_1 in 2013
  (a) 15000 (b) 4000 (c) 3500 (d) 2000
  (e) 2500

67. What is the average percentage increase in profit for company C_2 over all the years.
  (a) 49% (b) 32% (c) 23% (d) 38%
  (e) 35%

68. What was the approximate percent increase in percent increases of profit of company C_1 in the year 2014 from its previous year
  (a) 60% (b) 65% (c) 55% (d) 50%
  (e) 70%

69. If profit earned by company C_2 in 2014 is 27000 and by company C_3 in 2014 is 43500 then what is the total profit earned by them in year 2013?
  (a) 25,000 (b) 35,000
  (c) 40,000 (d) 50,000
  (e) None of these

DIRECTIONS (Qs. 70-74): *Study the following graph carefully and answer the questions given below.*

Number of students enrolled in Physics, Chemistry and Maths branches of five different colleges in the year 2018.

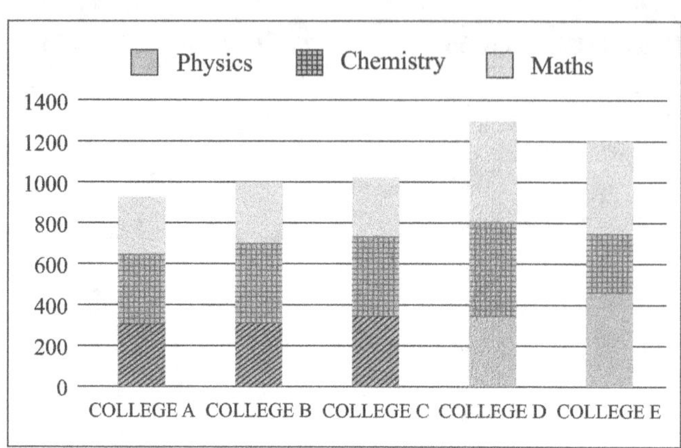

70. Ratio of number of male to female students in Chemistry discipline from college B is 16 : 9 and total professors from same college and same branch is 100/9% of total female students from the same branch and same college then, find total number of professor in Chemistry branch from college B.
  (a) 18 (b) 15
  (c) 20 (d) 22
  (e) 25

71. If number of male student in Maths branch from college D and male students in physics branch from college A are equal then what is the percentage of female students in physics branch of college A? Given that ratio of male to female students in Maths branch from college D is 13 : 12

  (a) $33\dfrac{1}{3}\%$ (b) $16\dfrac{2}{3}\%$

  (c) $13\dfrac{1}{3}\%$ (d) $\dfrac{22}{7}\%$

  (e) None of these

72. If 20% of students in Maths branch from college E are transferred to Maths branch of college C then find the ratio of students in Maths from college C to the total students from college E now.
  (a) 34/111 (b) 23/222
  (c) 23/111 (d) 34/113
  (e) None of these

73. Average of students in Chemistry branch from all colleges are what percent less/more than the average students in Maths branch from all colleges together? (Approximately)
  (a) 12% (b) 8%
  (c) 4% (d) 7%
  (e) 6%

74. If 20% of total students from College D are failed in yearly exam, 75% of total students are passed from college E in yearly exams then what will be total students in college D and E together in year 2018 if 400 more students are enrolled in 2019 from both colleges D and E together (consider both colleges were opened in 2018 and enrollment is cancelled when a student fails in exam)
  (a) 2340 (b) 2900
  (c) 2440 (d) 2800
  (e) None of these

DIRECTIONS (Qs. 75-79): *The following graph shows the percentage of discount offered on the total discount given in any years for 5 various products L, M, N, O and P in a given month by a shopkeeper.*

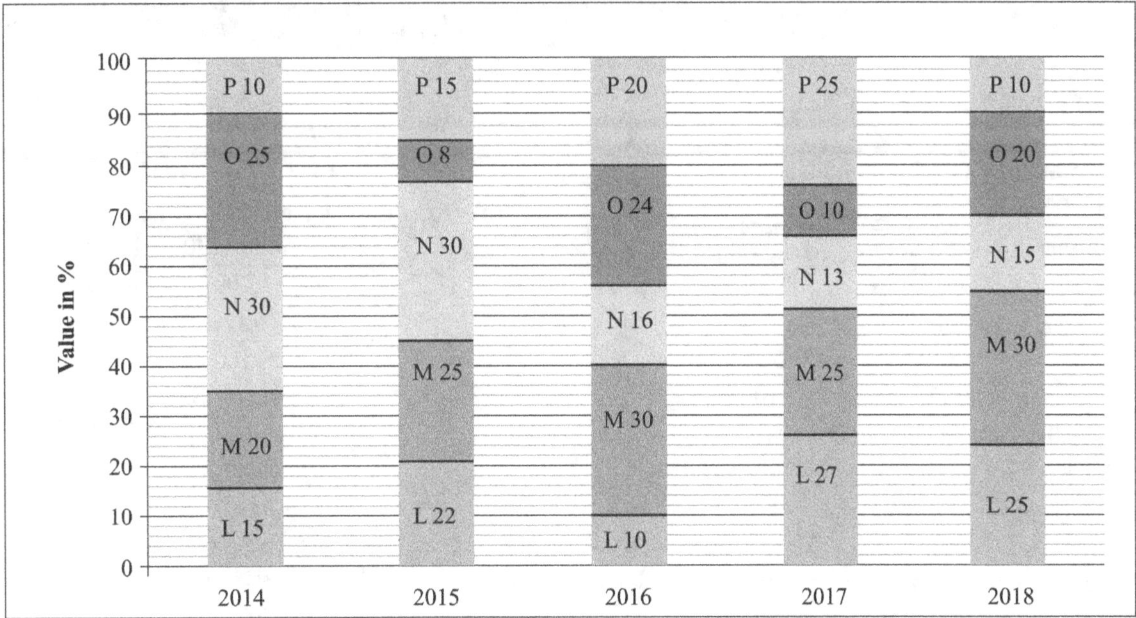

Condition 1: Total value of discount offered on all products increases by 10% every year.

Condition 2: Difference between the discount of N in 2014 and discount of O in 2017 is ₹333.8.

75. If total discount per year would have been increased by 20% instead of 10% as given above and condition 2 remains the same for new rate then, difference in value of discount of N in 2014 and P in 2015 according to new rate (approximately)
(a) 315
(b) 330
(c) 305
(d) 405
(e) 415

76. What is the cost price of article P in 2015 if ratio of cost price of P in 2015 and cost price of O in 2018 are in the ratio 6 : 5 and profit of O in 2018 is ₹343. (Approximately)
(a) 2400
(b) 2500
(c) 2000
(d) 1800
(e) 1500

77. Cost price of M in 2017 is what percent more or less than the cost price of N in 2014 if profit of M in 2017 is 280 and profit of N in 2014 is 20% more than the discount of P in 2016. (approximately)

(a) 98%
(b) 92%
(c) 109%
(d) 113%
(e) 102%

78. If 82 articles of N are sold in 2016 and Profit percent per article of N in 2016 is 25/4% more of the percent value of discount of N in 2016 then find the total profit in selling all articles. (approximately)
(a) 22500
(b) 17500
(c) 19250
(d) 24200
(e) 26300

79. If shopkeeper had 10 units of M type products in 2015 in which 2 articles are spoiled then he should sell the remaining articles at what price so that there is overall gain of 20% if there is a profit of 125/7% on selling a unit of M type product initially. (approximately)
(a) 2100
(b) 1800
(c) 1500
(d) 1400
(e) None of these

HINTS & SOLUTIONS

1. (d) Required percentage

$$= \frac{15000 + 30000}{5000 + 35000 + 15000 + 25000 + 30000 + 30000} \times 100$$

$$= \frac{45000}{140000} \times 100 = 32.14 \simeq 32\% \,(\text{Approx})$$

2. (e) In 2009

Total number of girls

$$= (20 + 20 + 5) \times \frac{38}{100} \times 1000 = \frac{45 \times 38 \times 1000}{100} = 17100$$

Total number of boys $= 45000 - 17100 = 27900$

Total number of boys who opted for Mathematics

$$= 27900 \times \frac{5}{45} = 3100$$

3. (a) Required Ratio $= (25 + 30) : (5 + 20) = 55 : 25 = 11 : 5$

4. (b) Required Percentage $= \dfrac{(15 + 10 + 15) \times 1000}{455030} \times 100$

$$= \frac{40 \times 1000}{455030} \times 100 = 8.79 \simeq 9\% \,(\text{Approx})$$

5. (e) Required total number of students

$$= (5 + 35 + 15 + 15 + 20 + 5) \times 1000$$
$$= 95 \times 1000 = 95000$$

6. (b) Post graduate engineers employed in company W
$$= 200$$

$$\therefore \quad \text{Required percentage} = \frac{200}{650} \times 100$$

$$\frac{400}{13} = 30\frac{10}{13}\%$$

7. (b) Average number of junior engineers

$$= \frac{100 + 100 + 150 + 250 + 250}{5} = \frac{850}{5} = 170$$

8. (c) Average number of assistant engineers

$$= \frac{200 + 350 + 200 + 200 + 100}{5}$$

$$= \frac{1050}{5} = 210$$

Required difference $= 210 - 170 = 40$

9. (d) In all companies:

Assistant engineers $= 200 + 350 + 200 + 200 + 100$
$$= 1050$$

Number after 37% increase

$$= \frac{1050 \times 137}{100} = 1438.5$$

Postgraduate engineers $= 100 + 200 + 350 + 500 + 350$
$$= 1500$$

Number after 20% decrease

$$= \frac{1500 \times 80}{100} = 1200$$

$\therefore$ Required percentage

$$= \frac{1438.5 - 1200}{1438.5} = \frac{238.5}{1438.5} \times 100 = 16.6\%$$

10. (b) Increase in the number of engineers:

Company V $\Rightarrow \dfrac{400 \times 130}{100} = 520$

Company X $\Rightarrow \dfrac{700 \times 135}{100} = 945$

Company Y $\Rightarrow \dfrac{950 \times 140}{100} = 1330$

Total engineers $= 520 + 945 + 1330 + 650 + 700$
$$= 4145$$

Total original number of engineers
$$= 400 + 650 + 700 + 950 + 700 = 3400$$

Percentage increase

$$= \frac{4145 - 3400}{3400} \times 100 = 21.9\%$$

$$\simeq 22\%$$

11. (a) Passengers of airline A
$$= (15 + 10 + 20 + 10 + 15 + 15) \text{ thousands}$$
$$= 85 \text{ thousands}$$

Passengers of airline C
$$= (15 + 15 + 15 + 10 + 20 + 10) \text{ thousands}$$
$$= 85 \text{ thousands}$$

Difference $= 85 - 85 = 0$

12. (b) Passengers of airline C who travelled to Delhi and Kolkata $= 30$ thousands

Required percentage $= \dfrac{30}{85} \times 100 \approx 35$

13. (c) Required ratio $= (15 + 10) : (15 + 10) = 25 : 25 = 1 : 1$

14. (d) Passengers of airline A who travelled to Chennai

First quarter $\Rightarrow 10000$

Second quarter $\Rightarrow 10000 \times \dfrac{150}{100} = 15000$

Third quarter $\Rightarrow \dfrac{15000 \times 100}{120} = 12500$

$$= \frac{12500 - 10000}{10000} \times 100 = \frac{250000}{10000} = 25$$

15. (d) Passengers of airline B who travelled to Bangaluru.

First quarter $\Rightarrow 10000$

Second quarter $\Rightarrow \dfrac{10000 \times 130}{100} = 13000$

Passengers of airline B who travelled to Kolkata

First quarter $\Rightarrow 10000$
Second quarter $\Rightarrow 14000$

$\therefore$ Required percentage $= \dfrac{20000}{27000} \times 100 \approx 74$

16. (c) The CO_2 emission in US, China and Japan after 2 years would be 918.75, 903.44 and 857.5 million ton respectively.
Similarly from the given condition the per capita income of US, China and Japan after 2 years would be 312.12, 292.03 and 254.61 respectively.
Hence the ratio of CO_2 emission to per capita income in US, China and Japan is 2.9, 3.1, 3.4 respectively.

17. (b) Since it is given that the ratio of CO_2 emission to per capita income is 0.75 hence the CO_2 emission of US and China should be 225 and 202.5 million ton respectively. The required reduction in CO_2 emission of US and China should be 975 and 977.5 million tons respectively. It is given that for every 1.25 units of carbon credit, 0.5 million ton of CO_2 emission is compensated.
So in a year, 26 million tons of CO_2 emission is compensated.
Then the number of years required are 977.5/26 = 38 years

18. (c) Total CO_2 emissions of these countries at the beginning = 450+450+350+400+400 = 2050
Since the ratio of CO_2 emissions to per capita income of each country becomes 50% of present value, hence total emission of these countries = 2050/2 = 1025
Total emissions of 5 countries = 350×5 = 1750
They can sell 1750-1025 = 725
In 3 years total CO_2 emissions they can sell
= 725×3 = 2175
Since for 0.5 emissions carbon credit is 1.25 hence for 2175 emissions it would be 2175×2.5= 5437. The actual value is less than this as we have ignored the percentage increase of 2%, 2.5% and 3.5% in per capita income.

19. (b) From eliminating options we will find that (B) is correct.

20. (d) Evaluate the given options we will get
The percentage increase in number of females in 2003 = 10%
That in 2006 = 9.38%.
Similarly in 2011 = 5.7%
in 2012 = 13.5%
Hence the highest percentage increase in females is in 2012.

21. (d) From the given data
The number of educated male in 2009 is = 302 million.
The number of uneducated female in 2009 is approximately 108 million.
The number of educated male in 2010 is approximately is 378 million.
The number of uneducated female in 2010 is approximately 168 million.
Hence the percentage change in female uneducated is (168-108)/108 × 100 = 55.5%

22. (c) From the given information in 2012 the number of people living in urban population is 68% of 600 = 408.
Then the rural population in 2012 = 900 − 408 = 492
The number of rural population in 2017 is
= 12×1100/55 = 240
Hence required ratio = 492/240= 2.05

23. (d) Let us eliminate the options one by one.
(A) → The statement is wrong as per the given information.
(B) → 3.2 MT of natural soda ash was built from 2015 to 2018 and that is the reason for the increase and hence the reason for change or increase in the trend of Tata. Hence it is not true.
(C) → Since the year is not mentioned hence the data given in this statement is incomplete.
(D) → The data given in above statement may be correct as Tata chemical might have acquired 0.3 MT of natural soda ash in 2017. Since there is no data given about the year 2016. So, depending on the data of production in 2016 it might have acquired 0.3MT of natural soda ash in 2017. So, this also leads to change in trend of Tata chemicals.

24. (d) This is one of the questions that could be solved by logic. Since it is given that trend of total global production is the same as Tata's synthetic production, and Tata has 0% increased from 2017 to 2018
Increase in global production = 0%.

25. (a) Let us evaluate given statement one by one
Statement 1: NS/SS in 2011 = 10/25 = 2/5
Also NS/SS in 2016 = 10/30 = 1/3
The proportion has decreased from 2/5 (i.e 40%) to 1/3 (i.e 33.33%)
Hence Statement 1 is true, 2 is false
Statement 3: SS/TS in 2015 = 0.9/0.9 = 1
SS/TS in 2017 = 2.2/2.5 = 22/25
And 22/25 <1 hence Proportion has decreased. And hence Statement 3 is true

26. (d) In order to find Tata Chemicals share of the global production in 2018, we require the global production in 2018. However, the data is given in question no 27 but it is mentioned that the data is for that particular question only.

27. (c) Given that Total Production = 40,

28. (b) Effort allocation of B → C, C → D, D → E
Hence we can say that new values of E are older values of B
So, rank of company 3, in order of effort of E is 3.

29. (a) In company 4, total effort for operations through B to F get evenly distributed.
So each gets the value of $\left(\dfrac{81.7}{5}\right)$
Initial percentage of E = 28.6
New percentage = 16.34
i.e Reduction of 12.3

30. (d) So B, C & D efforts will be removed & redistributed equally among any A, E and F.
It is clearly seen from the chart that E will show the maximum distribution of effort as E already shows the maximum distribution.

31. (b)

State	Rank				
MA	1	1	1	1	1
TN	2	2	2	2	2
GU	3	4	4	4	5
AP	4	3	3	3	3
KA	5	6	6	6	6
UP	6	5	5	5	4
WB	7	7	7	7	7

We see from table the required states are five MA, TN, AP, KA, WB

32. (b)

State	Rank				
MA	1	1	1	1	1
TN	2	2	2	2	2
GU	3	4	4	4	5
AP	4	3	3	3	3
KA	5	6	6	6	6
UP	6	5	5	5	4
WB	7	7	7	7	7

From above table we see that GU & UP are the states who change their relative rank two times but GU is not given in the options hence U.P will be the required state

33. (d) For Tamil Nadu,

$$\text{required \%} = \frac{8015 - 5604}{5604} \times 100 = 43\%$$

For Karnataka, $\text{required \%} = \dfrac{5413 - 3829}{3829} \times 100 = 41\%$

For Gujarat, $\text{required \%} = \dfrac{6300 - 4402}{4402} \times 100 = 43\%$

% share of A.P from 2013-2014 increased by

$$= \frac{7202 - 4728}{4728} \times 100 = 52\%$$

which is most among TN, KA, GU

34. (c) Growth rate in 2015-2016

$$= \frac{10,284 - 8067}{8067} \times 100 = 27.5\% \text{ approx.}$$

which is maximum in comparison to other pair of years

35. (a) In KA revenue increased from 2014 to 2016
= 4839 – 4265 = 574
& revenue increase from 2000 to 2001
= 5413 – 4839 = 574

36. (c)

State	Rank				
MA	1	1	1	1	1
TN	2	2	2	2	2
GU	3	4	4	4	5
AP	4	3	3	3	3
KA	5	6	6	6	6
UP	6	5	5	5	4
WB	7	7	7	7	7

From the table we see TN's rank is constant (MA and WB are not in options). Therefore its contribution to total tax collections will also have constant rank

37. (a) Comparing the operating income for 2017-18 in the 1st and the 3rd graph we can find that companies B and D are excluded from the graph 3.
As both B and D make loss in 2016-17, so the only possible answer is (a).

38. (c) This can be found out from the third chart at it gives the ratio of operating profit to operating income for the companies A, C, E and F. Clearly the highest point is the answer. On comparing the operating income from chart 1 we find it to be E.

39. (a) Option (a) talks about C (from chart 2) whose operating income is not lowest in 2017-18 (from chart 1)
Option (b) talks about D
Option (c) talks about B
Option (d) talks about A, C, E and F. Their operating incomes lies between 150 to 250 crore in 2017-18.

40. (d) Companies exceeding 10% profitability in 2017-18 are C and E. The operating profits (from chart 3) of C and E are 38 and 32.
Hence, the average operating profit

$$= \frac{(38 + 32)}{2} = 35 \text{ crore.}$$

41. (a) Fastest growing rate of population is in China

i.e., $\dfrac{22 - 16.5}{1000} \times 100 = 0.55\%$

Slowest growing rate of population is in France and U.K.

i.e., $\dfrac{1}{1000} \times 100 = 0.1\%$

$\therefore$ Required difference = 0.55 – 0.1 = 0.45%

42. (d) Total birth in USA $= \dfrac{25,00,00,000 \times 6}{1000} = 15,00,000$

Total deaths in Russia $= \dfrac{15,00,00,000 \times 2}{1000} = 3,00,000$

Difference = 15,00,000 – 3,00,000 = 12,00,000

$\therefore$ Required % $= \dfrac{12,00,000}{3,00,000} \times 100 = 400\%$

43. (b) Total birth in Japan in 2018 $= \dfrac{15,00,00,000 \times 9}{1000}$

$= 13,50,000$

Number of infants dying $= \dfrac{13,50,000 \times 3}{1000} = 4050$

Total death in Japan in 2018

$$= 15,00,00,000 \times \frac{6.5}{1000} = 975000$$

Now, required % $= \dfrac{4050}{975000} \times 100 = 0.415$

44. (d) It cannot be determined because population in 2018 is not given.

45. (c) Percentage growth rate of given countries:

USA : $\dfrac{1.5}{1000} \times 100 = 0.15\%$

UK : $\dfrac{1}{1000} \times 100 = 0.10\%$

India : $\dfrac{5}{1000} \times 100 = 0.50\%$

China : $\dfrac{5.5}{1000} \times 100 = 0.55\%$

Japan : $\dfrac{2.5}{1000} \times 100 = 0.25\%$

Russia : $\dfrac{1.5}{1000} \times 100 = 0.15\%$

France : $\dfrac{1}{1000} \times 100 = 0.10\%$

Hence, only two countries from all of the given countries have the rate of growth of population greater than 0.25%

46. (d) In 2012,
One dozen banana ≡ 0.8 kg cost ₹ 12

$\Rightarrow$ 1 kg cost = $\dfrac{12}{0.8} \times 1 = ₹15$

Cost of one kg of orange = ₹ 10

$\therefore \quad \dfrac{15-10}{15} \times 100 = 33\dfrac{1}{3}\%$

47. (c) Average cost of 1 kg of orange during (2012-18)

$\dfrac{10+12+14+16+18+20+22}{7} = 16$

Average cost of 1 kg of banana during (2012-18)

$= \left(\dfrac{12}{0.8} + \dfrac{13}{0.8} + \dfrac{14}{1} + \dfrac{15}{1.1} + \dfrac{16}{1.2} + \dfrac{17}{1.2} + \dfrac{18}{1.2}\right)\dfrac{1}{7}$

$= (15 + 16.25 + 14 + 13.63 + 13.33 + 14.16 + 15) \times \dfrac{1}{7}$

$= 14.48$
difference = 1.53

48. (a) In 2014, from graph it is clear

49. (d) Can not be found, data insufficient.

50. (d) In 2012 cost of one kg of banana = 15
In 2018 cost of 1 kg of banana = 15
Required % = 0

51. (c) Growth rate from 2006 to 2007 = (500 −380)/380 × 100 = 31.6% (we can approximate it to 30% as options given in the question are not very close)
Growth rate from 2004 to 2005
$= (270 - 180)/180 \times 100 = 50\%$
Hence required % change = (50−30)/50 × 100 = 40%
The actual value is less because we have reduced the growth from 2006 to 2007, only one option 35% is close to the 40% hence that is the answer.

52. (a) Percentage growth from 2006 to 2007 = (500-380)/380
$\times 100 = 31.6\%$

approx 30%
Since in the year 2008 subscription in Europe = 1.3 x 500 =650
Hence the required difference = 650–600=50

53. (a) Here again it is given in the question that we need to find the approximate value.
Let total number of subscriber in 2003 is 1000 (so that we can calculate the % increase /decrease easily), then number of men in 2003 = 600 and Women 400

YEAR	MEN	WOMEN
2003	600	400
2004	600 +30 = 630	400 + 40 =440
2005	661.5	484
2006	695	532.4
2007	730	585.6
2008	766	644
2009	804	708.6
2010	845	779

So in 2010 total number of subscriber = 845 + 779 = 1624
Hence 62.4% = approx 62%

54. (d) The gap between subscription revenues in US and Europe in 2003 = 410 – 110 = 300. The gap between subscription revenues in the US and Europe in 2004 = 525 – 185 = 340
The percentage change in the gap between subscription revenues in the US and Europe in the period of 2003–04 = (340–300)/300 = 40/300
Similarly in the period 2005-06 = (270-320)/320 = −50/320
In the period 2006- 07 = (210 – 270)/270 = −60/270
In the period 2008-09 = (110 −180)/180 = −70/180
In the period 2009-2010 = (100 −110)/110 = 10/110
Out of these 5 values the change in gap is highest in 2008-09

Sol. (55-59) :

55. (b) (SP/75 × 100 + SP/90 × 100 + SP/80 × 100)/3 = 7980
Solving this we will get SP = 6480
Then MP of soap by shop B = 6480/90 × 100 = ₹7200

56. (a) SP/85 × 100 – SP/95 × 100 = 1008

$SP = \dfrac{1008}{100} \times \dfrac{95 \times 85}{10} = 8138.6$

MP by shop C = (SP/70) × 100 = ₹11628

57. (e) (MP × 84)/100 + (MP × x)/100 = 7456   --- (1)
(MP × x)/100 + (MP × 72)/100 = 6736   --- (2)
Subtracting equation 1 from equation 2 we get
(MP × 12)/100 = 720
Thus MP = ₹6000
Then SP of shop C is 72% of MP which is ₹4320

58. (c) If discount is ₹1482 in shop B then SP of rice is
= (1482/15) × 85 = 8398
MP of rice by shop A (8398/65) × 100 = 12920
MP of rice by shop C = (8398/95) × 100 = 8840
Average of MP of these two shops = ₹10880

59. (d) Ratio of discount for sugar by shop B is 30%
According to given question discount by shop A will be 10%
Thus we have MP × 90/100 – MP × 70/100 = 1360
After solving this we have MP = ₹6800
And difference between SP of shop A and shop C is 1560
(i.e) 6800 × 90/100 – SP of shop C = 1560
SP by shop C is = 6120 – 1560 = 4560

Sol. (60-64):

60. (a) Part of the tank filled by pipe P in one minute = 1/24
Part of the tank filled by pipe Q in one minute = 1/30
Time taken by pipe T to fill the tank = 4/3 × 24 = 32 minutes
Part of the tank filled by pipe T in one minute = 1/36
Time taken by pipe U to fill the tank = 2/3 × 30 = 20 minutes
Part of the tank filled by pipe U in one minute = 1/20
Part of the tank emptied by pipe L in one minute = 1/36
Let required time = t minutes
According to the question

$$\frac{4}{24}+\frac{4}{30}+\frac{2}{36}-\frac{2}{36}+\frac{t}{20}=1$$

$$\frac{1}{6}+\frac{2}{15}+\frac{t}{20}=1$$

$$\frac{3}{10}+\frac{t}{20}=1$$

$$t=\frac{20\times7}{10}$$

t = 14 minutes

61. (c) Part of the tank filled by pipe P in one minute = 1/24
Part of the tank filled by pipe Z in one minute
  = 0.75/24 = 1/32
Part of the tank filled by pipe R in one minute = 1/20
Part of the tank emptied by pipe N in one minute = 1/48
Part of the tank emptied by pipe Y in one minute
  = 1.5/48 = 1/32
Part of the tank emptied by pipe M in one minute = 1/32
Part of the tank filled by pipe R and pipe Z in 3 minute
  = 3/20 + 3/32 = (24 + 15)/ 160 = 39/160
Let the required time taken = t minutes
t/32 + t/32 = 39/160 = 2t/32 = 39/160

$$t=\frac{39\times32}{160\times2}=\frac{39}{10}\text{ minutes}$$

62. (c) Time taken by pipe W to fill the tank = 5/4 x 16 = 20 minutes
Part of the tank filled by pipe W in one minute = 1/20
Time taken by pipe I to fill the tank = 20 x 120/100 = 24 minutes
Part of the tank filled by pipe I in one minute = 1/24
Time taken by pipe X to fill the tank = 10/9 x 36 = 40 minutes
Part of the tank filled by pipe X in one minute = 1/40
Part of the tank filled by pipe G in one minute = 2/40 = 1/20
Part of the tank filled by pipe S in one minute = 1/16
Part of the tank filled by pipe T in one minute = 1/36

Let the time taken by pipe I and pipe G to fill the tank = t minutes
And the time taken by pipe S and pipe T to fill the tank = k minutes
t/24 + t/20 = 1 = (5t + 6t)/120 = 1
= 11t/120 = 1 = t = 120/11 minutes
And k/16 + k/36 = 1
(9k + 4k)/144 = 1 = k = 144/13 minutes
Required percentage = (120/11)/ (144/13) x 100

$$=\frac{60\times13}{11\times72}\times100 = 98.48\%$$

63. (b) Part of the tank filled by pipe Q in one minute = 1/30
Time taken by pipe U to fill the tank = 2/3 × 30 = 20 minutes
Part of the tank filled by pipe U in one minute = 1/20
Part of the tank emptied by pipe K in one minute = 1/40
Part of the tank filled by pipe T in one minute = 1/36
Time taken by pipe V to fill the tank = 6/5 x 20 = 24 minutes
Part of the tank filled by pipe V in one minute = 1/24
Part of the tank emptied by pipe N in one minute = 1/48
Let the time taken by pipe Q, pipe U and pipe K together to fill the tank = t minutes
And the time taken by pipe T, pipe V and pipe N together to fill the tank = k minutes
t/30 + t/20 – t/40 = 1 = (4t + 6t – 3t)/120 = 1
  = 7t/120 = 1 = t = 120/7 minutes
And k/36 + k/24 – k/48 = 1
  = (4k + 6k – 3k)/144 = 1 = 7k/144 = 1
  = k = 144/7 minutes
Required ratio = 120/7 : 144/7 = 5 : 6

64. (b) Part of the tank filled by pipe P in one minute = 1/24
Part of the tank filled by pipe R in one minute = 1/20
Part of the tank filled by pipe T in one minute = 1/36
Part of the tank emptied by pipe K in one minute = 1/40
Part of the tank emptied by pipe N in one minute = 1/48
Time taken by pipe U to fill the tank = 2/3 x 30 = 20 minutes
Part of the tank filled by pipe U in one minute = 1/20
Time taken by pipe X to fill the tank = 10/9 x 36 = 40 minutes
Part of the tank filled by pipe X in one minute = 1/40
Let the required time taken = t minutes
4/24 + 4/20 + 4/36 – 2/40 – 2/48 + t/20 + t/40 = 1
= 1/6 + 1/5 + 1/9 – 1/20 – 1/24 + (2t + t)/40 = 1
= (60 + 72 + 40 – 18 – 15)/360 + 3t/40 = 1
= 139/360 + 3t/40 = 1 = 3t/40 = 1 – 139/360
= 3t/40 = (360 – 139)/ 360 = 3t/40 = 221/360

$$= t=\frac{221}{360}\times\frac{40}{3} = t=\frac{221}{27}$$

65. (a) Profit in 2013 = $2000\times\dfrac{130}{100}$ = 2600s

Total revenue = 50,000 + 2600 = 52600

66. (d) Profit of company C_1, in 2013 = $\dfrac{3000\times100}{150}$

$$= 2000$$

67. (e) Required average $= \dfrac{45 + 25 + 30 + 35 + 35 + 40}{6}$

$$= \dfrac{210}{6} = 35\%$$

68. (a) Required percentage $= \dfrac{40 - 25}{25} \times 100$

$$= \dfrac{15}{25} \times 100 = 60\%$$

69. (d) Profit earned by C_2 in 2013 $= \dfrac{27000 \times 100}{135}$

$$= 20,000$$

Profit earned by C_3 in 2013 $= \dfrac{43500 \times 100}{145}$

$$= 30,000$$

Total profit $= 50,000$

70. (b) Total number of professors $= \dfrac{1}{9} \times \dfrac{9}{25} \times 375 = 15$

71. (c) Number of male students in Physics branch from college A $= \dfrac{13}{25} \times 500 = 260$

Required percentage $= \dfrac{300 - 260}{300} \times 100$

$$= \dfrac{40}{3}\% = 13\dfrac{1}{3}\%$$

72. (a) 20% students from Maths branch in college

$E = \dfrac{20}{100} \times 450 = 90$

Total students of Maths branch in college C
$= 250 + 90 = 340$

Required ratio $= \dfrac{340}{1110} = \dfrac{34}{111}$

73. (e) Total students in Chemistry branch in all college
$= 350 + 375 + 375 + 450 + 325 = 1875$
Total students in Maths branch from all colleges
$= 275 + 300 + 250 + 500 + 450 = 1775$

Required percentage $= \dfrac{1875 - 1775}{1775} \times 100$

$$= 5.6\% \sim 6\% \text{ more}$$

74. (a) Total students in college D and E together in 2019 who are enrolled $= 1300 \times \dfrac{80}{100} + 1200 \times \dfrac{75}{100} + 400 = 2340$

Sol. (75–79):

Let total discount in 2014 $= x$
Then total discount in 2017 $= 1.331x$
According to question

$$\dfrac{30}{100}x - \dfrac{10}{100} \times 1.331x = 333.8$$

$3x - 1.331x = 3338$
$x = 2000$ (Total discount in 2014)
Total discount in 2015 $= 2200$
Total discount in 2016 $= 2420$
Total discount in 2017 $= 2662$
Total discount in 2018 $= 2928.2$

75. (a) According to new condition

$$\dfrac{30}{100}x - \dfrac{10}{100} \times 1.728x = 333.8$$

New $x \approx 2624$
Required difference

$$= \dfrac{30}{100} \times 2624 - \dfrac{15}{100} \times \dfrac{120}{100} \times 2624$$

$$= 787.2 - 472.32 \approx 315$$

76. (a) Marked price of O in 2018 $= 2928$

Selling price of O in 2018 $= 2928 - \dfrac{20}{100} \times 2928$

$$= 2928 - 585 = 2343$$

Cost price of O in 2018 $= 2343 - 343 = 2000$

Cost price of P in 2015 $= \dfrac{2000}{5} \times 6 = 2400$

77. (c) Cost price of M in 2017 $= 2662 - \dfrac{25}{100} \times 2662 - 80 \approx 1716$

Profit of N in 2014 $= \dfrac{120}{100} \times \dfrac{20}{100} \times 2420 \approx 580$

Cost price of N in 2014 $= 2000 - \dfrac{30}{100} \times 2000 - 580 \approx 820$

Required percentage $= \dfrac{896}{820} \times 100 \approx 109\%$

78. (d) Profit percent of N in 2016 $= \left(100\% + \dfrac{25}{4}\%\right)16\%$

$$= \left(1 + \dfrac{1}{16}\right)16\% = 17\%$$

Let cost price of N in 2016 $= x$

Then $\dfrac{117}{100}x = 2420 - \dfrac{16}{100} \times 2420$

$x \approx 1737$
Required value $\approx 82\,(295) \approx 24200$

79. (a) Cost price of M in 2015

$$= \left(2200 - \dfrac{25}{100} \times 2200\right) \times \left(1 + \dfrac{5}{28}\right) = 1400$$

Total cost price of 10 products $= 14000$

Required total selling price $= \dfrac{120}{100} \times 14000 = 16800$

New selling price per product $= \dfrac{16800}{8} = 2100$

2 LINE GRAPH

Line chart or time graph is a chart which shows the information of data point in series (Markers) connected by straight lines. In the time graph each marker denotes a different value and each marker is symbol of a different item / person / value etc. There are two types of line graph.

(i) **SINGLE DATA GRAPH :** In this type of graph, we described the single data series of data point.

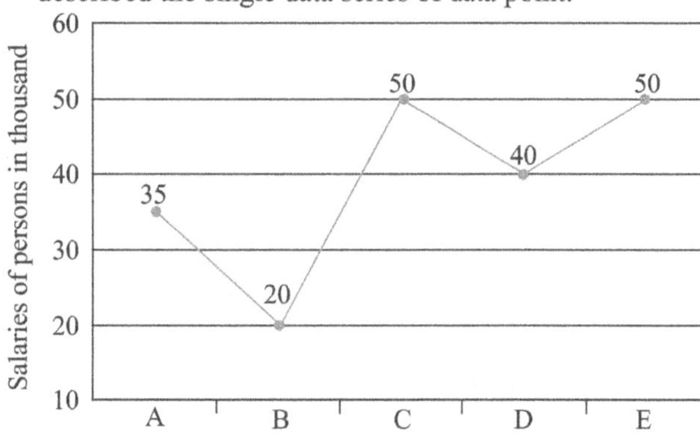

Example :

What is average salary of all persons together ?

Ans: Required average salary

$$= \frac{35000 + 20000 + 50000 + 40000 + 50000}{5} = \frac{195000}{5}$$

$$= 39000$$

(ii) **COMBINED DATA GRAPH**

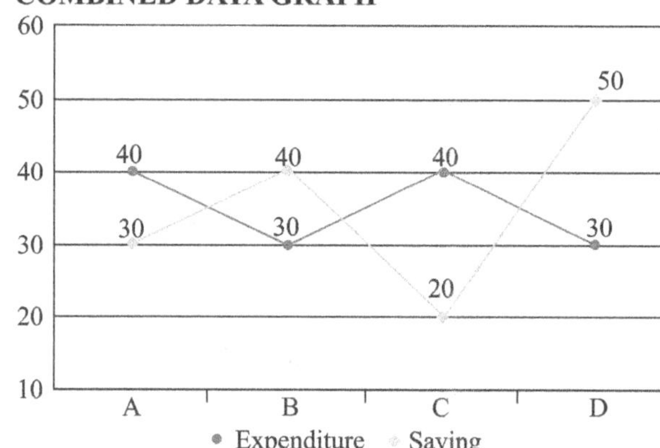

Example:

Salary of D is what percent more/less than that of A ?

Ans: Required %

$$= \frac{(50+30)-(40+30)}{40+30} \times 100 = \frac{10}{70} \times 100 = 14\frac{2}{7}\%$$

EXERCISE

Directions (Qs. 1-5) : *These questions are based on the graph given below.*

Solubility-Temperature relationships for various salts
[The Y-axis denotes solubility (kg / litre of water)]

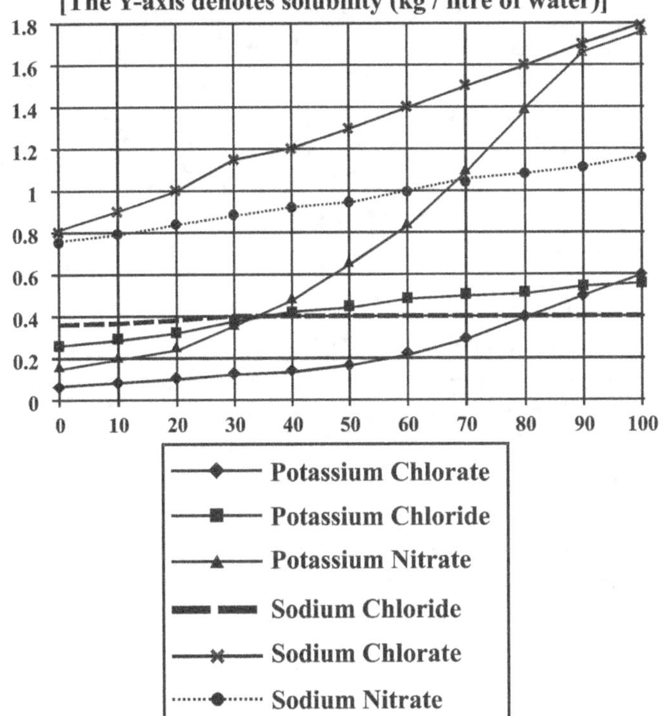

Potassium Chlorate

Potassium Chloride

Potassium Nitrate

Sodium Chloride

Sodium Chlorate

Sodium Nitrate

Temperature in °Celsius

1. Which of the following salts has greatest solubility?
   (a) Potassium Chlorate at 80°C
   (b) Potassium Chloride at 35°C
   (c) Potassium Nitrate at 39°C
   (d) Sodium Chloride at 85°C

2. Approximately, how many kg of Potassium Nitrate can be dissolved in 10 litres of water at 30°C?
   (a) 0.04　　(b) 0.4　　(c) 4　　(d) 0.35

3. By what % is the solubility of Potassium Chlorate in water increased as the water is heated from 30°C to 80°C?
   (a) 100　　(b) 200　　(c) 250　　(d) 300

4. If 1 mole of Potassium Chloride weighs 0.07456 kg, approximately. How many moles of Potassium Chloride can be dissolved in 100 litres of water at 36°C?
   (a) 700　　(b) 650　　(c) 480　　(d) 540

5. Which of the salts has greatest change in solubility in kg / litre of water between 15°C and 25°C?
   (a) Potassium Chlorate　　(b) Potassium Nitrate
   (c) Sodium Chlorate　　(d) Sodium Nitrate

DIRECTIONS (Qs. 6-10) : *These questions are based on the information and graph given below.*

Ghosh Babu has a manufacturing unit. The following graph gives the cost for various number of units. Given that Profit = Revenue – Variable Cost – Fixed Cost. The fixed cost remains constant upto 34 units after which additional investment is to be done in fixed assets. In any case production can not exceed 50 units.

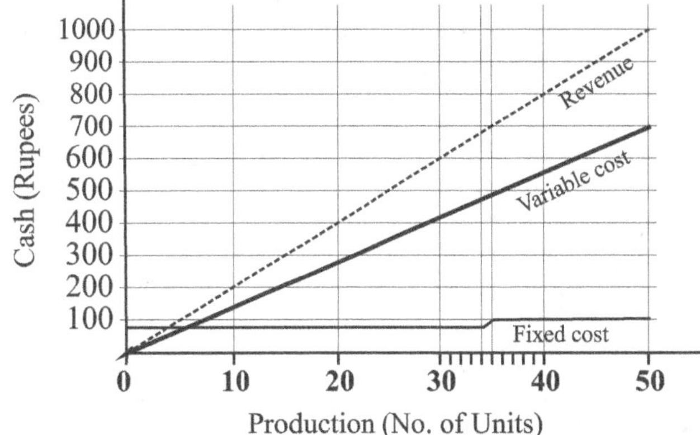

6. What is the minimum number of units that need to be produced to make sure that there was no loss?
   (a) 5　　　　　　　　　(b) 10
   (c) 20　　　　　　　　(d) indeterminable

7. How many units should be manufactured such that profit was atleast ₹ 50?
   (a) 20　　(b) 34　　(c) 45　　(d) 30

8. If at the most 40 units can be manufactured then what is the number of units that can be manufactured to maximize profit?
   (a) 40　　(b) 34　　(c) 35　　(d) 25

9. If the production can not exceed 45 units then what is the number of units that can maximise profit per unit?
   (a) 40　　(b) 34　　(c) 415　　(d) 35

10. If the fixed cost of production goes up by ₹ 40 then what is the minimum number of units that need to be manufactured to make sure that there is no loss
    (a) 10　　(b) 19　　(c) 15　　(d) 20

DIRECTIONS (Qs. 11-13) : *These questions are based on the figure given below.*

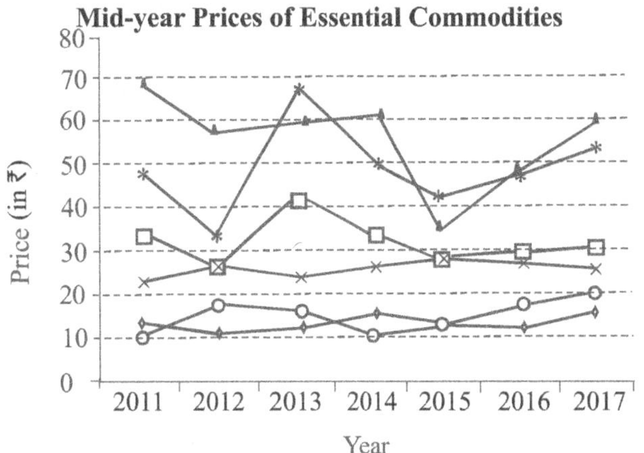

Mid-year Prices of Essential Commodities

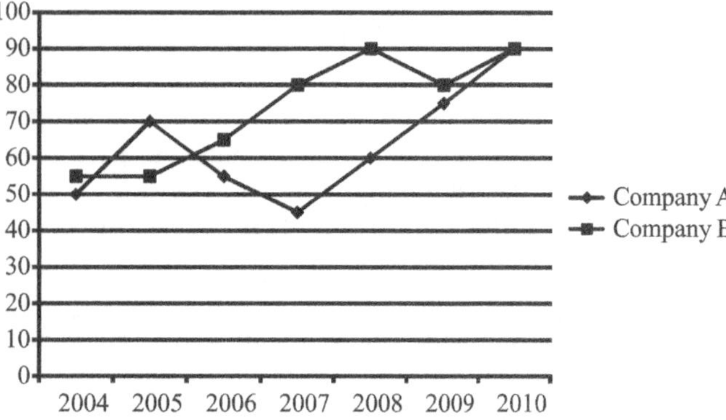

11. During 2011-2017, the number of commodities that exhibited a net overall increase and a net overall decrease, respectively, were
   (a) 3 and 3
   (b) 2 and 4
   (c) 4 and 2
   (d) 5 and 1

12. The number of commodities that experienced a price decline for two or more consecutive years is
   (a) 2
   (b) 3
   (c) 4
   (d) 5

13. For which commodities did a price increase immediately follow a price decline only once in this period?
   (a) Rice, Edible oil & Dal
   (b) Egg and Dal
   (c) Onion only
   (d) Egg and Onion

DIRECTIONS (Qs. 14-16) : *Study the following graph carefully to answer these questions.*

[SBI PO 2011]

The line graph below shows percent profit earned by two companies producing electronic goods over the years

% Profit = [Profit earned / Total Investment] × 100

Profit Earned = Total Income – Total Investment in the year

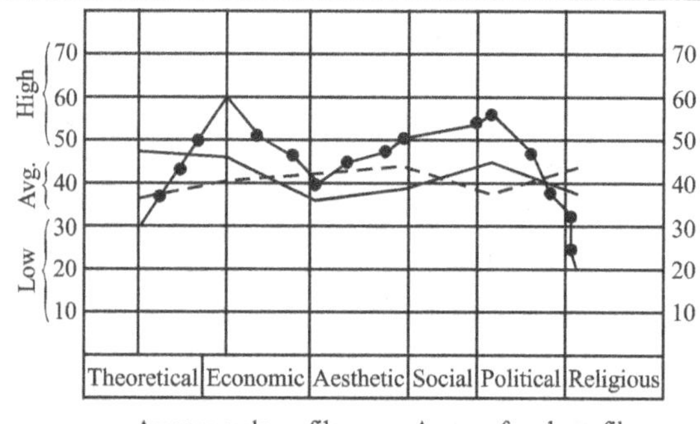

14. If the profit earned in 2006 by Company B was ₹8,12,500, what was the total income of the company in that year?
   (a) ₹12,50,000
   (b) ₹20,62,500
   (c) ₹16,50,000
   (d) None of these

15. If the amount invested by the two companies in 2005 was equal, what was the ratio of the total income of the company A to that of B in 2005?
   (a) 31 : 33
   (b) 33 : 31
   (c) 34 : 31
   (d) 14 : 11

16. If the total amount invested by the two companies in 2009 was ₹ 27 lakh while the amount invested by company B was 50% of the amount invested by Company A, what was the total profit earned by the two companies together?
   (a) ₹ 21.15 lakh
   (b) ₹ 20.70 lakh
   (c) ₹ 18.70 lakh
   (d) ₹ 20.15 lakh

DIRECTIONS (Qs. 17-21): *Study the following graph carefully and answer the questions that follow. Number of Girl students in '000s*

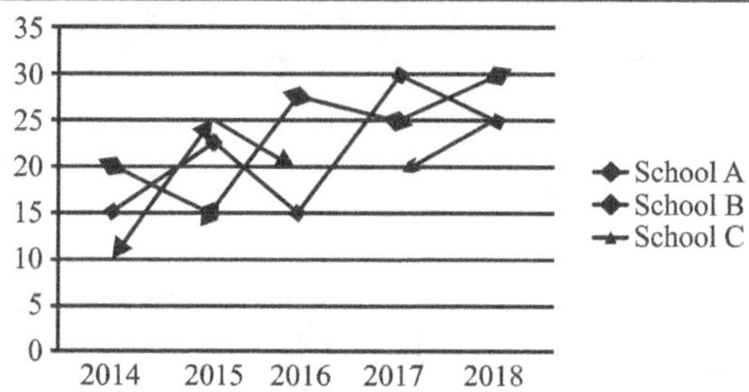

17. What was the ratio between the number girls enrolled in the school-C in the year 2017 and the total number of girls enrolled in school-A and school-B together in the same year?
   (a) 11 : 3
   (b) 3 : 11
   (c) 4 : 11
   (d) 4 : 7

18. In which school was the difference between the number of girls enrolled in the year 2018 and 2014 minimum?
   (a) Only school-A
   (b) Only School-B
   (c) Both school-A and school-B
   (d) Both school-A and school-C

19. What was the approximate average number of girls enrolled in the year 2016 in all the three schools together?
   (a) 20,800
   (b) 23,000
   (c) 20,000
   (d) 21,600

20. Total number of girls enrolled in all the three schools in the year 2014 was what percentage of the number of girls enrolled in school-C in the year 2017?
   (a) 208
   (b) 230
   (c) 200
   (d) 225

21. In which year was the total number of girls enrolled in all the three schools together second highest?
   (a) 2015
   (b) 2016
   (c) 2017
   (d) 2018

DIRECTIONS (Qs. 22-26) : *Use the graph given below to answer these questions : Given graph is the profile of values of a college student marked as personal profile. The normative profiles are given as average male profile and average female profile.*

22. Compare the three and state which of the given values is the highest in the personal profile of the student?
   (a) Theoretical
   (b) Religious
   (c) Social
   (d) Economic

23. In the given personal profile, which is the value with the lowest score?
   (a) Theoretical
   (b) Religious
   (c) Social
   (d) Aesthetic

24. In which values score, there exists maximum difference between average female profiles and personal profile?
    (a) Theoretical
    (b) Religious
    (c) Economic
    (d) Political

25. In which value score, there exists convergence between personal profile and average female profile?
    (a) Theoretical
    (b) Social
    (c) Aesthetic
    (d) None of the above

26. In which value score, there exists no difference state between the personal profile and average male profile?
    (a) Economic
    (b) Social
    (c) Aesthetic
    (d) None of the above.

DIRECTIONS (Qs. 27-29) : *Answer the questions on the basis of given information:*

The information are for the members of a society club "Bidhanpark Unayan Club" run by the residents of Bidhanpark. The club started its operation for social welfare and welfare for society on 1st January 2009. Every year after 2009, some new volunteers joined the club and still no one left the group from 2009 to 2014. All the values are recorded on the very second day of each year.

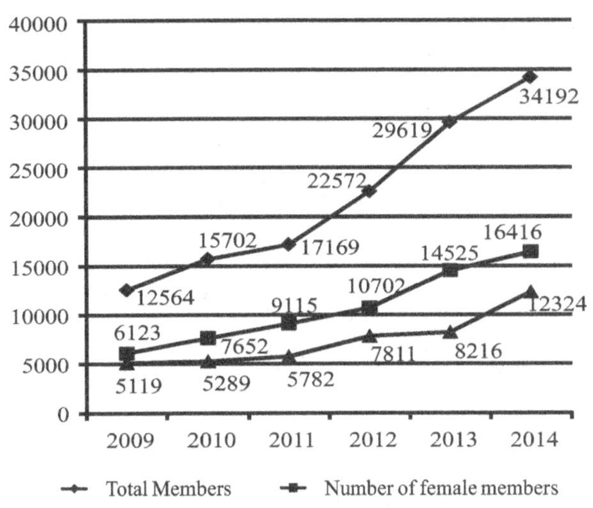

27. Which of the following years witnessed the highest % increase in new members over the previous years?
    (a) 2009
    (b) 2010
    (c) 2013
    (d) None of these

28. In which year women and men ratio is greatest?
    (a) 2011
    (b) 2012
    (c) 2013
    (d) None of these

29. The number of men who joined the club in 2010 was what % of the total number of people who joined the club in the same year?
    (a) 0.63
    (b) 0.75
    (c) 0.27
    (d) 0.11

DIRECTIONS (Qs. 30-34) : *In the following multiple graphs, the number of selected candidates for 6 different posts by three different companies A, B and C has been shown. Read the graph carefully and answer the questions.*

[SBI PO 2014]

Company A ⊸ ;   Company B ⊟ ;   Company C ⧍

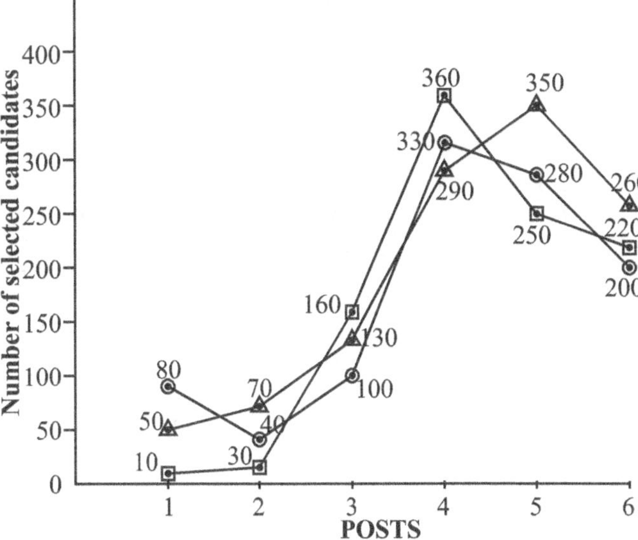
Number of Selected Candidates in three companies

POST 1 : HR officer
POST 2 : IT officer
POST 3 : Assistant Manager
POST 4 : Advertisement office Assistant
POST 5 : Office Assistant operatios
POST 6 : Junior office Administrator

30. What is the ratio between the number of all candidates selected for company A and that selected for the posts of assistant managers and junior office administrators in all three companies ?
    (a) 103 : 107
    (b) 102 : 107
    (c) 103 : 106
    (d) 113 : 117
    (e) None of these

31. The number of candidates recruited for the post of office assistant operations in company B is approximately what percent of total candidates recruited in that company ?
    (a) 28%
    (b) 24%
    (c) 30%
    (d) 31%
    (e) None of these

32. The number of candidates recruited for the posts of assistant manager and advertisement office assistant is what percent of the candidates recruited for the post of junior office administrator and HR officer by the company C ?
    (a) 115%   (b) 120%   (c) 135%   (d) 141%
    (e) None of these

33. The total number of candidates recruited for the post of HR officers in all the companies is what percent of the total candidates recruited by the company A for all posts ?
    (a) 16%   (b) 11%   (c) 12%   (d) 14%
    (e) None of these

34. What is the respective ratio between the average number of candidates selected for all the posts by company A and company C ?
    (a) 113 : 115
    (b) 115 : 113
    (c) 113 : 117
    (d) 117 : 113
    (e) 103 : 105

DIRECTIONS (Qs. 35-40) : *In the following multiple graphs production of wheat (in quintals) by three states - Bihar, Madhya Pradesh and Punjab have been given. Study the following graphs carefully to answer the questions.*

[SBI PO 2014]

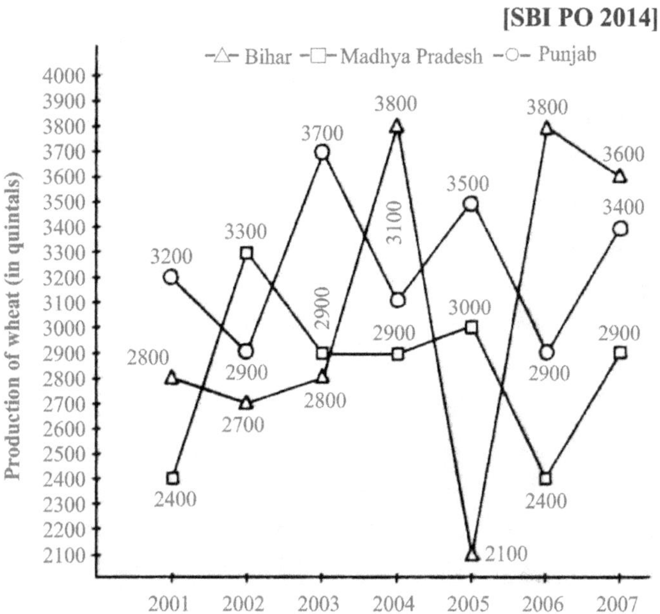

35. If the production of wheat by Madhya Pradesh in the years 2003, 2004, 2005 and 2007 increase by 30%, 40%, 45% and 40% respectively, what will be the overall percentage increase in the production of wheat in the state in the given years?
    (a) 22%   (b) 25%   (c) 35%   (d) 16%
    (e) 19%

36. What was the average production of wheat by all three states in the year 2005? (in quintals)
    (a) $2866\frac{1}{3}$ (b) $2866\frac{2}{3}$ (c) $2688\frac{2}{3}$ (d) $2688\frac{1}{3}$
    (e) None of these

37. In the given years, what is the average production of wheat in Bihar? (in quintals)
    (a) 3068   (b) 3076   (c) 3086   (d) 3088
    (e) None of these

38. If the productions of wheat in Bihar in the years 2001, 2002, 2003 and 2004 increase by 20%, 25%, 28% and 35% respectively; what will be the percentage increase in the average production of the state for the given years?
    (a) 35.7%   (b) 38.7%   (c) 40.7%   (d) 42.5%
    (e) None of these

39. By what per cent is the total production of wheat by three states in the year 2002, 2003 and 2004 more or less than that in the years 2005, 2006 and 2007?
    (a) 2.5%   (b) 2.6%   (c) 1.9%   (d) 1.09%
    (e) None of these

40. What was the total production of wheat by these three states in the year 2007? (in quintals)
    (a) 9900   (b) 9700   (c) 9980   (d) 8800
    (e) None of these

DIRECTIONS (Qs. 41-45): *Answer the questions based on the following two graphs, assuming that there is no fixed cost component and all the units produced are sold in the same year.*

[SBI PO Main 2015]

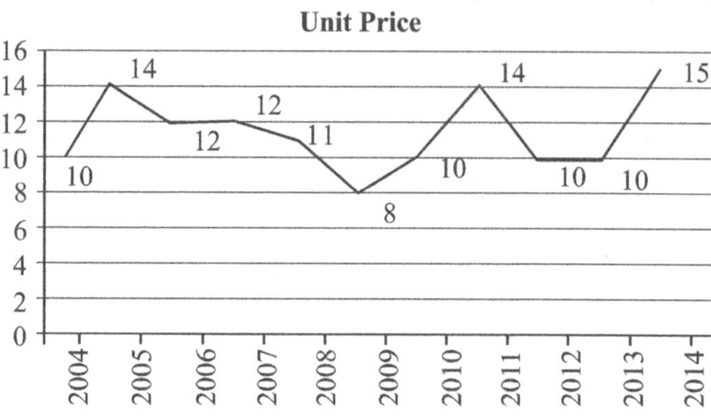

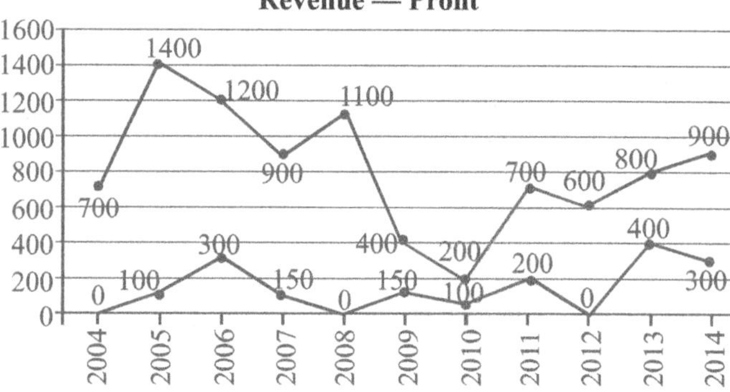

41. In which year per unit cost in highest?
    (a) 2006   (b) 2005   (c) 2009   (d) 2011
    (e) 2012

42. What is the approximate average quantity sold during the period 2004-2014?
    (a) 64 units   (b) 70 units
    (c) 77 units   (d) 81 units
    (e) 87 units

43. If volatility of a variable during 2000-2014 is defined as $\dfrac{\text{Maximum value} - \text{Minimum value}}{\text{Average value}}$, then which of the following is true?
    (a) Price per unit has highest volatility
    (b) Cost per unit has highest volatility
    (c) Total profit has highest volatility
    (d) Revenue has highest volatility
    (e) None of the above

44. If the price per unit decreases by 20% during 2004-2008 and cost per unit increases by 20% during 2009-2014, then during how many number of years there is loss?
    (a) 3 yr   (b) 4 yr   (c) 5 yr   (d) 7 yr
    (e) None of these

45. If the price per unit decrease by 20% during a 2004-2008 and cost per unit increase by 20% during 2009-2014, then the cumulative profit for the entire period 2009-2014 decrease by
    (a) ₹1650   (b) ₹1550
    (c) ₹1300   (d) ₹1250
    (e) Data inadequate

DIRECTIONS (Qs. 46-50): *Study the following information to answer the given questions*

[SBI PO Main 2016]

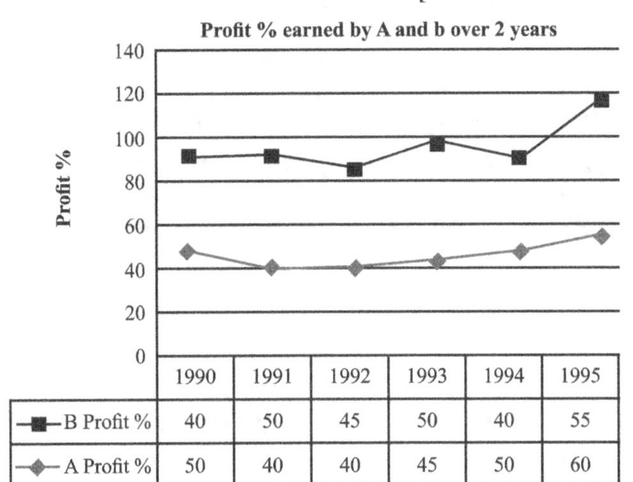

Profit % earned by A and b over 2 years

	1990	1991	1992	1993	1994	1995
—■— B Profit %	40	50	45	50	40	55
—◆— A Profit %	50	40	40	45	50	60

46. Expenditure of A in 1994 and 1995 are ₹12lakh and ₹14lakh. What was the total income of A in 1994 and 1995 together?
(a) ₹ 40.8 L   (b) ₹ 40.4 L
(c) ₹ 44 L   (d) ₹ 46.4 L
(e) None of these

47. Ratio of Expenditure of Companies A and B in 1993 was 4:5. What was the ratio of their incomes in the same year ?
(a) 58:75   (b) 75:58
(c) 78:55   (d) 72:55
(e) None of these

48. Total Expenditure of company B in all the years together was ₹ 125 L. What was the total income of the company in all the years together ?
(a) ₹ 185 L   (b) ₹ 520 L
(c) ₹ 250 L   (d) Cannot be determined
(e) None of these

49. If the incomes of the B in 1992 and 1993 were in the ratio 3:4, Find the ratio of Expenditures of that company in these 2 years ?
(a) 48 : 55   (b) 42 : 53
(c) 58 : 45   (d) 45 : 58
(e) None of these

50. If the expenditure of A and B in 1991 were equal and total income of A and B was ₹ 116L, what was the total expenditure of A and B in the same years ?
(a) ₹ 84 L   (b) ₹ 83 L
(c) ₹ 80 L   (d) ₹ 40 L
(e) None of these

DIRECTIONS (Qs. 51-55): *Two different finance Companies declare fixed annual rate of interests on the amounts deposited with them by the investers. The rate of interest offered by these Companies may differ from year to year depending on the variation in the financial status of the Company and the banks' rate of interest. The annual rate of interest offered by the two Companies P and Q over the years are shown by the graph provided below. Answer the questions based on this graph.*

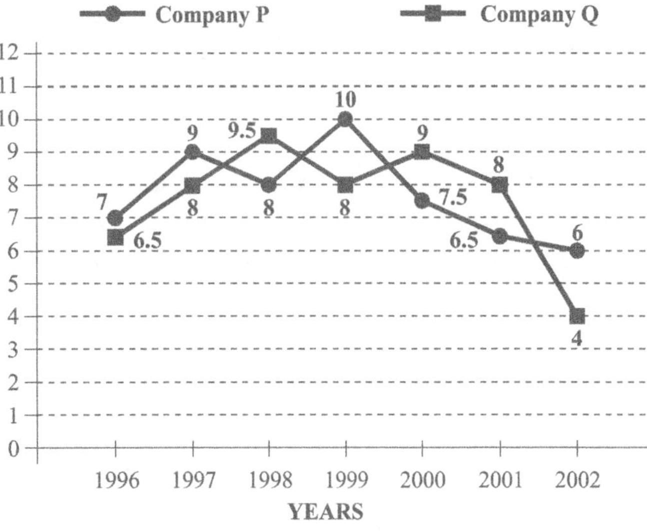

Annual Rate of Interest Offered by Two Finance Companies Over the Years

51. If two different amounts in the ratio 8 : 9 are invested in Companies P and Q respectively in 2002, then the amounts received after one year from Campanies P and Q are respectively in the ratio
(a) 2 : 3   (b) 3 : 4
(c) 6 : 7   (d) 4 : 3
(e) 9 : 8

52. In 2000, a part of ₹ 30 lakhs was invested in Company P and the rest was invested in Company Q for one year. The total interest received was ₹2.43 lakhs. What was the amount invested in Company P?
(a) ₹ 9 lakhs   (b) ₹ 11 lakhs
(c) ₹ 12 lakhs   (d) ₹ 14 lakhs
(e) ₹ 18 lakhs

53. A sum of ₹ 4.75 lakhs was invested in Company Q in 1999 for one year. How much more interest would have been earned if the sum was invested in Company P?
(a) ₹ 19000   (b) ₹ 14250
(c) ₹ 11750   (d) ₹ 9500
(e) ₹ 7500

54. An investor invested a sum of ₹ 12 lakhs in Company P in 1998. The total amount received after one year was reinvested in the same Company for one more year. The total appreciation received by the investor on his investment was
(a) ₹ 2,96,200   (b) ₹ 2,42,000
(c) ₹ 2,25,600   (d) ₹ 2,16,000
(e) ₹ 2,03,500

55. An investor invested ₹ 5 lakhs in Company Q in 1996. After one year, the entire amount along with the interest was transferred as investment to Company P in 1997 for one year. What amount will be received from Company P, by the investor?
(a) ₹ 594550   (b) ₹ 580425
(c) ₹ 579800   (d) ₹ 577500
(e) ₹ 575075

56. What is wrong about the following cumulative production graph?

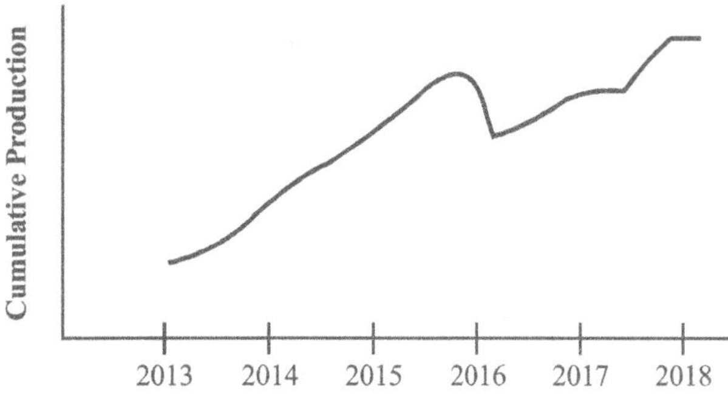

(a) No error
(b) Curve should be smooth
(c) Large variations are not possible
(d) Negative slope is not possible in cumulative data graph.

57. Find the equation of the graph shown below.

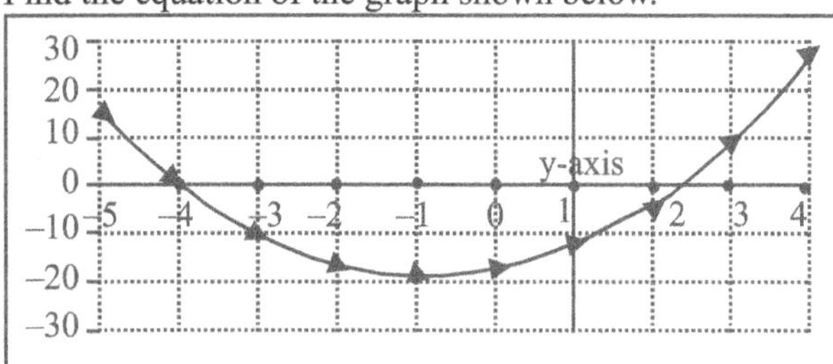

(a) $y = 3x - 4$
(b) $y = 2x^2 - 40$
(c) $x = 2y^2 - 40$
(d) $y = 2x^2 + 3x - 19$
(e) $x = 2y^2 + 3y - 19$

58. Interpret relationship between the returns of Stock X and Mutual Fund Y based on the following graph, where percentage return of Stock X and Mutual Fund Y are given for sixteen days of a month.

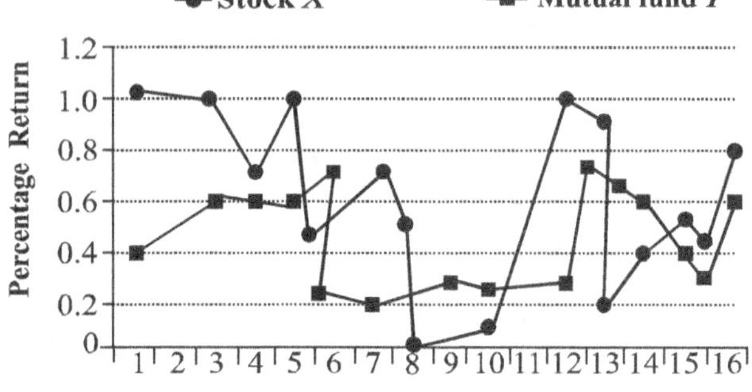

(a) Returns of Stock X are directly proportional to Mutual Fund Y.
(b) Average returns from Stock X and Mutual Fund Y are the same.
(c) Stock X is less volatile than Mutual Fund Y.
(d) Stock X is inversely proportional to Mutual Fund Y.
(e) Stock X is more volatile than Mutual Fund Y.

DIRECTIONS (Qs. 59-64) : *In the following chart, the inflation rate and the GNP figures are given for an island. Go through the following chart and then answer questions 63 to 68 based on that. Here, inflation is measured in % points and the values are shown on the left hand vertical axis. The GNP figures are in US $ (figures in millions) and the values are shown on the right hand vertical axis.*

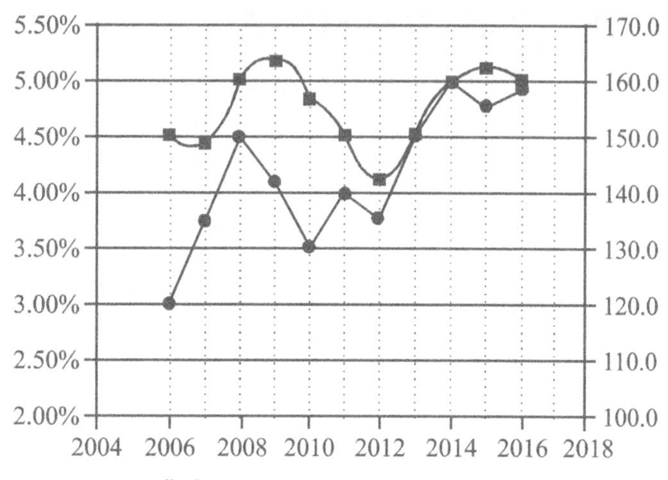

(In the above chart year 2006 refers to 2005-06. Other numbers are to be interpreted similarly.)

59. In which year the annual GNP growth rate was the maximum?
(a) 2006-07 (b) 2010-11 (c) 2012-13 (d) 2013-14

60. In which year, the GNP growth rate was the lowest?
(a) 2008-09   (b) 2009-2010
(c) 2011-12   (d) 2014-2015

61. In which of the following years, the inflation rate was higher than the growth rate in GNP?
(a) 2006-07 (b) 2010-11 (c) 2008-09 (d) 2013-14

62. In which of the following years, the average price level in the economy declined the most?
(a) 2007-08   (c) 2010-11
(c) 2015-16   (d) None of the above

63. In which of the following years, the direction of change in the inflation rate was exactly opposite that of the GNP?
(a) 2006-07 (b) 2007-08 (c) 2009-10 (d) 2012-2013

64. If it costs ₹ 250 to buy a basket of goods in 2006-07, then how much will it cost to buy the same basket of goods in 2010-11? Assume that the inflation rate captures the increase in the prices of this basket of goods.
(a) ₹ 302.46 (b) ₹ 280.35 (c) ₹ 319.50 (d) ₹ 328.87

DIRECTIONS (Qs. 65-69) : *Study the graph to answer these questions.*

The percentage profits of four leading airliners A, B, C and D for six years is shown in the line graph below.

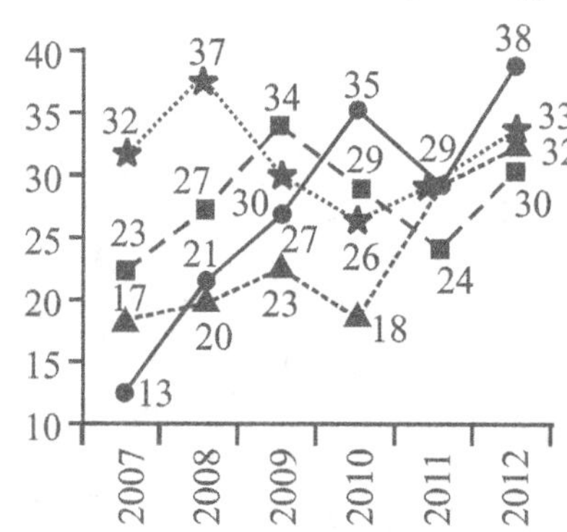

65. In 2007 company A invested ₹ 830 crore. Whereas C invested an amount which bears a ratio of 3 : 2 with that of A. The revenue generated by C in 2007 is
    (a) ₹ 1643.4 crore (b) ₹ 730.5 crore
    (c) ₹ 1456.7 crore (d) ₹ 647.5 crore

66. The total revenue generated by all the companies in 2010 is ₹ 3600 crore. The revenue of C is 30% of the total revenue. The revenue generated by A, B and D in the same year is $\dfrac{7}{25}, \dfrac{2}{5}$ and $\dfrac{8}{25}$ respectively of the remaining revenue. The maximum investment in that year is made by
    (a) A (b) C (c) B (d) D

67. In 2011, companies B and D invested a total amount of ₹ 946 crore. They earned their revenues by carrying passengers and goods. The profit earned by B through passenger traffic is 43% of part through goods traffic. The profit earned by D through goods traffic is 38% of the total profit earned by it and the remaining part of the profit is through passenger traffic. If the investment made by them are in the ratio 5 : 6, the actual profit of B through goods traffic is more/less than the passenger traffic of D by
    (a) less by ₹ 46.44 crore (b) more by ₹ 38.0808 crore
    (c) less by ₹ 33.9528 crore (d) more by ₹ 46.44 crore

68. In 2011, Airliner C invested an amount of ₹ 630 crore, $\dfrac{2}{3}$ of this amount was invested by B, A invested $\dfrac{3}{4}$ of the amount invested by B and D invested $1\dfrac{3}{5}$ of A in the same year. The revenue generated by A and D is more/less than that by B and C by
    (a) more by ₹ 276.99 crore (b) more by ₹ 48.09 crore
    (c) less by ₹ 48.09 crore (d) less by ₹ 276.99 crore

69. In 2012 investment made by A is ₹ 437 crore. B invests 20% more than A. C invests 20% less than B and D invests 20% more than C. If the profit earned by each is the average profit percent in 2012, who earns least revenue?
    (a) D (b) A (c) B (d) C

DIRECTIONS (Qs. 70-74): *Study the radar graph carefully and answer the questions that follow :*

[SBI PO 2013]

Number of students (in thousands) in two different universities in six different years Number of Students

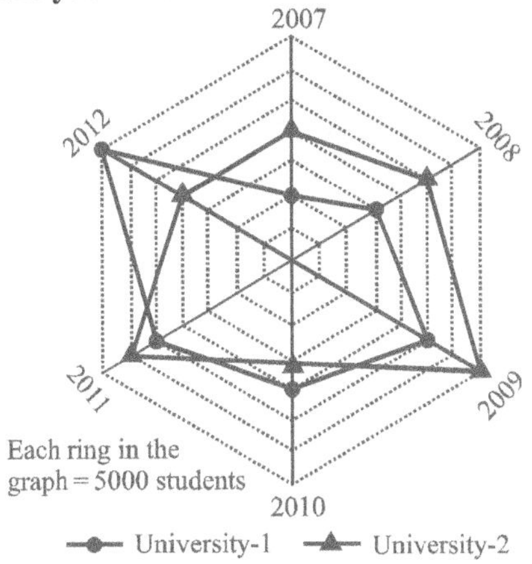

70. What was the difference between the number of students in university-1 in the year 2010 and the number of students in university-2 in the year 2012?
    (a) Zero (b) 5,000 (c) 15,000 (d) 10,000
    (e) 1,000

71. What is the sum of the number of students in university-1 in the year 2007 and the number of students in university-2 in the year 2011 together?
    (a) 50000 (b) 55000
    (c) 45000 (d) 57000
    (e) 40000

72. If 25% of the students in university-2 in the year 2010 were females, what was the number of male students in the university-2 in the same year?
    (a) 11250 (b) 12350
    (c) 12500 (d) 11500
    (e) 11750

73. What was the percent increase in the number of students in university-1 in the year 2011 as compared to the previous year?
    (a) 135 (b) 15 (c) 115 (d) 25
    (e) 35

74. In which year was the difference between the number of students in university-1 and the number of students in university-2 highest?
    (a) 2008 (b) 2009 (c) 2010 (d) 2011
    (e) 2012

DIRECTIONS (Qs. 75-79): *Read the following line graph and answer the following questions given below it –*

There are two car manufacturing companies (Company X and Company Y). The sale of cars by these two different companies is given in different years. **[SBI Po Prelim 2017]**

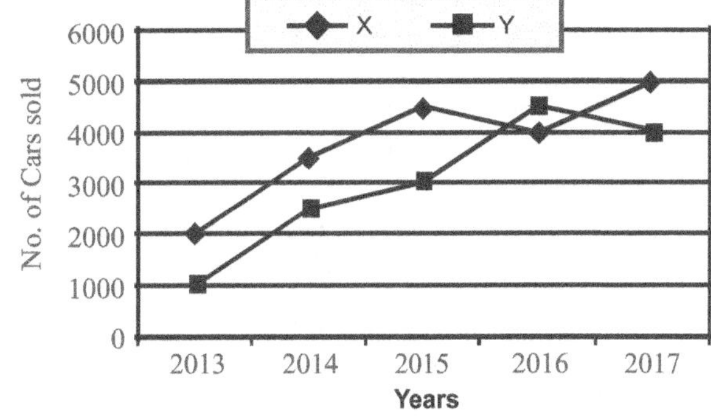

75. If the sale of company X in year 2018 is increased by 20% with respect to year 2017 and the sale of company Y in year 2018 with respect to year 2017 is decreased by 10% then find the total sale of the company X and Y together in year 2018?
    (a) 7200 (b) 9600 (c) 8400 (d) 5600
    (e) None of these

76. Find the ratio of the sales of company X in years 2013, 2015 and 2017 together to the total sale of company Y in year 2014 and 2016 together?
    (a) 23 : 14 (b) 14 : 23 (c) 11 : 29 (d) 29 : 11
    (e) None of these

77. Total cars sold by both companies in year 2014 are what percent more/less than the total cars sold by both companies in year 2015?
    (a) 28%   (b) 18%   (c) 25%   (d) 20%
    (e) None of these

78. Find the difference between the average number of cars sold by company X from 2013 to 2017 and the average number of cars sold by company Y from 2013 to 2017?
    (a) 750   (b) 900   (c) 800   (d) 850
    (e) None of these

79. Find the total number of cars sold by both companies from year 2014 to 2016?
    (a) 23000   (b) 21000   (c) 22500   (d) 21500
    (e) None of these

DIRECTIONS (Qs. 80-84): *Study the following Radar graph carefully and answer the questions given below.*

The number of students studying in different schools in a year (Number in Lac).

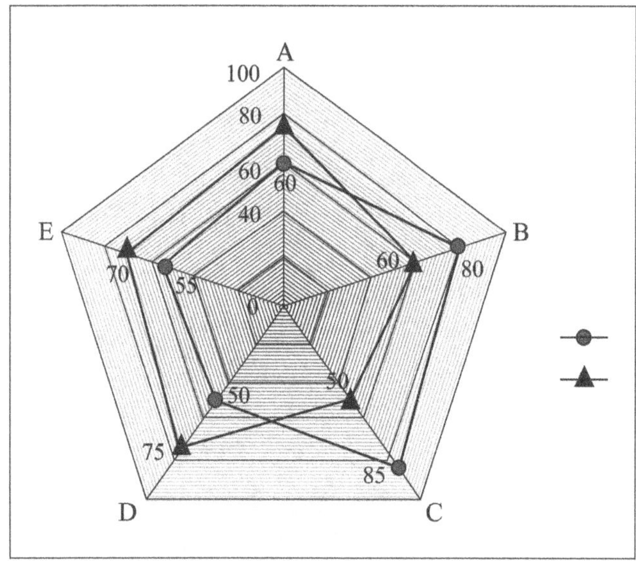

80. What is the average number of females in all the schools together?
    (a) 6600000   (b) 700000
    (c) 640000   (d) 6400000
    (e) None of these

81. What is the total number of students (males and females together) in school A and C together?
    (a) 2600000   (b) 2700000
    (c) 2800000   (d) 29000000
    (e) None of these

82. What is the respective ratio of the number of females from schools A and B together to the number of males in the schools C and E together?
    (a) 27 : 32   (b) 27 : 28   (c) 25 : 28   (d) 28 : 27
    (e) None of these

83. The number of males in school B is what per cent of the total number of students (males and females together) in school D?
    (a) 68%   (b) 62%   (c) 66%   (d) 64%
    (e) None of these

84. If the total number of males in school E increases by 50%, what would be the total number of students (males and females together) in that school?
    (a) 15052000   (b) 152500000
    (c) 15250000   (d) 150520000
    (e) None of these

DIRECTIONS (Qs. 85-89): *Study the graph carefully to answer the questions that follow.*

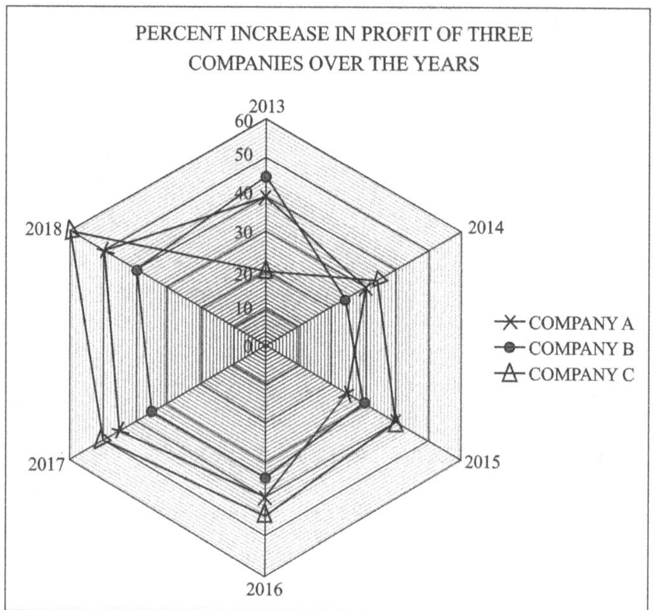

85. If profit for company B in 2014 is 4000 and expenditure in 2015 for company B is 100,000, then what is the total revenue in 2015 for B? Given that total revenue = expenditure + profit.
    (a) 105200   (b) 108400
    (c) 106560   (d) 111600
    (e) None of these

86. If profit in the year 2017 for company C is 6000 and profit of company A in 2015 is equal to profit of company C in 2017 then what is the profit of company A in 2015.
    (a) 3000   (b) 8000
    (c) 7000   (d) 4000
    (e) 5000

87. What is the average percentage increase in profit for company B over all the years?
    (a) 49%   (b) 32%   (c) 23%   (d) 38%
    (e) 35%

88. What was the approximate percent increase in profit of company A in the year 2016 from its previous year?
    (a) 60%   (b) 65%
    (c) 55%   (d) 50%
    (e) 70%

89. If profit earned by company B in 2016 is 54000 and by company C in 2016 is 87000 then what is the total profit earned by them in the year 2015?
    (a) 5,0000   (b) 70,000
    (c) 80,000   (d) 100,000
    (e) None of these

DIRECTIONS (Qs. 90-94): *Study the following graph carefully and answer the following question.*

The graph below represents the production (in tonnes) and sales (in tonnes) of a company M from 2013-2018

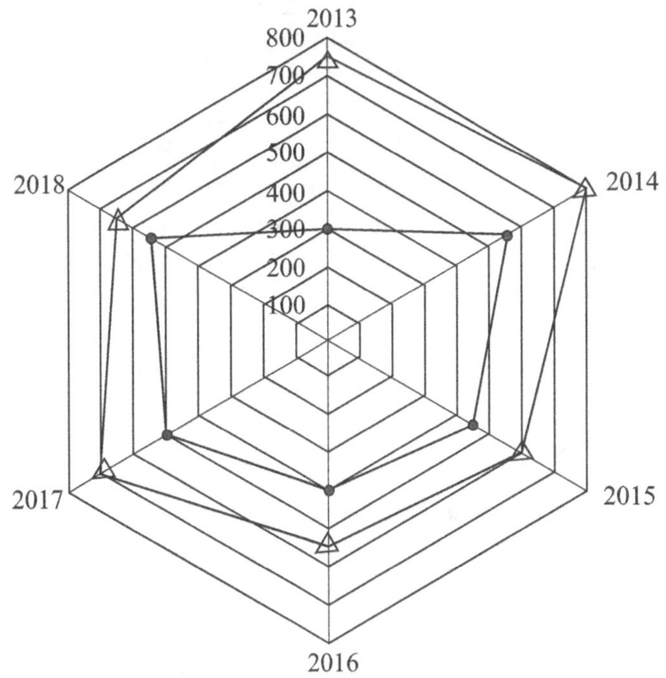

90. If the production of company M and another company N is in the ratio 14 : 13 in year 2017 then production of company N in 2017 is what percent more or less than production of company M in 2013.

 (a) $13\frac{1}{3}\%$ Less

 (b) $33\frac{1}{3}\%$ More

 (c) $66\frac{2}{3}\%$ Less

 (d) $16\frac{2}{3}\%$ Less

 (e) None of these

91. If the production of company M in 2019 is 120% of its production in 2018 then what is the ratio of sales of company M in 2013 to the production of company M in 2019.
 (a) 7/9 (b) 13/20 (c) 20/13 (d) 5/13
 (e) 7/13

92. If production cost is ₹1,500 per tonne and sale is at the rate of ₹2,800 per tonne over all years then what is the ratio of profit or loss of company M in 2016 to the profit or loss in year 2017. (Profit = Income through sales – Production cost)
 (a) 59/70
 (b) 20/23
 (c) 53/94
 (d) 27/38
 (e) None of these

93. If production cost in the year 2016 is 150 per tonne and production cost increases by 10% every year after 2016 then what is the average production cost of company M over all years after the year 2016?
 (a) 12,20,239
 (b) 1,16,737.5
 (c) 2,22,467
 (d) 1,33,647
 (e) None of these

94. If 35% of the production of company M in 2013 is added to the sale of company M in 2015 then the total sale of company M in 2015 is what percent of the total sale of company M over all the years now? (approximately)
 (a) 14% (b) 18%
 (c) 35% (d) 28%
 (e) 24%

DIRECTIONS (Qs. 95-99) : *The graph given here shows the percentage of literates in three different town in three years 2007, 2012 and 2017.*

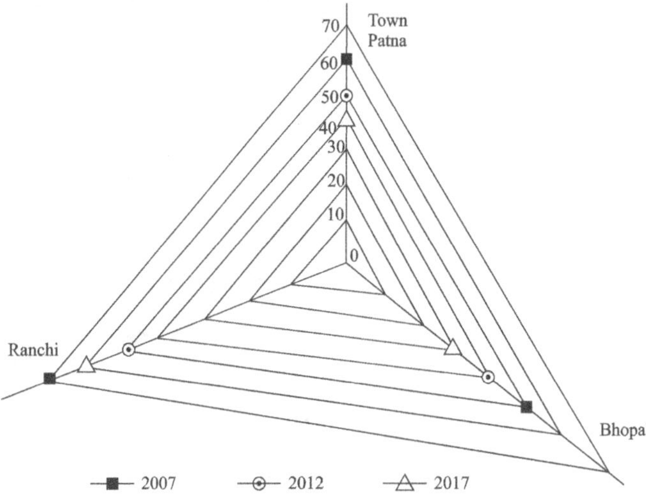

95. If population of Patna in 2007, 2012 and 2017 is in ratio 2 : 3 : 4 and average of literate in given three years be 42300. Then find the population of Patna in 2007.
 (a) 64000
 (b) 38000
 (c) 27000
 (d) 54000
 (e) None of these

96. Sum of literate from Ranchi in 2007 and 2012 is 45900 and sum of literates in 2012 and 2017 is 60300. If sum of literates from Ranchi in all the given years is 74700, then find population of Ranchi in 2012.
 (a) 63000
 (b) 31500
 (c) 44800
 (d) 28800
 (e) None of these

97. Population of Bhopal continuously decreases from 2007 to 2017 and it decreases by the same number in 2017 from 2012 as it decreased in 2012 from 2007. If Illiterates in Bhopal in 2012 and 2017 are same, then population of Bhopal in 2017 is what percent less than population of Bhopal in 2007.
 (a) 25%
 (b) 40%
 (c) 50%
 (d) 30%
 (e) None of these

98. If total population of three cities in year 2007 was 24000. And the population of three cities continuously increases by 5% in every next five years. The ratio of population of three cities Patna, Bhopal and Ranchi are 1 : 2 : 3 respectively in year 2017. Then find the average literates population of three cities in year 2017
 (a) 8820
 (b) 4116
 (c) 4611
 (d) 8280
 (e) None of these

99. Population of Ranchi in 2012 was 6000. Out of Literate population 40% are females. Then find the ratio of male literates population to illiterate population in 2012.
    (a) 3 : 4   (b) 4 : 5   (c) 3 : 5   (d) 2 : 5
    (e) None of these

DIRECTIONS (Qs. 100-104) : *Following Radar graph shows, the sales (in million) of smart phone and computer in the subsequent year 2012 to 2017. Based on the graph answer the question.*

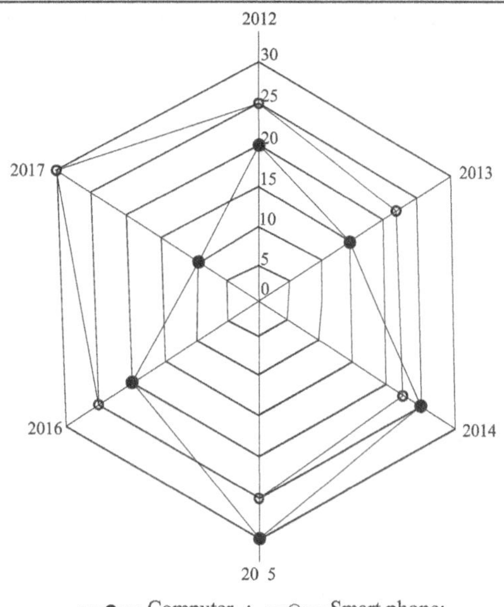

100. How many times do the sales of computer is less then the smartphone in the given years?
    (a) one   (b) two
    (c) three   (d) four
    (e) None of these

101. Find the ratio of the total number of smart phone sold to the total number of computers sold in all these years.
    (a) 5 : 6   (b) 6 : 5
    (c) 5 : 4   (d) 4 : 5
    (e) None of these

102. Which item and for which year shows the highest percentage increase in the sales from the previous year?
    (a) Computer, 2015   (b) Smart phone, 2015
    (c) Computer, 2014   (d) Smart phone, 2017
    (e) None of these

103. From the data series shown in the graph, how many years have shown the decrease in sales for both items in the same year?
    (a) one   (b) two   (c) three   (d) four
    (e) five

104. Which year shows the highest percentage decrease in the total sales of the two items?
    (a) 2013   (b) 2014
    (c) 2016   (d) 2017
    (e) None of these

DIRECTIONS (Qs.105-107) : *Line chart given below shows expense of five persons (in %) out of total income of two months. Income of persons is same in both months.*

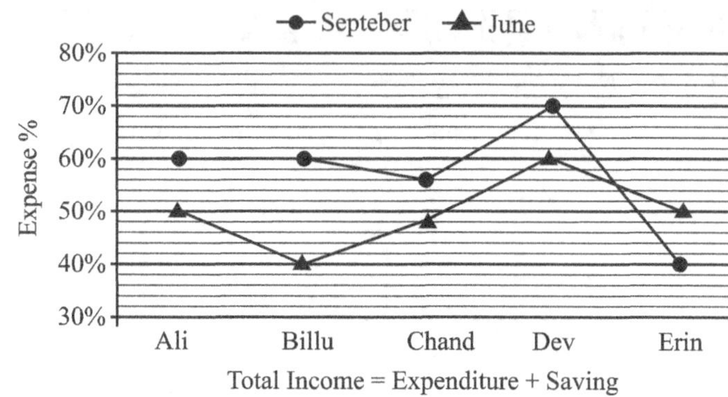

105. Find the difference between income of Dev and Erin?
    (I) Difference between expense of 'Dev' in September and saving of 'Erin' in June is ₹ 3200.
    (II) Difference between Saving of 'Dev' in June and Expense of 'Erin' in September is ₹ 8000.
    (a) Statement (I) alone is sufficient to answer the question but statement (II) alone is not sufficient to answer the question.
    (b) Statement (II) alone is sufficient to answer the question but statement (I) alone is not sufficient to answer the question.
    (c) Both the statements taken together are necessary to answer the questions, but neither of the statements alone is sufficient to answer the question.
    (d) Either statement (I) or statement (II) by itself is sufficient to answer the question.
    (e) Statements (I) and (II) taken together are not sufficient to answer the question.

106. Average saving of 'Chand' in both months is ₹ 19,200 while Ali's income is 20% more than Chand's income. Find expense of 'Ali' in the month of September
    (a) ₹ 9600   (b) ₹ 19200
    (c) ₹ 38400   (d) ₹ 24000
    (e) ₹ 28800

107. 'Billu' invested some amount of his saving in PPF account in September. Find the amount invested by 'Billu' in PPF account?
    (I) Amount invested by 'Billu' in PPF is 62.5% less than amount expend by 'Billu' in June while difference between amount expended by 'Billu' in September and June is ₹ 16,000.
    (II) Billu' invested 37.5% of his saving in PPF account while difference between saving of 'Billu' in September and June is ₹ 16,000.
    (a) Statement (I) alone is sufficient to answer the question but statement (II) alone is not sufficient to answer the question.
    (b) Statement (II) alone is sufficient to answer the question but statement (I) alone is not sufficient to answer the question.
    (c) Both the statements taken together are necessary to answer the question, but neither of the statements alone is sufficient to answer the question.
    (d) Either statement (I) or statement (II) by itself is sufficient to answer the question.
    (e) Statements (I) and (II) taken together are not sufficient to answer the question.

HINTS & SOLUTIONS

1. **(c)** At 39°C solubility of potassium nitrate = 0.48 kg/litre of water
   In other cases solubility is less than or equal to 0.4 kg/litre of water

2. **(c)** Solubility of potassium nitrate at 30°C = 0.38 kg /litre
   so in 10 litres of water it can be dissolved
   $= 10 \times 0.38 = 3.8 \text{kg} \cong 4$ (approx)

3. **(d)** Solubility of potassium chlorate at 30°C = 0.1
   Solubility of potassium chlorate at 80°C = 0.4
   % increase $= \dfrac{0.4 - 0.1}{0.1} \times 100 = 300\%$

4. **(d)** Solubility of Potassium chloride at 36°C = 0.4 kg/litre
   it means in 1 litre it can be dissolved = 0.4 kg
   In 100 litre it can be dissolved = 100 × 0.4 = 40 kg
   ∵ 0.07456 kg weighs 1 mole
   ∴ 40 kg weighs $\dfrac{1}{0.07456} \times 40 = 536$ (approx)

5. **(c)** It is clear from graph that greatest change in solubility between 15° and 25°C is of salt sodium chlorate and this change = 1.1 – 0.95 = 0.15 kg/litre

Sol. (6-10)
Profit = Revenue – variable cost – fixed cost
Fixed cost remains constant upto 34 units after which additional investment is to be done in fixed assets.
Maximum production = 50 units.

6. **(b)** For no loss
   Revenue = variable cost + Fixed cost and we can see from the graph that when production is equal to 10 units, Revenue = variable cost + Fixed cost and before this point there are losses and after this point, there are profits. Hence minimum number of units that must be produced to make sure that there are no losses is 10.
   At 10 units, Profit = 200 – 130 – 70 = 0.

7. **(a)** For 20 units,
   Profit = 400 – 280 – 70 = 50
   Below 20 units the profit will be less than 50. So a minimum of 20 units is to be manufactured.

8. **(b)**

Units	Revenue	Variable Cost	Fixed Cost	Profit	Profit / Unit
25	500	350	70	80	3.8
34	680	475	70	135	3.97
35	700	490	100	110	3.14
40	800	560	100	140	3.5

So, 34 units shall be manufactured to maximise profit/unit.

9. **(b)**

Units	Revenue	Variable Cost	Fixed Cost	Profit	Profit /Unit
45	900	630	100	170	3.77

So, from previous question it is clear that 34 units shall be manufactured.

10. **(b)** As per the question, Fixed Cost = 70 + 40 = 110 till 34 units.
    We know previously that there is no profit/loss at 10 units.

Units	Revenue	Variable Cost	Fixed Cost	Profit
15	300	210	110	–20
19	390	275	110	5
20	400	280	110	10

Hence, for no loss 19 units need to be manufactured.

11. **(c)** The graph shows that Rice, Onion, Egg and Chillies increase and Dal & Edible Oil decrease.

12. **(d)** Commodities showing price decline for 2 or more years consecutively – Rice, Dal, Chillies, Egg, Onion.

13. **(d)** The graph shows that only for Egg & onion, the price decline is followed by an increase in price, only once in the entire period.

14. **(b)** Let x be the investment, 65% of x = profit earned (8,12,500).
    x = 12,50,000
    then income = profit earned + investment = 20,62,500 (approx.).

15. **(c)** profit earned by Company A = $\dfrac{70}{100}$ x
    profit earned by Company B = $\dfrac{55}{100}$ x (where x is investments)
    required ratio = $\dfrac{170}{155} = 34 : 31$

16. **(b)** Let x be the sum invested by A
    So, $x + \dfrac{x}{2} = 27$, x = 18lakh.
    Profit : Company A = 75 % of 18lakh = 13.5lakh
    Company B = 80 % of 9 lakh = 7.2lakh

17. **(c)** 20 : (30 + 25) = 20 : 55 i.e. 4 : 11

18. **(c)** If we go through the line graph it is clearly evident that the difference is minimum in both School A and School B

19. **(a)** $\dfrac{(15000 + 20000 + 28000)}{3} = 21000 \approx 20800$

20. **(d)** $\dfrac{45}{20} \times 100 = 225\%$

21. **(c)**

22. **(d)** as we follow the graph we can clearly observe that personal profile is the highest.

23. **(b)**   24. **(b)**

25. **(c)**   26. **(d)**

Sol. (27-29)

27. (d) Since, 2009 is the year when the club is inaugurated.
So 2009 is rejected
Now, Check the % change

$$\% \text{ change in 2010} = \frac{15702 - 12564}{12564} \times 100$$
$$= 24.97\%$$

On similar way we observe that 2011 witnessed 9.34%, 2012 witnessed 31.46%, 2013 witnessed 31.22% and 2014 witnessed 15.43%.

28. (a) Lets find the ratio first

2009	6123 : 6441
2010	7652 : 8050
2011	9115 : 8054
2012	10702:11870
2013	14525 : 15094
2014	16416 : 17776

29. (c) Required % = $\dfrac{4}{1467} \times 100 = 0.27$

30. (a) Total number of candidates selected for company A
$= 80 + 40 + 100 + 330 + 280 + 200 = 1030$
Assistant Managers + Junior Office Administrators
$= (100 + 130 + 160) + (200 + 220 + 260)$
$= 390 + 680 = 1070$
Required ratio : 1030 : 1070 = 103 : 107

31. (b) Total candidates selected in company B
$= 10 + 30 + 160 + 360 + 250 + 220 = 1030$
$\therefore$ Required percentage = $\dfrac{250}{1030} \times 100 \approx 24\%$

32. (c) Company C
Assistant Manager + Advertisement Office Assistant
$= 130 + 290 = 420$
Junior Office Administrator + HR Officer
$= 260 + 50 = 310$
Required percentage = $\dfrac{420}{310} \times 100 \approx 135\%$

33. (d) Total number of HR officers selected
$= 80 + 10 + 50 = 140$
$\therefore$ Required percentage = $\dfrac{140}{1030} \times 100 \approx 14\%$

34. (e) Total candidates selected :
Company A $\Rightarrow$ 1030
Company C $\Rightarrow$ 1150
Required ratio = 1030 : 1150 = 103 : 115

35. (a) Increase in wheat production:
Year 2003 $\Rightarrow \dfrac{2900 \times 130}{100} = 3770$ quintals
Year 2004 $\Rightarrow \dfrac{2900 \times 140}{100} = 4060$ quintals
Year 2005 $\Rightarrow \dfrac{3000 \times 145}{100} = 4350$ quintals

Year 2007 $\Rightarrow \dfrac{2900 \times 140}{100} = 4060$ quintals
Total earlier production of wheat in Madhya Pradesh
$= 2400 + 3300 + 2900 + 2900 + 3000 + 2400 + 2800 = 19700$ quintals
New wheat production
$= 2400 + 3300 + 3510 + 4060 + 4350 + 2400 + 4060$
$= 24080$ quintals
Increase $= 24080 - 19700 = 4380$ quintals
Percentage increase $= \dfrac{4380}{19700} \times 100 = 22.23\% \approx 22\%$

36. (b) Required average production
$= \dfrac{3500 + 3000 + 2100}{3} = \dfrac{8600}{3} = 2866\dfrac{2}{3}$ quintals

37. (c) Average production of Bihar.
$= \dfrac{2800 + 2700 + 2800 + 3800 + 2100 + 3800 + 3600}{7}$
$= \dfrac{21600}{7} \Rightarrow 3086$

38. (e) Increase in wheat production in Bihar:
Year 2001 $\Rightarrow \dfrac{2800 \times 120}{100} = ₹ 3360$ quintals
Year 2002 $\Rightarrow \dfrac{2700 \times 125}{100} = ₹ 3375$ quintals
Year 2003 $\Rightarrow \dfrac{2800 \times 128}{100} = ₹ 3584$ quintals
Year 2004 $\Rightarrow \dfrac{3800 \times 135}{100} = ₹ 5130$ quintals
Total new production $= 3360 + 3375 + 3584 + 5130 + 2100 + 3800 + 3600 = 24949$ quintals
Total earlier production $= 2800 + 2700 + 2800 + 3800 + 2100 + 3800 + 3600 = 21600$ quintals
Increase $= 24949 - 21600 = 3349$ quintals
Average increase $= \dfrac{3349}{7}$ quintals
Required percentage increase
$= \dfrac{\dfrac{3349}{7}}{\dfrac{21600}{7}} \times 100 = 15.50\%$

39. (c) Wheat production by three states:
Year 2002 $\Rightarrow 3300 + 2900 + 2700 = 8900$ quintals
Year 2003 $\Rightarrow 2800 + 2900 + 3700 = 9400$ quintals
Year 2004 $\Rightarrow 2900 + 3100 + 3800 = 9800$ quintals
Total production in these years
$= 8900 + 9200 + 9800 = 28100$ quintals
Year 2005 $\Rightarrow 2100 + 3000 + 3500 = 8600$ quintals
Year 2006 $\Rightarrow 2400 + 2900 + 3800 = 9100$ quintals
Year 2007 $\Rightarrow 2900 + 3400 + 3600 = 9900$ quintals
Total production $= 8600 + 9100 + 9900 = 27600$ quintals
Required percentage $= \dfrac{28100 - 27600}{27600} \times 100 = 1.81\%$
$\approx 1.9\%$

40. (a) Total wheat production in the year 2007
$= (2900 + 3400 + 3600)$ quintals
$= 9900$ quintals

41. (b) Suppose x units are produced each year.
So, in the year 2006,
Total revenue $= 1200$
$\Rightarrow \quad 12 \times x = 1200$
$\Rightarrow \quad x = 100$
Profit $= 300$
$\therefore$ Cost price $= 1200 - 300 = 900$
$\therefore$ Cost per unit $= \dfrac{900}{100} = 9$
In the year 2005,
Total revenue $= 1400$
$\Rightarrow \quad 14 \times x = 1400$
$\qquad x = 100$
Profit $= 100$
$\therefore$ Cost price $= 1400 - 100 = 1300$
$\therefore$ Cost per unit $= \dfrac{1300}{100} = 13$
In the year 2009,
Total revenue $= 400$
$\Rightarrow \quad 8 \times x = 400 \quad \Rightarrow \quad x = 50$
Profit $= 150$
$\therefore$ Cost price $= 400 - 150 = 250$
$\therefore$ Cost per unit $= \dfrac{250}{50} = 5$
In the year 2011,
Total revenue $= 700$
$\Rightarrow \quad 14 \times x = 700 \quad \Rightarrow \quad x = 50$
Profit $= 200$
$\therefore$ Cost price $= 700 - 200 = 500$
$\therefore$ Cost per unit $= \dfrac{500}{50} = 10$

Thus, per unit cost is highest in the year 2005.

42. (b)

Years	Unit price	Revenue	Total units $= \dfrac{\text{Revenue}}{\text{Unit price}}$
2004	10	700	70
2005	14	1400	100
2006	12	1200	100
2007	12	900	75
2008	11	1100	100
2009	8	400	50
2010	10	200	20
2011	14	700	50
2012	10	600	60
2013	10	800	80
2014	15	900	60

Total $= 765$

$\therefore$ Average units $= \dfrac{765}{11} \simeq 70$ units

43. (c) Checking option (a),
Volatility per unit $= \dfrac{15-8}{\dfrac{126}{11}} = \dfrac{77}{126} = 0.611$
Checking of option (b),
Total cost $=$ Revenue $-$ Profit
$= (700 + 1400 + 1200 + 900 + 1100 + 400 + 200$
$+ 700 + 600 + 800 + 900) - (0 + 100 + 300 + 150 + 0$
$+ 150 + 100 + 200 + 0 + 400 + 300)$
$= 8900 - 1700 = 7200$
Average cost per unit $= \dfrac{7200}{11}$
Volatility cost per unit $= \dfrac{(1400-100)-(200-100)}{7200}$
$= \dfrac{1300-100}{7200} \times 11 = 1.833$
Checking option (c),
Average profit $= \dfrac{1700}{11}$
$\therefore$ Profit volatility $= \dfrac{400-0}{\dfrac{1700}{11}} = \dfrac{44}{17} = 2.588$
Checking option (d),
Average revenue $= \dfrac{8900}{11}$
$\therefore$ Revenue volatility $= \dfrac{1400-200}{\dfrac{8900}{11}}$
$= \dfrac{132}{89} = 1.483$
$\therefore$ Total profit has highest volatility.

44. (c)

Year	New revenue	Total cost = Old revenue – Profit
2004	80% of 700 – 560	700
2005	80% of 1400 = 1120	1300
2006	80% of 1200 = 960	900
2007	80% of 900 = 720	750
2008	80% of 1100 = 880	1100
2009	400	120% of 250 = 300
2010	200	120% of 100 = 120
2011	700	120% of 500 = 600
2012	600	120% of 600 = 720
2013	800	120% of 400 = 480
2014	900	120% of 600 = 720

In a year when total cost is more than new revenue then in that year there is loss.
These years are 2004, 2005, 2007, 2008 and 2012
So, there are total 5 yr.

45. (b) Total decrease in revenues
= 20% of (700 + 1400 + 1200 + 900 + 1100) = 1060
Total increase in cost
= 20% of (250 + 100 + 500 + 600 + 400 + 600) = 490
Decrease in cumulative profit
= Total decrease in revenues + Total increase in cost
= 1060 + 490 = ₹1550

46. (b) 1994 E = 12 L
% P = (I – E) × 100 / E
$$50 = (I - 12) \times \frac{100}{12}$$
I = 6 + 12 = 18 L
1995 E = 14L
$$60 = (I - 14) \times \frac{100}{14}$$
I = 22.4L
Total = 18 + 22.4 = 40.4L

47. (a) A : B = 40:50
$$45 = (I - 40) \times \frac{100}{40} \qquad \ldots (A)$$
I = 58L
$$50 = (I - 50) \times \frac{100}{50}$$
I = 75L $\ldots (B)$
A:B = 58:75

48. (d) Over all % is not known

49. (d) Income ⇒ 1992:1993 = 3:4 = 30:40
$$45 = (30 - E) \times \frac{100}{E}$$
$$\frac{45E}{100} = 30 - E$$
$$\frac{9E}{20} = 30 - E$$
9E = 600 – 20E
29E = 600
$$E = \frac{600}{29} \ldots\ldots\ldots\ldots 2012$$
$$50 = (40 - E) \times \frac{100}{E}$$
$$\frac{50E}{100} = 40 - E$$
E = 2(40 – E)
E = 80 – 2E
3E = 80
$$E = \frac{80}{3}$$
Ratio = (600/29) / (80/3) = 600*3 / 29*80
= 1800/2320 = 180/232 = 45/58

50. (c) For A
$$40 = (I - E) \times \frac{100}{E}$$
40E = (I – E)100
2E = 5I – 5E

5I = 7E
$$I = \frac{7E}{5}$$
For B
$$50 = (116\text{-}I - E) \times \frac{100}{E}$$
E = 2(116 - I - E)
E = 232 -2I - 2E
2I = 232 - 3E
$$I = \frac{232 - 3E}{2}$$
$$7/5E = \frac{-232 - 3E}{2}$$
14E = 1160 - 15E
29E = 1160
$$E = \frac{1160}{29} = 40$$
2E = 80

51. (d) Let the amounts invested in 2002 in Companies P and Q be ₹ 8x and ₹ 9x respectively.
Then interest received after one year from Company
$$P = ₹ (6\% \text{ of } 8x) = ₹ \left(\frac{48}{100}x\right)$$
and the interest received after one year from Company
$$P = ₹ (4\% \text{ of } 9x) = \left(\frac{36}{100}x\right).$$
$$\therefore \quad \text{Required ratio} = \left[\frac{\left(\frac{48}{100}x\right)}{\left(\frac{36}{100}x\right)}\right] = \frac{4}{3}.$$

52. (e) Let ₹ x lakhs be invested in Company P in 2000, then amount invested in Company Q in 2000 = ₹ (30 – x) lakhs.
Total interest received from the two Companies after one year
$$= ₹ [(7.5\% \text{ of } x) + \{9\% \text{ of } (30 - x)\}] \text{ lakhs}$$
$$= ₹ \left[2.7 - \left(\frac{1.5x}{100}\right)\right] \text{ lakhs}$$
$$\therefore \quad \left[2.7 - \left(\frac{1.5x}{100}\right)\right] = 2.43 \Rightarrow x = 18.$$
i.e. amount invested in Company P = ₹ 18 lakhs.

53. (d) Difference = ₹ [(10% of 4.75) – (8% of 4.75] lakhs = ₹ (2% of 4.75)lakhs = ₹ 0.095 lakhs = ₹ 9500.

54. (c) Amount received from Company P after one year (*i.e.* in 1999) on investing ₹ 12 lakhs in 1998 = ₹ [12 + (8% of 12)] lakhs = ₹ 12.96 lakhs.
Amount received from company P after one year on investing ₹ 12.96 lakh in the year 1999 = ₹[12.96 + (10% of 12.96)] lakh = ₹14.256
Appreciation received on investment during the period of two years = (14.256 – 12) lakhs = ₹ 2.256 lakhs

55. (b) Amount received from Company Q after one year on the investment of ₹ 5 lakhs in the year 1996

= ₹ [5 + (6.5% of 5)] lakhs = ₹ 5.325 lakhs.
Amount received from Company P after one year on investment of ₹ 5.325 lakhs in the year 1997 = ₹ [5.325 + (9% of 5.325)] lakhs = ₹ 5.80425 lakhs = ₹ 580425.

56. (d) The cumulative production goes on increasing and therefore a negative slope (as shown in the given graph between the years 2016 and 2017) is not possible.

57. (e) In the graph, y-axis is horizontal and x-axis is vertical (opposite of convention). The graph cuts y-axis at two places.
Hence, it will be quadratic equation for y. In the graph, at y = 0, the value of x is near to (–20)
Hence, required is $x = 2y^2 + 3y - 19$

58. (e)

59. (a) The GNP Growth for the given years : (2006-07) 120 to 135.(2010-11) 130 to 140. (2012-13) 135 to 150. (1013-14) 150 to 160. We see that maximum growth rate is in 2006-07 because growth is maximum and denominator (base) is least.

60. (b) The growth rate for the given years : (2008-09) 150 to 142.(2009-10) 142 to 130. (2011-12) 140 to 135. (2014-15) 160 to 155. So we see that in (2009-10) the growth reduces by 12 over a base of 142.

61. (c) In 2008-09, we see that inflation rate was 5.25% but GNP rate is negative, hence the answer is (c).

62. (d) Since inflation rate is always positive in all the years, prices increased in all the given years. It would be wrong to say that average price level declined in these years.

63. (a) Visual question. Simply check out on the graph and we say that it is the year 2006-07.

64. (a) The inflation rates for the year 2007-08, 2008-09, 2009-10, 2010-11 are 5%, 5.2%, 4.8% and 4.5% respectively. So increase 250 by 5%, 5.2%, 4.8% and 4.5% consecutively. Roughly, it is a 20% increase and hence we get a figure close to 300.

65. (a) Investment of C = $\dfrac{830 \times 3}{2}$ = ₹ 1245 crore

∴ Required revenue = $\dfrac{1245 \times 132}{100}$ = ₹ 1643.4 crore

66. (b) Revenue of C = $\dfrac{3600 \times 30}{100}$ = ₹ 1080 crore

∴ Remaining revenue = ₹ (3600 – 1080) crore
= ₹ 2520 croe

Revenue of A = $\dfrac{7}{25}$ × 2520 = ₹ 705.6 crore

Revenue of B = $\dfrac{2}{5}$ × 2520 = ₹ 1008 crore

Revenue of D = $\dfrac{8}{25}$ × 2520 = ₹ 806.4 crore

67. (c) Investment by company B = $\dfrac{5}{11}$ × 946 = ₹ 430 crore

Investment by company D = 946 – 430 = ₹ 516 crore

Total profit of company B = $\dfrac{430 \times 24}{100}$ = ₹ 103.2 crore

Total profit of company D = $\dfrac{516 \times 29}{100}$ = ₹ 149.64 crore

Profit of company B through goods traffic
= $\dfrac{103.2 \times 57}{100}$ = ₹ 58.824 crore

Profit of company D through passenger traffic
= $\dfrac{149.64 \times 62}{100}$ = ₹ 92.7768 crore

Difference = 92.7768 – 58.824 = ₹ 33.9528 crore

68. (d) Investment in 2011 :
C = ₹ 630 crore
B = ₹ 420 crore
A = $\dfrac{420 \times 3}{4}$ = ₹ 315 crore
D = $\dfrac{315 \times 8}{5}$ = ₹ 504 crore

Revenue generated by A and D
= $\dfrac{315 \times 129}{100} + \dfrac{504 \times 129}{100}$ = ₹ 1056.51 crore

Revenue generated by B = $\dfrac{420 \times 124}{100}$ = ₹ 520.8 crore

Revenue generated by C = $\dfrac{630 \times 129}{100}$ = ₹ 812.7 crore

Total = ₹ 1333.5 crore
Difference = 1333.5 – 1056.51 = ₹ 276.99 crore

69. (d) Investment by A = ₹ 437 crore
Investment by B = $\dfrac{437 \times 120}{100}$ = ₹ 524.4 crore

Investment by C = $\dfrac{524.4 \times 80}{100}$ = ₹ 419.52 crore

Investment by D = $\dfrac{419.52 \times 120}{100}$ = ₹ 503.424 crore

The profit % is the same for all.
∴ revenue would be least for the one whose investment is the least.

70. (a) Required difference = 20000 – 20000 = 0

71. (e) Required sum = 10000 + 30000 = 40000

72. (a) Required number of male students
= $\dfrac{15000 \times 75}{100}$ = 11250

73. (d) Total students :
University-1 (2011) ⇒ 25000
University-1 (2010) ⇒ 20000
Percentage increase = $\dfrac{5000}{20000}$ × 100 = 25

74. (e) Difference
Year 2008 ⇒ 10 thousand
Year 2009 ⇒ 10 thousand
Year 2010 ⇒ 5 thousand

Year 2011 $\Rightarrow$ 5 thousand
Year 2012 $\Rightarrow$ 15 thousand

75. (b) Required sale $= \dfrac{120}{100} \times 5000 + \dfrac{90}{100} \times 4000$

$\qquad = 6000 + 3600 = 9600$

76. (a) Required ratio
$\qquad = (2000 + 4500 + 5000) : (2500 + 4500)$
$\qquad = 11500 : 7000$
$\qquad = 115 : 70$
$\qquad = 23 : 14$

77. (d) Required % $= \dfrac{7500 - 6000}{7500} \times 100$

$\qquad = \dfrac{1500}{75} = 20\%$

78. (c) Required difference $= \dfrac{1}{5}(19000 - 15000)$

$\qquad = \dfrac{1}{5} \times 4000$

$\qquad = 800$

79. (e) Required no. of cars $= 6000 + 7500 + 8500$
$\qquad = 22000$

80. (a) Required No. $= \dfrac{75 + 60 + 50 + 75 + 70}{5} = \dfrac{330}{5}$ lakhs

$\qquad = 6600000$

81. (e) Required No. $(60 + 75 + 85 + 50) = 270$ lakhs

82. (b) Required Ratio $= (75 + 60) : (85 + 55)$
$\qquad = 27 : 28$

83. (d) Required % $= \dfrac{80}{50 + 75} \times 100 = 64\%$

84. (c) Required no. $= \left(55 \times \dfrac{150}{100}\right) + 70$

$\qquad = 152.5$ lakhs $= 15250000$

85. (a) Profit in 2015 $= 4000 \times \dfrac{130}{100} = 5200$

$\qquad$ Total revenue $= 100,000 + 5200 = 105200$

86. (d) Profit of company A in 2015 $= \dfrac{6000 \times 100}{150}$

$\qquad = 4000$

87. (e) Required average $= \dfrac{45 + 25 + 30 + 35 + 35 + 40}{6}$

$\qquad = \dfrac{210}{6} = 35\%$

88. (a) Required percentage $= \dfrac{40 - 25}{25} \times 100$

$\qquad = \dfrac{15}{25} \times 100 = 60\%$

89. (d) Profit earned by B in 2015 $= \dfrac{54000 \times 100}{135}$

$\qquad = 40,000$

Profit earned by C in 2015 $= \dfrac{87000 \times 100}{145}$

$\qquad = 60,000$

Total profit $= 100,000$

90. (a) Production of company N in 2017 $= \dfrac{700}{14} \times 13 = 650$

$\qquad$ Required percentage $= \dfrac{750 - 650}{750} \times 100 = \dfrac{100}{750} \times 100$

$\qquad = \dfrac{40}{3}\% = 13\dfrac{1}{3}\%$ less

91. (d) Production of company M in 2019 $= \dfrac{120}{100} \times 650 = 780$

$\qquad$ Required ratio $= \dfrac{300}{780} = \dfrac{5}{13}$

92. (a) Cost of production in 2016 $= 1500 \times 550 = ₹8,25,000$
$\qquad$ Total Income through sales $= 2800 \times 400 = ₹11,20,000$
$\qquad$ Profit in 2003 $= 11,20,000 - 8,25,000 = ₹2,95,000$
$\qquad$ Cost of production in 2017 $= ₹1500 \times 700$
$\qquad\qquad = ₹10,50,000$
$\qquad$ Total Income through sales $= ₹2800 \times 500$
$\qquad\qquad = ₹14,00,000$
$\qquad$ Profit in 2017 $= 3,50,000$

$\qquad$ Required ratio $= \dfrac{295}{350} = \dfrac{59}{70}$

93. (b) Total production cost in 2017 and 2018
$\qquad = 165 \times 700 + 181.5 \times 650 = 1,15,500 + 1,17,975$
$\qquad = 2,33,475$

$\qquad$ Required average $= \dfrac{2,33,475}{2} = 1,16,737.5$

94. (e) Total sale of company M in 2015

$\qquad = 450 + \dfrac{35}{100} \times 750 = 712.5$

$\qquad$ Required percentage

$\qquad = \dfrac{712.5}{300 + 550 + 450 + 400 + 500 + 550 + 262.5} \times 100$

$\qquad = \dfrac{712.5}{3012.5} \times 100 = 23.65\% \sim 24\%$

95. (b) C can't be the first part after the part given in bold as its connector 'but' doesn't correspond correctly with it; so, option (c) is eliminated. When we consider option (d) i.e. DBAC, we see that though D and B form a fair sequence; A and C fail to complete the sentence in a meaningful manner. So, option (d) is eliminated. Now, we are left with options (a), (b) and (e). A is in the same order in both options (a) and (b) so, we will ignore it and try to find the last or the penultimate part. By reading the sentence as per the sequences given in both the options, we can clearly find out that option (b) is making a meaningful sense. So, option (a) gets eliminated and option (b) with sequence BADC emerges as the correct answer.

96. (e) The parts of the sentence given in the question are in correct sequence.

97. (a) We will ignore part A as the first part after the part given in bold as none of the options starts with it. B can't be the last part as it ends with a comma; so, we can easily eliminate option (c) and (d) without even looking at their sequence. Now, we are left with option (a), (b) and (e). We will only try to find out the last or the second last part as A is in the same sequence in both of these options. When we read the sentence according to the sequence given in both options (a) and (b), we find that option (b) doesn't make a complete sense by ending with C; on the contrary, the sequence BACD in option (a) i.e. makes a complete sense, hence, it is the answer.

98. (c) After reading all the parts carefully, it is clear that part C should come ahead of the rest to make the sentence sound meaningful; thus, option (a) and (b) are eliminated as they start with D and B respectively. Now, we need to find the second part to follow C. A is the most appropriate part to follow C as it makes a correct continuation with C. So, option (d) gets eliminated. When we read the sentence according to the sequence given in option (c), the sentence becomes meaningful. Therefore option (c) i.e. CABD is the correct answer.

99. 10. (a); After reading all the parts carefully, we see that, part A follows the part given in bold most appropriately. Only one option starts with A; so, options (b), (c) and (d) are eliminated. Now, we have to choose either option (a) or (e) as the answer. When we read the sentence according to the sequence given in (a), the sentence becomes meaningful. Thus, option (a) i.e. ADBC is the answer.

100. (c) In the context of the sentence, 'prefers' will be followed by 'to' to make the sentence grammatically correct; so, part C will follow the part given in bold. So, options (a) and (b) get eliminated as they start with B. Further, part D makes a correct continuation with part C. Further, part B makes a correct continuation with part D and part A concludes the sentence meaningfully. So, the sequence CDBA in option (c) is the correct answer.

101. (d) The part given in bold ends with a comma so, we need to find the part which completes the part given in bold correctly. Considering all the parts, we find that only part B correctly matches with the comma so the first part will be B. So, option (b) and (c) are eliminated as they start with D and C respectively. Further, reading the sentence according to the sequence given in options (a) and (d), we find that only option (d) makes the sentence sound correct and logical thereby eliminating option (a). Thus, the correct answer is option (d) i.e. BDCA.

102. (a) In this sentence, all parts appear to logically follow the part given in bold. So, we will try to find the last part of the sentence. Reading all the parts carefully, we can easily pick that part A, B and C can't be the last part as they are incomplete in themselves. Moreover, part D clearly appears to be the last part. Now, we have only option (a) with sequence ending in D; and, the sentence according to this sequence is meaningful and logical. Hence the answer is option (a) BCAD.

103. (d) After reading all the parts carefully, we find C is the only logical follower of the part in boldface. Also, D and B are linked as a complementary pair. So, we can easily pick option (d) i.e. CDBA as the correct sequence.

104. (e) The parts of the sentence given in the question are in correct sequence.

105. (b) Let income of 'Dev' and 'Erin' is x and y respectively. We have to find the value of 'x – y'.

From (I)
$0.72x - 0.5y = 3200$
From (II)
$0.4x - 0.4y = 8000$
$$\Rightarrow x - y = \frac{8000}{0.4} = 20000$$

Hence, only (II) is sufficient to answer the question.

106. (e) Let Rs Chand's income is ₹ x
ATQ,
$$\frac{0.44x + 0.52x}{2} = 19200$$
$\Rightarrow\ x = 40,000$
Ali's income $= 1.2 \times 40,000 = ₹48,000$
Ali's expense in the month of September
$= \times 48000 = ₹28800$

107. (d) Let, income of Billu is ₹ x
From (I)
$0.6x - 0.4x = 16000$
$$\Rightarrow x = \frac{16000}{0.2} = 80,000$$
Amount invested by 'Billu' in PPF
$$= 80,000 \times \frac{40}{100} \times \frac{37.5}{100} = ₹12,000$$
From (II)
$0.6x - 0.4x = 16000$
$$\Rightarrow x = \frac{16000}{0.2} = 80,000$$
Amount invested by 'Billu' in PPF
$$= \frac{37.5}{100} \times \frac{40}{100} \times 80,000 = ₹12000$$

Hence, Either statement (I) or statement (II) by itself is sufficient to answer the question.

3

Pie chart or circular graph is a statistical graph which is divided into sectors or slices to illustrate numerical proportion. In a pie chart arc length of each sector (slice) represents the proportion of a different quantity.

Example:

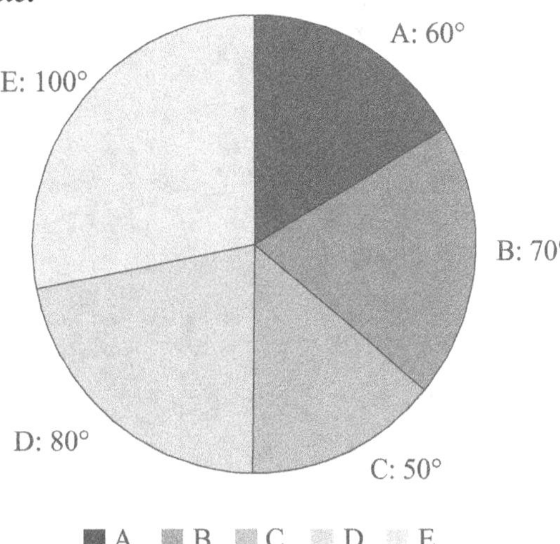

In this pie chart value of A is 60° and value of D is 80° then D is $\dfrac{80}{60}$ times to A

In a pie chart there are two medium to express the proportion: They are

(1) **BY ANGLE :** In this type of pie chart proportion is based on central angle of slice and sum of all angles is 360° (because of circle). If we have to find value of a slice then it will $\dfrac{\theta}{360} \times$ total value.

(2) **BY PERCENTAGE :** In this type of pie charts proportion is based on percentage of slice and sum of all values of slices is 100 (because %). If we have to find value of a slice then it will be $\dfrac{\%value}{100} \times$ total value.

Example:

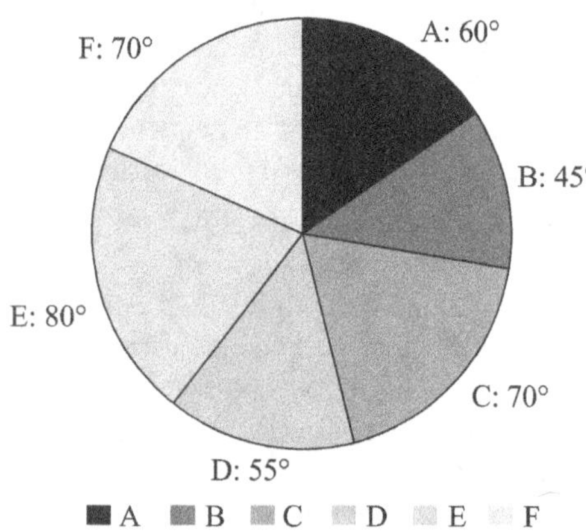

Q. If number of students in college A is 6000 then total number of students in all colleges = ?

Sol. We know total angle of all slices is 360° and angle of college A is 60° then, total value = $\dfrac{360}{60} \times 6000 = 36000$

Total number of students = 40000

Number of students in F is :

We know total value is 100% then value of F $= 40000 \times \dfrac{20}{100} = 8000$

Central angle of F $= 360 \times \dfrac{20}{100} = 72°$

EXERCISE

DIRECTIONS (Qs. 1-5): *Study the following pie- chart and answer the questions given below:*

[IBPS PO-2011]

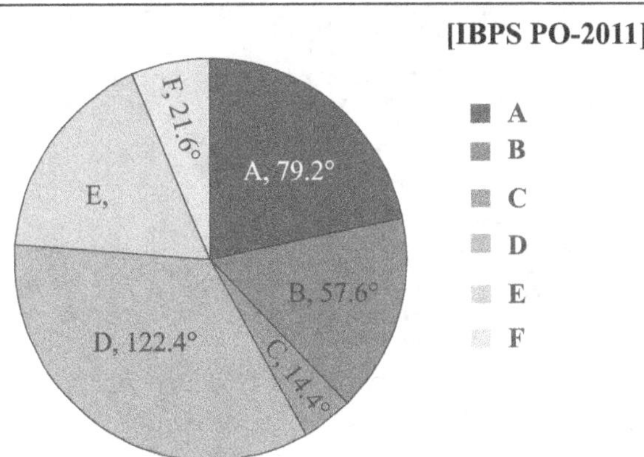

Preferences of students for six beverages A, B, C, D, E and F in terms of degrees of angle in the pie-chart

Total No. of students = 6800

1. What is the difference between the total numbers of students who prefer beverage A and C together and the total number of students who prefer beverages D and F together?
   (a) 959   (b) 955   (c) 952   (d) 954

2. What is the ratio of the number of students who prefer beverage F to the number of students who prefer beverage A?
   (a) 3 : 11   (b) 3 : 13   (c) 6 : 11   (d) 5 : 11

3. The number of students who prefer beverage E and F together is what percent of the total number of students?
   (a) 18   (b) 14   (c) 26   (d) 24

4. The number of students who prefer beverage C is approximately what percent of the number of students who prefer beverage D?
   (a) 7   (b) 12   (c) 18   (d) 22

5. How many students prefer beverage B and Beverage E together?
   (a) 2312   (b) 2313   (c) 2315   (d) 2318

DIRECTIONS (Qs. 6-10): *Study the following pie – chart carefully and answer the questions given below.*

[IBPS PO 2011]

Cost estimated by a family in renovation of their house

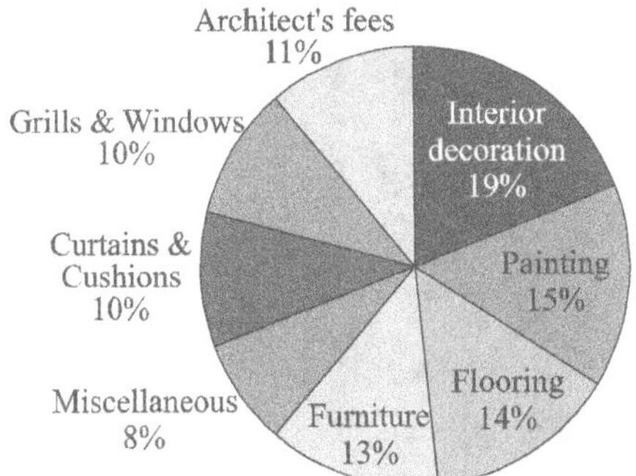

Cost estimated by a family in renovation of their house
Total Estimated cost is ₹1,20,000

6. What is the difference in the amount estimated by the family on interior decoration and that on architect's fees?
   (a) ₹ 10,000   (b) ₹ 9,500
   (c) ₹ 7,200   (d) None of these

7. During the process of renovation, the family actually incurred miscellaneous expenditure of ₹10,200. The percentage of the miscellaneous of the total estimated cost is?
   (a) 9.5%   (b) 9%   (c) 8.5%   (d) 10.55%

8. Other than getting the discount of 12% on the estimated cost of furniture and the actual miscellaneous expenditure being ₹ 10,200 instead of the estimated one, the family's estimated cost is correct. What is the total amount spent by the family in renovating its house?
   (a) ₹ 1,16,728   (b) ₹ 1,15,926
   (c) ₹ 1,19,500   (d) None of these

9. What is the cost estimated by the family on painting and flooring together?
   (a) ₹ 36,500   (b) ₹ 34,800
   (c) ₹ 36,000   (d) ₹ 34,500

10. The family gets a discount on furniture and pays 12% less than the estimated cost on furniture. what is the amount spent on furniture?
    (a) 13,200   (b) 14,526
    (c) 13,526   (d) 13,728

DIRECTIONS (Qs. 11-18) : *These questions are to be answered on the basis of the pie chart given below showing how a person's monthly salary is distributed over different expense heads.*

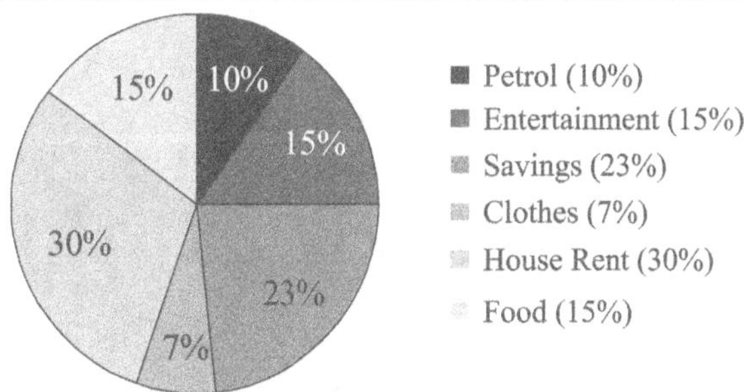

11. For a person, whose monthly salary is ₹ 6,000 p.m. how many items are there on which he has to spend more than ₹ 1,000 p.m. ?
    (a) 1   (b) 2   (c) 3   (d) 4

12. For the same person, an expenditure of ₹1,800 p.m. takes place on :
    (a) Petrol   (b) House Rent
    (c) Food   (d) Clothes

13. The annual savings for such a person will be approximately:
    (a) ₹ 5,000   (b) ₹ 10,000
    (c) ₹ 15,000   (d) ₹ 16,560

14. The monthly salary for a person who follows the same expense pattern, but has a petrol expense of ₹ 500 p.m is
    (a) ₹ 2,500
    (b) ₹ 3,000
    (c) ₹ 5,000
    (d) ₹ 6,500

15. The percentage of money spent on clothes and savings is equal to which other single item of expense?
    (a) Petrol
    (b) House Rent
    (c) Food
    (d) Entertainment

16. The angle made at the center of the pie chart by the sector representing the expense on petrol is :
    (a) 30°
    (b) 45°
    (c) 36°
    (d) 90°

17. Given that the pie chart is for a salary of ₹ 6,000 p.m., what would be the ratio of the radius of this pie chart to a pie chart for a person with a salary of ₹1,500 p.m. ?
    (a) 2 : 1
    (b) 1 : 2
    (c) $1 : \sqrt{2}$
    (d) $2\sqrt{2} : 1$

18. For a person with a salary of ₹ 1,500 p.m., the annual savings would be :
    (a) ₹ 4,140
    (b) ₹ 2,500
    (c) ₹ 2,100
    (d) ₹ 4,000

DIRECTIONS (Qs. 19-23): *Study the diagram given below and answer these questions.*

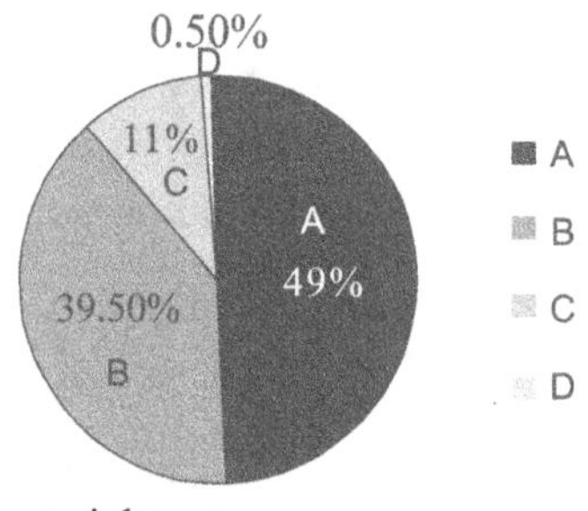

A = Raw material cost
B = Packing material cost
C = Fixed manufacturing expenses
D = Labour cost

19. If the total value in rupees of all the sectors is ₹ 128.3 lakh, then calculate the value of D in rupees,
    (a) ₹ 0.06 lakh
    (b) ₹ 0.6 lakh
    (c) ₹ 0.006 lakh
    (d) ₹ 6.0 lakh

20. If the total cost of production doubles in a period of one year, then what will be the value of D ?
    (a) ₹ 10.3 lakh
    (b) ₹ 1.3 lakh
    (c) ₹ 570 lakh
    (d) ₹ 50.7 lakh

21. If packing cost increased by 2% how much amount will be involved in packing cost ?
    (a) ₹ 25.6 lakh
    (b) ₹ 52.5 lakh
    (c) ₹ 52 lakh
    (d) ₹ 50 lakh

22. Packing and raw material costs together represent ₹……… of the total cost of production.
    (a) ₹ 86 lakh
    (b) ₹ 113 lakh
    (c) ₹ 115 lakh
    (d) ₹ 111 lakh

23. If the total cost of labour increases from 0.6 lakh to 2.4 lakh, then what percentage of increase does it represent ?
    (a) 75%
    (b) 25%
    (c) 200%
    (d) 300%

DIRECTIONS (Qs. 24-26): *These questions are based on the pie charts given below.*

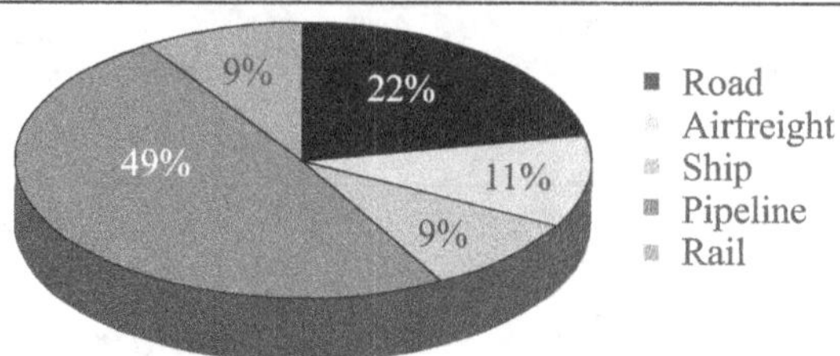

Chart 1: Volume transported

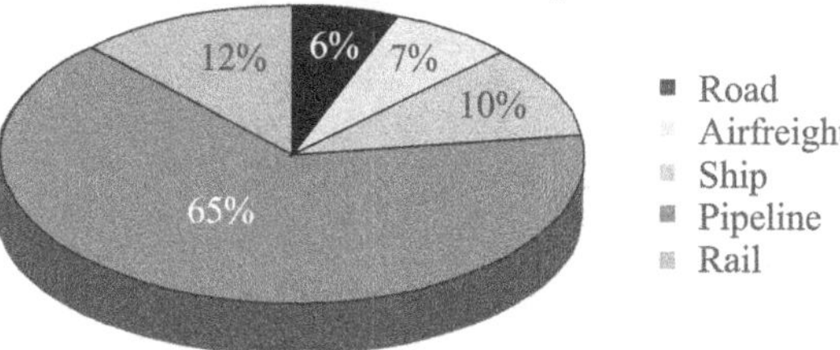

Chart 2: Cost of Transportation

Chart 1 shows the distribution of twelve million tonnes of crude oil transported through different modes over a specific period of time. Chart 2 shows the distribution of the cost of transporting crude oil. The total cost was ₹ 30 million.

24. The cost in rupees per tonne of oil moved by rail and road happens to be roughly
    (a) 3
    (b) 1.5
    (c) 4.5
    (d) 8

25. From the charts given, it appears that the cheapest mode of transport is
    (a) Road
    (b) Rail
    (c) Pipeline
    (d) Ship

26. If the costs per tonne of transport by ship, air and road are represented by P, Q and R respectively, which of the following is true?
    (a) R > Q > P
    (b) P > R > Q
    (c) P > Q > R
    (d) R > P > Q

DIRECTIONS (Qs. 27-31) : *Study the following pie-charts carefully and answer the questions given below :*

Disciplinewise Break up of Number of candidates appeared in Interview and Disciplinewise Break up of Number of Candidates selected by an organisation

Disciplinewise Break up of Number of candidates appeared in Interview by the organisation

Total Number of candidates Appeared In the Interview = 25780

Disciplinewise Break up of Number of candidates selected after Interview by the organisation

Total Number of candidates selected After Interview = 7390

27. What was the ratio between the number of candidates appeared in interview from other disciplines and number of candidates selected from Engineering discipline respectively (round off to the nearest integer) ?
 (a) 3609 : 813 (b) 3094 : 813
 (c) 3094 : 1035 (d) 4 125: 1035
 (e) 3981: 767

28. The total number of candidates appeared in interview from Management and other disciplines was what percent of number of candidates appeared from Engineering discipline?
 (a) 50 (b) 150
 (c) 200 (d) Cannot be determined
 (e) None of these

29. **Approximately** what was the difference between the number of candidates selected from Agriculture discipline and number of candidates selected from Engineering discipline?
 (a) 517 (b) 665
 (c) 346 (d) 813
 (e) 296

30. For which discipline was the difference in number of candidates selected to number of candidates appeared in interview the maximum ?
 (a) Management (b) Engineering
 (c) Science (d) Agriculture
 (e) None of these

31. **Approximately** what was the total number of candidates selected from Commerce and Agriculture discipline together?
 (a) 1700 (b) 1800 (c) 2217 (d) 1996
 (e) 1550

DIRECTIONS (Qs. 32-36): *In the following pie-charts, the percentage wise distribution of candidates who have applied for different subjects in a college and that of selected candidates has been given. Read the following pie-charts to answer the questions.*

Percentage of Candidates
Applied Number of candidates = 88000

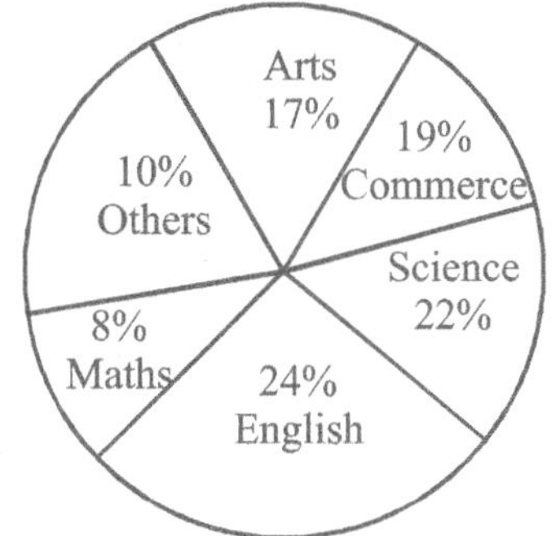

Percentage of Candidates Qualified
Number of candidates = 14400

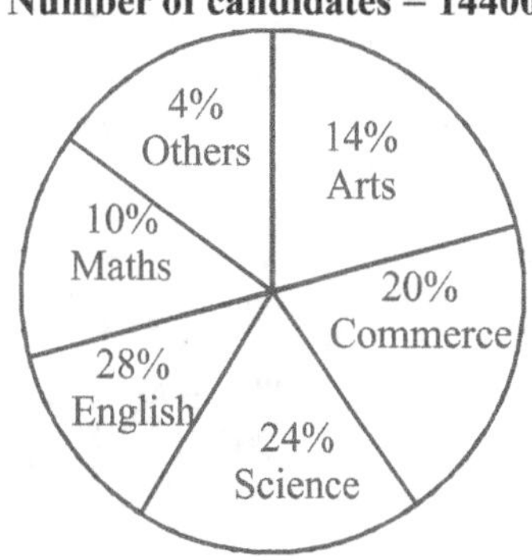

32. What is the difference between the total number of candidates who got selected in Science and the number of candidates who applied for the same ?
 (a) 15904 (b) 14904 (c) 15940 (d) 16940
 (e) None of these

33. What is the sum of the total number of candidates who applied for Arts and the number of candidates who got selected in Maths and English both ?
 (a) 19432 (b) 20432 (c) 20342 (d) 19432
 (e) None of these

34. What is the ratio between the number of candidates who qualified in Arts and commerce together and the number of candidates who qualified in English and Science ?
 (a) 17 : 25 (b) 17 : 29 (c) 17 : 26 (d) 29 : 17
 (e) None of these

35. What percent of candidates qualified in English of the total candidates applied for the same ?
 (a) 15 (b) 16 (c) 17 (d) 19
 (e) 22

36. Find the average number of candidates who got selected for English, Science and Arts.
 (a) 3618 (b) 3682 (c) 3628 (d) 3268
 (e) 3168

DIRECTIONS (Qs. 37-41): *Refer to Pie Charts and answer the following questions:*

Given Data: Total number of cars (both MUV & SUV) distributed by 8 dealers in 2016 = 56000

Total number of SUV cars distributed by 8 dealers in 2016 = 32000

Distribution of Cars   **Distribution of Cars**
(MUV & SUV)   **SUV**

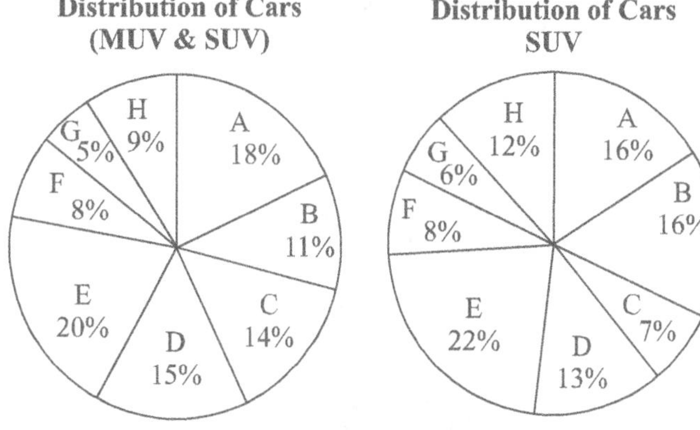

37. Total number of MUV cars sold by dealers C and H together is by what % less than total number of cars(both SUV and MUV) sold by stores F and H together?

(a) 27.58%   (b) 25.58%   (c) 26.58%   (d) 28.57%
(e) None of these

38. The number of cars(MUV and SUV) sold by store D is by what % more than total number of SUV cars distributed by dealers C, F and G together?
(a) 50%   (b) 25%   (c) 75%   (d) 605
(e) None of these

39. What is the average number of MUV cars delivered by dealers A, D, E, F and H together?
(a) 2892   (b) 3354
(c) 3634   (d)   3296
(e) None of these

40. What is the respective ratio between total no of SUV cars distributed by dealers A and B together and total number of cars (MUV and SUV) delivered by stores C and F together?
(a) 64:77   (b) 64:79   (c) 54:77   (d) 64:73
(e) None of these

41. If the number of cars distributed by stores A, D and E increased by 10%, 35% and 15% respectively from 2016-2017, what was the total number of MUV cars distributed by these three dealers in 2017?
(a) 14964   (b) 15964   (c) 13964   (d) 12964
(e) None of these

DIRECTIONS (Qs. 42-45): *These questions are based on the following pie-charts.*

Total Investment Funds = ₹11 crore 5 lakh.

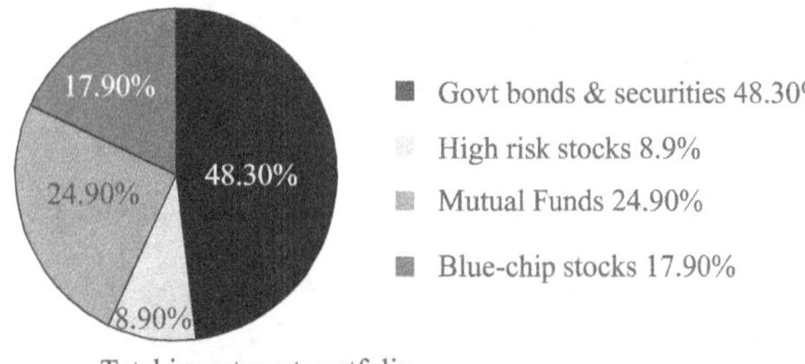

Total investment portfolio

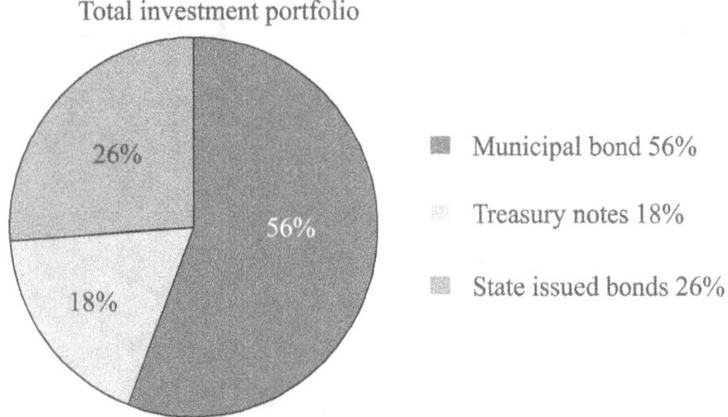

Government Bonds & securities

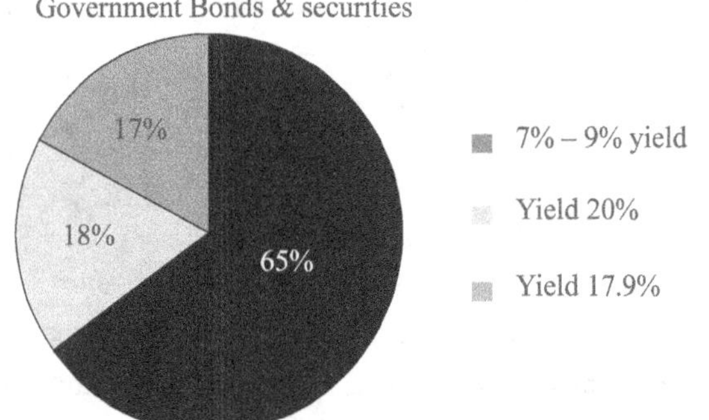

42. According to these graphs, approximately how much money from the investment portfolio was invested in high-risk stocks?
(a) ₹ 98,00,000   (b) ₹ 10,10,000
(c) ₹ 9,00,000   (d) None of these

43. Approximately how much money belonging to the investment portfolio was invested in State-issued bonds?
(a) ₹ 4,50,00,000
(b) ₹ 3, 39, 50,000
(c) ₹ 2,87,00,000
(d) None of these

44. Which of the following earned the least amount of money for the investment portfolio?
(a) Government bonds and securities
(b) State-issued bonds
(c) Municipal bonds
(d) None of the above

45. Which of the following was the greatest?
(a) The amount of money invested in high-risk stocks
(b) The amount of money invested in State-issued bonds
(c) The amount of money invested in municipal bonds which yielded between 7% and 9%
(d) The amount of money invested in municipal bonds which yielded over 9%

DIRECTIONS (Qs. 46-49): *Answer the questions based on the information provided in the pie-charts given below:*

Consider the information provided in the pie-charts given below relating to India's foreign trade in 2016-17 and the first eight months of 2017-18. Total trade with a region is defined as the sum of exports and imports from that region. Trade deficit is defined as the excess of imports over exports. Trade deficit may be negative.

A. U.S.A.   B. Germany
C. Other EU   D. U.K.
E. Japan   F. Russia
G. Other East Europe   H. OPEC
I. Asia   J. Other LDCs
K. Others

SOURCES OF IMPORTS
2016-17
Imports into India
$ 40,779 million

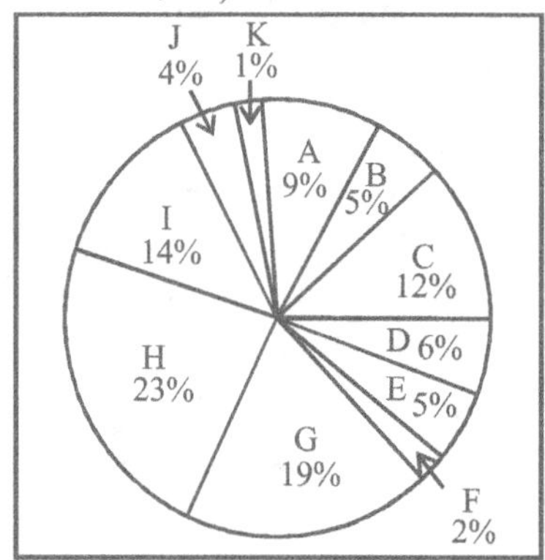

2017-18
Imports into India (April-Nov)
$ 28,126 million

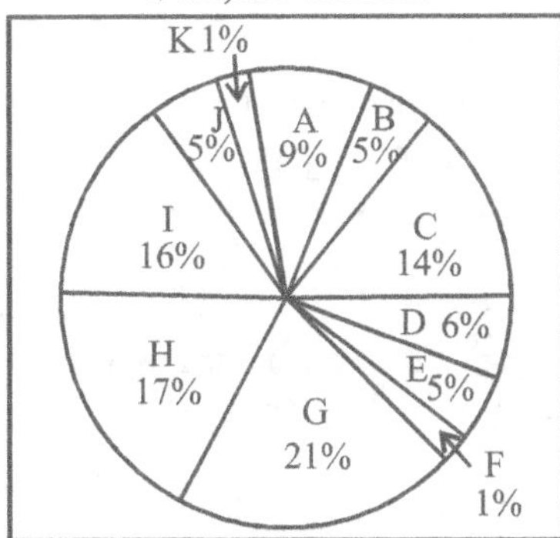

DESTINATION OF EXPORTS
2016-17
Exports from India
$ 33,979 million

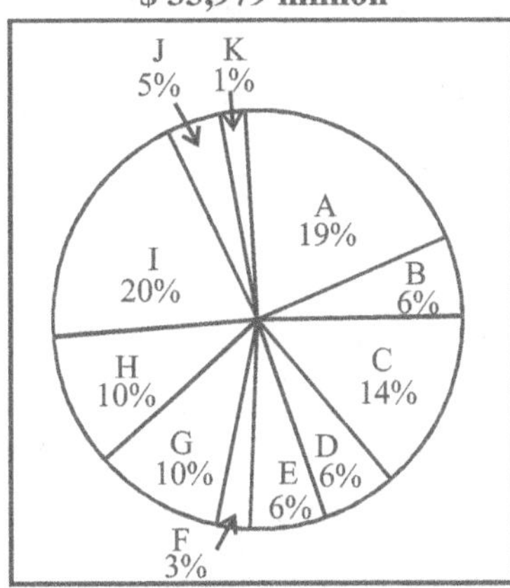

2017-18
Exports from India (April-Nov)
$ 21,436 million

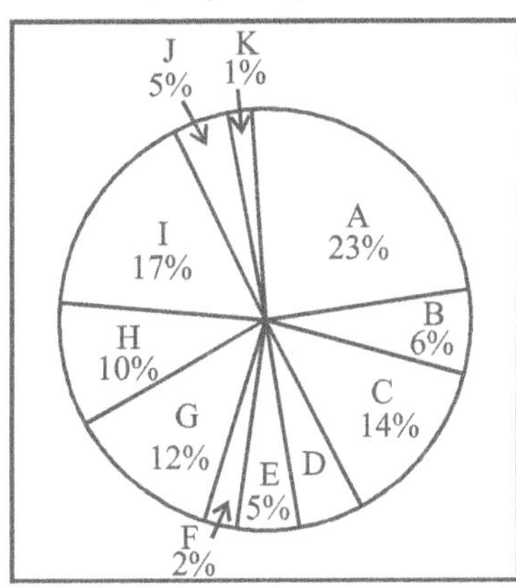

46. Which region had the lowest trade deficit with India in 2016-17?
    (a) Asia
    (b) Other EU
    (c) USA
    (d) Others

47. Approximate trade deficit (in billion US dollars) for the region with the highest trade deficit with respect to India during 2016-17, is
    (a) 7.5　　(b) 6.0　　(c) 4.5　　(d) 3.0

48. India had the highest total trade in 2016-17 with
    (a) OPEC
    (b) USA
    (c) Other EU
    (d) Others

49. The approximate amount of Indian exports during 2016-17 (in million US dollars) to the region with which India had the lowest trade during 2016-17 is
    (a) 220
    (b) 340
    (c) 440
    (d) 750

DIRECTIONS (Qs. 50-54) : *The following pie-chart represents the profits earned by a certain company in seven consecutive years. Study the pie-chart carefully and answer the question*

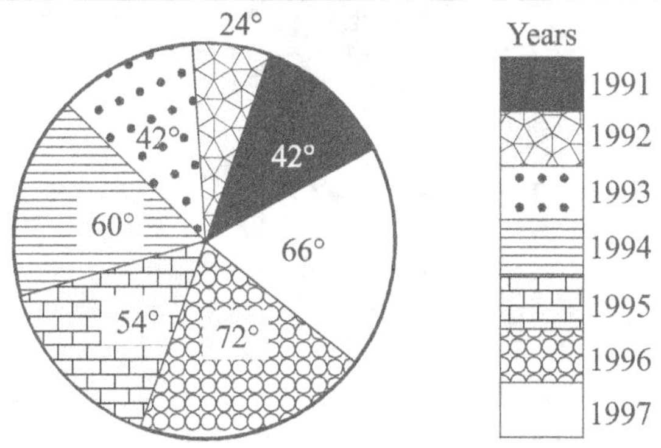

[*SSC CGL-2012*]

50. If the expenditure in the year 1993 was 30% more than the expenditure in the year 1991, then the income in the year 1993 exceeds the income in the year 1991 by 30% of
    (a) the income in the year 1991
    (b) the expenditure in the year 1993
    (c) the income in the year 1993
    (d) the expenditure in the year 1991

51. If $x\%$ of the total of profits earned in all the given years is same as the profit earned in the year 1994, then x is
    (a) $16\dfrac{2}{3}$　　　　(b) $33\dfrac{1}{3}$
    (c) $12\dfrac{1}{2}$　　　　(d) $11\dfrac{2}{3}$

52. The ratios of expenditures and incomes in the years 1992, 1994 and 1996 are given to be 6 : 5 : 8 and 2 : 3 : 4 respectively. The ratio of the income in the year 1996 to the total expenditure in the years 1992 and 1994 is
    (a) 40 : 11
    (b) 10 : 7
    (c) 20 : 11
    (d) 20 : 13

53. The year in which the profit is nearest to the average of the profits earned in all the given years is
    (a) 1991
    (b) 1995
    (c) 1993
    (d) 1994

54. If the income in the year 1997 was 5 times the expenditure made in the same year, then the ratio of the profit earned in the year 1991 to the expenditure in the year 1997 was
    (a) 11 : 28
    (b) 44 : 7
    (c) 28 : 11
    (d) 7 : 44

DIRECTIONS (Q. 55-556): *Based on the following information*

The following pie chart shows the percentage distribution of runs scored by a batsman in a test innings.

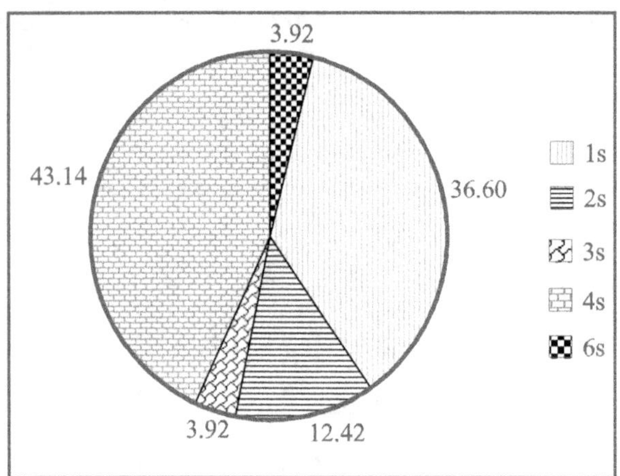

55. If the batsman has scored a total of 306 runs, how many 4s and 6s did he hit?
(a) 31 and 3 respectively   (b) 32 and 2 respectively
(c) 32 and 3 respectively   (d) 33 and 1 respectively
(e) 33 and 2 respectively

56. If 5 of the dot balls had been hit for 4s, and if two of the shots for which the batsman scored 3 runs each had fetched him one run instead, what would have been the central angle of the sector corresponding to the percentage of runs scored in 4s?
(a) 160   (b) 163   (c) 165   (d) 167
(e) 170

DIRECTIONS (Qs.57-61) : *Study the following pie-chart carefully to answer these questions.*

Percentagewise Distribution of Players Who Play Five Different Sports
Total Players are 4200 out of which Female Players are equal to 2000

Total Players = 4200
Percentage of Players who play different sports

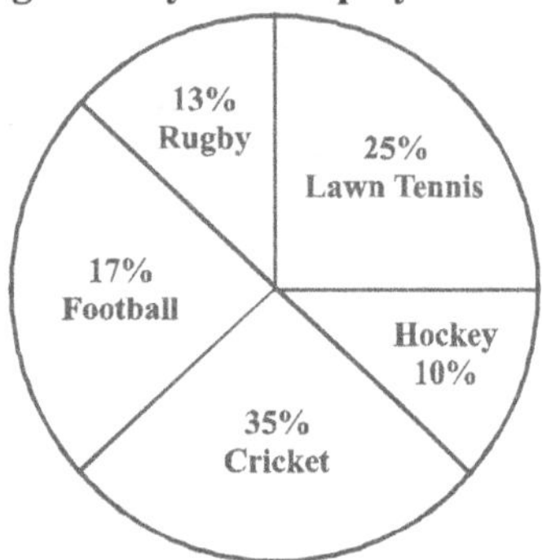

Female Players = 2000
Percentage of Female Players who play different sports

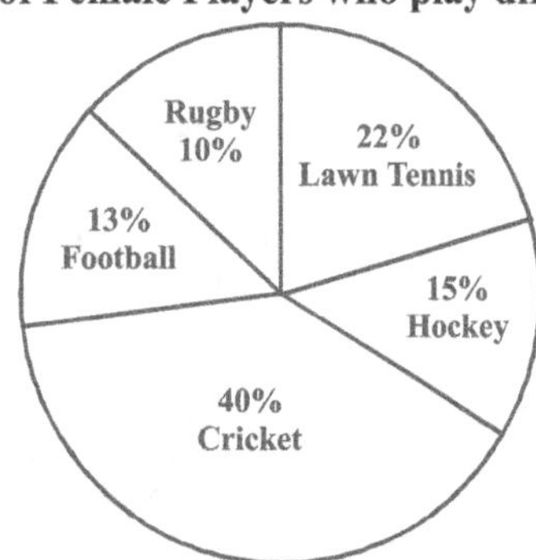

57. What is the average number of players (both male and female) who play football and rugby together?
(a) 620   (b) 357   (c) 230   (d) 630
(e) None of these

58. What is the difference between the number of the female players who play lawn tennis and the number of male players who play rugby?
(a) 94   (b) 84   (c) 220   (d) 240
(e) None of these

59. What is the respective ratio of the number of female players who play cricket and number of male players who play hockey?
(a) 20 : 7   (b) 4 : 21   (c) 20 : 3   (d) 3 : 20
(e) None of these

60. What is the total number of male players who play football, cricket and lawn tennis together ?
(a) 1,724   (b) 1,734   (c) 1,824   (d) 1,964
(e) None of these

61. Number of male players who play rugby is **approximately** what percentage of the total number of players who play lawn tennis ?
(a) 33   (b) 39   (c) 26   (d) 21
(e) 43

DIRECTIONS (Qs. 62-68) : *Study the following information carefully and answer the questions.*

[SBI PO Exam. 21.06.2014]

For a room, the rate of painting is ₹ 3200 per square metre. The rate of carpeting per square metre is 120% of that of tiling. The cost of decorating the room is 14 times to that of carpeting on the floor. The cost of electrification is 75% of that of carpeting the floor. The rate of tiling on the floor is 125% of that of painting. The dimensions of the room are 6 m × 6 m × 5m.

62. What is the ratio of the cost of painting the four walls of the room and that of decoration?
(a) 10 : 63   (b) 10 : 61
(c) 10 : 21   (d) 21 : 10
(e) None of these

63. What will be the total cost of decorating the room and tiling the floor when the four walls have also been tiled to a height of 0.25 metre?
(a) ₹ 5287200   (b) ₹ 2587200
(c) ₹ 25882000   (d) ₹ 2577200
(e) None of these

64. What will be the total cost of painting, carpeting, decoration and electrification of the room if the dimensions of the room be 21 m × 42 m × 27 m?
(a) ₹ 30888000   (b) ₹ 8388000
(c) ₹ 80388000   (d) ₹ 40888000
(e) None of these

65. What will be the cost of tiling the floor of the room if the rate of tiling be increased by 75% and the dimensions of the room be 51 m × 59 m × 84 m?
(a) ₹ 21163000   (b) ₹ 1263000
(c) ₹ 2163000   (d) ₹ 21063000
(e) None of these

66. If the length of the room be increased by 20%, breadth by 32% and height by 12%, then what will be the total cost of painting of the four walls of the room and tiling the floor?
    (a) ₹ 769996.80
    (b) ₹ 679996.80
    (c) ₹ 677796.80
    (d) ₹ 767796.80
    (e) None of these

67. What will be the total cost of carpeting, decoration, electrification and tiling the floor if the rate of painting be doubled?
    (a) ₹ 5771200
    (b) ₹ 5731200
    (c) ₹ 5371200
    (d) ₹ 7571200
    (e) None of these

68. What will be the cost of decoration of the room if its cost be increased by 25%?
    (a) ₹ 60480
    (b) ₹ 604800
    (c) ₹ 6048000
    (d) ₹ 6448000
    (e) None of these

DIRECTIONS (Qs. 69-73) : *Study the data given below and answer the following question. The pie charts shown below shows the distance covered by a boat moving upstream and downstream in different month of the year. And the table shows the speed of stream in km/hr. in different month of the year.*

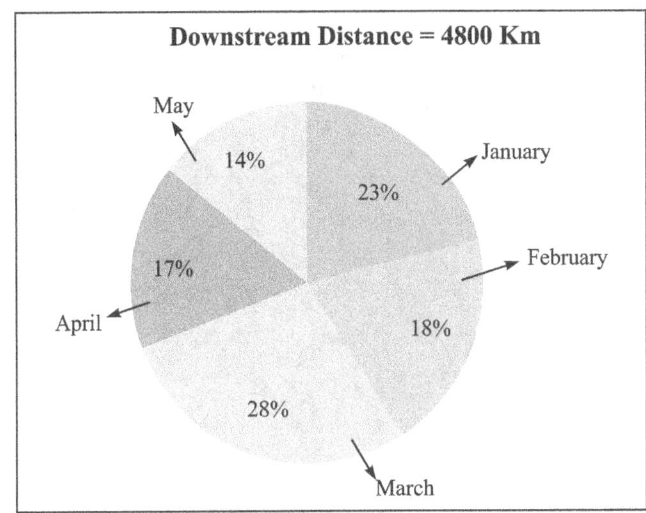

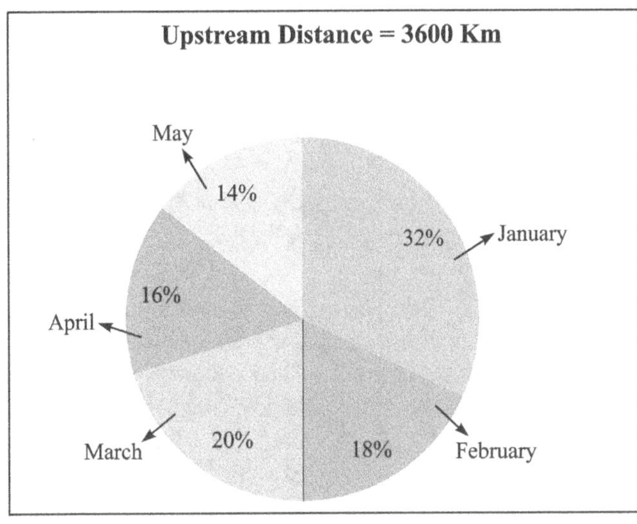

The table shows the speed of the stream in different days in the week and some data are missing.

Months	Speed of stream
January	16
February	–
March	24
April	–
May	8

69. If the time taken by boat to travel upstream in May is equal to the time taken by it to travel downstream in January and the speed of boat in still water in January is 30 kmph then find the speed of boat in still water in May?
    (a) 14.5 kmph
    (b) 15 kmph
    (c) 16.5 kmph
    (d) 12 kmph
    (e) None of these

70. If the speed of boat in still water on February was 20 kmph and the speed of boat in still water in March was 60% more than February and time taken to travel upstream in February is 12 hrs more than the time taken by it to travel downstream in March then find the speed of stream in February?
    (a) 2 kmph
    (b) 6 kmph
    (c) 4 kmph
    (d) 8 kmph
    (e) None of these

71. In April the speed of stream is $33\frac{1}{3}\%$ of the speed of the stream in March. If the time taken to cover upstream distance in April is 20% more than the downstream distance, what is the speed of boat in April ?
    (a) $30\frac{6}{7}$ kmph
    (b) $36\frac{6}{7}$ kmph
    (c) $24\frac{6}{7}$ kmph
    (d) $11\frac{6}{7}$ kmph
    (e) None of these

72. The speed of boat in January is 24 kmph more than the speed of stream on that month and time for upstream journey in May is same as time for upstream journey in January. What is the downstream journey time (approximate) in May?
    (a) 12 hours
    (b) 16 hours
    (c) 25 hours
    (d) 24 hours
    (e) 18 hours

73. In April ratio of speed of boat in still water in going upstream to downstream is 5:3 and also difference in speed of boat in still water in going upstream and downstream is 8 kmph. If the time taken by boat to cover upstream and downstream is same in April, find the speed of stream?
    (a) $6\frac{22}{29}$ kmph
    (b) $4\frac{22}{29}$ kmph
    (c) $8\frac{24}{19}$ kmph
    (d) $10\frac{26}{19}$ kmph
    (e) None of these

DIRECTIONS (Qs. 74-78) : *Percentage of students interested in studying different subjects (A Hindi, B English, C Computer, D Maths, E Science, F Sanskrit) in Pie chart I & percentage of girls interested in studying these subjects in pie chart II.*

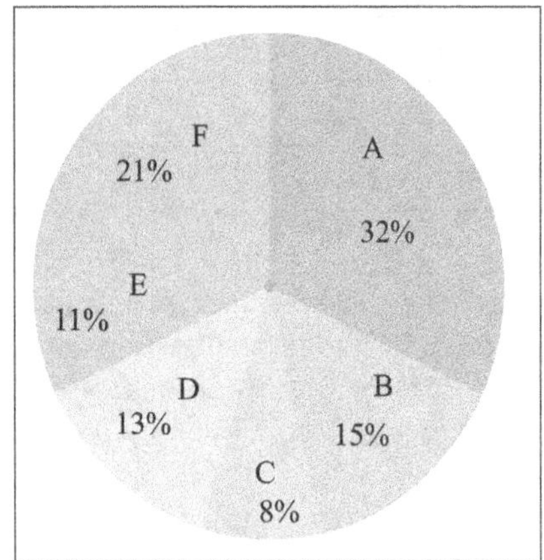

Pie-chart–I

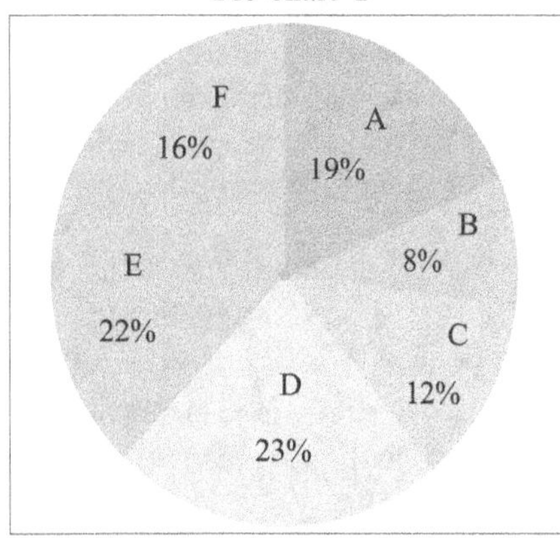

Pie-chart–II

RATIO OF BOYS : GIRLS = 5 : 3
TOTAL STUDENTS = 24000

74. For which of the subject, the ratio of percentage of student interested in that subject to the percentage of girls interested in that subject is minimum?
    (a) E   (b) C
    (c) D   (d) B
    (e) None of these

75. What is the difference between the no. of girls interested in studying C and that of E?
    (a) 0.75 thousand   (b) 1.1 thousand
    (c) 0.9 thousand   (d) 0.95 thousand
    (e) None of these

76. What is the ratio of the no. of boys interested in C and B together to that of girls interested in studying F and D together?
    (a) 124 : 117   (b) 128 : 119
    (c) 19 : 17   (d) 23 : 19
    (e) None of these

77. What is the ratio of the no. of students interested in studying D and F together to that interested in A and E together?
    (a) 23 : 32   (b) 34 : 43
    (c) 101 : 130   (d) 11 : 32
    (e) None of these

78. No. of girls studying A and B together is approximately what percent of the no. of boys studying the same subject?
    (a) 27%   (b) 30%
    (c) 17%   (d) 23%
    (e) 21%

DIRECTIONS (Qs. 79-83): *Study the following pie-chart and answer the following questions.*

Percentage distribution of income of 7 firms in year 2017 and 2018 is given below in pie-chart.

Percentage distribution of some firms is not given. You have to calculate these values if required to answer the questions.

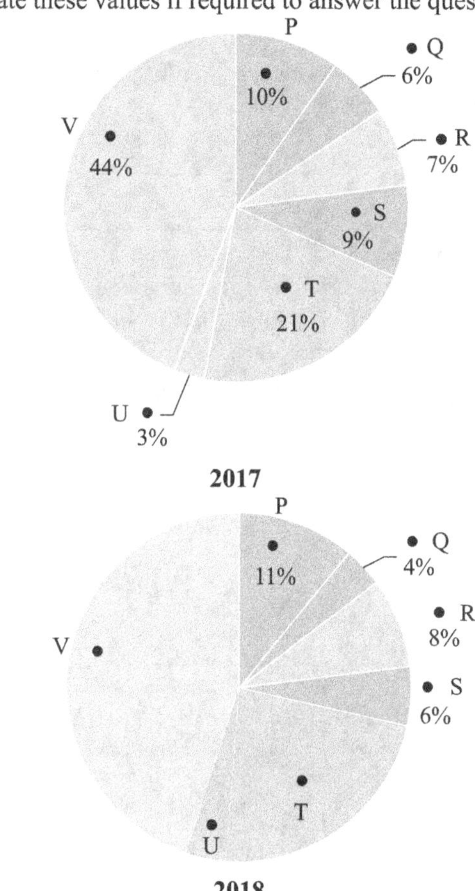

2017

2018

Note: Ratio of total income of all 7 firms in 2017 to 2018 is 5 : 7.

79. If expenditure of Q in 2017 is 80% of its income and expenditure of T in 2018 is 60% of its income and income of T in 2018 is 100/3% more than the income of T in 2017 then saving of Q in 2010 is what percent of saving of T in 2018.
    (a) 75/7%   (b) 38/9%
    (c) 100/3%   (d) 50/3%
    (e) None of these

80. If difference between the total income of all firms in 2017 and total income of all firms in 2018 is 'S', then what is the ratio of average income of firm P, Q and T together in 2017 to the average of income of firm Q, R and S together in 2018.
    (a) 203 : 201   (b) 133 : 123
    (c) 185 : 126   (d) 119 : 143
    (e) None of these

81. If income of firm T in 2018 is 400/7% of income of T in 2017 and ratio between percentage distribution of income of firm U and V is 11 : 8 in 2018 then what is the percentage distribution of income of firm V in 2018?
    - (a) 45/23%
    - (b) 133/7%
    - (c) 253/7%
    - (d) 255/103%
    - (e) 253/133%

82. Income of firm P, Q and T together in 2017 is what % more or less than income of firm R, S and T together if the income of firm T in 2018 is 50% more than income of firm P in 2017? (approximately)
    - (a) 7%
    - (b) 5%
    - (c) 5.1%
    - (d) 8%
    - (e) 48%

83. If income of firm P and Q together in 2018 is 120% of income of firm P and Q together in 2000 then income of firm P and Q together increase/decrease by what percent in 2000 with respect to 2017.
    - (a) 30%
    - (b) 23%
    - (c) 20%
    - (d) 25%
    - (e) 12%

HINTS & SOLUTIONS

Sol. (1-5)

	Degree	%	Value
A	79.2	22	1496
B	57.6	16	1088
C	14.4	4	272
D	122.4	34	2312
E	64.8	18	1224
F	21.6	6	408

1. (c) A prefer 22%, C prefer 4%, D prefer 34% and F prefer 6% therefore, A + C = 1496 + 272 = 1768 and D + F = 2312 + 408 = 2720

    2720 – 1768 = 952.

    Alternative Method :
    (A + C) = $79.2° + 14.4° = 93.6°$
    (D + F) = $122.4° + 21.6° = 144°$
    Difference = $144° – 93.6° = 50.4°$

    Then $\dfrac{50.4°}{360°} \times 6800 = 952$

2. (a) Ratio of F : A = 408 : 1496 i.e. 3 : 11

3. (d) People who prefer E and F together is 1224 + 408

    = 1632. Therefore, $\dfrac{1632}{6800} \times 100 = 24\%$

    Alternative Method :
    Let E + F = $64.8 + 21.6 = 86.4°$

    Required percentage = $\dfrac{86.4}{360} \times 100 = 24\%$

4. (b) C is $\dfrac{272}{2312} \times 100 = 11.76$ approx. 12% of D.

5. (a) B + E = 1088 + 1224 = 2312.

6. (d) Difference between the amount spent on Architect Fee's and Interior decoration is 22,800 – 13,200 = 9,600.

7. (c) Miscellaneous expenditure is 10,200. 10,200 is

    $\dfrac{10,200}{1,20,000} \times 100 = 8.5\%$ of the total estimated cost.

8. (d) According to question, 13% of 120000 + 8% of 120000
    = 25200 (which is estimated cost of furniture)
    Then actual cost of furniture is 15600 - 12% of 15600
    = 13728/-
    So total actual cost (furniture and miscellaneous)
    = 13728 + 10200 = 23928
    ∴ Total amount spent of renovating the house
    = 120000 – (25200 – 23928) = 118728

9. (b) the cost incurred on painting and flooring together is 18,000 + 16,800 = 34,800.

10. (d) Let, 12% discount on estimated cost of furniture is 12% of 15,600 = 1872. Then, The actual amount spent of furniture is 15600 – 1872 = 13728.

11. (b) On two items savings and house rent he has to invest more than ₹1000

12. (b) $\dfrac{1800}{6000} \times 100 = 30\%$. He invests ₹1800 on house rent.

13. (d) Saving per month = 6000 × 23% = ₹1380
    Annual saving = 1380 × 12 = ₹ 16560

14. (c) 10% = 500
    100% = ₹ 5000

15. (b) Money spent on clothes + saving = money spent on house rent.

16. (c) Angle made by sector Petrol = $\dfrac{360}{100} \times 10 = 36°$

17. (a) Let the two radii be r_1 and r_2

    Then required ratio = $\dfrac{\pi r_1^2}{\pi r_2^2} = \dfrac{6000}{1500}$

    $r_1 : r_2 = 2 : 1$

18. (a) Saving p.m. = 1500 $\dfrac{23}{100}$ = ₹ 345

    Annual saving = 345 × 12 = ₹ 4140

19. (b) D represents = 0.5%
    Share of D = 128.3 0.5% = 0.6 lakh (approximately)

20. (b) The value of D would be approximately = ₹1.3 lakh

21. (c) Packing cost after increase = (39.5 + 39.5 × 2%)
    = 40.29%
    ∴ Amount involved in packing cost = 128.3 × 40.29% = ₹ 51.69 = ₹52 lakh (approximately)

22. (b) Packing and raw material cost together = 88.5%
    128.3 × 88.5% = ₹113 lakh approximately

23. (d) % increase = $\dfrac{2.4 - 0.6}{0.6} \times 100 = 300\%$

24. (b) Volume transported by rail = 9% and by road = 22% so by both together it will be 9 + 22 = 31% of total volume transported = 31% of 12m = 31 × 12/100 = 3.72 million tonnes
    Cost of transportation by rail = 12% and by road = 6% so by both together it will be 12 + 6 = 18% of total cost of transportation = 18% of 30m = 18 × 12/100 = ₹ 5.4 million.
    Hence cost per tonne = 5.4/3.72 = 1.45 the closest option is 1.5

25. (a) Cost of transportation by Road = 6/22 3/11, by Rail = 12/9 = 4/3, by pipeline = 65/49 and by ship is 10/9, hence the cheapest way of transportation = Road

26. (c) From the answer of the previous question cost of transportation can be arrange as ship > Air > Road, hence P > Q > R

27. (b) Required ratio

$$= \frac{25780 \times 12}{100} : \frac{7390 \times 11}{100} = 3094 : 813$$

28. (b) Required percentage $= \frac{24}{16} \times 100 = 150$

29. (e) Required difference

$$= (11-7)\% \text{ of } 7390 = \frac{4 \times 7390}{100} = 296$$

30. (c) It is obvious from the Pie chart.

Science $\Rightarrow \dfrac{25780 \times 28}{100} - \dfrac{7390 \times 32}{100}$

$\approx 7218 - 2365 \approx 4853$

Engineering $\Rightarrow \dfrac{25780 \times 16}{100} - \dfrac{7390 \times 11}{100}$

$\approx 4124 - 813 \approx 3311$

Commerce $\Rightarrow \dfrac{25780 \times 18}{100} - \dfrac{7390 \times 16}{100}$

$\approx 4640 - 1182 \approx 3458$

31. (a) Required number of candidates

$$= 23\% \text{ of } 7390 = \frac{23 \times 7390}{100} \approx 1700$$

32. (a) Number of candidates who applied for Science

$$= 88000 \times \frac{22}{100} = 19360$$

Number of candidates selected for Science

$$= 14400 \times \frac{24}{100} = 3456$$

Required difference $= 19360 - 3456 = 15904$

33. (b) Number of candidates who applied for Arts

$$= 88000 \times \frac{17}{100} = 14960$$

Number of selected candidates in Maths and English

$$= 14400 \times \frac{38}{100} = 5472$$

Required sum $= 14960 + 5472 = 20432$

34. (c) Required ratio $= (14 + 20) : (28 + 24) = 34 : 52 = 17 : 26$

35. (d) Number of applicants for English $= 88000 \times \dfrac{24}{100}$

$$= 21120$$

Number of selected candidates $= \dfrac{14400 \times 28}{100} = 4032$

Required percentage $= \dfrac{4032}{21120} \times 100 \approx 19$

36. (e) Required average $= \dfrac{1}{3} \times \dfrac{14400 \times 66}{100} = 3168$

37. (d) Total no of MUV cars(C & H) = Total no of cars in MUV & SUV(C & H) – Total no of cars in SUV(C & H) = (14% + 9%) of 56000 – (7% + 12%) of 32000 = 6800
Total number of cars (both SUV and MUV) sold by stores F and H together = (8% + 9%) of 56000 = 9520
% = [(9520 - 6800)/9520]*100 = 28.57%

38. (b) Number of cars in MUV & SUV for D = 15% of 56000 = 8400
Total no of SUV cars(C,F,G)= 21% of 32000 = 6720
% = [(8400 – 6720)/6720)]*100= 25%

39. (d) Total no of MUV cars (A,D,E,F,H) = Total no of cars in MUV & SUV(A, D, E, F, H) – Total no of cars in SUV(A, D, E, F, H)
Total no of MUV cars(A, D, E, F, H) = 70% of 56000 – 71% of 32000 =16480 => Average = 16480/5 =3296

40. (a) Total no of SUV cars (A & B) : Total no of cars (MUV & SUV) for C & F
32% of 32000 : 22% of 56000
10240 : 12320 = 64:77

41. (b) In 2005, number of cars (MUV & SUV) for A, D, E = [110% of 18% of 56000 + 135% of 15% of 56000 + 115% of 20% of 56000] = 35308
In 2005, number of cars SUV for A, D, E = [110% of 16% of 32000 + 135% of 13% of 32000 + 115% of 22% of 30000] = 19344
Total number of MUV cars distributed by these three dealers in 2005 = 35308 – 19344 =15964

42. (a) Required investment in high-risk stock

$$= \frac{11,0500000 \times 8.9}{100} = ₹\,98,34500$$

43. (d) Required investment

$$= 11,05,00,000 \times \frac{48.3}{100} \times \frac{26}{100} = ₹1,38,76,590$$

44. (d) High-risk stocks

45. (c)

46. (c) We shall first prepare the table for the year 2016-17 as shown:

Region	Imports (in million US$)	Exports (in million US$)	Trade Deficit (Imports – Exports) (in million US$)	Total Trade (Imports + Exports) (in million US$)
A. USA	3670.11	6456.01	– 2785.90	10126.12
B. Germany	2038.95	2038.74	0.21	4077.69
C. Other EU	4893.48	4757.06	136.42	9650.54
D. UK	2446.74	2038.74	408.00	4485.48
E. Japan	2038.95	2038.74	0.21	4077.69
F. Russia	815.58	1019.37	– 203.79	1834.95

G. Other East Europe	7748.01	3397.90	4350.11	11145.91
H. OPEC	9379.17	3397.90	5981.27	12777.07
I. Asia	5709.06	6795.80	– 1086.74	12504.86
J. Other LDCs	1631.16	1698.95	– 67.79	3330.11
K. Others	407.79	339.79	68.00	747.58

From the above table, it is clear that USA had the lowest trade deficit with India in 2016-17.

47. (b) From the table in solution of Q. 48) it is clear that : OPEC had the highest trade deficit with respect to India during 2016-17.

This trade deficit = 5981.27 million US\$
$$= 5.98 \text{ billion US \$} \approx 6.0 \text{ billion US\$}$$

48. (a) From the table (in solution of Q. 48) it is clear that: India had the highest total trade of 12777.07 million US \$ with OPEC.

49. (b) From the table (in solution of Q. 48) it is clear that: India had the lowest trade with 'others' section in 2016-17. The amount of exports to this section (in 2016-17)
$$= 339.79 \text{ million US \$} \approx 340 \text{ million US \$}.$$

Sol. (50-54) :

Profit percentage in given years.

$$1991 \Rightarrow \frac{42}{360} \times 100 = 11.67\%$$

$$1992 \Rightarrow \frac{24}{360} \times 100 = 6.67\%$$

$$1993 \Rightarrow \frac{42}{360} \times 100 = 11.67\%$$

$$1994 \Rightarrow \frac{60}{360} \times 100 = 16.67\%$$

$$1995 \Rightarrow \frac{54}{360} \times 100 = 15\%$$

$$1996 = \frac{72}{360} \times 100 = 20\%$$

$$1997 = \frac{66}{360} \times 100 = 18.33\%$$

50. (d)

51. (a) x % of 100 = 16.67%
$$\Rightarrow x = 16\frac{2}{3}\%$$

52. (c)

53. (b) Average of year 1995
$$= \frac{11.67 + 6.67 + 11.67 + 16.67 + 15 + 20 + 18.33}{7}$$
$$= 14.28\% \approx 15\%$$
which is same as in year 1995.

54. (c)

55. (e) Out of 100 we get 306 run
$$\therefore \quad \text{For 43.14 we get } \frac{43.14 \times 306}{100} = 132.00 \text{ runs}$$
$$\therefore \quad \text{No. of 4} = \frac{132}{4} = 33$$

For 3.92 we get $\dfrac{3.92 \times 306}{100} = 12$ runs

$$\therefore \quad \text{No. of 6s} = \frac{12}{6} = 2$$

Hence (e) is the correct option

56. (e) According to the question total runs = 306 + 20 – 4 = 322
From previous question runs scored in fours = 132
So, runs scored in fours = 132 + 20 = 152

So, central angle = $\dfrac{152}{322} \times 360 = 169.93 \simeq 170°$

Hence (e) is the correct option

57. (d) Average number of players who play Football and Rugby
$$= \frac{1}{2}[(17 + 13)\% \text{ of } 4200]$$
$$= \frac{1}{2} \times 4200 \times \frac{30}{100} = 630$$

58. (a) Number of players who play Rugby
$$= 4200 \times \frac{13}{100} = 546$$
Number of female players who play Rugby
$$= 2000 \times \frac{10}{100} = 200$$
$\therefore$ Number of male players who play Rugby
$$= 546 – 200 = 346$$
Number of female players who play Lawn Tennis.
$$= 2000 \times \frac{22}{100} = 440$$
$\therefore$ Required difference = 440 – 346 = 94

59. (c) Number of female cricketers
$$= 2000 \times \frac{40}{100} = 800$$
Number of male Hockey players
$$= \frac{4200 \times 10}{100} - \frac{2000 \times 15}{100} = 420 – 300 = 120$$
$\therefore$ Required ratio = 800 : 120 = 20 : 3

60. (b) Number of male players who play Football, Cricket and Lawn Tennis
$$= (17 + 35 + 25)\% \text{ of } 4200 – (13 + 40 + 22)\% \text{ of } 2000$$
$$= 4200 \times \frac{77}{100} - 2000 \times \frac{75}{100} = 3234 – 1500 = 1734$$

61. (a) Number of male players who play Rugby
$$= 4200 \times \frac{13}{100} - 200 = 346$$

Number of players who play Lawn Tennis

$$= 4200 \times \frac{25}{100} = 1050$$

$\therefore$ Required percentage $= \frac{346}{1050} \times 100 \approx 33$

62. (a) Area of the four walls of the room $= 2 \times 5 \, (6 + 6)$
$= 10 \times 12 = 120$ sq. metre
$\therefore$ Expenditure on painting $= ₹(120 \times 3200)$
Area of the floor $= 6 \times 6 = 36$ sq. metre
$\therefore$ Expenditure on decoration $= ₹ (36 \times 4800 \times 14)$
$\therefore$ Require ratio $= (120 \times 3200):(36 \times 4800 \times 14) = 10:63$

63. (b) Area of tiles on the walls $= 2 \times 0.25 \, (6 + 6)$
$= 12 \times 0.5 = 6$ sq. metre
$\therefore$ Required total cost $= ₹ \, [(36 + 6) \times 4000 + 36$
$\times 4800 \times 14]$
$168000 + 2419200 = ₹ \, 2587200$

64. (c) Area of the four walls of room $= 2 \times 27 \, (21 + 42)$
$= 2 \times 27 \times 63 = 3402$ sq. metre
Area of the floor $= 21 \times 42 = 882$ sq. metre
Painting $\Rightarrow (3402 + 882) \times 3200 = ₹ \, 13708800$
Carpeting $\Rightarrow 4800 \times 882 = ₹ \, 4233600$
Decoration $\Rightarrow 4233600 \times 14 = ₹ \, 59270400$
Electrification $\Rightarrow \dfrac{4233600 \times 75}{100} = ₹ \, 3175200$
$\therefore$ Total expenditure
$= ₹ \, (13708800 + 4233600 + 59270400 + 3175200)$
$= ₹ \, 80388000$

65. (d) Area of the floor $= 51 \times 59 = 3009$ sq. metre
Rate of tiling $= \dfrac{4000 \times 175}{100} = ₹ \, 7000$
$\therefore$ Total cost $= ₹ \, (3009 \times 7000) = ₹ \, 21063000$

66. (a) New length of the room $= \dfrac{6 \times 120}{100} = 7.2$ metre
Breadth $= \dfrac{6 \times 132}{100} = 7.92$ metre
Height $= \dfrac{5 \times 112}{100} = 5.6$ metre
Area of the four walls $= 2 \times 5.6(7.2 + 7.92)$
$= 2 \times 5.6 \times 15.12 = 169.344$ sq. metre
Area of the floor $= 7.2 \times 7.92 = 57.024$ sq. metre
Painting $\Rightarrow 3200 \times 169.344 = ₹ \, 541900.8$
Tiling $\Rightarrow 57.024 \times 4000 = ₹ \, 228096$
Total cost $= ₹ \, (541900.8 + 228096) = ₹ \, 769996.8$

67. (b) Carpeting $\Rightarrow 6 \times 6 \times 9600 = ₹ \, 345600$
Decoration $\Rightarrow 36 \times 9600 \times 14 = ₹ \, 4838400$
Electrification $\Rightarrow \dfrac{345600 \times 75}{100} = ₹ \, 259200$
Tiling $\Rightarrow 6 \times 6 \times 8000 = ₹ \, 288000$
Total cost $= 345600 + 4838400 + 259200 + 288000$
$= ₹ \, 5731200$

68. (c) Expenditure on decoration of the room
$= \dfrac{4838400 \times 125}{100} = ₹ \, 6048000$

Sol. (69–73) :

Month	Upstream distance	Downstream distance	Speed of stream
January	1152	1104	16
February	648	864	–
March	720	1344	24
April	576	816	–
May	504	672	8

69. (e) $\dfrac{504}{b-8} = \dfrac{1104}{30+16}$
$b = 29$ kmph

70. (a) Speed of boat on February $= 20$ kmph
Speed of boat on March $= 20 * 160/100 = 32$ kmph
Upstream distance on February $= 648$ km
Downstream distance on March $= 1344$ km
Speed of stream on March $= 24$ kmph
$\dfrac{648}{20 - S_F} - \dfrac{1344}{32 + 24} = 12$
$\dfrac{648}{20 - S_F} - 24 = 12$
$20 - S_F = \dfrac{648}{24 + 12}$
$20 - S_F = 18$
$S_F = 2$ kmph

71. (a) Speed of the stream on April $= 24 * 100/300 = 8$ kmph
$120/100$ (Downstream journey time) $=$ upstream journey time
$120/100 \, (816/(b + 8)) = 576/ \, (b - 8)$
$6/5 \, (1021 \, (b + 8)) = 72/(b - 8)$
$7b = 216$
$b = 216/7 = 30\dfrac{6}{7}$ kmph

72. (c) Speed of stream on January $= 16$ kmph
Speed of boat on January $= 16 + 24 = 40$ kmph
Upstream journey on January $= \dfrac{1152}{40 - 16} = 48$ hours
Stream speed on May $= 8$ kmph
Upstream journey time on May $= 48$ hours
$504/b - 8 = 48$
$b = 18.5$ kmph
Downstream journey time on May $= 672 \, (8 + 18.5)$
$= 25$ hours (Approximately)

73. (a) Difference $5x - 3x = 8$
$2x = 8$
$x = 4$
Speed of boat in still water in upstream $= 5 \, (4) = 20$ kmph
Speed of boat in still water in downstream $= 3 \, (4)$
$= 12$ kmph
Distance of downstream on April $= 816$
Distance of upstream on April $= 576$
$408/(12 + w) = 288/20 - w$
$w = 6\dfrac{22}{29}$ kmph

74. (a) Required ratio

$$= \frac{\text{Percentage of total student interested in a subject}}{\text{Percentage of females interested in some subject}}$$

For E $= \dfrac{11}{22} = 0.5$

For C $= \dfrac{8}{12} = 0.66$

For D $= \dfrac{13}{23} = 0.565$

For B $= \dfrac{15}{8} = 1.875$

For A $= \dfrac{32}{19} = 1.684$

For F $= \dfrac{21}{16} = 1.3125$

∴ Ratio for E is minimum

75. (c) Total no. of girls studying

$$= \frac{3}{8} \times 24 \text{ thousands} = 9 \text{ thousands}$$

Difference between no. of girls interested in studying computer and that of science

$$= 10\% \text{ of } 9 \text{ thousand} = 0.9 \text{ thousand}$$

76. (a) Boys interested in C

$$= \frac{8}{100} \times 24 - \frac{12}{100} \times 9 = 0.84 \text{ thousand}$$

Boys interested in B

$$= \frac{15}{100} \times 24 - \frac{8}{100} \times 9 = 2.88 \text{ thousand}$$

Girls interested in F $= \dfrac{16}{100} \times 9 = 1.44$ thousand

Girls interested in D $= \dfrac{23}{100} \times 9 = 2.07$ thousands

∴ Required ratio $= \dfrac{2.88 + 0.84}{1.44 + 2.07} = \dfrac{124}{117}$

77. (b) Required ratio $= \dfrac{21 + 13}{11 + 32} = 34 : 43$

78. (a) No. of boys studying A

$$= \frac{32}{100} \times 24 - \frac{19}{100} \times 9 = 7.68 - 1.71 = 5.97$$

No. of boys studying B $= \dfrac{15}{100} \times 24 - \dfrac{8}{100} \times 9$

$$= 3.6 - 0.72 = 2.88$$

∴ Required percentage

$$= \frac{2.43}{8.85} \times 100 \approx 27.457 = 27\%$$

79. (a) Let total income in 2017 and 2018 is $5x$ and $7x$

Saving of Q in 2017 $= \dfrac{20}{100} \times \dfrac{5x}{100} \times 6 = \dfrac{6x}{100}$

Income of T in 2018 $= \dfrac{4}{3} \times \dfrac{5x}{100} \times 21 = \dfrac{7x}{5}$

Saving of T in 2018 $= \dfrac{2}{5} \times \dfrac{7x}{5} = \dfrac{14x}{25}$

Required % $= \dfrac{\frac{6x}{100}}{\frac{14x}{25}} \times 100 = \dfrac{75}{7}\%$

80. (c) Given $7 - 5 \rightarrow S$

∴ $1 \rightarrow \dfrac{S}{2}$

Total income of all firm in 2017 $= \dfrac{5}{2}S$

Total income of all firm in 2018 $= \dfrac{7}{2}S$

Average of income of firm P, Q and T in 2017

$$= \frac{50 \times 37}{2 \times 100 \times 3}$$

Average of income of firm Q, R and S together in 2018

$$= \frac{70 \times 18}{2 \times 100 \times 3}$$

Required ratio $= 185 : 126$

81. (c) Income of firm T in 2018 $= \dfrac{4}{7} \times \dfrac{5x}{100} \times 21 = \dfrac{3x}{5}$

% income of T in 2018 $= \dfrac{\frac{2x}{5}}{7x} \times 100 = \dfrac{60}{7}\%$

% income of firm U and V together

$$= \left[100 - \left(11 + 4 + 8 + 6 + \frac{60}{7} \right) \right] = \frac{437}{7}\%$$

% income of firm U in 2018 $= \dfrac{437}{7} \times \dfrac{11}{19} = \dfrac{253}{7}\%$

82. (a) Income of P, Q and T together in 2017 $= 37 \times \dfrac{5x}{100} = \dfrac{185}{100}x$

Income of T in 2018 $= \dfrac{3}{2} \times \dfrac{5x}{100} \times 10 = \dfrac{3}{4}x$

Income of R, S and T together in 2018

$$= \frac{7x}{100} \times 14 + \frac{3}{4}x = \frac{173}{100}x$$

Required % $= \dfrac{\left(\frac{185}{100}x - \frac{173}{100}x \right)}{\frac{173}{100}x} \times 100 = \dfrac{12}{173} \times 100$

$$\approx 7\%$$

83. (d) Income of firm P and Q in 2018 $= \dfrac{7x}{100} \times 15 = \dfrac{105}{100}x$

Income of firm P and Q in 2016 $= \dfrac{105}{100} \times \dfrac{100}{120}x = \dfrac{7x}{8}$

Income of firm P and Q in 2017 $= \dfrac{5x}{100} \times 14 = \dfrac{70}{100}x = \dfrac{7}{10}x$

Required % $= \dfrac{\frac{7}{8}x - \frac{7}{10}x}{\frac{7}{10}x} \times 100 = 25\%$ increase

Mixed chart or Mixed graph is not a single statistical figure. It is the comparative study of two different type of graphs which are complementary pair of graphs. In these type of questions both graphs are necessary to determine the answer of given questions.

There are many type of mix graph like :

(i) **PIE-TABLE :**

Example: Total no. of workers = 36000

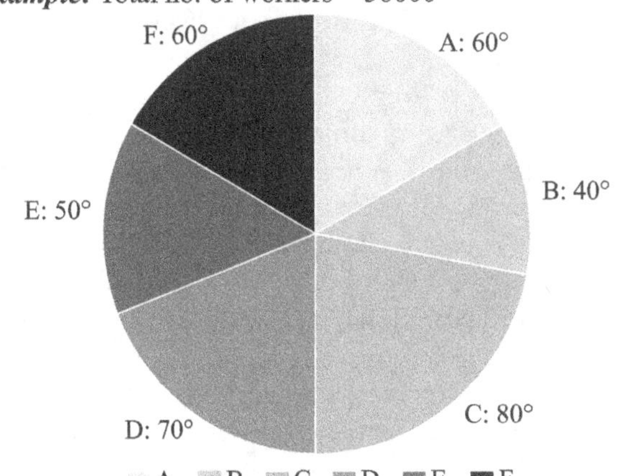

Works	A	B	C	D	E	F
Trained : Untrained	2 : 1	5 : 3	3 : 5	3 : 4	3 : 2	3 : 1

What is number of untrained workers in C ?

$$\text{Answer} = 36000 \times \frac{80}{360} \times \frac{5}{8} = 5000$$

(ii) **PIE - BAR :**

Example : Total marks = 360

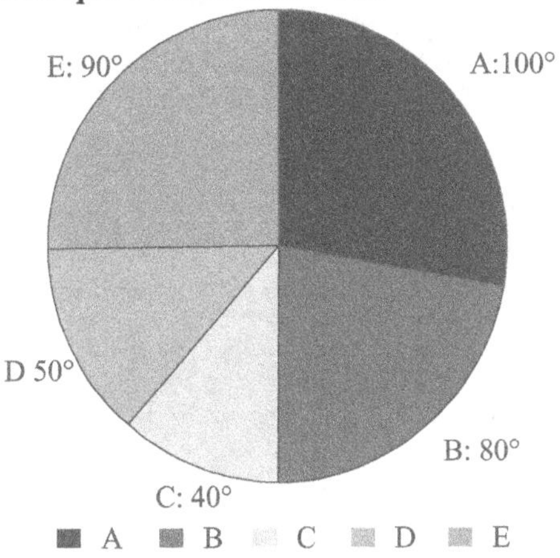

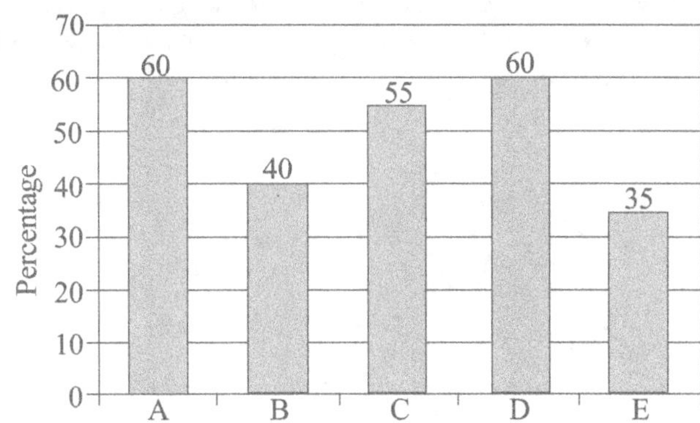

What is marks obtained in C ?

$$\text{Obtained marks in C} = 360 \times \frac{40}{360} \times \frac{55}{100} = 22$$

(iii) **BAR LINE**

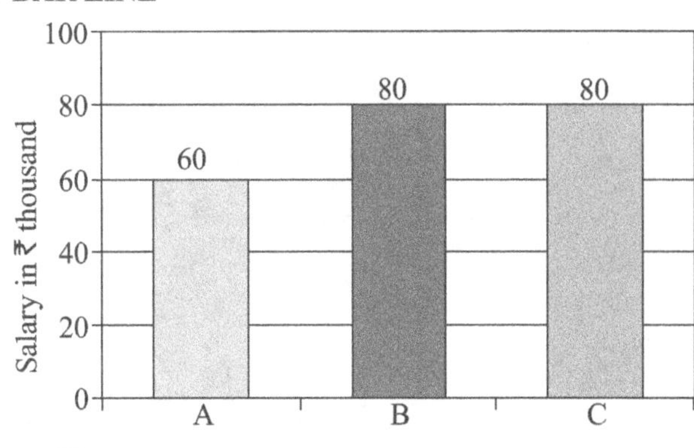

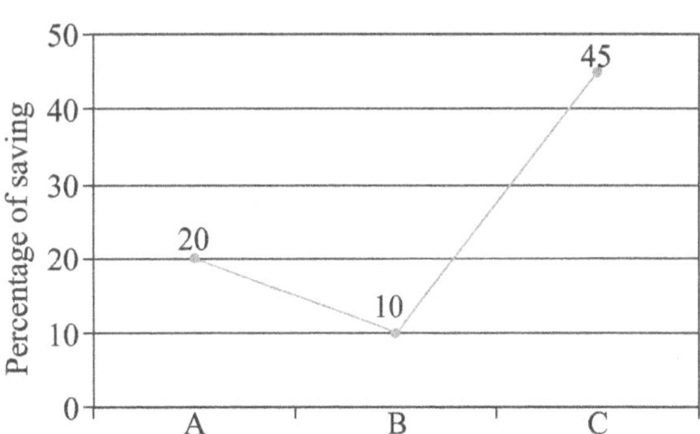

What is expenditure of C ?

$$\text{Expenditure of C} = 80000 \times \frac{45}{100} = 36000$$

EXERCISE

DIRECTIONS (Qs. 1-3): *A marketing survey team visited five different colleges of Kolkata where the respective students of Asutosh college, South Point college, St. Xavier's college, Lady Bovine and South Kolkata Government college have given their votes for their favorite Actors. The number of male voters of South point exceed to that of St. Xavier by 40500.*

Voters according to their Colleges

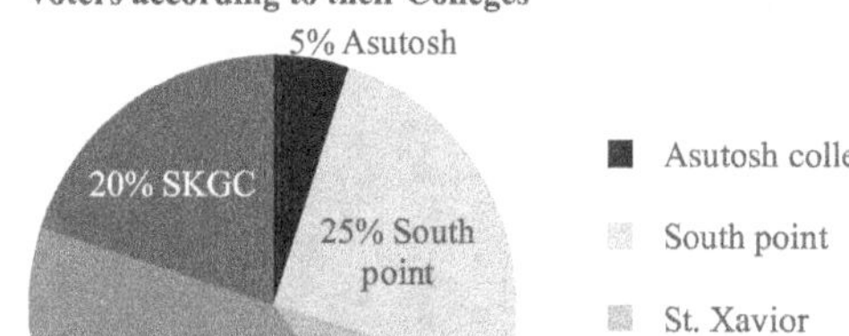

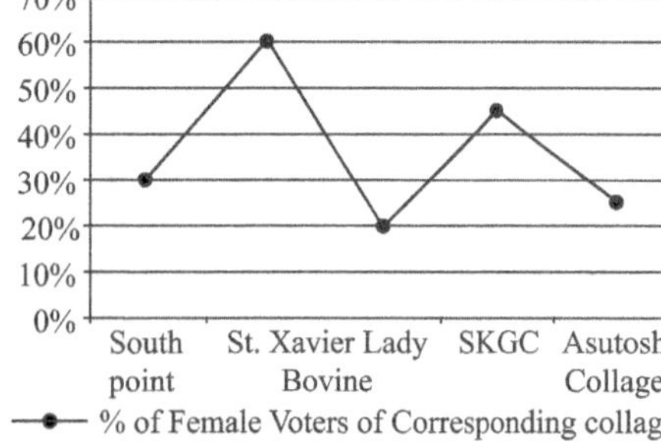

1. Find the ratio of number of voters from SKGC to the number of male voters from St. Xavier?
   (a) 5 : 3   (b) 5 : 1
   (c) 13 : 9   (d) None of these

2. What percentage of the total voters would have been from Lady Bovine, if the number of voters from south point increased by 15%?
   (a) 38.61%   (b) 38.55%   (c) 34.45%   (d) 34.55%

3. Find the difference between the number of female voters from Lady Bovine and the number of male voters from Asutosh?
   (a) 24000   (b) 17750   (c) 12750   (d) 11250

DIRECTIONS (Qs. 4-7): *The following table gives the amount of loans disbursed by the various banks in the year 2013-2017. The bank which disburses the maximum amount in a particular year is said to be a market leader.*

Constituents of others in 2017

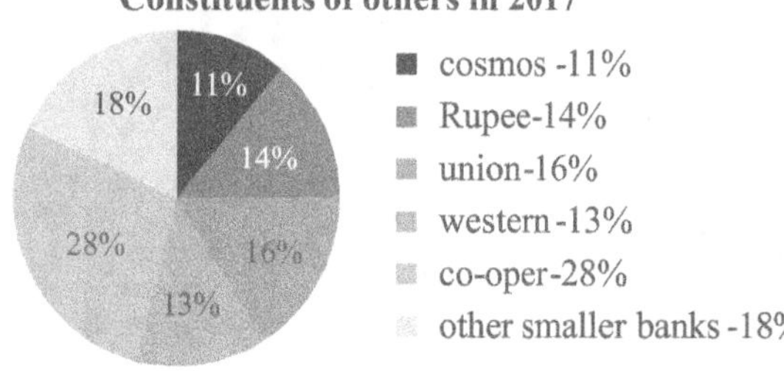

BANK	2013	2014	2015	2016	2017
ICICI	88	98	113	129	146
HDFC	98	118	128	138	130
CBI	47	43	53	49	58
SBI	78	83	88	94	103
BOM	46	53	48	59	71
OTHERS	89	111	123	133	145

4. In 2015 all the major banks had same percentage share in auto-finance as their respective shares in total loan disbursement. How much was the share of HDFC greater than the share of SBI if the total auto-finance market was of 180 Crore?
   (a) 8.8 cr   (b) 11 cr   (c) 13 cr   (d) 15.6 cr

5. In the year 2018, all the banks retained their respective market shares as they had in 2017. The merger of which of the following three banks would make them the market leader?
   (a) CBI, cosmos, jan kalian (b) CBI, Rupee, Union
   (c) Cosmos, Rupee, SBI   (d) Rupee,union,SBI

6. If in 2017, the Rupee and western banks go bankrupt on account of increasing non-performing assets then the market Shares of these banks gets equally distributed to other banks. What is the percentage increase in the market share of ICICI bank?
   (a) 5.2%   (b) 8.3%
   (c) 11.2%   (d) Indeterminable

7. By what percentage did the total market of loan disbursement increase in the year 2015 with respect to 2014?
   (a) 8.08%   (b) 9.28%
   (c) 13.5%   (d) Indeterminable

DIRECTIONS (Qs. 8-17): *Study the following pie- charts and table to answer these questions.*

[RBI GRADE B OFFICER 2009]

Statewise Details of the adult population of a country

Graduate and Above
Total No. = 24 Lakhs

Upto XII STD pass
Total No. = 32 Lakhs

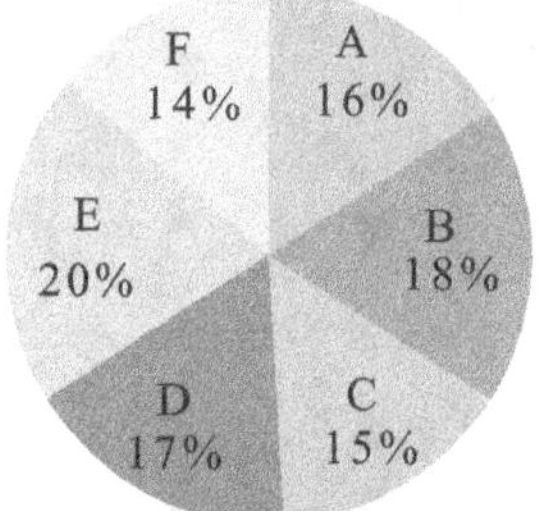

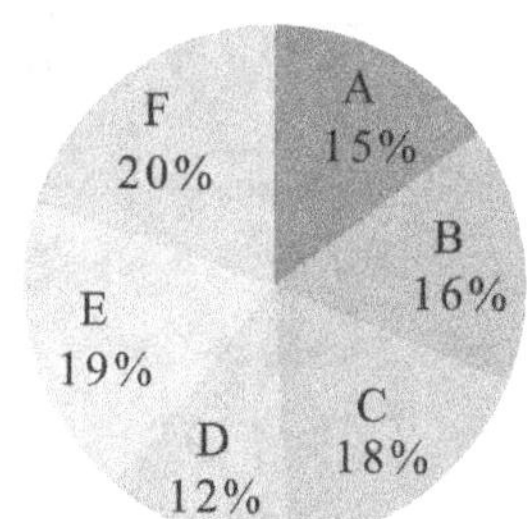

Male: Female ratio

State	Graduate & Above	Upto XII Std Pass
	M : F	M : F
A	7 : 5	7 : 9
B	5 : 3	3 : 5
C	5 : 4	4 : 5

D	9 : 8	5 : 7
E	9 : 7	9 : 10
F	4 : 3	3 : 2

8. What is the difference between the Graduate male population and XII Std male population from State 'A'?
   (a) 24,000
   (b) 14,000
   (c) 28,000
   (d) 36,000

9. What is the ratio of the Graduate female population of State E to Std XII female population of State D?
   (a) 7 : 5 (b) 5 : 7 (c) 16 : 15 (d) 15 : 16

10. The graduate female population of State C is what percent of the Std XII population of all the states together?
    (a) 4%
    (b) 6.25%
    (c) 5%
    (d) 5.25%

11. The STD XII male population of State C is what percent of the total STD XII population of all the states together?
    (a) 8% (b) 12% (c) 11% (d) 9%

12. What is the ratio of the Graduate male population of State E to Std XII female population of that State?
    (a) 28 : 35
    (b) 35 : 28
    (c) 32 : 45
    (d) None of these

13. Total graduate population of State F is what per cent of the total Std XII population of State A?
    (a) 56
    (b) 72
    (c) 68
    (d) None of these

14. Std XII male population of State E is what per cent of the Std XII male population of State F?
    (a) 70 (b) 75 (c) 68 (d) 72

15. What is the ratio of the total Graduate and Std XII male population of State A to the total Graduate and Std XII female population of that state?
    (a) 215 : 216
    (b) 214 : 215
    (c) 217 : 215
    (d) 215 : 217

16. What is the ratio of the total; Graduate population of State D to the total Std XII population of that State?
    (a) 17 : 16
    (b) 16 : 17
    (c) 64 : 51
    (d) 51 : 48

17. The Graduate female population of State B is what per cent of the Graduate female population of state E? (rounded off to the nearest integer)
    (a) 129 (b) 82 (c) 77 (d) 107

DIRECTIONS (Qs. 18-27): *Study the following graph and answer these questions given below it.*

Tea in India (In Million kg)

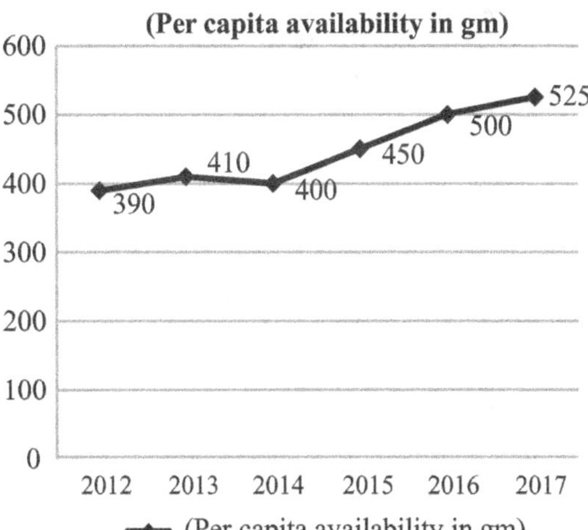

18. Which year shows the maximum percentage of export with respect to production?
    (a) 2013
    (b) 2014
    (c) 2017
    (d) 2016

19. The population of India in 2014 was:
    (a) 800 million
    (b) 1080 million
    (c) 985 million
    (d) 900 million

20. If the area under tea production was less by 10% in 2015 than in 2014, then the approximate rate of increase in productivity of tea in 1994 was:
    (a) 97.22
    (b) 3
    (c) 35
    (d) Cannot be determined

21. The average proportion of tea exported to the tea produced over the period is:
    (a) 0.87
    (b) 0.47
    (c) 0.48
    (d) 0.66

22. What is the first half decade's average per capita availability of tea?
    (a) 475g
    (b) 535g
    (c) 446g
    (d) 430g

23. In which year was the per capita availability of tea minimum?
    (a) 2017
    (b) 2015
    (c) 2012
    (d) None of these

24. In which year was there minimum percentage of export with respect to production?
    (a) 2012
    (b) 2013
    (c) 2014
    (d) 2015

25. In which year we had maximum quantity of tea for domestic consumption?
    (a) 2015
    (b) 2012
    (c) 2014
    (d) 2017

26. What approximately was the average quantity of tea available for domestic consumption during the period?
    (a) 324.3 million Kg
    (b) 400 million kg
    (c) 410.3 million kg
    (d) 320.3 million kg

27. What was approximately the average population during the period?
    (a) 625 million
    (b) 624 million
    (c) 600 million
    (d) 757 million

DIRECTIONS (Qs. 28-30): *Refer to the given line graph and the pie-charts and answer these questions: (1000 hectars)*

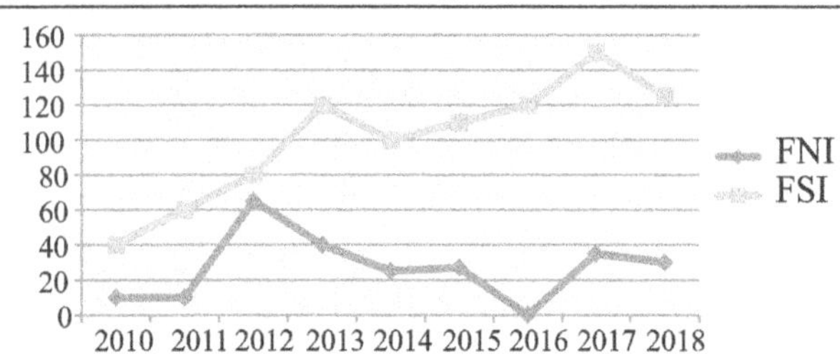

FNI – Distribution of Forest Land in North India

FSI – Distribution of Forest Land in South India

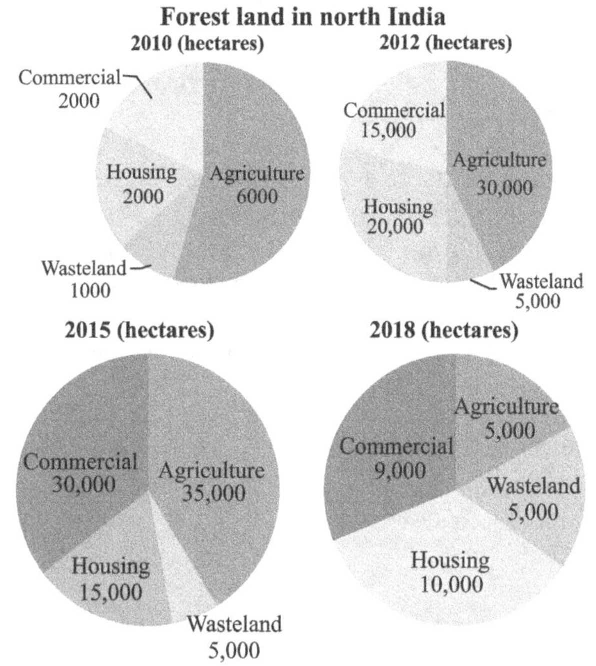

28. How many hectares of FSI has been distributed between 2010–2018?
    (a) 3,00,500 (b) 2,77,500 (c) 6,57,000 (d) 9,00,000

29. How many years witnessed a decline in FNI and an increase in FSI?

    (a) 2   (b) 3   (c) 4   (d) 5

30. During 2010-2018 the greatest proportion of FNI was put to commercial use in:
    (a) 2018   (b) 2010   (c) 2015   (d) 2012

DIRECTIONS (Qs. 31-35): *Study the following figures to answer these questions:*

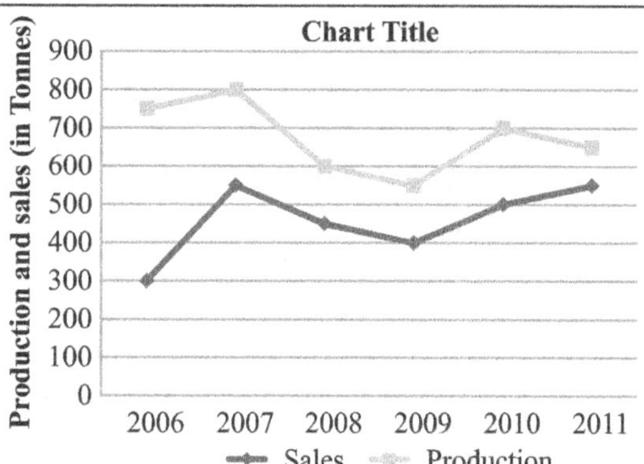

31. What is the approximate percentage increase in the production of Company A (in tonnes) from the year 2009 to the production of Company A (in tonnes) in the year 2010?
    (a) 18%   (b) 38%   (c) 23%   (d) 27%

32. The sales of company A in the year 2009 was approximately what per cent of the production of Company A in the same year?
    (a) 65%   (b) 73%   (c) 79%   (d) 83%

33. What is the average production of Company A (in tonnes) form the year 2006 to the year 2011?
    (a) 574   (b) 649   (c) 675   (d) 593

34. What is the ratio of the total production (in tonnes) of Company A to the total sales (in tonnes) of Company A?
    (a) 81 : 64   (b) 64 : 55   (c) 71 : 81   (d) 81 : 55

35. What is the ratio of production of Company A (in tonnes) in the year 2006 to production of Company A (in tonnes) in the year 2008?
    (a) 2 : 5   (b) 4 : 5   (c) 5 : 4   (d) 3 : 5

DIRECTIONS (Q. 36): *On the basis of the data given in the chart.*

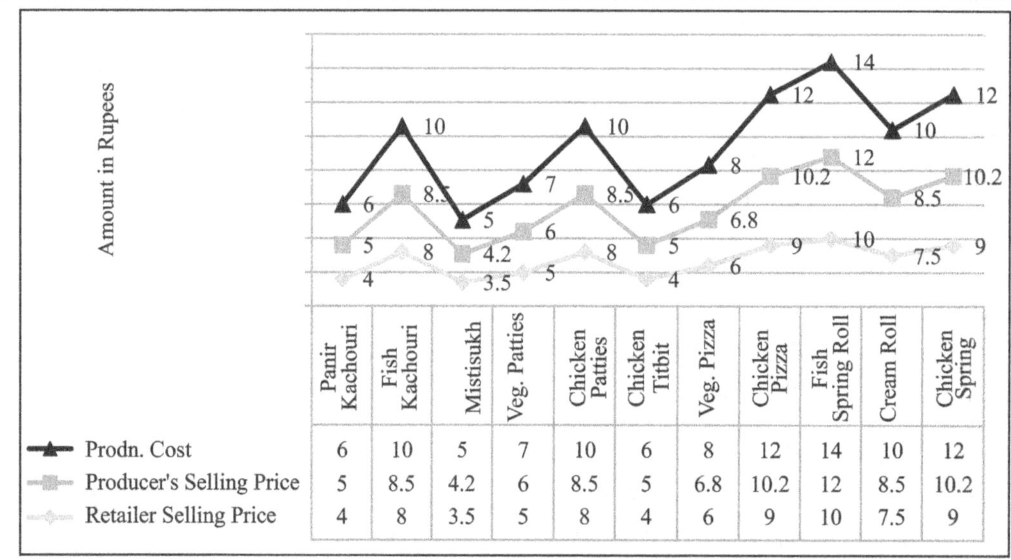

	Panir Kachouri	Fish Kachouri	Mistisukh	Veg. Patties	Chicken Patties	Chicken Titbit	Veg. Pizza	Chicken Pizza	Fish Spring Roll	Cream Roll	Chicken Spring
Prodn. Cost	6	10	5	7	10	6	8	12	14	10	12
Producer's Selling Price	5	8.5	4.2	6	8.5	5	6.8	10.2	12	8.5	10.2
Retailer Selling Price	4	8	3.5	5	8	4	6	9	10	7.5	9

36. Which of the following conclusion can be drawn from the above diagram?
    (a) Retailer's selling price for mistisukh was more than producer's selling price for chicken titbit.
    (b) Difference between retailer's selling price and producer's selling price for fish kachouri was more than that of cream roll.
    (c) There are three types of margins for all items.
    (d) Of all the margins, both for retailer and producer, producer's margin for chicken pizza was the maximum.
    (e) The three lines that connect different points, in the diagram above are superfluous.

DIRECTIONS (Qs. 37-41): *Two pie charts are given. First pie chart shows the number of workers in six different companies in 2015 and second pie chart shows the number of trained workers in those companies in 2016. Study the given data carefully and answer the related questions.*

Total no. of workers in 2015 = 21600   Total no. of trained workers in 2016 = 12000

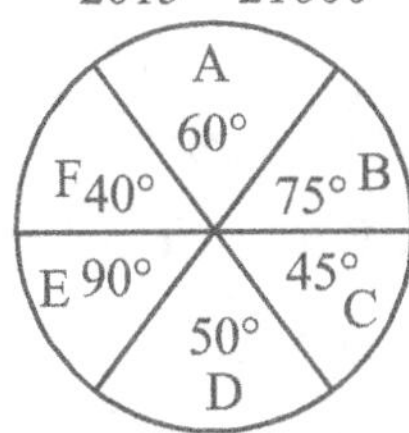

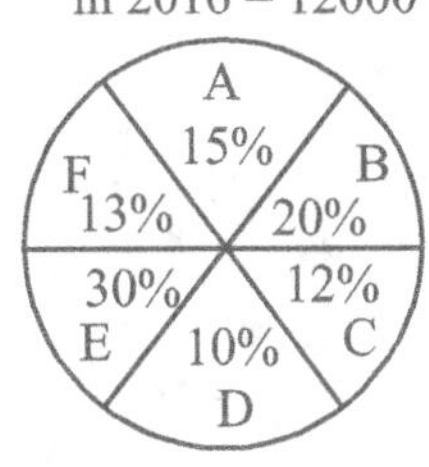

37. Number of workers is increased by 20% in B in 2016 from 2015 and respective ratio of number of male workers to that of female workers in 2016 is 5 : 4. If number of trained female workers is 30% of number as total trained workers then number of trained male worker is what percent of total number of male workers in 2016?
    (a) 56%   (b) 44%   (c) 46%   (d) 52%
    (e) None of these

38. Total number of workers in C in 2015 is 10% less than that of C in 2016 and number trained workers in C in 2016 is 10% less than that of C in 2015 then what is increment/decrement recorded in number of untrained workers in C in 2016 from 2015?
    (a) 40.8%   (b) 41.8%   (c) 38.8%   (d) 39.8%
    (e) None of these

39. If 20% of total number of workers are trained in D in 2016 and number of trained worker in D in 2016 is 20% less than that of trained workers in D in 2015 then what is respective ratio of number of untrained workers in 2015 and 2016 in D?
    (a) 5:12   (b) 8:13   (c) 5:16   (d) 16:5
    (e) None of these

40. Respective ratio of no of male workers and that of female workers in F is 5:3 in 2015. Number of male and female workers are increased by 20% and 40% respectively in 2016 from 2015 then what is difference between number of trained workers and that of untrained worker in 2016 in F?
    (a) 300   (b) 500
    (c) 600   (d) 60
    (e) None of these

41. Total no of workers is increased by 20% in A in 2016 from 2015 and total no of workers is decreased by 20% in E in 2016 from 2015 then what is respective ratio of number of untrained workers in A and E in 2016?
    (a) 5:3   (b) 2:7   (c) 4:5   (d) 8:3
    (e) None of these

DIRECTIONS (Qs. 42-46): *Two pie charts are given. First pie chart shows the number of Persons living in different cities and second pie chart the number of Female Children in those cities. Study the given data carefully and answer the related questions.*

Total population = 1080000   Total no. of female children = 150000

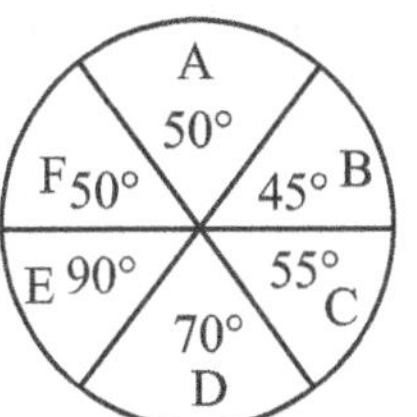

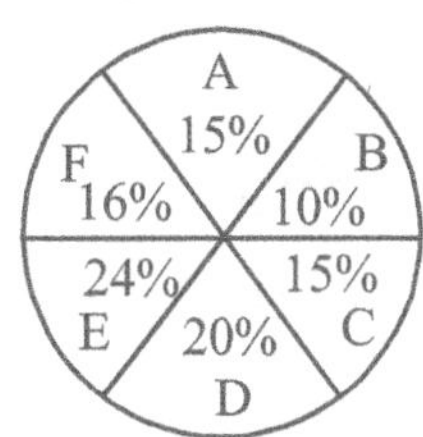

42. If number of female children is 30% of total female population and total number of children is 25% of total population of city A then number of adult males is what percent of total male population?
    (a) 20%   (b) 60%
    (c) 80%   (d) 75%
    (e) None of these

43. Number of male children is 20% more than that of female children in B and number of male children in this city is 30% of total number of males then number of adult males is what percent more/less than that of females?
    (a) 20%   (b) 25%
    (c) 18%   (d) 30%
    (e) None of these

44. If number of male children in city D is 25% more than that of female children and respective ratio of number of adult males and adult female is 9 : 10 in this city then what is respective ratio of no. of males to that of females in city D?
    (a) 3 : 2   (b) 2 : 1
    (c) 1 : 2   (d) 3 : 4
    (e) None of these

45. No. of males in city F is 50% more than that of females and 20% of total population of this city are children then what is difference between no. of adult males and that of adult females in this city?
    (a) 48000   (b) 24000
    (c) 8000   (d) 20000
    (e) None of these

46. Respective ratio of no. of male children and that of female children in city C is 4 : 3 and Number of female children in city E is 25% of total female population of this city. If number of male children in city C is 40% of total male population then what is respective ratio of number of males in cities C and E?
    (a) 42 : 25   (b) 25 : 42
    (c) 18 : 25   (d) 25 : 21
    (e) None of these

DIRECTIONS (Qs. 47-51): *One pie chart is followed by two tables. Pie chart shows the number of persons living in different cities. First table shows the respective ratio of number of adult to no. of children in each city and second table shows the respective ratio of number of employed males and that of employed females. Study the given data carefully and answer the related questions.*

Total no. of persons = 2880000

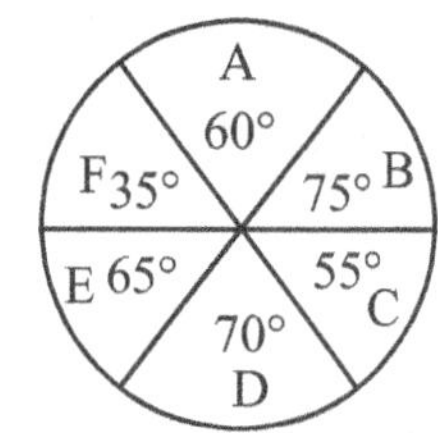

Cities	No. of adults : No. of children
A	3 : 1
B	2 : 1
C	8 : 3
D	5 : 2
E	10 : 3
F	4 : 1

Cities	No. of employed males : No. of employed females
A	3 : 2
B	2 : 1
C	1 : 3
D	1 : 1
E	7 : 6
F	2 : 3

47. If 70% of total population is unemployed in city B and 40% of adult population is number of adult females then number of unemployed adult males is what percent more/less than that of unemployed adult females?

(a) 20%   (b) 25%   (c) $16\frac{2}{3}\%$ (d) $33\frac{1}{3}\%$

(e) None of these

48. Total no. of children in all cities together is what percent of total no. of adults in all cities together?
(a) 32.97%   (b) 36.88%
(c) 37.68%   (d) 41.28%
(e) None of these

49. If 20% of female population and 30% of male population are employed in city D then what is difference between number of males and that of females in this city?
(a) 50000   (b) 120000   (c) 112000   (d) 121000
(e) None of these

50. If 45% of total number of adults are males and respective ratio of number of male children to that of female children is 2 : 1 in city A then what is respective ratio of no. males to that of females in this city?
(a) 123 : 119   (b) 119 : 121
(c) 117 : 119   (d) 121 : 119
(e) None of these

51. What is difference between average no. of males and that of females in all cities together?
(a) 50000   (b) 100000
(c) 70000   (d) Can't be determined
(e) None of these

DIRECTIONS (Qs. 52-56): *One pie chart is followed by a bar graph. Pie chart shows the food expenditure of different persons and Bar-graph shows the various expenditures of those persons. Study the given data carefully and answer the related questions.*

Total food expenditure = 252000

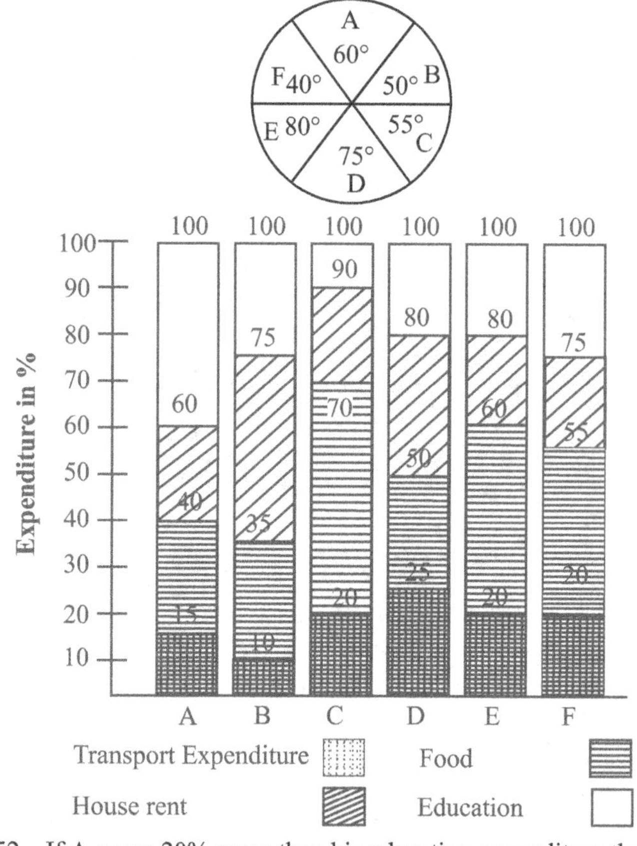

52. If A saves 20% more than his education expenditure then his saving is what percent of his total expenditure?
(a) 48%   (b) 49%   (c) 50%   (d) 45%
(e) None of these

53. Saving of D is two times of the difference of his transport expenditure and education expenditure then what is respective ratio of his total expenditure to his total saving?
(a) 1 : 10   (b) 10 : 1   (c) 2 : 5   (d) 5 : 2
(e) None of these

54. If food expenditure of F is 20% less than his saving then what is difference between his saving and house rent?
(a) 21000   (b) 12000
(c) 19000   (d) 25000
(e) None of these

55. If saving of C is 20% of his salary and education expenditure of E is 16% of his salary then what is respective ratio of their savings?
(a) 20 : 11   (b) 11 : 10
(c) 11 : 19   (d) 11 : 20
(e) None of these

56. If saving of F is 50% more than that of B who saves 25% of his salary then salary of F is what percent more/less than that of B?
    (a) 21% (b) 29% (c) 27% (d) 32%
    (e) None of these

DIRECTIONS (Qs. 57-61): *One pie chart is followed by a line graph. Pie chart shows the number of students in different schools in 2015 and line graph shows the percentage of number of girls in 2015 and 2016. Study the given graphs carefully and answer the related questions:*

Total no. of students in 2015 = 43200

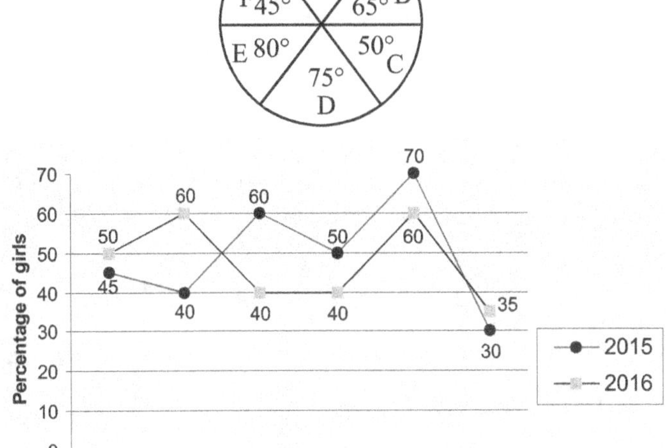

57. No. of boys is decreased by 20% in school B in 2016 from 2015 then what is increment recorded in number of girls in 2016 from 2015?
    (a) 80% (b) 75% (c) 60% (d) 84%
    (e) None of these

58. Number of girls in E in 2015 is 80% of the number of girls in 2016 then what is increment recorded in number of students in 2016 from 2015 in E?
    (a) 43.83% (b) 47.83% (c) 41.83% (d) 60.83%
    (e) None of these

59. Number of students is increased by 40% in C in 2016 from 2015 and 40% of total students are failed in 2015 in C. If respective ratio of number of passed girls in 2015 and that of passed girls in 2016 is 5 : 6 and respective ratio of number of passed boys and that of passed girls in 2015 was 2 : 1 then what is difference between number of passed boys in this school in these years?
    (a) 1000 (b) 2000
    (c) 2500 (d) Can't be determined
    (e) None of these

60. What is respective ratio of number of boys and that of girls in all schools together in 2015?
    (a) 2201 : 2299 (b) 2121 : 2199
    (c) 2201 : 2929 (d) 2021 : 2299
    (e) None of these

61. 40% of total number of boys and 30% of total number of girls were passed in D in 2015 and 60% of total no. of boys and 70% of total number of girls were passed in F in 2015 then what is respective ratio of number of failed students in D and F in 2015?
    (a) 212 : 325 (b) 111 : 325
    (c) 325 : 111 (d) 311 : 125
    (e) None of these

DIRECTIONS (Qs. 62-66): *One pie chart is followed by a table. In the pie chart data is given about population of different cities and table shows the respective ratio of different groups. Study the given data carefully and answer the related questions.*

Total population = 324000

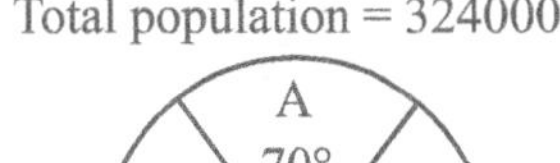
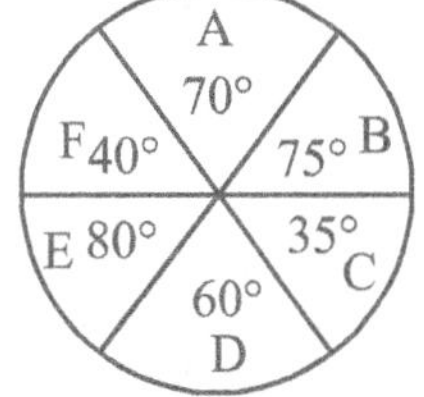

Cities	No. of Adult males : No. of Adult females	No. of male children : No. of female children
A	3 : 2	4 : 5
B	2 : 1	1 : 2
C	2 : 1	4 : 3
D	3 : 4	2 : 1
E	7 : 9	7 : 5
F	2 : 3	4 : 1

62. If number of children is 1/3rd of total population of city B and 40% of total adult males and 50% of total adult females are married than what is respective ratio of number of unmarried males to that of unmarried females?
    (a) 8 : 5 (b) 5 : 8 (c) 3 : 5 (d) 8 : 7
    (e) None of these

63. Respective ratio of number of males to that of females in city C is 5 : 3 then what is difference between number of adults and number of children in this city?
    (a) 3139 (b) 3839 (c) 3938 (d) 4039
    (e) None of these

64. Number of male children is 25% of total number of adult males in D then what is difference between total no. of males and that of females in this city?
    (a) 3900 (b) 4700 (c) 5000 (d) 4800
    (e) None of these

65. 40% of adult male population and 55% of adult female population are married in city E. If 48% of total adult population is married then what is number of children in this city?
    (a) 15400 (b) 16000 (c) 12600 (d) 14400
    (d) None of these

66. Respective ratio of number of males to that of females in city A is 4 : 3 and number of children in city F is 25% of total population of the city then total no. of males in city A is what percent of that of males in city F?
    (a) 280.3% (b) 208.3% (c) 201.3% (d) 218.3%
    (e) None of these

DIRECTIONS (Qs. 67-71) : *The following Pie chart shows the percentage number of the candidates passed in examination from States A, B, C, D, E, F of a country in 2016. The Bar graph shows the percentage of fresh candidates who passed their graduation in 2016.*

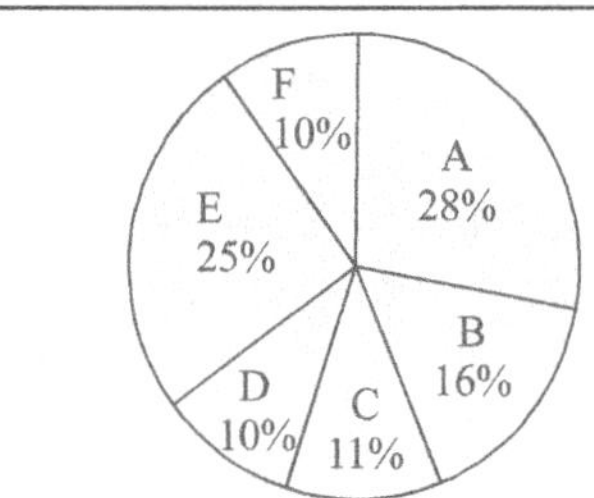

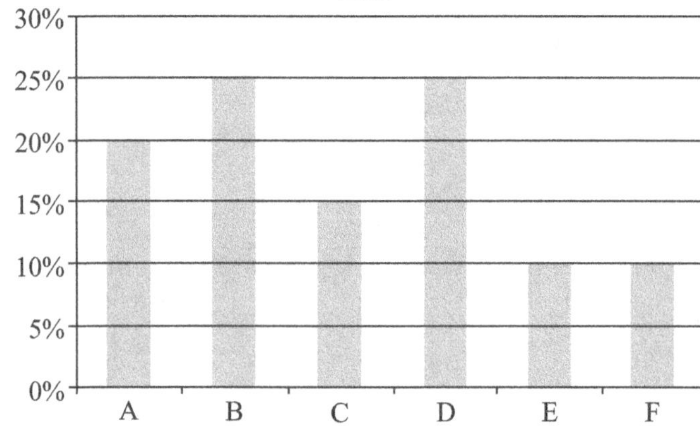

67. If in 2016, the total passed candidates from states A, B, C, D, E and F was 650, then percentage of non-fresher candidates from State A who passed the examination in 2016 is
    (a) 95%   (b) 86%   (c) 80%   (d) 70%
    (e) None of these

68. If in 2016, the total number of freshers from state D was 160, then how many non-fresher candidates passed the exam from State E?
    (a) 1430   (b) 1240   (c) 1420   (d) 1440
    (e) None of these

69. If total passed candidates from state B in 2016 was 112. what is the ratio between the number of freshers from state A and that of non-freshers from state C?
    (a) 39:65   (b) 38:65   (c) 43:65   (d) 41:65
    (e) None of these

70. If there is an increase of 10% and 20% candidates from state A and state B in the year 2017 respectively and the number of total passed candidates from state C in 2016 was 77, what would be the approximate total no of passed candidates from state A and State B in 2017?
    (a) 400   (b) 350   (c) 450   (d) 380
    (e) None of these

71. If the non-fresher candidates from state B in 2016 were 60, how many candidates passed the exam from all the states?
    (a) 600   (b) 400   (c) 500   (d) 350
    (e) None of these

DIRECTIONS (Qs. 72-76): *Study the graph to answer the following Questions*

4000 posts of different cadres have to be filled up by six different banks (A, B, C, D, E, F). Chart - I shows the breakup of vacant posts in these banks. Chart - II shows the percentage breakup of the requirement of personnel in the different cadres in a bank. Assume that these percentages are the same for all the banks.

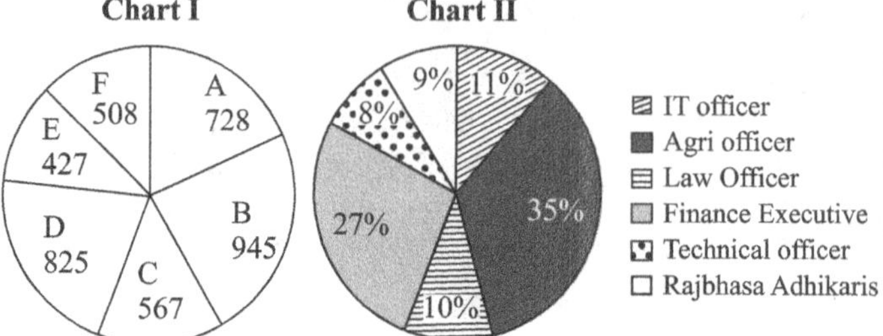

72. Banks A and C recruited IT officers as per given requirement. After few days some of the newly employed IT officers left A and Joined C. The number of new requirements of IT officers in A and C have now become equal. The approximate percentage of new recruits who left A is
    (a) 11%   (b) 15%   (c) 22%   (d) 20%
    (e) None of these

73. By what % is the number of recruitments of law officers more/less in C, E and F taken together than in A, B and D taken together?
    (a) More by 40%   (b) More by 20%
    (c) less by 40%   (d) less by 20%
    (e) None of these

74. What is the ratio of requirement of Finance Executives in C and E taken together with D and F taken together?
    (a) 1333:994 (b) 633:991 (c) 799:998 (d) 994:1333
    (e) None of these

75. Banks D and F hired 15% of Rajbhasha Adhikaris than their own requirement(%). After 1 year the total strength of the staff was brought down to the original strength through retrenchments of some employees. What is the difference between the initial strength and the current strength of employees?
    (a) 80   (b) 60   (c) 50   (d) 30
    (e) None of these

76. In Bank E, about how many more technical officers should be employed than the required number so that the ratio of technical officers to that of finance executives becomes 2:3?
    (a) 63   (b) 33   (c) 43   (d) 53
    (e) None of these

DIRECTIONS (Qs. 77-81): *Answer the following questions, based on the following two graphs, assuming that there is no fixed component and all the units produced are sold in the same year.*

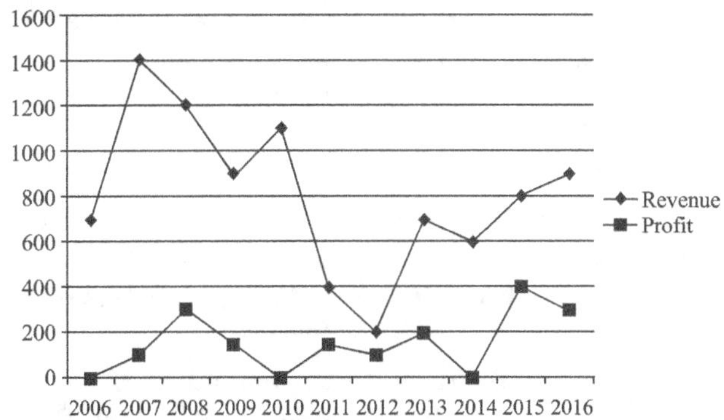

77. In which year per unit cost is lowest?
(a) 2008   (b) 2009   (c) 2012   (d) 2013
(e) None of these

78. In which year per unit cost is highest?
(a) 2007   (b) 2009   (c) 2012   (d) 2013
(e) None of these

79. What is the approximate average quantity sold during the period 2006-2016?
(a) 50%   (b) 60%   (c) 81%   (d) 70%
(e) None of these

80. What is the average number of total units sold in the years of 2008, 2009, 2010, 2011 and 2014 together?
(a) 88   (b) 66   (c) 77   (d) 44
(e) None of these

81. If the price per unit decrease by 10% during 2006-2010 and cost per unit increase by 10% during 2011-2016, then the cumulative profit for the entire period 2006-2016 decreases by?
(a) 700   (b) 500   (c) 565   (d) 775
(e) None of these

DIRECTIONS (Qs. 82-86): *Answer the questions based on the following two graphs, assuming that there is no fixed cost component and all the units produced are sold in the same year.*

[SBI Bank PO Main 2015]

Unit Price

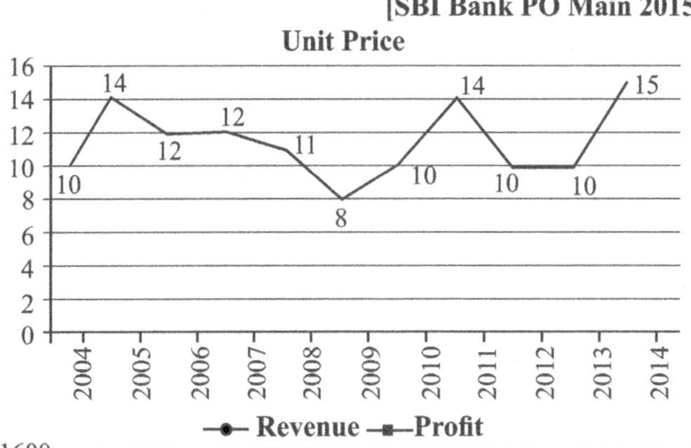

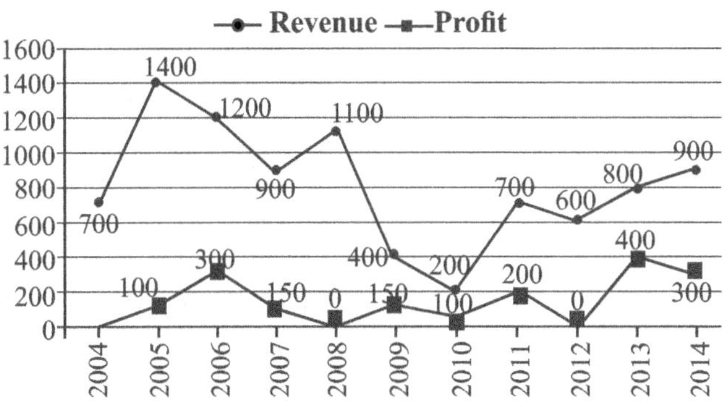

82. In which year per unit cost in highest?
(a) 2006   (b) 2005   (c) 2009   (d) 2011
(e) 2012

83. What is the approximate average quantity sold during the period 2004-2014?
(a) 64 units   (b) 70 units
(c) 77 units   (d) 81 units
(e) 87 units

84. If volatility of a variable during 2000-2014 is defined as $\dfrac{\text{Maximum value} - \text{Minimum value}}{\text{Average value}}$, then which of the following is true?
(a) Price per unit has highest volatility
(b) Cost per unit has highest volatility
(c) Total profit has highest volatility
(d) Revenue has highest volatility
(e) None of the above

85. If the price per unit decrease by 20% during 2004-2008 and cost per unit increase by 20% during 2009-2014, then during how many number of years there is loss?
(a) 3 yr   (b) 4 yr   (c) 5 yr   (d) 7 yr
(e) None of these

86. If the price per unit decrease by 20% during 2000-2004 and cost per unit increase by 20% during 2005-2010, then the cumulative profit for the entire period 2000-2010 decrease by
(a) ₹1650   (b) ₹1550
(c) ₹1300   (d) ₹1250
(e) Data inadequate

DIRECTIONS (Qs. 87-91) : *Study the following bar graph and table carefully and answer the following questions given below.*

[IBPS RRB Officer Scale-I 2016]

Time taken to travel (in hours) by six vehicles on two different days.

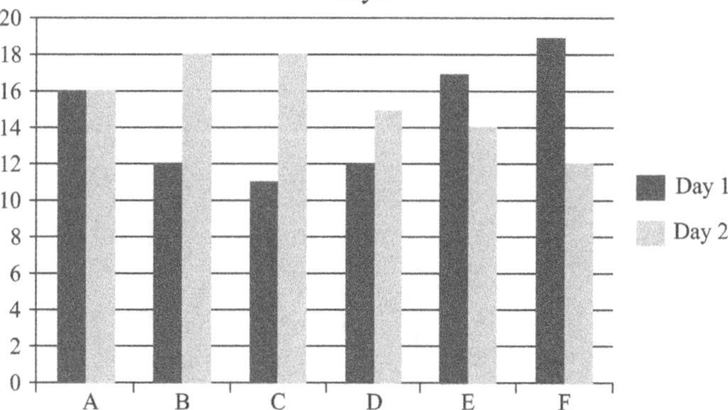

Distance covered by six vehicles on each day

Vehicle	Day 1	Day 2
A	832	864
B	516	774
C	693	810
D	552	765
E	935	546
F	703	636

87. Which of the following vehicles travelled at the same speed on both the days?
    (a) Vehicle A   (b) Vehicle B
    (c) Vehicle C   (d) Vehicle D
    (e) None of these

88. What was the difference between the speed of vehicle A on day 1 and the speed of the vehicle C on the same day?
    (a) 22 kmph   (b) 11 kmph
    (c) 10 kmph   (d) 13 kmph
    (e) None of these

89. What was the speed (in m/s) of vehicle C on day 2?
    (a) 12.5 m/s   (b) 11.5 m/s
    (c) 10.5 m/s   (d) 9.5 m/s
    (e) None of these

90. The distance travelled by vehicle F on day 2 was approximately what % of the distance travelled by it on day 1?
    (a) 90%   (b) 95%   (c) 94%   (d) 98%
    (e) None of these

91. What is the ratio of speeds of vehicle D and Vehicle E on day 2?
    (a) 14:15   (b) 17:13   (c) 15:16   (d) 13:17
    (e) 17 : 15

DIRECTIONS (Qs. 92-96): *Study the following pie chart and answer the following questions:*

Production of rice in different states.
Total production = 50lac tones

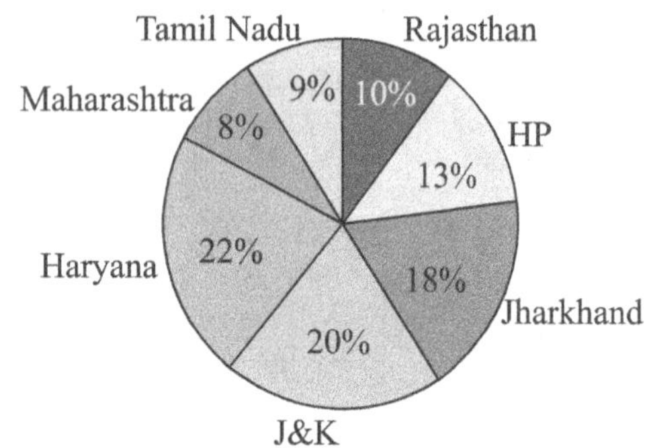

Production: Machine v/s manual

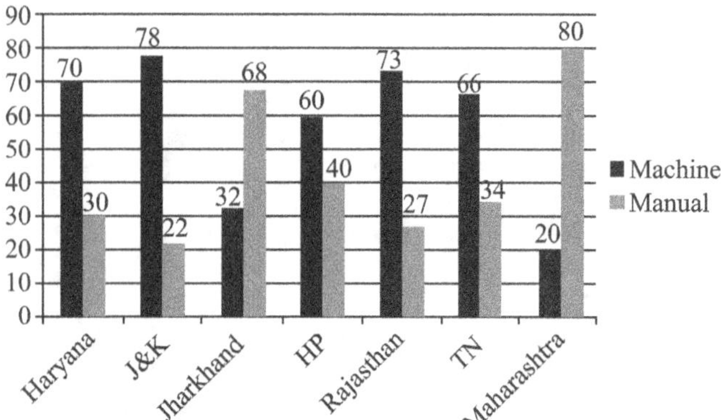

92. What is the difference between the production by machine and manual method in Rajasthan?
    (a) 2.5 lakh   (b) 2.3 lakh
    (c) 2.8 lakh   (d) 2.7 lakh
    (e) None of these

93. What is the ratio of production by manual method in TN to that of machine method in J&K?
    (a) 9:40   (b) 99:260
    (c) 51:260   (d) 33:130
    (e) None of these

94. What is the average production of wheat by machine method for all states?
    (a) 4.24   (b) 4.28   (c) 4.32   (d) 4.46
    (e) None of these

95. The production by machine method in Haryana is approximately what percent greater than the production by manual method in Maharashtra?
    (a) 130%   (b) 135%
    (c) 140%   (d) 145%
    (e) None of these

96. The production of tea in HP by manual method is approximately how many times the production in Jharkhand by machine method?
    (a) 1.2   (b) 1.5
    (c) 0.9   (d) 1
    (e) 1.3

DIRECTIONS (Qs. 97-101) : *Study the data given below and answer the following questions. The pie charts shown below shows the distance covered by a boat moving upstream and downstream in different days of a week. And the table shows the speed of stream in km/hr. in different days of a week.*

[SBI PO 2017 Main]

Total distance covered upstream = 1800 km

Saturday 10% · Sunday 18% · Friday 15% · Monday 15% · Thursday 12% · Wednesday 14% · Tuesday 16%

Total distance covered downstream = 1500 km

Saturday 18% · Sunday 10% · Friday 15% · Monday 16% · Thursday 12% · Wednesday 15% · Tuesday 14%

Day	Speed of stream (km/hr)
Monday	2
Tuesday	3
Wednesday	—
Thursday	1
Friday	2
Saturday	—
Sunday	4

97. If the time taken by boat to travel upstream on Thursday is equal to the time taken by it to travel downstream on Monday and the speed of boat in still water on Monday is 16 kmph then find the speed of boat in still water on Thursday?
    (a) 16.2 kmph   (b) 17.2 kmph
    (c) 15.4 kmph   (d) 12.5 kmph
    (e) None of these

98. If the time taken by boat to travel upstream on Monday is $\frac{45}{11}$ hrs. more than the time taken by it to travel downstream on the same day, then find the speed of boat in still water on Monday?
    (a) 22 kmph   (b) 18 kmph
    (c) 20 kmph   (d) 19 kmph
    (e) None of these

99. If the speed of boat in still water on Tuesday was 15 km/hr and the speed of boat in still water on Wednesday was $66\frac{2}{3}\%$ more than that of Tuesday and time taken to travel upstream on Wednesday is $\frac{9}{10}$ times than time taken by it to travel downstream on Tuesday, then find the speed of stream (in kmph) on Wednesday?
    (a) 1.5   (b) 2.5   (c) 2   (d) 1
    (e) None of these

100. The speed of boat in still water on Saturday was 21 km/hr. and that on Sunday was $28\frac{4}{7}\%$ less than that on Saturday, if the time taken by boat to travel upstream on Saturday is $1\frac{3}{16}$ times than time taken to travel downstream on Sunday, then find the time taken by the boat to cover a distance of 57.6 km upstream when the speed of stream is same as that of Saturday.
    (a) 3 hrs.   (b) 2 hrs.
    (c) 4 hrs.   (d) 2.5 hrs.
    (e) None of these

101. If the time taken by boat to travel upstream on Sunday is 2 hours more than the time taken by it to travel downstream on Thursday and the speed of boat in still water on Thursday is 17 kmph, then find the upstream speed of boat on Sunday?
    (a) 27 kmph   (b) 22 kmph   (c) 20 kmph   (d) 25 kmph
    (e) None of these

DIRECTIONS (Qs. 102-106) : *A, B, C, D and E are five persons employed to complete a job X. Line graph shows the data regarding the time taken by these persons to complete the job X. Table shows the actual time for which every one of them worked on the job X.*

Note 1: All the persons worked on the job X for 'whole number' days.

Note 2: Two jobs Y and Z are similar to job X and require same effort as required by job X.

102. A and C worked on job Y working alternatively for 10 days. B and D then worked together for 'x' days. If $\frac{1}{36}$ of the job was still remained, then find the value of 'x'?
    (a) 2 days   (b) $1\frac{1}{4}$ days   (c) $1\frac{1}{3}$ days   (d) $1\frac{1}{7}$ days
    (e) 1 day

103. E worked on job 'Z' for 5 days and the remaining job was completed by A, B and D who worked on alternate days starting with A followed by B and D in that order. Find the no. of days B worked for?
    (a) 2   (b) 4   (c) 9   (d) 3
    (e) None of these

104. If A, C and E worked on job Z for 2 days each and the remaining job was done by B and D. If the ratio of no. of days for which B and D worked is 20 : 21, then find the number of days for which B worked?
    (a) 50 days   (b) $4\frac{1}{2}$ days   (c) $5\frac{1}{2}$ days   (d) 4 days
    (e) None of these

105. If the ratio of number of days for which B and D worked on job X is 4 : 3, then find the difference between number of days for which B and D worked?
    (a) 2   (b) 3   (c) 1   (d) 4
    (e) None of these

106. If C worked on job Y with $\frac{5}{4}$ times his given efficiency and was assisted by B every 3rd day, then find the time taken by C to complete the job Y?
    (a) 13 days   (b) $12\frac{1}{6}$ days
    (c) $13\frac{1}{2}$ days   (d) 12 days
    (e) None of these

DIRECTIONS (Qs. 107–111) : *Study the graphs carefully to answer the questions that follow :*

Total number of children in 6 different schools and the percentage of girls in them   [SBI & Its Associates PO 2010]

[SBI PO Main 2017]

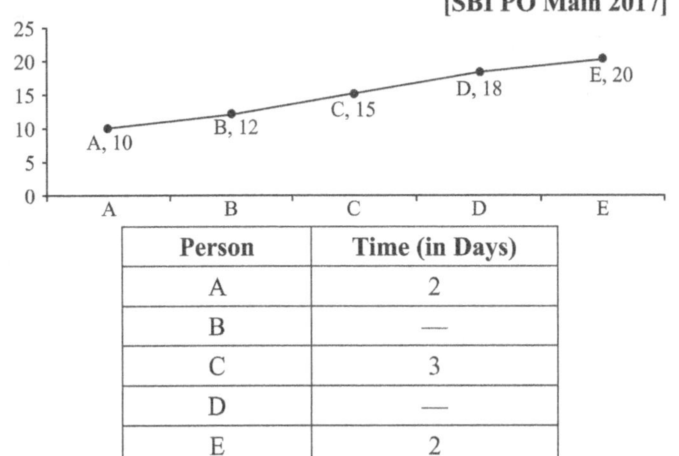

Person	Time (in Days)
A	2
B	—
C	3
D	—
E	2

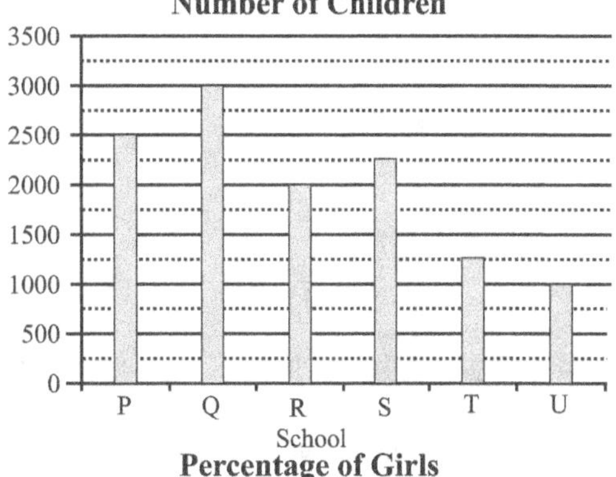

Percentage of Girls

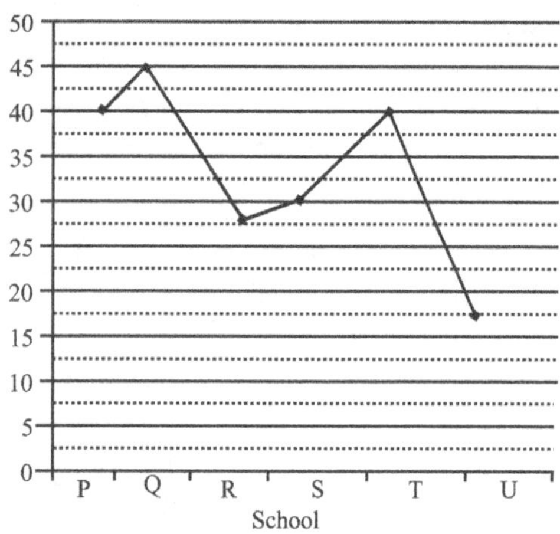

107. What is the total percentage of boys in schools R and U together (rounded off to two digits after decimal)
(a) 78.55   (b) 72.45   (c) 76.28   (d) 75.83
(e) None of these

108. What is the total number of boys in School T ?
(a) 500   (b) 600   (c) 750   (d) 850
(e) None of these

109. The total number of students in school R, is approximately what percent of the total number of students in school S ?
(a) 89   (b) 75   (c) 78   (d) 82
(e) 94

110. What is the average number of boys in schools P and Q together ?
(a) 1425   (b) 1575   (c) 1450   (d) 1625
(e) None of these

111. What is the respective ratio of the number of girls in school P to the number of girls in school Q ?
(a) 27 : 20   (b) 17 : 21
(c) 20 : 27   (d) 21 : 17
(e) None of these

DIRECTIONS (Qs. 112–116) : *Study the following pie-charts carefully and answer the questions given below :*

Disciplinewise Break up of Number of candidates appeared in Interview and Disciplinewise Break up of Number of Candidates selected by an organisation

Disciplinewise Break up of Number of candidates appeared in Interview by the organisation **[SBI & Its Associates PO 2010]**

Total Number of candidates Appeared In the Interview = 25780

Disciplinewise Break up of Number of candidates selected after Interview by the organisation

Total Number of candidates selected After Interview = 7390

112. What was the ratio between the number of candidates appeared in interview from other disciplines and number of candidates selected from Engineering discipline respectively (round off to the nearest integer) ?
(a) 3609 : 813   (b) 3094 : 813
(c) 3094 : 1035   (d) 4 125: 1035
(e) 3981: 767

113. The total number of candidates appeared in interview from Management and other disciplines was what percent of number of candidates appeared from Commerce discipline?
(a) 50   (b) 150
(c) 200   (d) Cannot be determined
(e) None of these

114. Approximately what was the difference between the number of candidates selected from Agriculture discipline and number of candidates selected from Engineering discipline?
(a) 517   (b) 665
(c) 346   (d) 813
(e) 296

115. For which discipline was the difference in number of candidates selected to number of candidates appeared in interview the maximum ?
(a) Management   (b) Engineering
(c) Science   (d) Agriculture
(e) None of these

116. Approximately what was the total number of candidates selected from Commerce and Agriculture discipline together?
(a) 1700   (b) 1800
(c) 2217   (d) 1996
(e) 1550

DIRECTIONS (Qs. 117-118) : *Contribution of different sources of water to fulfil the requirement in Delhi and consumption of water for different uses by two major sources.*

Total consumption of water = 720 million litres

[SBI PO Exam 2011]

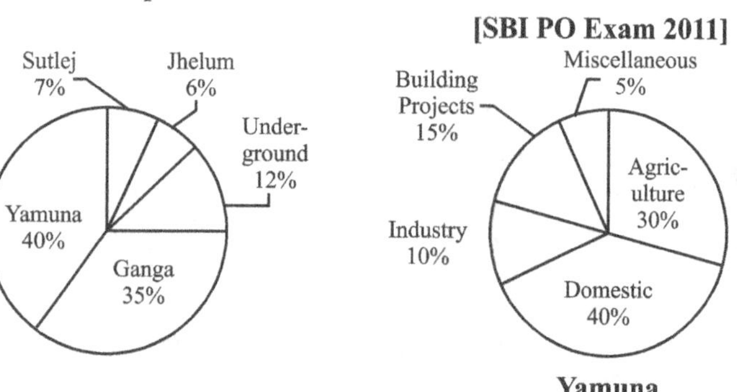

Yamuna

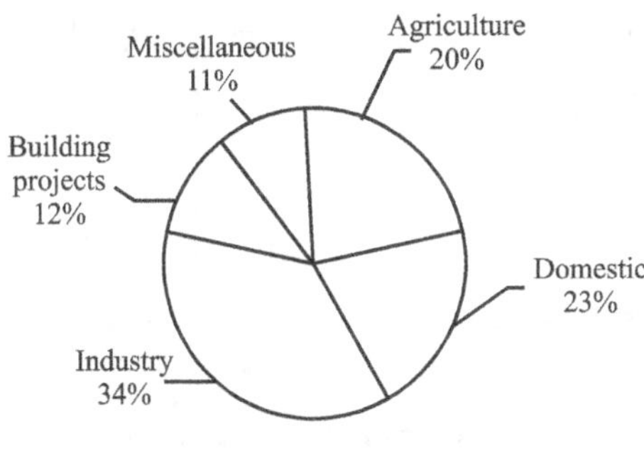

Ganga

117. How many litres of Yamuna water is consumed for building projects in Delhi?
    (a) 39.9m litre
    (b) 43.2 m litre
    (c) 47.3 m litre
    (d) 51.9 m litre
    (e) None of these

118. What is the ratio of supply of Jehlum water and underground water together to consumption of Yamuna water for domestic purposes and Ganga water for Agriculture purposes together?
    (a) 17 : 23
    (b) 5 : 8
    (c) 17 : 22
    (d) 18 : 23
    (e) None of these

DIRECTIONS (Qs. 119-123) : *Study the following data carefully and answer accordingly.*

Following chart shows the number of students in different universities

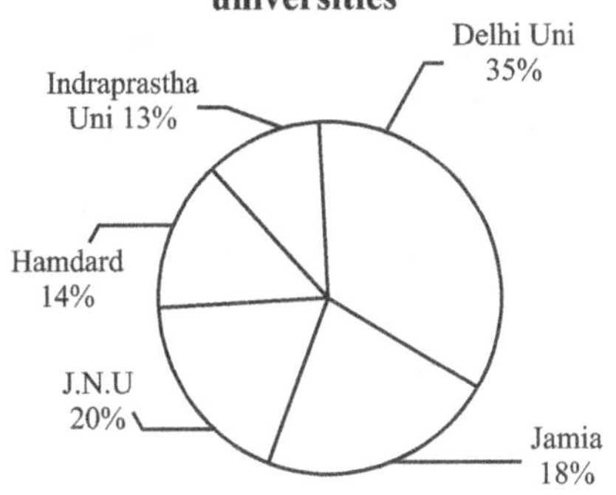

Total no. of students = 120,000

Percentage of listeners of different FM channels in National Capital Region

Universities ↓	FM Channels				
	Radio Mirchi	Radio City	Red FM	FM Gold	Rainbow
Indraprastha	76%	72%	46%	54%	48%
Hamdard	63%	64%	59%	47%	53%
JNU	52%	65%	64%	51%	54%
DU	82%	44%	32%	35%	45%
Jamia	75%	32%	36%	52%	64%

[SBI PO 2011]

119. How many students of JNU listen to Radio city?
    (a) 15200
    (b) 15600
    (c) 14400
    (d) 14600
    (e) None of these

120. The no. of Indraprastha students listening to Rainbow is what per cent of the no. of Jamia students listening FM Gold?
    (a) 65
    (b) 56
    (c) 68
    (d) 58
    (e) None of these

121. From which of the following universities, the no. of students liking Red FM is minimum?
    (a) Indraprastha
    (b) Jamia
    (c) JNU
    (d) DU
    (e) Hamdard

122. How many students of Indraprastha and Jamia together listen to Red FM?
    (a) 12562
    (b) 12872
    (c) 14952
    (d) 14272
    (e) None of these

123. Which of the following channels is the most popular among the students of Hamdard and JNU?
    (a) Radio Mirchi
    (b) Radio city
    (c) Red FM
    (d) FM Gold
    (e) Rainbow

DIRECTIONS (Qs. 124-128) : *Study the following information and answer the questions that follow :*

The graph given below represents the production (in Tonnes and sales (in Tonnes) of company a from 2006-2011

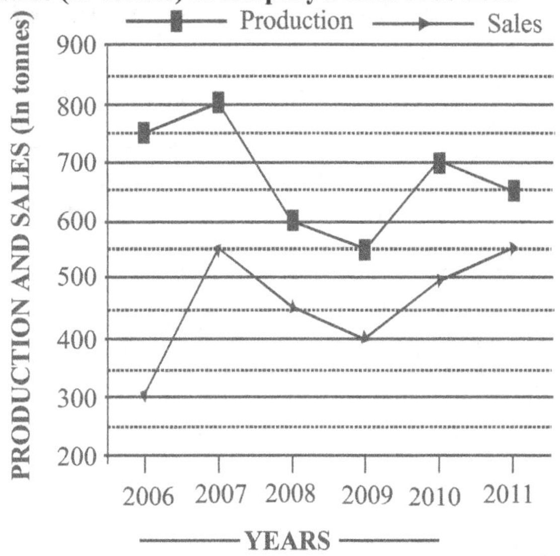

[IBPS PO 2012]

The table given below represents the respective ratio of the production (in tonnes) of Company A to the production (in tonnes) of Company B, and the respective ratio of the sales (in tonnes) of Company A to the sales (in tonnes) of Company B.

Year	Production	Sales
2006	5:4	2:3
2007	8:7	11:12
2008	3:4	9:14
2009	11:12	4:5
2010	14:13	10:9
2011	13:14	1:1

124. What is the approximate percentage increase in the production of Company A (in tonnes) from the year 2009 to the production of Company A (in tonnes) in the year 2010 ?
(a) 18   (b) 38   (c) 23   (d) 27
(e) 32

125. The sales of Company A in the year 2009 was approximately what percent of the production of Company A in the same year ?
(a) 65   (b) 73
(c) 79   (d) 83
(e) 69

126. What is the average production of Company B (in tonnes) from the year 2006 to the year 2011 ?
(a) 574   (b) 649
(c) 675   (d) 593
(e) 618

127. What is the respective ratio of the total production (in tonnes) of Company A to the total sales (in tonnes) of Company A ?
(a) 81 : 64   (b) 64 : 55
(c) 71 : 81   (d) 71 : 55
(e) 81 : 55

128. What is the respective ratio of production of Company B (in tonnes) in the year 2006 to production of Company B (in tonnes) in the year 2008 ?
(a) 2 : 5   (b) 4 : 5   (c) 3 : 4   (d) 3 : 5
(e) 1 : 4

DIRECTIONS (Qs. 129-133) : *Study the following table to answer these questions.*

Plan of Public Sector Under Various
Plans Sector-wise Expenditure out of that total expenditure
(in million)

Plan	I	II	III	IV	V	VI
Public sector plan expenditure	19600	46720	85770	157240	394260	975000
Social service	4180	7440	12960	24620	63720	14035
Education	1530	2730	5890	7860	13360	25240
Health	980	2140	2260	3370	7610	18210
Family Planning	—	20	250	2780	4920	10100
Housing and urban services	330	800	1280	2470	11500	24880
Water supply and sanitation	—	—	1060	4740	10920	39220
Social welfare and related area	1340	1750	2220	3400	15410	22700

[IBPS PO 2013]

129. Which of the following graphs explain best the expenditure on water supply and sanitation?

(a) 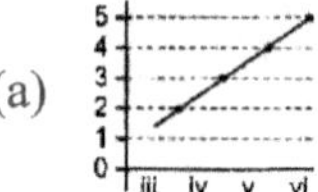   (b) 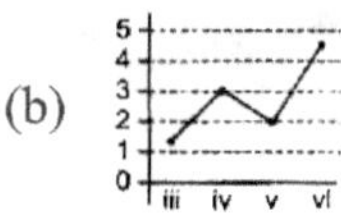

(c) 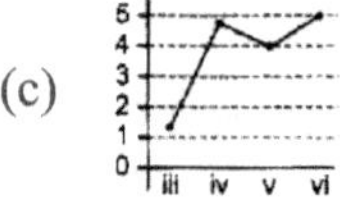   (d) 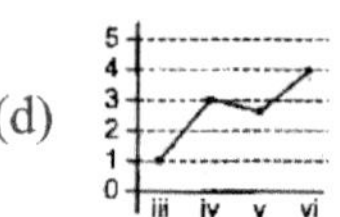

(e) None of these

130. The ratio of public sector expenditure to the expenditure on social services was highest in which plan?
(a) I   (b) VI   (c) V   (d) II
(e) None of these

131. In the successive plans in the ratio of public sector expenditure there was a continuous decrease in which sector?
(a) In no sector   (b) Health
(c) Education   (d) Social services
(e) Social welfare and related areas

132. For plan VI out of public sector expenditure, what per cent of expenditure is on Housing and Urban services?
(a) 0.35   (b) 25   (c) 25.5   (d) 2.5
(e) 20.5

133. For all the given plans, what was the difference in expenditure on education and health?
(a) ₹ 220400000   (b) ₹ 224000000
(c) ₹ 22040000000   (d) ₹ 220400000000
(e) None of these

DIRECTIONS (Qs. 134-138) : *Study the following pie chart carefully to answer the questions.*

Degree Wise Break-up of Employees Working in Various Departments of an Organization and the ratio of Men to Women

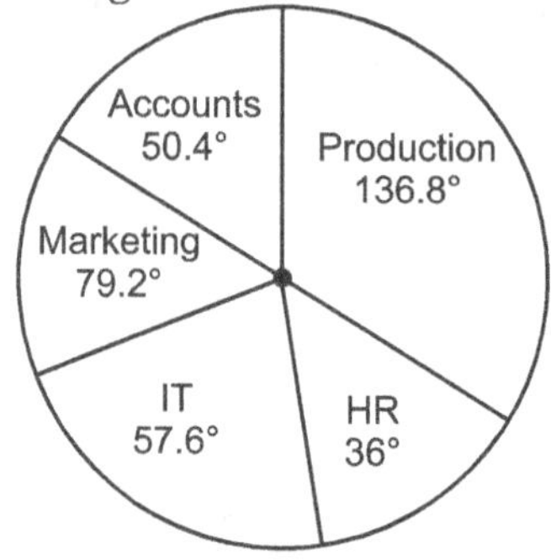

Total number of employees = 3250
Respective Ratio of Men to Women in each Department

Department	Men	Women
Production	4	1
HR	12	13
IT	7	3
Marketing	3	2
Accounts	6	7

[IBPS PO 2013]

134. What is the number of men working in the Marketing department?
(a) 462   (b) 454   (c) 418   (d) 424
(e) None of these

135. What is the respective ratio of the number of women working in the HR department to the number of men working in the IT department?
(a) 11:12   (b) 17:29   (c) 13:28   (d) 12:35
(e) None of these

136. The number of men working in the production department of the organisation forms what per cent of the total number of employees working in that department?
(a) 88%   (b) 90%   (c) 75%   (d) 65%
(e) None of these

137. The number of women working in the IT department of the organization forms what per cent of the total number of employees in the organization from all departments together?
(a) 3.2%   (b) 4.8%
(c) 6.3%   (d) 5.6%
(e) None of these

138. What is the total number of men working in the organization?
(a) 2198   (b) 2147
(c) 2073   (d) 2236
(e) None of these

DIRECTIONS (Qs. 139-143) : *Study the following pie-chart and table carefully and answer the questions given below :*

PERCENTAGE WISE DISTRIBUTION OF THE NUMBER OF MOBILE PHONES SOLD BY A SHOPKEEPER DURING SIX MONTHS
Total number of mobile phones sold = 45,000

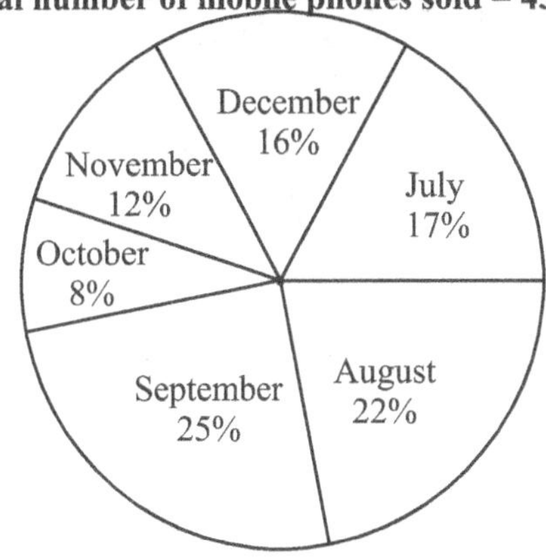

The respective ratio between the number of mobile phones sold of company A and company B during six months

Month	Ratio
July	8:7
August	4:5
September	3:2
October	7:5
November	7:8
December	7:9

139. What is the respective ratio between the number of mobile phones sold of company B during July and those sold during December of the same company ?
(a) 119:145   (b) 116:135
(c) 119 :135   (d) 119:130
(e) None of these

140. If 35% of the mobile phones sold by company A during November were sold at a discount, how many mobile phones of company A during that month were sold without a discount?
(a) 882   (b) 1635   (c) 1638   (d) 885
(e) None of these

141. If the shopkeeper earned a profit of ₹433/- on each mobile phone sold of company B during October, what was his total profit earned on the mobile phones of that company during the same month ?
(a) ₹ 6,49,900/-   (b) ₹ 6,45,900/-
(c) ₹ 6,49,400/-   (d) ₹ 6,49,500/-
(e) None of these

142. The number of mobile phones sold of company A during July is approximately what percent of the number of mobile phones sold of company A during December ?
(a) 110   (b) 140   (c) 150   (d) 105
(e) 130

143. What is the total number of mobile phones sold of company B during August and September together ?
(a) 10,000   (b) 15,000   (c) 10,500   (d) 9,500
(e) None of these

DIRECTIONS (Qs. 144-148): *Study the following graph and answer the given questions.*

[IBPS IT Officer 2016]

Number of Vehicles Manufactured By Two Companies during Six Years (in thousands)

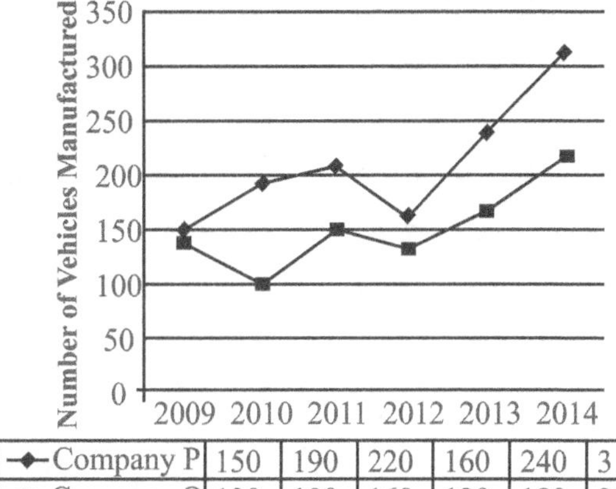

	2009	2010	2011	2012	2013	2014
Company P	150	190	220	160	240	310
Company Q	130	100	160	120	180	210

144. What is the difference between total number of vehicles manufactured by company P in 2011, 2012 and 2014 together and company Q in 2012, 2013 and 2014 together? (in thousands)
(a) 120   (b) 210   (c) 100   (d) 270
(e) 180

145. What is the average number of vehicles manufactured by company Q over six years? (in thousands)
(a) 170   (b) 150   (c) 90   (d) 60
(e) 130

146. What is the percentage decrease in number of vehicles manufactured by company from 2011 to 2012?
(a) $45\frac{3}{11}\%$ (b) $33\frac{3}{11}\%$ (c) $26\frac{6}{19}\%$ (d) $27\frac{3}{11}\%$
(e) $33\frac{4}{11}\%$

147. Out of the number of vehicles manufactured by company P in 2013, 15000 pieces were found defective and out of the number of vehicles manufactured by company Q in 2014, 10000 pieces were found defective. What is the respective ratio of non-defective vehicles manufactured by company P in 2013 and Q in the 2014?
(a) 9 : 8   (b) 11 : 4   (c) 3 : 8   (d) 5 : 8
(e) 7 : 4

148. In year 2015, there was an increase of 30% in number of vehicles manufactured by company P as compared to vehicles manufactured by same company in the year 2010. What is the total number of vehicles manufactured by the same company in the year 2015?
(a) 247   (b) 297   (c) 211   (d) 310
(e) 283

DIRECTIONS (Qs. 149-153): *Refer to the pie-chart and the table and answer the given questions.*

% Distribution of Total Number of Cellular Phones i.e. 11200 (Both Nokia and Samsung) **Sold by Six Stores in October**

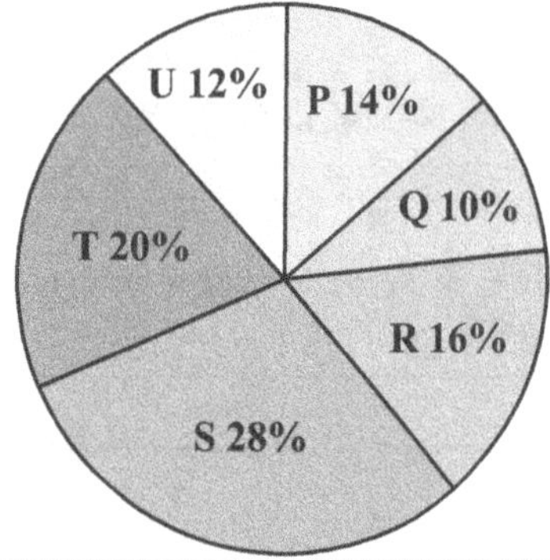

Store	Respective Ratio of Number of Nokia Cellular Phone Sold to the Number of Samsung Cellular Phone Sold
P	4 : 3
Q	3 : 1
R	5 : 4
S	7 : 6
T	1 : 4
U	11 : 10

[IBPS (I.T.) Officer 2016]

149. What is the average number of Nokia cellular phones sold by stores P, R, S and T together?
(a) 1007   (b) 1048   (c) 3908   (d) 1006
(e) 996

150. Number of Nokia cellular phones sold by store R is what percent more than the total number of Samsung cellular phones sold by stores P and Q together?
(a) $23\frac{1}{17}\%$ (b) $19\frac{5}{17}\%$ (c) $20\frac{3}{17}\%$ (d) $17\frac{11}{17}\%$
(e) $4\frac{74}{119}\%$

151. What is the central angle corresponding to total number of cellular phones (both Nokia and Samsung) sold by store S?
(a) 99.2°   (b) 93.6°   (c) 100.8°   (d) 97.4°
(e) 101.2°

152. What is the respective ratio between number of Nokia cellular phones sold by store S and total number of Samsung cellular phones sold by stores T and U together?
(a) 43 : 72   (b) 49 : 76   (c) 43 : 76   (d) 49 : 72
(e) None of these

153. Total number of cellular phones (both Nokia and Samsung) sold by stores Q increased by 15% from October to November and total number of cellular phones (both Nokia and Samsung) sold by store T increased by 5% from October to November. What was the total number of cellular phones sold by stores Q and T together in November?
(a) 3540   (b) 3720   (c) 3640   (d) 3420
(e) 3880

DIRECTIONS (Qs. 154-158) : *One pie chart and two tables are given. In the pie chart distribution of educated females is given and first table shows the respective ratio of number of educated males to that of females. Second table shows the respective ratio of number of educated persons to number of uneducated persons in each city. Study the graphs carefully and answer the related questions.*

Number of educated females = 360000

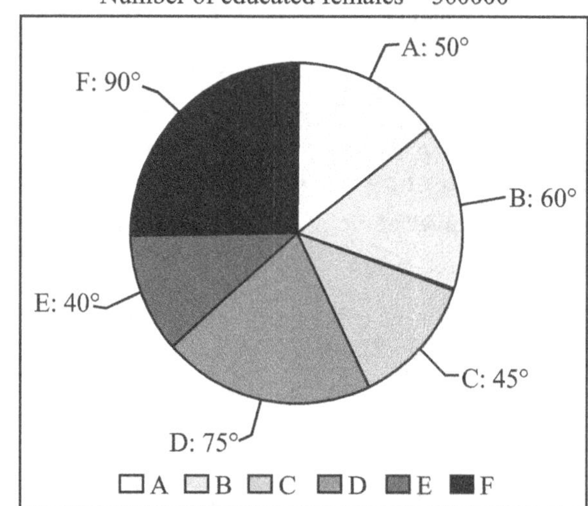

Cities	Educated females : Educated males		No. of males : No. of females
A	5 : 8	A	4 : 3
B	2 : 3	B	8 : 5
C	3 : 4	C	2 : 3
D	5 : 6	D	1 : 1
E	2 : 5	E	5 : 3
F	3 : 5	F	9 : 5

154. If No. of educated males is two times of the number of uneducated males in city A then what percent of number of females is uneducated in this city ?
(a) 71.2%   (b) 72.9%   (c) 73.7%   (d) 72.2%
(e) None of these

155. If number of uneducated males is 50% more than number of educated males in C then what is the respective ratio of number of educated females to number of uneducated females?
(a) 4 : 1   (b) 1 : 4   (c) 2 : 5   (d) 3 : 4
(e) None of these

156. If 40% of total population is educated in city F and 30% of total population is educated in city B then what is the respective ratio of Number of educated persons in cities B and F ?
(a) 5 : 8   (b) 4 : 7   (c) 3 : 8   (d) 8 : 5
(e) None of these

157. If 60% females are educated in city D then what is difference between number of males and number of females in this city?
(a) 50000   (b) 100000   (c) 45000   (d) 60000
(e) None of these

158. If 35% of total population is educated in city E then what is difference between number of educated males and number of uneducated males ?
(a) 100000   (b) 75000   (c) 50000   (d) 25000
(e) None of these

DIRECTIONS (Qs. 159 - 163) : *One pie chart is followed by a table. Pie chart shows the distribution of Number of passed boys in different schools and table shows the respective ratio of number of passed , failed and absented boys from those schools.*

Total number of passed boys = 43200

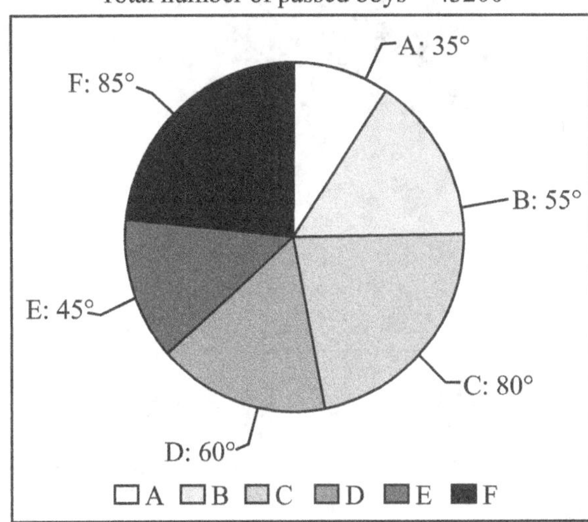

	Passed boys : Failed boys : Absent boys
A	7 : 8 : 1
B	5 : 4 : 3
C	4 : 5 : 2
D	5 : 3 : 1
E	9 : 11 : 5
F	5 : 2 : 2

159. Number of passed boys from school C is what percent of number of appeared students in this school ?
(a) 40.4%   (b) 38.4%   (c) 44.4%   (d) 45.4%
(e) None of these

160. Number of students in school E is what percent more/less than that of school B ?
(a) 5.3%   (b) 6.3%   (c) 7.3%   (d) 8.3%
(e) None of these

161. What is respective ratio of Number of passed and failed boys from all schools together ?
(a) 12 : 13   (b) 13 : 15   (c) 17 : 19   (d) 12 : 17
(e) None of these

162. What is average number of absented students from all schools together ?
(a) 3000   (b) 2980
(c) 2960   (d) 2920
(e) None of these

163. What is respective ratio of number of students in schools D and F ?
(a) 5 : 7   (b) 9 : 11   (c) 13 : 17   (d) 12 : 17
(e) None of these

DIRECTIONS (Qs. 164-168) : *One pie chart is followed by a table. Pie chart shows the number of students who passed the exam of different subjects in year 2015. And table shows the respective ratio of total number of students in 2015 and 2016 study the given data carefully and answer the related questions.*

Number of passed students in 2015 = 9000

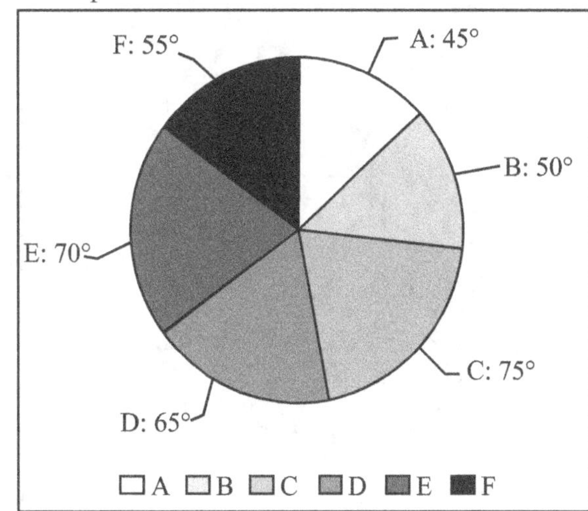

Students	No. of students in 2015 :No. of students in 2016
A	4 : 5
B	3 : 5
C	15:23
D	13:15
E	07:10
F	11:14

164. If 30% students are passed in subject A in 2015 and 40% students are passed in 2016 in this subject then what is the increment percent in number of passed students in 2016 ?
(a) 25%   (b) 30%   (c) 40%   (d) 50%
(e) None of these

165. If number of passed students in D in 2016 is 20% more than that in 2015 then number of passed students is what percent of number of failed students in 2016 in this subject ?
(a) 40%   (b) 50%
(c) 70%   (d) Can't be determined
(e) None of these

166. Total number of students in C in 2015 and 2016 together is 19000 then what is the respective ratio of number of passed and failed students in 2015 in this subject ?
(a) 3 : 1   (b) 1 : 3   (c) 4 : 3   (d) 5 : 3
(e) None of these

167. If pass percentage of students in subject F in 2015 and 2016 was 40% and 50% respectively and difference between number of passed students in these years was 390 then what is difference between number of students in these years ?
    (a) 450   (b) 600   (c) 750   (d) 1050
    (e) None of these

168. If 40% of total number of students passed in subject B in 2015 then what is the average number of students in this subject in both years ?
    (a) 4400   (b) 4267   (c) 4167   (d) 4067
    (e) None of these

DIRECTIONS (Qs. 169-173) : *One pie chart is followed by a table. Pie chart shows the distribution of males in different cities and table shows the respective ratio of number of males and females in those cities. Study the given data carefully and answer the related questions.*

Number of males = 129600

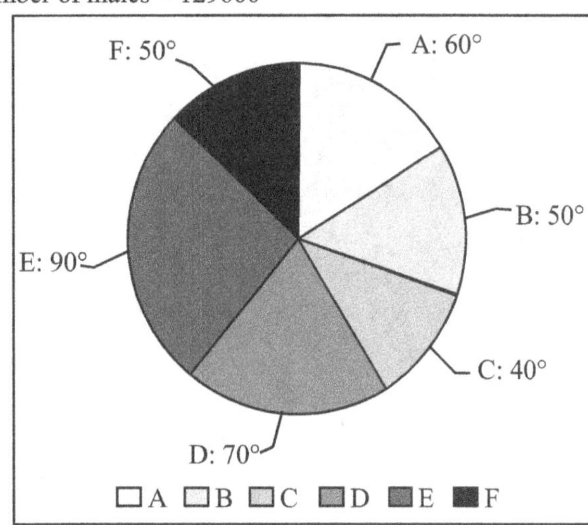

City	No. of males : No. of females
A	2 : 3
B	5 : 4
C	4 : 3
D	7 : 6
E	5 : 4
F	2 : 5

169. If number of males and females increase by 40% and 30% respectively in city D then what is increment percent in total population ?
    (a) 38.35%   (b) 38.53%
    (c) 33.58%   (d) 35.38%
    (e) None of these

170. What is average population of all the cities ?
    (a) 44720   (b) 46920   (c) 46620   (d) 47620
    (e) None of these

171. If number of males increase by 20% and number of females increase by 50% in city B then what would be difference between number of males and females in this city?
    (a) 20000   (b) 40000   (c) 25000   (d) 50000
    (e) None of these

172. What is respective ratio of the population of city B and city F ?
    (a) 18 : 35   (b) 35 : 18   (c) 1 : 1   (d) 5 : 4
    (e) None of these

173. Number of females in city C is what percent of that in city D ?
    (a) 100%   (b) 50%
    (c) 200%   (d) 150%
    (e) None of these

DIRECTIONS (Qs. 174-178) : *In a pie chart data is given about the distribution of salaries of different persons. Pie chart is followed by a bar graph which shows the percentage of expenditure and saving. Study the given data carefully and answer the related questions*

Total salary = 500000

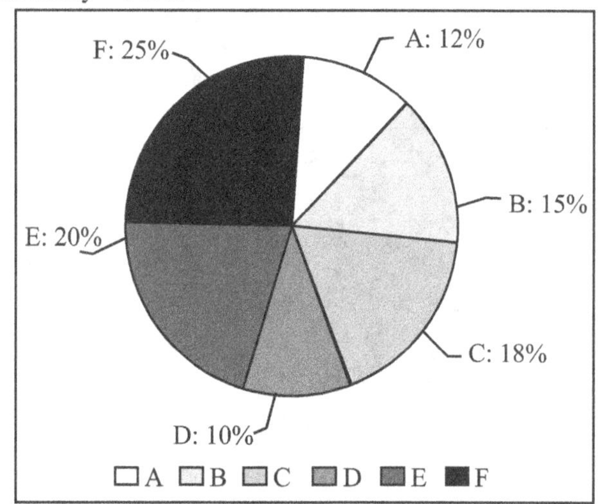

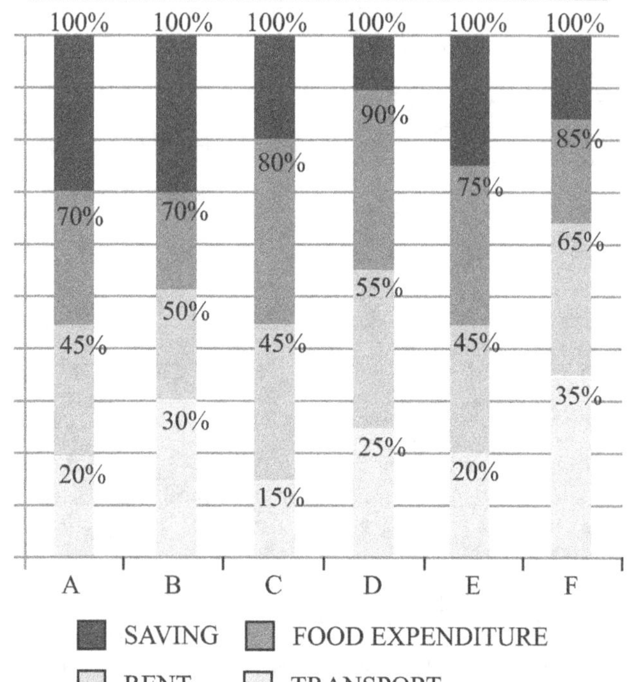

174. What is average saving of all the persons together ?
    (a) 17775   (b) 18775
    (c) 17825   (d) 17875
    (e) None of these

175. Food expenditure of E is what percent more/ less than that of F ?
    (a) 10% (b) 25%
    (c) 20% (d) $33\frac{1}{3}\%$
    (e) None of these

176. What is the percentage of overall transport expenditure ?
    (a) 23.75% (b) 28.35%
    (c) 24.15% (d) 29.25%
    (e) None of these

177. What is respective ratio of rent expenditure of A to that of C ?
    (a) 5 : 9 (b) 9 : 5 (c) 4 : 5 (d) 9 : 4
    (e) None of these

178. What is the difference between total expenditure of A and D ?
    (a) 2000 (b) 3000
    (c) 5000 (d) 12000
    (e) None of these

DIRECTIONS (Qs. 179-183): *In the pie chart distribution of girls participants is given from different schools. Pie chart is followed by a table which shows the respective ratio of number of girl participants and number of boy participants. Study the given data carefully and answer the related questions.*

Total number of girl participants = 2160

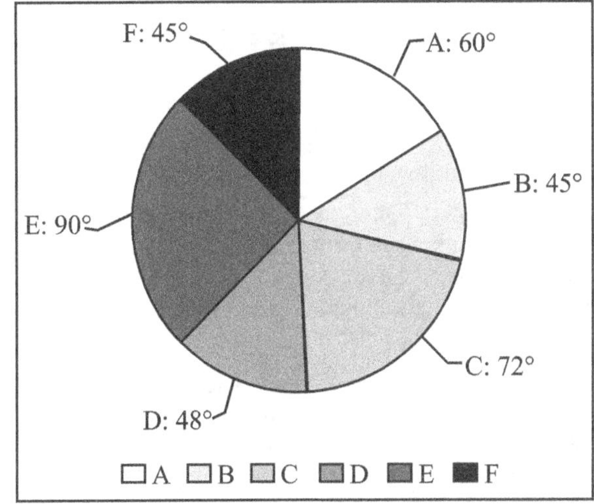

City	No. of girls participants : No. of boys participants
A	3 : 4
B	1 : 2
C	8 : 9
D	12 : 7
E	9 : 5
F	3 : 7

179. If 20% of number of girls and 30% of number of boys are participating in B in games then number of girls in what percent of number of boys in this school ?
    (a) 50% (b) 60%
    (c) 75% (d) 80%
    (e) None of these

180. What is average number of participants in all the schools ?
    (a) 894 (b) 764
    (c) 774 (d) 794
    (e) None of these

181. If 30% of number of girls and 15% of number of boys are participating in school E then what is difference between number of boys and girls in this schools ?
    (a) 500 (b) 250
    (c) 400 (d) 300
    (e) None of these

182. If 20% of total students are participating in school E and respective ratio of number of boys and girls is 4 : 3 the what is respective ratio of No. of boys and girls who are not participating ?
    (a) 5 : 3 (b) 3 : 5
    (c) 1 : 1 (d) 2 : 3
    (e) None of these

183. What is the respective ratio of number of participants in school B and school F ?
    (a) 10 : 9 (b) 9 : 10
    (c) 1 : 1 (d) 2 : 3
    (e) None of these

DIRECTIONS (Qs. 184-188) : *A pie chart is followed by another pie chart and two tables. First pie-chart shows the number of passed boys in different schools and second pie chart shows the number of absent girls in those schools. First table shows the respective ratio of number of passed, failed and absent boys from all schools and second table shows that of girls in those schools.*

Number of passed boys = 21600

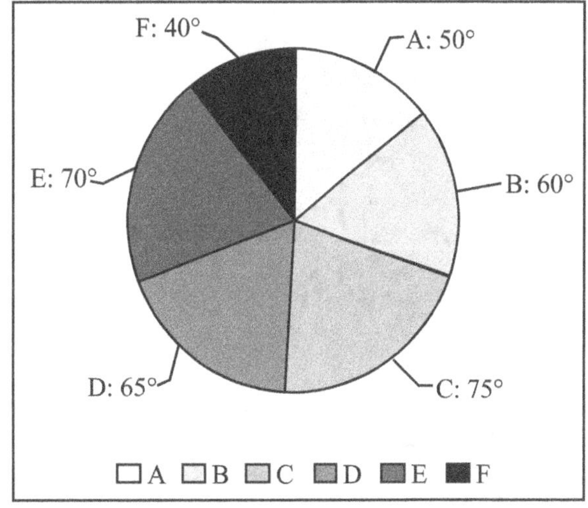

	No. of passed boys : failed boys : absent boys
A	5 : 8 : 2
B	3 : 4 : 1
C	5 : 4 : 1
D	13 : 15 : 2
E	7 : 10 : 3
F	4 : 3 : 1

Number of absent girls = 6000

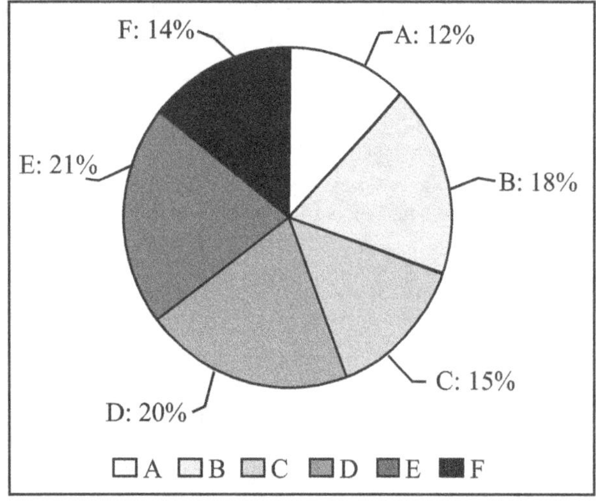

Total number of persons = 1440000

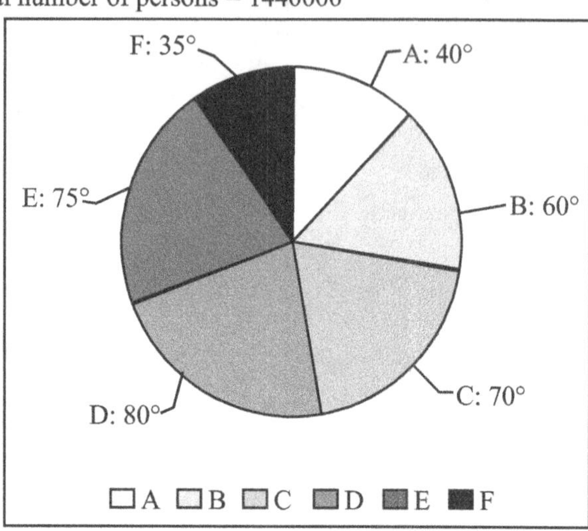

	No. of passed girls : failed girls : absent girls
A	4 : 5 : 2
B	5 : 8 : 3
C	2 : 3 : 1
D	5 : 8 : 2
E	7 : 5 : 3
F	6 : 3 : 2

	No. of males : No. of females		Male children : female children
A	3 : 5	A	2 : 3
B	7 : 5	B	3 : 5
C	4 : 3	C	3 : 4
D	7 : 9	D	1 : 1
E	8 : 7	E	2 : 1
F	19 : 16	F	3 : 2

184. Number of boys in school C is what percent of number of student in this school ?
 (a) 50%
 (b) 40%
 (c) 62.5%
 (d) 37.5%
 (e) None of these

185. What is difference between average number of absent boys and girls from all schools together ?
 (a) 300
 (b) 200
 (c) 100
 (d) 50
 (e) None of these

186. Number of failed boys in school E is what percent of that of girls in this school ?
 (a) 100%
 (b) 200%
 (c) 185%
 (d) 255%
 (e) None of these

187. What is respective ratio of number of boys to that of girls in school C ?
 (a) 5 : 3
 (b) 3 : 5
 (c) 5 : 4
 (d) 4 : 5
 (e) None of these

188. What is respective ratio of number of boys to that of girls from all schools together ?
 (a) 292 : 445
 (b) 445 : 292
 (c) 392 : 445
 (d) 492 : 545
 (e) None of these

189. If number of children in city D is 20% of the population of this city then number of male children is what percent of male population ?
 (a) 19.85%
 (b) 21.75%
 (c) 22.85%
 (d) 25%
 (e) None of these

190. If 20% of total population of city A are children then what is difference between number of male voters and that of female voters ?
 (a) 2400
 (b) 80800
 (c) 41200
 (d) 39600
 (e) None of these

191. What is difference between average number of males and females living in all cities together ?
 (a) 40000
 (b) 48000
 (c) 36000
 (d) 54000
 (e) None of these

192. What is respective ratio of number of males in city C and that of city E ?
 (a) 1 : 1
 (b) 2 : 1
 (c) 3 : 2
 (d) 4 : 5
 (e) None of these

193. Number of females in city F is what percent more/less than that of city B ?
 (a) 32%
 (b) 36%
 (c) 64%
 (d) 40%
 (e) None of these

DIRECTIONS (Qs. 189-193) : *One pie chart is followed by two tables. Pie chart shows the number of persons living in different cities. First table shows the respective ratio of number of males and females and second table shows the respective ratio of number of minors in those cities. Study the given data carefully and answer the related questions.*

DIRECTIONS (Qs. 194-198) : *One pie chart is followed by a table. Pie chart shows the salary distribution of different persons. Table shows the respective ratio of their expenditure and saving. Study the given data carefully and answer the related questions.*

Total salary of all persons = 900000

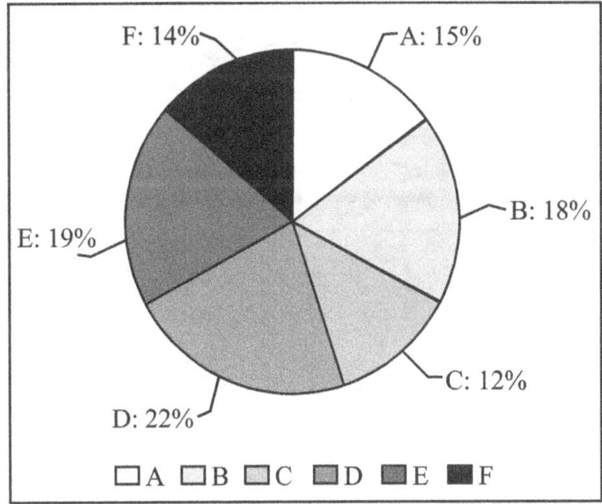

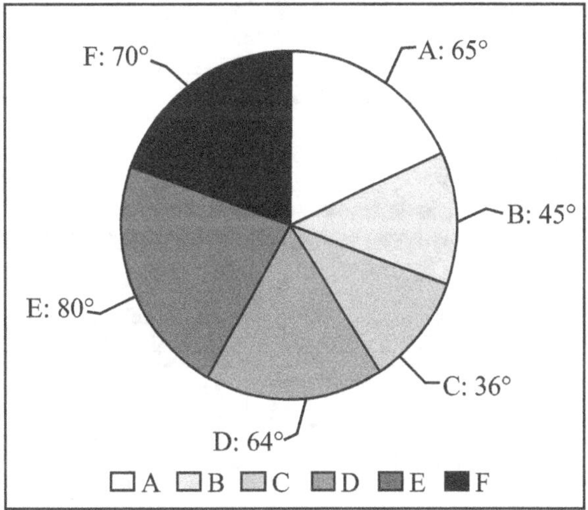

	Expenditure : Saving
A	3 : 2
B	5 : 1
C	3 : 1
D	8 : 3
E	13 : 6
F	5 : 2

	No. of trained workers : No. of untrained workers
A	5 : 7
B	3 : 5
C	4 : 3
D	2 : 5
E	4 : 1
F	7 : 2

194. Expenditure of B is what percent of Salary of A ?

(a) 50% (b) $66\dfrac{2}{3}\%$

(c) 100% (d) 80%
(e) None of these

195. What is respective ratio of total expenditure and total saving of all persons ?
(a) 11 : 18 (b) 18 : 11
(c) 7 : 18 (d) 18 : 7
(e) None of these

196. What is difference between savings of E and F ?
(a) 18000 (b) 36000
(c) 54000 (d) 72000
(e) None of these

197. Total savings of all persons is what percent of total salary of all persons ?
(a) 30% (b) 25%
(c) 32% (d) 35%
(e) None of these

198. What is average salary of all six persons ?
(a) 120000 (b) 150000
(c) 180000 (d) 75000
(e) None of these

199. What is average number of workers in all companies together?
(a) 42825 (b) 42925
(c) 43625 (d) 43925
(e) None of these

200. What is difference between average number of trained and untrained workers in all companies ?
(a) 1875 (b) 1925
(c) 2425 (d) 2925
(e) None of these

201. Number of untrained workers in B is what percent more/ less than that of D ?
(a) 53.1% (b) 52.5%
(c) 63.1% (d) 45.1%
(e) None of these

202. What is respective ratio of number of workers in E and F ?
(a) 8 : 9 (b) 9 : 10
(c) 10 : 9 (d) 9 : 8
(e) None of these

203. Number of trained workers is what percent of total number of workers in all companies together ?
(a) 49.5% (b) 51.2%
(c) 46.7% (d) 42.8%
(e) None of these

DIRECTIONS (Qs. 199-203) : *A pie chart is followed by a table. Pie chart shows the distribution of number of trained workers and table shows the respective ratio of number of trained and untrained workers in all companies. Study the given data carefully and answer the related questions.*

Number of trained workers = 126000

DIRECTIONS (Qs. 204-208) : *Study the following information carefully and answer the given questions:*

The line graph shows that total number of manufacturing parts produced by five different companies in the year 2017 and 2018.

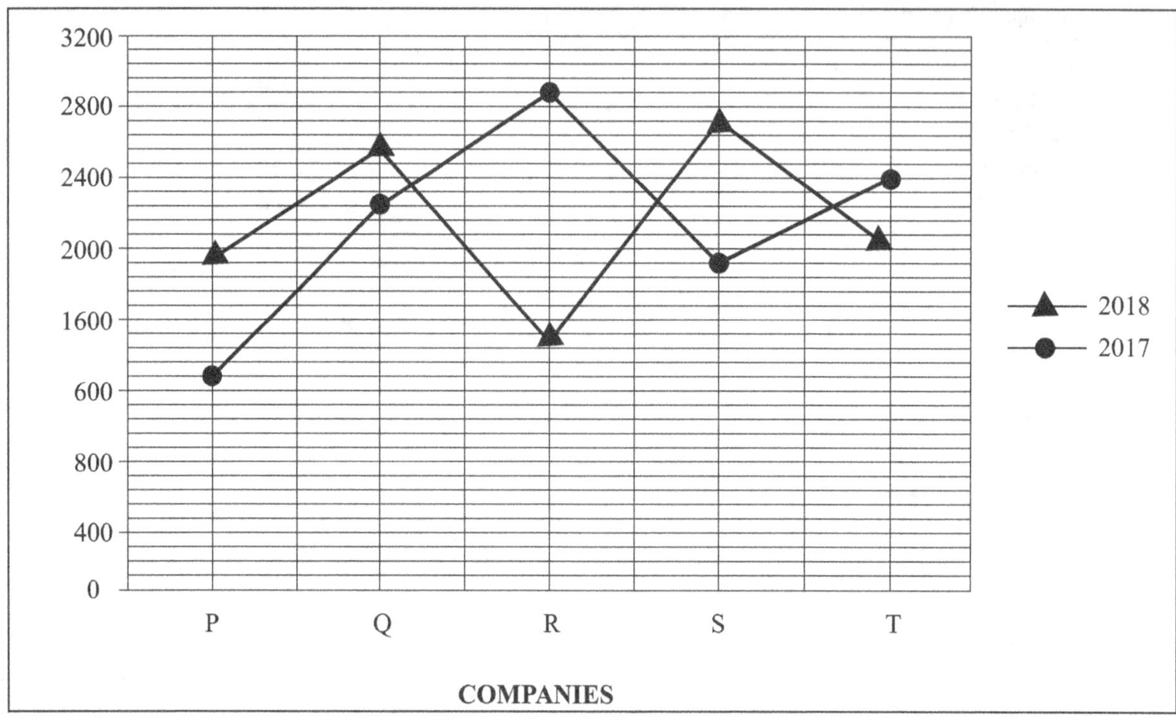

The table shows that percentage of Defective parts and percentage of non-defective parts that are not passed the quality test in the year 2017

Companies	% of Defective parts	% of non-defective that are not passed the quality test
P	15%	50%
Q	30%	25%
R	25%	10%
S	20%	25%
T	28%	50%

204. If both the years the percentage of defective parts from company S is equal, and in 2018 only 10% of non-defective parts are not passed the quality test for company S, then what is the total number of non-defective parts that are passed the quality test in both years from company S?
(a) 3312   (b) 612   (c) 3111   (d) 3332
(e) None of those given as option

205. What is the ratio of Non-defective parts that are not passed by quality test from company Q and R in 2017 to the Non-defective parts that are passed by quality test from the same companies together in 2018 if the percentage of Non-defective parts that are not passed by quality test from company Q and R are equal in both the years?
(a) 3 : 7   (b) 53 : 52   (c) 4 : 9   (d) 19 : 17
(e) Cannot be determined

206. In 2018, the percentage of defective parts from company P, Q and T are 20%, 25% and 15% respectively, then the total number of Non-defective parts that are passed from quality test from company R and S in 2017 is approximately what percentage more or less than that of the total number of Non-defective parts from P, Q and T together in 2018?
(a) 38% More   (b) 50% less
(c) 28% More   (d) 40% less
(e) None of those given as option

207. What is the average number of non-defective parts that are not passed the quality test from all the company except S in 2017?
(a) 508
(b) 496
(c) 440
(d) None of those given as option
(e) 504

208. What is the difference between the non-defective parts that are passed the quality test from Company Q and R together in 2017 to the non-defective parts that are not passed the quality test from Company P, S and T together in 2017?
(a) 1328   (b) 1572
(c) 1088   (d) 1368
(e) None of those given as option

Directions (Qs. 209-213): *Given below is table which shows the ratio of efficiency of both Ramu and Shyamu on different days and total time taken by Ramu and Shyamu to complete the work if they complete whole work with the efficiency of different days.*

Days	Efficiency of Ramu and Shyamu	Time taken by both to complete work (hours)
Monday	3:2	3
Tuesday	3:2	4
Wednesday	7:9	6
Thursday	8:9	5
Friday	5:4	8

There is also the line graph which shows the time taken by Abinav to complete another work if it completes whole work with efficiency of different days.

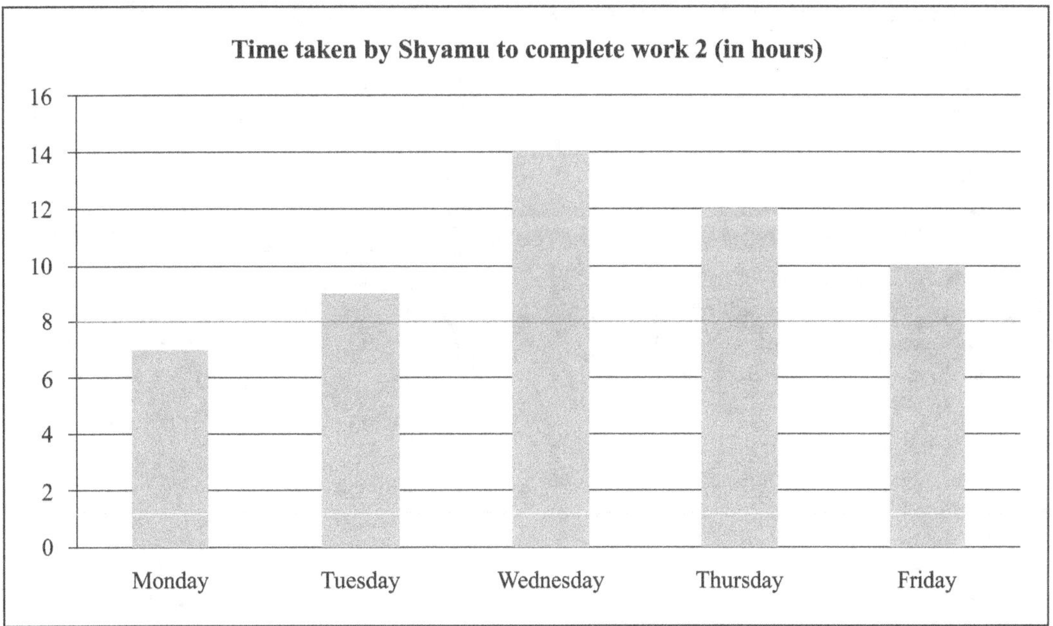

Note: The ratio of efficiency of Ramu and Shyamu to do work 2 on different days is same as data given in the table for work 1.

209. Ramu and Shyamu both started to complete work 1 on Tuesday but Ramu left after working for 2 hours. Another person Bhanu whose efficiency is 60% of the efficiency of Ramu (as of Tuesday) joins with Shyamu. Shyamu leaves 2 hours before the completion of work then Bhanu alone finishes the remaining work. What is the total time in which work 1 is completed.
(a) 115/2 hours (b) 111/13 hours
(c) 108/19 hours (d) 110/19 hours
(e) 110/13 hours

210. If a part of work 2 completed by 4 women in 5 hours equals to the part of work 2 done by Shyamu on Wednesday in 7 hours and ratio of efficiency of a woman and a children to complete work 2 is 5 : 3 then in what time work 2 will be completed by 3 children.
(a) 120/9 hours (b) 200/9 hours
(c) 100/11 hours (d) 210/11 hours
(e) 150/21 hours

211. x can complete a work in $(n-m)$ hours while y can complete the same work in $(n+m)$ hours where m is the time taken by Ramu to complete work 2 on Tuesday and n is time taken by Ramu to complete work w on Friday. Find the time in which x and y together can complete the work
(a) 3/2 hours (b) 7/4 hours
(c) 7/5 hours (d) 8/3 hours
(e) 9/5 hours

212. Ramu and Shyamu started to complete work 1, alternatively starting from shyamu on first hour on Monday. Then time taken by Ramu and Shyamu in completing 80% of work 1, alternatively on Monday what percent more or less than time taken by Ramu and Shyamu together to complete work 2 together on Friday.
(a) 3% (b) 5% (c) 8% (d) 15%
(e) 6%

213. If Shyamu with another person Vikram works on work 2 on Friday for 2 hours than 80% of work 2 is completed then, time taken by Vikram alone to finish work 2 is what percent to time taken by Shyamu to finish work 1 with efficiency of Friday.
(a) 500/27% (b) 400/13% (c) 300/17% (d) 400/21%
(e) 500/21%

DIRECTIONS (Qs. 214-218) : *The following bar graph shows the no. of persons who got affected by 'Dengue' in five different countries. Also, the table shows ratio of male to female in them.*

Study the graphs carefully to answer the related questions.

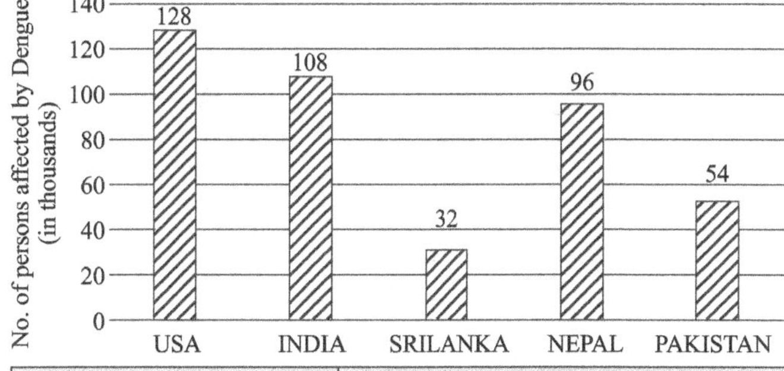

States	Ratio of male to female		
	Male	**:**	**Female**
USA	5	:	3
INDIA	5	:	4
SRI LANKA	3	:	1
NEPAL	7	:	5
PAKISTAN	2	:	1

214. Total no. of male persons affected by Dengue in India are what percent more or less than that of male persons from USA who were affected by Dengue?
(a) 25% less (b) 25% more
(c) 30% less (d) 30% more
(e) 20% more

215. Find the average No. of females who were affected by Dengue in all the five countries
(a) 28400 (b) 25200 (c) 32400 (d) 20800
(e) 24400

216. If 50/3% out of total affected Males in Nepal are of age group (21-25) years, 100/3% out of total affected males are of age group (26-30) years and rest are of age group above 30 years from the same state, then find total no. of males from Nepal who are affected by Dengue, having age of (21-25) years and (26-30) years together.
(a) 32000   (b) 28000   (c) 24000   (d) 36000
(e) 20000

217. What is the difference between total no. of males in India, Sri Lanka and Pakistan together and total no. of females in USA, Sri Lanka and Nepal together who are affected by Dengue.
(a) 30000   (b) 26000   (c) 28000   (d) 24000
(e) 36000

218. Total no. of females in India who are affected by Dengue is what percent more than that of females from Nepal who are affected by Dengue?
(a) 20%   (b) 30%   (c) 15%   (d) 25%
(e) 22%

DIRECTIONS (Qs. 219-223): *The following pie-chart shows the percentage distribution of test series of different coaching institutes and the bar graph shows the percentage of these test series sold by two e-commerce sites-M and N. Study the graph carefully to answer the following questions.*

Total no. of test series launched by different institutes = 10, 00, 000

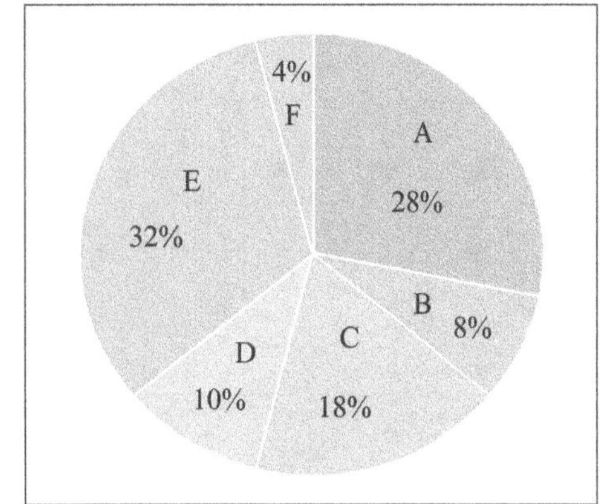

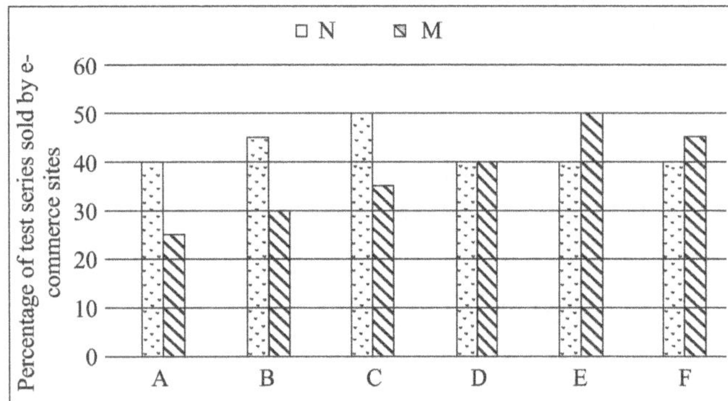

219. What is the total no. of test series remained unsold of A, C and D together?
(a) 130600   (b) 145000
(c) 145800   (d) 142480
(e) 146080

220. Total no. of test series sold by B and F through both e-commerce companies is approximately what percent of total no. of test series of A which remained unsold?

(a) 99%   (b) 92%   (c) 96%   (d) 86%
(e) 88%

221. Total no. of test series of E sold by both sites is approximately what percent of total no. of test series of all institutes except E sold by N?
(a) 98%   (b) 94%   (c) 89%   (d) 92%
(e) 86%

222. What is the ratio of no. of test series of E to that of A which remained unsold?
(a) 49 : 16   (b) 16 : 49   (c) 33 : 49   (d) 32 : 49
(e) 11 : 16

223. Total no. of test series of C and D together sold by N is what percent more or less than the total no. of test series of E sold by M?
(a) 1.875% less   (b) 17.85% more
(c) 187.5% less   (d) 18.75% more
(e) 18.75% less

DIRECTIONS (Qs. 224-228): *Study the graphs carefully to answer the questions that follow.*

Total number of children in 6 different colleges and the percentage of girls in them

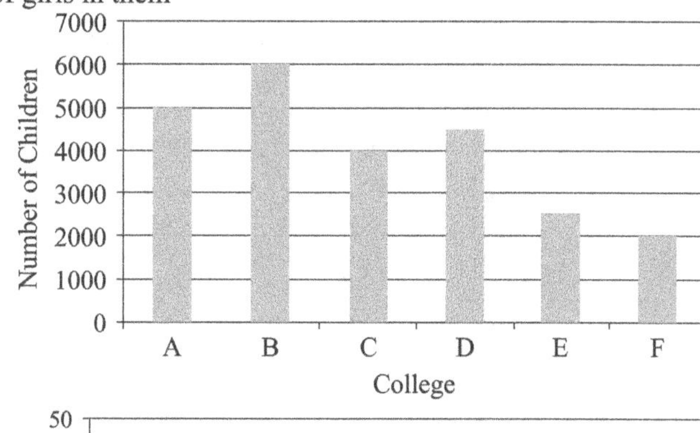

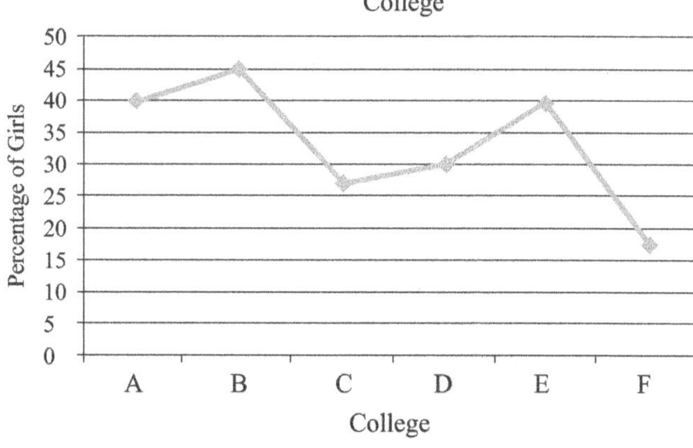

224. What is the total percentage of boys in colleges C and F together? (rounded off to two digits after decimal)
(a) 78.55%   (b) 72.45%
(c) 76.28%   (d) 75.83%
(e) None of these

225. What is the total number of boys in college E?
(a) 1000   (b) 1200   (c) 1500   (d) 1700
(e) None of these

226. The total number of students in college C, is approximately what per cent of the total number of students in college D?
(a) 89%   (b) 75%   (c) 78%   (d) 82%
(e) 94

227. What is the average number of boys in college A and B together?
 (a) 1425　(b) 1575　(c) 1450　(d) 1625
 (e) None of these

228. What is the respective ratio of the number of girls in college A to the number of girls in college B?
 (a) 27 : 20　(b) 17 : 21　(c) 20 : 27　(d) 21 : 17
 (e) None of these

DIRECTIONS (Qs. 229-233): *The bar graph shows the sales of six different car-manufacturers in 2018 (in thousands of units) in America. The pie-chart shows the break-up of sales of Brand JAMA in 2018 in different states of America.*

Note → All manufactured cars are sold in these given 7 states.

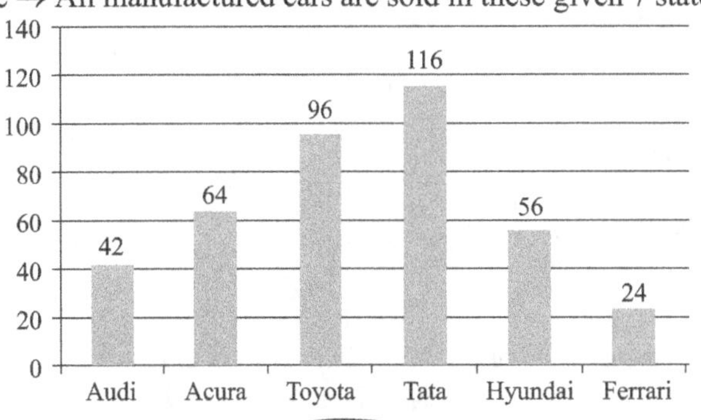

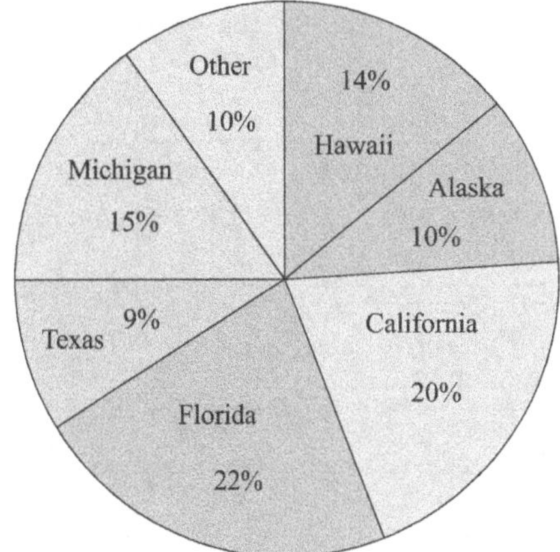

State-wise sale of Brand Tata in 2018

229. What is the difference between the sales of Tata in California and that in Texas?
 (a) 101200　(b) 12760
 (c) 13134　(d) 12440
 (e) None of these

230. By what percent should the sales of brand Tata be increased so that it sales volume in Hawaii becomes 30000, while the volume of sales in all other state remains the same (approximately)
 (a) 10%　(b) 9%
 (c) 7%　(d) 13%
 (e) 12%

231. If in 2019, the total sale of Brand Tata increase by 12%, while its sale in Alaska is increased by 34% and in Florida by 22%, what is the approximate sales increase in the rest of the states.
 (a) 4000　(b) 3000
 (c) 4400　(d) 5000
 (e) 4100

232. Total sale of Audi, Acura and Toyota in 2018 is what percent of the total sales of Tata in all states together in that year, 2018. (approximately)
 (a) 100%　(b) 113%
 (c) 190%　(d) 175%
 (e) 150%

233. If total sale of all brands together increases by 20% in 2019 and sale of Tata in California increase by 10% keeping % percentage distribution of Tata in these seven states same as previously then, what is the total sale of all cars in 2019 of all brands except brand Tata.
 (a) 350000　(b) 300000
 (c) 400000　(d) 200000
 (e) None of these

DIRECTIONS (Qs. 234-238): *Study the following graphs carefully to answer the questions that follow. Number of employees (in hundred) of three categories in 5 factories.*

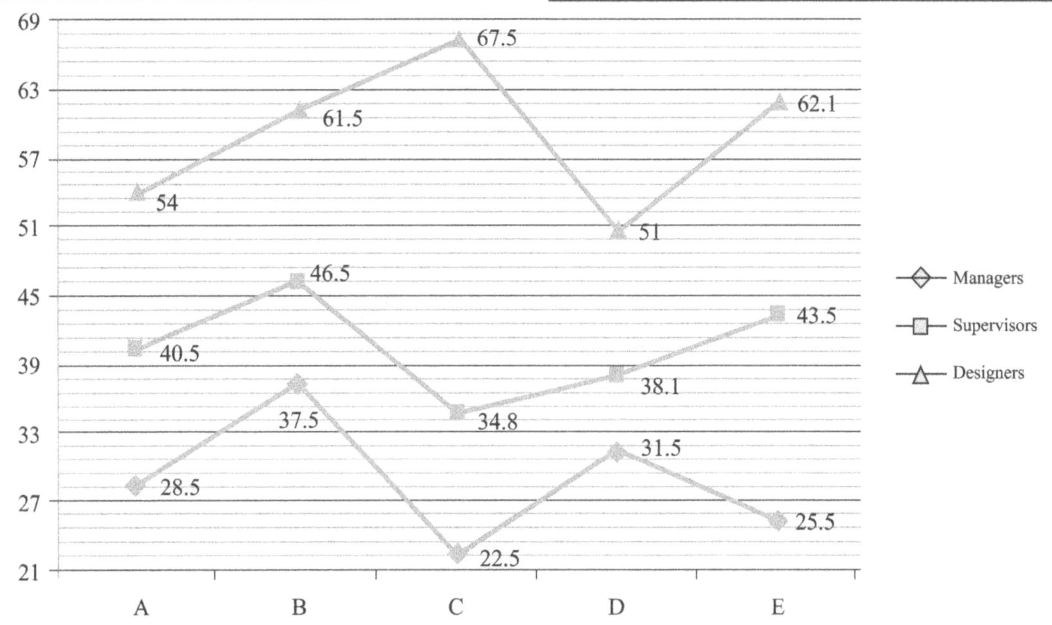

Percentage of females in each group

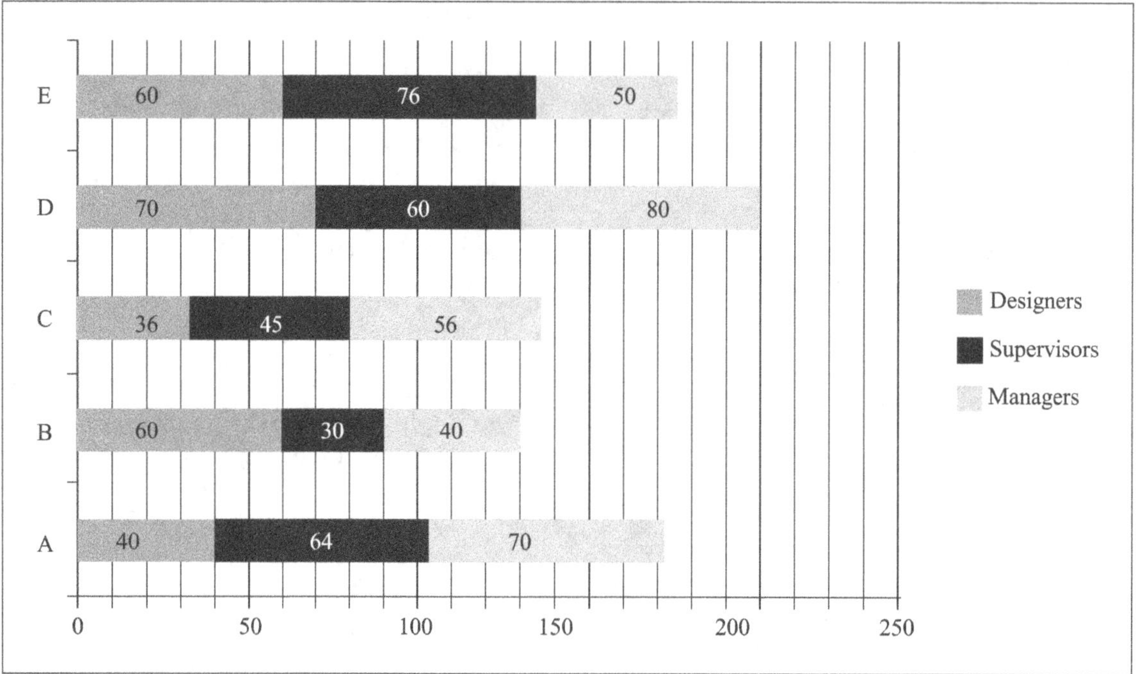

234. The females in Manager post in company C can finish a certain piece of work in 20 days. After they began to work, 60 females left the work after every 5 days. Find the number of days required to complete the work.

(a) $21\dfrac{3}{17}$ days

(b) $21\dfrac{13}{17}$ days

(c) $21\dfrac{13}{19}$ days

(d) $20\dfrac{13}{17}$ days

(e) None of these

235. Find the average number of males in Manager post in all factories together.
(a) 915   (b) 975
(c) 1350   (d) 1200
(e) None of these

236. By what percent the males in the Designer post in factories C and D together are more or less than the females on Supervisor post in factories A and B together?
(a) 45.8%   (b) 46.7%
(c) 42.3%   (d) 44.2%
(e) 40.2%

237. The average age of male designers in factory D is 74 years. Two-fifth of them have average age of 76 years, 50% of remaining have average age 4 years less that of all male designers. Find the average age of remaining male designers.
(a) 74 year 5 month
(b) 72 year 4 month
(c) 75 year 4 month
(d) 75 year 6 month
(e) None of these

238. Find the ratio of total female designers in factories C and D together and female Managers in factory B.
(a) 3 : 2   (b) 4 : 1
(c) 3 : 1   (d) 2 : 1
(e) None of these

DIRECTIONS (Qs. 239-242) : *Given table shows the % range of commission earned on all sold books and commission earned by five shop in Rupees.*

Shop	Range of commission (%)	Commission earned Rupees
PP	0-16	3200
QQ	16-32	-
RR	-	3500
SS	-	-
TT	0-20	4000

Note: - Commission percent is on selling price.

Note: - Some values are missing, you have to calculate them according to question.

Note: - Range of commission are in integral values.

239. Shop 'PP' sells 480 books and only 3 types of books it have, their number are in ratio 1 : 2 : 3 and their selling prices are 200, 300 and 100 respectively and commission charged on them have difference of 1 percent in sequence (least number of articles sold have least commission percent) respectively, then find the highest commission% of books.
(a) 14.375%   (b) 12.375%
(c) 15.45%   (d) 16.375%
(e) None of these

240. Shop RR sells 3 products in equal numbers (105) and equal commission percent. If their selling price (in Rupees.) are 20, 30 and 40. Then what is the commission percent.

(a) $\dfrac{1200}{27}\%$

(b) $\dfrac{900}{27}\%$

(c) $\dfrac{1150}{27}\%$

(d) $\dfrac{1000}{27}\%$

(e) $\dfrac{1040}{27}\%$

241. Shop SS sold 3 books each in number 100 and each have S.P. of ₹ 80 and commission % for each is in A.P. with common difference of 5. If total commission earned by Shop SS is 14 $\dfrac{2}{7}\%$ more than that of Shop RR, find the minimum range of commission%?

(a) $(11-22)$ (b) $(16-23)$

(c) $(05-08)$ (d) $(14-24)$

(e) $(07-10)$

242. If Shop RR have only one type of book and number of book and its S.P is equal which is (≥ 100 & < 110) then find the % range of commission?

(a) $(27.5-30)$ (b) $(34-37.7)$

(c) $(17.4-26.8)$ (d) $(29.4-35)$

(e) $(28-36.6)$

HINTS & SOLUTIONS

Sol. (1-3):

Let the total number of voters be x

as from the question, we came to know that 70% of 25% of x – 40% of 10 % of x = 40500 or, x = 300,000

1. **(b)** Total number of voters from SCGC = 20% of 300000
   Then the number of male voters of St. xavier = 40% of 10% of 300000
   Required ratio = 0.2/ 0.04 = 5:1

2. **(b)** Total number of voters from Lady bovine = 40% of 300000
   New addition to the total number of voters = 15% of 25% of 300000
   New total number of voters be = 300000 + 15% of 25% of 300000
   Hence, required %
   $$= \frac{40\% \text{ of } 300000}{300000 + 15\% \text{ of } 25\% \text{ of } 300000} \times 100$$
   $$= 38.55\%$$

3. **(c)** The number of female voters from lady Bovine = 20% of 40% of 300000 = 24000
   The number of male voters from asutosh college = 75% of 5% of 300000 = 11250
   Required difference = 24000 – 11250 = 12750.

4. **(c)** In 2015 HDFC and SBI disbursed 128 crore and 88 crore respectively. So their market share for loans were 128 / 553 = 23.14% and 88/553 = 15.9% respectively. So the difference between their shares is 23.14 – 15.9 = 7.2%. Auto finance market in 2015 was of 180 crore, so 7.2% of 180 crore is approximately 13 crore. Hence, the answer is (c).

5. **(d)** Market Share of Rupee, Union and SBI = 103 + (14 % + 16 %) of 145 is 146.5 crore, which is more than ICICI, the market leader. Hence, the answer is (d).

6. **(d)** Since we do not know the total number of banks, the answer is indeterminable. Hence, the answer is (d).

7. **(b)** Total amount disbursed in the year 2014 was 506 crore and for the year 2015 it was 553 crore, hence percentage increase = (553 – 506) × 100/506 = 9.28%. Out of the given answer option, the most appropriate answer is (b).

8. **(b)** The difference between the male graduates and XII pass male candidates are 224000 – 210000 = 14000.

9. **(d)** The ratio of female graduates in state E and XII pass female candidates of state D is 210000 : 224000 = 15 : 16

10. **(c)** Female graduates of state C is $\dfrac{160000}{3200000} \times 100 = 5\%$ of XII pass population of all the states together.

11. **(a)** Std XII male candidates of state C is $\dfrac{256000}{3200000} \times 100$ = 8% of Std XII population of all the states together

12. **(d)** The ratio of Male graduate of state E and XII pass female candidate of the same state is 270000 : 320000 = 27 : 32

13. **(d)** Total Graduates in state F is $\dfrac{336000}{480000} \times 100 = 70\%$ of total Std XII population of state A.

14. **(b)** XII male population of state E is $\dfrac{288000}{384000} \times 100 = 75\%$ of the XII male population of state F.

15. **(c)** Required Ratio
   $$= \frac{(\text{graduate} + \text{XII}) \text{ male}}{(\text{graduate} + \text{XII}) \text{ female}}$$
   $$= \frac{\left(24 \times 16\% \times \dfrac{7}{12}\right) + \left(32 \times 15\% \times \dfrac{7}{16}\right)}{\left(24 \times 16\% \times \dfrac{5}{12}\right) + \left(32 \times 15\% \times \dfrac{9}{16}\right)}$$
   $$= 217 : 215$$

16. **(d)** The ratio of total graduate population in state D and total XII population in state D = 4,08,000 : 3,84,000 = 51 : 48

17. **(c)** Female graduates in state B is $\dfrac{162000}{210000} \times 100 = 77\%$ (approx.) of the female graduates in state E.

18. **(c)** 2017 shows maximum percentage of 68.18% export with respect to production.

19. **(b)** Tea available in India in 2014 = 720 – 288 = 432 and Per capita availability in 2014 = 0.4kg. therefore, the population in India is $\dfrac{432}{0.4} = 1080$.

20. **(d)** Cannot be determined since there is no data given about area.

21. **(b)** Tea exported over the period = 96 + 180 + 288 + 340 + 400 + 450 = 1754 million kg and tea produced over the period = 480 + 540 + 720 + 700 + 600 + 660 = 3700 million kg. The average proportion = $\dfrac{1754}{3700} = 0.47$

22. **(d)** The average per capita availability of tea is
   $$\frac{390 + 410 + 400 + 450 + 500}{5} = 430g$$

23. **(c)** It is clearly evident from the graph that 2012 has the minimum per capita availability of tea.

24. **(a)** There was minimum percentage of export with respect to production is in 2012.

25. (c) Quantity of tea for domestic consumption in the following years:-
$2012 \Rightarrow 480 - 96 = 384$
$2014 \Rightarrow 720 - 288 = 432$
$2015 \Rightarrow 700 - 340 = 360$
$2017 \Rightarrow 660 - 450 = 210$

26. (a) The average quantity of tea available for domestic consumption is $384 + 432 + 360 + 210 + 360 + 200 =$
$$\frac{1946}{6} = 324.3 \text{ million kg}$$

27. (d) Population of all the years :-
$$2012 \Rightarrow \frac{480 - 96}{0.39} = 985 \text{ million}$$
$$2013 \Rightarrow \frac{540 - 180}{0.41} = 878 \text{ million}$$
$$2014 \Rightarrow \frac{720 - 288}{0.4} = 1080 \text{ million}$$
$$2015 \Rightarrow \frac{700 - 340}{0.45} = 800 \text{ million}$$
$$2016 \Rightarrow \frac{600 - 400}{0.5} = 400 \text{ million}$$
$$2017 \Rightarrow \frac{660 - 450}{0.525} = 400 \text{ million}$$
Therefore, the average population
$$\frac{985 + 878 + 1080 + 800 + 400 + 400}{6} = 757 = \text{million}$$

28. (d) $40 + 60 + 80 + 120 + 100 + 110 + 120 + 150 + 120 = 9,00,000$ hectares of FSI has been distributed between 2010-2018.

29. (a) It is clearly visible from the graph that the common years which witnessed a decline in FNI and increase in FSI is 2013 and 2016

30. (c) The greatest proportion of FNI in commercial use is in
$2015 = \dfrac{30000}{30000} = 1$ and the rest are lower than this.

31. (d) Production of Company A in the year 2009 = 550 and Production of Company A in the year 2010 = 700.
Required percentage $= (700 - 550)/550 \times 100 = 27.27\%$ or approximately 27%

32. (b) Sales of Company A in 2009 = 400 and production = 550
Required percentage $= 400/550 \times 100 = 72.72$ of approximately 73%

33. (c) Sum of production $= (750 + 700 + 800 + 600 + 650 + 550) = 4050$
$\therefore$ Average $= 4050/6 = 675$

34. (d) Required ratio = total production of company A : total sales of company A = 4050 : 2750 = 81 : 55.

35. (c) Production of company B in the year 2006 and 2008 are 750 and 600 respectively
Required ratio = 750 : 600 = 5 : 4

36. (e) Again we will eliminate the options one by one. Option

A - Retailer's S.P. for Mistisukh is 3.5 which is lower than producer's S.P. for Chicken titbits which is 5
Hence, option 'A' is wrong
Option B- Producer's S.P. (Fish kachori) – Retailer's S.P. (Fish kachori) = 0.5
And Producer's S.P. (Cream roll) – Retailer's S.P. (Cream roll) = 1
As 0.5 is less than 1, hence option 'B' is wrong.
Option C As there are only 2 types of margins, 'C' is wrong.
Option D Producer's margin for Chicken pizza is 13.33% which is not the maximum; hence, D is also wrong
Option E- it Is correct.

37. (a) Total no of workers in B in 2015 $= 21600 \times \dfrac{75}{360} = 4500$
Total no of workers in B in 2016 $= 4500 \times \dfrac{120}{100} = 5400$
No of male workers in B in 2016 $= 5400 \times \dfrac{5}{9} = 3000$
Total no of trained workers in B in 2016
$= 12000 \times \dfrac{20}{100} = 2400$
Total no of trained male workers in B in 2016
$= 2400 \times \dfrac{70}{100} = 1680$
Req. % $= \dfrac{1680}{3000} \times 100 = 56\%$

38. (b) Total no of workers in C in 2015 $= 21600 \times \dfrac{45}{360} = 2700$
Total no of workers in C in 2016 $= 2700 \times \dfrac{100}{90} = 3000$
Total no of trained workers in C in 2016
$= 12000 \times \dfrac{12}{100} = 1440$
Total no of trained workers in C in 2015
$= 1440 \times \dfrac{100}{90} = 1600$
Total no of untrained workers in C in 2015
$= 2700 - 1600 = 1100$
Total no of untrained workers in C in 2016
$= 3000 - 1440 = 1560$
Req. % $= \dfrac{1560 - 1100}{1100} \times 100 = \dfrac{460}{110} \times 100 = 41.8\%$

39. (c) Total no of workers in D in 2015
$= 21600 \times \dfrac{50}{360} = 3000$
Total no of trained workers in D in 2016
$= 12000 \times \dfrac{10}{100} = 1200$
Total no of workers in D in 2016 $= 1200 \times \dfrac{100}{20} = 6000$

Total no of trained workers in D in 2015

$$= 1200 \times \frac{100}{80} = 1500$$

Required ratio $= (3000 - 1500) : (6000 - 1200)$
$$= 1500 : 4800 = 5 : 16$$

40. (d) Total no of workers in F in 2015 $= 21600 \times \dfrac{40}{360}$
$$= 2400$$

Total no of male workers in F in 2015 $= 2400 \times \dfrac{5}{8}$
$$= 1500$$
Total no of female workers in F in 2015 $= 2400 - 1500$
$$= 900$$

Total no of male workers in F in 2016 $= 1500 \times \dfrac{120}{100}$
$$= 1800$$

Total no of female workers in F in 2016 $= 900 \times \dfrac{140}{100}$
$$= 1260$$
Total no of workers in F in 2016 $= 1800 + 1260 = 3060$

Total no of trained workers in F in 2016 $= 12000 \times \dfrac{13}{100}$
$$= 1560$$
Total no of untrained workers in F in 2016
$$= 3060 - 1560 = 1500$$
Req. difference $= 1560 - 1500 = 60$

41. (e) Total no of workers in A in 2015 $= 21600 \times \dfrac{60}{360} = 3600$

Total no of workers in A in 2016 $= 3600 \times \dfrac{120}{100} = 4320$

Total no of trained workers in A in 2016
$$= 12000 \times \frac{15}{100} = 1800$$

Total no of untrained workers in A in 2016
$$= 4320 - 1800 = 2520$$

Total no of workers in E in 2015 $= 21600 \times \dfrac{90}{360} = 5400$

Total no of workers in E in 2016 $= 5400 \times \dfrac{80}{100} = 4320$

Total no of trained workers in E in 2016
$$= 12000 \times \frac{30}{100} = 3600$$

Total no of untrained workers in E in 2016
$$= 4320 - 3600 = 720$$
Req. ratio $= 2520 : 720 = 7 : 2$

42. (c) Total population of city A
$$= 1080000 \times \frac{50}{360} = 150000$$

Total number of children in city A
$$= 150000 \times \frac{25}{100} = 37500$$

Total number of female children in city A
$$= 150000 \times \frac{15}{100} = 22500$$

Total number of male children in city A

$$= 37500 - 22500 = 15000$$

Total no. of females in city A $= \dfrac{22500 \times 100}{30} = 75000$

Total no. of males in city A $= 150000 - 75000 = 75000$
Total no. of adult males in city A
$$= 75000 - 15000 = 60000$$

Req. % $= \dfrac{60000}{75000} \times 100 = 80\%$

43. (d) Total population of city B
$$= 1080000 \times \frac{45}{360} = 135000$$

Total no. of female children in city B
$$= 150000 \times \frac{10}{100} = 15000$$

Total no. of male children in city B
$$= 15000 \times \frac{120}{100} = 18000$$

Total no. of males in city B $= 18000 \times \dfrac{100}{30} = 60000$

Total no. of adult males in city B
$$= 60000 - 18000 = 42000$$
Total no. of females in city B $= 135000 - 60000 = 75000$
Total no. of adult females in city B
$$= 75000 - 15000 = 60000$$

Req. % $= \dfrac{60000 - 42000}{60000} \times 100 = \dfrac{18000}{60000} \times 100 = 30\%$

44. (e) Total population of city D
$$= 1080000 \times \frac{70}{360} = 210000$$

Total no. of female children $= 150000 \times \dfrac{20}{100} = 30000$

Total no. of male children in city D
$$= 30000 \times \frac{125}{100} = 37500$$

Total no. of children in city D $= 30000 + 37500 = 67500$
Total no. of adults in city D $= 210000 - 67500 = 142500$

No. of adult males in city D $= 142500 \times \dfrac{9}{19} = 67500$

Total no. of males in city D $= 37500 + 67500 = 105000$
Total no. of females in city D $= 210000 - 105000$
$$= 105000$$
Req. ratio $= 105000 : 105000 = 1 : 1$

45. (a) Total population in city F
$$= 1080000 \times \frac{50}{360} = 150000$$

No. of males in city F : No. of females in city F
$$= 150 : 100 = 3 : 2$$

Total no. of males in city F $= 150000 \times \dfrac{3}{5} = 90000$

Total no. of females in city F $= 150000 - 90000 = 60000$

Total no. of children in city F $= 150000 \times \dfrac{20}{100} = 30000$

Total no. of female children in city F

$$= 150000 \times \frac{16}{100} = 24000$$

Total no. of male children in city F
$$= 30000 - 24000 = 6000$$
Required difference $= (90000 - 6000) - (60000 - 24000)$
$$= 84000 - 36000 = 48000$$

46. (b) Total population of city C $= 1080000 \times \dfrac{55}{360} = 165000$

No. of female children in city

$$C = 150000 \times \frac{15}{100} = 22500$$

No. of male children in city C $= 22500 \times \dfrac{4}{3} = 30000$

Total no. of males in city C $= 30000 \times \dfrac{100}{40} = 75000$

Total population of city E $= 1080000 \times \dfrac{90}{360} = 270000$

No. of female children in city

$$E = 150000 \times \frac{24}{100} = 36000$$

Total no. of females in city E $= 36000 \times \dfrac{100}{25} = 144000$

Total no. of males in city E $= 270000 - 144000 = 126000$
Required ratio $= 75000 : 126000 = 25 : 42$

47. (a) Total population of city B $= 2880000 \times \dfrac{75}{360} = 600000$

Total no. of unemployed persons in city B
$$= 600000 \times \frac{70}{100} = 420000$$

Total no. of employed persons in city B
$$= 600000 - 420000 = 180000$$
Total no. of employed males in city B
$$= 180000 \times \frac{2}{3} = 120000$$

Total no. of employed females in city B
$$= 180000 - 120000 = 60000$$

Total no. of adults in city B $= 600000 \times \dfrac{2}{3} = 400000$
Total no. of adult females in city B
$$= 400000 \times \frac{40}{100} = 160000$$

Total no. of adult males in city B
$$= 400000 - 160000 = 240000$$
Total no. of unemployed adult males incity B
$$= 240000 - 120000 = 120000$$
Total no. of unemployed adult females in city B
$$= 160000 - 60000 = 100000$$

Req. % $= \dfrac{120000 - 100000}{100000} \times 100 = 20\%$

48. (b) Total no. of children in city A
$$= 2880000 \times \frac{60}{360} \times \frac{1}{4} = 120000$$

Total no. of children in city B
$$= 2880000 \times \frac{75}{360} \times \frac{1}{3} = 200000$$
Total no. of children in city C
$$= 2880000 \times \frac{55}{360} \times \frac{3}{11} = 120000$$
Total no. of children in city D
$$= 2880000 \times \frac{70}{360} \times \frac{2}{7} = 160000$$
Total no. of children in city E
$$= 2880000 \times \frac{65}{360} \times \frac{3}{13} = 120000$$
Total no. of children in city F
$$= 2880000 \times \frac{35}{360} \times \frac{1}{5} = 56000$$

Total no. of children in all cities together
$$= 120000 + 200000 + 120000 + 160000 + 120000$$
$$+ 56000 = 776000$$
Total no. of adults in all cities together
$$= 2880000 - 77600 = 2104000$$
Req. % $= \dfrac{776000 \times 100}{2104000} = 36.88\%$

49. (c) Let no. of employed males and no. of employed females be x and x respectively in city D.
No. of males in city D : No. of females in city D
$$= x \times \frac{100}{30} : x \times \frac{100}{20} = 2 : 3$$

Required difference $= 2880000 \times \dfrac{70}{360} \times \dfrac{1}{5}$
$$= 560000 \times \frac{1}{5} = 112000$$

50. (d) Total population of city A
$$= 2880000 \times \frac{60}{360} = 480000$$

Total no. of children in city A $= 480000 \times \dfrac{1}{4} = 120000$

Total no. of male children in city A
$$= 120000 \times \frac{2}{3} = 80000$$

Total no. of adult persons in city A
$$= 480000 - 120000 = 360000$$
Total no. of adult males in city A
$$= 360000 \times \frac{45}{100} = 162000$$

Total no. of males in city A $= 162000 + 80000 = 242000$
Total no. of females in city
$$A = 480000 - 242000 = 238000$$
Req. ratio $= 242000 : 238000 = 121 : 119$

51. (d) Here nothing is given about no. of males or females Hence, can't be determined.

52. (a) Food expenditure of A $= 252000 \times \dfrac{60}{360} = 42000$

Education expenditure of A

$$= \frac{42000}{40-15} \times (100-60)$$

$$= \frac{42000}{25} \times 40 = 67200$$

Saving of A $= 67200 \times \dfrac{120}{100} = 80640$

Total expenditure of A $= \dfrac{42000}{40-15} \times 100 = 168000$

Required % $= \dfrac{80640}{168000} \times 100 = 48\%$

53. (b) Food expenditure of D $= 252000 \times \dfrac{75}{360} = 52500$

Transport expenditure of D $= \dfrac{52500}{50-25} \times 25 = 52500$

Education expenditure of

$$D = \frac{52500}{25} \times (100-80) = 42000$$

Saving of D $= (52500 - 42000)2 = 21000$

Total expenditure of D $= \dfrac{52500}{25} \times 100 = 210000$

Required ratio $= 210000 : 21000 = 10 : 1$

54. (c) Food expenditure of F $= 252000 \times \dfrac{40}{360} = 28000$

Saving of F $= 28000 \times \dfrac{100}{80} = 35000$

House rent of F $= \dfrac{28000}{(55-20)} \times (75-55)$

$$= \frac{28000}{35} \times 20 = 16000$$

Required difference $= 35000 - 16000 = 19000$

55. (d) Food expenditure of C $= 252000 \times \dfrac{55}{360} = 38500$

Total expenditure of C $= \dfrac{38500 \times 100}{70-20} = 77000$

Salary of C $= 77000 \times \dfrac{100}{80} = 96250$

Saving of C $= 96250 - 77000 = 19250$

Food expenditure of E $= 252000 \times \dfrac{80}{360} = 56000$

Total expenditure of E

$$= \frac{56000}{60-20} \times 100 = \frac{56000 \times 100}{40} = 140000$$

Education expenditure of E

$$= 140000 \times \frac{100-80}{100} = 28000$$

Salary of E $= \dfrac{28000 \times 100}{16} = 175000$

Saving of E $= 175000 - 140000 = 35000$

Required ratio $= 19250 : 35000 = 11 : 20$

56. (e) Food expenditure of B $= 252000 \times \dfrac{50}{360} = 35000$

Total expenditure of B $= \dfrac{35000}{35-10} \times 100 = 140000$

Salary of B $= \dfrac{140000 \times 100}{75} = \dfrac{560000}{3}$

Food expenditure of F $= 252000 \times \dfrac{40}{360} = 28000$

Total expenditure of F

$$= 28000 \times \frac{100}{55-20} = 28000 \times \frac{100}{35} = 80000$$

Saving of F $= \left(\dfrac{560000}{3} (140000) \right) \times \dfrac{125}{100}$

$$= \frac{140000}{3} \times \frac{125}{100} = \frac{175000}{3}$$

Salary of F $= 80000 + \dfrac{175000}{3} = \dfrac{415000}{3}$

Req % $= \dfrac{\dfrac{560000}{3} - \dfrac{415000}{3}}{\dfrac{560000}{3}} \times 100$

$$= \frac{145000}{560000} \times 100 = 25.89\%$$

57. (a) Total no. of students in B in 2015 $= 43200 \times \dfrac{65}{360} = 7800$

Total no. of girls in B in 2015 $= 7800 \times \dfrac{40}{100} = 3120$

Total no. of boys in B in 2015 $= 7800 - 3120 = 4680$

Total no. of boys in B in 2016 $= 4680 \times \dfrac{80}{100} = 3744$

Total no. of students in B in 2016 $= 3744 \times \dfrac{100}{40} = 9360$

Total no. of girls in B in 2016 $= 9360 - 3744 = 5616$

Required % $= \dfrac{5616 - 3120}{3120} \times 100 = \dfrac{2496}{3120} \times 100 = 80\%$

58. (e) Total no. of students in E in 2015 $= 43200 \times \dfrac{80}{360} = 9600$

Total no. of girls in E in 2015 $= 9600 \times \dfrac{70}{100} = 6720$

Total no. of girls in E in 2016 $= 6720 \times \dfrac{100}{80} = 8400$

Total no. of students in E in

$$2016 = 8400 \times \frac{100}{60} = 14000$$

Required % $= \dfrac{14000 - 9600}{9600} \times 100$

$$= \frac{4400}{9600} \times 100 = 45.83\%$$

59. (d) Here, we can't find number of passed boys in 2016
Hence, can't be determined.

60. (b) Total number of students in A in 2015
$$= 43200 \times \frac{45}{360} = 5400$$

Total no. of girls in A in 2015 $= 5400 \times \frac{45}{100} = 2430$

Total no. of girls in B in 2015
$$= 43200 \times \frac{65}{360} \times \frac{40}{100} = 3120$$

Total no. of girls in C in 2015
$$= 43200 \times \frac{50}{360} \times \frac{60}{100} = 3600$$

Total no. of girls in D in 2015
$$= 43200 \times \frac{75}{360} \times \frac{50}{100} = 4500$$

Total no. of girls in E in 2015
$$= 43200 \times \frac{80}{360} \times \frac{70}{100} = 6720$$

Total no. of girls in F in 2015
$$= 43200 \times \frac{45}{360} \times \frac{30}{100} = 1620$$

Total no. of girls in all schools together in 2015
$$= 2430 + 3120 + 3600 + 4500 + 6720 + 1620$$
$$= 21990$$
Total no. of boys in all schools together in 2015
$$= 43200 - 21990 = 21210$$
Required ratio $= 21210 : 21990 = 2121 : 2199$

61. (c) Total no. of students in D in 2015
$$= 43200 \times \frac{75}{360} = 9000$$

Total no. of girls in D in 2015 $= 9000 \times \frac{50}{100} = 4500$

Total no. of boys in D in 2015 $= 9000 - 4500 = 4500$
Total no. of failed students in D in 2015
$$= 4500 \times \frac{60}{100} + 4500 \times \frac{70}{100} = 2700 + 3150 = 5850$$

Total no. of students in F in
$$2015 = 43200 \times \frac{45}{360} = 5400$$

Total no. of girls in F in 2015 $= 5400 \times \frac{30}{100} = 1620$

Total no. of boys in F in 2015 $= 5400 - 1620 = 3780$
Total no. of failed students in F in 2015
$$= 1620 \times \frac{30}{100} + 3780 \times \frac{40}{100} = 486 + 1512 = 1998$$

Required ratio $= 5850 : 1998 = 325 : 111$

62. (a) Total population of city B $= 324000 \times \frac{75}{360} = 67500$

Total no. of children in city B $= 67500 \times \frac{1}{3} = 22500$

Total no. of adults in city B $= 67500 - 22500 = 45000$

Total no. of adult males in city B $= 45000 \times \frac{2}{3} = 30000$

Total no. of adult females in city B
$$= 45000 - 30000 = 15000$$

Required ratio $= 30000 \times \frac{40}{100} : 15000 \times \frac{50}{100} = 8 : 5$

63. (c) Total population of city C $= 324000 \times \frac{35}{360} = 31500$

Let number of adult males and adult females be 2x and x respectively
Let number of male children and female children be 4y and 3y respectively
According to the question.
$$\frac{2x + 4y}{x + 3y} = \frac{5}{3}$$

$\Rightarrow$ $6x + 12y = 5x + 15y$ $\therefore$ $x = 3y$
Total no. of males : Total no. of females $= 2 \times 3y + 4y$:
$3y + 3y = 5 : 3$
Total no. of adults : Total no. of children
$$= 3 \times 3y : 4y + 3y = 9 : 7$$

Required difference $= 31500 \times \frac{2}{16} = 3937.5 \approx 3938$

64. (e) Let total no. of adult males and adult females be 3x and 4x respectively in D
Let total no. of male children and female children be 2y and y respectively in D

According to the question $3x \times \frac{25}{100} = 2y$

$\Rightarrow$ $3x = 8y$ $\therefore$ $x : y = 8 : 3$
Total no. of males : Total no. of females $= 3 \times 8 + 2 \times$
$3 : 4 \times 8 + 3 = 30 : 35 = 6 : 7$

Total population of city D $= 324000 \times \frac{60}{360} = 54000$

Required difference $= 54000 \times \frac{1}{13} = 4153.8 \cong 4154$

65. (d)

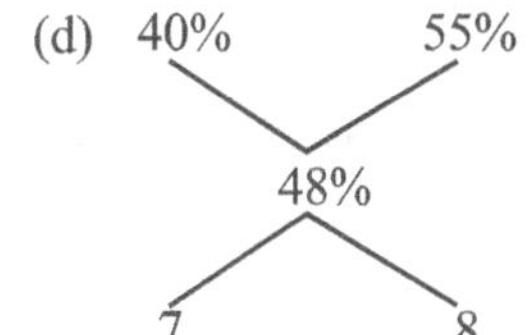

Number of males : No. of females $= 7 : 8$
Let no. of adult males and adult females be 7x and 9x respectively
Let no. of male children and females children be 7y and 5y respectively
According to the question
$$\frac{7x + 7y}{9x + 5y} = \frac{7}{8}$$ $\Rightarrow$ $56x + 56y = 63x + 35y$

$\Rightarrow$ $7x = 21y$ $\therefore$ $x : y = 3 : 1$
Total no. of adults : Total no. of children
$$= 16 \times 3 : 12 \times 1 = 4 : 1$$

Total no. of children $= 324000 \times \frac{80}{360} \times \frac{1}{5} = 14400$

66. (b) Total no. of males in city A

$$= 324000 \times \frac{70}{360} \times \frac{4}{7} = 36000$$

Let no. of adult males and adult females in city F be 2x and 3x respectively

Let no. of male children and female children in city F be 4y and y respectively

According to the question

$$5x \times \frac{25}{100} = 5y \qquad \therefore \quad x : y = 4 : 1$$

Total no. of males : Total no. of females
= 2 × 4 + 4 × 1 : 3 × 4 + 1 = 12 : 13

Total no. of males in city F

$$= 324000 \times \frac{40}{360} \times \frac{12}{25} = 17280$$

Required % $= \dfrac{36000}{17280} \times 100 = 208.3\%$

67. (c) Percentage of non-fresher candidates from State A who passed the examination in 2006 = 100% - students fresher = 100-20 = 80%

68. (d) x-Total students appeared from D
Total no of freshers from D = 25% of x = 160
$\Rightarrow$ x = 640
y – Total students appeared from all states
10% of y = 640 $\Rightarrow$ y = 6400
Non-fresher candidates (%) passed the exam from State E = 100 – 10 = 90
Total no of non-fresher candidates
= 90*1600/100 = 1440

69. (a) Total no of candidates =16% of x = 112 $\Rightarrow$ x=700
Students passed from state A = 28% of 700 =196
Freshers from state A = 20% of 196 = 39
Students passed from C state = 11% of 700 = 77
Non-freshers from state C = 85% of 77 = 65
$\Rightarrow$ 39:65

70. (b) Total no of candidates in 2006 = 700
No of candidates from state A in 2006 = 28% of 700 = 196
No of candidates from state B in 2006 = 16% of 700 = 112
No of candidates from state A in 2007
= 110% of 196 = 216
No of candidates from state B in 2007
= 120% of 112 = 134
Total no of passed candidates from state A and State B in 2007 = 350

71. (c) Total no of candidates passed from state B in 2006
= 75% of x = 60 => x= 80
Total no of candidates passed from all states = 16% of y = 80 => y=500

72. (a) Total no of IT officers recruitment in Bank A = 11% of 728 = 80 (approx)
Total no of IT officers recruitment in Bank C = 11% of 567 = 62 (approx)
Difference between A & C = 18
Some of the newly employed IT officers left A and

Joined C. The number of new requirements of IT officers in A and C have now become equal.
i.e. 9 IT officers left from Bank A and joined Bank C
The approximate percentage of new recruits who left A = (9/80) + 100 = 11% (approx)

73. (c) Total law officers in C, E, F = 10% of (567+427+508)
= 150(approx)
Total law officers in A, B, D = 10% of (728+945+825)
= 250(approx)
Law officers in C, E, F are less than A, B, D
= [250 – 150/250] × 100 = 40%

74. (d) Ratio = [27% of (567 + 427)/27% of (825 + 508)]
= 994:1333

75. (a) Initially
Requirement of Rajbhasha Adhikaris in D = 15% of 825 = 124 (approx)
Requirement of Rajbhasha Adhikaris in F = 15% of 508 = 76 (approx)
Total strength=200
After 1 year (current strength)
Requirement of Rajbhasha Adhikaris in D = 9% of 825 = 74 (approx)
Requirement of Rajbhasha Adhikaris in F = 9% of 508 = 46 (approx)
Total strength=120
Difference = 80

76. (c) Total technical officers = 8% of 427 = 34 (approx)
Total Financial executives = 27% of 427 = 115 (approx)
Additional technical officers - x
34 + x/115 = 2/3 $\Rightarrow$ x = 43 (approx)

77. (c) In the years 2008, 2009, 2012, 2013

Unit(x) = Total Revenue/Price	Profit	Cost Price = Revenue-Profit	Cost Per Unit = Cost Price/ Unit
x = 1200/12 $\Rightarrow$ x = 100	300	1200 – 300 = 900	900/100 = 9
x = 900/12 $\Rightarrow$ x = 75	150	900 – 150 = 750	750/75 = 10
x = 200/10 $\Rightarrow$ x = 20	100	200 – 100 = 100	100/20 = 5
x = 700/14 $\Rightarrow$ x = 50	200	700 – 200 = 500	500/50 = 10

78. (a) In the years 2007, 2009, 2012, 2013

Unit (x) = Total Revenue/Price	Profit	Cost Price = Revenue-Profit	Cost Per Unit = Cost Price/ Unit
x = 1400/14 $\Rightarrow$ x=100	100	1400 – 100 = 1300	1300/100 = 13
x = 900/12 $\Rightarrow$ x=75	150	900 – 150 = 750	750/75 = 10
x = 200/10 $\Rightarrow$ x=20	100	200 – 100 = 100	100/20 = 5
x = 700/14 $\Rightarrow$ x=50	200	700 – 200 = 500	500/50 = 10

79. (d)

Years	Unit Price	Revenue	Total Units = Revenue/ Unit Price
2006	10	700	70
2007	14	1400	100
2008	12	1200	100
2009	12	900	75
2010	11	1100	100
2011	8	400	50
2012	10	200	20
2013	14	700	50
2014	10	600	60
2015	10	800	80
2016	15	900	60
Total = 765-> Avg =765/11 =70 (approx)			

80. (c) Average of total units sold in the years of 2008, 2009, 2010, 2011 and 2014 = $100 + 75 + 100 + 50 + 60/5 = 77$

81. (d) Total decrease in revenue = 10% of $(700 + 1400 + 1200 + 900 + 1100) = 530$

Total decrease in cost = 10% of $(250 + 100 + 500 + 600 + 400 + 600) = 245$

The cumulative profit for the entire period 2006-2016 decrease by = Total decrease in revenue + Total increase in cost = $530 + 245 = 775$

82. (b) Suppose x units are produced each year.

So, in the year 2006,

Total revenue = 1200

$\Rightarrow 12 \times x = 1200 \Rightarrow x = 100$

Profit = 300

$\therefore$ Cost price = $1200 - 300 = 900$

$\therefore$ Cost per unit = $\dfrac{900}{100} = 9$

In the year 2005,

Total revenue = 1400

$\Rightarrow 14 \times x = 1400$

$x = 100$

Profit = 100

$\therefore$ Cost price = $1400 - 100 = 1300$

$\therefore$ Cost per unit = $\dfrac{1300}{100} = 13$

In the year 2009,

Total revenue = 400

$\Rightarrow 8 \times x = 400 \Rightarrow x = 50$

Profit = 150

$\therefore$ Cost price = $400 - 150 = 250$

$\therefore$ Cost per unit = $\dfrac{250}{50} = 5$

In the year 2011,

Total revenue = 700

$\Rightarrow 14 \times x = 700 \Rightarrow x = 50$

Profit = 200

$\therefore$ Cost price = $700 - 200 = 500$

$\therefore$ Cost per unit = $\dfrac{500}{50} = 10$

Thus, per unit cost is highest in the year 2005.

83. (b)

Years	Unit price	Revenue	Total units = $\dfrac{\text{Revenue}}{\text{Unit price}}$
2004	10	700	70
2005	14	1400	100
2006	12	1200	100
2007	12	900	75
2008	11	1100	100
2009	8	400	50
2010	10	200	20
2011	14	700	50
2012	10	600	60
2013	10	800	80
2014	15	900	60
			Total = 765

$\therefore$ Average units = $\dfrac{765}{11} \simeq 70$ units

84. (c) Checking option (a),

Volatility per unit = $\dfrac{15-8}{\dfrac{126}{11}} = \dfrac{77}{126} = 0.611$

Checking of option (b),

Total cost = Revenue – Profit

$= (700 + 1400 + 1200 + 900 + 1100 + 400 + 200 + 700 + 600 + 800 + 900) - (0 + 100 + 300 + 150 + 0 + 150 + 100 + 200 + 0 + 400 + 300)$

$= 8900 - 1700 = 7200$

Average cost per unit = $\dfrac{7200}{11}$

Volatility cost per unit $= \dfrac{(1400-100)-(200-100)}{7200} \times 11$

$= \dfrac{1300-100}{7200} \times 11 = 1.833$

Checking option (c),

Average profit = $\dfrac{1700}{11}$

$\therefore$ Profit volatility = $\dfrac{400-0}{\dfrac{1700}{11}} = \dfrac{44}{17} = 2.588$

Checking option (d),

Average revenue = $\dfrac{8600}{11}$

$\therefore$ Revenue volatility = $\dfrac{1400-200}{\dfrac{8600}{11}} = \dfrac{132}{86} = 1.535$

$\therefore$ Total profit has highest volatility.

85. (c)

Year	New revenue	Total cost = Old revenue – Profit
2004	80% of 700 = 560	700
2005	80% of 1400 = 1120	1300
2006	80% of 1200 = 960	900
2007	80% of 900 = 720	750
2008	80% of 1100 = 880	1100
2009	400	120% of 250 = 300
2010	200	120% of 100 = 120
2011	700	120% of 500 = 600
2012	600	120% of 600 = 720
2013	800	120% of 400 = 480
2014	900	120% of 600 = 720

In a year when total cost is more than new revenue then in that year there is loss.

These years are 2004, 2005, 2006, 2007 and 2008

So, there are total 5 yr.

86. (b) Total decrease in revenues

= 20% of (700 + 400 + 1200 + 900 + 1100) = 1060

Total increase in cost

= 20% of (250 + 100 + 500 + 600 + 400 + 600) = 490

Decrease in cumulative profit

= Total decrease in revenues + Total increase in cost

= 1060 + 490 = ₹1550

87. (b) Speed of vehicle A on day 1 = 832/16 = 52kmph

Speed of vehicle A on day 2 = 864/16 = 54kmph

Speed of vehicle B on day 1 = 516/12 = 43kmph

Speed of vehicle B on day 2 = 774/18 = 43kmph

Speed of vehicle C on day 1 = 693/11 = 63kmph

Speed of vehicle C on day 2 = 810/18 = 45kmph

Speed of vehicle D on day 1 = 552/12 = 46kmph

Speed of vehicle D on day 2 = 765/15 = 51kmph

Vehicle B travelled at the same speed on both the days

88. (b) Speed of vehicle A on day 1 = 832/16 = 52kmph

Speed of vehicle C on day 1 = 693/11 = 63kmph

Difference = 63-52 = 11kmph

89. (a) Speed of vehicle C on day 2 = 810/18 = 45kmph

Speed of vehicle C on day 2 = 45 × (5/18) = 12.5 m/s

90. (a) Percentage = (636/703)*100 = 90%

91. (b) Speed of vehicle D on day 2 = 51kmph

Speed of vehicle E on day 2 = 39kmph

Ratio = [Speed of vehicle D on day 2/Speed of vehicle E on day 2] = 51/39 = 17:13

92. (b) Rajasthan = (10/100)*50*(73 -27)/100 = 2.3

93. (c) Ratio => (9/100)*50*(34/100) : (20/100)*50*(78/100)

= 51/260

94. (a) Rajasthan = (10/100)*50*(73/100) = 3.65 similarly,

HP = 3.9 Jharkhand = 2.88 J&K = 7.8 Haryana = 7.7

Maharashtra = 0.8 TN = 2.97

Total = 29.7, so average = 29.7/7 = 4.24

95. (c) Production in Haryana by machine method = 7.7 and production of Maharashtra by manual method = 3.2,

So % greater = [(7.7 - 3.2)/3.2]*100 = 140%

96. (c) Production in HP by manual method = 2.6 and production in Jharkhand by machine method = 2.88

x = 2.6/2.88 = 0.9

97. (b) Let speed of boat in still water on Thursday = x

According to question,

$$\frac{12\times18}{x-1}=\frac{16\times15}{16+2}$$

$$=\frac{12\times18\times18}{16\times15}=x-1$$

x – 1 = 16.2

x = 17.2 kmph

∴ Speed of boat in still water on Thursday = 17.2 kmph

98. (c) Let speed of boat in still water on Monday = x

According to question,

$$\frac{15\times18}{x-2}=\frac{45}{11}+\frac{16\times15}{x+2}$$

$$15\left(\frac{18}{x-2}-\frac{16}{x+2}\right)=\frac{45}{11}$$

$$\frac{18}{x-2}-\frac{16}{x+2}=\frac{3}{11}$$

If we put x = 20

Then it satisfy the above equation

∴ x = 20 kmph

99. (d) Speed of boat in still water on Tuesday = 15 km/hr

∵ $66\dfrac{2}{3}\%=\dfrac{2}{3}$

Speed of boat in still water on Wednesday

$$= 15+\frac{2}{3}\times15$$

= 25 km/hr

According to question,

$$\frac{14\times18}{25-x}=\frac{14\times15}{(15+3)}\times\frac{9}{10}$$

$$\frac{6}{25-x}=\frac{5}{18}\times\frac{9}{10}$$

$$\frac{6}{0.25}=25-x$$

25 – x = 24

x = 1 km/hr

∴ Speed of boat in still water on wednesday = 1 km/hr

100. (a) Given

Speed of boat in still water on Saturday = 21 km/hr

∵ $28\dfrac{4}{7}\%=\dfrac{2}{7}$

∴ Speed of boat in still water on Sunday

$$= 21-\frac{2}{7}\times21 = 21 - 6 = 15 \text{ kmph}$$

According to question,

$$\frac{10\times18}{21-x}=\frac{19}{16}\times\frac{10\times15}{15+4}$$

$$x = 1.8$$

$$\text{Required time} = \frac{57.6}{21-1.8}$$

$$= \frac{57.6}{19.2} = 3 \text{ hrs.}$$

101. (a) According to question,

$$\frac{18 \times 18}{x-4} = 2 + \frac{12 \times 15}{17+1}$$

$$18 \times 18 = 12\,(x-4)$$

$$x - 4 = 27$$

$$x = 31 \text{ kmph}$$

Required upstream speed $= 31 - 4 = 27$ kmph

102. (e) As per given condition

$$\frac{5}{10} + \frac{5}{15} + \frac{x}{12} + \frac{x}{18} = \left(1 - \frac{1}{36}\right)$$

$$\frac{5x}{36} = \frac{35}{36} - \frac{5}{6}$$

$$x = \frac{36}{5}\left(\frac{35-30}{36}\right)$$

$$= 1 \text{ day.}$$

103. (d) Part of work completed by $E = \dfrac{5}{20} = \dfrac{1}{4}$

3 days work by $(A + B + D)$

$$= \frac{1}{10} + \frac{1}{12} + \frac{1}{18}$$

$$= \frac{18+15+10}{180} = \frac{43}{180}$$

9 days work $= (3A + 3B + 3D) = \dfrac{129}{180}$

Remaining work $= \dfrac{3}{4} - \dfrac{129}{180}$

$$= \frac{135-129}{180} = \frac{6}{180} = \frac{1}{30}$$

This will be done by A in

$$= \frac{1}{30} \times 10 = \frac{1}{3} \text{ days}$$

So B worked for 3 days.

104. (d) Work done by A. C and E on job Z

$$= \frac{2}{10} + \frac{2}{15} + \frac{2}{20}$$

$$= \frac{12+8+6}{60}$$

$$= \frac{26}{60} = \frac{13}{30}$$

Remaining work done by B and D in $20x$ and $21x$

$$\frac{20x}{12} + \frac{21x}{18} = \frac{17}{30}$$

$$\frac{60x+42x}{36} = \frac{17}{30} \Rightarrow 102x = 17 \times \frac{36}{30}$$

$$x = \frac{6}{30} = \frac{1}{5}$$

Required days $= 20 \times \dfrac{1}{5} = 4$ **days**

105. (c) According to question,

$$\frac{2}{10} + \frac{4x}{12} + \frac{3}{15} + \frac{3x}{18} + \frac{2}{20} = 1$$

$$\Rightarrow \frac{1}{5} + \frac{x}{3} + \frac{1}{5} + \frac{x}{6} + \frac{1}{10} = 1$$

$$\frac{6+10x+6+5x+3}{30} = 1$$

$$15x + 15 = 30$$

$$x = 1$$

Required difference $= 4x - 3x$

$$= 4 - 3 = 1$$

106. (d) With new efficiency C will complete job in $= 12$ days

3 days work of C and 1 day work of B $= 1/3$

Days required $= 9$ days

107. (d)

School	Number of Girls	Number of Boys
P	1000	1500
Q	1350	1650
R	550	1450
S	675	1575
T	500	750
U	175	825

Number of boys in schools R and U together

$$= (1450 + 825) = 2275$$

$\therefore$ Required percentage

$$= \frac{2275}{3000} \times 100 = 75.83$$

108. (c) Number of boys in school T $= 750$

109. (a) Required percentage

$$= \frac{2000}{2250} \times 100 = 89$$

110. (b) Required average

$$= \frac{1}{2}\,(1500 + 1650) = 1575$$

111. (c) Required ratio $= 20 : 27$

112. (b) Required ratio

$$= \frac{25780 \times 12}{100} : \frac{7390 \times 11}{100} = 3094 : 813$$

113. (e) Required percentage

$$= \frac{24}{18} \times 100 = 133.3$$

114. (e) Required difference

$$= (11-7)\% \text{ of } 7390 = \frac{4 \times 7390}{100} = 296$$

115. (c) It is obvious from the Pai chart.

$$\text{Science} \Rightarrow \frac{25780 \times 28}{100} - \frac{7390 \times 32}{100}$$

$$\approx 7218 - 2365 \approx 4853$$

$$\text{Engineering} \Rightarrow \frac{25780 \times 16}{100} - \frac{7390 \times 11}{100}$$

$$\approx 4124 - 813 \approx 3311$$

$$\text{Commerce} \Rightarrow \frac{25780 \times 18}{100} - \frac{7390 \times 16}{100}$$

$$\approx 4640 - 1182 \approx 3458$$

116. (a) Required number of candidates

$$= 23\% \text{ of } 7390$$

$$= \frac{23 \times 7390}{100} \approx 1700$$

117. (b) Required answer

$$= 720 \times \frac{40}{100} \times \frac{15}{100} = 43.2 \text{ million litres}$$

118. (d) Total supply from Jhelum and underground water

$$= 720 \times \frac{(12+6)}{100} = 129.6 \text{ million litres}$$

Consumption of Yamuna water for domestic purposes

$$= 720 \times \frac{40}{100} \times \frac{40}{100} = 115.2$$

Consumption of Ganga water for agriculture purposes

$$= 720 \times \frac{35}{100} \times \frac{20}{100} = 50.4$$

$\therefore$ Required ratio

$$= \frac{129.6}{(115.2 + 50.4)} = \frac{18}{23} = 18 : 23$$

$$[3 \times 3 \times 2 \times 2 \times 2 \text{ is common.}]$$

119. (b) No. of students (of JNU) listening to Radio City

$$= 120000 \times \frac{20}{100} \times \frac{65}{100} = 15600$$

120. (e) The no. of Indraprastha students listening to FM Rainbow = $120000 \times 13\% \times 48\%$
The no. of Jamia students listening to FM Gold = $120000 \times 18\% \times 52\%$

$\therefore$ reqd percentage

$$= \frac{120000 \times 13\% \times 48\%}{120000 \times 18\% \times 52\%} \times 100 = 66.66\%$$

121. (a) Indraprastha University

122. (c) The no. of Indraprastha students listening to

$$\text{Red FM} = 120000 \times \frac{13}{100} \times \frac{46}{100} = 12 \times 598$$

The no. of Jamia students listening to Red FM

$$= 120000 \times \frac{18}{100} \times \frac{36}{100} = 12 \times 648$$

$\therefore$ Total students $= (12 \times 598) + (12 \times 648)$

$$= 12 \times 1246 = 14952$$

123. (b) Radio City

124. (d) Percentage increase

$$= \frac{700 - 550}{550} \times 100 = 27.2 \approx 27\%$$

125. (b) Percent of production

$$= \frac{400}{550} \times 100 = 72.72 \approx 73\%$$

126. (c)

Year	Production of B
2006	600
2007	700
2008	800
2009	600
2010	650
2011	700

$$= \frac{600 + 700 + 800 + 600 + 650 + 700}{6} = 675$$

127. (e) Total production of company $A = 4050$
Total sales of company $A = 2750$
Required ratio $\Rightarrow 4050 : 2750 = 81 : 55$

128. (c) Required ratio = production of B in the year 2006 : Production of B in the year 2008
$\Rightarrow$ $600 : 800 \Rightarrow 3 : 4$

129. (a) From table we can say that expenditure on water supply and sanitation are increasing in every plan. So, the graph represent in option (a) is best explain of it.

130. (b) By watching table, we see that the ratio of public sector expenditure to the expenditure on social service was highest in the VIth plan.

131. (a) From table, we can say that in all the sector, there is no continuous decrease.

132. (d) Required percentage

$$= \frac{24880}{975000} \times 100\%$$

$$= 2.551\% = 2.5\%$$

133. (c) Total expenditure on education in all the plans
$$= 1530 + 2730 + 5890 + 7860 + 13360 + 25240$$
$$= 56610 \text{ million}$$
Total expenditure on health in all the plans
$$= 980 + 2140 + 2260 + 3370 + 7610 + 18210$$
$$= 34570 \text{ million}$$

$\therefore$ Required difference
$$= (56610 - 34570)$$
$$= 22040 \text{ million}$$
$$= ₹ \, 22040 \times 1000000$$
$$= ₹ \, 22040000000$$

134. (e) Number of men working in the marketing department

$$3250 \times \frac{79.2°}{360°} \times \frac{3}{5} = 429$$

135. (c) $\therefore$ Required ratio $= \dfrac{3250 \times \dfrac{36°}{360°} \times \dfrac{13}{25}}{3250 \times \dfrac{57.6°}{360°} \times \dfrac{7}{10}} = 13 : 28$

136. (e) Number of men working in the production department

$$= 3250 \times \frac{136.8°}{360°} \times \frac{4}{5} = 988$$

Total number of employees in production department

$$3250 \times \frac{136.8°}{360°} = 1235$$

Required percentage

$$= \frac{988}{1235} \times 100\% = 80\%$$

137. (b) Number of women working in IT department

$$= 3250 \times \frac{57.6°}{360°} \times \frac{3}{10} = 156$$

Total number of employees = 3250

Required percentage $\frac{156}{3250} \times 100\% = 4.8\%$

138. (b) Number of men working in accounts department

$$= 3250 \times \frac{50.4°}{360°} \times \frac{6}{13} = 210$$

Number of men working in marketing department

$$= 3250 \times \frac{79.2°}{360°} \times \frac{3}{5} = 429$$

Number of men working in IT department

$$= 3250 \times \frac{57.6°}{360°} \times \frac{7}{10} = 364$$

Number of men working in HR department

$$= 3250 \times \frac{36°}{360°} \times \frac{12}{25} = 156$$

Number of men working in production department

$$= 3250 \times \frac{136.8°}{360°} \times \frac{4}{5} = 988$$

Hence, total number of men working in the organization
$$= 210 + 429 + 364 + 156 + 988 = 2147$$

Sol. (139-143) :

	Total number of Mobiles Sold	Total Number of Mobiles Sold of Company A	Total Number of Mobiles Sold of Company B
July	7650	4080	3570
August	9900	4400	5500
September	11250	6750	4500
October	3600	2100	1500
November	5400	2520	2880
December	7200	3150	4050

139. (c) Number of mobiles sold of company B in July = 3570
Number of mobiles sold of company B in December
= 4050
Required Ratio = 3570 : 4050 = 119 : 135

140. (c) Total mobiles sold by company A during November
= 2520

Total mobiles sold by this company at discount
= 35% of 2520 = 882
Total mobiles sold by company A without discount
= 2520 – 882 = 1638

141. (d) Mobile phones sold of company B during October
= 1500
Total profit earned on the mobile phones
= ₹(433 × 1500) = ₹ 6,49,500

142. (e) Number of mobile phones sold of company
A during July = 4080
Number of mobile phones sold by company A during
December = 3150
Required percentage

$$= \frac{4080}{3150} \times 100 = 129.5 \approx 130\%$$

143. (a) Mobile phones sold of company B during August
= 5500
Mobile phones sold of company B during September
= 4500
Total number of mobile phones
= 5500 + 4500 = 10,000

144. (e) Total number of vehicles produced by P in 2011, 2012
and 2014 = 690
Produced by Q in year 2012 , 2013 and 2014 = 510
Difference = 690 – 510 = 180 thousands

145. (b) Average number of vehicles by company

$$Q = \frac{130 + 100 + 160 + 120 + 180 + 210}{6}$$

$$= \frac{900}{6} = 150 \text{ thousands}$$

146. (c) Total number of vehicles in 2011 = 380
Total number of vehicles produced in 2012 = 280

Percentage Decrease $= \frac{380 - 280}{380} \times 100$

$$= \frac{500}{19} = 26\frac{6}{19}\%$$

147. (a) Total vehicles produced by P in 2013 = 240 thousand
Defective = 15 thousand
Non - defective = 225 thousand
Total vehicles produced by Q in 2014 = 210 thousand
Defectives = 10000
Non - defective = 200 thousand
Ratio = 225 : 200 = 9 : 8

148. (a) Number of vehicles produced by P in the year 2010
= 190

Number of vehicles produced in 2015 $= 190 \times \frac{130}{100} = 247$

149. (a) Number of Nokia phones sold by store

$$P = \frac{4}{7} \times 14 \times \frac{11200}{100} = 8 \times \frac{11200}{100} = 896$$

Number of Nokia phones sold by store

$$R = \frac{5}{9} \times 16 \times \frac{11200}{100} = \frac{80 \times 112}{9} = 996$$

Number of Nokia phones sold by store

$$S = \frac{7}{13} \times \frac{28}{100} \times 11200 = 14 \times 112 = 1688 \text{ approx}$$

Number of Nokia phones sold by store

$$T = \frac{1}{5} \times \frac{20}{100} \times 11200 = 448$$

Total Nokia phones sold by
$(P + R + S + T) = 896 + 996 + 1688 + 448 = 4028$

$\therefore$ Required average $= \dfrac{4028}{4} = 1007$

150. (e) Samsung phone sold by store

$$P = \frac{3}{7} \times \frac{14}{100} \times 11200 = 672$$

Samsung phone sold by store

$$Q = \frac{1}{4} \times \frac{10}{100} \times 11200 = 280$$

Total Samsung phone sold by $(P + Q)$
$= 672 + 280 = 952$
Total Nokia phone sold by $R = 996$
Difference $= 996 - 952 = 44$
Required percentage

$$= \frac{44}{952} \times 100 = \frac{44 \times 25}{238} = \frac{22 \times 25}{119}$$

$$= \frac{550}{119} = 4\frac{74}{119}$$

151. (c) We know, $100\% = 360°$
So, $1\% = 3.6°$
So, $28\% = 28 \times 3.6 = 100.8°$

152. (e) Number of Nokia phones sold by store S
$= 1688(\text{approx})$
Total Number of Samsung phone sold by store T

$$= \frac{4}{5} \times \frac{20}{100} \times 11200 = 1792$$

Total Number of Samsung phone sold by store U

$$= \frac{10}{21} \times \frac{12}{100} \times 11200 = 640$$

$\therefore$ Required ratio
$= 1688 : (1792 + 640)$
$= 1688 : 2432 = 211 : 304$

153. (c) Total Number of cellular phones sold by stores Q in October

$$= \frac{10}{100} \times 11200 = 1120$$

Sold in November

$$= 1120 \times \frac{115}{100} = 1288$$

Total Number of cellular phone by T in October

$$= \frac{20}{100} \times 11200 = 2240$$

Sold in November $= 2240 \times \dfrac{105}{100} = 2352$

Total Phone sold $= 2352 + 1288 = 3640$

154. (d) No. of males in city A

$$= 360000 \times \frac{50}{360} \times \frac{8}{5} \times 3 = 240000$$

No. of females in city A

$$= 240000 \times \frac{3}{4} = 180000$$

No. of uneducated females

$$= 180000 - 360000 \times \frac{50}{360} = 130000$$

No. of uneducated males

$$= 240000 - 360000 \times \frac{50}{360} \times \frac{8}{5} = 160000$$

Required %

$$= \frac{130000}{180000} \times 100 = \frac{650}{9} = 72.2\%$$

155. (b) Number of females in city C

$$= 360000 \times \frac{45}{360} \times \frac{4}{3} \times \frac{250}{100} \times \frac{3}{2} = 225000$$

Number of educated females in city C

$$= 360000 \times \frac{45}{360} = 45000$$

Required ratio $= 45000 : 180000 = 1 : 4$

156. (a) Required ratio

$$= 60 \times \frac{5}{2} : 90 \times \frac{8}{3} = 5 : 8$$

157. (e) Required difference $= 1 - 1 = 0$

158. (c) Required difference

$$= \left(360000 \times \frac{40}{360} \times \frac{7}{2} \times \frac{100}{35} \times \frac{5}{8} - 360000 \times \frac{40}{360} \times \frac{5}{2} \right)$$

$$- 360000 \times \frac{40}{360} \times \frac{5}{2} = (250000 - 100000) - 100000$$

$$= 50000$$

159. (c) Required % $= \dfrac{4}{9} \times 100 = 44.4\%$

160. (a) Required %

$$= \frac{55 \times \dfrac{12}{5} - 45 \times \dfrac{25}{9}}{55 \times \dfrac{12}{5}} \times 100$$

$$= \frac{132 - 125}{132} \times 100 = \frac{700}{132}$$

$$= 5.3\%$$

161. (e) Required ratio

$$= 360 : \left(35 \times \frac{8}{7} + 55 \times \frac{4}{5} + 80 \times \frac{5}{4} + 60 \times \frac{3}{5} + 45 \times \frac{11}{9} + 85 \times \frac{2}{5} \right)$$

$$= 360 : 309 = 120 : 103$$

162. (b) Total angle for absented students

$$= 35 \times \frac{1}{7} + 55 \times \frac{3}{5} + 80 \times \frac{2}{4} + 60 \times \frac{1}{5} + 45 \times \frac{5}{9} + 85 \times \frac{2}{5}$$

$$= 149°$$

Required average $= \dfrac{43200}{6} \times \dfrac{149}{360} = 2980$

163. (d) Required ratio

$$= 60 \times \frac{9}{5} : 85 \times \frac{9}{5} = 12 : 17$$

164. (e) Increment

$$= 9000 \times \frac{45}{360} \times \frac{100}{30} \times \frac{5}{4} \times \frac{40}{100} - 9000 \times \frac{45}{360}$$

$$= 1875 - 1125 = 750$$

Required % $= \dfrac{750}{1125} \times 100 = 66\dfrac{2}{3}\%$

165. (d) Can't be determined

166. (b) Required ratio

$$= 9000 \times \frac{75}{360} : \left(19000 \times \frac{15}{38} - 9000 \times \frac{75}{360} \right)$$

$$= 1875 : (7500 - 1875)$$

$$= 1875 : 5625$$

$$= 1 : 3$$

167. (a) $14 \times \dfrac{50}{100} x - 11 \times \dfrac{40}{100} x = 390$

$$\frac{260}{100} \, x \Rightarrow 390$$

$$\therefore \quad x \Rightarrow 150$$

Required difference $= 3 \times 150 = 450$

168. (c) Required average

$$= 9000 \times \frac{50}{360} \times \frac{100}{40} \times \frac{8}{3} \times \frac{1}{2} = \frac{12500}{3}$$

$$= 4167$$

169. (d) Required %

$$= \frac{7 \times \dfrac{40}{100} + 6 \times \dfrac{30}{100}}{13} \times 100 = \frac{460}{13} = 35.38\%$$

170. (c) $\dfrac{129600}{360} \times$

$$\frac{\left(60 \times \dfrac{5}{2} + 50 \times \dfrac{9}{5} + 40 \times \dfrac{7}{4} + 70 \times \dfrac{13}{7} + 90 \times \dfrac{9}{5} + 50 \times \dfrac{7}{2} \right)}{6}$$

$$= \frac{360}{6} \times (150 + 90 + 70 + 130 + 162 + 175)$$

$$= 60 \times 777 = 46620$$

171. (e) Required difference

$$= 5 \times \frac{120}{100} - 4 \times \frac{150}{100} = 0$$

172. (a) Required ratio

$$= 50 \times \frac{9}{5} : 50 \times \frac{7}{2} = 18 : 35$$

173. (b) Required % $= \dfrac{40 \times \dfrac{3}{4} \times 100}{70 \times \dfrac{6}{7}}$

$$= \frac{30 \times 100}{60} = 50\%$$

174. (d) Required average

$$= \frac{500000 \times \dfrac{12}{100} \times \dfrac{30}{100} + 500000 \times \dfrac{15}{100} \times \dfrac{30}{100}}{6}$$

$$+ \frac{500000 \times \dfrac{18}{100} \times \dfrac{20}{100} + 500000 \times \dfrac{10}{100} \times \dfrac{10}{100}}{6}$$

$$+ \frac{500000 \times \dfrac{20}{100} \times \dfrac{25}{100} + 500000 \times \dfrac{25}{100} \times \dfrac{15}{100}}{6}$$

$$= \frac{18000 + 22500 + 18000 + 5000 + 25000 + 18750}{6}$$

$$= \frac{107250}{6} = 17875$$

175. (c) Required %

$$= \frac{500000 \times \dfrac{20}{100} \times \dfrac{30}{100} - 500000 \times \dfrac{25}{100} \times \dfrac{20}{100}}{500000 \times \dfrac{25}{100} \times \dfrac{20}{100}} \times 100$$

$$= \frac{5000}{25000} \times 100 = 20\%$$

176. (e) $12 \times \dfrac{20}{100} + 15 \times \dfrac{30}{100} + 18 \times \dfrac{15}{100} +$

$$10 \times \frac{25}{100} + 20 \times \frac{20}{100} + 25 \times \frac{35}{100}$$

$$2.4 + 4.5 + 2.7 + 2.5 + 4 + 8.75$$

$$= 24.85\%$$

177. (a) Required ratio $= 12 \times \dfrac{25}{100} : 18 \times \dfrac{30}{100}$

$$= 5 : 9$$

178. (b) Required difference

$$= 500000 \times \frac{10}{100} \times \frac{90}{100} - 500000 \times \frac{12}{100} \times \frac{70}{100}$$

$$= 45000 - 42000 = 3000$$

179. (c) Required %

$$= \frac{2160 \times \dfrac{45}{360} \times \dfrac{100}{20}}{2160 \times \dfrac{45}{360} \times \dfrac{2}{1} \times \dfrac{100}{30}} \times 100 = 75\%$$

180. (d) Required average

$$= \frac{2160 \times \dfrac{60}{360} \times \dfrac{7}{3} + 2160 \times \dfrac{45}{360} \times \dfrac{3}{1}}{6}$$

$$+ \frac{2160 \times \dfrac{72}{360} \times \dfrac{17}{8} + 2160 \times \dfrac{48}{360} \times \dfrac{19}{12}}{6}$$

$$= \dfrac{2160 + \dfrac{90}{360} \times \dfrac{14}{9} + 2160 \times \dfrac{45}{360} \times \dfrac{10}{3}}{6}$$

$$= \dfrac{840 + 810 + 918 + 456 + 840 + 900}{6}$$

$$= \dfrac{4764}{6} = 794$$

181. (e) Required difference

$$= 2160 \times \dfrac{90}{360} \times \dfrac{5}{9} \times \dfrac{100}{15} - 2160 \times \dfrac{90}{360} \times \dfrac{100}{30}$$

$$= 2000 - 1800 = 200$$

182. (a) Required ratio

$$= \left(2160 \times \dfrac{90}{360} \times \dfrac{14}{9} \times \dfrac{4}{7} \times \dfrac{100}{20} - 2160 \times \dfrac{90}{360} \times \dfrac{5}{9} \right)$$

$$: \left(2160 \times \dfrac{90}{360} \times \dfrac{14}{9} \times \dfrac{100}{20} \times \dfrac{3}{7} - 2160 \times \dfrac{90}{360} \right)$$

$$= (2400 - 300) : (1800 - 540)$$

$$= 2100 : 1260 = 5 : 3$$

183. (b) Required ratio $= 45 \times \dfrac{3}{1} : 45 \times \dfrac{10}{3} = 9 : 10$

184. (c) $\dfrac{21600 \times \dfrac{75}{360} \times \dfrac{10}{5}}{21600 \times \dfrac{75}{360} \times \dfrac{10}{5} + 6000 \times \dfrac{15}{100} \times \dfrac{6}{1}} \times 100$

$$= \dfrac{9000}{9000 + 5400} \times 100 = \dfrac{9000}{14400} \times 100$$

$$= \dfrac{1000}{16} = 62.5\%$$

185. (d) Required difference

$$= \dfrac{21600 \times \dfrac{50}{360} \times \dfrac{2}{5} + 21600 \times \dfrac{60}{360} \times \dfrac{1}{3}}{6}$$

$$+ \dfrac{21600 \times \dfrac{75}{360} \times \dfrac{1}{5} + 21600 \times \dfrac{65}{360} \times \dfrac{2}{13}}{6}$$

$$+ \dfrac{21600 \times \dfrac{70}{360} \times \dfrac{3}{7} + 21600 \times \dfrac{40}{360} \times \dfrac{1}{4}}{6}$$

$$= \dfrac{1200 + 1200 + 900 + 600 + 1800 + 600 - 6000}{6}$$

$$= \dfrac{6300 - 6000}{6} = \dfrac{300}{6} = 50$$

186. (e) Required %

$$= \dfrac{21600 \times \dfrac{70}{360} \times \dfrac{10}{7}}{6000 \times \dfrac{21}{100} \times \dfrac{5}{3}} \times 100$$

$$= \dfrac{6000}{2100} \times 100 = \dfrac{2000}{7}$$

$$= 285.7\%$$

187. (a) Required ratio

$$= 21600 \times \dfrac{75}{360} \times \dfrac{10}{5} : 6000 \times \dfrac{15}{100} \times \dfrac{6}{1}$$

$$= 9000 : 5400 = 5 : 3$$

188. (b) Required ratio

$$= \left(21600 \times \dfrac{50}{360} \times \dfrac{15}{5} + 21600 \times \dfrac{75}{360} \times \dfrac{10}{5} \right)$$

$$+ \left(\begin{array}{l} 21600 \times \dfrac{65}{360} \times \dfrac{30}{13} + 21600 \times \dfrac{70}{360} \times \dfrac{20}{7} \\ + 21600 \times \dfrac{40}{360} \times \dfrac{8}{4} + 21600 \times \dfrac{60}{360} \times \dfrac{8}{3} \end{array} \right)$$

$$: \left(6000 \times \dfrac{12}{100} \times \dfrac{11}{2} + 6000 \times \dfrac{18}{100} \times \dfrac{16}{3} \right)$$

$$+ \left(\begin{array}{l} 6000 \times \dfrac{20}{100} \times \dfrac{15}{2} + 6000 \times \dfrac{21}{100} \times \dfrac{15}{3} \\ + 6000 \times \dfrac{14}{100} \times \dfrac{11}{2} + 6000 \times \dfrac{15}{100} \times 6 \end{array} \right)$$

$$= (9000 + 9600 + 9000 + 9000 + 12000 + 4800)$$

$$: (3960 + 5760 + 5400 + 9000 + 6300 + 4620)$$

$$= 53400 : 35040 = 445 : 292$$

189. (c) Required %

$$= \dfrac{1440000 \times \dfrac{80}{360} \times \dfrac{20}{100} \times \dfrac{1}{2}}{1440000 \times \dfrac{80}{360} \times \dfrac{7}{16}} \times 100$$

$$= \dfrac{32000}{140000} \times 100 = \dfrac{160}{7} = 22.85\%$$

190. (d) Required difference

$$= \left(1440000 \times \dfrac{40}{360} \times \dfrac{3}{8} - 1440000 \times \dfrac{40}{360} \times \dfrac{20}{100} \times \dfrac{2}{5} \right)$$

$$- \left(1440000 \times \dfrac{40}{360} \times \dfrac{5}{8} - 1440000 \times \dfrac{40}{360} \times \dfrac{20}{100} \times \dfrac{3}{5} \right)$$

$$= (60000 - 12800) - (100000 - 19200)$$

$$= 41200 - 80800 = 39600$$

191. (e) Required difference $= \dfrac{1440000}{360} \times$

$$\left[\dfrac{\left(40 \times \dfrac{2}{8} + 60 \times \dfrac{2}{12} + 70 \times \dfrac{1}{7} \right)}{6} \right.$$

$$\left. + \dfrac{\left(80 \times \dfrac{2}{16} + 75 \times \dfrac{1}{15} + 35 \times \dfrac{3}{35} \right)}{6} \right]$$

$$= \dfrac{4000 \times 48}{6} = \dfrac{192000}{6} = 32000$$

192. (a) Required ratio

$$= 70 \times \dfrac{4}{7} : 75 \times \dfrac{8}{15} = 40 : 40 = 1 : 1$$

193. (b) Required %

$$= \frac{60 \times \dfrac{5}{12} - 35 \times \dfrac{16}{35}}{60 \times \dfrac{5}{12}} \times 100$$

$$= \frac{9}{25} \times 100$$

$$= 36\%$$

194. (c) Required %

$$= \frac{900000 \times \dfrac{18}{100} \times \dfrac{5}{6}}{900000 \times \dfrac{15}{100}} \times 100$$

$$= \frac{135000}{135000} \times 100$$

$$= 100\%$$

195. (d) Required ratio

$$= \left(15 \times \dfrac{3}{5} + 18 \times \dfrac{5}{6} + 12 \times \dfrac{3}{4} + 22 \times \dfrac{8}{11} + 19 \times \dfrac{13}{19} + 14 \times \dfrac{5}{7}\right)$$

$$: \left(15 \times \dfrac{2}{5} + 18 \times \dfrac{1}{6} + 12 \times \dfrac{1}{4} + 22 \times \dfrac{3}{11} + 19 \times \dfrac{6}{19} + 14 \times \dfrac{2}{7}\right)$$

$$= (9 + 15 + 9 + 16 + 13 + 10) : (6 + 3 + 3 + 6 + 6 + 4)$$

$$= 72 : 28 = 18 : 7$$

196. (a) Required difference

$$= 900000 \times \dfrac{19}{100} \times \dfrac{6}{19} - 900000 \times \dfrac{14}{100} \times \dfrac{2}{7}$$

$$= 54000 - 36000 = 18000$$

197. (e) Required %

$$= 15 \times \dfrac{2}{5} + 18 \times \dfrac{1}{6} + 12 \times \dfrac{1}{4} + 22 \times \dfrac{3}{11} + 19 \times \dfrac{6}{19} + 14 \times \dfrac{2}{7} = 28\%$$

198. (b) Required average

$$= \frac{900000}{6} = 150000$$

199. (d) Required average

$$= \frac{126000 \times \dfrac{65}{360} \times \dfrac{12}{5} + 126000 \times \dfrac{45}{360} \times \dfrac{8}{3}}{6}$$

$$+ \frac{126000 \times \dfrac{36}{360} \times \dfrac{7}{4} + 126000 \times \dfrac{64}{360} \times \dfrac{7}{2}}{6}$$

$$+ \frac{126000 \times \dfrac{80}{360} \times \dfrac{5}{4}}{6} + \frac{126000 \times \dfrac{70}{360} \times \dfrac{9}{7}}{6}$$

$$= \frac{54600 + 42000 + 22050}{6}$$

$$+ \frac{78400 + 35000 + 31500}{6}$$

$$= \frac{263550}{6} = 43925$$

200. (b) Required difference

$$= \frac{126000}{360 \times 6}$$

$$\left\{\left(65 \times \dfrac{7}{5} + 45 \times \dfrac{5}{3} + 36 \times \dfrac{3}{4} + 64 \times \dfrac{5}{2} + 80 \times \dfrac{1}{4} + 70 \times \dfrac{2}{7}\right) - 360\right\}$$

$$= \frac{350}{6} \times (393 - 360) = \frac{350}{6} \times 33 = 1925$$

201. (a) Required %

$$= \frac{64 \times \dfrac{5}{2} - 45 \times \dfrac{5}{3}}{64 \times \dfrac{5}{2}} \times 100$$

$$= \frac{85}{160} \times 100 = 53.1\%$$

202. (c) Required ratio

$$= 80 \times \dfrac{5}{4} : 70 \times \dfrac{9}{7}$$

$$= 100 : 90$$

$$= 10 : 9$$

203. (e) Required %

$$= \frac{360}{360 + 393} \times 100 = \frac{360}{753} \times 100$$

$$= 47.8\%$$

Sol. (204-208) :

Companies	Total number of Manufacturing Parts in 2017	% of Defective parts	Defective parts	Non Defective parts	% of non defective parts that are not passed the quality test	Non defective parts that are not passed the quality test	Non defective parts that are passed the quality test
P	1280	15%	192	1088	50%	544	544
Q	2240	30%	672	1568	25%	392	1176
R	2880	25%	720	2160	10%	216	1944
S	1920	20%	384	1536	25%	384	1152
T	2400	28%	672	1728	50%	864	864

204. (c) Total number of manufacturing parts from company S
in 2018 = 2720
From the given question there 20% parts that are
defective in 2018 from company S = 2720 * 20/100
= 272 × 2 = 544
Non defective parts = 2 (1360 – 272) = 2176
10% of non-defective parts are not passed the quality
test for company S = 10% of 2176 = 217.6 ≈ 217
Non-defective parts that are passed the quality test for
company S = 2176 – 217 = 1959

The total number of non-defective parts that are passed
the quality test in both years from company S
= 1152 + 1959
= 3111 parts

205. (e) There is no such information to find out the defective
and non-defective parts from Company Q and Company
R in 2018. So we are not able to find out the Non-
defective parts that are passed by quality test from
company Q and Company R in 2018. So cannot be
determined is the answer.

206. (d) In 2018,

Companies	Total number of Manufacturing Parts	% of Defective parts	Defective parts	Non Defective parts
P	1920	20%	384	1538
Q	2560	25%	640	1920
T	2000	15%	300	1700

The total number of Non-defective parts that are passed
from quality test from company R and S in 2017
= (1944 + 1152) = 3096
Total number on Non-defective parts from P, Q and T
together in 2018 = 1538 + 1920 + 1700 = 5158
Required percentage = (5158–3096) / 5158 * 100
= 39.97% = 40% less

207. (e) The average numbers of non-defective parts that are
not passed the quality test from all the company except
S in 2017

$$= \frac{(544 + 392 + 216 + 864)}{4} = 504$$

208. (a) The non-defective parts that are passed the quality test
from Company Q and R together in 2017
= (1176+1944) = 3120
The non-defective parts that are not passed the quality
test from Company P, S and T together in 2017
= (544 + 384 + 864) = 1792
Difference = 3120 – 1792 = 1328

Sol. (209-213) :

209. (c) Let Ramu and Shyamu can do 3x and 2x unit of work
1 in one hour respectively.
So, total work 1 done by both
= (3x + 2x) * 4 = 20x
Ramu alone will complete work 1
= 20x/3x = 20/3 hours
Shyamu alone will complete work 1
= 20x/2x = 10 hours
Ratio of efficiency of Ramu and Bhanu = 5 : 3
Ratio of time taken by Ramu and Bhanu = 3 : 5.
Bhanu alone will complete work 1
= 20/(3 × 3) × 5 hours = 100/9 hours
Let total time taken in completing work 1 is y
So, 2/(20/3) + (y – 2)/10 + (y – 2)/(100/9) = 1
(y – 2)/10 + 9 (y – 2)/100 = 7/10
10y – 20 + 9y – 18 = 70
y = 108/19 hours

210. (b) Part of work 2 done by Shyamu on Wednesday in 7
hours = 7/14 = 1/2
This part of work done by 4 women in 5 hours
So whole work will be completed by 4 women in
= 10 hours
One women will complete it in
= 40 hours
3 childern will complete it in
= 40 × 5/3 × 3 = 200/9 hours

211. (b) Ratio of efficiency of Ramu and Shyamu on Tuesday
= 3 : 2
Let Ramu and Shyamu does 3x and 2x work in one
hour
And Shyamu completes work 2 in 9 hours
So, total work = 9 × 2x = 18x
Ramu will complete work 2 in 18x/3x = 6 hours
So, m = 6
Similarly n = 10 × 4x/5x = 8
Total x and y will complete the work in
= (8 – 6) (8 + 6)/ (8 – 6) + (8 + 6)
= 28/16 = 7/4 hours

212. (b) Let Ramu and Shyamu can do 3x and 2x work in one
hour on Monday
Then 80% of total work 1
= 4/5 (3x + 2x) × 3 = 12x
In 4 hours 10x work 1 is completed, working
alternatively and remaining 2x is complete by Ramu
on 5th hour
So total time = (4 + 2x/3x) hours = 14/3 hours
Ratio of efficiency on Friday is 5 : 4
Ratio of time taken to complete work will be 4 : 5
But Shyamu completes work 2 in 10 hours on Friday
So, Ramu will complete work 2 in 8 hours on Friday
Together they will complete work 2 in = 8 × 10/18
= 40/9 hours
Required percentage = (14/3 – 40/9)/(40/9) × 100
= ((42 – 40)/9)/ (40/9) × 100
= 2/40 × 100 = 5%

213. (a) Let Bhanu complete work 2 in x hours
According to question, $2/10 + 2/x = 4/5$
$2/x = 4/5 - 1/5$
$2/x = 3/5$
$x = 10/3$
Time taken by Shyamu to finish work 1 on Friday
$= (5 + 4) * 8/4 = 18$ hours
Required percentage $= 10/(3 \times 18) \times 100 = 500/27\%$

Sol. (214-218) :

214. (a) No. of male persons affected by Dengue in India
$$= \frac{5}{9} \times 108 = 60 \text{ thousand}$$
No. of male persons affected by Dengue in USA
$$= \frac{5}{8} \times 128 = 80 \text{ thousand}$$
Required percentage
$$= \frac{80 - 60}{80} \times 100 = 25\% \text{ less}$$

215. (c) Required average no.
$$\frac{1}{5} \times \left(\frac{3}{8} \times 128 + \frac{4}{9} \times 108 + \frac{1}{4} \times 32 + \frac{5}{12} \times 96 + \frac{1}{3} \times 54 \right) \text{thousand}$$
$$= \frac{1}{5} \times \left(48 + 48 + 8 + 40 + 18 \right) \text{ thousand}$$
$$= \frac{1}{5} \times 162000 = 32400$$

216. (b) $\therefore 16\dfrac{2}{3}\% \rightarrow \dfrac{1}{6}$
$$33\frac{1}{3}\% \rightarrow \frac{1}{3}$$
Required answer
$$= \frac{7}{12} \times \left[\frac{1}{6} + \frac{1}{3} \right] \times 96$$
$$= \frac{7}{12} \times \frac{1}{2} \times 96 = 28000$$

217. (d) Total males in India, Sri Lanka and Pakistan together who are affected by Dengue
$$= \frac{5}{9} \times 108 + \frac{3}{4} \times 32 + \frac{2}{3} \times 54$$
$$= 60 + 24 + 36 = 120 \text{ thousand}$$
Total no females in USA, Sri Lanka and Nepal together who are affected by Dengue
$$= \frac{3}{8} \times 128 + \frac{1}{4} \times 32 + \frac{5}{12} \times 96$$
$$= 48 + 8 + 40$$
$$= 96 \text{ thousand}$$
$\therefore$ Required difference $= (120 - 96)$ thousand
$$= 24000$$

218. (a) Total females in India who are affected by Dengue
$$= \frac{4}{9} \times 108 \text{ thousand} = 48000$$
Total no. of females in Nepal affected by Dengue
$$= \frac{5}{12} \times 96 \text{ thousand} = 40000$$

$\therefore$ Required percentage
$$= \frac{48000 - 40000}{40000} \times 100 = 20\%$$

Sol. (219-223) :
Test launched by Various institutes
$A \rightarrow 28 \times 10000 = 2,80,000$
$B \rightarrow 8 \times 10000 = 80000$
$C \rightarrow 18 \times 10000 = 180000$
$D \rightarrow 10 \times 10000 = 100000$
$E \rightarrow 32 \times 10000 = 320000$
$F \rightarrow 4 \times 10000 = 40000$

219. (b) Required no. of test series which remained unsold
$$= \frac{35}{100} \times 280000 + \frac{15}{100} \times 180000 + \frac{20}{100} \times 100000$$
$$= (24500 + 6750 + 5000) \, 4$$
$$= 145000$$

220. (c) Total no. of test series of B and F which were sold by both sites
$$= \frac{75}{100} \times 80000 + \frac{85}{100} \times 40000$$
$$= (15000 + 8500) \times 4 = 94000$$
No. of test series of A which remained unsold
$$= \frac{35}{100} \times 280000 = 98000$$
$\therefore$ Required percentage
$$= \frac{94000}{98000} \times 100 \approx 96\%$$

221. (a) Total no. of test series of E sold by both sites
$$= \frac{90}{100} \times 320000$$
$$= 288000$$
Total no. of series of all other institutes except E sold by N
$$= (40 \times 700 + 45 \times 200 + 50 \times 450 + 40 \times 250 + 40 \times 100) \, 4$$
$$= (28000 + 9000 + 22500 + 10000 + 4000) \, 4$$
$$= 294000$$
$\therefore$ Required percentage $= \dfrac{288000}{294000} \times 100 \approx 98\%$

222. (b) Required ratio
$$= \frac{(10 \times 800)4}{(35 \times 700)4} = \frac{16}{49}$$

223. (e) Total test series of C & D sold by N
$$= (50 \times 450 + 40 \times 250) \, 4$$
$$= 130000$$
No. of test series of E sold by M
$$= (50 \times 800) \, 4$$
$$= 160000$$
$\therefore$ Required percentage
$$= \frac{160000 - 130000}{160000}$$
$$= 18.75\% \text{ less}$$

224. (d) Number of boys in college C and F together

$$= \frac{4000 \times 72.5}{100} + \frac{2000 \times 82.5}{100} = 2900 + 1650$$

$$= 4550$$

$\therefore$ Required percentage

$$= \frac{4550}{6000} \times 100 = 75.83\%$$

225. (c) Number of boys in college E

$$= \frac{2500 \times 60}{100} = 1500$$

226. (a) Total number of students in college C = 4000

Total number of students in college D = 4500

$\therefore$ Required percentage

$$= \frac{4000}{4500} \times 100 \approx 89$$

227. (e) Required average

$$= \frac{1}{2}\left(\frac{5000 \times 60}{100} + \frac{6000 \times 55}{100}\right)$$

$$= \frac{1}{2}(3000 + 3300) = 3150$$

228. (c) Required ratio

$$= \frac{5000 \times 40}{100} : \frac{6000 \times 45}{100}$$

$$= 25 \times 40 : 30 \times 45 = 100 : 135 = 20 : 27$$

229. (b) Total sale of Tata cars in California

$$= \frac{116}{100} \times 20 = 23.2 \text{ thousands } = 23200$$

Total sale of Tata car in Texas

$$= 116 \times \frac{9}{100} = 10440$$

Required difference = 23200 – 10440 = 12760

230. (e) Sales of tata cars in Hawaii

$$= \frac{116}{100} \times 14 = 16.24 \text{ thousands } = 16240$$

Increase in volume

$$= 30000 - 16240 = 13760$$

Percentage increase

$$= \frac{13760}{116000} \times 100 \approx 12\%$$

231. (c) Total sale of Tata in 2019

$$= \frac{112}{100} \times 116000 = 129920$$

New total sale in Alaska

$$= \frac{134}{100} \times \frac{10}{100} \times 116000 = 15544$$

New total sale in Florida

$$= \frac{122}{100} \times \frac{22}{100} \times 116000$$

$$\approx 31134.4 \approx 31134$$

Total new sale in these two states = 46678

Previous overall sale in all state except Florida and

Alaska $= \dfrac{68}{100} \times 116000 = 78880$

Required increase in sale in other states

$$= (129920 - 46678) - 78880 = 4362$$

$$\approx 4400$$

232. (d) Required % $= \dfrac{101}{58} \times 100 \approx 175\%$

233. (a) Net total sale

$$= \frac{120}{100} \times 398000 = 477600$$

New sale of Tata in California

$$= \frac{110}{100} \times \frac{20}{100} \times 116000$$

$$= 25520$$

New total sale of Tata

$$= \frac{25520}{20} \times 100 = 127600$$

Required total sale

$$= 477600 - 127600 = 350000$$

234. (b) Number of females

$$= \frac{56}{100} \times 2250 = 1260$$

$\therefore$ $1260 \times 20 = 1260 \times 5 + 1200 \times 5 + 1140 \times 5$

$$+ 1080 \times 5 + 1020 \times x$$

$\Rightarrow$ $x = 1\dfrac{13}{17}$

$\therefore$ Total required days

$$= 5 + 5 + 5 + 5 + 1\frac{13}{17} = 21\frac{13}{17} \text{ days.}$$

235. (d) Required average

$$= \frac{1}{5}\left(\begin{array}{c}\dfrac{30}{100} \times 2850 + \dfrac{60}{100} \times 3750 + \dfrac{44}{100} \times 2250 + \dfrac{20}{100} \\ \times 3150 + \dfrac{50}{100} \times 2550\end{array}\right)$$

$$= \frac{1}{5} \times 6000 = 1200$$

336. (b) Designer

$$= \frac{64}{100} \times 6750 + \frac{30}{100} \times 5100 = 4320 + 1530 = 5850$$

Female supervisors

$$= \frac{64}{100} \times 4050 + \frac{30}{100} \times 4650 = 3987$$

$\therefore$ Required percentage

$$= \frac{(5850 - 3987)}{3987} \times 100 \approx 46.7\%$$

237. (c) Number of male designers

$$= \frac{30}{100} \times 5100 = 1530$$

$\therefore$ $1530 \times 74 = 612 \times 76 + 459 \times 70 + 459 \times x$

or, $x = 75$ yr. 4 months.

238. (b) Required ratio

$$= \frac{\dfrac{36}{100} \times 6750 + \dfrac{70}{100} \times 5100}{\dfrac{40}{100} \times 3750} = \frac{2000}{500}$$

$$= 4 : 1$$

239. (c) Selling price of book I $\Rightarrow 20 \times 200 = 4000$
II $\Rightarrow 40 \times 300 = 12000$
III $\Rightarrow 60 \times 100 = 6000$
Let commission % be (a–1), a and (a+1) respectively.
ATQ,

$$4000 \frac{(a-1)}{100} + \frac{12000(a)}{100} + \frac{6000(a+1)}{100} = 3200$$

$a = 14.45\%$
highest commission $= 15.45\%$

240. (d) Total commission earned by shop RR = ₹ 3500
Total selling price of Book I = 105×20 = ₹ 2100
Total selling price of Book II = 105×30 = ₹ 3150
Total selling price of Book III = 105×40 = ₹ 4200
Let commission percent = x%

$$(2100 + 3150 + 4200) \times \frac{x}{100}$$

$$= 3500 = \frac{1000}{27} \%$$

241. (a) Total commission of SS

$$= \frac{3500 \times 8}{7} = ₹ 4000.$$

S.P. of each product = 100×80 = ₹ 8000

Let commission % charged on 3 products be (x – 5) %, x% and (x+5)%.
So,

$$8000 \frac{(x-5)}{100} + 8000 \frac{(x)}{100} + 8000$$

$$= \frac{(x+5)}{100} \, 4000$$

$240x = 4000$

$$x = \frac{400}{24} = \frac{100}{6} \%$$

$$x = 16\frac{2}{3} \%$$

Least range could be $= 16 - 5 = 11\%$
$16 + 6 = 22\% = (11 - 22)$

242. (d) Let total books = x
So S.P. = x
Now total commission $\Rightarrow 3500$
Minimum values of x = 100
Maximum value of x = 109
Let 'a' be commission %
So, Max value of 'a' could be

$$(100 \times 100) \times \frac{a}{100} = 3500$$

$a = 35\%$
Minimum value could be

$$109 \times 109 \times \frac{a}{100} = 3500 \approx 29.45$$

Range = $(29.4 - 35)$

5 TABULATIONS

Collection of statistical data in the tabular form is called tabulation. Tabulation is generally used to show the tax, trading or these types of values. In these days two types of questions are important for exams:

(i) COMPLETE DATA TABULATION

In these types of tables we need to calculate the data given in tabular form.

For example

Students	Hindi FM-200	English FM-150	Math FM-100	Science FM-200	SST FM-200	Sanskrit FM-150
A	75%	60%	90%	65%	50%	50%
B	80%	50%	70%	85%	65%	80%
C	55%	60%	85%	75%	55%	60%
D	60%	70%	75%	80%	75%	60%

1. Overall marks obtained by B is what percent of overall marks obtained by D in all subjects together?
   (a) 97.5% (b) 103.5%
   (c) 105% (d) 111.1%
   (e) None of these

For example:

Items	Cost Price	Selling Price	Market Price	Profit %	Loss %	Discount %	Profit Amount	Loss Amount	Discount Amount
TV	–	–	–	20%	–	25%	1800	–	–
AC	–	–	40,000	–	25%	25%	–	–	–
Laptop	–	50,000	–	25%	–	–	–	–	10,000
PC	25000	–	–	–	–	40%	5,000	–	–

2. What is profit of shopkeeper if he sells all items at marked price?
   (a) 44.2% (b) 42.8%
   (c) 47.6% (d) 41.1%
   (e) None of these

Ans. (a) Cost price of TV $= 1800 \times \dfrac{100}{20} = 9000$

Market price of TV $= 9000 \times \dfrac{120}{75} = 14400$

Cost price of AC $= 40000 \times \dfrac{75}{75} = 40000$

Market Price of AC $= 40000$

Ans: (b) Total marks obtained by B in all subjects together

$$= 200 \times \frac{80}{100} + 150 \times \frac{50}{100} + 100 \times \frac{70}{100} +$$
$$200 \times \frac{85}{100} + 200 \times \frac{65}{100} + 150 \times \frac{80}{100}$$
$$= 160 + 75 + 70 + 170 + 130 + 120 = 725$$

Total marks obtained by D in all subjects together

$$= 200 \times \frac{60}{100} + 150 \times \frac{70}{100} + 100 \times \frac{75}{100} +$$
$$200 \times \frac{80}{100} + 200 \times \frac{75}{100} + 150 \times \frac{60}{100}$$
$$= 120 + 105 + 75 + 160 + 150 + 90 = 700$$

Required % $= \dfrac{725}{700} \times 100 = 103.5\%$

(ii) MISSING DATA TABULATION

In these types of tabulation we need to find some hidden values for the answer of given questions. In these days these type of questions are most important for the competitive exams.

Cost price of Laptop $= 50000 \times \dfrac{100}{125} = 40000$

Market price of Laptop $= 50000 + 10000 = 60000$

Cost price of PC $= 25000$

Market price of PC $= (25000 + 5000)\dfrac{100}{60} = 50000$

Total cost price of all items together
$= 9000 + 40000 + 40000 + 25000 = 114000$

Total market price of all items together
$= 14400 + 40000 + 60000 + 50000 = 164400$

Profit $= 164400 - 114000 = 50400$

Required % $= \dfrac{50400 \times 100}{114000} = 44.2\%$

EXERCISE

DIRECTIONS (Qs. 1-5): *Answer these question based on the table given below.*

The Hotel Company of India (HCI) owns seven Hotels with the same capacity. The occupancy rates across the seven hotels are given in the following table.

Hotel Name	Pleasant Stay	Dessert Palace	Black Lagoon	Lake View	Classic	Radiant	Plaza
2017	65%	55%	70%	49%	71%	47%	59%
2016	43%	72%	76%	46%	64%	64%	63%
2015	63%	71%	65%	61%	58%	66%	65%
2014	72%	68%	60%	64%	61%	72%	49%
2013	81%	67%	64%	63%	59%	69%	45%

1. In which year did HCI witness the highest occupancy rate?
   (a) 2016 (b) 2015
   (c) 2013 (d) 2014

2. Which one of the following statements is true ?
   (a) The lowest average occupancy rate was in the year 2016.
   (b) The average occupancy rate in 2013 was greater than that in the year 2014.
   (c) There is a gradual decrease in the average occupancy rate over the years.
   (d) The highest average occupancy rate was witnessed in 2013.

3. Which of the following statement(s) is/are false ?
   (a) The average occupancy rate of Plaza was greater than that of Lake View.
   (b) The greatest average occupancy rate was witnessed in Pleasant Stay.
   (c) The average occupancy rate for Dessert Palace is greater than that of Black Lagoon.
   (d) All of the above statements are false.

4. In which year was the rate of growth in occupancy rate the highest ?
   (a) 2013 (b) 2014
   (c) 2015 (d) 2016

5. Every year HCI gives special awards to the managers of those hotels that had achieved the best and the second best occupancy rates. Which of the hotels has won this award at least twice ?
   (a) Pleasant Stay and Lake View
   (b) Dessert Palace and Classic
   (c) Black Lagoon and Radiant
   (d) Lake View and Plaza

DIRECTIONS (Qs. 6-10) : *Study the following table, showing monthly sales of cars of five types by five automobile shops to answer these questions.*

Type	Automobile shops				
	P	Q	R	S	T
A	1250	3500	1360	2240	210
B	2100	3080	3700	4200	920
C	3460	4400	4860	4860	4760
D	900	680	700	1120	600
E	300	440	1200	1250	280

6. Which shop has the lowest sales of both type B and type E as compared to other shops ?
   (a) P (b) Q (c) R (d) T

7. Which shop has a share of 15% sales of the total type D sold by all the shops ?
   (a) P (b) Q
   (c) R (d) T

8. Which shop has the highest sale of cars of all the types ?
   (a) P (b) Q
   (c) R (d) None of these

9. Which shop sales cars of type B seven times to that of type E sold by it ?
   (a) Only P (b) Only Q
   (c) Both P and Q (d) Only T

10. Among all the shops the lowest sale of type A is the highest sale of which of the following types ?
    (a) B (b) C
    (c) D (d) No such type exists

DIRECTIONS (Qs. 11-15) : *Refer to the table given below to answer these questions.*

Participation in Elections (Persons in Millions)

Characteristics	1984		1988		1992	
	Persons of voting age	Percent voted	Persons of voting age	Percent voted	Persons of voting age	Percent voted
Total	330	69	348	68	408	63
Male	156	72	162	70	192	64
Female	174	67	186	66	216	62
Urban	96	57	102	60	126	55
Rural	234	75	246	71	282	66
Age 18 -24	30	51	36	50	75	50
25 - 44	135	69	138	67	147	63
45 - 64	114	76	120	75	126	71
65 years and above	51	66	54	66	60	63

11. Which of the following groups had the highest percentage of voters in 1988?
    (a) Male (b) 25 – 44 years
    (c) Rural (d) 65 years and above

12. In 1992 approximately what per cent of persons of voting age were females ?
    (a) 42   (b) 53   (c) 60   (d) 64

13. In 1988 how many males of voting age voted ?
    (a) 113,400,000   (b) 114,400,000
    (c) 123,400,000   (d) 134,000,000

14. How many persons of 65 years and above did not vote in 1992 ?
    (a) 37,000,000   (b) 37,800,000
    (c) 23,000,000   (d) 22,200,000

15. If X be the number of persons (in million) of voting age 25 – 44 living in rural areas in 1984, then which of the following includes all possible values and only possible values of X?
    (a) $0 \leq X \leq 145$ (b) $39 \leq X \leq 135$
    (c) $39 \leq X \leq 234$ (d) $135 \leq X \leq 234$

DIRECTIONS (Qs. 16-18): *Use the data in the table given below to answer these questions*

	% of protein	% of carbohydrate	% of fat	Cost per 100g
Food A	10	20	30	₹ 1.80
Food B	20	15	10	₹ 3.00
Food C	20	10	40	₹ 2.75

16. What will be the cost of purchasing x grams of food A, y grams of food B and z grams of food C ?
    (a) $₹ (0.3^2 x + 1.8^2 y + 2.57 z)$
    (b) $₹ (1.8x + 0.3z + 2.75y)$
    (c) $₹ \left(\dfrac{0.9}{50} x + \dfrac{0.3}{10} y + \dfrac{0.11}{4} z \right)$
    (d) $₹ (x + y + z)$

17. Which of the following diets would supply the most grams of protein ?
    (a) 500 g of A   (b) 250 g of B
    (c) 350 g of C   (d) 200 g of B and 200 g of C

18. All the following diets would supply at least 75 g of fat. Which of the diets costs the least ?
    (a) 300 g of A
    (b) 200 g of C
    (c) 150 g of A and 100 g of B
    (d) 500 g of B and 100 g of A

DIRECTIONS (Qs. 19-22): *The following table gives the frequency distribution of the final grades of 100 students in Mathematics and Physics. Analyse the data presented to answer these questions.*

Mathematics Grade (Row wise) and Physics Grade (Column wise)

	40-49	50-59	60-69	70-79	80-89	90-99
90 - 99				4	2	5
80 - 89			2	3	7	2
70 - 79			1	7	6	3
60 - 69	2	5	9	8	5	
50 - 59	3	3	6	1		
40 - 49	2	7	7			

19. How many students received grades 80 and above in Mathematics ?
    (a) 20   (b) 30   (c) 23   (d) 25

20. How many students would qualify for admission to a prime Engineering College that stipulates above 80% in Mathematics and Physics ?
    (a) 9   (b) 12   (c) 16   (d) 18

21. The School Trust provides scholarships for higher studies to students who secure 90% and above in Mathematics and Physics. How many students are eligible for scholarships for higher studies?
    (a) 5   (b) 3   (c) 7   (d) 4

22. What percentage of students got less than 70% in both Mathematics and Physics ?
    (a) 34   (b) 43   (c) 39   (d) 44

DIRECTIONS (Qs. 23-26): *Answer the following questions based on the information given below:*

A health-drink company's R & D department is trying to make various diet formulations, which can be used for certain specific purposes. It is considering a choice of 5 alternative ingredients (O, P, Q, R and S), which can be used in different proportions in the formulations. The table below gives the composition of these ingredients. The cost per unit of each of these ingredients is O:150, P: 50, Q: 200, R: 500, S:100.

Ingredient	Composition			
	Carbohydrate (%)	Protein (%)	Fat (%)	Minerals (%)
O	50	30	10	10
P	80	20	0	0
Q	10	30	50	10
R	5	50	40	5
S	45	50	0	5

23. Which among the following is the formulation having the lowest cost per unit for a diet having 10% fat and at least 30% protein? The diet has to be formed by mixing two ingredients.
    (a) P and Q   (b) P and S   (c) R and S   (d) Q and S

24. In what proportion P, Q and S should be mixed to make a diet having at least 60% carbohydrate at the lowest per unit cost?
    (a) 2:1:3   (b) 4:1:2   (c) 2:1:4   (d) 4:1:1

25. The company is planning to launch a balanced diet required for growth needs of adolescent children. This diet must contain at least 30% each of carbohydrate and protein, no more than 25% fat and at least 5% minerals. Which one of the following combination of equally mixed ingredients is feasible?
    (a) O and P   (b) R and S
    (c) P and S   (d) None of these

26. For a recuperating patient, the doctor recommended a diet containing 10% minerals and at least 30% protein. In how may different ways can we prepare this diet by mixing at least two ingredients?
    (a) One   (b) Two   (c) Three   (d) Four

DIRECTIONS (Qs. 27-31): *On the basis of the information given below.*

In a Class X Board examination, ten papers are distributed over five Groups of PCB, Mathematics, Social Science, Vernacular and English. Each of the ten papers is evaluated out of 100. The final score of a student is calculated in the following manner. First the Group Scores are obtained by averaging marks in the papers within the Group. The final score is the simple average of the Group Scores. The data for the top ten students are presented below. (Dipan's score in English Paper II has been intentionally removed in the table).

Name of the student	PCB Group			Social Science Group			Vernacular Group		English Group		Final Score
	Phy.	Chem.	Bio.	Mathematics Group	Hist.	Geo.	Paper I	Paper II	Paper I	Paper II	
Ayesha (G)	98	96	97	98	95	93	94	96	96	98	96.2
Ram (B)	97	99	95	97	95	96	94	94	96	98	96.1
Dipan (B)	98	98	98	95	96	95	96	94	96	??	96.0
Sagnik (B)	97	98	99	96	96	98	94	97	92	94	95.9
Sanjiv (B)	95	96	97	98	97	96	92	93	95	96	95.7
Shreya (G)	96	89	85	100	97	98	94	95	96	95	95.5
Joseph (B)	90	94	98	100	94	97	90	92	94	95	95.0
Agni (B)	96	99	96	99	95	96	82	93	92	93	94.3
Pritam (B)	98	98	95	98	83	95	90	93	94	94	93.9
Tirna (G)	96	98	79	99	85	94	92	91	87	96	93.7

Note: B or G against the name of a student respectively indicates whether the student is a boy or a girl.

27. How much did Dipan get in English Paper II?
    (a) 94
    (b) 96.5
    (c) 97
    (d) 98

28. Students who obtained Group Scores of at least 95 in every group are eligible to apply for a prize. Among those who are eligible, the student obtaining the highest Group Score in Social Science Group is awarded this prize. The prize was awarded to:
    (a) Shreya
    (b) Ram
    (c) Ayesha
    (d) Dipan

29. Among the top ten students, how many boys scored at least 95 in at least one paper from each of the groups?
    (a) 1
    (b) 2
    (c) 3
    (d) 4

30. Each of the ten students was allowed to improve his/her score in exactly one paper of choice with the objective of maximizing his/her final score. Everyone scored 100 in the paper in which he or she chose to improve. After that, the topper among the ten students was:
    (a) Ram
    (b) Agni
    (c) Pritam
    (d) Dipan

31. Had Joseph, Agni, Pritam and Tirna each obtained Group Score of 100 in the Social Science Group, then their standing in decreasing order of final score would be:
    (a) Pritam, Joseph, Tirna, Agni
    (b) Joseph, Tirna, Agni, Pritam
    (c) Pritam, Agni, Tirna, Joseph
    (d) Joseph, Tirna, Pritam, Agni

DIRECTIONS (Qs. 32-36): *Study the following table to answer the given questions.*

Centrewise and Postwise number of candidates

Post → Specialist Centre ↓	Officer	Clerk	Field Officer	Supervisor	Specialist officer
Bangalore	2000	5000	50	2050	750
Delhi	15000	17000	160	11000	750
Mumbai	17000	19500	70	7000	900
Hyderabad	3500	20000	300	9000	1150
Kolkata	14900	17650	70	1300	1200
Lucknow	11360	15300	30	1500	650
Chennai	9000	11000	95	1650	500

32. In Kolkata, number of Specialist Officers is approximately what per cent of Officers?
    (a) 8.7
    (b) 9
    (c) 6.5
    (d) 8
    (e) 6.9

33. What is the difference between total number of Officers and Clerks?
    (a) 29680
    (b) 34180
    (c) 32690
    (d) 28680
    (e) None of these

34. In Chennai, the number of Clerks is approximately how much per cent more than that of Officers?
    (a) 18
    (b) 22
    (c) 20
    (d) 2
    (e) 13

35. Which centre has 300% more number of Clerks as compared to those in Bangalore?
    (a) Lucknow
    (b) Mumbai
    (c) Hyderabad
    (d) Chennai
    (e) None of these

36. Which centre has the highest number of candidates?
    (a) Delhi
    (b) Kolkata
    (c) Hyderabad
    (d) Mumbai
    (e) None of these

DIRECTIONS (Qs. 37-41): *Read the following table and answer the following question.*

Total number of visitors and Percentage of male out of these visitors are given.

Districts	Museum	
	Total visitors (Male and Female)	Percentage of male out of total visitors
A	250	40%
B	350	44%
C	375	60%
D	450	56%
E	300	55%
F	525	32%

[SBI PO Prelim 2017]

37. Total number of female visitors from district B and C together to see the museum are how much more/less than total number of male visitors from district C and D together to see the museum?
 (a) 142 (b) 126 (c) 128 (d) 131
 (e) None of these

38. Average number of visitors from district A, B and C together to see the museum are approximately what percent of the average number of visitors from district D, E and F together to see the museum.
 (a) 71%
 (b) 76%
 (c) 78%
 (d) 74%
 (e) 85%

39. Find the ratio of the male visitors from district E and F together to see the museum to the female visitors form district C and D together to see the museum?
 (a) 107 : 117
 (b) 116 : 111
 (c) 111 : 116
 (d) 117 : 107
 (e) None of these

40. Male visitors from district C to see the museum are what percent more/less than the female visitors from district E to see the museum? (Calculate up to two decimal points)
 (a) $33\frac{1}{3}\%$ (b) $33\frac{2}{3}\%$
 (c) $66\frac{1}{3}\%$ (d) $66\frac{2}{3}\%$
 (e) None of these

41. Find the difference between the total number of male visitors from district B, C and D together to see the museum and the total number of female visitors from district D, E and F together to see the museum?
 (a) 25 (b) 75
 (c) 60 (d) 50
 (e) None of these

DIRECTIONS (Qs. 42-46) : *Study the following table carefully to answer these questions.*

Production (in lakh tonnes) of product by six companies over the given years

Year/ Company	2013	2014	2015	2016	2017	2018
A	487	565	648	734	848	765
B	522	378	725	673	729	695
C	746	483	679	499	685	720
D	398	526	498	580	617	732
E	415	680	840	689	780	637
F	632	775	580	720	670	746

42. Production of Company *B* in 2015 was what per cent of the total production of all the companies together for that year (rounded off to the nearest integer)?
 (a) 17 (b) 20 (c) 22 (d) 18
 (e) None of these

43. During which year was the percentage increase/decrease in production from the previous year the lowest for Company *A*?
 (a) 2018 (b) 2014 (c) 2016 (d) 2015
 (e) None of these

44. What was the difference between the total productions of companies *E & F* (in lakh tonnes) in the given years?
 (a) 78 (b) 86 (c) 76 (d) 72
 (e) None of these

45. Approximately what was the average production of all the six companies (in lakh tonnes) in the year 2014?
 (a) 590 (b) 550 (c) 570 (d) 450
 (e) 620

46. What was the percent fall in production of Company 'C' in 2016 over that in 2015 (rounded off to two digits after decimal)?
 (a) 25. 61 (b) 26. 51 (c) 36. 07 (d) 37. 16
 (e) None of these

DIRECTIONS (Qs. 47-51) s: *Study the following table and answer the following questions carefully. Following table shows the percentage population of six states below poverty line and the proportion of male and female*

State	Percentage population below proverty line	Proportion of male and female	
		Below poverty line M : F	Above poverty line M : F
A	12	3:02	4:03
B	15	5:07	3:04
C	25	4:05	2:03
D	26	1:02	5:06
E	10	6:05	3:02
F	32	2:03	4:05

47. The total population of state *A* is 3000, then what is the approximate no. of females above poverty line in state *A*?
 (a) 1150 (b) 2112 (c) 1800 (d) 1950
 (e) 2025

48. If the total population of *C* and *D* together is 18000, then what is the total no. of females below poverty line in the above stated states?
    - (a) 5000
    - (b) 5500
    - (c) 4800
    - (d) Data inadequate
    - (e) None of these

49. If the population of males below poverty line in state A is 3000 and that in state E is 6000, then what is the ratio of the total population of state A and E?
    - (a) 3 : 4
    - (b) 4 : 5
    - (c) 1 : 2
    - (d) 2 : 3
    - (e) None of these

50. If the population of males below poverty line in state B is 500 then what is the total population of that state?
    - (a) 14400
    - (b) 6000
    - (c) 8000
    - (d) 7600
    - (e) None of these

51. If in state E population of females above poverty line is 19800 then what is the population of males below poverty line in that state?
    - (a) 5500
    - (b) 3000
    - (c) 2970
    - (d) Data inadequate
    - (e) None of these

DIRECTIONS (Qs. 52-56): *In the table data is given about the obtained marks of some different students in some different subjects. Some data is given and some data is missing. Study the table carefully and answer the related questions.*

Students	Obtained marks in Math out of 200	Obtained marks in Hindi out of 200	Obtained marks in English out of 100	Obtained marks in Science out of 150	Obtained marks in Sanskrit out of 100	Average obtained marks in all subjects
A	130	–	55	–	75	100
B	–	95	–	85	70	–
C	–	–	45	75	85	90
D	–	–	60	105	45	–
E	–	140	–	120	–	100

52. Total marks obtained by A in Hindi is 50% more than marks obtained by him in science then what is percentage of marks obtained by A in science?
    - (a) 64%
    - (b) 60%
    - (c) 56%
    - (d) 72%
    - (e) None of these

53. If marks obtained by C in Science is 25% less than marks obtained by C in Hindi then what is respective ratio of marks obtained by C in Math and Hindi?
    - (a) 20 : 29
    - (b) 29 : 20
    - (c) 24 : 29
    - (d) 29 : 21
    - (e) None of these

54. If marks obtained by D in Hindi is 60% of full marks of science and his average score in all subjects together is 10% less than that of A then what is percentage of marks obtained by him in Math?
    - (a) 50%
    - (b) 60%
    - (c) 75%
    - (d) 80%
    - (e) None of these

55. If A scored 20% more marks than C in Science then what is average percentage of marks scored by all students together in Science?
    - (a) 62.3%
    - (b) 61.1%
    - (c) 71.1%
    - (d) 63.3%
    - (e) None of these

56. Marks obtained by E in Sanskrit is 50% more than marks obtained by him in English and marks obtained by E in Math is equal to marks obtained by him in English and Sanskrit together then what is his obtained marks in Math?
    - (a) 72
    - (b) 105
    - (c) 110
    - (d) 125
    - (e) None of these

DIRECTIONS (Qs. 57-61): *In the table some data is given about workers of different companies. Study the given data carefully and answer the related questions.*

Companies	No of male workers	No of trained males : No of untrained males	No of males : No of females	No of trained females : No of untrained females	Salary of trained workers : Salary of untrained workers	Salary of a untrained worker
A	800	5:11	2:3	1:2	9:5	2500
B	200	3:2	2:5	2:3	2:1	2000
C	450	4:11	9:4	1:3	3:2	3000
D	300	1:2	2:1	3:7	5:4	4000
E	600	7:13	3:2	2:3	10:7	3500

57. What is respective ratio of total salary of trained workers and untrained workers in B?
    - (a) 13 : 9
    - (b) 9 : 32
    - (c) 19 : 32
    - (d) 19 : 16
    - (e) None of these

58. Total no of trained workers in all companies together is what percent of total no workers in all companies?
    - (a) 43.47%
    - (b) 44.37%
    - (c) 37.44%
    - (d) 34.47%
    - (e) None of these

59. What is average salary of all workers of company A?
    - (a) 3350
    - (b) 3250
    - (c) 3150
    - (d) 3050
    - (e) None of these

60. What is difference between average no of male workers and that of female workers in all companies together?
 (a) 50 (b) 20
 (c) 100 (d) 200
 (e) None of these

61. What is respective ratio of average salary of a worker of D and that of a worker of E?
 (a) 7780 : 7299 (b) 7299 : 7780
 (c) 8077 : 9972 (d) 8707 : 9792
 (e) None of these

DIRECTIONS (Qs. 62-66) : *In the table some data is given about an electronic shop which sells different electronic goods. Study the given data carefully and answer the related questions.*

	C.P.	S.P.	M.P.	Profit %	Loss %	Discount %	Amount of Profit	Amount of Loss	Amount of Discount
T.V.	20000			20%		40%			
P.C.			40000			25%	10000		
Mobile				20%		20%	6000		
Laptop		35000			30%				15000
Music system	20000					50%		5000	
Mixer			10000	50%			2500		

62. If all six electronic goods are sold at their marked price then what is profit percentage of seller?
 (a) 45.8% (b) 48.2%
 (c) 49.6% (d) 39.8%
 (e) None of these

63. Marked price of laptop is what percent of that of Music system?
 (a) 116.7% (b) 150% (c) 66.7% (d) 166.7%
 (e) None of these

64. If seller sells Mixer at successive discounts of 30% and 20% then what would be the profit/loss?
 (a) 12% loss (b) 10% profit
 (c) 15% profit (d) 20% loss
 (e) None of these

65. What is respective ratio of average cost price and average selling price of all items together?
 (a) 58 : 59 (b) 59 : 58
 (c) 60 : 61 (d) 59 : 61
 (e) None of these

66. What is respective ratio of total profit and total discount on all items together?
 (a) 1 : 8 (b) 8 : 27 (c) 1 : 27 (d) 27 : 1
 (e) None of these

DIRECTIONS (Qs. 67-71) : *In the table data is given about some electronic goods produced by a company. Some data is given and some data is missing. Study the given data carefully and answer the related questions.*

	Total production	No. of unsold items	C.P.	M.P.	Discount %	Profit %	Loss %
T.V.	5000	500	13500		10%	20%	
Music system		1000	20000	40000	20%	20%	
P.C.	10000		20000	30000	25%	0%	0%
A.C.		500	25000	40000	30%		20%
Laptop	8000	1000	25000	50000	10%		

67. Marked price of T.V. is what percent more than its cost price?
 (a) 48.14% (b) 44.18%
 (c) 41.84% (d) 46.5%
 (e) None of these

68. What is total cost price of the stock of music system?
 (a) 8000000 (b) 80000000
 (c) 10000000 (d) 12000000
 (e) None of these

69. What is average cost price of all items together. If he sells A.C at M.P. then his profit is 20%?
 (a) 15000 (b) 19000
 (c) 27000 (d) 41000
 (e) None of these

70. What is respective ratio of total no. of music system and total no. of A.C.'s produced by company?
 (a) 2 : 3 (b) 1 : 2 (c) 2 : 1 (d) 3 : 2
 (e) None of these

71. Total no. of unsold items is what percent of total production?
 (a) 47.11% (b) 17.14% (c) 11.47% (d) 14.17%
 (e) None of these

DIRECTIONS (Qs. 72-76) : *Study the following tables carefully and answer the questions given below:*

Number & Percentage of Candidates Qualified in a Competitive Examination:
Number of Candidates appeared in a Competitive Examination From Five Centres Over The Years

Centre → Year ↓	Mumbai	Delhi	Kolkata	Hyderabad	Chennai
2010	35145	65139	45192	51124	37346
2011	17264	58248	52314	50248	48932
2012	24800	63309	56469	52368	51406
2013	28316	70316	71253	54196	52315
2014	36503	69294	69632	58360	55492
2015	29129	59216	64178	48230	57365
2016	32438	61345	56304	49178	58492

Approximate Percentages of Candidates Qualified To Appeared In the Competitive Examination From Five Centres Over the year

Centre → Year ↓	Mumbai	Delhi	Kolkata	Hyderabad	Chennai
2010	12	24	18	17	9
2011	10	28	12	21	12
2012	15	21	23	25	10
2013	11	27	19	24	8
2014	13	23	16	23	13
2015	14	20	21	19	11
2016	16	19	24	20	14

72. In which of the following years was the difference in number of candidates appeared from Mumbai over the previous year the minimum ?
(a) 2013   (b) 2015   (c) 2016   (d) 2011
(e) None of these

73. In which of the following years was the number of candidates qualified from Chennai, the maximum among the given years ?
(a) 2016   (b) 2015   (c) 2014   (d) 2012
(e) None of these

74. Approximately what was the total number of candidates qualified from Delhi in 2011 and 2015 together ?
(a) 27250   (b) 25230
(c) 30150   (d) 28150
(e) 26250

75. Approximately how many candidates appearing from Kolkata in 2013 qualified in the competitive examination?
(a) 13230   (b) 13540
(c) 15130   (d) 15400
(e) 19240

76. Approximately what was the difference between the number of candidates qualified from Hyderabad in 2010 and 2011?
(a) 1680   (b) 2440   (c) 1450   (d) 2060
(e) 1860

DIRECTIONS (Qs. 77-81) : *In the following table the production of different kinds of toys by a company in different years has been given. Read the table carefully and answer the questions.*   **[SBI PO 2014]**

Production of 5-different Toys and Percentage of Defective Toys in Various Years

Toys → Years ↓	Type-A Production	% defective toys	Type-B Production	% defective toys	Type-C Production	% defective toys	Type-D Production	% defective toys	Type-E Production	% defective toys
2006	18000	06	20000	06	12000	04	22000	07	23000	08
2007	21000	05	15000	05	15000	08	20000	08	18000	06
2008	16000	08	18000	04	17000	05	18000	05	17000	05
2009	22000	09	19000	06	20000	07	24000	06	20000	04
2010	24000	04	21000	09	24000	09	27000	08	24000	08
2011	28000	05	20000	05	28000	05	28000	05	27000	09
2012	26000	07	28000	08	31000	02	30000	05	30000	05

77. Find the approximate average number of defect free A, C and E types of toys manufactured in 2007.
(a) 16890   (b) 16980   (c) 16880   (d) 17890
(e) None of these

78. How many defect free C-type of toys were manufactured in 2008?
(a) 16250   (b) 16150   (c) 16350   (d) 16450
(e) None of these

79. Find the difference between the number of E-type of toys manufactured in 2008 and the total number of A type and B type of toys manufactured in 2009.
(a) 26000   (b) 23000   (c) 24000   (d) 18000
(e) None of these

80. In which year was the maximum number of defective toys of type-A manufactured ?
(a) 2010   (b) 2008   (c) 2012   (d) 2009
(e) None of these

81. Find the ratio between the number of defective toys of type A in 2006 and that of defective toys of type-E in 2007 ?
(a) 3 : 2   (b) 2 : 3   (c) 1 : 2   (d) 2 : 1
(e) 1 : 1

DIRECTIONS (Qs. 82-86): *Study the following table carefully and answer the questions that follow:*

The percentage marks obtained by seven students in six different subjects

Subject → Student ↓	A (Out of 75)	B (Out of 150)	C (Out of 100)	D (Out of 50)	E (Out of 150)	F (Out of 75)
P	85	68	76	92	89	82
Q	78	72	84	80	64	70
R	66	75	79	88	72	66
S	74	62	91	74	70	74
T	90	75	67	68	69	78
V	86	80	69	78	82	80
W	82	68	81	85	76	72

82. What total percentage marks 'R' did secure in all the six subjects together?
(a) 75.73   (b) 74.33
(c) 73.75   (d) 74.75
(e) None of these

83. What is the difference between the marks obtained by 'P' in the subjects 'B', 'D' and 'E' together and by 'T' in the same subjects?
    (a) 32.5   (b) 31.5   (c) 37   (d) 34
    (e) None of these

84. What is the average of marks obtained by all the students in subject 'B'? (up to two decimal places)
    (a) 107.14   (b) 71.4
    (c) 114.07   (d) 73.14
    (e) None of these

85. What is the average percentage of marks obtained by all the students in the subjects 'C' and 'D' together?
    (a) 78   (b) 80.71
    (c) 79.43   (d) 77.53
    (e) None of these

86. What is the total marks obtained by all the students in subject 'F'?
    (a) 422   (b) 398.5   (c) 522   (d) 391.5
    (e) None of these

DIRECTIONS (Qs. 87-91): *Study the following table carefully and answer the questions that follow:*

Investment (in ₹ crores) by six units of XYZ Company from 2011 to 2016

Year → Unit ↓	2011	2012	2013	2014	2015	2016	Total
A	85	132	125	116	142	138	738
B	105	140	145	148	142	144	824
C	114	137	138	136	150	152	827
D	98	125	132	145	158	152	810
E	82	128	141	152	149	165	817
F	108	150	145	156	154	162	875
Total	592	812	826	853	895	913	4891

87. In which of the following years the investment of unit 'C' was minimum per cent of the investment of all the units taken together in the same year?
    (a) 2012   (b) 2013   (c) 2014   (d) 2016
    (e) None of these

88. In the year 2012 the investment of which of the following units is the maximum per cent of the investment during the given years?
    (a) A   (b) F   (c) C   (d) B
    (e) None of these

89. What is the increase per cent in the investment of unit 'D' from 2011 to 2014?
    (a) 26.75   (b) 21.55
    (c) 21.60   (d) 27.55
    (e) None of these

90. How much more/less is the investment by units A, B and C in the year 2013 than the investment by the same three units in the year 2014?
    (a) ₹ 10 crores less   (b) ₹ 8 crores more
    (c) ₹ 8 crores less   (d) ₹ 10 crores more
    (e) None of these

91. What is the ratio between the total investment of unit A, B and C in the year 2013 and the total investment of units D, E and F in the year 2014?
    (a) 36 : 51   (b) 51 : 36
    (c) 26 : 43   (d) 43 : 26
    (e) None of these

DIRECTIONS (Qs. 92-96) : *Study the table carefully to answer the questions that follow.*

[SBI Bank PO Main 2015]

Number of people Liking Eight Different Teams in IPL-5 and the percentages of Men, Women and Children Liking these Teams

Teams	Total number of people	Percentage of		
		Men	Women	Children
CSK	45525	20	44	36
DD	36800	39	33	28
DC	56340	45	30	25
MI	62350	38	28	34
RR	48300	21	44	35
RCB	35580	15	35	50
KXI	56250	24	36	40
KKR	64000	16	54	30

92. What is the approximate average number of women liking all the teams?
    (a) 16707   (b) 16686
    (c) 16531   (d) 16668
    (e) None of these

93. The total number of women liking RR forms approximately what per cent of the total number of women liking all the teams?
    (a) 11   (b) 15   (c) 20   (d) 20
    (e) None of these

94. What is the total number of children liking CSK?
    (a) 14085   (b) 16389   (c) 20031   (d) 14850
    (e) None of these

95. What is the ratio of total number of men liking DD to those liking RR?
    (a) 69 : 49   (b) 7 : 5   (c) 208 : 147   (d) 70 : 52
    (e) None of these

96. The number of men liking DC forms what per cent of those liking RCB? (Rounded off to two digits after decimal).
    (a) 21.05%   (b) 475.04%
    (c) 25.56%   (d) 25%
    (e) None of these

DIRECTIONS (Qs. 97-101): *Study the following table carefully and answer the questions given below it:*

Statewise and Disciplinewise Number of Candidates Appeared (App.) and Qualified (Qual.) at a competitive Examination

State →	A.P.		U.P.		Kerala		Orissa		M.P.		W.B.		Total	
Discipline ↓	App.	Qual.	App.	Qual.	App.	Qual.	App.	Qual.	App.	Qual.	App.	Qual.	App.	Qual.
Arts	5420	1840	4980	1690	2450	845	3450	1200	7500	2000	4800	1500	28600	9075
Commerce	8795	2985	6565	2545	3500	2040	4800	2200	8400	2400	7600	2700	39660	14870
Science	6925	2760	8750	3540	4250	2500	4500	1950	6850	3000	8500	3200	39775	16950
Engineering	1080	490	2500	1050	1200	450	1850	850	2500	750	3400	1400	12530	4990
Agriculture	2040	850	1085	455	700	200	450	150	1500	475	1200	500	5775	2130
Total	23060	8425	23880	9280	12100	6035	15050	6350	26750	8625	25500	9300	126340	48015

97. For which of the following disciplines the proportion of qualifying candidates to the appeared candidates from U.P. State is the lowest?
    (a) Arts (b) Commerce
    (c) Science (d) Engineering
    (e) Agriculture

98. For which of the pair of States, the qualifying percentage from Agriculture discipline is exactly the same?
    (a) A.P. & U.P. (b) A.P. & West Bengal
    (c) U.P & West Bengal (d) Kerala & Orissa
    (e) None of these

99. For which of the following states the percentage of candidates qualified to appeared is the minimum for commerce discipline?
    (a) AP (b) UP (c) Kerala (d) Orissa
    (e) MP

100. Approximately what is the ratio between total qualifying percentage of UP and that of MP?
    (a) 15 : 16 (b) 13 : 14 (c) 14 : 13 (d) 19 : 16
    (e) 17 : 16

101. The qualifying percentage for which of the following states is the lowest for Science discipline?
    (a) AP (b) UP
    (c) Kerala (d) West Bengal
    (e) None of these

DIRECTIONS (Qs. 102-106): *Study the following information to answer the given questions*

[IBPS PO Main 2016]

Dept	STAFF		STUDENTS	
	Number	M : F	Number	M : F
ECE	120	13 : 11	1800	7 : 11
EEE	80	9 : 7	1500	7 : 8
CES	150	17 : 13	2200	9 : 13
IT	90	4 : 5	600	7 : 5
ME	140	4 : 3	1600	17 : 15
EIE	70	18 : 17	1200	9 : 11

102. What is the ratio of total number of staff in ECE, EEE to the total no of students in CSE and IT ?
    (a) 14:1 (b) 1:14 (c) 1:12 (d) 1:17
    (e) None of these

103. The total no of male staff in IT and EIE is what % of the total number of staff in these 2 dept ?
    (a) 44.5% (b) 45.7% (c) 47.5% (d) 45.00%
    (e) None of these

104. Total no of female students in CSE is what % more than the male students in the same Dept ?
    (a) 44.45% (b) 40.76% (c) 40.75% (d) 40.66%
    (e) None of these

105. Find the number of female students in ME dept ?
    (a) 850 (b) 650 (c) 150 (d) 750
    (e) None of these

106. Find the average of total no of staff in all the dept ?
    (a) 103.8 (b) 108.3 (c) 108.2 (d) 108
    (e) None of these

DIRECTIONS (Qs. 107-111): *There are five shop owners A, B, C, D and E. They are selling five different items given in the table.*

In the table, Discount (as a percentage) is given on mark price of these five products by different sellers. Study the table and answer the following questions:

	Item I	Item II	Item III	Item IV
A	18%	32%	36%	—
B	22%	—	33%	40%
C	—	16%	14%	15%
D	28%	28%	16%	—
E	—	8%	—	7%

Note:

1. Some values are missing. You have to calculate these values as per data given in the questions.

2. Mark price of a particular item is same for all of the shop owners.

107. If the profit percentage of seller A after selling item II is s% and that of seller C for the same item is (2s - 4)% and the ratio of cost price of item II by seller A and seller C is 17 : 21 then find the value of s?
    (a) 2 (b) 3 (c) 4 (d) 5
    (e) None of these

108. For seller Difference between the selling price of item II and that of item III is ₹ 420 if the sum of the mark price of item II and item III by the same seller is 6000 then the Mark price (in ₹) of item II is what percent more/less than that of item III by the same seller ? (Selling price of item II is greater than that of item III)
    (a) 50% (b) 40% (c) 30% (d) 35%
    (e) 45%

109. Average SP of item II by seller A and B is ₹ 3888, by seller B and C is ₹ 4320. Find the SP (in ₹) of item III by seller C.
    (a) 4536 (b) 3656 (c) 5430 (d) 4150
    (e) None of these

110. If the selling price of item I and item III by seller E are in the ratio of 5 : 6. If the seller earned a profit of 25% which is ₹ 750 on item I and 20% on item III then find the total profit (in ₹) by selling item I and item III together by the same seller?
(a) 750   (b) 2000   (c) 1750   (d) 1250
(e) 1500

111. Cost price of item III is ₹ 60 for all of the sellers and all of them marked the same product at higher than the cost price, then to get a total profit of ₹ 80 by all of the five sellers after selling item III, what is the minimum discount should be provided by seller E on item III.
(a) 21%   (b) 19%
(c) 17%   (d) 25%
(e) None of these

DIRECTIONS (Qs. 112-116) : *Study the following table to answer the given questions :*

[SBI PO Exam 2011]

Each company produces two types of steel. In table I the total production (in lakh tonnes) of both types of steel together of six companies over the years is given. In table II the ratio of production of two types A and B (A : B) over the years is given.

Yrs. → Com. ↓	1997	1998	1999	2000	2001	2002	Total
BS	424	390	258	756	319	427	2574
TIS	339.5	663	812	598	663	782	3857.5
SAI	532	576	364	936	595	665	3668
MPI	620	850	876	1045	1274	1296	5961
ES	612	806	627	406	874	760	4085
LTS	840	836	776	748	384.72	816	4400.72
Total	3367.5	4121	3713	4489	4109.72	4746	24546.22

Table-I

Yrs. → Com. ↓	1997	1998	1999	2000	2001	2002
BS	3 : 5	8 : 7	1 : 2	4 : 5	6 : 5	5 : 2
TIS	1 : 2.5	9 : 8	13 : 15	7 : 6	6 : 7	14 : 9
SAI	13 : 15	7 : 9	1 : 3	11 : 7	10 : 7	62 : 71
MPI	41 : 59	17 : 8	100 : 119	53 : 42	24 : 25	7 : 9
ES	2 : 7	12 : 19	6 : 5	3 : 11	10 : 13	19 : 21
LTS	13 : 11	21 : 23	5 : 3	4 : 7	1 : 1.29	7 : 5

Table-II

112. The production of steel A by company MPI in 1999 is approximately what per cent of production in 2001?
(a) 51 %   (b) 53%
(c) 55%   (d) 60%
(e) 64%

113. In 2001, in how many companies production of A type steel is more than that of B type steel?
(a) No company   (b) Two
(c) Three   (d) Cannot be determined
(e) None of these

114. For how many companies did the production of steel A increase every year and the production of steel B decrease every year together from that of the previous year?
(a) No company   (b) One
(c) Two   (d) Three
(e) None of these

115. Production of TIS increases by 10% in 2003 and production of SAI decreases by 10% in 2003 in comparison to 2002. If the ratio of production remains the same as in 2002, find the ratio of production of A type to B type steel for both the companies together.
(a) 8026 : 6561   (b) 7026 : 7561
(c) 8097 : 6061   (d) 8026 : 5061
(e) None of these

116. If the profit ratio per unit tonne of steel A and B is 3 : 4 for company BS, what is the actual profit ratio of the company BS for the year 1998 for steel A and B?
(a) 6 : 7   (b) 3 : 4
(c) 8 : 7   (d) Can't be determined
(e) None of these

DIRECTIONS (Qs. 117-121) : *Study the following table carefully and answer the questions given below it :*

[SBI PO Exam 2011]

Area and Population of different states

States	Area (in sq kilometres)	Population (in lakhs)
A	6230	1122
B	2540	838
C	8135	649
D	7436	572
E	4893	711
F	3718	286
G	4297	860

117. Among the given states, in case of how many states the area of that state was more than 15 per cent of the total areas taken together?
(a) One   (b) Three   (c) two   (d) Can't say
(e) None of these

118. For which two states the density of population is approximately equal?
(a) No state   (b) A and G   (c) D and F   (d) C and F
(e) None of these

119. Approximately how much more is the density of population of state B in comparison to that of state A?
(a) 15000   (b) 18000   (c) 13000   (d) 14000
(e) 17000

120. In case of how many states the density of population was more than 12 thousand per square kilometre?
(a) Two   (b) Five   (c) Three   (d) Four
(e) None of these

121. What is the approximate ratio of the areas of state B to the areas of state A and G together.
(a) 1 : 3.8   (b) 1 : 3.5   (c) 1 : 5.2   (d) 1 : 4.5
(e) 1 : 4.1

122. The surface area of a spherical part of a bowl with a flat circular detachable cover, excluding the cover, is 616 sq cm. The area of the cover is 38.5 sq cm. What is the volume of the bowl?
    - (a) 1339 cm^3
    - (b) 1430 cm^3
    - (c) 1570 cm^3
    - (d) Cannot be determined
    - (e) None of these

DIRECTIONS (Qs. 123-129): *Study the following table carefully and answer the questions which follow.*

[SBI Po exam 2011]

Number of Candidates found Eligible and the Number of Candidates Shortlisted for Interview for a recent Recruitment Process for Six Posts from

Different States
E-Eligible S- Short listed

Post	1		II		III		IV		V		VI	
State	E	S	E	S	E	S	E	S	E	S	E	S
A	2500	65	7200	240	5200	76	3600	200	4600	110	5400	380
B	3200	220	8500	420	8400	190	6200	320	5800	180	6200	430
C	2800	280	4500	350	7600	160	8200	440	7300	310	3700	250
D	2400	85	4800	200	2600	55	7500	350	3900	160	4800	360
E	3000	120	5600	280	3800	75	6800	280	6100	260	7800	520
F	4800	325	6400	320	4400	220	4700	180	4900	220	8800	640
G	6500	550	7000	140	6000	325	5500	220	8100	410	2700	200

123. From State B, which post had the highest percentage of candidates shortlisted?
    - (a) V
    - (b) IV
    - (c) VI
    - (d) II
    - (e) None of these

124. What is the average number of candidates (approximately) found eligible for Post III from all states?
    - (a) 6700
    - (b) 6200
    - (c) 4200
    - (d) 4500
    - (e) 5500

125. What is the overall percentage (rounded off to one digit after decimal) of candidates shortlisted over the total number of candidates eligible for Post I from all the States together?
    - (a) 9.5%
    - (b) 12.5%
    - (c) 7.2%
    - (d) 6.5%
    - (e) None of these

126. What is the ratio of the total number of candidates shortlisted for all the posts together from State E to that from state G?
    - (a) 307 : 369
    - (b) 73 : 79
    - (c) 6 : 5
    - (d) 9 : 7
    - (e) None of these

127. The total number of candidates found eligible for Post I from all states together is approximately what per cent of the total number of candidates found eligible for Post VI from all States together?
    - (a) 45%
    - (b) 50%
    - (c) 60%
    - (d) 55%
    - (e) 63.9%

128. Which state had the lowest percentage of candidates short listed with respect to candidate eligible for Post IV?
    - (a) G
    - (b) F
    - (c) E
    - (d) C
    - (e) None of these.

129. What is the ratio of the total number of candidates short listed for post V to that for post VI from all states together?
    - (a) 6 : 7
    - (b) 55 : 96
    - (c) 165 : 278
    - (d) 16 : 25
    - (e) None of these

DIRECTIONS (Qs. 130-134) : *Study the table carefully to answer the questions that follow :*

IBPS PO/MT exam 2011

Percentage of Marks Obtained by Different Students in Different Subjects of MBA

Students	SUBJECTS (Maximum Marks)					
	Strategic Management (150)	Brand Management (100)	Compensation Management (150)	Consumer Behaviour (125)	Service Marketing (75)	Training & Development (50)
Anushka	66	75	88	56	56	90
Archit	82	76	84	96	92	88
Arpan	76	66	78	88	72	70
Garvita	90	88	96	76	84	86
Gunit	64	70	68	72	68	74
Pranita	48	56	50	64	64	58

130. How many marks did Anushka get in all the subjects together?
    - (a) 369
    - (b) 463
    - (c) 558
    - (d) 496
    - (e) None of these

131. Who has scored the highest total marks in all the subjects together ?
    - (a) Archit
    - (b) Gunit
    - (c) Pranita
    - (d) Garvita
    - (e) Arpan

132. Marks obtained by Garvita in Brand Management are what percent of marks obtained by Archit in the same subject ? (rounded off to two digits after decimal)
    - (a) 86.36
    - (b) 101.71
    - (c) 115.79
    - (d) 133.33
    - (e) None of these

133. How many students have scored the highest marks in more than one subject ?
    - (a) Three
    - (b) Two
    - (c) One
    - (d) None
    - (e) None of these

134. What are the average marks obtained by all students together in Compensation Management ?
    - (a) 116
    - (b) 120
    - (c) 123
    - (d) 131
    - (e) None of these

DIRECTIONS (Qs. 135-139) : *Study the following table carefully and answer the questions given below :*

[IBPS PO Exam 2013]

Number of books of different prices bought over the months.

Price \ Months	January	March	May	July	September	November
More than ₹ 5,000	50	106	2	30	25	75
₹ 4,000-₹ 5,000	105	1000	40	105	400	375
₹ 3,000-₹ 3,999	70	100	80	115	200	240
₹ 2,000-₹ 2,999	300	500	100	216	135	300
₹ 1,000-₹ 1,999	140	370	200	225	175	470
₹ 500-₹ 999	200	700	15	400	75	530
Less than ₹ 500	65	135	111	118	25	65

135. In which month maximum number of books were bought?
   (a) March   (b) November
   (c) July   (d) September
   (e) None of these

136. In which price range maximum books were bought in the given months taken together?
   (a) ₹ 500 - ₹ 999   (b) ₹ 2000 - ₹ 2999
   (c) ₹ 1000 - ₹ 1999   (d) ₹ 3000 - ₹ 3999
   (e) None of these

137. In the price range of ₹ 1000 - ₹ 1999 the number of books bought in January is what percent of the number of books bought in May in the same price range ?
   (a) 30   (b) 70   (c) 142.86   (d) 60
   (e) None of these

138. What is the difference between the number of books bought in September and November ?
   (a) 244   (b) 776
   (c) 1020   (d) 1310
   (e) None of these

139. What is the ratio between the number of books in price range ₹ 4000 – ₹ 5000 bought in January and March ?
   (a) 1 : 10   (b) 15 : 100
   (c) 930 : 2911   (d) 21 : 200
   (e) None of these

DIRECTIONS (Qs. 140-149) : *Study the table carefully to answer the questions that follow.*

[IBPS PO Exam 2013]

Total number of 24500 people who are engaged in given professions and (of these) percentage of females and males

Professions	Percentage of People	Percentage Females	Percentage Males
Medical	11	60	40
Engineering	18	30	70
Law	24	45	55
Teaching	21	80	20
Banking	16	35	65
Management	10	44	56

140. What is the respective ratio of the total males in Medical and Teaching profession together to the total number of females in the same professions together ?
   (a) 117 : 43   (b) 29 :183   (c) 183 : 29   (d) 43:117
   (e) None of these

141. The total number of people in Teaching profession is what percent of the total number of people in law profession?
   (a) 87.5   (b) 93   (c) 68   (d) 79.5
   (e) None of these

142. What is the total number of males from all the professions together?
   (a) 11472   (b) 12784   (c) 12348   (d) 12453
   (e) None of these

143. Females in Engineering profession are what per cent of the males in Management profession? (Rounded off to two digits after decimal)
   (a) 71.71   (b) 96.43   (c) 83.16   (d) 68.54
   (e) None of these

144. What is respective ratio of the number of males in Banking profession to the number of males in Engineering profession?
   (a) 17 : 7   (b) 28 : 55   (c) 7 : 11   (d) 52 : 63
   (e) None of these

DIRECTIONS (Qs. 145-149) : *Study the table carefully to answer the questions that follow:*

[SBI PO Exam 2013]

Monthly Bill (in rupees) of landline phone, electricity, laundry and mobile phone paid by three different people in five different months.

Month	Monthly Bills											
	Landline Phone			Electricity			Laundry			Mobile Phone		
	Ravi	Dev	Manu	Ravi	Dev	Manu	Ravi	Dev	Manu	Ravi	Dev	Manu
March	234	190	1s13	145	245	315	93	323	65	144	234	345
April	124	234	321	270	220	135	151	134	35	164	221	325
May	156	432	211	86	150	98	232	442	132	143	532	332
June	87	123	124	124	150	116	213	324	184	245	134	125
July	221	104	156	235	103	131	413	532	143	324	432	543

145. What is the total amount of bill paid by Dev in the month of June for all the four commodities?
 (a) ₹ 608/- (b) ₹ 763/-
 (c) ₹ 731/- (d) ₹ 683/-
 (e) ₹ 674/-

146. What is the average electricity bill paid by Manu over all the five months together?
 (a) ₹ 183/- (b) ₹ 149/-
 (c) ₹ 159/- (d) ₹ 178/-
 (e) ₹ 164/-

147. What is the difference between the mobile phone bill paid by Ravi in the month of May and the laundry bill paid by Dev in the month of March?
 (a) ₹ 180/- (b) ₹ 176/- (c) ₹ 190/- (d) ₹ 167/-
 (e) ₹ 196/-

148. In which months respectively did Manu pay the second highest mobile phone bill and the lowest electricity bill?
 (a) April and June (b) April and May
 (c) March and June (d) March and May
 (e) July and May

149. What is the respective ratio between the electricity bill paid by Manu in the month of April and the mobile phone bill paid by Ravi in the month of June?
 (a) 27 : 49 (b) 27 : 65
 (c) 34 : 49 (d) 135 : 184
 (e) 13 : 24

DIRECTIONS (Qs. 150-154): *Study the table carefully to answer the questions that follow:*

[SBI PO Exam 2013]

Station Name	Arrival time	Departure time	Halt time (in minutes)	Distance travelled from origin (in km)	No. of Passengers boarding the train at each station
Dadar	Starting point	12.05 am	-	0 km	437
Vasai Road	12.53 am	12.56 am	3 minutes	42 km	378
Surat	4.15 am	4.20 am	5 minutes	257 km	458
Vadodara	6.05 am	6.10 am	5 minutes	386 km	239
Anand Jn.	6.43 am	6.45 am	2 minutes	422 km	290
Nadiad Jn.	7.01 am	7.03 am	2 minutes	440km	132
Ahmedabad	8.00 am	8.20 am	20 minutes	486 km	306
Bhuj	5.40 pm	Ending point	–	977 km	None

150. What is the distance travelled by the train from Surat to Nadiad Jn.?
 (a) 176 km (b) 188 km
 (c) 183 km (d) 193 km
 (e) 159 km

151. How much time does the train take to reach Ahmedabad after departing from Anand Jn. (Including the halt time)?
 (a) 1 hr. 59 min (b) 1 hr. 17 min.
 (c) 1 hr. 47 min. (d) 1 hr. 45 min.
 (e) 1 hr. 15 min.

152. What is the respective ratio between the number of passengers boarding from Vasai Road and from Ahmedabad in the train?
 (a) 21 : 17 (b) 13 : 9 (c) 21 : 19 (d) 15 : 13
 (e) 13 : 15

153. If halt time (stopping time) of the train at Vadodara is decreased by 2 minutes and increased by 23 minutes at Ahmedabad. At what time will the train reach Bhuj?
 (a) 6.10 am (b) 6.01 pm
 (c) 6.05 am (d) 6.50 pm
 (e) 6.07 pm

154. Distance between which two stations is second lowest?
 (a) Nadiad Jn. to Ahmedabad
 (b) Anand Jn. to Nadiad Jn.
 (c) Dadar to Vasai Road
 (d) Anand Jn. to Vadodara
 (e) Vasai Road to Surat

DIRECTIONS (Qs. 155-159): *Study the following information carefully and answer the given questions:*

The following table shows the number of classes taken by each tutors in different days and the total amount given to the tutor per class for the certain course is also given

Tutors	Number of classes taken on Monday, Tuesday and Wednesday by each	Number of classes taken on Thursday and Friday by each	Salary per class (In ₹)
L	2	0	10000
M	3	–	16000
N	1	3	12000
O	2	2	8000

Note:

Saturday and Sunday are holidays

"–" is missing value, we have to find the value according to the question.

155. Find the ratio of the number of lectures taken by L to that of the number of lectures taken by O in a week?
 (a) 3 : 5 (b) 4 : 7 (c) 5 : 9 (d) 11 :13
 (e) None of these

156. Find the earnings made by N if he teaches for 6 weeks?
 (a) 612000 (b) 564000 (c) 696000 (d) 648000
 (e) None of these

157. Find the difference between the earnings made by N for 3 weeks to that of the earnings made by O for 2 weeks?
   (a) ₹ 148000   (b) ₹ 132000
   (c) ₹ 164000   (d) ₹ 140000
   (e) None of these

158. If M takes 2 classes each on Thursday and Friday, then how much he can earn in a week?
   (a) 232000   (b) 208000
   (c) 190000   (d) 176000
   (e) None of these

159. If the amount of ₹6.24 lakhs was given to the tutor M for 3 weeks, then find the number of class/classes taken by the tutor M in Thursday and Friday each?
   (a) 2   (b) 4   (c) 3   (d) 1
   (e) None of these

DIRECTIONS (Qs. 160-164): *Follow the given instruction to give the answer of the followings questions.*

Total number who attended the workshop = Number of Literates + Number of illiterates

Month	No. of literates (males+Females)	Overall ratio (illiterate : literates) (out of those who attended)	Number of (literates + illiterates) out of those who attended
January	840	5:6	500
February	700	3:5	480
March	640	5:4	640
April	600	5:4	600
May	840	2:3	640

160. The total number of people (literates + illiterates) who attended the workshop in January was what % more than those who attended in May?
   (a) 12%   (b) 10%   (c) 15%   (d) 18%
   (e) None of these

161. In May, if 384 illiterate males attended the workshop, what was the number of literate females who attended the workshop in that month?
   (a) 584   (b) 600
   (c) 550   (d) 560
   (e) None of these

162. In June, if the number of illiterates (males + females) increased by 40% and that of literates (males + females) reduced by 20%, as compared February what was the difference between the number of literates and illiterates who attended the workshop in June?
   (a) 24   (b) 28   (c) 30   (d) 36
   (e) None of these

163. What is the average number of illiterates (males +females) who attended the workshop January, March and April?
   (a) 780   (b) 800
   (c) 600   (d) 740
   (e) None of these

164. What is the ratio of the total number of males (Literates + Illiterates) who attended the workshop on February and May together to that of females (literates and Illiterates) who attended the workshop on the same months together?
   (a) 5 :9   (b) 9 : 7   (c) 7 : 9   (d) 1 : 3
   (e) None of these

DIRECTIONS (Qs.165-169) : *Study the information carefully to answer the followings questions.*

In the following table there are five university in which total student and percentage of arts students and the ratio of civil and mechanical engineering students are given. Calculate the missing data if necessary:

University	Total number of students	Percentage of arts students	Ratio of civil to mechanical engineering students
P	3000	35%	–
Q	–	40%	–
R	–	–	7:3
S	4200	–	3:2
T	3500	–	–

165. If the ratio of boys and girls in university P for civil engineering students are 4 : 1 and the civil engineering students are 50% more than the mechanical engineering students. Then find the difference of boys and girls in civil department?
   (a) 240   (b) 860   (c) 702   (d) 640
   (e) 540

166. If the total engineering student in university T is 1050 and students in civil department are less than the students in mechanical department and the engineering student in university S is 1470. Then find ratio of civil engineering student in university S and T?
   (a) 445 : 247   (b) 441 : 243
   (c) 453 : 247   (d) 441 : 245
   (e) 441 : 249

167. If arts student in university P is 750 less than arts student in university Q. Then the total student in university S is what percent more or less than the total students in university Q.
   (a) $5\frac{1}{7}\%$ (b) $8\frac{1}{7}\%$ (c) $2\frac{1}{7}\%$ (d) $7\frac{1}{7}\%$
   (e) $1\frac{1}{7}\%$

168. If total student in university R is 2760 and total arts student in university R is equal to the total students in engineering. And the ratio of boys and girls in university R in arts is 5 : 1. If 20% of boys are transferred to university T, then find the total students in university T.
   (a) 3092   (b) 2912   (c) 3170   (d) 3730
   (e) 3374

169. Suppose there is another university X in which arts students are 2/5th of arts student in university P and engineering student in university X is 40% of total students of university S then what is the total students in X?
   (a) 2100   (b) 2410   (c) 3280   (d) 3100
   (e) 9040

DIRECTIONS (Qs. 170-174) : *The following table shows the profit percentage earned by five different stores on Funskool different products. Study the table carefully to answer the following questions.*

Note: In table, some data are missing. Find these data if they are required in any question and then proceed.

Products	Different stores which sell funskool products				
	A	B	C	D	E
Toy 1	40%	–	–	25%	20%
Toy 2	–	$33\frac{1}{3}\%$	–	25%	$16\frac{2}{3}\%$
Toy 3	25%	–	10%	24%	30%
Toy 4	20%	30%	–	–	15%
Toy 5	–	40%	20%	–	25%

170. If cost price of Toy 1 at A is 25% more than cost price of Toy 1 at B. Find profit earned by B on Toy 1 if selling price of Toy 1 at B is 80% of that of A
    (a) 35% (b) 40% (c) 45% (d) 30%
    (e) 24%

171. If average of profit percentage earned on Toy 3 by all the five stores is 23%. Find the percentage profit earned by B on Toy 3
    (a) 16% (b) 36 % (c) 26% (d) 28%
    (e) 32%

172. If ratio of cost price of Toy 5 by C to E is 3 : 5. Find the ratio of selling price of Toy 5 by C to E.
    (a) 25 : 49 (b) 9 : 11 (c) 77 : 125 (d) 72 : 125
    (e) 125 : 77

173. If ratio of cost price of Toy 3 to Toy 4 for A are 2 : 5. Find profit percent on Toy 3 and Toy 4 together by A
    (a) $21\frac{3}{7}\%$ (b) $11\frac{5}{8}\%$ (c) 25% (d) 27%
    (e) $33\frac{1}{3}\%$

174. If cost price of one Toy 2 by B, D and E was ₹450, 384 and 360 respectively the find total profit earned by these three stores together on Toy 2 (in ₹)
    (a) ₹603 (b) ₹206 (c) ₹306 (d) ₹406
    (e) ₹340

DIRECTIONS (Qs. 175-179): *Refer to the table given below and answer the given questions:*

Table shows the 5 countries and total population and percentage of males, females and children in each country in year 2016.

Some data are missing, find the missing data to answer the given questions.

Country	Total population	Percentage of males	Percentage of females	Percentage childrens
P	1200	25%	–	–
Q	–	–	40%	20%
R	–	50%	20%	–
S	400	–	–	16%
T	–	–	24%	36%

Note: Don't treat children as male or female. Treat them separately.

175. If the ratio of population of females and children in country P in year 2016 is 3 : 7, and female in country P in year 2017 is increased by 20% from that of year 2016. Then find the total number of males and children in country P in year 2017 so that overall population in year 2017 is same as in year 2016?
    (a) 876 (b) 926 (c) 1376 (d) 1600
    (e) 764

176. If number of children in country R in year 2016 is 180 and ratio of male and females in country S in year 2016 is 1 : 2. Then find the difference of males in country R and country S?
    (a) 196 (b) 186 (c) 188 (d) 185
    (e) 192

177. If total population of country Q and country R together in year 2016 is 25% more than the total population of country P in year 2016 and ratio of total population of country Q and country R in year 2016 is 2 : 3. Then find the ratio of males in country Q to children in country R in year 2016?
    (a) 9 : 8 (b) 8 : 9
    (c) 2 : 3 (d) 3 : 5
    (e) 3 : 2

178. If ratio of males of country S in year 2016 to the females in country P in year 2016 is 2 : 5 and population of children in country P is increased by 20% in year 2017 from year 2016. Then find the total population of children in year 2017 in country P?
    (a) 2000 (b) 1200
    (c) 1500 (d) cannot be determined
    (e) None of these

179. If ratio of total population of country R to country T in year 2016 is 5 : 4. Then number of males in country T in year 2016 is what percent more or less than the number of children in country R in year 2016?
    (a) 5.67% (b) 12%
    (c) 10% (d) 3.334%
    (e) 6.67%

DIRECTIONS (Qs. 180-184) : *In the following table, the Investment and profit of three Companies in different states is given.*

	Investment (in mn $)			Profit (in mn $)		
State	X	Y	Z	X	Y	Z
TN	30000	–	50000	–	16000	25000
AP	–	14000	16000	–	–	28000
UP	8000	10000	8000	–	–	–
MP	18000	20000	–	9000	12000	–
JK	–	–	34000	40000	60000	80000

Note: Some values are missing. You have to calculate these values as per data given in the questions:

180. If X invested his amount in TN state for 9 years and Z invested his amount in the same state for 10 years then find the total profit made by all of them from TN
(a) $ 58500 mn   (b) $ 48500 mn
(c) $ 54500 mn   (d) $ 62400 mn
(e) None of these

181. If the total profit earned from AP by all of them is $ 64750 mn and each invested for 9 years then find the ratio of investment of X in AP to the profit of Y from TN?
(a) 16 : 7   (b) 7 : 16   (c) 8 : 13   (d) 13 : 8
(e) None of these

182. If X, Y and Z invested in UP for 5 years, 8 years and 6 years respectively then profit earned by Z form UP is what% of the profit earned by X and Y together from the same state, if total profit earned by all of them from UP state is 17400 mn $.
(a) 45%   (b) 50%   (c) 55%   (d) 40%
(e) None of these

183. In JK state total Investment of X and Y is $ 170000 mn, while X and Y invested their amount for 4 years and 6 years respectively in the same state, then find the number of years that Z invested his amount?
(a) 8 years   (b) 9 years
(c) 20 years   (d) Can't be determined
(e) None of these

184. Average Investment made by all of them in MP is $ 20000 mn and average profit earned by all of them from the same state is $ 12000 mn, then profit earned by Z in the same country is what percent more/less than the amount invested by Z in the same state?
(a) $35\frac{1}{8}\%$ (b) $37\frac{6}{7}\%$ (c) $32\frac{7}{11}\%$ (d) $33\frac{7}{11}\%$
(e) $31\frac{9}{11}\%$

DIRECTIONS (Qs. 185-189) : *A person purchased 5 Products from a shop and sold them online. Given below is the data showing cost price, selling price and profit/loss percentage.*

	C.P. (in ₹)	Profit/Loss%	S.P. (in ₹)
P_1	64890	–	81112.5
P_2	–	Profit-15%	81880
P_3	44300	Loss-12%	–
P_4	56590	–	62280
P_5	–	Profit-25%	14150

185. Cost price of P_2 is what percent of selling price of P_3? (approximate)
(a) 138%   (b) 182%   (c) 142%   (d) 154%
(e) 186%

186. If there has been a profit of 12% on P_3 instead of 12% loss. Then the new S.P. is how much more than the original S.P.?
(a) 10432   (b) 10792   (c) 10672   (d) 10632
(e) None of these

187. Profit percentage on P_4 is what percent more/less than profit percentage on P_2?
(a) 50% more   (b) 33.34% less
(c) 33.67% more   (d) 50% less
(e) 150% less

188. What is the ratio between profit percentage of P5 to profit percentage of P_1?
(a) 5 : 3   (b) 3 : 2   (c) 3 : 5   (d) 2 : 5
(e) None of these

189. What is the overall profit/loss percentage? (approximate)
(a) 22.12% profit   (b) 12.12% profit
(c) 14.14% profit   (d) 33.12% loss
(e) 15.15% loss

DIRECTIONS (Qs. 190-194): *Study the table and answer the given questions.*

Data related to the number of employees in five different companies in January 2017

Company	Total Number of Employees	Out of total number of employees		
		Percentage of B.Sc. Graduates	Percentage of B.Com. Graduates	Percentage of B.A. Graduates
A	2100	32%	–	–
B	1400	–	31%	40%
C	–	30%	30%	–
D	–	–	40%	20%
E	–	35%	50%	–

Note: (I) Employees of the given companies can be categorised only in three types: B.Sc. graduates, B.Com. graduates and B.A. graduates

(II) A few values are missing in the table (indicated –). A candidate is expected to calculate the missing value, if it is required to answer the given question, on the basis of the given data and information.

190. What is the difference between the number of BA graduate employees and B.Sc. graduate employees in Company B?
(a) 174   (b) 178   (c) 154   (d) 162
(e) 146

191. The average number of BA graduate employees and B.Com. graduate employees in Company E was 312. What was the total number of employees in Company E?
(a) 920   (b) 960   (c) 1120   (d) 1040
(e) 1080

192. If the ratio of the number of B.Com. graduate employees to that of BA graduate employees in Company A was 10 : 7, what was the number of BA graduate employees in A?
(a) 588 (b) 432 (c) 560 (d) 616
(e) 644

193. The total number of employees in Company B increased by 20% from January 2017 to January 2018. If 20% of the total number of employees in Company B in January 2018 were B.Sc. graduates, what was the number of B.Sc. graduate employees in company B in January 2018?
(a) 448 (b) 532 (c) 588 (d) 504
(e) 336

194. The total number of employees in Company D was 3 times the total number of employees in Company C. If the difference between the number of BA graduate employees in Company D and that in Company C was 180, what was the total number of employees in Company C?
(a) 1200 (b) 1440 (c) 720 (d) 900
(e) 1080

DIRECTIONS (Qs. 195-199): *A team of 5 players participated in a tournament and played four matches (1 to 4). The following table gives partial information about their individual scores and the total runs scored by the team in each match.*

Each column has two values missing. These are runs scored by the two lowest scores in that match. None of the two missing values is more than 10% of runs scored by player the total runs scored in that match.

Name	Match-1	Match-2	Match-3	Match-4
Ajay		100		53
Pradeep	88	65		52
Chanchal			110	
Deepak	72	75	20	56
Vivek	60		78	
Total	270	300	240	200

195. What is the maximum possible percentage contribution of Ajay in the total runs scored in the four matches (approximately)?
(a) 20% (b) 22%
(c) 17% (d) 23%
(e) Cannot be determined

196. What is the maximum possible percentage contribution of Vivek in the total runs scored in the four matches?
(a) 18% (b) 19.9%
(c) 18.6% (d) 20.2%
(e) Cannot be determined

197. If the absolute difference between the total runs scored by Ajay and Chanchal in the four matches is minimum possible then what is the ratio of Ajay and Chanchal's total runs scored by them in the four matches.
(a) 187 : 189 (b) 189 : 187
(c) 183 : 187 (d) 189 : 188
(e) Cannot be determined

198. If the absolute difference between the total runs scored by Ajay and Chanchal in the four matches is minimum possible then what is the absolute difference between total runs scored by Pradeep and Vivek in the four matches?
(a) 32 (b) 37
(c) 35 (d) 27
(e) Cannot be determined

199. The players are ranked 1 to 5 on the basis of the total runs scored by them in the four matches, with the highest scorer getting Rank 1. If it is known that no two players scored the same number of total runs, how many players are there whose ranks can be exactly determined?
(a) 0 (b) 1 (c) 3 (d) 5
(e) Cannot be determined

DIRECTIONS (Qs. 200-204): *Study the following data related to the performance of 6 batsmen in a tournament.*

Batsman	No. of matches played	Average runs scored	Total balls faced	Strike rate
Akhtar	8	—	—	129.6
Balaji	20	81	—	—
Cheteshwar	—	38	400	114
Dhawan	—	—	—	72
Eeshan	28	55	1280	—
Fawad	—	—	—	66

Note:

(i) Strike rate $= \dfrac{\text{Total runs scored}}{\text{Total balls faced}} \times 100$

(ii) All given batsman bat in all the given matches played by them.

200. The respective ratio between the total number of balls faced by Dhawan and that of Fawad in the tournament is 3 : 4. The total number of runs scored by Fawad in the tournament is what percent more than the total runs scored by Dhawan in the tournament?
(a) $33\dfrac{1}{3}\%$ (b) $22\dfrac{2}{9}\%$
(c) $22\dfrac{1}{9}\%$ (d) 22%
(e) None of these

201. If the runs scored by Eeshan in Last 3 matches of the tournament are not considered, his average runs scored in the tournament decreased by 9. If the runs scored by Eeshan in 26th and 27th match are below 128 and no two scores among these 3 scores are equal, then what are the minimum possible runs scored by Eeshan in the 28th match?
  (a) 133   (b) 135   (c) 137   (d) 140
  (e) None of these

202. In the tournament, the total number of balls faced by Akhtar is 74 less than the total number of runs scored by him. What is the average run scored by Akhtar in the tournament?
  (a) 42.5   (b) 40   (c) 41.8   (d) 40.5
  (e) None of these

203. In the tournament Cheteshwar and Dhawan played same number of matches. Dhawan scored 24 runs more than that scored by Fawad when Fawad faced equal number of balls which was faced by Cheteshwar. Find the difference in the total runs scored and total ball faced by Dhawan.
  (a) 118   (b) 112   (c) 122   (d) 108
  (e) None of these

204. If the average number of the match played by all players is 19, and the maximum possible runs scored by Fawad is 3 times the match played by him when he faced a total number of balls less than 151, then find the minimum possible matches played by Dhawan.
  (a) 12   (b) 10   (c) 13   (d) 8
  (e) None of these

DIRECTIONS (Qs. 205-209): *There are five students who appeared for CAT exam. Paper consists of 100 questions with 1 mark for each correct answer and 0.25 mark for each wrong answer.*

	Questions attempted	Right Questions	Wrong Questions	Marks obtained
Raghuvir	78	–	–	70.5
Mahavir	92	76	–	–
Rajvir	98	–	36	–
Dharamvir	–	30	–	27.25
Satyavir	56	–	–	53.50

205. Difference between total right number of questions of all students together and total wrong no. of questions of all students together is
  (a) 141   (b) 161   (c) 223   (d) 156
  (e) None of these

206. Marks obtained by Raghuvir and Mahavir together is what % of the marks obtained by Dharamvir, Satyavir and Rajvir together? (rounded off to 2 decimal places)

(a) 106.54%   (b) 91.16%
(c) 95.20%   (d) 96.71%
(e) 101.71%

207. If the penalty of the wrong answer is 0.33 then marks obtained by Raghuvir, Rajvir and Mahavir together is
  (a) 192.21   (b) 224.19
  (c) 190.86   (d) 219.14
  (e) 194.22

208. If the passing % marks in the exam is 50 marks than at least how many questions has to be answered right by Mahavir? (He attempted 92 questions)
  (a) 58   (b) 56   (c) 59   (d) 55
  (e) 60

209. What is the percent of marks obtained by all of them together?
  (a) 59.03%   (b) 53.15%
  (c) 52.53%   (d) 45.05%
  (e) 55.25%

DIRECTIONS (Qs. 210-214): *Study the given table and answer the following questions.*

Percentage profit or loss for following fruits is based on the sum of cost price and transportation cost.

Name of Product	CP	SP	Cost of transpor-tation	Profit	Loss	Profit or loss % (on total c.p.)
Apple	1800		600			5%
Banana		1600	0		600	
Grapes	4000		1000	500		
Mango		10000	0			5% Loss
Orange	12000		800			7% Profit

210. The percentage profit on Apple is 5%. What will be its selling price?
  (a) 2000   (b) 2500
  (c) 2520   (d) 2400
  (e) 2320

211. The selling price of Grapes is what percent of the cost price of Banana?
  (a) 200%   (b) 250%
  (c) 280%   (d) 255%
  (e) 240%

212. What is the ratio of the loss on Mango to that on Banana?
  (a) 49 : 58   (b) 50 : 57
  (c) 50 : 59   (d) 40 : 47
  (e) None of these

213. What is the difference between the selling price of Orange and that of Grapes?
  (a) 8196   (b) 8200
  (c) 8000   (d) 8396
  (e) 7996

214. If the loss on Apple is 10% then its selling price is what percentage less than the selling price of Orange?
    (a) 89%
    (b) 92%
    (c) 94%
    (d) 84%
    (e) 88%

DIRECTIONS (Qs. 215-218): *Given table shows the % range of commission earned on all sold books and commission earned by five shop in Rupees.*

Shop	Range of commission (%)	Commission earned Rupees
PP	0-16	3200
QQ	16-32	-
RR	-	3500
SS	-	-
TT	0-20	4000

Note : Commission percent is on selling price.

Note : Some values are missing, you have to calculate them according to question.

Note : Range of commission are in integral values.

215. Shop 'PP' sells 480 books and only 3 types of books it have, their number are in ratio 1 : 2 : 3 and their selling prices are 200, 300 and 100 respectively and commission charged on them have difference of 1 percent in sequence (least number of articles sold have least commission percent) respectively, then find the highest commission% of books.

    (a) 14.375%
    (b) 12.375%
    (c) 15.45%
    (d) 16.375%
    (e) None of these

216. Shop RR sells 3 products in equal numbers (105) and equal commission percent. If their selling price (in Rupees.) are 20, 30 and 40. Then what is the commission percent.

    (a) $\dfrac{1200}{27}\%$
    (b) $\dfrac{900}{27}\%$
    (c) $\dfrac{1150}{27}\%$
    (d) $\dfrac{1000}{27}\%$
    (e) $\dfrac{1040}{27}\%$

217. Shop SS sold 3 books each in number 100 and each have S.P. of ₹ 80 and commission % for each is in A.P. with common difference of 5. If total commission earned by Shop SS is $14\dfrac{2}{7}\%$ more than that of Shop RR, find the minimum range of commission%?

    (a) $(11 - 22)$
    (b) $(16 - 23)$
    (c) $(05 - 08)$
    (d) $(14 - 24)$
    (e) $(07 - 10)$

218. If Shop RR have only one type of book and number of book and its S.P is equal which is (≥ 100 & < 110) then find the % range of commission?

    (a) $(27.5 - 30)$
    (b) $(34 - 37.7)$
    (c) $(17.4 - 26.8)$
    (d) $(29.4 - 35)$
    (e) $(28 - 36.6)$

HINTS & SOLUTIONS

1. (b) HCI encountered the highest occupancy rate in 2015.

2. (b) Is true. The average occupancy rate in 2013 was 64 % and 2014 was 63.71%

3. (d) All the statements were false.

4. (c) The rate of growth is highest in 2015.

5. (c) It is visible that Black Lagoon and Radiant won this award atleast twice.

6. (d) Shop T has the lowest sales of 920 and 280 in both B and E.

7. (d) 15% of 4000 = 600

8. (d) S has the highest sale of cars i.e., 13670.

9. (c) Both P & Q sells 300 × 7 = 2100 & 440 × 7 = 3080.

10. (b)

11. (c) Rural has the highest percentage of voters i.e. 71%

12. (b) $\dfrac{216}{408} \times 100 = 53\%$ (approx..)

13. (a) 70% of 162 million = 113,400,000

14. (d) $(100 - 63)\% = 37\%$ didn't vote. Therefore, 37% of 60 million = 22,200,000

15. (b)

16. (c) Let Cost of purchasing x gm of food A, y gm of food B and z gm of food C (convert it into one gram)
$$= \frac{1.80}{100}x + \frac{3}{100}y + \frac{2.75}{100} = \frac{0.9}{50}x + \frac{0.3}{10}y + \frac{0.11}{4}z$$

17. (d) From the table, Protein in 500 g of A = 500 × 10% = 50
250 g of B = 250 × 20 % = 50
350 g of C = 350 × 20 % = 70
200 g of B and 200 g of C = 200 × 20 % +
$\qquad\qquad\qquad\qquad\qquad = 200 \times 20\% = 80$
Hence (d) provides the maximum protein.

18. (a) The cost of 300 g of A = $\dfrac{1.8}{100} \times 300 = 5.40$

The cost of 200 g of C = $\dfrac{2.75}{100} \times 200 = 5.5$

The cost of 150 g of A and 100 g of B
$$= \frac{1.8}{100} \times 150 + \frac{3}{100} \times 100 = 5.7$$
500 g of B and 100 g of A
$$= \frac{3}{100} \times 500 + \frac{1.8}{100} \times 100 = 16.8$$
The cost of 300 gm of A is least.

19. (b) $(2 + 7 + 6 + 5 + 5 + 2 + 3) = 30$

20. (c) $(2 + 7) + (5 + 2) = 16$

21. (a)

22. (d) Only 44 % of students score less than 70%.

23. (d) Given condition is diet must contain Fat -10% and Protein ≥ 30%
We will eliminate option one by one to get the correct combination from the given options.
(a) P and Q is mixed, to get Fat 10% we have to mix them in the ratio of 4:1 and then the protein content would be 110/500 < 30 hence this option is eliminated.
(b) P & S, None of them contain Fat hence this option also eliminated.
(c) R & S, they must be mixed in the ratio of 1:3 to get 10% fat, then protein content will be (150 + 50)/400½ >30% hence this combination is also allowed
The cost per unit in this case = 800/400 = 2
(d) Q & S they must be mixed in the ratio of 1:4 to get 10% Fat, in that case protein content = 230/500 > 30 hence this combination is allowed and then cost per unit would be (200 + 4x100)/500 = 6/5 hence option 4 gives us the minimum cost

24. (d) Here we want higher % of carbohydrate and lower cost both of this given by P, it has the highest Carbohydrate % and the lowest cost, hence in the mixture P should be maximum
(a) 2:1:3, P is not the highest hence eliminated
(b) 4:1:2, then content of carbohydrate
= (4×80 + 10 + 2×45)/ 700 = 420/700 = 0.6
= 60% and cost per unit = (200 + 200 + 200)/700
= 600/7
(c) 2:1:4 again P is not the highest hence eliminated
(d) 4 : 1 :1, carbohydrate content = (4 × 80 + 10 + 45) /600 =375/600 > 60%
Cost per unit = (200 + 200 + 100)/6 = 500/6
Hence cost in option (d) (i.e 500/6) is less than that of option (b) (600/7)

25. (d) The given condition is Carbohydrate ≥ 30%
Protein ≥ 30%
Fat ≤ 25%
Minerals ≥ 5%
Now we will evaluate and eliminate the options one by one.
(a) protein content = (30+20)/200 × 100
$\qquad\qquad = 25\% < 30\%$ hence eliminated.
(b) carbohydrate < 30% hence eliminated
Similarly option

(c) doesn't satisfy the Mineral content.

(d) Hence, correct option is (d).

26. (a) Here in this question Diet must contain Minerals 20% and protein $\geq$ 30%

The only one combination that gives 10% minerals is O and Q in 1:1 ratio, no other combination can give us minerals 10%

27. (c) From the table it is given that average score of Dipan in PCB group is 98 and his average scores in Mathematics, Social Science, and Vernacular groups are 95, 95.5 and 95 respectively. Let the average score in English group be x then total average = (98+95+95.5+95+x)/5 = 96 as 96 is the total average, then x = 96.5 so total score in English is 96.5 × 2= 193. Score of Dipan in English 1 = 96 hence his score in English 2= 193 – 96 = 97.

28. (d) From the table we can observe that only Dipan is eligible to apply for the prize as he is the only one who satisfy the condition of at least 95 in every group. So Dipan gets the prize.

29. (a) From the table we can observe that only Dipan scored at least 95 in at least one paper from each of the groups

30. (d) In order to maximize scores, each student would choose to improve score in the paper which would affect the group score the most or in the group that has minimum average.

STUDENT	Change in Group	Change in Group Avg	Change in Avg	Final Average
Ram	94 to 100 (Vern. Grp)	6/2 = 3	3/5 = 0.6	96.1 + 0.6 = 96.7
Agni	82 to 100 (Vern paper I)	18/2 = 9	9/5 = 1.8	94.3 + 1.8 = 96.1
Pritam	83 to 100 (History)	17/2 = 8.5	8.5/5 = 1.7	93.9 + 1.7 = 95.6
Ayesha	93 to 100 (geo.)	7/2 = 3.5	3.5/5 = 0.7	96.2 + 0.7 = 96.9
Dipan	95 to 100 (Math.)	5/1 = 5	5/5 = 1	96 + 1 = 97

Hence from the table Dipan has the highest score.

31. (a) Group scores of Joseph, Agni, Pritam and Tirna in Social Science Group are 95.5, 95.5, 89 and 89.5 respectively. Their final scores are 95, 94.3, 93.9, 93.7 respectively. If their group scores in social science change to hundred their final scores will be affected by For Joseph (100-95.5)/5 = 4.5/5 = 0.9 and final score 95.9
For Agni (100 – 95.5)/5 = 4.5/5 = 0.9, and final score = 94.3 + 0.9 = 95.2

For Pritam (100 – 89)/5 = 11/5 = 2.2 and final score = 93.9 + 2.2 = 96.1

For Tirna (100 – 89.5)/5 = 10.5/5 = 2.1and final score = 93.7 + 2.1 = 95.8

Their standing in decreasing order of final score would be Pritam, Joseph, Tirna, Agni.

32. (d) Reqd. % $= \dfrac{1200}{14900} \times 100 \approx 8\%$

33. (c) Total no. of Officers = 2000 + 15000 + 17000 + 3500 + 14900 + 11360 + 9000 = 72760

Total no. of Clerks = 5000 + 17000 + 19500 + 20000 + 17650 + 15300 + 11000 = 105450

Reqd. difference = 105450 – 72760 = 32690

34. (b) Reqd. more % $= \dfrac{11000 - 9000}{9000} \times 100 \approx 22\%$

35. (c) 300% more means four times the number of Clerks in Bangalore, which is in Hyderabad.

36. (d) No. of candidates in different centres:

Bangalore = 3550; Mumbai = 44470; Delhi = 43910;

Hyderabad = 33950, Kolkata = 35120;

Lucknow = 28840; Chennai= 22245

37. (d) Required no. of visitors = (225) + (252) – 196 – 150 = 131

38. (b) Required % $= \dfrac{\frac{1}{3}(975)}{\frac{1}{3}(1275)} \times 100 \approx 76\%$

39. (c) Required ratio = 333 : 348 = 111 : 116

40. (d) Required % $= \dfrac{225 - 135}{135} \times 100 = 66\dfrac{2}{3}\%$

41. (e) Required difference
= (198 + 135 + 357) – (154 + 225 + 252)
= 690 – 631 = 59

42. (d) Total production by all the companies together
= 648 + 725 + 679 + 498 + 840 + 580 = 3970

Reqd. % $= \dfrac{725}{3970} \times 100 \simeq 18\%$

43. (a) % increase/decrease for company A 2014 = 16.01%, 2015 = 14.69%, 2016 = 13.27%, 2017 = 15.53%, 2018 = 9.78%

44. (e) Total production of E
= 415 + 680 + 840 + 689 + 780 + 637 = 4041
Total production of F
= 632 + 775 + 580 + 720 + 670 + 746 = 4123
Reqd. difference = 4123 – 4041 = 82 lakh tonnes

45. (c) $\text{Avg} = \dfrac{565 + 378 + 483 + 526 + 680 + 775}{6}$

$\simeq 570$ lakh tonnes

46. (b) $\%\ \text{fall} = \dfrac{679 - 499}{679} \times 100 = 26.51\%$

47. (a) No. of females above poverty line in state A

$= 3000 \times (100 - 12)\% \times \dfrac{3}{7} \approx 1150$

48. (d) Since, we cannot find the population of states C and D separately, we can't find the required value.

49. (e) Population of state A below poverty line

$= 3000 \times \dfrac{5}{3} = 5000$

$\therefore$ Total population of state A $= \dfrac{5000}{12} \times 100$

and the population of state E below poverty line

$= 6000 \times \dfrac{11}{6} = 11000$

Total population of state E $= \dfrac{11000}{10} \times 100$

Required ratio $= \dfrac{5}{12} \times \dfrac{10}{11} = \dfrac{25}{66}$

50. (c) Total population of state B $= 500 \left(\dfrac{12}{5}\right)\left(\dfrac{100}{15}\right) = 8000$

51. (b) Population of state E $= 19800 \left(\dfrac{5}{2}\right)\left(\dfrac{100}{100-10}\right) = 55000$

$\therefore$ Population of males below poverty line

$= 55000 \left(\dfrac{10}{100}\right)\left(\dfrac{6}{11}\right) = 3000$

52. (a) Let marks obtained by A in Science be x

Marks obtained by A in Hindi $= x \times \dfrac{150}{100} = \dfrac{3x}{2}$

Total marks obtained by A in all subjects together
$= 5 \times 100 = 500$

According to question

$x + \dfrac{3x}{2} + 130 + 55 + 75 = 500$

$\dfrac{5x}{2} = 500 - 260 = 240$

$\therefore \quad x = \dfrac{240 \times 2}{5} = 96$

Req. % $= \dfrac{96}{150} \times 100 = 64\%$

53. (b) Marks obtained by C in Science $= 75$

Marks obtained by C in Hindi $= 75 \times \dfrac{100}{75} = 100$

Marks obtained by C in Math
$= 90 \times 5 - (100 + 45 + 75 + 85)$
$= 450 - 305 = 145$
Required ratio $= 145 : 100 = 29 : 20$

54. (c) Average score of D in all subjects together

$= 100 \times \dfrac{90}{100} = 90$

Total score of D in all subjects together $= 90 \times 5 = 450$

Score of D in Hindi $= 150 \times \dfrac{60}{100} = 90$

Score of D in Math
$= 450 - (90 + 60 + 105 + 45) = 450 - 300 = 150$

Required % $= \dfrac{150}{200} \times 100 = 75\%$

55. (d) Marks obtained by A in Science $= 75 \times \dfrac{120}{100} = 90$

Total marks obtained by all students together in Science
$= 90 + 85 + 75 + 105 + 120 = 475$

Average obtained marks of all students together in Science

$= \dfrac{475}{5} = 95$

Required % $= \dfrac{95}{150} \times 100 = \dfrac{190}{3} = 63.3\%$

56. (e) Let marks obtained by E in English be x

Marks obtained by E in Sanskrit $= x \times \dfrac{150}{100} = \dfrac{3x}{2}$

Marks obtained by E in Math $= x + \dfrac{3x}{2} = \dfrac{5x}{2}$

According to question

$x + \dfrac{3x}{2} + \dfrac{5x}{2} + 140 + 120 = 100 \times 5$

$5x = 500 - 260 \qquad \therefore \quad x = \dfrac{240}{5} = 48$

Marks obtained by E in Math $= \dfrac{5}{2} \times 48 = 120$

57. (e) Total no of male workers in B $= 200$

No of trained male workers in B $= 200 \times \dfrac{3}{5} = 120$

Total no of female workers in B $= 200 \times \dfrac{5}{2} = 500$

No of trained female workers in B $= 500 \times \dfrac{2}{5} = 200$

Total no of workers in B $= 200 + 500 = 700$
Total no of trained workers in B $= 120 + 200 = 320$
Total no of untrained workers in B $= 700 - 320 = 380$
Salary of a untrained worker of B $= 2000$

Salary of a trained worker of B $= 2000 \times \dfrac{2}{1} = 4000$

Required ratio $= 320 \times 4000 : 380 \times 2000 = 32 : 19$

58. (d) Total no of workers in A $= 800 + 800 \times \dfrac{3}{2} = 2000$

Total no of workers in B $= 200 + 200 \times \dfrac{5}{2} = 700$

Total no of workers in C $= 450 + 450 \times \dfrac{4}{9} = 650$

Total no of workers in D $= 300 + 300 \times \dfrac{1}{2} = 450$

Total no of workers in E $= 600 + 600 \times \dfrac{2}{3} = 1000$

Total no of workers in all companies together
$= 2000 + 700 + 650 + 450 + 1000 = 4800$

Total no of trained workers in A
$= 800 \times \dfrac{5}{16} + 1200 \times \dfrac{1}{3} = 650$

Total no of trained workers in B
$= 200 \times \dfrac{3}{5} + 500 \times \dfrac{2}{5} = 320$

Total no of trained workers in C
$= 450 \times \dfrac{4}{15} + 200 \times \dfrac{1}{4} = 170$

Total no of trained workers in D
$= 300 \times \dfrac{1}{3} + 150 \times \dfrac{3}{10} = 145$

Total no of trained workers in E
$= 600 \times \dfrac{7}{20} + 400 \times \dfrac{2}{5} = 370$

Total no of trained workers in all companies together
$= 650 + 320 + 170 + 145 + 370 = 1655$

Required % $= \dfrac{1655 \times 100}{4800} = 34.47\,\%$

59. (c) No of male workers in A $= 800$

No of trained male workers in A $= 800 \times \dfrac{5}{16} = 250$

No of female workers in A $= 800 \times \dfrac{3}{2} = 1200$

No of trained female workers in A $= 1200 \times \dfrac{1}{3} = 400$

Total no of workers in A $= 800 + 1200 = 2000$
Total no of trained workers in A $= 250 + 400 = 650$
Total no of untrained workers in A $= 2000 - 650 = 1350$
Total Salary of all workers of A
$= 650 \times 2500 \times \dfrac{9}{5} + 1350 \times 2500$
$= 2925000 + 3375000 = 6300000$

Average Salary of all workers of A
$= \dfrac{6300000}{2000} = 3150$

60. (b) Total no of male workers in all companies together
$= 800 + 200 + 450 + 300 + 600 = 2350$
Total no of female workers in all companies together
$= 800 \times \dfrac{3}{2} + 200 \times \dfrac{5}{2} + 450 \times \dfrac{4}{9}$

$+ 300 \times \dfrac{1}{2} + 600 \times \dfrac{2}{3} = 1200 + 500$

$+ 200 + 150 + 400 = 2450$

Required difference $= \dfrac{2450}{5} - \dfrac{2350}{5} = 490 - 470 = 20$

61. (a) Total no of workers in D

$= 300 + 300 \times \dfrac{1}{2} = 300 + 150 = 450$

Total no of trained workers in D

$= 300 \times \dfrac{1}{3} + 150 \times \dfrac{3}{10} = 145$

Total no of untrained workers in D $= 450 - 145 = 305$
Salary of a untrained worker of D $= 4000$

Salary of a trained worker of D $= 4000 \times \dfrac{5}{4} = 5000$
Total Salary of all workers of D
$= 145 \times 5000 + 305 \times 4000 = 1945000$
Total no of workers in E

$= 600 + 600 \times \dfrac{2}{3} = 600 + 400 = 1000$

Total no of trained workers in E

$= 600 \times \dfrac{7}{20} - 400 \times \dfrac{2}{5} = 370$

Total no. of a untrained worker in E $= 1000 - 370 = 630$
Salary of a untrained worker of E $= 3500$

Salary of a trained worker of E $= 3500 \times \dfrac{10}{7} = 5000$
Total salary of all workers of E
$= 370 \times 5000 + 630 \times 3500 = 1850000 + 2205000$
$= 4055000$

Required ratio $= \dfrac{1945000}{450} : \dfrac{4055000}{1000} = 7780 : 7299$

62. (b) Cost price of T.V. $= 20000$

Marked price of T.V. $= 20000 \times \dfrac{120}{60} = 40000$

Cost price of P.C. $= 40000 \times \dfrac{75}{100} - 10000$
$= 30000 - 10000 = 20000$

Marked price of P.C. $= 40000$

Cost price of Mobile $= 6000 \times \dfrac{100}{20} = 30000$

Marked price of Mobile $= 30000 \times \dfrac{120}{80} = 45000$

Cost price of laptop $= 35000 \times \dfrac{100}{70} = 50000$

Marked price of laptop $= 35000 + 15000 = 50000$
Cost price of Music system $= 20000$

Marked price of Music system

$$= (20000 - 5000)\,\frac{100}{50} = 30000$$

Cost price of Mixer $= 2500 \times \dfrac{100}{50} = 5000$

Marked price of Mixer $= 10000$

Total cost price of all items $= 20000 + 20000 + 30000$
$$+ \; 50000 + 20000 + 5000 = 145000$$

Total Marked price of all items $= 40000 + 40000$
$$+ \; 45000 + 50000 + 30000 + 10000 = 215000$$

Total profit $= 215000 - 145000 = 70000$

Req. % $= \dfrac{70000}{145000} \times 100 = 48.2\%$

63. (d) Marked price of laptop $= 35000 + 15000 = 50000$
Marked price of Music system

$$= (20000 - 5000) \times \frac{100}{50} = 30000$$

Req. % $= \dfrac{50000}{30000} \times 100 = 166.7\%$

64. (e) Cost price of Mixer $= 2500 \times \dfrac{100}{50} = 5000$

Marked price of Mixer $= 10000$

Selling price of Mixer after discounts

$$= 10000 \times \frac{70}{100} \times \frac{80}{100} = 5600$$

Profit $= 5600 - 5000 = 600$

Req. % $= \dfrac{600}{5000} \times 100 = 12\%$ Profit

65. (a) Cost price of T.V. $= 20000$

Selling price of T.V. $= 20000 \times \dfrac{120}{100} = 24000$

Cost price of P.C. $= 40000 \times \dfrac{75}{100} - 10000 = 20000$

Selling price of P.C. $= 20000 + 10000 = 30000$

Cost price of Mobile $= 6000 \times \dfrac{100}{20} = 30000$

Selling price of Mobile $= 30000 + 6000 = 36000$

Cost price of laptop $= 35000 \times \dfrac{100}{70} = 50000$

Selling price of laptop $= 35000$
Cost price of Music system $= 20000$
Selling price of Music system $= 20000 - 5000 = 15000$

Cost price of Mixer $= 2500 \times \dfrac{100}{50} = 5000$

Selling price of Mixer $= 5000 + 2500 = 7500$
Total cost price of all items $= 20000 + 20000 + 30000$
$$+ \; 50000 + 20000 + 5000 = 145000$$

Total selling price of all items $= 24000 + 30000 + 36000$
$$+ \; 35000 + 15000 + 7500 = 147500$$

Required ratio $= \dfrac{145000}{5} : \dfrac{147500}{5} = 58 : 59$

66. (c) Total cost price of all items together $= 145000$
Total selling price of all items together $= 147500$
Total Marked price of all items together $= 215000$
Total profit $= 147500 - 145000 = 2500$
Total discount $= 215000 - 147500 = 67500$
Req. ratio $= 2500 : 67500 = 1 : 27$

67. (a) Total cost price of stock of T.V.
$$= 5000 \times 13500 = 67500000$$
Total selling price of stock of T.V.

$$= 67500000 \times \frac{120}{100} = 81000000$$

Selling price of one T.V. $= \dfrac{81000000}{4500} = 18000$

Marked price of one T.V. $= 18000 \times \dfrac{100}{90} = 20000$

Req. % $= \dfrac{20000 - 13500}{13500} \times 100$

$$= \frac{6500}{13500} \times 100 = 48.14\%$$

68. (b) Let no. of music system in stock be x
Cost price of one music system $= 20000$
Selling price of one music system

$$= 40000 \times \frac{80}{100} = 32000$$

According to the question

$$x \times 20000 \times \frac{120}{100} = (x - 1000)32000$$

$$x \times 24000 = (x - 1000)\,32000$$
$$3x = 4x - 4000 \qquad \therefore \quad x = 4000$$
Total cost of stock of music system
$$= 4000 \times 20000 = 80000000$$

69. (e) Let, total no. of A.C's in stock be x
According to the question,

$$x \times 25000 \times \frac{120}{100} = (x - 500)40000$$

$$3x = 4x - 2000 \qquad \therefore \quad x = 2000$$
Average cost price
$$= \frac{\begin{array}{l}5000 \times 13500 + 4000 \times 20000 + 10000 \times 20000 + \\ 2000 \times 25000 + 8000 \times 25000\end{array}}{5000 + 4000 + 10000 + 2000 + 8000}$$

$$= \frac{\begin{array}{l}67500000 + 80000000 + 200000000 \\ + 50000000 + 200000000\end{array}}{29000}$$

$$= 20603.4$$

70. (c) Required ratio $= 4000 : 2000 = 2 : 1$

71. (d) Total no. of unsold items

$$= 500 + 1000 + \frac{10000}{9} + 500 + 1000 = \frac{37000}{9}$$

Required % $= \dfrac{37000}{9 \times 29000} \times 100 = 14.17\%$

72. (c) The difference was minimum in the year 2016.

In the year 2016

Difference = 32438 – 29129

$\qquad$ = 3309

73. (a) Number of candidates passed from Chennai

Year 2014 $\Rightarrow \dfrac{55492 \times 13}{100} = 7214$

Year 2016 $\Rightarrow \dfrac{58492 \times 14}{100} = 8189$

74. (d) Number of candidates passed from Delhi in 2011 and 2015

$= \dfrac{58248 \times 28}{100} + \dfrac{59216 \times 20}{100} = 16309 + 11843$

$= 28152 \approx 28150$

75. (b) Required number of passed candidates.

$= \dfrac{71253 \times 19}{100} \approx 13540$

76. (e) Required difference

$= \dfrac{50248 \times 21}{100} - \dfrac{51124 \times 17}{100}$

$\approx 10551 - 8691 = 1860$

77. (a) Required number of defect free toys

$= \dfrac{21000 \times 95}{100} + \dfrac{15000 \times 92}{100} + \dfrac{18000 \times 94}{100}$

$= 19950 + 13800 + 16920 = 50670$

Required average $= \dfrac{50670}{3} = 16890$

78. (b) Required answer $= \dfrac{17000 \times 95}{100} = 16150$

79. (c) Required difference = 22000 + 19000 – 17000 = 24000

80. (d) Number of defective toys of type – A :

Year 2010

$\Rightarrow \dfrac{24000 \times 4}{100} = 960$

Year 2008

$\Rightarrow \dfrac{16000 \times 8}{100} = 1280$

Year 2009

$\Rightarrow \dfrac{22000 \times 9}{100} = 1980$

Year 2012

$\Rightarrow \dfrac{26000 \times 7}{100} = 1820$

So in the year 2009 maximum number of defective toys of type A were manufactured

81. (e) Required ratio

$= \dfrac{18000 \times 6}{100} : \dfrac{18000 \times 6}{100} = 1 : 1$

82. (c) Marks obtained by R in different subjects

A	B	C	D	E	F
49. 50	112.5	79	44	108	49. 50

Total marks obtained by R out of 600 marks

$= 49.50 + 112.50 + 79 + 44 + 108 + 49.50 = 442.5$

$\therefore$ Required % marks $= \dfrac{442.5 \times 100}{600} = 73.75\%$

83. (b) Marks of P and T in the subjects 'B, 'D' and 'E'

Sub → Students ↓	B	D	E	Total
P	102	46	133.5	281.5
T	112.5	34	103.5	250

Hence required difference $= 281.5 - 250 = 31.5$

84. (a) Total marks obtained by all the students in subject B

$= \dfrac{150 \times (68 + 72 + 75 + 62 + 75 + 80 + 68)}{100}$

$\therefore$ Required average $= \dfrac{750}{7} = 107.14$

85. (c) $\dfrac{\text{Total in C} + \text{Total in D}}{1400} \times 100$

$= \dfrac{547 + 565}{14} = 79.43\%$

86. (d) Required total marks

$= \dfrac{75 \times (82 + 70 + 66 + 74 + 78 + 80 + 72)}{100}$

$= \dfrac{75 \times 522}{100} = 391.5$

87. (c) Investment per cent of unit C as a fraction of the total investment of all the units in

2011	2012	2013	2014	2015	2016
19.26%	16.87%	16.71%	15.94%	16.76%	16.65%

88. (a) Investment percent in 2012 as a fraction of the total investment in all the given years together of each unit is as follows:

	A	B	C	D	E	F
Investment	132	140	137	125	128	150
Out of	738	824	827	810	817	875
In per cent	17.89%	16.99%	16.57%	15.43%	15.67%	17.14%

89. (e) Required % increase $= \dfrac{(145 - 98)}{98} \times 100 = 47.96\%$

90. (b) Investment by units A, B and C in 2013

$= 125 + 145 + 138 = 408$ crores

Investment by units A, B and C in 2014

$= 116 + 148 + 136 = 400$ crores

Thus, required difference

$= 408 - 400 = 8$ crores (more)

91. (e) Total investment of units A, B and C in the year 2013

$$= 125 + 145 + 138 = 408 \text{ crores}$$

Investment by the units D, E and F in the years 2014

$$= 145 + 152 + 156 = 453 \text{ crores}$$

Hence required ratio $= \dfrac{408}{453} = 136:151$

92. (e) Number of women liking

CSK = 44% of 45525 = 20031

DD = 33% of 36800 = 12144

DC = 30% 0f 56340 = 16902

MI = 28% of 62350 = 17458

RR = 44% of 48300 = 21252

RCB = 35% of 35580 = 12453

KXI = 36% of 56250 = 20250

KKR = 54% of 64000 = 34560

Total = 155050

$\therefore$ Required average $= \dfrac{155050}{8} = 19381.25 \approx 19381$

93. (e) Required percentage

$$= \dfrac{\text{Number of women liking RR}}{\text{Number of women liking all teams}} \times 100$$

$$= 21252/155050 \times 100 = 13.7\%$$

94. (b) Required number $= 45525 \times 36/100 = 16389$

95. (c) Required ratio $= (36800 \times 39):(48300 \times 21) = 208:147$

96. (b) Number of men liking DC = 45% 56340 = 25353

Number of men liking RCB = 15% of 35580 = 5337

$\therefore$ Required percentage $= \dfrac{25353}{5337} \times 100 = 475.04\%$

97. (a) UP (Qua/App)

Arts	Commerce	Science	Engg.	Agr.
0.34	0.39	0.4	0.42	0.42

Alternative Approach: $\dfrac{\text{Qual.}}{\text{App.}}$ should be the least.

$\Rightarrow \dfrac{\text{App.}}{\text{Qual.}}$ should be the maximum.

Now, for Arts, if we divide (4980 ») 5000 by (1690 ») 1700 we find the value of quotient near about 3. But in other cases the quotient is just more than 2. So, our answer is Arts.

98. (b)

A.P.	U.P.	W.B.	Kerala	Orissa	M.P.
41.67	41.93	41.67	28.57	33.34	31.66

99. (e) Percentage of students qualified in commerce

A.P.	U.P.	Kerala	Orissa	M.P.
33.9	38.7	58.2	45.8	28.5

100. (d) Qualifying percentage of UP $= \dfrac{9280}{23880} \times 100 = 38.86$

Qualifying percentage of MP $= \dfrac{8625}{26750} \times 100 = 32.24$

Ratio $= 38:32 = 19:16$

101. (d) Qualifying percentage for Science

A.P.	U.P.	W.B.	Kerala	Orissa	M.P.
39.9	40.5	37.7	58.8	43.3	43.8

102. (b) Staff = 200

Students = 2800

200: 2800 = 2:28 = 1:14

103. (c) IT = 90 => 4:5 => 40 (male)

EIE = 70 => 18:17 => 36 (male)

40 + 36 = 76

Total = 90 + 70 = 160

76 × 100/160 = 47.5%

104. (a) 2200 => 9:13 => 900:1300

$$400 \times \dfrac{100}{900} = 44.45\%$$

105. (d) 1600 => 17:15 => 850 : 750(f)

106. (b) $\dfrac{(120 + 80 + 150 + 90 + 140 + 70)}{6} = \dfrac{650}{6} = 108.3$

107. (c) Let MP of item - II by seller A = 100x

$\therefore$ MP of item - II by seller C = 100x

$$\dfrac{\dfrac{100}{100+s} \times 68x}{\dfrac{100}{100+2s-4} \times 84x} = \dfrac{17}{21}$$

$$\dfrac{68}{84} \times \dfrac{96+2s}{100+s} = \dfrac{17}{21}$$

$$\dfrac{96+2s}{100+s} = \dfrac{1}{1}$$

$$96 + 2s = 100 + s$$

$$s = 4$$

108. (b) Let mark price of item II = 100x

Let mark price of item III = 100y

$\therefore$ 100x + 100y = 6000

$x + y = 60$ ...(i)

And, 72x − 84y = 420

$6x − 7y = 35$ ...(ii)

From (i) and (ii)

$y = 25$

$x = 35$

$\therefore$ M.P of item II = 3500

M.P. of item III = 2500

$$\text{Required \%} = \frac{3500 - 2500}{2500} \times 100 = \frac{1000}{25} = 40\%$$

109. (a) Let M.P. of item II = 100a

$\therefore$ S.P. of item II by seller A = 68a

S.P. of item II by seller B = (100 − x) a

Then (168 − x) a = (3888) × 2

(184 − x) a = 4320 × 2

$\therefore \quad \dfrac{168 - x}{184 - x} = \dfrac{9}{10}$

(10 × 168) − 10x = 9 × 184 − 9x

x = 24

a = 54

Now S.P. of item II by seller C = ₹4536

110. (e) Let S.P. of item I = 500

$\therefore$ S.P. of item III = 600

$$\text{C.P. of item I} = \frac{100}{125} \times 500 = 400$$

$$\text{C.P. of item II} = \frac{100}{120} \times 600 = 500$$

Profit on item I = 500 − 400 = 100

$\therefore \quad 100 \to 750$

$I \to 7.5$

(200) $\leftrightarrow$ (200 × 7.5) = ₹ 1500

111. (a) C.P. = ₹ 60

$$\text{M.P.} = \frac{200}{300} \times 60 + 60 = 40 + 60 = 100$$

Total C.P. = 60 × 5 = 300

Total selling price should be = 380

S.P. of item III by seller E

= (380 − 64 − 67 − 86 − 84) = 79

$\therefore$ Minimum required discount = (100 − 79) = 21%

112. (e) $\dfrac{\dfrac{100}{219} \times 876}{\dfrac{24}{49} \times 1274} \times 100 = \dfrac{400}{624} \times 100 \approx 64\%$

113. (b)

114. (a) From the table it can be observed.

115. (a) In 2003, TIS total production

$$= 782\left(\frac{110}{100}\right) = 860.2$$

$$\text{SAI total production} = 665\left(\frac{90}{100}\right) = 598.5$$

$$\text{Total of A-type steel} = \left(\frac{860.2}{23} \times 14\right) + \left(\frac{598.5}{133} \times 62\right)$$

$$= (523.6) + (279) = 802.6$$

$$\text{Total of B-type steel} = \left(\frac{860.2}{23} \times 9\right) + \left(\frac{598.5}{133} \times 71\right)$$

$$= (336.6) + (319.5) = 656.1$$

Required ratio = 8026 : 6561

116. (a) Required ratio = $\dfrac{3}{4} \times \dfrac{8}{7} = \dfrac{6}{7}$ or 6 : 7

Sol. (117-121) :

Following table can be made easily :

Total area = 37249 sq kilometres

State	Density of population (in thousands)s	Approx % area
A	$\dfrac{112200}{6230} = 18$ (approx)	16.7
B	$\dfrac{83800}{2540} = 33$ (approx)	6.8
C	$\dfrac{64900}{8135} = 8$ (approx)	21.8
D	$\dfrac{572}{7436} = \dfrac{1}{13} \times 100 = 7.69$ (approx)	20
E	$\dfrac{71100}{4893} = 14.5$ (approx)	13
F	$\dfrac{286}{3718} = \dfrac{1}{13} \times 100 = 7.69$ (approx)	10
G	$\dfrac{86000}{4297} = 20$ (approx)	11.5

[**Note :** Density of population is the population per square kilometre.]

117. (b) From the above (column 3) it can be answered. States A, C and D have more than 15 per cent of total areas.

118. (c) States D and F have same population density.

119. (a) Required answer = (33 − 18 =) 15 thousand.

120. (d) For state A, B, E and G, ie for 4 states.

121. (e) Required answer = 2540 : (6230 + 4297)

$$= \frac{2540}{10527} = \frac{1}{4.1}$$

122. (d)

The radius of the spherical part of the bowl can't be determined. Hence volume cannot be calculated.

123. (c) $\dfrac{430}{6200} \times 100 = 6.9\%$

124. (e) Required average

$$= \frac{5200 + 8400 + 7600 + 2600 + 3800 + 4400 + 6000}{7}$$

$$= \frac{38000}{7} = 5428.5 \approx 5500$$

125. (d) Number of candidates eligible for post I
$$= 100 (25 + 32 + 28 + 24 + 30 + 48 + 65) = 25200$$
Number of candidates shortlisted for post I
$$= 65 + 220 + 280 + 85 + 120 + 325 + 550 = 1645$$
Required answer $= \dfrac{1645}{25200} \times 100 = 6.52\%$

126. (a) Number of candidates shortlisted from state E for all the posts $= 120 + 280 + 75 + 280 + 260 + 520 = 1535$
Number of candidates shortlisted from state G for all posts $= 550 + 140 + 325 + 220 + 410 + 200 = 1845$
Required answer $= \dfrac{1535}{1845} = \dfrac{307}{369}$

127. (e) Total number of candidates eligible form all states for post I $= 25200$
Total number of candidates eligible form all states for post VI $= 39400$
Required answer $= \dfrac{25200}{39400} \times 100 = 63.9\%$

128. (b)

129. (c) Total candidates shortlisted for post V $= 1650$
Total candidates shortlisted for post VI $= 2780$
Required ratio $= \dfrac{1650}{2780} = \dfrac{165}{278}$

130. (b) Marks scored by Anushka
$$= 150 \times \frac{66}{100} + 100 \times \frac{75}{100} + 150 \times \frac{88}{100}$$
$$+ 125 \times \frac{56}{100} + 75 \times \frac{56}{100} + 50 \times \frac{90}{100}$$
$$= 99 + 75 + 132 + 70 + 42 + 45 = 463$$

131. (d) Marks scored by Archit
$$= 150 \times \frac{82}{100} + 100 \times \frac{76}{100} + 150 \times \frac{84}{100} + 125 \times$$
$$\times \frac{96}{100} + 75 \times \frac{92}{100} + 50 \times \frac{88}{100}$$
$$= 123 + 76 + 126 + 120 + 69 + 44 = 558$$
Marks scored by Arpan
$$= 150 \times \frac{76}{100} + 100 \times \frac{66}{100} + 150 \times \frac{78}{100} + 125 \times$$
$$\times \frac{88}{100} + 75 \times \frac{72}{100} + 50 \times \frac{70}{100}$$
$$= 114 + 66 + 117 + 110 + 54 + 35 = 496$$
Marks scored by Garvita
$$= 150 \times \frac{90}{100} + 100 \times \frac{88}{100} + 150 \times \frac{96}{100} + 125 \times$$
$$\times \frac{76}{100} + 75 \times \frac{84}{100} + 50 \times \frac{86}{100}$$
$$= 135 + 88 + 144 + 95 + 63 + 43 = 568$$
Marks scored by Gunit.
$$= 150 \times \frac{64}{100} + 100 \times \frac{70}{100} + 150 \times \frac{68}{100} + 125 \times$$

$$\times \frac{72}{100} + 75 \times \frac{68}{100} + 50 \times \frac{74}{100}$$
$$= 96 + 70 + 102 + 90 + 51 + 37 = 446$$
Marks scored by Pranita
$$= 150 \times \frac{48}{100} + 100 \times \frac{56}{100} + 150 \times \frac{50}{100} + 125 \times$$
$$\times \frac{64}{100} + 75 \times \frac{64}{100} + 50 \times \frac{58}{100}$$
$$= 72 + 56 + 75 + 80 + 48 + 29 = 360$$
Hence, highest total marks scored by Garvita.

132. (c) Required percentage $= \dfrac{88}{76} \times 100 = 115.79\%$

133. (b) Two students i.e. Garvita strategic management brand management & compensation management and Archit consumer behaviour & service marketing.

134. (a) Required Average Marks
$$= \frac{(88+84+78+96+68+50) \times 150}{100 \times 6} = \frac{464 \times 150}{600} = 116$$

135. (a) Number of books bought in :
January $\Rightarrow 50+105+70+300+140+200+65 = 930$
March $\Rightarrow 106+1000+100+500+370+700+135 = 2911$
May $\Rightarrow 2+40+80+100+200+15+111 = 548$
July $\Rightarrow 30+105+115+216+225+400+188 = 1279$
September $\Rightarrow 25+400+200+135+175+75+25 = 1035$
November $\Rightarrow 75+375+240+300+470+530+65 = 2055$
So maximum number of books were bought in March.

136. (e) Number of books in the price range :
More than ₹ 5000 $\Rightarrow 50 + 106 + 2 + 30 + 25 + 75 = 288$
₹ 4000 − ₹ 5000 $\Rightarrow 105 + 1000 + 40 + 105 + 400 + 375 = 2025$
₹ 3000 − ₹ 3999 $\Rightarrow 70 + 100 + 80 + 115 + 200 + 240 = 805$
₹ 2000 − ₹ 2999 $\Rightarrow 300 + 500 + 100 + 216 + 135 + 300 = 1551$
₹ 1000 − ₹ 1999 $\Rightarrow 140 + 370 + 200 + 225 + 175 + 470 = 1580$
₹ 500 − ₹ 999 $\Rightarrow 200 + 700 + 15 + 400 + 75 + 530 = 1920$
Less than ₹ 500 $\Rightarrow 65 + 135 + 111 + 188 + 25 + 65 = 589$
So maximum number of books bought in price range of ₹ 4000 − 5000.

137. (b) Required percentage $= \dfrac{140}{200} \times 100 = 70$

138. (c) Number of books bought in September
$$= (25 + 400 + 200 + 135 + 175 + 75 + 25) = 1035$$
Number of books bought in November
$$= (75 + 375 + 240 + 300 + 470 + 530 + 65) = 2055$$
So Required difference $= 2055 − 1035 = 1020$.

139. (d) Required ratio $= 105 : 1000 = 21 : 200$

140. (d) Number of people in medical profession
$$= 24500 \times \frac{11}{100} = 2695$$

Number of males $= 2695 \times \dfrac{40}{100} = 1078$

Number of females $= 2695 - 1078 = 1617$
Number of people in teaching profession
$$= 24500 \times \frac{21}{100} = 5145$$

Number of males $= 5145 \times \dfrac{1}{5} = 1029$

Number of females $= 5145 - 1029 = 4116$

∴ Required ratio $= (1078 + 1029) : (1617 + 4116)$
$$= 2107 : 5733 = 43 : 117$$

141. (a) Number of people in teaching profession $= 5145$
Number of people in law profession
$$= 24500 \times \frac{24}{100} = 5880$$

∴ Required percentage $= \dfrac{5145}{5880} \times 100 = 87.5$

Alternative
Percentage of people in teaching profession $= 21$
Percentage of people in law profession $= 24$

∴ Required percentage $= \dfrac{21}{24} \times 100 = 87.5$

142. (c) Number of males :
Medical $\Rightarrow 1078$

Engineering $\Rightarrow 24500 \times \dfrac{18}{100} \times \dfrac{70}{100} = 3087$

Law $\Rightarrow 24500 \times \dfrac{24}{100} \times \dfrac{55}{100} = 3234$

Teaching $\Rightarrow 1029$

Banking $\Rightarrow 24500 \times \dfrac{16}{100} \times \dfrac{65}{100} = 2548$

Management $\Rightarrow 24500 \times \dfrac{10}{100} \times \dfrac{56}{100} = 1372$

∴ Total number of males
$$= 1078 + 3087 + 3234 + 1029 + 2548 + 1372$$
$$= 12348$$

143. (b) Number of females in Engineering profession
$$= 24500 \times \frac{18}{100} \times \frac{30}{100} = 1323$$

Number of males in Management $= 1372$

Required percentage $= \dfrac{1323}{1372} \times 100 = 96.43$

144. (d) Required ratio $= 2548 : 3087 = 52 : 63$

145. (c) Total amount paid by Dev in June for all commodities
$$= 123 + 150 + 324 + 134 = ₹\ 731$$

146. (c) Average electricity bill paid by Manu in all five months
$$= 315 + 135 + 98 + 116 + 131 = \frac{795}{5} = ₹\ 159$$

147. (a) Mobile phone bill paid by Ravi in May $= ₹\ 143$
Laundry bill paid by Dev in March $= ₹\ 323$
Difference $= 323 - 143 = ₹\ 180$

148. (d)

149. (a) Electricity bill paid by Manu in April $= 135$
Mobile bill paid by Ravi in June $= 245$
Ratio $= 135 : 245 = 27 : 49$

150. (c) Distance travelled by train from Surat to Nadiad Jn.
$$= 440 - 257 = 183\ kms$$

151. (e) Time taken to reach Ahmedabad
$$= 8 : 00\ Am - 6 : 45\ Am = 1\ hour\ 15\ min.$$

152. (a) Ratio between No. of passengers boarding from Vasai
Road and from Ahmedabad $= 378 : 306 = 21 : 17$

153. (b) Total time increase $= 23 - 2 = 21$ min.
∴ Train will reach Bhuj at $= 5{:}40$ pm $+ 21$ min
$$= 6{:}01\ pm$$

154. (d) Distance between Anand Jn. to Vadodara is second lowest.

Sol. (155 – 159) :

155. (a) The number of lectures taken by L in a week
$$= (2 * 3) + (0 * 2) = 6$$
The number of lectures taken by O in a week
$$= (2 * 3) + (2 * 2) = 6 + 4 = 10$$
Required ratio $= 6 : 10 = 3 : 5$

156. (d) The number of lectures taken by N in a week
$$= (1 * 3) + (3 * 2) = 3 + 6 = 9$$
The number of lectures taken by N in 6 weeks
$$= 9 * 6 = 54$$
The earnings made by N if he teaches for 6 weeks
$$= 54 * 12000 = ₹\ 324000 \times 2 = 648000$$

157. (c) The number of lectures taken by N in a week
$$= (1 * 3) + (3 * 2) = 3 + 6 = 9$$
The earnings made by N for 3 weeks
$$= 9 * 3 * 12000 = 324000$$
The number of lectures taken by O in a weeks
$$= (2 * 3) + (2 * 2) = 6 + 4 = 10$$
The earnings made by O for 2 weeks
$$= 10 * 2 * 8000 = 160000$$
Required difference $= 324000 - 160000 = 164000$

158. (b) M takes 2 classes each on Thursday and Friday
The number of classes taken by M in a week
$$= (3 * 3) + (2 * 2) = 9 + 4 = 13$$
M is earning in a week $\Rightarrow\ 13 * 16000 = 208000$

159. (a) Total number of classes taken by the professor M in 3
weeks $= 624000/16000 = 39$ classes
According to the question,
$(9 * 3) + 3 *$ (Friday + Thursday) $= 39$
$3 *$ (Friday + Thursday) $= 39 - 27$
$3 *$ (Friday + Thursday) $= 12$
Tuesday + Thursday $= 4$ classes
2 classes each taken by the tutor M in Thursday and Friday

Sol. (160-164) :

160. (b) Total number of people who attended the workshop in January = 840 * (11/6) = 1540

Total number of people who attended the workshop in May = 840 * (5/3) = 1400

Required % = (1540 – 1400)* 100/1400 = 10%

161. (a) Number of Literate males in May = 640 – 384 = 256

Literate female in May 840 – 256 = 584

162. (b)

163. (d) Required average = {(840 * 5/6 + 640 * 5/4 + 600 * 6/5)}/3 = (700 + 800 + 720)/3 = 740

164. (c) Number of illiterate (male + female) in February = 700 * 3/5 = 420

Number of illiterate (male + females) in May = 640 * (5/4) = 800

Number of females (literate + illiterate) in February = (700 + 420 – 480 = 640)

Similarly on May = (640 + 800 – 640) = 800

Required ratio = (480 + 640) : (640 + 800) = 7 : 9

Sol. (165-169) :

165. (c) Total number of engineering student in university P = (100 – 35)% of 3000 = (65/100)* 3000 = 1950

Given that the civil engineering students are 50% more than the mechanical engineering students.

Let x be the number of mechanical engineering students in university P.

Then number of civil engineering students in college P = x + 50% of x = 150% of x

So, x + (150/100) x = 1950

(250/100) x = 1950

x = 780

So, the no of mechanical engineering students = 780

The number of civil engineering students = 1170

Given that the ratio of boys and girls in university P for civil engineering students = 4 : 1

So, the difference of boys and girls in civil students = (3/5) * 1170 = 702

166. (d) Given that, the total engineering student in university T = 1050

Let the number of mechanical engineering students in university T be X.

Then the number of civil engineering student in university T = X – 12% of X = 87 % of X

Therefore, X + 87 % of X = 1050

187% of X = 1050

X = 560

So, the number of mechanical engineering students in university T = 560

And the number of civil engineering students in university T = 1050 – 560 = 490

The number of engineering student in university S = 1470

The number of civil engineering in university S = (3/5) * 1470 = 882

Required ratio = 882 : 490 = 441 : 245

167. (d) Number of arts student in university P = (35/100)* 3000 = 1050

Number of arts student in university Q = 1050 + 750 = 1800

Let the total number of students in university Q be X. We know that, there are 40% of students in university Q are arts.

So, (40/100)* X = 1800 $\Rightarrow$ X = 4500

(i.e) Total number of students in university Q = 4500

Required percent = [(4500 – 4200)/ 4200]* 100 = $7\dfrac{1}{7}$%

168. (d) Given that, total student in university R = 2760 and total arts student in university R = total engineering students in university R

So, total arts students + total engineering student = 2760

Therefore, total arts student = 1380

Number of arts boys in university R = (5/6) * 1380 = 1150

If 20% of boys are transferred to university T, then the total

Students in university T = 3500 + (20/100) * 1150 = 3730

169. (a) Total students in X= [(2/5)* (35/100)* 3000] + [(40/100) * 4200] = 420 + 1680 = 2100

Sol. (170-174) :

170. (b) Let C.P. of Toy 1 at A is ₹100

$\therefore$ S.P. of Toy 1 at A = ₹140

$\therefore$ C.P. of Toy 1 at B = $100 \times \dfrac{100}{125} = 80$

S.P. of Toy 1 at B = $140 \times \dfrac{80}{100} = 112$

$\therefore$ Required percentage profit

$= \dfrac{112 - 80}{80} \times 100 = 40\%$

171. (c) Let profit percentage of B on Toy 3 is x%

$\therefore$ x + 25 + 10 + 24 + 30 = 5 × 23

$\Rightarrow$ x = 26%

172. (d) Required ratio of selling prices = $\dfrac{3 \times \dfrac{120}{100}}{5 \times \dfrac{125}{100}} = \dfrac{72}{125}$

173. (a) Let C.P. of Toy 3 for A = $2x$

So, C.P. of Toy 4 = $5x$

Total C.P. of both items for A = $2x + 5x = 7x$

S.P. of Toy 3 for A = $2x \times \dfrac{125}{100} = 2.5x$

S.P. of Toy 4 for A = $5x \times \dfrac{120}{100} = 6x$

Total S.P. of both items by A = $6x + 2.5x = 8.5x$

Required Profit % = $\dfrac{8.5x - 7x}{7x} \times 100 = 21\dfrac{3}{7}\%$

174. (c) Required total profit

$$= 450 \times \frac{100}{300} + 384 \times \frac{25}{100} + 360 \times \frac{50}{300}$$

$$= 150 + 96 + 60$$

$$= 306 \text{ rupees}$$

Sol. (175-179) :

175. (a) Let population of females and children in country P be $3x$ and $7x$ respectively.

$$\therefore 10x = \frac{75}{100} \times 1200$$

$$x = 90$$

No. of females in country P in year 2017

$$= 270 \times \frac{120}{100} = 324$$

$\therefore$ Required no. of males and children together in country P in 2017 $= 1200 - 324 = 876$

176. (c) Total no. of males in country R

$$= \frac{50}{100} \times \frac{100}{30} \times 180 = 300$$

No. of males in country S $= \frac{1}{3} \times \frac{84}{100} \times 400 = 112$

$\therefore$ Required difference $= 300 - 112 = 188$

177. (b) Total population of males in country Q

$$= \frac{40}{100} \times \frac{2}{5} \times \frac{125}{100} \times 1200 = 240$$

And that of children in country R

$$= \frac{30}{100} \times \frac{3}{5} \times \frac{125}{100} \times 1200 = 270$$

$\therefore$ Required ratio $= \dfrac{240}{270} = 8 : 9$

178. (d) Let males in country S $= 2x$

Females in country P $= 5x$

Let population of children in country P $= a\%$

$\therefore$ No. of children in country P in 2017 $= \dfrac{6a}{5}\%$

From here we cannot find the required answer

179. (e) Let total population of country R $= 5x$

& that of country T $= 4x$

Required percent

$$= \frac{0.4 \times 4x - 0.3 \times 5x}{0.3 \times 5x} \times 100 = \frac{100}{15}\% = 6.67\%$$

Sol. (180-184) :

180. (c) $\dfrac{30000 \times 9}{50000 \times 10} = \dfrac{x}{25000}$

$$\frac{27}{50} = \frac{x}{25000}$$

$$x = 13500$$

$\therefore$ Required profit $= 13500 + 16000 + 25000$

$$= \$ 54500 \text{ mn}$$

181. (b) $\dfrac{14000}{16000} = \dfrac{P_Y}{28000}$

$P_Y = 24500$ mn

$P_Y = 64750 - 24500 - 28000$

$P_Y = 12250$

Let investment of X in

AP $= x$

$\therefore \quad \dfrac{x}{14000} = \dfrac{12250}{24500}$

$x = \$ 7000$

Required Ratio $= 7000 : 16000 = 7 : 16$

182. (a)

$$\begin{array}{ccc} X & Y & Z \end{array}$$

Profit : $(8000 \times 5) : (10000 \times 8) : (9000 \times 6)$

$$\qquad 20 \quad : \quad 40 \quad : \quad 27$$

$\therefore P_X = \dfrac{20}{87} \times 17400 = 4000$ mn

$P_Y = \dfrac{40}{87} \times 17400 = 8000$

$P_Z = 5400$

Required %

$$= \frac{5400}{12000} \times 100 = 45\%$$

> **Trick :**
> Required value $=$
> $$\frac{27}{40 + 20} \times 100 = 45\%$$

183. (c) $\dfrac{x \times 4}{(170000 - x)6} = \dfrac{40,000}{60,000}$

$$\frac{2x}{3(170000 - x)} = \frac{2}{3}$$

$6x = 2 \times 3 \times 170000 - 6x$

$12x = 6 \times 170000$

$x = 85000$

$I_X = 85000$

$\therefore I_Y = 85000$

Let Required Years $= y$

$\therefore \dfrac{85000 \times 6}{34000 \times y} = \dfrac{60000}{80000}$

$y = 20$ years

184. (e) $I_z = 60000 - 18000 - 20000 = 22000$

$P_z = 36000 - 9000 - 12000 = 15000$

Required % $= \dfrac{22000 - 15000}{22000} \times 100$

$$= 31\frac{9}{11}\%$$

185. (b) Let cost price of $P_2 = x$

$$x \times \frac{(100 + 15)}{100} = 81880$$

$$x = 71200$$

Selling price of $P_3 = 44300 \times \dfrac{(100 - 12)}{100} = 38984$

Required percentage $= \dfrac{71200}{38984} \times 100 \approx 182\%$

186. (d) Original S.P. $= 44300 \times \dfrac{88}{100} = 38984$

New S.P. $= 44300 \times \dfrac{(100+12)}{100} = 49616$

Difference $= 49616 - 38984 = 10632$

187. (b) Percentage profit on P_4

$= \dfrac{62280 - 56590}{56590} \times 100 = 10.05\%$

Profit percentage on $P_2 = 15\%$

Required percentage

$= \dfrac{(15-10)}{15} \times 100 = \dfrac{100}{3} = 33.34\%$ less

188. (e) Profit percentage on P_1

$= \dfrac{81112.5 - 64890}{64890} \times 100 = 25\%$

Profit percentage on $P_5 = 25\%$

Required Ratio $= 1 : 1$

189. (b) Overall cost price of all items together $= 64890 + 71200 + 44300 + 56590 + 11320 = 248300$

Overall selling price of all items together $= 81112.5 + 81880 + 38984 + 62280 + 14150 = 278406.5$

Profit percentage $= \dfrac{278406.5 - 248300}{248300} \times 100$

$\approx 12.12\%$ profit

190. (c) Total number of employees in company B $= 1400$

Percentage of B.Sc. graduate employees

$= [100 - (31 + 40)] = 29\%$

Now, percentage difference between BA graduate and B.Sc. graduate employees $= (40 - 29)\% = 11\%$

11% of $1400 = 154$

Therefore, difference $= 154$

191. (b) The percentage of BA graduate employees in Company E $= 100 - 35 - 50 = 15\%$

Now, The percentage of BA graduate employees and B.Com. $= 50 + 15 = 65\%$

Average $= 312$

Therefore, the total number of employees in B.Com. and BA $= 2 * 312 = 624$

Let the total employees in Company E be x

Then, 65% of $x = 624$

$x = 960$

192. (a) The percentage of B.Com. graduate and BA graduate employees in company A $= 100 - 32 = 68\%$

Now, the percentage of BA graduate employees

$= \dfrac{68 \times 7}{17} = 28\%$

The percentage of B.com. graduate employees

$= \dfrac{68 \times 10}{17} = 40\%$

The number of B.A. graduate employees in company

$A = \dfrac{2100 \times 28}{100} = 588$

193. (e) The number of employees in company B in January 2017 $= 1400$

The number of employees in company B in January 2018 $= \dfrac{1400 \times 120}{100} = 1680$

Number of B.Sc. graduate employees in company B in January 2018

$= \dfrac{20 \times 1680}{100} = 336$

194. (d) The percentage of BA graduate employees in company C $= 100 - 30 - 30 = 40\%$

The percentage difference between BA graduate employees in company C and D $= 40 - 20 = 20\%$

Now, let the number of employees in company C be x

Then $x \times 20\% = 180$

$x = 900$

195. (a) Maximum possible runs scored by Ajay in Match-1 $= 27$

Maximum possible runs scored by Ajay in Match-3 $= 24$

Maximum possible percentage contribution:

$\dfrac{27 + 100 + 24 + 53}{270 + 300 + 240 + 200} \times 100\% = \dfrac{204}{1010} \times 100\%$

$= 20.19\% = 20\%$ approx.

196. (c) Maximum possible runs scored by Vivek in Match-2 $= 30$

Maximum possible runs scored by Vivek in Match-4 $= 20$

Maximum possible percentage contribution:

$\dfrac{60 + 30 + 78 + 20}{270 + 300 + 240 + 200} \times 100\% = \dfrac{188}{1010} \times 100\%$

$= 18.6\%$

197. (b) Maximum possible total runs scored by Chanchal in the four matches $= 27 + 30 + 110 + 20 = 187$.

Total runs scored by Ajay in the four matches is in the range of 189 to 204

Hence,

In such a case minimum possible

Total runs scored by Ajay in the four matches

$= 23 + 100 + 13 + 53 = 189$

Difference $= 189 - 187 = 2$ (minimum possible)

So required ratio is $189 : 187$

198. (b) Maximum possible total runs scored by Chanchal in the four matches $= 27 + 30 + 110 + 20 = 187$.

In such a case minimum possible total runs scored by Ajay in the four matches $= 23 + 100 + 13 + 53 = 189$.

Difference $= 189 - 187 = 2$ (minimum possible)

Subsequently total runs scored by Pradeep in the four
matches $= 88 + 65 + 19 + 52 = 224$.

Also, total runs scored by Vivek in the four matches
$$= 60 + 30 + 78 + 19 = 187$$
Absolute difference $= 224 - 187 = 37$

199. (c) Individual ranges for total score:

Ajay　　　:　189 – 204

Pradeep　:　218 – 224

Chanchal:　182 – 187

Deepak　:　223

Vivek　　:　187 – 188

Least total will be of Chanchal (Rank 5)

2nd least will be Vivek (Rank 4)

Rank 3 must be of Ajay

It is not possible to determine the exact ranks of Pradeep
and Deepak.

200. (b) Runs scored by Dhawan $= \dfrac{72 \times 3x}{100} = 2.16x$

Runs scored by Fawad $= \dfrac{66 \times 4x}{100} = 2.64x$

$\therefore$ Required percentage $= \dfrac{0.48x}{2.16x} \times 100 = 22\dfrac{2}{9}\%$

201. (c) Total runs scored by Eeshan $= 28 \times 55 = 1540$

If last 3 matches are not considered, then his total runs
$$= 25 \times 46 = 1150$$

Maximum possible runs in 26th and 27th match is 126
and 127.

$\therefore$ Minimum possible run in 28th match
$$= 1540 - 1150 - 126 - 127 = 137$$

202. (d) Let total runs scored by x

$\therefore$ Total balls faced $= x - 74$

So, $129.6 = \dfrac{x}{x - 74} \times 100$

$\Rightarrow 29.6x = 9590.4 \quad \Rightarrow \quad x = 324$

$\therefore$ Required average runs scored $= \dfrac{324}{8} = 40.5$

203. (b) Total runs scored by Cheteshwar $= \dfrac{114 \times 400}{100} = 456$

$\therefore$ Total matches played $= \dfrac{456}{38} = 12$

Runs scored by Fawad $= \dfrac{66 \times 400}{100} = 264$

So, total balls faced by Dhawan $= \dfrac{264 + 24}{72} \times 100 = 400$

So, required difference $= 400 - 288 = 112$

204. (c) Number of matches played by Dhawan and Fawad
together $= 19 \times 6 - (8 + 20 + 12 + 28) = 46$

Max. Possible runs of Fawad $= \dfrac{66 \times 150}{100} = 99$

$\therefore$ Matches played by him $= \dfrac{99}{3} = 33$

So, required min. no. of matches played by Dhawan
$$= 46 - 33 = 13$$

205. (c) Required difference
$$= (72 + 76 + 62 + 30 + 54) - (6 + 16 + 36 + 11 + 2)$$
$$= 294 - 71 = 223$$

206. (a) Required % $= \dfrac{70.5 + 72}{53 + 27.25 + 53.50} \times 100 = 106.54\%$

207. (c) Required marks $= (72 + 76 + 62) - 0.33 (6 + 16 + 36)$
$$= 190.86$$

208. (c) By options

Let right questions $= 59$

$\therefore$ Marks $= 59 - \dfrac{1}{4}(92 - 59) = 50.75$

209. (e) Required % $= \dfrac{70.5 + 72 + 53 + 27.25 + 53.50}{500} \times 100$
$$= 55.25\%$$

210. (c) CP of Apple $= ₹ 1800$

Transportation cost $= ₹ 600$

$\therefore$ Total CP $= 1800 + 600 = 2400$

Given Profit percent $= 5\%$

$\therefore$ SP $= 2400 \times \dfrac{105}{100} = ₹ 2520$

211. (b) SP of Grapes $=$ (CP + Transportation cost + Profit)
$$= 4000 + 1000 + 500 = 5500$$

$\therefore$ CP of Banana $=$ SP + Loss $= 1600 + 600 = 2200$

Required percentage $= \dfrac{5500}{2200} \times 100 = 250\%$ of the CP
of Banana

212. **(b)** Loss on Mango
$$= 10000 \times \dfrac{100}{95} - 10000 = 10000 \left[\dfrac{5}{95}\right] \times 2$$

Loss on Banana $= ₹ 600$

$\therefore$ Required Ratio $= \dfrac{10000 \times 5}{95 \times 600} = 50 : 57$

213. (a) SP of Orange $=$ CP + Cost of Transportation + Profit
$$= 12000 + 800 + 7\% \text{ of } (12000 + 800) = 107\% \text{ of } 12800$$
$$= ₹ 13696$$

Selling Price of Grapes $= 4000 + 1000 + 500 = 5500$

$\therefore$ Desired Difference $= 13696 - 5500 = 8196$

214. (d) CP of Apple $= 1800 + 600 = 2400$

Given Loss % $= 10\%$ $\therefore$ 10% of $2400 = 240$

$\therefore$ SP of Apple $= 2400 - 240 = (1080) \times 2 = 2160$ and

SP of Orange $= 107\%$ of $12800 = (6848) \times 2 = 13696$

Required Percentage
$$= \dfrac{13696 - 2160}{13696} \times 100 = \dfrac{11536}{13696} \times 100 \approx 84\%$$

215. (c) Selling price of book I $\Rightarrow 20 \times 200 = 4000$

II $\Rightarrow 40 \times 300 = 12000$

III $\Rightarrow 60 \times 100 = 6000$

Let commission % be (a–1), a and (a+1) respectively.

ATQ,

$$4000\frac{(a-1)}{100} + \frac{12000(a)}{100} + \frac{6000(a+1)}{100} = 3200$$

a = 14.45%

Highest commission = 15.45%

216. (d) Total commission earned by shop RR

= ₹ 3500

Total selling price of Book I

= $105 \times 20 = ₹ 2100$

Total selling price of Book II

= $105 \times 30 = ₹ 3150$

Total selling price of Book III

= $105 \times 40 = ₹ 4200$

Let commission percent = x%

$$(2100 + 3150 + 4200) \times \frac{x}{100} = 3500 = \frac{1000}{27} \%$$

217. (a) Total commission of SS

$$= \frac{3500 \times 8}{7} = ₹ 4000.$$

S.P. of each product = $100 \times 80 = ₹ 8000$

Let commission % charged on 3 products be (x – 5) %, x% and (x+5)%.

So,

$$8000\frac{(x-5)}{100} + 8000\frac{(x)}{100} + 8000 = \frac{(x+5)}{100} 4000$$

240x = 4000

$$x = \frac{400}{24} = \frac{100}{6}\%$$

$$x = 16\frac{2}{3}\%$$

Least range could be = 16 – 5 = 11%

16 + 6 = 22% = (11 – 22)

218. (d) Let total books = x

So S.P. = x

Now total commission $\Rightarrow$ 3500

Minimum values of x = 100

Maximum value of x = 109

Let 'a' be commission %

So, Max value of 'a' could be

$$(100 \times 100) \times \frac{}{100} = 3500$$

a = 35%

Minimum value could be

$$109 \times 109 \times \frac{a}{100} = 3500 \approx 29.45$$

Range = (29.4 – 35)

6 CASELETS

Caselets are known as mathematical puzzles. In the caselets generally we evaluate the values based on a given paragraph for the solution of the questions. The questions of caselets based on a paragraph but number of questions may be differ with paragraphs.

For example: Salary of A is 25% more than that of B who saves 40% of his salary. Salary of B is 20% less than that of D who saves 40% more than C. Respective ratio of saving of C and E is 4:5 and C saves 20% less than his expenditure. Respective ratio of expenditure of A and that of D is 5: 6. Difference between expenditures of A and D is 12000. A saves 40% of his salary. E spends 50% of his salary.

(1) Salary of C is what percent of that of D?

(a) $33\dfrac{1}{3}\%$ (b) 50%

(c) 45%   (d) 55%

(e) None of these

(2) Saving of B is what % of expenditure of E?

(a) 128%

(b) 108%

(c) 86%

(d) 88%

(e) None of these

Persons	Salary	Expenditure	Saving	Notes
A	$60000 \times \dfrac{100}{60}$ $= 100000$	12000×5 $= 60000$	$100000 - 60000$ $= 40000$	Difference between expenditures of A and that of D is 12000. Respective ratio of expenditures of A and D is 5 : 6 A saves 40% of his salary.
B	$100000 \times \dfrac{100}{125}$ $= 80000$	$80000 - 32000$ $= 48000$	$80000 \times \dfrac{40}{100}$ $= 32000$	Salary of A is 25% more than that of B. B saves 40% of his salary
C	$20000 + 25000$ $= 45000$	$20000 \times \dfrac{100}{80}$ $= 25000$	$28000 \times \dfrac{100}{140}$ $= 20000$	D saves 40% more than C C saves 20% less than his expenditure
D	$80000 \times \dfrac{100}{80}$ $= 100000$	12000×6 $= 72000$	$100000 - 72000$ $= 28000$	Difference between expenditures of A and D is 12000 Respective ratio of expenditures of A and that of D is 5:6 Salary of B is 20% less than that of D.
E	$25000 \times \dfrac{100}{50}$ $= 50000$	$50000 - 25000$ $= 25000$	$20000 \times \dfrac{5}{4}$ $= 25000$	Respective ratio of saving of C and E is 4:5 E spends 50% of his salary.

Ans (1) (c) Salary of C = ₹ 45000
Salary of D = ₹ 100000
Required % = $\dfrac{45000}{100000} \times 100$
= 45%

Ans (2) (a) Saving of B = ₹ 32000
Expenditure of E = ₹. 25000
Required % = $\dfrac{32000}{25000} \times 100$
= 128%

EXERCISE

DIRECTIONS (Qs. 1-5): *Study the information carefully to answer the questions that follow:*

A school consisting of a total of 1560 students has boys and girls in the ratio of 7 : 5 respectively. All the students are enrolled in different types of hobby classes, viz: Singing, Dancing and Painting. One-fifth of the boys are enrolled in only Dancing classes. Twenty percent of the girls are enrolled in only Painting classes. Ten percent of the boys are enrolled in only Singing classes. Twenty four percent of the girls are enrolled in both Singing and Dancing classes together. The number of girls enrolled in only Singing classes is two hundred percent of the boys enrolled in the same. One-thirteenth of the boys are enrolled in all the three classes together. The respective ratio of boys enrolled in Dancing and Painting classes together to the girls enrolled in the same is 2 : 1 respectively. Ten percent of the girls are enrolled in only Dancing classes whereas eight percent of the girls are enrolled in both Dancing and Painting classes together. The remaining girls are enrolled in all the three classes together. The number of boys enrolled in Singing and Dancing classes together is fifty percent of the number of girls enrolled in the same. The remaining boys are enrolled in only Painting classes.

1. What is the total number of boys who are enrolled in dancing?
   (a) 318   (b) 364
   (c) 292   (d) 434
   (e) None of these

2. Total number of girls enrolled in singing is **approximately** what percent of the total number of students in the school?
   (a) 37%   (b) 19%
   (c) 32%   (d) 14%
   (e) 26%

3. What is the total number of students enrolled in all the three classes together ?
   (a) 135   (b) 164
   (c) 187   (d) 142
   (e) None of these

4. Number of girls enrolled in only dancing classes is what percent of the boys enrolled in the same ? (rounded off to two digits after decimal)
   (a) 38.67%   (b) 35.71%
   (c) 41.83%   (d) 28.62%
   (e) None of these

5. What is the respective ratio of the number of girls enrolled in only painting classes to the number of boys enrolled in the same?
   (a) 77 : 26   (b) 21 : 73   (c) 26 : 77   (d) 73 : 21
   (e) None of these

DIRECTIONS (Qs. 6–10): *Study the following information carefully and answer the questions that follow :*

An Organisation consists of 2400 employees working in different departments, viz; HR, Marketing, IT, production and Accounts. The ratio of male to female employees in the Organisation is 5 : 3 respectively. Twelve per cent of the males work in the HR department. Twenty four per cent of the females work in the Accounts department. The ratio of males to females working in the HR department is 6 : 11 respectively. One-ninth of the females work in the IT department. Forty two percent of the males work in the production department. Number of females working in the production department is ten percent of the males working in the same. The remaining females work in the Marketing department. The total number of employees working in the IT department is 285. Twenty two percent of the males work in the Marketing department and the remaining work in the Accounts department.

6. The number of males working in the IT department forms **approximately** what percent of the total number of males in the organisation ?
   (a) 5%   (b) 12%
   (c) 21%   (d) 8%
   (e) 18%

7. How many males work in the Accounts department ?
   (a) 170   (b) 165
   (c) 185   (d) 160
   (e) None of these

8. The total number of employees working in the accounts department forms what percent of the total number of employees in the organisation ? (rounded off to two digits after decimal)
   (a) 19.34%
   (b) 16.29%
   (c) 11.47%
   (d) 23.15%
   (e) None of these

9. The number of females working in the production department forms what percent of the total number of females in the organisation ?
   (a) 7%   (b) 12%
   (c) 4%   (d) 15%
   (e) None of these

10. What is the total number of females working in the HR and marketing department together ?
    (a) 363   (b) 433
    (c) 545   (d) 521
    (e) None of these

DIRECTIONS (Qs. 11-13): *Study the information carefully and answer the questions that follow :*

The students of a school have an option to study only Hindi, only Sanskrit or a composite subject Hindi and Sanskrit. Out of, the 175 students in the school, boys and girls are in the ratio of 3 : 4 respectively. 40% of boys have opted for only Hindi. 44% of the students have opted for only Sanskrit. Out of the total number of girls 32% have opted for the composite subject. The number of boys who opted for only Sanskrit and that for composite subject are in the ratio of 2 : 1 respectively.

11. What is the ratio between the number of boys who have opted for only Hindi and the number of girls who have opted for the composite subject respectively?
    (a) 15 : 16　　　　　(b) 10 : 7
    (c) 10 : 9　　　　　(d) 11 : 12
    (e) None of these

12. How many boys have opted for the composite subject?
    (a) 30　　　　　(b) 15
    (c) 21　　　　　(d) 32
    (e) None of these

13. How many girls have opted for only Sanskrit?
    (a) 72　　　　　(b) 47
    (c) 51　　　　　(d) 77
    (e) None of these

DIRECTIONS (Qs. 14-18): *Answer these questions on the basis of the information given below:*

(i) In a class of 80 students the girls and the boys are in the ratio of 3:5. The students can speak only Hindi or only English or both Hindi and English.

(ii) The number of boys and the number of girls who can speak only Hindi is equal and each of them is 40% of the total number of girls.

(iii) 10% of the girls can speak both the languages and 58% of the boys can speak only English.

14. How many girls can speak only English?
    (a) 12　　(b) 29　　(c) 18　　(d) 15
    (e) None of these

15. In all how many boys can speak Hindi?
    (a) 21　　　　　(b) 9
    (c) 24　　　　　(d) Data inadequate
    (e) None of these

16. What percentage of all the students (boys and girls together) can speak only Hindi?
    (a) 24　　(b) 40　　(c) 50　　(d) 30
    (e) None of these

17. In all how many students (boys and girls together) can speak both the languages?
    (a) 15　　(b) 12　　(c) 9　　(d) 29
    (e) None of these

18. How many boys can speak either only Hindi or only English?
    (a) 25　　(b) 38　　(c) 41　　(d) 29
    (e) None of these

DIRECTIONS (Qs. 19-23): *Study the following information to answer the questions given below:*

(i) The ratio of the populations of males, females and children (10 years old and above is) 11 : 10 : 9 in a state . Out of which 40% males or 8800 males are literate, 20% children (10 year old and above) are illiterate while 30% females are literate.

(ii) The number of children below 10 years of age is 10% of the number of females. 5% of the total population of the state are below poverty line and 80% of them are illiterate.

19. What is the number of illiterate persons below the poverty line?
    (a) 2480　　　　　(b) 3100
    (c) 620　　　　　(d) Cannot be determined
    (e) None of these

20. What is the total population of the State?
    (a) 60,000　　　　　(b) 62,000
    (c) 42,000　　　　　(d) 40,000
    (e) None of these

21. What is the number of literate children of age 10 years and above?
    (a) 14400%　　　　　(b) 14800%
    (c) 16200%　　　　　(d) 12600%
    (e) None of these

22. Total number of women is what percentage of the total population of the State? (rounded off to two places of decimal)
    (a) 28.86%　　　　　(b) 30.25%
    (c) 32.86%　　　　　(d) 32.26%
    (e) None of these

23. How many women are illiterate?
    (a) 20000　　　　　(b) 6000
    (c) 14400　　　　　(d) 16800
    (e) None of these

DIRECTIONS (Qs. 24-27): *Study the given information and answer the questions that follow:*

The students of a school have an option to study either only English, only maths or both. Out of 175 students in the school, boys and girls are in the ratio of 3:4 respectively. 40% percent of the boys opted only for English. 44% of the students opted only for maths. Out of the number of girls 32% opted for both the subjects. The number of boys who opted for only maths and both subjects are in the ratio of 2:1 respectively.

24. What is the ratio of the number of boys who have opted for only English and the number of girls who have opted both subjects?
    (a) 14:17　　　　　(b) 15:16
    (c) 12:13　　　　　(d) 16:19
    (e) None of these

25. How many boys have opted for both subjects?
    (a) 21　　　　　(b) 32
    (c) 30　　　　　(d) 15
    (e) None of these

26. How many girls are opted for only maths?
    (a) 32   (b) 20
    (c) 47   (d) 15
    (e) None of these

27. The number of boys who opted for only maths is what percent less than number of girls who opted for maths?
    (a) 32%   (b) 33%
    (c) 36%   (d) 38%
    (e) 39%

DIRECTIONS (Qs. 28-33): *Study the following charts and answer the following questions:*

In a school there are total of 240 staff members and 1600 students. 65 percent of the numbers of staff members are teachers and the remaining staff members are administrative officials. Out of the total number of the students 45 percent are girls. Twenty percent of the number of girls can speak only English. The remaining girls can speak both Hindi and English. Three-fourths of the number of boys can speak only English. The remaining boys can speak both Hindi and English. Two-thirds of the numbers of teachers are males. Five-fourteens of the number of the administrative officials are females.

28. What is the difference between the number of boys (students) who can speak both Hindi and English and the number of girls (students) who can speak both Hindi and English?
    (a) 346   (b) 356
    (c) 376   (d) 400
    (e) None of these

29. The total number of girls students is what percent of the total number of staff members in the school?
    (a) 100%   (b) 200%
    (c) 300%   (d) 400%
    (e) None of these

30. Sum of the number of female administrative officials and female teachers is how many greater than the number of male administrative officials?
    (a) 14   (b) 22   (c) 28   (d) 30
    (e) None of these

31. What is the ratio of the total number of teachers to the number of boys (students) who can speak English only?
    (a) 13:53   (b) 13:55
    (c) 13:56   (d) 13:57
    (e) None of these

32. What is the total number of male administrative officials, female teachers and girls (students) who can speak English only?
    (a) 125   (b) 225
    (c) 250   (d) 300
    (e) None of these

33. What is the ratio of the number of male administrative staff to the number of girls students who speak only English?
    (a) 5:8   (b) 3:11
    (c) 3:7   (d) 3:8
    (e) None of these

DIRECTIONS (Qs. 34-38): *Study the following information carefully and answer the given questions.*

Among 800 cricket players, 45% played in IPL –1 and 6.25% played only in IPL –1. Again, 57.5% players played in IPL –2 and 11.25% players played only in IPL –2. Again, 72.5% players played in IPL –3 and 27.5% players played only in IPL –3. Twenty per cent players played in all three IPL tournaments.

34. How many players are there who played in IPL –1 and IPL –2 but not in IPL –3?
    (a) 210   (b) 190
    (c) 120   (d) 220

35. What is the percentage of players who played in IPL –2 and IPL –3 but not in IPL –1?
    (a) 65%   (b) 56.25%
    (c) 75%   (d) 55%

36. What is the percentage of the number of players who played in at least two IPL tournaments?
    (a) 30%   (b) 35%
    (c) 45%   (d) 55%

37. The number of players who played only in either IPL –1 or IPL –2 is what percentage of number of players who played in all the three IPL?
    (a) 72%   (b) 75%
    (c) 87%   (d) 87.5%

38. The number of players who played in at most one IPL tournament is what percentage more/less than the number of players who played in at least one IPL?
    (a) 55% more   (b) 55% less
    (c) 40% more   (d) 40% less

DIRECTIONS (Qs. 39-43): *Study the following information carefully to answer the questions that follow:*

A company produces 4 different products, viz AC, fans, refrigerators and ovens, each product of two different qualities i.e, Quality A and Quality B. The company produces a total of 500 products. One-fifth of total number of products are fans, out of which 35% are of Quality B. Fifteen percent of the total number of products are AC. Two-thirds of the ACs are of Quality A. Twenty five per cent of the total number of products are refrigerators, out of which 40 are of quality B. Ten per cent of the number of ovens are of Quality B.

39. What is the total number of AC and ovens of Quality B and fans and refrigerators of Quality A together made by the company?
    (a) 165   (b) 205
    (c) 155   (d) 195

40. What is the average number of products of Quality A made by the company?
    (a) 90   (b) 75   (c) 80   (d) 95

41. What is the ratio of the number of ovens of Quality B to the number of fans of Quality A?
    (a) 5 : 2   (b) 4 : 13   (c) 5 : 13   (d) 4 : 9

42. What is the difference between the number of ACs of Quality A and Quality B?
    (a) 25   (b) 50
    (c) 35   (d) 40

43. The number of refrigerators of Quality A is approximately what percentage of the total number of ovens (both Quality A and B together)?
    (a) 39   (b) 31
    (c) 35   (d) 43

DIRECTIONS (Qs. 44-48): *Study the information carefully to answer the questions that follow.*

A company produced five different products, viz mobile phone, pen drive, calculator, television and washing machine. The total number of all the five products is 1650. 24% of the total number of products is mobile phones. One-sixth of the total number of products is pen drives. 14% of the total number of products is calculators. Remaining products are either television or washing machine. The number of washing machines is 50 more than the number of televisions produced.

44. What is the ratio of the number of washing machines to the number of calculators produced by the company?
    (a) 17 : 11   (b) 19 : 11
    (c) 11 : 17   (d) 19 : 13

45. If 24 per cent of the pen drives are defective, what is the number of pen drives which are not defective?
    (a) 209   (b) 215
    (c) 219   (d) 225

46. The number of televisions produced is approximately what per cent of the total number of calculators and washing machines produced together?
    (a) 63   (b) 55
    (c) 59   (d) 51

47. What is the difference between the total number of televisions and mobile phones together and the number of calculators produced?
    (a) 534   (b) 524
    (c) 514   (d) 523

48. What is the total number of pen drives, calculators and washing machines produced by the company?
    (a) 907
    (b) 917
    (c) 925
    (d) 905

DIRECTIONS (Qs. 49-53): *These questions are based on the following data. Study it carefully and answer the questions that follow.*

In a school having 400 students, boys and girls are in the ratio of 3 : 5. The students speak Hindi, English or both the languages. 12% of the boys speak only Hindi. 22% of the girls speak only English. 24% of the total students speak only Hindi and the number of boys speaking both the languages is six times the number of boys speaking only Hindi.

49. How many boys speak Hindi?
    (a) 18   (b) 126   (c) 108   (d) 26

50. How many girls speak only Hindi?
    (a) 55   (b) 117
    (c) 96   (d) 78

51. How many students speak English?
    (a) 304   (b) 79
    (c) 225   (d) 117

52. The number of girls speaking only Hindi is what per cent of the total number of students speaking only Hindi?
    (a) 38.2%   (b) 71.8%
    (c) 31.2%   (d) None of these

53. What is the ratio of the number of boys to the number of girls speaking both the languages?
    (a) 23 : 25   (b) 12 : 25
    (c) 12 : 13   (d) 25 : 13

DIRECTIONS (Qs. 54-58): *For solving these questions we summarise the given information as below:*

Certain number of students passed from five colleges P, Q, R, S and T. Total students passed in College P is 18% of total passed students from all colleges. Ratio of total passed students from College Q to total passed students from College R is 11:10 and their average value is 840. From College S, 600 students passed which is 15% of total passed students and students passed in College T is 5/4th of number of total passed students of College R. Ratio of boys to girls passed from College P is 13 : 5. Number of passed boys in College Q is 240% of number of passed girls from College P. Ratio of total passed in College R to number of girls passed in College R is 20:11. Number of girls passed in College S is 40% more than the number of passed boys in College S or 40% more than the 25% of total students passed in College T. Average of boys passed in all five colleges is 462.

54. What is the average of total girls passed in all colleges?
    (a) 274   (b) 372
    (c) 338   (d) 369

55. What is the ratio of passed boys and girls of college T?
    (a) 5 : 3   (b) 4 : 3
    (c) 7 : 3   (d) 7 : 5

56. Number of boys passed in college Q is how much percentage more than the number of passed girls in college Q?
    (a) 20%   (b) 30%
    (c) 40%   (d) 45%

57. Number of girls passed in college P is what percent of number of passed boys in college S?
    (a) 60%   (b) 70%
    (c) 80%   (d) 40%

58. In which college the percentage of girls passed with respect to its total passed students is maximum?
    (a) P   (b) Q
    (c) R   (d) S

DIRECTIONS (Qs. 59-63): *Study the following information carefully and answer the given questions.*

In a UN conference there were 400 delegates. Out of them 45% delegates speak English. The ratio between number of people speaking French and number of people speaking Latin is 5 : 7. Difference between the number of people speaking English and number of people speaking Latin is 10% of the total number of delegates. Among these three languages English speaking people are maximum. 30 delegates are there who can speak English and French but cannot speak Latin and it is 25% more than the number of people who can speak French and Latin. 5% of the delegates can speak all three languages. Number of people who can speak English and Latin but cannot speak French is 10.

59. How many delegates are there who can speak only one language out of English, French and Latin?
    (a) 224   (b) 248
    (c) 221   (d) 280

60. How many delegates are there who can not speak any of three language out of English, French, Latin?
    (a) 64   (b) 48
    (c) 44   (d) 36

61. How many delegates can speak at least two languages out of English, French, and Latin?
    (a) 64   (b) 80
    (c) 88   (d) 104

62. How many delegates are there who can speak exact two languages out of English, French, and Latin?
    (a) 24   (b) 36
    (c) 40   (d) 44

63. How many delegates are there who can speak at most two languages?
    (a) 316   (b) 380
    (c) 248   (d) 296

DIRECTIONS (Qs. 64-68): *Study the following information and answer the questions that follow:*

The premises of a bank are to be renovated. The renovation is in terms of flooring. Certain areas are to be floored either with marble or wood. All rooms/halls and pantry are rectangular. The area to be renovated comprises a hall for customer transaction measuring 23m by 29m, the branch manager's room measuring 13m by 17m, a pantry measuring 14m by 13m, a record keeping-cum-server room measuring 21m by 13 m and locker area measuring 29m by 21m. The total area of the bank is 2000 square metres. The cost of wooden flooring is ₹170 per square metre and the cost of marble flooring is ₹ 190 per square metre. The locker area, record keeping-cum-server room and pantry are to be floored with marble. The branch manager's room and the hall for customer transaction are to be floored with wood. No other area is to be renovated in terms of flooring.

64. What is the ratio of the total cost of wooden flooring to the total cost of marble flooring?
    (a) 1879 : 2527   (b) 1887 : 2386
    (c) 1887 : 2527   (d) 1829 : 2527

65. If the four walls and ceiling of the branch manager's room (the height of the room is 12 metres) are to be painted at the cost of ₹190 per square metre, how much will be the total cost of renovation of the branch manager's room, including the cost of flooring?
    (a) ₹ 1,36,800   (b) ₹ 2,16,360
    (c) ₹ 1,78,790   (d) ₹ 2,11,940

66. If the remaining area of the bank is to be carpeted at the rate of ₹110 per square metre, how much will be the increment in the total cost of renovation of bank premises?
    (a) ₹ 5,280   (b) ₹ 4,848
    (c) ₹ 3,689   (d) ₹ 6,690

67. What is the percentage area of the bank that is not to be renovated?
    (a) 2.2%   (b) 2.4%
    (c) 4.2%   (d) 4.4%

68. What is the total cost of renovation of the hall for customer transaction and the locker area?
    (a) ₹ 2,29,100   (b) ₹ 2,30,206
    (c) ₹ 2,16,920   (d) ₹ 2,42,440

DIRECTIONS (Qs. 69-73): *Study the following information carefully to answer the questions that follow:*

There are two trains, Train A and Train B. Both trains have four different types of coaches, viz General, Sleeper, First Class and AC. In Train A, there are total 700 passengers. Train B has thirty per cent more passengers than Train A. Twenty per cent of the passengers of Train A are in General Coach. One-fourth of the total number of passengers of Train A are in AC coach. Twenty three per cent of the passengers of Train A are in Sleeper Coach. Remaining passengers of Train A are in First Class Coach. The total number of passengers in AC Coach in both the trains together is 480. Thirty per cent of the numbers of passengers of Train B are in Sleeper Coach. Ten per cent of the total passengers of Train B are in First Class Coach. The remaining passengers of Train B are in General Coach.

69. What is the ratio of the number of passengers in First Class Coach of Train A to the number of passengers in Sleeper Coach of Train B?
    (a) 13 : 7   (b) 7: 13
    (c) 32 : 39   (d) Data Inadequate

70. What is the total number of passengers in the General Coach of Train A and the AC Coach of Train B together?
    (a) 449   (b) 459
    (c) 435   (d) 445

71. What is the difference between the number of passengers in the AC Coach of Train A and the total number of passengers in Sleeper and First Class Coach together of Train B?
    (a) 199   (b) 178
    (c) 187   (d) None of these

72. The total number of passengers in General Coaches of both the trains together is approximately what percentage of the total number of passengers in Train B?
    (a) 35   (b) 42   (c) 46   (d) 38

73. If the cost per ticket of First Class coach is ₹ 450, what will be the total amount generated from First Class Coach of Train A?
  (a) ₹ 1,00,080
  (b) ₹ 1,08,000
  (c) ₹ 1,00,800
  (d) ₹ 10,800

DIRECTIONS (Qs. 74-78): *In the paragraph some data is given about some different workshops. Study the paragraph carefully and answer the related questions.*

In workshop A number of workers is 20% more than that of D, where number of male workers is 40% less than that of female workers. Number of workers in workshop E is 50% more than that of C and in E number of male workers is equal to the number of female workers. Respective ratio of number of workers in A, C and B is 12 : 10 : 9. Number of female workers in B is 60% of total number of workers in this workshop. Number of male workers in A is two times of the number of male workers in B. Number of female workers in A is 25% more than male workers in C. Difference between number of male workers and female workers in B is 360.

74. Total number of male workers in all workshops together is what percent more/less than total number of female workers in all workshops together?
  (a) 14%
  (b) 12%
  (c) 19%
  (d) 24%
  (e) None of these

75. If 60% of male workers and 70% female workers are trained workers in workshop E then what is percentage of trained workers in this workshop?
  (a) 55%
  (b) 65%
  (c) 80%
  (d) 60%
  (e) None of these

76. If average salary of a worker of workshop C is 6000 and respective ratio of salary of a male worker and salary of a female worker in this workshop is 5 : 4 then what is salary of a male worker in C?
  (a) 5264
  (b) 7853
  (c) 6843
  (d) 4368
  (e) None of these

77. Number of female workers in D is what percent more/less than average number of female workers in all workshops together?
  (a) 5.49%
  (b) 8.73%
  (c) 4.22%
  (d) 3.78%
  (e) None of these

78. What is respective ratio of number of male workers in workshop C and number of female workers in workshop D?
  (a) 62 : 81
  (b) 71 : 89
  (c) 68 : 87
  (d) 34 : 53
  (e) None of these

DIRECTIONS(Qs. 79–83): *In the paragraph some information is given about income and expenditure of some different persons. Study the given information carefully and answer the related questions.*

Income of A is 25% more than his expenditure and his saving is two times of the saving of C who saves 40% of his income. Saving of B is 50% of his expenditure and his salary is 50% more than that of E. Saving of E is 50% less than that of A. Expenditure of D is 25% less than that of B and his saving is 40% more than that of C. Expenditure of A is 36000 more than his saving. E saves 30% of his salary.

79. Total saving of all persons together is what percent of total income of all persons together?
  (a) 32.37%
  (b) 31.67%
  (c) 33.33%
  (d) 16.67%
  (e) None of these

80. If income of B is increase by 40% and he increases his expenditure by 30% then what is increment recorded in his saving?
  (a) 50%
  (b) 35%
  (c) 45%
  (d) 60%
  (e) None of these

81. What is respective ratio of average expenditure and average saving of all persons together?
  (a) 112 : 165
  (b) 256 : 121
  (c) 265 : 112
  (d) 112 : 265
  (e) None of these

82. Saving of E is what percent of average saving of all persons together?
  (a) 75.70%
  (b) 70.75%
  (c) 71.75%
  (d) 68.75%
  (e) None of these

83. What is difference between average income of A & E and average income of B, C & D?
  (a) 17200
  (b) 22800
  (c) 23500
  (d) 12800
  (e) None of these

DIRECTIONS (Qs. 84–88): *In the paragraph some information is given about some different trains. Study the given paragraph carefully and answer the related questions.*

Train A starts its journey at 5 A.M and reaches its destination at 7 P.M same day. Train D covers 25% more distance than train A in 50% more time than A. B covers a distance equal to total distance covered by A and D together and it takes 2 hrs more than A. Distance covered by train E is 20% less than train D. Speed of train C is five times of the time taken by train B and it takes equal time as train A. Train C coveres 12% more distance than train A. Speed of train C is 20% less than that of train E.

84. What is respective ratio of speeds of train C and that of train A?
  (a) 5 : 8
  (b) 25 : 28
  (c) 28 : 25
  (d) 13 : 17
  (e) None of these

85. If speed of train D is increased by 20% then what is time required to cover a distance covered by A?
  (a) 12 hrs   (b) 10 hrs   (c) 20 hrs   (d) 7 hrs
  (e) None of these

86. What is average distance covered by A, C and E together?
    - (a) 1210 km
    - (b) 960 km
    - (c) 1020 km
    - (d) 1040 km
    - (e) None of these

87. What is respective ratio of speed of B and that of D?
    - (a) 189 : 80
    - (b) 80 : 89
    - (c) 80 : 189
    - (d) 180 : 89
    - (e) None of these

88. What is average speed of all trains together?
    - (a) 82.86 km/h
    - (b) 88.26 km/h
    - (c) 76.56 km/h
    - (d) 89.86 km/h
    - (e) None of these

DIRECTIONS (Qs. 89–93): *In the paragraph some information is given about a shopkeeper who sells different things. Study the information carefully and answer the related questions.*

A shopkeeper sells some different electronic goods. T.V is sold at 10% loss after a discount of 20%. Respective ratio of selling price of T.V and A.C is 2 : 5 and A.C is sold at 20% profit after 20% discount. Profit occurred on P.C is 50% of that of A.C which is 5 times of that of cooler which is sold at 30% profit after a discount of 35%.

Cost price of Music system is 50% more than that of cooler and its selling price is 30% of the cost price of A.C. Marked price of Music system is equal to average marked price of all other electronic goods. Profit amount on A.C is 12000. P.C is sold at 20% Profit after a discount of 40%.

89. If all electronic goods were sold at marked price than what would be the profit of shopkeeper?
    - (a) 77.8%
    - (b) 78.7%
    - (c) 82.4%
    - (d) 66.6%
    - (e) None of these

90. What is respective ratio of total profit amount and total discount amount for all electronic goods together?
    - (a) 32 : 55
    - (b) 23 : 87
    - (c) 54 : 89
    - (d) 78 : 97
    - (e) None of these

91. What is difference between profit occurred on A.C and profit occurred on P.C?
    - (a) 12000
    - (b) 6000
    - (c) 4000
    - (d) 8000
    - (e) None of these

92. What is discount given by shopkeeper for all electronic goods together?
    - (a) 57.34%
    - (b) 31.52%
    - (c) 34.57%
    - (d) 31.45%
    - (e) None of these

93. If 10% additional discount is allowed on T.V and 20% additional discount is allowed on P.C then what would be the respective ratio of selling price of T.V to that of P.C?
    - (a) 7 : 9
    - (b) 8 : 9
    - (c) 10 : 9
    - (d) 9 : 10
    - (e) None of these

DIRECTIONS (Qs. 94–98): *In the paragraph some information is given about some different schools. Study the given information carefully and answer the related questions.*

Respectives ratio of number of boys and that of girls in school A is 5 : 4 and 50% of total student are passed. Number of students in school C is 20% more than that of school E. Respective ratio of number of girls in schools B, C and D is 5 : 6 : 4. Number of boys in school E is 20% more than that of school A and number of boys in school C is 25% more than that of girls in this school. In school D number of boys is 25% less than that of girls in this school. Number of boys in school B is 20% more than number of boys in school A. Difference between number of students in school A and school E is 720. Number of students in school A is 20% less than that of E.

94. What is respective ratio of total number of boys and total number of girls in all schools together?
    - (a) 110 : 97
    - (b) 97 : 110
    - (c) 11 : 9
    - (d) 121 : 95
    - (e) None of these

95. If 40% of total number of girls are failed in school C and 50% of total number of boys are passed in school C then what is pass percentage of students in this school?
    - (a) 50.44%
    - (b) 54.4%
    - (c) 51.4%
    - (d) 57.4%
    - (e) None of these

96. If 20% boys are absent from exam in school D and 10% students are absent from school E then what is difference between number of students who attended exam from schools D and E?
    - (a) 1240
    - (b) 1352
    - (c) 1192
    - (d) 1760
    - (e) None of these

97. If 50% boys and 60% girls are failed in exam from school B then number of passed students in A is what percent to the number of passed students from school B?
    - (a) 116.7%
    - (b) 66.7%
    - (c) 110%
    - (d) 90%
    - (e) None of these

98. Average number of boys in schools A, C, E is what percent more/less than average number of girls in schools B and D?
    - (a) 27%
    - (b) 31%
    - (c) 45%
    - (d) 12%
    - (e) None of these

DIRECTIONS (Qs. 99-103): *In the paragraph some information is given about some different workshops. Study the given information carefully and answer the related questions.*

Number of workers in workshop A is 50% more than number of workers in workshop D where number of workers is 20% less than the number of workers in workshop B. Number of male workers in B is 20% more than number of male workers in workshop E where Number of male worker is equal to number of female workers in this workshop. Number of workers in workshop C is 25% more than number of workers in workshop D where number of male workers is 50% of number of female workers in this workshop. Respective ratio of number of male workers and female workers in A is 2 : 1. Number of female workers in C is 45% of total number of workers in this workshop.

99. 50% of male worker and 40% female workers are trained in workshop B and respective ratio of salary of a trained worker and that of a untrained worker is 2 : 1, then what percent of total amount is received by untrained workers in this workshop?
(a) 32%   (b) 34%
(c) 43%   (d) 49%
(e) None of these

100. What is difference between average number of male workers and that of female workers in all workshops together?
(a) 405   (b) 316
(c) 305   (d) 302
(e) None of these

101. Number of trained workers is 50% of total number of workers in A and number of trained workers is 60% in workshop C then what is respective ratio of number of untrained workers in A and C?
(a) 1 : 2   (b) 2 : 3
(c) 3 : 2   (d) 2 : 1
(e) None of these

102. If salary of a male worker is 5000 and salary of a female worker is 4500 in workshop D then what is respective ratio of expenditure of workshop for the salary of male workers and that of female workers ?
(a) 4 : 9   (b) 4 : 5
(c) 9 : 5   (d) 5 : 9
(e) None of these

103. Number of male workers in workshop A is what percent of average number of workers in all workshops together?
(a) 75.82%   (b) 89%
(c) 59%   (d) 80%
(e) None of these

DIRECTIONS (Qs. 104–108): *In the paragraph some information is given about some different students who attended exam from different schools. Study the given informations carefully and answer the related questions.*

A gets 20% more marks than C and B gets 25% less marks than C. D gets 60% of full marks. Marks of E is 20% more than that of C. In Math C gets 25% more marks than D who gets 60% marks in this subject. Full marks of Math, Hindi and English are 200, 200 and 100 respectively. Marks obtained by A in math is 40% more than D who obtained 25% less marks than E. Respective ratio of marks obtained by B in Math, Hindi and English is 6 : 4 : 5. B obtained 75% marks in English which is 15 more than marks obtained by B in Hindi. A gets 60% marks in Hindi. A obtained 20% more marks than C in English. Respective ratio of marks obtained by D in Math and Hindi is 4 : 3. Marks obtained by D in English is 50% more than marks obtained by E is this subject.

104. What is difference between total marks obtained by B and that of D?
(a) 75   (b) 50   (c) 60   (d) 90
(e) None of these

105. What is overall percentage of marks obtained by all students together in English?
(a) 75%   (b) 78%
(c) 82%   (d) 63%
(e) None of these

106. What is difference between average marks obtained by all students together in Math and Hindi?
(a) 35.8   (b) 37.6
(c) 38.4   (d) 42.2
(e) None of these

107. What is overall percentage of marks obtained by A in all subjects together?
(a) 61%   (b) 77%
(c) 72%   (d) 68%
(e) None of these

108. What is respective ratio of total marks obtained by all students together is Hindi and total marks obtained by all students together in English?
(a) 500 : 367   (b) 500 : 397
(c) 400 : 257   (d) 500 : 357
(e) None of these

DIRECTIONS (Qs. 109–113): *In the paragraph some data is given about Income and expenditure of some different persons. Study the paragraph carefully and answer the related questions.*

A spends 80% of his salary. Salary of C is twice of the expenditure of D who saves 40% of his salary. Salary of E is 50% more than that of A and his expenditure is 25% more than that of D. Saving of A is 20% less than that of B who saves 25% of his salary. Saving of C is two times of that of A. Saving of C is 40% less than his expenditure.

109. What is difference between average expenditure of all the persons together and average saving of all the persons together?
(a) 24800   (b) 32600
(c) 22800   (d) 32800
(e) None of these

110. What is respective ratio of average salary of A, B and E together to that of C an D together?
(a) 15 : 8   (b) 105 : 82
(c) 77 : 92   (d) 105 : 93
(e) None of these

111. Average salary of all persons together is what percent more/ less than salary of B?
(a) 8.9%   (b) 9.1%   (c) 9.5%   (d) 8.7%
(e) None of these

112. Expenditure of C is what percent of total saving of A, B, D and E together?
(a) 42.1%   (b) 24.1%   (c) 41.2%   (d) 46.7%
(e) None of these

113. What is respective ratio of average salary of all the persons together to average expenditure of all the persons together?
    (a) 911 : 655　　(b) 752 : 915
    (c) 615 : 982　　(d) 982 : 615
    (e) None of these

DIRECTIONS (Qs. 114-118): *In the paragraph some information is given about some different students who attended final exam of different subjects. Study the paragraph carefully and answer the related questions:*

A obtained 60% marks in all three subjects together. Full marks of Maths, Hindi and English are 200, 150 and 150 respectively. B obtained 20% less marks than C who obtained 25% more marks than A in all subjects together. Respective ratio of overall marks obtained by B, D and E is 6 : 8 : 7. Marks obtained by B in Math is 25% more than that of Hindi and marks obtained by him in English is equal to that of Hindi. Marks obtained by D in Math is 75% of full marks and respective ratio of marks obtained by D in Hindi and English is 4 : 5. Difference between marks obtained by C and A is 75. Respective ratio of marks obtained by C in Math, English and Hindi is 6 : 4 : 5. A obtained 80% marks in English and 40% marks in Hindi. Marks obtained by E in Math is 25% more than that of A and marks obtained by him in Hindi is 20% less than that of C.

114. What is average percentage of marks obtained by all students together in English?
    (a) 73.48%　　(b) 74.38%
    (c) 78.43%　　(d) 84.73%
    (e) None of these

115. What is respective ratio of total marks obtained by A and that of C in all subjects together?
    (a) 5 : 4　　(b) 4 : 5
    (c) 3 : 2　　(d) 2 : 3
    (e) None of these

116. Overall marks obtained by D in all subjects together is what percent more/less than overall marks obtained by E in all subjects together?
    (a) 12.48%　　(b) 18.42%
    (c) 14.28%　　(d) 15.67%
    (e) None of these

117. What is difference between average marks obtained by all students together in Math and English?
    (a) 32.86　　(b) 62.86
    (c) 28.66　　(d) 26.86
    (e) None of these

118. What is average percentage of marks obtained by all students in all subjects together?
    (a) 59 %　　(b) 79 %
    (c) 81 %　　(d) 65 %
    (e) None of these

DIRECTIONS (Qs. 119-123): *In the paragraph some information is given about income and expenditure of some different persons. Study the paragraph carefully and answer the related questions.*

A spends 75% of his income. Income of B is 25% less than C which is 25% more than that of E. D spends 70% of his income and his saving is 50% more than saving of A. Respective ratio of expenditure of A and that of B is 6 : 5 and respective ratio of expenditure and saving of B is 5 : 3. Difference between saving of D and that of A is Rs. 36000. Expenditure of E is two times of the saving of B. Expenditure of C is 25% less than income of B.

119. Average expenditure of all persons together is what percent of average income of all persons together?
    (a) 70.57%　　(b) 69.67%
    (c) 64.31%　　(d) 62.77%
    (e) None of these

120. Transport expenditure of C is 25% of his total expenditure and Food expenditure of C is 20% of his total income then what is respective ratio of transport expenditure and Food expenditure of C?
    (a) 7 : 8　　(b) 9 : 8
    (c) 64 : 45　　(d) 45 : 64
    (e) None of these

121. What is difference between average expenditure and average saving of all persons together?
    (a) 106650　　(b) 105660
    (c) 106560　　(d) 122660
    (e) None of these

122. If income of A and E is increase by 20% and 30% respectively then income of E is what percent more/less than that of A?
    (a) 16.35%　　(b) 18.40%
    (c) 19%　　(d) 19.56%
    (e) None of these

123. What is respective ratio of average income of A, C and E together and that of B and D together?
    (a) 136 : 135　　(b) 135 : 136
    (c) 125 : 127　　(d) 127 : 135
    (e) None of these

DIRECTIONS (Qs. 124-128): *In the paragraph some information is given about a shop. Study the paragraph carefully and answer the related questions.*

Cost price of a bed is 25% less than its selling prices and its marked price is 50% more than its cost price. Cost price a sofa is 20% less than that of bed and it is sold at 20% profit after a discount of 20%. Respective ratio of cost price of bed and that of dining set is 3 : 4 and respective ratio of marked price of sofa and dining set is 5 : 8. Dining set is sold at 20% profit. Cost price of a dressing table is 50% of that of sofa and its marked price is 60% of that of bed and it is sold at 25% discount. Cost price of a bookself is 60% of that dressing table and it is sold at 40% profit after 30% discount. Profit occurred on bed is Rs. 18000.

124. If all items were sold at marked price then what would be the percentage of profit?
    (a) 59 %　　(b) 55 %
    (c) 49 %　　(d) 69 %
    (e) None of these

125. What is respective ratio of total profit amount and total discount amount of all items together?
    (a) 3287 : 3393
    (b) 3393 : 3287
    (c) 3293 : 3387
    (d) 3387 : 3293
    (e) None of these

126. What is overall percentage of profit on all items together?
    (a) 28.87%
    (b) 31.27%
    (c) 29.97%
    (d) 22.97%
    (e) None of these

127. Profit occurred on bed is what percent more/less than that of dining set?
    (a) 35%
    (b) $33\frac{1}{3}\%$
    (c) 20%
    (d) 25%
    (e) None of these

128. What is difference between average marked price and average selling price of all items together?
    (a) 11200
    (b) 11800
    (c) 13200
    (d) 12500
    (e) None of these

DIRECTIONS (Qs. 129-133): *In the paragraph some information is given about some different trains. Study the paragraph carefully and answer the related questions.*

Train A starts at 10 AM on Monday and completes its journey at 8 AM on Tuesday. Train D covers 25% less distance than train A and it takes 50% less time than train A. Respective ratio of speed of train D and that of train E is 4 : 5 . Respective ratio of speed of trains A, C and B is 5 : 6 : 8. Speed of train A is 60 km/h on first day and it runs with $\frac{5}{6}$ th of its original speed on second day.

Running time of train A is 10% more than that of B. Respective ratio of time taken by D and that of E is 1 : 2. Respective ratio of distance covered by train C and train D is 4 : 3.

129. What is average speed of all the trains together?
    (a) 80.79 km/h
    (b) 79.80 km/h
    (c) 97.80 km/h
    (d) 89.07 km/h
    (e) None of these

130. Average speed of train A is what percent more/less than of E?
    (a) 52.6%
    (b) 46.6%
    (c) 54.7%
    (d) 58.6%
    (e) None of these

131. If train B crosses a 200 m platform in 20 sec and train D crosses a person standing on platform in 18 sec then what is respective ratio of length of train B and that of train D?
    (a) 6 : 5
    (b) 7 : 8
    (c) 11 : 17
    (d) 42 : 55
    (e) None of these

132. If destination of train A and C is interchanged then what is difference between their running time?
    (a) 4 hrs
    (b) 2.7 hrs
    (c) 4.5 hrs
    (d) 3.7 hrs
    (e) None of these

133. What is average distance covered by all trains together?
    (a) 1597.72 km
    (b) 1707.72 km
    (c) 1507.72 km
    (d) 1102.77 km
    (e) None of these

DIRECTIONS (Qs. 134-138): *In the paragraph some information is given about the number of workers in different workshops. Study the paragraph carefully and answer the related questions.*

Number of workers in workshop B is 25% more than that of workers in workshop E. Respective ratio of number of workers in workshops A and C is 5 : 6 and number of worker in workshop A is 20% more than number of workers in workshop B. Number of workers in workshop D is 20% more than that of workers in workshop A. Respective ratio of number of male workers and that of female workers in workshop A is 3 : 2. Respective ratio of number of male workers in workshop A and that of male workers in workshop C is 6 : 7. Number of female workers in workshop D is 20% less than that of male workers in this workshop. Number of workers in workshop C is 900 more than that workers in workshop A. Number of female workers in B is 50% more than number of male workers in this workshop. Respective ratio of number of male workers and that of female workers in workshop E is 1 : 2.

134. What is difference between average number of male workers and that of female workers in all workshops together?
    (a) 130
    (b) 560
    (c) 590
    (d) 630
    (e) None of these

135. 50% male workers and 40% female workers are trained in workshop D and salary of a trained worker is 25% more than that of an untrained worker then total salary of all trained workers of D is what percent of salary of all workers in D?
    (a) 47.2%
    (b) 51.12%
    (c) 67.8%
    (d) 71.1%
    (e) None of these

136. What is respective ratio of total number of male workers and total number of female workers in all workshops together?
    (a) 62 : 95
    (b) 61 : 97
    (c) 74 : 67
    (d) 67 : 73
    (e) None of these

137. Respective ratio of salary of a male worker and that of a female worker in C is 5 : 4 then total salary of male workers is what percent more/less than total salary of female workers in this workshop?
    (a) 25%
    (b) 85%
    (c) 75%
    (d) 50%
    (e) None of these

138. What is respective ratio of average number of workers in workshops A, C and E and that of workers in workshops B and D?
    (a) 178 : 213
    (b) 182 : 173
    (c) 183 : 172
    (d) 172 : 183
    (e) None of these

DIRECTIONS (Qs. 139-143): *In the paragraph some information is given about some different runners. Study the paragraph carefully and answer the related questions:*

Five runners are participating in a race of 1 km. In a race of 200 m A can beat D by 10 sec. C is 25% more as fast runner as E. If A and E are running in a 100 m race then E looses by 20 m or 5 sec. B crosses a 200 m long train in 50 sec when train is standing on the platform.

139. If A and B are running on circular race track in same direction and length of track is 500 m then they will meet at starting point after:-
    (a) 500 sec
    (b) 1000 sec
    (c) 250 sec
    (d) 100 sec
    (e) None of these

140. What is average speed of all runners together in the race of 1 km?
    (a) 3.44 m/s
    (b) 4. 34 m/s
    (c) 5 m/s
    (d) 4.8 m/s
    (e) None of these

141. If A crosses a train standing on platform in 20 sec and D. Crosses a bridge in 30 sec then what is respective ratio of length of train to length of bridge?
    (a) 4 : 5
    (b) 6 : 5
    (c) 5 : 6
    (d) 3 : 5
    (e) None of these

142. If A and C are running in a 200 metre race then A can win by
    (a) 10 sec
    (b) 5 sec
    (c) 15 sec
    (d) 20 sec
    (e) None of these

143. A 300 m long train is moving with certain speed. C is running parallel to train in same direction. If train crosses C in 12 sec then what is speed as the train?
    (a) 20 m/s
    (b) 25 m/s
    (c) 27 m/s
    (d) 30 m/s
    (e) None of these

DIRECTIONS (Qs. 144-148): *In the paragraph some information is given about the population of some different cities. Study the paragraph carefully and answer the related question:*

Total population of city A is 20% more than that of city D. 40% of total population of city A is population of females and 30% of male population and 20% of female population of this city are minors. Respective ratio of total population of cities B, D and E is 5 : 4 : 8 and population of city D is 20% less than total population of city C. 28% of total population of city C are minors where 25% of male population and 30% of female population are minors. Male population of city D is 25% more than female population of this city and 20% male population and 18% of total population are minors in this city. Respective ratio of male population and female population of city B is 3 : 2 and 25% of total population of city B are minors. Difference between total male population and total female population of city B is 25200. Respective ratio

of female population in cities B and E is 1 : 2. Respective ratio of number of male minors to that of female minors in city E is 5 : 4 and 20% of total population of this city are minors.

144. What is respective ratio of total number of adult persons in cities B and D?
    (a) 75 : 82
    (b) 137 : 253
    (c) 91 : 47
    (d) 56 : 95
    (e) None of these

145. Total number of minors in all cities together is what percent of total population of all cities together?
    (a) 24.10%
    (b) 22.30%
    (c) 32.20%
    (d) 23.20%
    (e) None of these

146. What is difference between average male population and average female population in all cities together?
    (a) 7870
    (b) 7780
    (c) 7078
    (d) 7178
    (e) None of these

147. 50% males and 25% females are employed in city A and child employment is not allowed then what percent of total population of city A is employed?
    (a) 30%
    (b) 40%
    (c) 50%
    (d) 45%
    (e) None of these

148. What is difference between adult population of cities C and D?
    (a) 8064
    (b) 6480
    (c) 6840
    (d) 8180
    (e) None of these

DIRECTIONS (Qs. 149-153): *In the paragraph some information is given about some different schools. Study the paragraph carefully and answer the related questions :*

Number of students in school A is 50% more than of in school C where respective ratio of number of boys and that of girls is 3 : 2. 30% boys and 40% girls are failed in the exam from school C. Number of boys in school E is 40% more than the Number of boys in school C and respective ratio of number of boys and that of girls in school E 7 : 6. Number of students in school D is 50 % more than that of in school A. 28% of total students are passed the exam from school E and 30% boys and 27% girls are passed in this school. Respective ratio of number of students in schools D and B is 5 : 8 and respective ratio of number of boys and that of girls in school B is 3 : 2. 50% boys and 75% girls are passed the exam from school B. Difference between Number of students in schools A and C is 6300. Number of boys and that of girls is equal in school A. Respective ratio of number of boys and that of girls in school D is 5 : 4. 30% of total students are failed in school A. 40% students are failed in school D.

149. What is passing percentage of students from all schools together?
    (a) 57.08%
    (b) 59.6%
    (c) 61.02%
    (d) can't be determined
    (e) None of these

150. What is difference between average number of boys and that of girls in all schools together?
  (a) 3270   (b) 3251
  (c) 3357   (d) 3421
  (e) None of these

151. What is respective ratio of passing percentage of students in schools A and E?
  (a) 3 : 5   (b) 2 : 5   (c) 5 : 2   (d) 4 : 5
  (e) None of these

152. What is respective ratio of number of passed students and that of failed students in school B?
  (a) 5 : 4   (b) 3 : 4
  (c) 2 : 3   (d) 3 : 2
  (e) None of these

153. What is difference between number of passed students and that of failed students in school D?
  (a) 5510   (b) 5160
  (c) 5480   (d) 6290
  (e) None of these

DIRECTIONS (Qs. 154-158) : *Study the following information carefully and answer the given questions:*

There are three states P, Q and R. Certain Number of Projects are allocated to these states under Scheme L, Scheme M and Scheme N in 2018.

Scheme L : The Number of Projects in State Q is 2/3rd of the Number of projects in State Q under Scheme M. The Number of Projects in State R is 4/5th of the Number of projects in State R under Scheme N. The Total Number of Projects in State P and State R is equal under Scheme L.

Scheme M : The Total Number of Projects under Scheme M is 750. The Number of Projects in State Q is 150 less than that of number of projects in State P and R together. The Number of Projects in State P is 5/6th of the number of projects in State P under Scheme N.

Scheme N : The Number of Projects under Scheme N is 4/5th of the number of Projects under Scheme M. The Number of Projects in State P is equal to the number of projects in State Q under Scheme M. The Number of Projects in State R under Scheme M and Scheme N is Equal.

154. In 2019, the projects allocated for State Q under Scheme M increases by 30%, and the project allocated for State R under scheme N decreases by 45%, then the total number of projects in 2019 for State Q under scheme M and State R under Scheme N is equal to total number of projects in which of the following States in 2018?
  (a) State R under Scheme L and State P under scheme N together
  (b) State Q under Scheme L and State R under scheme L together
  (c) State P under Scheme M and State Q under scheme N together
  (d) State R under Scheme M and State P under scheme N together
  (e) None of those given as options

155. What is the average number of projects under Scheme M and Scheme N for State R and State Q together?
  (a) 150   (b) 160
  (c) 200   (d) 300
  (e) None of those given as option

156. If the cost of each project is 15 crore for scheme L, and 19 crore for Scheme M, and 17 crore for Scheme N, then how much fund is allocated for State R under these three schemes (In Million)?
  (a) 96000   (b) 7600
  (c) 9600   (d) 108000
  (e) None of those given as option

157. What is the total number of projects under Scheme L and Scheme M together?
  (a) 560
  (b) 675
  (c) 720
  (d) None of those given as option
  (e) 635

158. In State X, The number of projects allocated under L is 20% more than that of number of projects allocated for State R under scheme L, and the number of projects allocated under scheme M is 40% less than that of number of projects allocated for state Q under scheme M and the total number of projects in State X is 600, then how many projects are allocated for state X under scheme N?
  (a) 308   (b) 200
  (c) 188   (d) 228
  (e) None of those given as option

DIRECTIONS (Qs.159-163): *Study the information carefully to answer the followings questions.*

Data regarding number of employees working in various departments in Company P and Q in the year 2018. Both Companies have six departments namely Production, HR, Finance, R&D, Marketing and Accounts. The total number of employees in company P is 18000. In Company P, number of employees in production, HR and finance together is 60% of the total number of employees. The number of employees in R&D, Marketing and Accounts were 2600, 2880 and 1720 respectively. The number of employees in Production department was 25% more than that of finance department. In company Q the number of employees in Marketing was 1800 and they constituted 12% of the total number of employees. Also the number of employees in Marketing was 40% less than that of HR department. The number of employees in production from company Q was 10% less than the same department from Company P. The number of employees in accounts is 1000. Number of employees in finance and R&D department is same. Total Number of employees in finance and R&D together were double the total Number of employees in Marketing and accounts together.

159. What is the difference between the total Number of employees in Marketing and Accounts together in Company P and that in the same courses together in Company Q?
  (a) 1400   (b) 400   (c) 800   (d) 1200
  (e) 1800

160. 3/4th of the number of R&D employees in Company P was female. If the number of female R&D employees in Company P is less than that of Company Q by 350, what is the number of male R&D employee in Company Q?
    (a) 1200
    (b) 800
    (c) 1000
    (d) 200
    (e) 1600

161. What is the respective ratio between the total number of employees in Finance and Production together in Company P and that in the same courses together in company Q?
    (a) 1 : 9
    (b) 7 : 3
    (c) 4 : 9
    (d) 9 : 8
    (e) 3 : 2

162. Number of HR employees in Company Q is what percent less than that in Company P?
    (a) 10/4%
    (b) 50/3%
    (c) 26/7%
    (d) 12/6%
    (e) 43/6%

163. Total number of employees in Company P, is what percent to that of in Company Q?
    (a) 120%
    (b) 160%
    (c) 216%
    (d) 567%
    (e) 230%

DIRECTIONS (Qs. 164-168) : *Read the given information carefully to answer the questions that follow:*

A college consisting of '3120' students has boys and girls in the ratio of 7:5 respectively. All the students enrolled for different country vis china, Canada and USA. One fifth of the boys are enrolled for only Canada tour. Twenty percent of the girls are enrolled for only USA tour. Ten percent of the boys are enrolled for only China four. Twenty four percent of the girls are enrolled for both China and Canada tour together. The number of girls enrolled for only China tour is two hundred percent of the boys enrolled in the same. One-thirteenth of the boys enrolled for all the three tour together. The respective ratio of boys enrolled for Canada and USA tour together to the girls enrolled for the same is 2:1 respectively. Ten percent of the girls are enrolled for only Canada tour whereas eight percent of the girls are enrolled for both Canada and USA together. The remaining girls are enrolled for all the three tours together. The number of boys enrolled for China and Canada tour together is fifty percent of the same. The remaining boys are enrolled for only USA tour.

164. Numbers of girls enrolled for only Canada, China and USA tour together is what percent of the boys together enrolled for the same.
    (a) 37.57%
    (b) 57.29%
    (c) 61.93%
    (d) 55.22%
    (e) None of these

165. What is the sum of the total number of boys who enrolled for Canada and the total number of girls who enrolled for same tour together?
    (a) 1872
    (b) 1454
    (c) 1772
    (d) 1544
    (e) None of these

166. What is the respective ratio of the number of girls enrolled for only USA tour and number of boys enrolled for Canada tour together to the number of boys enrolled for the USA tour and number of girls enrolled for Canada tour together?
    (a) 77 : 52
    (b) 75 : 52
    (c) 52 : 75
    (d) 52 : 77
    (e) None of these

167. What is the total number of students enrolled for all the three tours and number of girls enrolled for Canada and China tour together and number of boys enrolled for Canada and USA tour together?
    (a) 790
    (b) 830
    (c) 770
    (d) 580
    (e) None of these

168. Total number of girls enrolled for China is approximately what percent of students in the college?
    (a) 37%
    (b) 29%
    (c) 32%
    (d) 28%
    (e) 26%

DIRECTIONS (Qs. 169-173) : *The citizen Bank has total 4100 account holder. Accounts are of five different types viz current account, saving account, recurring account, NRI account and senior citizenship accounts. Two fifth of the total number of accounts is current account. 18% of the total accounts are NRI accounts. And 25% are saving accounts. Remaining accounts are either senior citizenship account or recurring accounts. The number of recurring accounts is 137 more than the number of senior citizenship account.*

169. Find the difference between the total number of senior citizenship and saving accounts together and the number of recurring accounts.
    (a) 1080
    (b) 678
    (c) 888
    (d) 976
    (e) None of these

170. Find the total number of senior citizenship, current and NRI accounts together.
    (a) 2658
    (b) 2568
    (c) 2865
    (d) 1868
    (e) None of these

171. The number of NRI accounts is approximately what percent of the total number of saving accounts and current accounts together?
    (a) 24%
    (b) 23%
    (c) 25.4%
    (d) 30000%
    (e) None of these

172. If 30% of current accounts are non-operative. What is the number of current accounts which are operative?
    (a) 1336
    (b) 1228
    (c) 1184
    (d) 1148
    (e) None of these

173. Find the ratio of the total number of current accounts to the total number of recurring and senior citizenship accounts together.
    (a) 1640 : 670
    (b) 1640 : 697
    (c) 697 : 1640
    (d) 670 : 1640
    (e) None of these

DIRECTIONS (Qs. 174-175) : *Population of two small cities A and C are 16,000 and 12,800 respectively. Ratio of population of city A to that of B is 4 : 5. Three manufacturers, X, Y and Z supply cycles in these three cities. These manufacturer manufactured cycles in the ratio of 22 : 19 : 20 (X : Y : Z) by assuming that each person will buy one cycle and 60%, 75% and 80% of the cycles manufactured by X, Y and Z respectively are sold and selling price of each cycle is ₹ 8,000.*

(a) Supply $= \dfrac{\text{Revenue}}{\text{Selling price of a cycle}}$

(b) Demand %

$= \dfrac{\text{Number of cycles ordered by customers}}{\text{Total number of cycles remainded with manufacturer}} \times 100$

(c) Revenue = 8000 × number of cycles supplied

(d) Use the above information to answer the following questions.

174. What is the revenue generated from city B, if each person of city A and C purchased a cycle?
  (a) 8.424 crore
  (b) 4.768 crore
  (c) 6.348 crore
  (d) 9.00 crore
  (e) 10.246 crore

175. What is the profit earned by manufacturer Z from city A, if total revenue earned by all three manufacturers in city A is 9.6 crore and number of cycles supplied by all of them are equal and cost price of each cycle is 6000?
  (a) 90 lakh
  (b) 50 lakh
  (c) 75 lakh
  (d) 80 lakh
  (e) 43 lakh

HINTS & SOLUTIONS

Sol. (1-5):

Total number of boys $= \dfrac{1560 \times 7}{12} = 910$

Total number of girls $= 1560 - 910 = 650$

Hobby	Boys	Girls
Painting only	385	130
Singing only	91	182
Dancing only	182	65
Dancing and Singing	78	156
Dancing and Painting	104	52
Dancing, Painting and Singing	70	65

1. (d) Total number of boys enrolled in dancing class.
   $= 182 + 78 + 104 + 70 = 434$

2. (e) Number of girls enrolled in singing class
   $= 156 + 182 + 65 = 403$
   $\therefore$ Required percentage
   $= \dfrac{403}{1560} \times 100 = 26\%$

3. (a) Required number of students
   $= 70 + 65 = 135$

4. (b) Required percentage
   $= \dfrac{65}{182} \times 100 = 35.71\%$

5. (c) Required ratio $= 130 : 385 = 26 : 77$

Sol. (6-10) :

Department	Males	Females
HR	180	330
Marketing	330	191
IT	185	100
Production	630	63
Accounts	175	216

6. (b) Required percentage
   $= \dfrac{185}{1500} \times 100 = 12\%$

7. (e) Number of males in Accounts department $= 175$

8. (b) Required percentage
   $= \dfrac{(175 + 216)}{2400} \times 100 = 16.29\%$

9. (a) Required percentage
   $= \dfrac{63}{900} \times 100 = 7\%$

10. (d) Number of females is HR and marketing department
    $= 330 + 191 = 521$

Sol. (11-13):

No. of boys $= \dfrac{3}{7} \times 175 = 75$

No. of girls $= 175 - 75 = 100$

No. of boys who opt only Hindi $= 40\%$ of $75 = 30$

Remaining boys $= 75 - 30 = 45$

No. of boys who opt only Sanskrit
$= \dfrac{2}{3} \times 45 = 30$

No. of boys who opt composite subjects
$= 45 - 30 = 15$

Total no. of students who opt only Sanskrit
$= 44\%$ of $175 = 77$

No. of girls who opt only Sanskrit
$= 77 - 30 = 47$

No. of girls who opt composite subjects $= 32$

No. of girls who opt Hindi only
$= 100 - (32 + 47) = 21$

11. (a) Req. ratio $= 30 : 32 = 15 : 16$

12. (b)   13. (b)

Sol. (14-18): No of boys in the class
$= \dfrac{5}{8} \times 80 = 50$

$\therefore$ No of girls in the class $= 80 - 50 = 30$

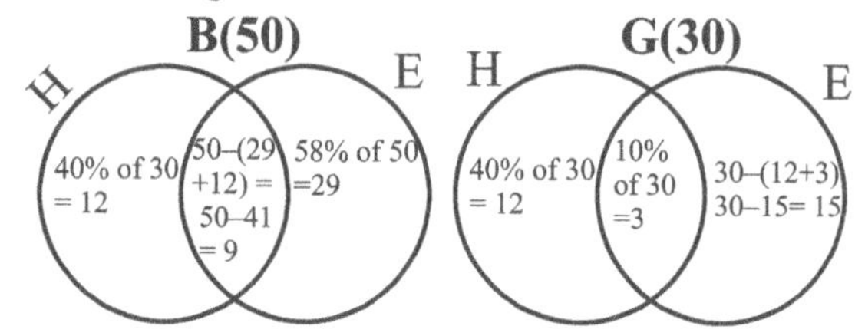

14. (d)   15. (a)   16 (d)   17. (b)

18. (c)

Sol. (19-23):

40% of males $= 8800$ males

$\therefore$ **No. of total males**
$= \dfrac{8800}{40} \times 100 = 22{,}000$

Ratio of males, females and children (10 years old and above)
$= 11 : 10 : 9$

Hence, **no. of total females**
$= \dfrac{22{,}000}{11} \times 10 = 20{,}000$

No. of total children (10 yrs old and above)
$= \dfrac{22{,}000}{11} \times 9 = 18{,}000$

No. of literate males $= 8800$

No. of illiterate males $= 22{,}000 - 8800 = 13{,}200$

No. of literate females

$$= \frac{20,000 \times 30}{100} = 6,000$$

No. of illiterate females $= 20,000 - 6,000 = 14,000$

The number of children below 10 years of age $= 10\%$ of the number of females

$$= \frac{20,000 \times 10}{100} = 2000$$

No. of total children $= 18000 + 2000 = 20,000$

No. of illiterate children (10 years old and above)

$$= \frac{18000 \times 20}{100} = 3600$$

No. of literate children (10 years old and above)
$= 18000 - 3600 = 14400$

No. of persons below poverty line
$= 5\%$ of $(22,000 + 20,000 + 20,000)$

$$= \frac{5 \times 62000}{100} = 3100$$

Illiterate persons among these 3100 persons

$$= 80\% \text{ of } 3100 = \frac{80 \times 3100}{100} = 2480$$

19. (a)   **20.** (b)   **21.** (a)

22. (d)   Required %

$$= \frac{20,000}{62,000} \times 100 = 32.26\%$$

23. (e)   14000

Sol. (24-27)

Boys = 75 (only English = 30, only maths = 30, both subjects = 15)

Girls = 100 (only English = 21, only maths = 47, both subjects = 32)

24. (b) $30:32 = 15:16$

25. (d)   **26.** (c)

27. (c) $[(47-30)/47] \times 100 = 36.17 = 36$

Sol. (28-33) :

Staff members = 240 [Teachers = 156 (male = 104. Females = 52) and Administrative staff = 84 (Male = 54, female = 30)] Students = 1600 [Boys = 880 (only English = 660, both Hindi and English = 220)], Girls = 720 (only English = 144, both Hindi and English = 576)]

28. (b) $576 - 220 = 356$

29. (c) $(720/240) \times 100 = 300\%$

30. (c) $30 + 52 - 54 = 28$

31. (b) $156:660 = 13:55$

32. (c) $54 + 52 + 144 = 250$

33. (d) $54:144 = 3:8$

Sol. (34-38):

Among 800 cricket players, 45% played in IPL –1 and 6.25% played only in IPL –1. Again, 57.5% players played in IPL –2 and 11.25% players played only in IPL –2. Again, 72.5% players played in IPL –3 and

27.5% players played only in IPL –3. Twenty per cent players played in all three IPL tournaments.

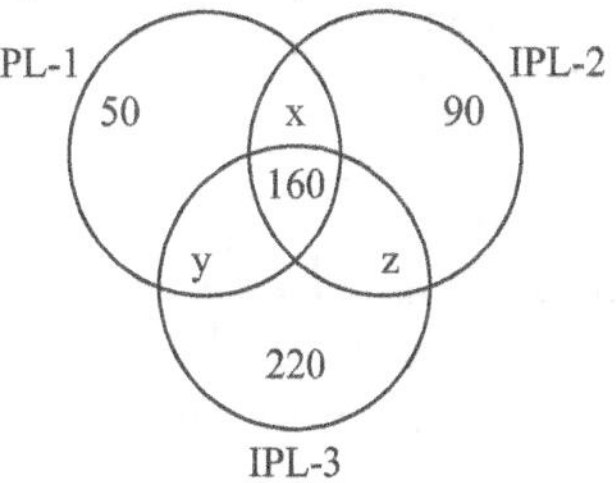

$x + y = (360 - 210) = 150$ ...(i)

$x + z = (460 - 250) = 210$ ...(ii)

$y + z = (580 - 380) = 200$ ...(iii)

$\Rightarrow$ adding (i) + (ii) + (iii), we get

$2(x + y + z) = 560$

$x + y + z = 280$

$x = 80, y = 70$ and $z = 130$

34. (d)   Required number of players $= 50 + 90 + 80 = 220$

35. (d)   Required number of players
$= 90 + 130 + 220 = 440$
Required % $= (440/800) \times 100 = 55\%$

36. (d)   Number of players who played at least two IPL
$= 80 + 70 + 130 + 160 = 440$
Required % $= (440/800) \times 100 = 55\%$

37. (d)   Only IPL 1 = 50, only IPL 2 = 90
Total = 140
Required % $= (140/160) \times 100 = 87.5\%$

38. (b)   At least one IPL = 800
At most one IPL $= 50 + 90 + 220 = 360$
Required less %
$= (800 - 360)/800 \times 100$
$= 55\%$ less

Sol. (39-43) :

39. (d)   Required total $= 25 + 20 + 65 + 85 = 195$

40. (d)   Required average no. of products

$$= \frac{349}{231 + 399} \times 100 = \frac{349}{630} \times 100$$

41. (b)   **42.** (a)

43. (d)   Required percentage

$$= \frac{85}{200} \times 100 \approx 43 = 43$$

Sol. (44-48):

Number of mobile phones

$$= \frac{1650 \times 24}{100} = 396$$

Number of pen drives

$$= 1650 \times \frac{1}{6} = 275$$

Number of calculators

$$= 1650 \times \frac{14}{100} = 231$$

Number of televisions and washing machines = 748
Number of washing machines = T + 50
T + W = 748

$T + T + 50 = 748$

$2T = 748 - 50 = 698$

$\therefore \quad T = \dfrac{698}{2} = 349$

Washing machines = $349 + 50 = 399$

44. (b) Ratio $= \dfrac{399}{231} = \dfrac{133}{77} = \dfrac{19}{11} = 19 : 11$

45. (a) Number of pen drives which are not defective

$= 275 \times \dfrac{76}{100} = 275 \times 76 = 209$

46. (b) Required %

$= \dfrac{349}{231 + 399} \times 100 = \dfrac{349}{630} \times 100$

$= 55.39\% = 55\%$

47. (c) Difference $= 349 + 396 - 231$

$= 745 - 231 = 514$

48. (d) Total number of pen drives, calculators and washing machines = $275 + 231 + 399 = 905$

Sol. (49-53):

	Eng. only	Hindi only	Both	Total
Boys	24	18	108	150
Girls	55	78	117	250
Total	79	96	225	400

49. (b)   50. (d)   51. (a)   52. (d)   53. (c)

Sol. (54-58)

College	Total passed	Boys	Girls
P	720	520	200
Q	880	480	400
R	800	360	440
S	600	250	350
T	1000	700	300
Total	4000	2310	1690

54. (c) Required average = 1690/5 = 338

55. (c) Required ratio = 700/300 = 7 : 3

56. (a) Required percentage = [(480 – 400)/400] ×100 = 20%

57. (c) Number of girls passed in College P = 200
Number of passed boys in College S = 250
Required percentage = (200/250) ×100 = 80%

58. (d) College S has the percentage of girls passed with respect to its total passed students is maximum.

Sol. (59-63):

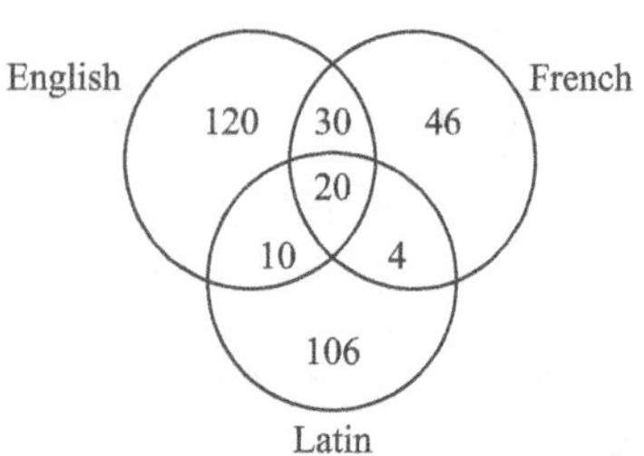

59. (c) Required delegates = 120 + 46 + 106 = 272

60. (a) Required delegates = 64

61. (a) Required delegates = 30 + 10 + 20 + 4 = 64

62. (d) Required delegates = 30 + 10 + 4 = 44

63. (b) Required delegates = 400 – 20 = 380

Sol. (64-68):

64. (c) Total flooring area with marble
= locker area + record keeping + pantry
= 182 + 273 + 609 = 1064 sqm
Cost of flooring = 1064 × 190
Total flooring area with wooden
= Branch Manager room + Hal
= 221 + 667 = 888 sqm
Cost of flooring = 888 × 170
Ratio = 888 × 170 : 1064 × 190
= 888 × 17 : 1064 × 19
= 1887 : 2527

65. (b) Cost of flooring of branch manager room
= 221 × 170 = ₹ 37570
Cost of painting
= [2(17 × 12 + 13 × 12) + 13 × 17] × 190
= [2(204 + 156) + 221] × 190
= (2 × 360 + 221) × 190
= (720 + 221) × 190
= 941 × 190 = ₹ 178790
Total cost = 178790 + 37570
= ₹ 216360

66. (a) Total area of bank = 2000 sq m
Total flooring area = 1952 sq m
Remaining area
= 2000 – 1952 = 48 sq m
So Cost of carpeting
= 48 × 110 = ₹ 5280

67. (b) Area not to be renovated = 48 sq m

Required % $= \dfrac{48}{2000} \times 100 = 2.4\%$

68. (a) Cost of renovation of hall + locker area
= 667 × 170 + 609 × 190
= 113390 + 115710
= ₹ 229100

Sol. (69-73):

	Train A (700)	Train B (910)
General coaches	140	241
Sleeper coaches	161	273
First Class	224	91
AC coaches	175	305

69. (c)   70. (d)

71. (c)   72. (b)

73. (c)

Sol. (74–78) :

Workshops	No. of workers	No. of male workers	No. of female workers	Notes
A	$\dfrac{1800 \times 12}{9}$ $= 2400$	720×2 $= 1440$	$2400 - 1440$ $= 960$	Respective ratio of number of workers in A, C and B is 12 : 10 : 9. Number of male workers in A is two times of number of male workers in B.
B	$\dfrac{360 \times 100}{60 \times 40}$ $= 360 \times 5$ $= 1800$	$1800 - 1080$ $= 720$	$\dfrac{1800 \times 60}{100}$ $= 1080$	Number of female workers in B is 60% of total number of workers in this workship Difference between number of male workers and female workers in B is 360
C	$\dfrac{1800 \times 10}{9}$ $= 2000$	$\dfrac{960 \times 100}{125}$ $= 768$	$2000 - 768$ $= 1232$	Respective ratio of number of workers in A, C and B is 12 : 10 : 9 Number of female workers in A is 25% more than number of male workers in C.
D	$\dfrac{2400 \times 100}{100 + 20}$ $= \dfrac{2400 \times 100}{120}$ $= 2000$	$\dfrac{2000 \times 60}{100 + 60}$ $= \dfrac{2000 \times 60}{160}$ $= 750$	$2000 - 750$ $= 1250$	Number of workers in workshop A is 20% more than that of D. Number of male workers is 40% less than that of female workers.
E	$\dfrac{2000 \times 150}{100}$ $= 3000$	$\dfrac{3000 \times 1}{2}$ $= 1500$	$3000 - 1500$ $= 1500$	Number of workers in E is 50% more than that of C. Number of male workers in equal to number of female workers in E.

74. (a) Total number of male workers in all workshops together
$$= 1440 + 720 + 768 + 750 + 1500 = 5178$$
Total number of female workers in all workshops together
$$= 960 + 1080 + 1232 + 1250 + 1500 = 6022$$
Difference $= 6022 - 5178 = 844$
Required %
$$= \frac{844 \times 100}{6022} = 14.01\% = 14\%$$

75. (b) Total number of workers in workshop E = 3000
Number of trained male workers in workshop
$$E = \frac{1500 \times 60}{100} = 900$$
Number of trained female workers in workshop
$$E = \frac{1500 \times 70}{100} = 1050$$
Total number of trained workers in workshop
$$E = 900 + 1050 = 1950$$
Required %
$$= \frac{1950 \times 100}{3000} = 65\%$$

76. (c) Let salary of a male worker in workshop C be 5x and salary of a female worker in workshop C be 4x.
Total salary of all workers in workshop

$C = 2000 \times 6000 = 12000000$.
According to the question,
$$768 \times 5\,x + 1232 \times 4\,x = 12000000$$
$$\Rightarrow \quad 3840\,x + 4928\,x = 12000000$$
$$\Rightarrow \quad 8768\,x = 12000000$$
$$\therefore \quad x = \frac{12000000}{8768} = 1368.6$$
$\therefore$ Salary of a male worker in C
$$= 5 \times 1368.6 = 6843.0$$

77. (d) Total number of female workers in all workshops together
$$= 960 + 1080 + 1232 + 1250 + 1500$$
$$= 6022$$
Average number of female workers in all workshops together $= \dfrac{6022}{5}$
Number of female workers in D = 1250
$$\text{Difference} = 1250 - \frac{6022}{5} = \frac{6250 - 6022}{5} = \frac{228}{5}$$
Required %
$$= \frac{228}{5} \times 100 \times \frac{5}{6022} = 3.78\%$$

78. (e) Required ratio
$$= 768 : 1250 = 384 : 625$$

Sol. (79–83)

Persons	Income	Expenditure	Saving	Notes
A	$\dfrac{36000 \times 5}{4 \times 1}$ $= 60000$	$\dfrac{60000 \times 4}{5}$ $= 48000$	$60000 - 48000$ $= 12000$	Expenditure of A is 36000 more than his saving. Income of A is 25% more than his Expenditure. Ratio of income and expenditure of A = 5 : 4.
B	$\dfrac{20000 \times 150}{100}$ $= 30000$	$\dfrac{30000 \times 100}{100 + 50}$ $= 20000$	$30000 - 20000$ $= 10000$	Income of B is 50% more than that of E. Saving of B is 50% of his expenditure.
C	$\dfrac{6000 \times 100}{40}$ $= 15000$	$15000 - 6000$ $= 9000$	$\dfrac{12000}{2} = 6000$	Saving of A is two times of that of C. C saves 40% of his income.
D	$15000 + 8400$ $= 23400$	$\dfrac{20000 \times 75}{100}$ $= 15000$	$\dfrac{6000 \times 140}{100}$ $= 8400$	Saving of D is 40% more than that of C. Expenditure of D is 25% less than that of B.
E	$\dfrac{6000 \times 100}{30}$ $= 20000$	$20000 - 6000$ $= 14000$	$\dfrac{12000 \times 50}{100} = 6000$	Saving of E is 50% less than that of A. E saves 30% of his salary.

79. (e) Total income of all persons together
$= 60000 + 15000 + 30000 + 23400 + 20000$
$= 148400$
Total saving of all persons together
$= 12000 + 6000 + 10000 + 8400 + 6000$
$= 42400$
Required %
$= \dfrac{42400}{148400} \times 100 = 28.57\%$

80. (d) Income at B after increment
$= \dfrac{30000 \times 140}{100} = 42000$

Expenditure of B after increment
$= \dfrac{20000 \times 130}{100} = 26000$

Saving of B after increment
$= 42000 - 26000 = 16000$
Increment in saving $= 16000 - 10000 = 6000$
Required
$= \dfrac{6000}{10000} \times 100 = 60\%$

81. (e) Total expenditure of all persons together
$= 48000 + 9000 + 20000 + 15000 + 14000$
$= 106000$
Total saving of all persons together
$= 12000 + 6000 + 10000 + 8400 + 6000$
$= 42400$

Required ratio
$= \dfrac{106000}{5} : \dfrac{42400}{5} = 265 : 106$

82. (b) Total saving of all persons together
$= 42400$
Average saving of all persons together
$= \dfrac{42400}{5} = 8480$
Saving of E $= 6000$
Required %
$= \dfrac{6000}{8480} \times 100 = 70.75\%$

83. (a) Total income of A and E
$= 60000 + 20000 = 80000$
Average income of A and E
$= \dfrac{80000}{2} = 40000$
Total income of B, C and D
$= 15000 + 30000 + 23400$
$= 68400$
Average income of B, C and D
$= \dfrac{68400}{3} = 22800$
Required difference
$= 40000 - 22800 = 17200$

Sol. (84–88):

Trains	Speed	Time	Distance	Notes
A	$\dfrac{1000}{14} = \dfrac{500}{7}$ Km/h	14 hrs	$\dfrac{1120 \times 100}{112}$ $= 1000$ km	Trains A starts its journey at 5 A.M and reaches its destination at 7 P.M. same day. Train C covers 12% more distance than train A
B	$\dfrac{2250}{16} = \dfrac{1125}{8}$ Km/h	14 + 12 hrs $= 16$ hrs	$1000 + 1250$ $= 2250$ Km	Train B takes 2 hrs more than train A Train B covers equal to the distance covered by trains A and D together
C	$16 \times 5 = 80$ Km/h	14 hrs	$80 \times 14 = 1120$ Km	Speed of train C is five times of the time taken by train B. Train C takes equal time as train A
D	$\dfrac{1250}{21}$ Km/h	$\dfrac{14 \times 150}{100} = 21$ hrs	$\dfrac{1000 \times 125}{100} = 1250$ Km	Train D takes 50% more time than A Train D covers 25% more distance than train A
E	$\dfrac{80 \times 100}{80}$ $= 100$ Km/h	$\dfrac{1000}{100} = 10$ hrs	$\dfrac{1250 \times 80}{100} = 1000$ Km	Distance covered by train E is 20% less than train D Speed of train C is 20% less than that of train E

84. (c) Speed of train C = 80 Km/h

Speed of train A = $\dfrac{500}{7}$ Km/h

Required ratio = $80 : \dfrac{500}{7} = 28 : 25$

85. (e) Speed of train D after increment

$= \dfrac{1250}{21} \times \dfrac{120}{100} = \dfrac{500}{7}$ Km/h

Required time = $\dfrac{1000}{\dfrac{500}{7}} = 14$ hrs

86. (d) Total distance covered by A, C and E together

$= 1000 + 1120 + 1000$

$= 3120$ Km

Required average = $\dfrac{3120}{3} = 1040$ Km

87. (a) Speed of B = $\dfrac{1125}{8}$ Km/h

Speed of D = $\dfrac{1250}{21}$ Km/h

Required ratio

$= \dfrac{1125}{8} : \dfrac{1250}{21} = 189 : 80$

88. (b) Total distance covered by all trains together

$= 1000 + 2250 + 1120 + 1250 + 1000$

$= 6620$ Km

Total time taken by all trains together

$= 14 + 16 + 14 + 21 + 10$

$= 75$ hrs

Required average speed

$= \dfrac{6620}{75} = 88.26$ Km/h

Sol. (89–93):

Electronic goods	Cost Price	Selling Price	Marked Price	Notes
T.V	$\dfrac{28800 \times 100}{90}$ $= 32000$	$\dfrac{72000 \times 2}{5}$ $= 28800$	$\dfrac{28800 \times 100}{80}$ $= 36000$	Respective ratio of selling price of T.V and A.C is 2 : 5. T.V. is sold at 10% loss after 20% discount
A.C	$\dfrac{12000 \times 100}{20}$ $= 60000$	$\dfrac{60000 \times 120}{100}$ $= 72000$	$\dfrac{72000 \times 100}{80}$ $= 90000$	Profit amount on A.C is 12000. A.C is sold at 20% Profit after 20% discount
P.C	$\dfrac{12000 \times 50}{100} \times \dfrac{100}{20}$ $= 30000$	$\dfrac{30000 \times 120}{100}$ $= 36000$	$\dfrac{36000 \times 100}{60}$ $= 60000$	Profit occurred on P.C is 50% of that of A.C. P.C is sold at 20% Profit after a discount of 40%.
Cooler	$\dfrac{12000}{5} \times \dfrac{100}{30}$ $= 8000$	$\dfrac{8000 \times 130}{100}$ $= 10400$	$\dfrac{10400 \times 100}{65}$ $= 16000$	Profit on A.C is 5 times of that of cooler. Cooler is sold at 30% Profit after 35% discount.

Music system	$\dfrac{8000 \times 150}{100}$ $= 12000$	$\dfrac{60000 \times 30}{100}$ $= 18000$	$\dfrac{36000 + 90000 + 60000 + 16000}{4}$ $= \dfrac{202000}{4} = 50500$	Cost price of music system is 50% more than that of cooler. Selling price of music system is 30% of the cost price of A.C. M.P of Music system is equal to average marked Price of all other goods.

89. (a) Total cost price of all items together
$$= 32000 + 60000 + 30000 + 8000 + 12000$$
$$= 142000$$
Total marked price of all items together
$$= 36000 + 90000 + 60000 + 16000 + 50500$$
$$= 252500$$
Profit = 252500 – 142000 = 110500
Required %
$$= \dfrac{110500 \times 100}{142000} = 77.8\%$$

90. (e) Total cost price of all items = 142000
Total selling price of all items
$$= 28800 + 72000 + 36000 + 10400 + 18000$$
$$= 165200$$
Total marked price of all items = 252500

Total discount = 252500 – 165200 = 87300
Total profit = 165200 – 142000 = 23200
Required ratio = 23200 : 87300 = 232 : 873

91. (b) Profit on A.C = 72000 – 60000 = 12000
Profit on P.C = 36000 – 30000 = 6000
Required difference = 12000 – 6000 = 6000

92. (c) Total marked price of all goods together = 252500
Total selling price of all goods together = 165200
Total discount = 252500 – 165200 = 87300
Required % $= \dfrac{87300 \times 100}{252500} = 34.57\%$

93. (d) Required ratio
$$= 28800 \times \dfrac{90}{100} : 36000 \times \dfrac{80}{100} = 9:10$$

Sol. (94-98) :

Schools	No. of students	No. of boys	No. of girls	Notes
A	$\dfrac{720}{20} \times 80$ $= 2880$	$\dfrac{2880 \times 5}{9}$ $= 1600$	$2880 - 1600$ $= 1280$	Respective ratio of number of boys and girls in school A is 5 : 4. Difference between number of students in schools A and E is 720. Number of students in school A is 20% less than that of E. 50% of the total students of the school A are passed.
B	$1920 + 1600$ $= 3520$	$\dfrac{1600 \times 120}{100}$ $= 1920$	$\dfrac{1920 \times 5}{6}$ $= 1600$	Respective ratio of number of girls in schools B, C and D is 5 : 6 : 4 Number of boys in school B is 20% more than number of boys in school A
C	$\dfrac{3600 \times 120}{100}$ $= 4320$	$\dfrac{4320 \times 125}{100 + 125}$ $= \dfrac{4320 \times 5}{9}$ $= 2400$	$4320 - 2400$ $= 1920$	Number of students in school C is 20% more than that of school E Number of boys in school C is 25% more than that of girls in this school.
D	$960 + 1280$ $= 2240$	$\dfrac{1280 \times 75}{100}$ $= 960$	$\dfrac{1920 \times 4}{6}$ $= 1280$	Respective ratio of number of girls in schools B, C and D is 5 : 6 : 4 In school D number of boys is 25% less than that of girls in this school
E	$\dfrac{2880 \times 100}{80}$ $= 3600$	$\dfrac{1600 \times 120}{100}$ $= 1920$	$3600 - 1920$ $= 1680$	Number of students in school A is 20% less than that of E Number of boys in school E is 20% more than that of A.

94. (a) Total no. of boys in all schools together
$$= 1600 + 1920 + 2400 + 960 + 1920 = 8800$$
Total no. of girls in all schools together
$$= 1280 + 1600 + 1920 + 1280 + 1680 = 7760$$
Required ratio = 8800 : 7760 = 110 : 97

95. (b) Number of passed boys in school
$$C = \dfrac{2400 \times 50}{100} = 1200$$

Number of passed girls in school
$$C = \dfrac{1920 \times 60}{100} = 1152$$
Total number of students in school C = 4320
Total number of passed students in school
C = 1200 + 1152 = 2352
Required % $= \dfrac{2352 \times 100}{4320} = 54.4$

96. (c) Number of absent students from school

$$D = \frac{960 \times 20}{100} = 192$$

Number of present students from school

$$D = 2240 - 192 = 2048$$

Number of present students from school

$$E = \frac{3600 \times 90}{100} = 3240$$

Required difference $= 3240 - 2048 = 1192$

97. (d) Total number of passed students in

$$A = \frac{2880 \times 50}{100} = 1440$$

Total number of passed students in

$$B = \frac{1920 \times 50}{100} + \frac{1600 \times 40}{100} = 960 + 640 = 1600$$

$$\text{Required \%} = \frac{1440}{1600} \times 100 = 90\%$$

98. (e) Total number of boys in schools A, C and E
$$= 1600 + 2400 + 1920 = 5920$$

Average number of boys in schools A, C and E $= \dfrac{5920}{3}$

Total number of girls in schools B and D
$$= 1600 + 1280 = 2880$$

Average number of girls in schools B and

$$D = \frac{2880}{2} = 1440$$

$$\text{Difference} = \frac{5920}{3} - 1440 = \frac{1600}{3}$$

$$\text{Required \%} = \frac{1600}{3} \times \frac{100}{1440} = \frac{1000}{27} = 37\%$$

Sol. (99-103):

Workshop	Number of workers	Number of male workers	Number of female workers	Notes
A	$\dfrac{5184 \times 150}{100}$ $= 7776$	$\dfrac{7776 \times 2}{3}$ $= 5184$	$7776 - 5184$ $= 2592$	Number of workers in A is 50% more than number of workers in D. Respective ratio of number of male workers and female workers in A is 2 : 1
B	$\dfrac{1080 \times 120}{20}$ $= 6480$	$\dfrac{2700 \times 120}{100}$ $= 3240$	$6480 - 3240$ $= 3240$	Number of male workers in B is 20% more than number of male workers in E.
C	$\dfrac{5184 \times 125}{100}$ $= 6480$	$6480 - 2916$ $= 3564$	$\dfrac{6480 \times 45}{100}$ $= 2916$	Number of workers in C is 25% more than number of workers in D. Number of female workers in C is 45% of total number of workers in this workshop.
D	$\dfrac{6480 \times 80}{100}$ $= 5184$	$\dfrac{5184 \times 50}{100 + 50}$ $= 1728$	$5184 - 1728$ $= 3456$	Number of workers in D is 20% less than number of workers in B. Number of male workers is 50% of number of female workers in D.
E	$\dfrac{1080 \times 100}{20}$ $= 5400$	$\dfrac{5400 \times 1}{2}$ $= 2700$	$5400 - 2700$ $= 2700$	Number of male workers in B is 20% more than number of male workers in E. Number of male workers is equal to number of female workers in E.

99. (e) Total number of workers in B $= 6480$

Total number of trained workers in

$$B = \frac{3240 \times 50}{100} + \frac{3240 \times 40}{100} = 1620 + 1296 = 2916$$

Total number of untrained workers in
$$B = 6480 - 2916 = 3564$$

Respective ratio of total salary of trained and untrained workers
$$= 2916 \times 2 : 3564 \times 1 = 1458 : 891 = 18 : 11$$

$$\text{Required \%} = \frac{11}{29} \times 100 = \frac{1100}{29} = 37.93\%$$

100. (d) Total number of male workers in all workshops together
$$= 5184 + 3240 + 3564 + 1728 + 2700 = 16416$$

$$\text{Average} = \frac{16416}{5} = 3283.2$$

Total number of female workers in all workshops together $= 2592 + 3240 + 2916 + 3456 + 2700 = 14904$

$$\text{Average} = \frac{14904}{5} = 2980.8$$

Required difference $= 302.4 = 302$

101. (c) Total no. of workers in A $= 7776$

Total no. of workers in C $= 6480$

$$\text{Required ratio} = \frac{7776 \times 50}{100} : \frac{6480 \times 40}{100} = 3 : 2$$

102. (d) Required ratio $= 1728 \times 5000 : 3456 \times 4500 = 5 : 9$

103. (e) Total number of workers in all workshops together

$$= 7776 + 6480 + 6480 + 5184 + 5400$$

$$= 31320$$

Average number of workers in all workshops together

$$= \frac{31320}{5} = 6264$$

Number of male workers in A = 5184

$$\text{Required } \% = \frac{5184}{6264} \times 100 = 82.75\%$$

Sol. (104-108):

Students	Hindi	Math	English	Notes
A	$\frac{200 \times 60}{100} = 120$	$\frac{120 \times 140}{100} = 168$	$\frac{225 \times 100}{75} \times \frac{120}{100}$ $(120 + 168)$ $= 360 - 288 = 72$	A gets 60% marks in Hindi A gets 20% more marks than C Marks obtained by A in Math is 40% more than D. A obtained 20% more marks than C in English
B	$\frac{75 \times 4}{5} = 60$	$\frac{75 \times 6}{5} = 90$	$\frac{15 \times 5}{5 - 4} = 75$	B gets 25% less marks than C B obtained 15 more marks in English than Hindi Respective ratio of marks obtained by B in Math, Hindi and English is 6 : 4 : 5 B obtained 75% marks in English
C	$\frac{225 \times 100}{75} - (150 + 60)$ $= 300 - 210 = 90$	$\frac{120 \times 125}{100} = 150$	$\frac{72 \times 100}{120} = 60$	C gets 25% more marks than D in Math A obtained 20% more marks than C in English
D	$\frac{120 \times 3}{4} = 90$	$\frac{200 \times 60}{100} = 120$	$\frac{500 \times 60}{100} \times (90 + 120)$ $= 300 - 210 = 90$	D gets 60% marks in Math D gets 60% of full marks Respective ratio of marks obtained by D in Math and Hindi is 4 : 3
E	$\frac{300 \times 120}{100} \times (160 + 60)$ $= 360 - 220 = 140$	$\frac{120 \times 100}{75} = 160$	$\frac{90 \times 100}{150} = 60$	D obtained 25% less marks than E in Math. Marks of E is 20% more than that of C Marks obtained by D in English is 50% more than that marks obtained by E in this subject.

Full marks of Maths, Hindi and English are 200, 200 and 100 respectively.

104. (a) Total marks obtained by B = 60 + 90 + 75 = 225
Total marks obtained by D = 90 + 120 + 90 = 300
Required difference = 300 − 225 = 75

105. (e) Total marks obtained by all students together in English
$$= 72 + 75 + 60 + 90 + 60 = 357$$
$$\text{Required } \% = \frac{357}{5 \times 100} \times 100 = 71.4\%$$

106. (b) Total marks obtained by all students together in Math
$$= 168 + 90 + 150 + 120 + 160 = 688$$
Total marks obtained by all students together is Hindi
$$= 120 + 60 + 90 + 90 + 140 = 500$$

Required average $= \dfrac{688}{5} - \dfrac{500}{5} = \dfrac{188}{5} = 37.6$

107. (c) Total marks obtained by A in all subjects together
$$= 120 + 168 + 72 = 360$$
Full marks of all subjects together
$$= 200 + 200 + 100 = 500$$
$$\text{Required } \% = \frac{360}{500} \times 100 = 72\%$$

108. (d) Total marks obtained by all students together in Hindi
$$= 120 + 60 + 90 + 90 + 140 = 500$$
Total marks obtained by all students together in English
$$= 72 + 75 + 60 + 90 + 60 = 357$$
Required ratio = 500 : 357

Sol. (109-113):

Persons	Salary	Expenditure	Saving	Notes
A	$\frac{135000 \times 100}{150}$ $= 90000$	$\frac{90000 \times 80}{100}$ $= 72000$	$90000 - 72000$ $= 18000$	Saving of A is 20% less than that of B Salary of E is 50% more than that of A A spends 80% of his salary
B	$\frac{22500 \times 100}{50}$ $= 90000$	$90000 - 22500$ $= 67500$	$\frac{18000 \times 100}{80}$ $= 22500$	Saving of A is 20% less than that of B B saves 25% of his salary

C	$60000 + 36000$ $= 96000$	$\dfrac{36000 \times 100}{60}$ $= 60000$	18000×2 $= 36000$	Salary of C is twice of the expenditure of D Saving of C is two times of that of A Saving of C is 40% less than his expenditure
D	$\dfrac{48000 \times 100}{60}$ $= 80000$	$\dfrac{96000}{2}$ $= 48000$	$80000 - 48000$ $= 32000$	Salary of C is twice of the expenditure of D D saves 40% of his salary
E	$\dfrac{45000 \times 100 + 50}{100 - 50}$ $= 135000$	$\dfrac{48000 \times 125}{100}$	$1350000 - 60000$	Salary of E is 50% more than that of A Expenditure of E is 25% more than that of D

109. (a) Total expenditure of all persons together
$= 72000 + 67500 + 60000 + 48000 + 60000$
$= 307500$
Total saving of all persons together
$= 18000 + 22500 + 36000 + 32000 + 75000$
$= 183500$
Required difference
$= \dfrac{307500 - 183500}{5} = \dfrac{124000}{5} = 24800$

110. (e) Total salary of A, B and E together
$= 90000 + 90000 + 135000 = 315000$

Average salary of A, B and E $= \dfrac{315000}{3} = 105000$

Total salary of C and D together $= 96000 + 80000$
$= 176000$

Average salary of C and D $= \dfrac{176000}{2} = 88000$

Required average
$= 105000 : 88000 = 105 : 88$

111. (b) Total salary of all persons together
$= 90000 + 90000 + 96000 + 80000 + 135000 = 491000$

Average salary of all persons $= \dfrac{491000}{5} = 98200$

Salary of B $= 90000$
Difference $= 98200 - 90000 = 8200$

Required % $= \dfrac{8200 \times 100}{90000} = 9.1\%$

112. (e) Expenditure of C $= 60000$
Total saving of A, B, D and E together
$= 18000 + 22500 + 32000 + 75000 = 147500$

Required % $= \dfrac{60000}{147500} \times 100 = 40.6\%$

113. (d) Average salary of all the persons together $= 98200$
Total expenditure of all the persons together
$= 72000 + 67500 + 60000 + 48000 + 60000 = 307500$

Average expenditure of all persons $= \dfrac{307500}{5} = 61500$

Required ratio $= 98200 : 61500 = 982 : 615$

Sol. (114-118) :

Student	Math F.M – 120	Hindi F.M – 150	English F.M – 150	Notes
A	$500 \times \dfrac{60}{100} - (120 + 60)$ $= 120$	$150 \times \dfrac{40}{100} = 60$	$150 \times \dfrac{80}{100} = 120$	A obtained 60% marks in all three subjects together. A obtained 80% marks in English and 40% marks in Hindi. Difference between marks obtained by C and A is 75.
B	$500 \times \dfrac{80}{100} \times \dfrac{75}{100} \times \dfrac{5}{13}$ $= \dfrac{1500}{13}$	$\dfrac{1200}{13}$	$\dfrac{1200}{13}$	B obtained 20% less marks than C. Marks obtained by B in Math is 25% more than that of Hindi and marks obtained by him in Hindi is equal to that of English.
C	$500 \times \dfrac{75}{100} \times \dfrac{6}{15} = 150$	$500 \times \dfrac{75}{100} \times \dfrac{5}{15} = 125$	$500 \times \dfrac{75}{100} \times \dfrac{4}{15} = 100$	C obtained 25% more marks than A in all subjects together. Respective ratio of marks obtained by C in Math, Hindi and English is 6 : 5 : 4.
D	$200 \times \dfrac{75}{100} = 150$	$\left(500 \times \dfrac{60}{100} \times \dfrac{8}{6} - 150\right)$ $\dfrac{4}{9} = \dfrac{1000}{9}$	$\left(500 \times \dfrac{60}{100} \times \dfrac{8}{6} - 150\right)$ $\dfrac{5}{9} = \dfrac{1250}{9}$	Respective ratio of overall marks obtained by B, D and E is 6 : 8 : 7. Marks obtained by D in Math is 75% of full marks Respective ratio of marks obtained by D in Hindi and English is 4 : 5.
E	$120 \times \dfrac{125}{100} = 150$	$120 \times \dfrac{80}{100} = 100$	$300 \times \dfrac{7}{6} - (150 + 100)$ $= 100$	Respective ratio of overall marks obtained by B, D and E is 6 : 8 : 7. Marks obtained by E in Math is 25% more than that of A. Marks obtained by E in Hindi is 20% less than that of C.

114. (a) Total marks obtained by all students together in English
$$= 120 + 92.3 + 100 + 138.8 + 100 = 551.1$$
$$\text{Required\%} = \frac{551.1}{5 \times 150} \times 100 = \frac{1102.2}{15} = 73.48\%$$

115. (b) Total marks obtained by A in all subjects together
$$= 120 + 60 + 120 = 300$$
Total marks obtained by C in all subjects together
$$= 150 + 125 + 100 = 375$$
Required ratio $= 300 : 375 = 4 : 5$

116. (c) Total marks obtained by D in all subjects together
$$= 150 + \frac{1000}{9} + \frac{1250}{9} = 400$$
Total marks obtained by E in all subjects together
$$= 150 + 100 + 100 = 350$$
Difference $= 400 + 350 = 50$
$$\text{Required \%} = \frac{50}{350} \times 100 = 14.28\%$$

117. (d) Total marks obtained by all students together in Math
$$= 120 + 115.4 + 150 + 150 + 150 = 685.4$$
Total marks obtained by all students together in English
$$= 120 + 92.3 + 100 + 138.8 + 100 = 551.1$$
Required difference
$$= \frac{685.4 - 551.1}{5} = \frac{134.3}{5} = 26.86$$

118. (e) Total marks obtained by A $= 120 + 60 + 120 = 300$
$$\text{Total marks obtained by B} = \frac{1500}{13} + \frac{1200}{13} + \frac{1200}{13}$$
$$= 300$$
Total marks obtained by C $= 150 + 125 + 100 = 375$
$$\text{Total marks obtained by D} = 150 + \frac{1000}{9} + \frac{1250}{9} = 400$$
Total marks obtained by E $= 150 + 100 + 100$
$$= 350$$
Average overall obtained marks of all students
$$= \frac{300 + 300 + 375 + 400 + 350}{5}$$
$$= \frac{1725}{5} = 345$$
$$\text{Req. \%} = \frac{345}{500} \times 100 = 69\%$$

Sol. (119–123) :

Persons	Income	Expenditure	Saving	Notes
A	$72000 \times \dfrac{100}{25} = 288000$	$288000 - 72000 = 216000$	$36000 \times \dfrac{100}{150 - 100}$ $= 36000 \times \dfrac{100}{50} = 72000$	A spends 75% of his income. Saving of D is between saving of D and that of A is Rs. 36000.
B	$180000 + 108000$ $= 288000$	$216000 \times \dfrac{5}{6} = 180000$	$180000 \times \dfrac{3}{5} = 108000$	Respective ratio of expenditure of A and that of B is 6 : 5. Respective ratio of expenditure and saving of B is 5 : 3.
C	$288000 \times \dfrac{100}{75} = 384000$	$288000 \times \dfrac{75}{100} = 216000$	$384000 - 216000 = 168000$	Income of B is 25% less than that of C Expenditure of C is 25% less than income of B.
D	$108000 \times \dfrac{100}{30} = 360000$	$360000 - 108000 = 252000$	$72000 \times \dfrac{150}{100} = 108000$	D spends 70% of his income and saving of D is 50% more than saving of A.
E	$384000 \times \dfrac{100}{125} = 307200$	$108000 \times 2 = 216000$	$307200 - 216000 = 91200$	Income of C is 25% more than that of E. Expenditure of E is two times of the saving of B.

119. (e) Total expenditure of all persons together
$$= 216000 + 180000 + 216000 + 252000 + 216000$$
$$= ₹1080000$$
Total income of all persons together
$$= 288000 + 288000 + 384000 + 360000 + 307200$$
$$= ₹1627200$$
$$\text{Required\%} = \frac{1080000}{1627200} \times 100 = 66.37\%$$

120. (d) Total expenditure of C $= ₹216000$
$$\text{Transport expenditure of C} = 216000 \times \frac{25}{100}$$
$$= ₹ 54000$$

Income of C $= ₹ 384000$
$$\text{Food expenditure of C} = 384000 \times \frac{20}{100} = 76800$$
Required ratio $= 54000 : 76800 = 45 : 64$

121. (c) Total expenditure of all persons together $= 1080000$
Total income of all persons together $= 1627200$
Total saving of all persons together
$$= 1627200 - 1080000 = 547200$$
Required difference
$$= \frac{1080000 - 547200}{5} = \frac{532800}{5}$$
$$= 106560$$

122. (e) Income of A = 288000

Income of A after increase = $288000 \times \dfrac{120}{100} = 345600$

Income of E = 307200

Income of E after increase

$$= 307200 \times \dfrac{130}{100} = 399360$$

Difference in income of E

$$= 399360 - 345600 = 53760\%$$

Required percentage

$$= \dfrac{53760}{345600} \times 100 = 15.55\%$$

123. (a) Total income of A, C and E together

$$= 288000 + 384000 + 307200$$
$$= 979200$$

Average income of A, C and E = 326400

Total income of B and D together

$$= 288000 + 360000$$
$$= 648000$$

Average income of B and D

$$= \dfrac{648000}{2} = 324000$$

Required ratio = 326400 : 324000
$$= 136 : 135$$

Sol. (124–128) :

Items	Cost Price	Selling Price	Marked Price	Notes
Bed	$18000 \times \dfrac{75}{25} = 54000$	$18000 \times \dfrac{100}{25} = 72000$	$54000 \times \dfrac{150}{100} = 81000$	Cost price of bed is 25% less than its selling price and its marked price is 50% more than its cost price. Profit accrued on bed is 18000.
Sofa	$54000 \times \dfrac{80}{100} = 43200$	$43200 \times \dfrac{120}{100} = 51840$	$43200 \times \dfrac{120}{80} = 64800$	Cost price of sofa is 20% less than that of bed. Sofa is sold at 20% profit after a discount of 20%
Dining set	$54000 \times \dfrac{4}{3} = 72000$	$72000 \times \dfrac{120}{100} = 86400$	$64800 \times \dfrac{8}{5} = 103680$	Respective ratio of cost price of bed and that of dining set is 3 : 4. Respective ratio of marked price of sofa and dining set is 5 : 8 Dining set is sold at 20% profit.
Dressing table	$43200 \times \dfrac{50}{100} = 21600$	$48600 \times \dfrac{75}{100} = 36450$	$81000 \times \dfrac{60}{100} = 48600$	Cost price of dressing table is 50% of that of sofa and its marked price is 60% of that of bed. Dressing table is sold at 25% discount
Book self	$21600 \times \dfrac{60}{100} = 12960$	$12960 \times \dfrac{140}{100} = 18144$	$12960 \times \dfrac{140}{70} = 25920$	Cost price of a book self is 60% of that of dressing table and it is sold at 40% Profit after 30% discount.

124. (a) Total cost price of all items together

$$= 54000 + 43200 + 72000 + 21600 + 12960$$
$$= 203760$$

Total marked price of all items together

$$= 81000 + 64800 + 103680 + 48600 + 25920$$
$$= 324000$$

Difference = 324000 – 203760 = 120240

Required profit%

$$= \dfrac{120240}{203760} \times 100 = 59\%$$

125. (b) Total cost price of all items together = 203760

Total selling price of all items together

$$= 72000 + 51840 + 86400 + 36450 + 18144 = 264834$$

Total marked price of all items together = 324000

Required ratio = (264834 – 203760) :
$$(324000 - 264834) = 61074 : 59166 = 3393 : 3287$$

126. (c) Total cost price of all items together = 203760

Total selling price of all items together = 264834

Total profit = 264834 – 203760 = 61074

$$\text{Required\%} = \dfrac{61074}{203760} \times 100 = 29.97\%.$$

127. (d) Cost price of bed = 54000

Selling price of bed = 72000

Profit = 72000 – 54000 = 18000

Cost price of dining set = 72000

Selling price of dining set = 86400

Profit = 86400 – 72000 = 14400

$$\text{Required \%} = \dfrac{18000 - 14400}{14400} \times 100$$

$$= \dfrac{3600 \times 100}{14400} = 25\%$$

128. (e) Total amount of discount = 59166

$$\text{Required average} = \dfrac{59166}{5} = ₹\ 11833.2$$

$$\text{Average marked price} = \dfrac{324000}{5} = ₹\ 64800$$

Average selling price

$$= \dfrac{264834}{5} = ₹\ 52966.80$$

Difference = 64800 – 52966.80
$$= ₹\ 11833.20$$

Sol. (129–133) :

Trains	Speed	Time	Distance	Notes
A	$\dfrac{1240}{22}$ = 56.36 km/h	22 hrs	$60 \times 14 - 50 \times 8$ $= 840 + 400$ $= 1240$ km	Speed of train A is 60 km/h on first day and it runs with $\dfrac{5}{6}$ th of its original speed on second day. Train A starts at 10 A.M on Monday and completes its journey at 8 A.M on Tuesday.
B	$\dfrac{1240}{22} \times \dfrac{8}{5}$ = 90.18 km/h	$22 \times \dfrac{100}{110} = 20$ hrs	$\dfrac{1240 \times 8}{110} \times 20$ $= 1803.6$ km	Respective ratio of speed of trains A, C and B is 5 : 6 : 8. Running time of train A is 10% more than that of B
C	$\dfrac{1240}{22} \times \dfrac{6}{5}$ = 67.6 km/h	$\dfrac{1240 \times 110}{1240 \times 6} = 18.3$ hrs	$930 \times \dfrac{4}{3}$ $= 1240$ km	Respective ratio of speed of trains A, C and B is 5 : 6 : 8 Respective ratio of distance covered by train C and train D is 4 : 3.
D	$\dfrac{930}{11}$ = 84.5 km/h	$22 \times \dfrac{50}{100} = 11$ hrs	$1240 \times \dfrac{75}{100}$ $= 930$ km	Train D covers 25% less distance than train A. Train D takes 50% less time than train A.
E	$\dfrac{930}{11} \times \dfrac{5}{4}$ = 105.68 km/h	$\dfrac{11 \times 2}{1} = 22$ hrs	$\dfrac{930 \times 5}{44} \times 22$ $= 2325$ km	Respective ratio of speed of train D and that of train E is 4 : 5. Respective ratio of time taken by D and that of E is 1 : 2.

129. (a) Total distance covered by all trains together
$$= 1240 + 1803.6 + 1240 + 930 + 2325 = 7538.6 \text{ km}$$
Total time taken by all trains together
$$= 22 + 20 + 18.3 + 11 + 22 = 93.3 \text{ hrs}$$
Required average speed $= \dfrac{7538.6}{93.3} = 80.79$ km/h

130. (b) Average speed of train A = 56.36 km/h
Average speed of train E = 105.68 km/h
Difference = 105.68 – 56.36 = 49.32 km/h
Required% $= \dfrac{49.32}{105.68} \times 100 = 46.6\%$

131. (e) Distance covered by train B in 20 sec
$$= 90.18 \times \dfrac{5}{18} \times 20 = 501 \text{ m}$$

length of train B = 501 – 200 = 301 m
length of train D = $84.5 \times \dfrac{5}{18} \times 18 = 422.5$ m
Required ratio = 301 : 422.5 = 602 : 845

132. (d) According to the question
Distance covered by train A = 1240 km
Time = 22 hrs
Distance covered by train C = 1240 km
Time = 18.3 hrs
Since distance covered by train A and train B are same, therefore required difference = 22 – 18.3 = 3.7 hrs

133. (c) Total distance covered by all trains together = 7538.6 km
Required average distance $= \dfrac{7538.6}{5} = 1507.72$ km

Sol. (134–138) :

Workshop	Number of workers	Number of male workers	Number of female workers	Notes
A	$900 \times \dfrac{5}{6-5} = 4500$	$4500 \times \dfrac{3}{5} = 2700$	$4500 - 2700 = 1800$	Respective ratio of number of workers in workshops A and C is 5 : 6. Respective ratio of number of male workers and that of female workers in workshop A is 3 : 2
B	$4500 \times \dfrac{100}{120} = 3750$	$3750 - 2250$ $= 1500$	$3750 \times \dfrac{150}{150+100}$ $= 3750 \times \dfrac{3}{5} = 2250$	Number of workers in workshop A is 20% more than number of workers in workshop B. Number of female workers in workshop B is 50% more than number of male workers in this workshop.
C	$4500 \times \dfrac{6}{5} = 5400$	$2700 \times \dfrac{7}{6} = 3150$	$5400 - 3150 = 2250$	Number of workers in workshop C is 900 more than that of workers in workshop A. Respective ratio of number of workers in workshops A and C is 5 : 6 Respective ratio of number of male workers in workshops A and C is 6 : 7.

D	$4500 \times \dfrac{120}{100} = 5400$	$5400 \times \dfrac{100}{100+80}$ $= 3000$	$5400 - 3000 = 2400$	Number of workers in workshop D is 20% more than that of workers in workshop A. Number of female workers in workshop D is 20% less than that of male workers in this workshop.
E	$3750 \times \dfrac{100}{125} = 3000$	$3000 \times \dfrac{1}{3} = 1000$	$3000 - 1000 = 2000$	Number of workers in workshop B is 25% more than that of workers in workshop E. Respective ratio of number of male workers and that of female workers is 1 : 2.

134. (a) Total number of male workers in all workshop together
= 2700 + 1500 + 3150 + 3000 + 1000 = 11350
Average number of male workers in all workshop
$= \dfrac{11350}{5} = 2270$
Total number of female workers in all workshops together
= 1800 + 2250 + 2250 + 2400 + 2000 = 10700
Average number of female workers in all workshops
$= \dfrac{10700}{5} = 2140$
Required difference = 2270 – 2140 = 130

135. (b) Total number of workers in workshop D = 5400
Total number of trained workers in workshop D
$= 3000 \times \dfrac{50}{100} + 2400 \times \dfrac{40}{100} = 1500 + 960$
$= 2460$
Let salary of a worker of D be x then salary of a trained worker of workshop D
$= x \times \dfrac{125}{100} = 1.25\,x$
Total salary of all trained workers in workshop D
$= 2460 \times 1.25\,x = 3075\,x$
Total salary of all workers of workshop D
$= 2940 \times x + 2460 \times 1.25x = 2940x + 3075x = 6015x$
Required %
$= \dfrac{3075x}{6015x} \times 100 = 51.12\%$

136. (e) Total number of male workers in all workshop together
= 11350
Total number of female workers in all workshop together = 10700
Required ratio = 11350 : 10700 = 227 : 214

137. (c) Let salary of a male worker of workshop C be 5x, then salary of a female worker of workshop C be 4x
Total salary of male workers of C = $3150 \times 5x = 15750x$
Total salary of female workers of C
$= 2250 \times 4x = 9000x$
Difference = $15750x - 9000x = 6750x$
Required %
$= \dfrac{6750x}{9000x} \times 100 = 75\%$

138. (d) Total number of workers in workshops A, C and E together
= 4500 + 5400 + 3000 = 12900
Average number of workers in workshops A, C and E
$= \dfrac{12900}{3} = 4300$
Total number of workers in workshops B and D together
= 3750 + 5400 = 9150
Average number of workers in workshops B and D
$= \dfrac{9150}{2} = 4575$
Required ratio
= 4300 : 4575 = 172 : 183

Sol. (139–143):

Persons	Distance	Time	Speed	Notes
A	1 km = 1000 m	$250 - 5 \times 10 = 200$ sec.	$\dfrac{1000}{200} = 5$ m/s	If A and E are running in a 100 m race then E loses by 20 m or 5 sec.
B	1 km = 1000 m	$\dfrac{1000}{4} = 250$ sec.	$\dfrac{200}{50} = 4$ m/s	B crosses a 200 m long train in 50 sec. when train is standing on the platform
C	1 km = 1000 m	$\dfrac{1000}{5} = 200$ sec.	$4 \times \dfrac{125}{100} = 5$ m/s	C is 25% more as fast runner as E.
D	1 km = 1000 m	$200 + 10 \times 5 = 250$ sec.	$\dfrac{1000}{250} = 4$ m/s	In a race of 200 m A can beat D by 10 sec.
E	1 km = 1000 m	$\dfrac{1000}{4} = 250$ sec.	$\dfrac{20}{5} = 4$ m/s	If A and E are running in a 100 m race then E loses by 20 m or 5 sec.

139. (a) Time for A for complete a round of track

$$= \frac{500}{5} = 100 \text{ sec.}$$

Time for B for complete a round of track

$$= \frac{500}{4} = 125 \text{ sec.}$$

Required time = L.C.M. of 100 sec and 125 sec
= 500 sec.

140. (b) Total distance covered by all persons = 5×1000
= 5000 m

Total time taken by all persons together
= 200 + 250 + 200 + 250 + 250 = 1150 sec.

Required speed = $\dfrac{5000}{1150}$ = 4.34 m/s

141. (c) Speed of A = 5 m/s
Time = 20 sec.
length of train = $5 \times 20 = 100$ m
speed of D = 4 m/s
Time = 30 sec
length of bridge = $4 \times 30 = 120$ m
Required ratio = 100 : 120 = 5 : 6

142. (e) Required time = $\dfrac{200}{5} - \dfrac{200}{5} = 0$

143. (d) Let speed of train be x m/s
Relative speed = $(x - 5)$ m/s
According to the question
$(x - 5) \, 12 = 300$

$$x - 5 = \frac{300}{12} \qquad x - 5 = 25$$

$\therefore \quad x = 30$ m/s

Sol. (144–148)

Cities	Number of males	Number of females	Total Population	Notes
A	$120960 - 48384$ $= 72576$	$120960 \times \dfrac{40}{100}$ $= 48384$	$100800 \times \dfrac{120}{100}$ $= 120960$	Total population of city A is 20% more than that of city D. 40% of total population of city A is population of females. 30% of the male population and 20% of female population of city A are minors.
B	$126000 \times \dfrac{3}{5}$ $= 75600$	$126000 - 756000$ $= 50400$	$100800 \times \dfrac{5}{4}$ $= 126000$	Respective ratio of total population of cities B,D and E is 5 : 4 : 8. Respective ratio of male population and female population of city B is 3 : 2. 25% of total population of city B are minors. Difference between total male population and total female population of city B is 25200.
C	$126000 \times \dfrac{2}{3+2}$ $= 50400$	$126000 \times \dfrac{3}{3+2}$ $= 75600$	$\dfrac{5}{4} \times 100800$ $= 126000$	28% of total population of city C are minors where 25% of male population and 30% of female population are minors.
D	$100800 \times \dfrac{125}{100+125}$ $= 100800 \times \dfrac{5}{9}$ $= 56000$	$100800 - 56000$ $= 44800$	$126000 \times \dfrac{80}{100}$ $= 100800$	Population of city D is 20% less than population of city C. Male population of city D is 25% more than female population of this city. 20% of male population and 18% of total population are minors in city D.
E	$201600 - 100800 =$ 100800	$50400 \times \dfrac{2}{1}$ $= 100800$	$100800 \times \dfrac{8}{4}$ $= 201600$	Respective ratio of number of male numbers to that of female minors in city E is 5:4 Respective ratio of total population of cities B, D and E is 5 : 4 : 8. Respective ratio of female population of cities B and E is 1 : 2. 20% of total population of city E are minors. Respective ratio of number of male minors to that of female minor in E is 5 : 4

144. (e) Total population of city B = 126000

Total adult population of city B = $126000 \times \dfrac{75}{100} = 94500$

Total population of city D = 100800
Total number of minors in city D

$$= 100800 \times \frac{18}{100} = 18144$$

Total adult population of city D = $100800 - 18144$
$$= 82656$$
Required ratio = 94500 : 82656 = 375 : 328

145. (d) Total number of minors in city A

$$= 72576 \times \frac{30}{100} + 48384 \times \frac{20}{100} = 31449.6 = 31450$$

Total number of minors in city B

$$= 126000 \times \frac{25}{100} = 31500$$

Total number of minors in city C

$$= 126000 \times \frac{28}{100} = 35280$$

Total number of minors in city D

$$= 100800 \times \frac{18}{100} = 18144$$

Total number of minors in city E

$$= 201600 \times \frac{20}{100} = 40320$$

Total number of minors in all cities together

$$= 31450 + 31500 + 35280 + 18144 + 40320$$
$$= 156694$$

Total population of all cities together

$$= 120960 + 126000 + 126000 + 100800 + 201600$$
$$= 675360$$

Required % $= \dfrac{156694}{675360} \times 100 = 23.20\%$

146. (c)   Total male population of all cities together

$$= 72576 + 75600 + 50400 + 56000 + 100800$$
$$= 355376$$

Total female population of all cities together

$$= 48384 + 50400 + 75600 + 44800 + 100800$$
$$= 319984$$

Required difference $= \dfrac{355376 - 319984}{5} = \dfrac{35392}{5}$
$$= 7078.4 = 7078$$

147. (b)   Total number of employed persons in city A

$$= 72576 \times \frac{50}{100} + 48384 \times \frac{25}{100} = 48384$$

Required % $= \dfrac{48384 \times 100}{120960} = 40\%$

148. (a)   Total population of city C = 126000
Total number of minors in city C = 35280
Total number of adults in city C = 126000 − 35280
$$= 90720$$
Total population of city D = 100800
Total number of minors in city D = 18144
Total number of adults in city D
$$= 100800 - 18144$$
$$= 82656$$
Required difference
$$= 90720 - 82656 = 8064$$

Sol. (149-153) :

Schools	Number of Students	Number of boys	Number of girls	Notes
A	$6300 \times \dfrac{150}{150-100}$ $= 18900$	$18900 \times \dfrac{1}{2}$ $= 9450$	$18900 - 9450$ $= 9450$	Difference between number of students in schools A and C is 6300. Number of students in school A is 50% more than that of in school C. Number of boys and that of girls is equal in school A. 30% of total students are failed in school A.
B	$28350 \times \dfrac{8}{5}$ $= 45360$	$45360 \times \dfrac{3}{5}$ $= 27216$	$45360 - 27216$ $= 18144$	Respective ratio of number of students in schools D and B is 5 : 8. Respective ratio of number of boys and that of girls in school B is 3 : 2 50% boys and 75% girls are passed the exam from school B.
C	$18900 \times \dfrac{100}{150}$ $= 12600$	$12600 \times \dfrac{3}{5}$ $= 7560$	$12600 - 7560$ $= 5040$	Number of students in school A is 50% more than that of in school C. Respective ratio of number of boys and that of girls in school C is 3 : 2 30% boys and 40% girls are failed in the exam from school C.
D	$18900 \times \dfrac{150}{100}$ $= 28350$	$28350 \times \dfrac{5}{9}$ $= 15750$	$28350 - 15750$ $= 12600$	Number of students in school D is 50% more than that of in school A. Respective ratio of number of boys and that of girls in school D is 5 : 4. 40% students are failed in school D.
E	$10584 + 9072$ $= 19656$	$7560 \times \dfrac{140}{100}$ $= 10584$	$\dfrac{10584 \times 6}{7}$ $= 9072$	28% of total students are passed the exam from school E. 30% boys and 27% girls are passed in the school E. Number of boys in school E is 40% more than the number of boys in school C. Respective ratio of number of boys and that of girls in school E is 7 : 6

149. (a)   Total number of passed students in A

$$= 18900 \times \frac{70}{100} = 13230$$

Total number of passed students in school B

$$= 27216 \times \frac{50}{100} + 18144 \times \frac{75}{100} = 27216$$

Total number of passed students in school C

$$= 7560 \times \frac{70}{100} + 5040 \times \frac{60}{100} = 8316$$

Total number of passed students in school D

$$= 28350 \times \frac{60}{100} = 17010$$

Total number of passed students in school E

$$= 19656 \times \frac{28}{100} = 5503.6 = 5504$$

Total number of passed students in all school together
$$= 13230 + 27216 + 8316 + 17010 + 5504 = 71276$$
Total number of students $= 18900 + 45360 + 12600 + 28350 + 19656 = 124866$

Required % $= \dfrac{71276}{124866} \times 100 = 57.08\%$

150. (b) Total number of boys in all schools together
$$= 9450 + 27216 + 7560 + 15750 + 10584 = 70560$$
Total number of girls in all schools together
$$= 9450 + 18144 + 5040 + 12600 + 9072 = 54306$$

Required difference $= \dfrac{70560 - 54306}{5} = \dfrac{16254}{5}$
$$= 3250.8 = 3251$$

151. (c) Passing percentage of students in A
$$= \frac{13230}{18900} \times 100 = 70$$
Passing percentage of students in E = 28%
Required ratio = 70 : 28 = 5 : 2

152. (d) Number of students in B = 45360
Number of passed students in B = 27216
Number of failed students in B = 45360 − 27216 = 18144
Required ratio = 27216 : 18144 = 3 : 2

153. (e) Total number of students in D = 28350
Number of passed students in D = 17010
Number of failed students in D = 28350 − 17010
$$= 11340$$
Required difference = 17010 − 11340 = 5670

Sol. (154-158):

City/Schemes	Scheme L	Scheme M	Scheme N
State P	160	250	300
State Q	200	300	100
State R	160	200	200
Total	520	750	600

154. (d) In 2019, The projects allocated for State Q under Scheme M increases by 30% = 300 * 130/100
$$= (195) \times 2 = 390$$
The project allocated for State R under scheme N decreases by 45% = 200 * 55/100 = 110
Thus the total number of projects in 2019 for State Q under scheme M and State R under Scheme N = 500
From the given options 500 projects obtained only from option D.

155. (c) The average number of projects under Scheme M and Scheme N for State R and State Q together = (300 + 200 + 100 + 200)/4 = 800/4 = 200

156. (a) Fund allocated for State R under these three schemes = (15 * 160) + (200 * 19) + (200 * 17) = 9600 crores = 96000 Millions

157. (d) The total number of projects under Scheme L and Scheme M together = 520 + 750 = 1270 Projects

158. (d) The number of Projects allocated under scheme L is 20% more than that of number of projects allocated for State R under
Scheme L = 160 * 120/100 = 96 × 2 = 192
The number of projects allocated under scheme M is 40% less than that of number of projects allocated for State Q under
Scheme M = 300 * 60/100 = 180
The total number of projects in State X is 600
Then number of projects allocated for State X under scheme N = 600 − 192 − 180 = 228 projects

Sol. (159-163) :

Subject	Company P (18000)	Company Q (15000)
R&D	2600	2800
Marketing	2880	1800
Accounts	1720	1000
Production	4000	3600
HR	3600	3000
Finance	3200	2800

159. (e) Total Number of employees in Marketing and Accounts together (in P) = 2880 + 1720 = 4600
Total Number of employees in Marketing and Accounts together (in Q) = 1800 + 1000 = 2800
Required difference = 4600 − 2800 = 1800

160. (a) The number of female R&D employee in company P = (3/4 * 2600) = 1950
The number of female R&D employees in company Q = 1950 − 350 = 1600
The number of male R&D employees in company Q = 2800 − 1600 = 1200

161. (d) Total number of employees in Finance and Production together in P = 4000 + 3200 = 7200
Total number of employees in Finance and Production together in Q = 2800 + 3600 = 6400
Required ratio = 7200 : 6400 = 9 : 8

162. (b) Number of HR employees in company Q = 3000
Number of HR employees in company P = 3600
Required percentage = {(3600 − 3000) * 100}/3600 = 50/3%

163. (a) Total number of employees in company P = 18000
Total number of employees in company Q = 15000
Required percentage = {18000 * 100}/15000 = 120%

Sol. (164-168):

Total number of boys $= 3120 \times \dfrac{7}{12} = 1820$

Number of girls $= 3120 - 1820 = 1300$

Countries	Boys	Girls
USA	770	260
China	182	364
Canada	364	130
China & Canada	156	312
Canada & USA	208	104
China, Canada & USA	140	130

164. (b) Number of girls for only Canada, China and USA tour
$= 260 + 364 + 130 = 754$
Number of boys for only Canada, China and USA tour
$= 770 + 182 + 364 = 1316$.
$\therefore$ Required percent $= \dfrac{754}{1316} \times 100 = 57.29\%$

165. (d) Total number of boys enrolled for Canada four
$= 364 + 156 + 208 + 140 = 868$
Number of girls $= 130 + 312 + 104 + 130 = 676$
$\therefore$ Required answer $= 868 + 676 = 1544$

166. (c) Required ratio $= (260 + 364) : (770 + 130)$
$= 52 : 75$

167. (a) Required number of students
$= (140 + 130) + 312 + 208 = 790$

168. (e) Number of girls for China $= 312 + 364 + 130 = 806$
Required percent $= \dfrac{806}{3120} \times 100 = 26\%$

Sol. (169-173):

Number of current accounts $= 4100 \times \dfrac{2}{5} = 1640$

Number of saving accounts $= 4100 \times \dfrac{25}{100} = 1025$

Number of NRI accounts $= 4100 \times \dfrac{18}{100} = 738$

Number of senior citizenship and recurring accounts
$= (4100 - 1640 - 1025 - 738) = 697$
and number of recurring accounts = Number of senior citizenship accounts $+ 137$.
$\therefore$ $2 \times$ Number of senior citizenship accounts $+ 137$
$= 697$
Number of senior citizenship accounts
$= \dfrac{697 - 137}{2} = 280$
and, Number of recurring account $= 280 + 137 = 417$.

169. (c) Difference $= 280 + 1025 - 417 = 888$.

170. (a) Total of senior citizenship + NRI + current accounts.
$= 280 + 738 + 1640 = 2658$.

171. (e) Required percent
$= \dfrac{738}{(1640 + 1025)} \times 100 = 27.69\% \approx 28\%$

172. (d) Number of current accounts that are operative
$= 1640 \times \left(1 - \dfrac{30}{100}\right) = 1640 \times \dfrac{70}{100} = 1148$

173. (b) Required ratio $= (1640) : (697)$

174. (b) Total population in A and C is 16000 and 12800
Population in B $\Rightarrow \dfrac{16000}{4} \times 5 = 20{,}000$
Cycle manufactured by X, Y and Z
$= 16000 + 12800 + 20000 = 48800$
Total cycle manufactured by X
$= \dfrac{48800}{61} \times 22 = 17600$
By Y $= \dfrac{48800}{61} \times 19 = 15200$
By Z $= \dfrac{48800}{61} \times 20 = 16000$
Cycle supplied by X $= \dfrac{60}{100} \times 17600 = 10560$
By Y $= \dfrac{75}{100} \times 15200 = 11400$
By Z $= \dfrac{80}{100} \times 16000 = 12800$
Cycle supplied by B
$= 10560 + 11400 + 12800 - 16000 - 12800 = 5960$
Revenue $= 8000 \times 5960 = 47680000 = 4.768$ cr.

175. (d) Total revenue $= 9.6$ cr
Total cycle supplied $= \dfrac{\text{Revenue}}{8000}$
$= \dfrac{9.6 \text{ cr}}{8000} = 12000$
Cycles supplied by Z $= \dfrac{12000}{3} = 4000$
Total profit $= 4000 \times (8000 - 6000) = 80$ lakh

DATA ANALYSIS

Comparison between two different values, quantities etc is called data analysis. Two quantities are generally coded as x and y or quantity1 and quantity2. There are two types of questions in data analysis.

(i) SINGLE QUESTIONS BASED ANALYSIS : In this type of questions one or more questions are asked for two different codes.

For example :

Q. Find the values of x and y and answer as

(a) If $x > y$ (b) If $x < y$

(c) If $x = y$ (d) If $x \geq y$ or $x \leq y$

(e) If can't be determined

x = Cost price of an article which is sold at 20% profit after 40% discount. Marked price of this artical is 1200.

y = Cost price of an article which is sold at 20% profit after 20% discount and its marked price is 900.

Answer: (c) $x = 1200 \times \dfrac{60}{120} = 600$

$y = 900 \times \dfrac{80}{120} = 600$

Hence, $x = y$

(ii) PARAGRAPH BASED ANALYSIS : These type of questions are based on paragraph like caselets. Generally five questions are asked based on a paragraph.

For example :

In the paragraph some information is given about some different schools. Two different values are coded as x and y. Study the paragraph carefully for the values of x and y then answer as

(a) If $x > y$ (b) If $x < y$

(c) If $x = y$ (d) If $x \geq y$ or $x \leq y$

(e) If can't be determined

Number of students is school A is 25% more than number of students in school C where number of boys is 25% more than number of girls in this school. Number of girls in school B is 20% more than number of boys in school A. Respective ratio of number of boys and that of girls in school A is 7 : 5. Difference between number of students in schools A and C is 1800. Number of girls in school B is 60% of total number of students in this school.

Q. x = Average number of boys in all schools together

y = Average number of girls in all schools together

Schools	Number of students	Number of boys	Number of girls	Notes
A	$1800 \times \dfrac{125}{25}$ $= 9000$	$9000 \times \dfrac{7}{12} = 5250$ $= 3750$	$9000 - 5250$	Difference between number of students in school A and C is 1800. Respective ratio of number of boys and girls in school A is 7 : 5. Number of students is school A is 20% more than school C.
B	$6300 \times \dfrac{100}{60}$ $= 10500$	$10500 - 6300 =$ 4200	$5250 \times \dfrac{120}{100}$ $= 6300$	Number of girls in school B is 20% more than number of boys in school A. Number of girls in school B is 60% of total number of students in this school.
C	$9000 \times \dfrac{100}{125}$ $= 7200$	$7200 \times \dfrac{125}{100+125}$ $7200 \times \dfrac{5}{9} = 4000$	$7200 - 4000$ $= 3200$	Number of students in school A is 25% more than school C. Number of boys is 25% more than number of girls in school C.

Ans (a) x = Average number of boys in all schools together

$$= \dfrac{5250 + 4200 + 4000}{3} = \dfrac{13450}{3}$$

y = Average number of girls in all schools together

$$= \dfrac{3750 + 6300 + 3200}{3} = \dfrac{13250}{3}$$

Hence, $x > y$

EXERCISE

DIRECTIONS (Qs. 1-10) : *In the following questions two values are coded as X and Y. Find the values of X and Y then answer as*

(a) If X > Y   (b) If X < Y
(c) If X = Y   (d) If X ≥ Y or X ≤ Y
(e) If relation can't be established between X and Y

1. A train is moving with uniform speed. Another train is moving with 50% more speed than first train in opposite direction. They crosses a person in 20 sec and 15 sec respectively then
X = Length of first train
Y = Length of second train

2. A, B and C are running together on a race track. In a 200m race A beets B by 10 sec and C by 40 m. If A gives a start of 50 m to B then they finish at same time then:
X = Speed of B
Y = Speed of C

3. A train is moving with uniform speed of 60 km/h. Another train is moving in opposite direction to the first train and both trains cross each other in 30 sec. A person feels the first train crosses him in 18 sec then
X = Length of first train
Y = Length of second train

4. Respective ratio of lengths of two trains is 4 : 5. First train crosses a person standing on platform in 20 sec and second train crosses a telegraph pole is 30 sec then
X = Speed of first train
Y = Speed of second train

5. A person is running with a uniform speed of 9 km/h. Person crosses a train standing on platform in 1 min and another train crosses the same train in 18 sec with a speed of 60 km/h then
X = Length of first train
Y = Length of second train

6. X = Cost price of the cooler which marked price is 1500 and it is sold at 20% profit after a discount of 40%.
Y = Cost price of a cooler which marked price is 1000 and it is sold at 20% profit after a discount of 10%.

7. Respective ratio of marked price of a T. V and marked price of a Mobile is 3 : 4. T.V is sold at 20% Profit after a discount of 30% and Mobile is sold at cost price after two discounts of 25% and 20% then
X = Cost price of T.V
Y = Cost price of Mobile

8. X = Profit amount when a Laptop is sold at 12000 after a discount of 20% and seller got 20% profit on it.
Y = Discount amount on same Laptop.

9. Respective ratio of cost price and selling price of a Mixer is 4 : 5 and it is sold after 2500 discount. Its marked price is 15000.
X = Profit amount
Y = Discount amount

10. X = Total discount when two successive discounts are allowed on marked of 2500 are 30% and 10%
Y = Total discount when two successive discounts of 20% and 20% are allowed on marked price of 2500.

DIRECTIONS (Qs. 11-15) : *In the paragraph some informations are given about selling of some different items. Two different values are coded as X and Y in the questions based on paragraph. Study the paragraph carefully and answer the questions as*

(a) If X > Y   (b) If X < Y
(c) If X = Y   (d) If X ≥ Y or X ≤ Y
(e) If can't be established relation between X and Y

A T.V is sold at 10% profit after a discount of 20%. Cost price of a mobile is 20% more than cost price of T.V and 40% less than cost price of laptop. Selling price of Mobile is 5 times of that of a mixer which is sold at 20% profit after a discount of 20% at marked price. Selling price of A.C is 50% more than its cost price and 50% less than its marked price. Amount of Profit on T.V is Rs. 3000. Mobile is sold at 25% loss after a discount of 50%. Selling price of laptop is two times of that of T.V and cost price of laptop is 40% less than its marked price. Selling price of A.C is 100% more than cost price of T.V.

11. X = Total cost price of T.V and laptop together
Y = Marked price of A.C

12. X = Cost price of Mobile
Y = Marked price of Mixer

13. X = Cost price of T.V and A.C together
Y = Cost price of Laptop

14. X = Average Profit amount on all items together
Y = Average discount amount on all items together

15. X = Marked price of Laptop
Y = Total selling price of T.V, mobile and A.C

DIRECTIONS (Qs. 16-20) : *In the paragraph given below some informations are given about some different trains. Two different values are coded as X and Y in the questions based on paragraph. Study the paragraph carefully for exact values of X and Y and answer as :*

(a) If X > Y   (b) If X < Y
(c) If X = Y   (d) If X ≥ Y or X ≤ Y
(e) If can't be established relation between X and Y.

Train A starts at 7 AM and reaches its destination at 5 PM same day. Speed of train D is 50% more than speed of train A which runs 2 hr less than train E for same distance. Train C covers 50% more distance than train A which coveres 20% more distance than train B, Train C covers 400 km more than B. Train D covers 50% more distance than total distance covered by trains A and C together. Running time of train B is 20% of that of D. Time taken by train C is equal to total time taken by trains A and B together, then

16. X = Total time taken by A and C together.
     Y = Time taken by train D.

17. X = Speed of train B
     Y = Speed of train D

18. X = Total distance covered by trains B and D together
     Y = Total distance covered by trains A, C and E together

19. X = Average speed of all trains together
     Y = Speed of train C

20. X = Average distance of all trains together
     Y = Distance covered by train E

DIRECTIONS (Qs. 21-25) : *In each of the following questions two values are coded as X and Y. Find the exact values of X and Y and answer as following.*

  (a) If X > Y   (b) If X < Y
  (c) If X = Y   (d) If X ≤ Y or X ≥ Y
  (e) If can't be established relation between X and Y

21. A is 20% more efficient worker than B. B is 20% less efficient worker than C. If A, B and C can complete a piece of work in 25 days then:
     X = Number of days required for A to complete whole work alone.
     Y = Number of days required for C to complete whole work alone.

22. 5 men and 9 boys can complete a piece of work in 12 days. 9 men and 5 boys can complete same piece of work in 15 days then
     X = daily wages of 30 men
     Y = Daily wages of 90 boys

23. A can complete a piece of work in 25 days. B can complete same piece of work is 20% less time than A. If A, B and C can complete the same work in 10 days then
     X = Time taken by B for whole work
     Y = Time taken by C for whole work

24. A, B and C are working together. If A and B together completed $\dfrac{11}{25}$ of work and B and C together complete $\dfrac{17}{25}$ of work. They got Rs. 2500 for the work then
     X = Share of B
     Y = Share of C

25. A and B together is 3 times work efficient than C. A and C is 3 times efficient than B then
     X = Time required for A for whole work
     Y = Time required for C and B together for whole work

DIRECTIONS (Qs. 26-30) : *In the paragraph some informations are given about some different persons. Study the paragraph carefully for values of X and Y and answer as :*

  (a) If X > Y   (b) If X < Y
  (c) If X = Y   (d) If X ≥ Y or X ≤ Y
  (e) Can't be established relation between X and Y

Salary of A is 20% more than that of B who saves 25% of his salary. E saves 25% more than D who saves one third of his salary. Respective ratio of savings of A and E is 3 : 5 and salary of C is equal to total expenditures of A and E together. Expenditures of A and E are 50% and 60% of their salaries respectively. Saving of C is 50% of his expenditure. Expenditure of D is 24000.

26. X = Difference between salaries of D and E
     Y = Difference between Expenditures of D and E

27. X = Saving of A
     Y = Total saving of B and C together

28. X = Salary of B
     Y = Average salary of all persons together

29. X = Average salary of A and E together
     Y = Total saving of B, C and D together

30. X = Average expenditure of all persons together
     Y = Average saving of A and E together

DIRECTIONS (Qs. 31-35) : *In the paragraph some data is given about some different schools. Study the given data carefully and answer the related questions as below where two different values are coded as X and Y.*

  (a) If X > Y   (b) If X < Y
  (c) If X = Y   (d) If X ≥ Y or X ≤ Y
  (e) Can't be established relation between X and Y

Number of students in school C is 50% more than that of E. Number of boys in school A is 20% less than number of girls in same school. Number of boys in school B is 20% less than that of D but number of girls in school B is 25% more than that of girls in D. Respective ratio of number of boys and that of girls in school D is 4 : 5 and difference between number of boys in school B and D is 160. Number boys in school A is 20% more than that of boys is school B. Number of boys in school C is equal to number of girls in school E where number of boys is 50% of total number of students. Number of girls in school D is 25% more than that of E. Number of girls in school C is 60% of total number of students in this school.

31. X = Difference between number of students in school C and D
     Y = Difference between number of students in school D and E

32. X = Average number of students in school A and C
     Y = Average number of students in school B and D

33. X = Total no. of boys in schools C, D and E together
     Y = Total no. of girls in schools A and B together

34. X = Number of boys in school D
     Y = Number of girls in school E

35. X = Average number of students in all school together
     Y = Total number of students in school B

DIRECTIONS (Qs. 36-40) : *In the paragraph some informations are given about the workers of some different companies. In the questions based on paragraph two different values are coded as X and Y. Study the paragraph carefully for exact values of X and Y and answer as*

  (a) If X > Y   (b) If X < Y
  (c) If X = Y   (d) If X ≤ Y or X ≥ Y
  (e) If can't be established relation between X and Y

Total number of workers in company D is 50% less than that of A which is 20% less than that of E. Respective ratio of number of trained workers is B, C and D is 4 : 7 : 5. Number of trained workers in B is 20% less than number of untrained workers in this company. Number of trained workers in company D is 40% of total number of workers in this company. Number of untrained workers in companies A and C are 60% and 50% of total number of employees in these companies respectively. Difference between number of trained workers and untrained workers in D is 400. Number of trained workers in C is 20% less than number of untrained workers in E then

36. X = Number of untrained workers in B
    Y = Number of trained workers in D

37. X = Average number of trained workers in all companies together
    Y = Average number of untrained workers in all companies together

38. X = Difference between number of trained workers and untrained workers in E
    Y = Total number of workers in C

39. X = Difference between total number of workers in companies A and E
    Y = Difference between total number of workers in companies B and C

40. X = Number of female workers in all companies together
    Y = Number of male workers in all companies together

DIRECTIONS (Qs. 41-63) : *In the following questions two values are coded as X and Y. Find the values of X and Y then answer as*

(a) If X > Y   (b) If X < Y
(c) If X = Y   (d) If X ≥ Y or X ≤ Y
(e) If relation can't be established between X and Y

41. Three pipes are connected in a tank. First pipe is 50% more fast than other pipe and third is a outlet pipe. Third pipe can empty the tank in 30 hrs. If all three are working together then they can fill the tank in 15 hrs then
    X = Time taken by first pipe to fill the tank.
    Y = Time taken by third pipe to empty the tank.

42. Three persons are working together. A is 50% more efficient than B. C is 60% efficient to A and B. If A, B and C can complete a piece of work in 30 days then
    X = No of days required for A to complete whole work.
    Y = No of days required for C to complete whole work.

43. A, B and C can complete a piece of work in 30 days. If A and B start the work and they left after 10 days then $\frac{3}{4}$ work is remaining for C. If B works alone for 30 days then $\frac{1}{2}$ work is remaining for A and C then
    X = No of days required for A for whole work
    Y = No of days required for C for whole work

44. Respective ratio of ages of Meera and her mother is 3:8. 8 years hence age of Meera's brother is half of her mother. If Meera is 6 years younger than her brother than ;
    X = Sum of ages of Meera and her brother
    Y = Age of mother

45. A person is 6 years elder than his wife. Age of person is 5 times of that of son and age of mother is 4 time of daughter then

X = Sum of ages of father and daughter
Y = Sum of ages of mother and son

46. Two cars are moving with uniform speeds from A and B respectively. Distance between A and B is 500 km. If both cars reach their destination (B and A) in 16 hrs. and 25 hrs. after meeting then
    X = speed of car moving from A to B
    Y = speed of car moving from B to A

47. A starts a business by investing some amount. B joins here after 4 months investing 50% more amount than A. C joins them for last 4 months by investing amount equal to 60% of total amount of A and B together. If they got annual profit of Rs 100000, then
    X = difference between shares of A and B
    Y = difference between shares of B and C

48. A and B started a business together. They invested 150000 and 120000 respectively. After 4 months B invested another 25% and A withdraws 25% if they got annual profit of 212000 then
    X = share of A in profit
    Y = share of B in profit

49. A can complete a piece of work in 50 days. A is 25% more efficient than B. If A and B can complete the same work in 10 days with the help of C then
    X = number of days required for B to complete whole work alone
    Y = number of days required for C to complete whole work alone

50. Three persons A, B and C are working together. A and B completed $\frac{7}{15}$ of the whole work and B and C completed $\frac{11}{15}$ of whole work together then;
    X = working efficiency of A
    Y = working efficiency of C

51. Speed of boat in still water is 2 times to speed of current. If a person covers 50 km in 10 hrs in upstream then;
    X= time required to cover 40 km in downstream
    Y = time required to cover 30 km in upstream

52. A, B and C can complete a piece of work in 50 days. A is 25% more work efficient than B. B and C can complete the work in 60 days alone then;
    X = Number of days required for C to complete the whole work alone.
    Y = Number of days required for B to complete the whole work alone.

53. X = Square of least two digits number completely divisible by 6, 5, 10, 9 and 15
    Y = Square of highest two digits number which is completely divisible by 30,15, 18 and 45.

54. Two trains are moving in same direction. First train crosses a 120m platform in 20 sec and second train crosses a 100m long platform in 30 sec.
    X = speed of first train.
    Y = speed of second train.

55. First train crosses a 150m long platform in 25 sec and second train crosses a person standing on same platform in 20 sec. If speed of both trains are 60 km/h and 45 km/h respectively then
X = length of first train.
Y = length of second train.

56. A person sells a T.V. and a music system. T.V. is sold by him in Rs. 20000 and cost price of music system is Rs. 15000. He got 20% profit on music system after 10% discount and he allow 25% discount on T.V.
X = Marked price of music system.
Y = Selling price of T.V.

57. X = number of sides of a regular polygon which each exterior angle is 18°
Y = number of sides of a regular polygon which has 170 diagonals

58. Area of a rectangle is 1200 sq m and respective ratio of its length and breadth is 3:4. Area of a square is 25 sq m more than that of rectangle then
X = perimeter of rectangle
Y = perimeter of square

59. First train crosses a 200m long platform in 15 sec and 400m long bridge in 25 second. Another train crosses a person standing on same platform in 20 sec. If speed of second train is 36 km/h then;
X = length of first train
Y = length of second train

60. Marked price of a fan is 50% more than its cost price and it is sold with 30% discount then seller's profit is ₹ 50. A bookself is sold at 10% profit for ₹ 1100 then;
X = cost price of fan
Y = cost price of bookself

61. X = Area of in circle of square which side is 20 cm
Y = Area of square which each side is 12 cm

62. Two cars are moving with uniform speeds from A and B respectively. Distance between A and B is 1000 km. If both cars reach their destination (B and A) in 36 hrs. and 64 hrs. after meeting then
X = speed of car moving from A to B
Y = speed of car moving from B to A

63. A starts a business with a investment of 75000. Capital of A is 25% less than that of B who joins 2 month after starting. C got $\frac{11}{30}$ of total profit. C joined business with A then
X = Capital of C
Y = Capital of A

(a) If X > Y   (b) If X < Y
(c) If X = Y   (d) If X ≥ Y or X ≤ Y
(e) Can't be determined

Respective ratio of the number of boys and girls in school A is 5 : 7 Average number of students in schools A, B, C, D and E is 4800. Total number of students in school E is 25% of total number of students in all schools and number of girls is 40% of total number of students in this school. Number of students in school B is 20% less than the number of students in school E and respective ratio of number of boys and girls in school B is 9 : 7. Respective ratio of number of students is school B and school D is 5 : 4 and number of boys in school B is 10% less than that of school D. Number of girls is school C is equal to number of girls in school A and respective ratio of number of students in school A and school C is 20 : 19.

64. X = Number of student in school A
Y = number of students in school B

65. X = Number of boys in school C
Y = Number of girls in school E

66. X = Average number of boys in all schools
Y = Average number of girls in all schools

67. X = Average number of boys in schools A, C and E
Y = Average number of girls in school B and D

68. X = Difference between number of students in schools A and C
Y = Difference between number of students in schools E and B

(a) If X > Y   (b) If X < Y
(c) If X = Y   (d) If X ≥ Y or X ≤ Y
(e) Can't be determined

Train A is running with a speed of 60 km/h. Distance covered by train D is 40% more than distance covered by train E and speed of train E is 20% more than train A. Train C starts at 7AM and reaches its destination at 5 PM. Its speed is 80% of the speed of train D which speed is 50% more than the speed of train A. Respective ratio of distance covered by trains A, B and C is 5 : 7 : 3. Time taken by train A is equal to the time taken by train E and 20% more than train D. Speed of train B is 4 times to number of hrs taken by E.

69. X = Time taken by A
Y = Time taken by B

70. X = Speed of C
Y = Speed of E

71. X = Average distance covered by trains A, C and E
Y = Average distance covered by trains B and D

72. X = total distance covered by A and C together
Y = total distance covered by B and D together

73. X = Speed of C
Y = total number of hrs taken by A, B, C and E together

(a) If X > Y   (b) If X < Y
(c) If X ≥ Y   (d) If X ≤ Y
(e) If X = Y or any other options

A shopkeeper has some electronic goods in his shop. Cost price of T.V is 40% less than the selling price of A.C which is sold at 20% profit after a discount of 20%. Selling price of cooler is 50% less than the cost price of T.V and it is sold at 10% profit with a discount of 20%. T.V is sold at 20% profit with a discount of 40% and amount of discount on T.V is ₹ 24000. Laptop is sold at 30% discount and its cost price is two times to selling price of Mobile which is sold at 50% gain and 25% discount. Selling price of Laptop is 50% more than the selling price of A. C and person got 20% profit on it.

74. X = Average cost price of A.C and Mobile
    Y = cost price of Laptop

75. X = Average profit amount of all items
    Y = average discount amount of all items.

76. X = cost price of Cooler
    Y = profit amount of Laptop

77. X = Profit amount of Mobile
    Y = Discount amount of Mobile

78. X = Marked price of Laptop
    Y = Marked price of A. C

DIRECTIONS (Qs. 79-83): *In the paragraph some information are given about the income expenditure and savings of some different persons. Study the given information's carefully and answer the related questions as below where two values are coded as X and Y*

(a) If X > Y	(b) If X < Y
(c) If X = Y	(d) If X ≤ Y
(e) If X ≥ Y	

Five persons A, B, C, D and E are working in 5 different fields. Salary of D is 20% less than that of B and 50% less than that of A. Expenditure of C is 80% of the expenditure of E who spends 80% of his salary. Respective ratio of savings of A and E is 8 : 5 and A saves 25% of his salary. Savings of B and D are 40% and 20% of their salaries respectively. Salary of C is 20% less than average salary of all others. Saving of E is 10000.

79. X = Salary of B
    Y = Expenditure of A

80. X = Average salary of all persons together
    Y = Salary of D

81. X = Total expenditure of all persons together
    Y = Total salary of A, D and E together

82. X = Saving of A
    Y = Saving of C

83. X = Total saving of all persons together
    Y = Salary of A

DIRECTIONS (Qs. 84-88): *In the paragraph some information is given about income and expenditure of some different persons. Two different values are coded as X and Y. Study the paragraph carefully for the values of X and Y and answer as:*

(a) If X > Y	(b) If X < Y
(c) If X = Y	(d) If X ≥ Y or X ≤ Y
(e) If can't be determined.	

Income of B is 20% less than D who saves 30% of his income. C saves 25% of his income and his transport expenditure in 40% of his total expenditure. C spends 18000 on transport. Income of A is 25% more than that of C and his expenditure is 20% less than C. Respective ratio of income of A and that of B is 3:4. Respective ratio of expenditure and saving of B is 5:3. Income of E is equal to total saving of B and D together and E saves 60% of his income.

84. X = Difference between expenditure of A and that of E.
    Y = Difference between saving of B and that of D.

85. X= Average salary of A, C and E.
    Y = Average salary of B and D.

86. X= Percentage of expenditure of C.
    Y = Percentage of expenditure of A.

87. X = Average expenditure of all persons together.
    Y = Average saving of all persons together.

88. X = Average income of all persons.
    Y = Income of C.

DIRECTIONS (Qs. 89–93): *In the paragraph some information is given about production and selling of some different electronic goods of a company . Two different values are coded as X and Y. Study the paragraph carefully for the values of X and Y and answers as.*

(a) If X > Y	(b) If X < Y
(c) If X = Y	(d) If X ≥ Y or X ≤ Y
(e) If can't be determined.	

10% of total number of T.V. are defective and 20% of remaining are unsold. Number of produced A.C. is 25% less than number of produced T.V. 10% of total number of produced A.C. is remain unsold. Number of produced laptops is 20% more than T.V. and number of defective laptops is 50% more than that of T.V. Number of unsold laptops is 50% of that of T.V. Respective ratio of number of produced T.V, P.C. and music system is 8 : 5 : 10. 10% of total number of music system remain unsold and respective ratio of number of defective music system and unsold music system is 3 : 2. Number of unsold T.V. is 9000. There is no defective or unsold P.C.

89. X = Average number of defective pieces of all items together.
    Y = Average number of unsold pieces of all items together.

90. X = Total number of sold T.V.
    Y = Total number of sold Music System.

91. X = Total number of A.C produced by company.
    Y = Total number of Music System produced by company.

92. X = Total number of defective items.
    Y = Average number items

93. X = Total number of unsold T.V and A. C
    Y = Total number of unsold Laptop and Music system.

DIRECTIONS (Qs. 94-98): *In the paragraph some information is given about some different trains. Two values are coded as X and Y. Study the paragraph carefully for the values of X and Y answer and as*

(a) If X > Y	(b) If X < Y
(c) If X = Y	(d) If X ≥ Y or X ≤ Y
(e) If, can't be determined.	

Train C starts at 5 A.M and reaches its destination at 5 P.M same day. Respective ratio of speed of trains A and D is 7 :

9 and respective ratio of time taken to these trains is 3 : 2. Speed of train B is 20% more than that of E which speed is 25% less than that of A. Train B covers 10% less distance than train C. Speed of train D is 20% more than that of C. Time taken by train C is 20% more than that of D. Difference between distance covered to trains A and D is 90 km. Time taken by train A is 50% more than that of B. Time taken by train E is 40% of total time taken by A and B together.

94. X = Total time taken by all trains together.
    Y = Speed of train A.

95. X = Average speed of all trains together
    Y = Total time taken by A, B and E together

96. X = Average distance covered by all trains together
    Y = Distance covered by train C.

97. Train C crosses a man standing on platform in 27 sec. and train E crosses a telegraph pole in 36 sec. then
    X = length of train C
    Y = length of train E

98. X = Time taken by train B
    Y = Time taken by train D

DIRECTIONS (Qs. 99–103): *In the paragraph some information is given about some different runners. Two different values are coded as X and Y. Study the paragraph carefully for the values of X and Y and answers as*

  (a) If X > Y   (b) If X < Y
  (c) If X = Y   (d) If X ≥ Y or X ≤ Y
  (e) If can't be determined

A beats C by 20 m in the race of 200 m. Five runners are running in a race of 1 Km. B beats E by 10 sec. in a race of 500 m. If B and C are running in 100 m race C wins by 5 sec. and B is 20 m behind him. D is 25% more as fast runner as B.

99. X = Time taken by A for 5 Km race
    Y = Time taken by D for 4 Km race.

100. X = Average speed of all runners together for 1 Km race
    Y = Speed of C.

101. X = Distance covered by D is 10 min.
    Y = Distance covered by E is 15 min.

102. X = Difference between speeds of A and E
    Y = Difference between speeds B and D.

103. X = Speed of B
    Y = Speed of E

DIRECTIONS (Qs.104-108): *In the paragraph some information is given about some different schools. Two different values are coded as X and Y. Study the paragraph carefully for the value of X and Y and answer as*

  (a) If $X > Y$ (b) If $X < Y$
  (c) If $X = Y$ (d) If $X \geq Y$ or $X \leq Y$
  (e) If can't be determined.

In school A number of boys is 25% less than that of C where number of boys is 25% more than that of girls. Number of boys in school B is 20% more than that of A and number of girls in school B is 20% less than that of C. Number boys in school D is 45% less than total number of students in this school. Respective ratio of number of students in schools.

A, D and E is 4 : 5 : 8. Number of boys in school E is 50% more than that of girls in this school. Difference between number of boys and that of girls in school D is 600. Number of students in school C is 25% less than number of students in school E.

104. X = Average number of boys in all schools together.
    Y = Average number of girls in all schools together.

105. X = Number of passed girls in school B.
    Y = Number of failed boys in school B.

106. If 50% boys and 40% girls are passed the exam from school C and 40% boys and 70% girls are passed the exam from school E. Then
    X = Number of failed students from school C.
    Y = Number of failed students from school E.

107. X = Total number of boys in schools A and D together.
    Y = Total number of girls in schools B and E together.

108. X = Percentage of boys in school C
    Y = Percentage of boys in school A

DIRECTIONS (Qs. 109-113): *In the paragraph some information is given about some different trains. Two different values are coded as X and Y. Study the paragraph carefully for the values of X and Y and answer as*

  (a) If X > Y   (b) If X < Y
  (c) If X = Y   (d) If X ≥ Y or X ≤ Y
  (e) If can't be determined

Train A covers 20% more distance than train D. Train E starts at 10 AM and reaches its destination at 8 PM same day. Distance covered by train E is 50% more than that of A. Respective ratio of speeds of trains D, B and C is 4 : 8 : 9. Train D takes 20% more time than train E and difference between speed of train B and C is 10 km/h. Respective ratio of time taken by train A and that of train D is 3 : 4. Respective ratio of distance covered by train C and that of train E is 5 : 4. Train B covers 50% more distance than train D.

109. X = Average speed of all trains together
    Y = Speed of train E

110. X = Distance covered by train C
    Y = Average distance covered by all trains together

111. X = Length of train B
    Y = Length of train D

112. Train A crosses a person standing on platform in 18 sec and Train E crosses a tree in 12 sec.
    X = Length of train A
    Y = Length of train E

113. X = Time taken by train B for 800 km
    Y = Time taken by train A for 1000 km

DIRECTIONS (Qs. 114–118): *In the paragraph some information is given about income and expenditure of some different persons. Two different values are coded as X and Y. Study the paragraph carefully for the values of X and Y and answer as:*

  (a) If X > Y   (b) If X < Y
  (c) If X = Y   (d) If X ≥ Y or X ≤ Y
  (e) If can't be determined.

Expenditure of B is three times of the saving of E who spends 80% of his income. Income of A is 20% more than that of C who saves 20% more than D. Respective ratio of expenditure of B and that of D is 4 : 5. Income of E is 25% more than that of A and difference of their income is 18000. D saves 25% more than E. Respective ratio of expenditure of B and saving of A is 3 : 1. Expenditure of B is 50% more than his saving.

114. X = Income of C.
Y = Income of E.

115. X = Difference between average expenditure and average saving of all persons together.
Y = Average saving of all persons together.

116. X = Difference between income of B and that of E.
Y = Difference between income of C and that of A.

117. X = Percentage of expenditure of B.
Y = Percentage of expenditure of D.

118. X = Income of A, B and E together.
Y = Total expenditure of all persons together.

DIRECTIONS (Qs. 119–123): *In the paragraph some information is given about a shop. Two values are coded as X and Y. Study the paragraph carefully for the values of X and Y and answer as:*

  (a) If X > Y   (b) If X < Y
  (c) If X = Y   (d) If X ≥ Y or X ≤ Y
  (e) If can't be determined

A laptop is sold at 50% profit after a discount of 25%. Cost price of a T.V is 50% less than that of an A.C. which is sold at 20% profit. Selling price of A.C. is equal to average of its cost price and market price. Cost price of a P.C is 20% more than cost price of T.V and its market price is 50% less than marked price of laptop. Cost price of a music system is 25% less than that of T.V and it is sold at 20% profit after 10% discount. Amount of profit on music system is ₹ 3600. Marked price of laptop is two times of cost price of A.C. P.C. is sold at 25% profit and respective ratio of cost price of T.V. and marked price of T.V is 2 : 5 and it is sold at 50% profit.

119. X = Average profit amount of all items together.
Y = Average discount amount of all items together.

120. X = Difference between marked price and cost price of A.C.
Y = Difference between marked price and cost price of P.C.

121. X = Average cost price of A.C, T.V and Music system.
Y = Average marked price of P.C and Laptop.

122. X = Profit on T.V.
Y = Discount on music system.

123. X = Cost price of laptop.
Y = Marked price of T.V.

DIRECTIONS (Qs. 124–128): *In the paragraph some information is given about some different workshops. Two different values are coded as X and Y. Study the paragraph carefully for values of X and Y and answer as:*

  (a) If X > Y   (b) If X < Y
  (c) If X = Y   (d) If X ≥ Y or X ≤ Y
  (e) If can't be determined

In workshop A number of workers is 50% more than number of workers in workshop D where 60% workers are male. Number of workers in workshop B is 20% less than that of workers in C where number of workers is 25% more than that of A. Number of workers in workshop B is 50% more than number of female workers in this workshop. Difference between number of male workers and that of female workers in D is 1200. Number of male workers in A is 25% more than number of female workers in this workshop. Respective ratio of number male workers and female workers in C is 4 : 5. Number of female workers in B is 20% more than number of female workers in E where number of male workers is equal to that of A.

124. X = Average number of male workers in all workshops together.
Y = Average number of female workers in all workshops together.

125. X = Difference between number of male workers in A and E.
Y = Difference between number of workers in B and D.

126. X = Percentage of male workers in C.
Y = Percentage of female workers in D.

127. 50% of total number of male workers are trained in C and 60% of total number of workers are trained in this workshop then
X = Total number of untrained male workers in C.
Y = Total number of trained female workers in C.

128. X = Total number of workers in A and E together.
Y = Total number of workers in B, C and D together.

DIRECTIONS (Qs. 129–133): *In the paragraph some information is given about car production of some different companies. Two values are coded as X and Y. Study the paragraph carefully for the values of X and Y and answer as:*

  (a) If X > Y   (b) If X < Y
  (c) If X = Y   (d) If X ≤ Y or X ≥ Y
  (e) If can't be determined

Number of cars produced by company B is 25% more than that of C. Respective ratio of number of cars produced by companies C, A and E is 8 : 5 : 9. Number of cars produced by company E is 10% less than that of D. 60% of total number of cars produced by company A are air-conditioned. Respective ratio of number of air-conditioned cars and general cars produced by B is 5 : 7. Company C produced 6000 less cars than E. Number of air-conditioned cars produced by company E is 20% less than number of general cars produced by this company. Company C produced equal number of air-conditioned and general cars. Numbers of air-conditioned cars produced by company A is 50% less than that of D.

129. X = Total number of air conditioned cars produced by all companies together.
Y = Total number of general cars produced by all companies together.

130. X = Difference between total number of cars produced by A and E.
Y = Difference between total number of cars produced by B and D.

131. X = Average number of cars produced by A, C and E.
     Y = Average number of cars produced by B and D.

132. X = Number of general cars produced by B.
     Y = Number of air conditioned cars produced by D.

133. X = Number of cars produced by A.
     Y = Number cars produced by B.

DIRECTIONS (Qs. 134-138): *In the paragraph some information is given about some different students who attended final exam. The different values are coded as X and Y Study the paragraph carefully for values of X and Y and answer as.*

(a) If X > Y
(b) If X < Y
(c) If X = Y
(d) If X ≥ Y or X ≤ Y
(e) If can't be determined

A obtained 60% marks in all subjects together. B obtained 20% less marks than E who obtained 25% more marks than A in all subjects together. Respective ratio of total marks obtained by C and that of D is 4 : 5. B obtained 50% and 45% marks in Hindi and English respectively. Full marks in the exam is 500 and respective ratio of full marks of Hindi, English and Math is 2 : 1 : 2. A obtained 20% more marks than B in English and 25% more marks than B in Hindi. Respective ratio of marks obtained by E in Hindi, English and Math is 5 : 3 : 7. Total marks obtained by A is equal to that of C. Respective ratio of marks obtained by C in Hindi, English and Math is 7 : 5 : 8. D obtained 20% more marks than E in English and 20% less marks than E in Math.

134. X = Percentage of marks obtained by B in Hindi.
     Y = Percentage of marks obtained by E in Math.

135. X = Average percentage of marks obtained by all students in English.
     Y = Average percentage of marks obtained by all students in Hindi.

136. X = Total marks obtained by A in all subjects together.
     Y = Total marks obtained by D in all subjects together.

137. X = Difference between total marks obtained by B and C in all subjects together.
     Y = Difference between total marks obtained by A and E in all subjects together.

138. X = Total marks obtained by all students together in Math.
     Y = Total marks obtained by all students together in Hindi.

DIRECTIONS (Qs. 139-143): *In the paragraph some information is given about the workers of some different workshops. Two different values are coded as X and Y. Study the information carefully for the values of X and Y and answer as*

(a) If X > Y
(b) If X < Y
(c) If X = Y
(d) If X ≥ Y or X ≤ Y
(e) If can't be determined

Number of workers in workshop B is 50% more than that of A where number of male workers is 20% more than that of female workers and 40% of male workers and 50% female workers are trained in this workshop. Number of workers in workshop D is 25% more than that of E where respective ratio of number of male workers and that of female workers is 3 : 2. Respective ratio of number of workers in B and C is 3 : 2. Number of male workers is 50% less than that of female workers in B. Difference between number of male workers and that of female workers in B is 3600. Respective ratio of number of workers in A and E is 9 : 10.
Number of male workers in C is 25% more than member of male workers in B. Number of female workers in A is 20% less than number of female workers in E. Number of male and female workers in workshop D are equal.

139. X = Number of workers in workshop C
     Y = Number of workers in workshop A

140. X = Average number of male workers in all workshops together
     Y = Average number of female workers in all workshops together

141. X = Total number of trained workers in workshop B
     Y = Total number of trained workers in workshop D

142. X = Total number of workers in B and E together
     Y = Total number of male workers in A, C and D together

143. X = Percentage of trained workers in A
     Y = Percentage of trained workers in D

DIRECTIONS (Qs. 144-148): *In the questions given below two different values are coded as X and Y. Find the values of X and Y and answer as*

(a) If X > Y
(b) If X < Y
(c) If X = Y
(d) If X ≥ Y or X ≤ Y
(e) If can't be determined

144. X = Square of highest two digits number which is completely divisible by 5, 9, 18 and 45.
     Y = Square of least number which is completely divisible by 2, 9, 18 and 30.

145. A boat goes 50 Km in downstream in 2 hrs and 54 Km is 4 hrs in upstream. A swimmer can cover 30 Km in 2 hrs upstream and 64 Km in downstream in 4 hrs then
     X = Speed of boat in still water
     Y = Speed of swimmer in still water

146. X = C.P of Fan which is sold at 20% profit after 20% discount and its marked price is 1800.
     Y = Cost price of a Fan which is sold at 50% profit for 1800.

147. A train is running with a uniform speed of 60 Km/h. A man is running with 6 Km/h uniform speed in same direction. Train crosses the man is 15 sec. and a platform is 27 sec. then
     X = Length of train
     Y = Length of platform.

148. A sum of money is lent at 20% per annum interest for 2 years
     X = Interest accrued when compounded annually
     Y = Interest accrued when compounded semi annually

DIRECTIONS (Qs. 149-153): *In the paragraph some information is given about some different persons. Two different values are coded as X and Y. Study the paragraph carefully for the values of X and Y answer as:*

(a) If X > Y
(b) If X < Y
(c) If X = Y
(d) If X ≥ Y or X ≤ Y
(e) If can't be determined

Salary of A is 50% more than that of B who saves 20% of his salary and respective ratio of expenditure and saving of E is 14 : 9. E saves 25% more amount than B. Respective ratio of expenditure of D and that of A is 5 : 8. Transport expenditure of A is 20% of his salary and 30% of his expenditure. Expenditure of C is 25% more than average expenditure of four other persons. Salary of C is two times of the expenditure of B. Saving of A is 36000. Respective ratio of food expenditure, transport expenditure and education expenditure of D is 4 : 5 : 3. Expenditure of D is 50% more than his saving.

149. X = Average expenditure of all persons together.
   Y = Expenditure of C.

150. X = Difference between expenditure and saving of B.
   Y = Difference between expenditure and saving of D.

151. X = Percentage of expenditure of C.
   Y = Percentage of expenditure of A.

152. If transport expenditure of E is 20% of his total expenditure then
   X = Transport expenditure of D
   Y = Transport expenditure of E

153. X = 50% of income of C and income of D together.
   Y = 75% of total expenditure of A and E together.

DIRECTIONS (Qs. 154-158): *In the paragraph some information is given about some different schools. Two different values are coded as X and Y. Study the paragraph carefully for the values of X and Y answer as:*

(a) If X > Y
(b) If X < Y
(c) If X = Y
(d) If X ≥ Y or X ≤ Y
(e) If can't be determined

Respective ratio of the number of boys and girls in school A is 5 : 7. Average number of students in schools A, B, C, D and E is 7200. Total number of students in school E is 25% of total number of students in all schools together and number of girls is 40% of total number of students in this school. Number of students in school B is 20% less than the number of students in school E and respective ratio of number of boys and that of girls in school B is 9 : 7. Respective ratio of number of students in school B and school D is 4 : 5 and number of boys in school B is 10% less than that of in school D. Number of girls in school C is equal to number of girls in school A and respective ratio of number of students in school A and school C is 5 : 4.

154. X = Number of students in school D.
   Y = Number of students in school E.

155. X = Number of boys in school C.
   Y = Number of girls in school E.

156. X = Average number of boys in all schools together.
   Y = Average number of girls in all schools together.

157. X = Average number of boys in schools A, C and E.
   Y = Average number of girls in schools B and D.

158. X = Difference between number of students in schools A and C.
   Y = Difference between number of students in schools E and B.

DIRECTIONS (Qs. 159-163): *In the paragraph some information is given about a shop. Two different values are coded as X and Y. Study the paragraph carefully for the values of X and Y and answer as:*

(a) If X > Y
(b) If X < Y
(c) If X = Y
(d) If X ≥ Y or X ≤ Y
(e) If can't be determined

Cost price of Bookshelf is 50% less than that of T.V which cost price is 25% more than that of P.C. Marked price of Laptop is 75% more than its cost price and it is sold with 20% discount. Selling price of Laptop is 25% less than that of A.C which is sold at 20% profit and respective ratio of its cost price and marked price is 2 : 3. Respective ratio of cost price of P.C and that of Laptop is 5 : 9. Respective ratio of selling price of Bookshelf, T.V and PC is 2 : 4 : 5 and discounts on these things are 20%, 10% and 25% respectively. Marked price of Laptop is 70000 and Bookshelf is sold at 20% profit.

159. X = cost price of Laptop.
   Y = Average cost price of all things.

160. X = Average selling price of all items.
   Y = Total profit accrued on all things.

161. X = Marked price of Bookshelf.
   Y = Selling price of PC.

162. X = Profit amount on A.C.
   Y = Profit amount on Laptop.

163. X = Average profit amount on all items together.
   Y = Average discount amount on all items together.

DIRECTIONS (Qs. 164-168): *In the paragraph some information is given about some different workshops. Two different values are coded as X and Y. Study the paragraph carefully for the values of X and Y and answer as:*

(a) If X > Y
(b) If X < Y
(c) If X = Y
(d) If X ≥ Y or X ≤ Y
(e) If can't be determined

Total number of workers in workshop C is 20% more than that of workers in workshop E. Number of workers in workshop A is 50% more than that of workers in workshop D. Respective ratio of number of workers in workshop B, A and C is 6 : 5 : 4. Respective ratio of number of male workers and that of female workers is A is 3 : 2 where 40% male workers and 45% female workers are trained. Number of male worker in B is equal to that of male workers in A. 30% of total workers and 25% of male workers are trained in B. Number of female workers in C is 25% less than that of male workers in D. Number of female workers in E is 25% more than number of female workers in A. Number of female workers in A is 3000. Number of male workers in C is 60% of total number of workers in E.

164. X = Number of male workers in A.
   Y = Number of female workers in B.

165. X = Average number of male workers in all workshops together.
   Y = Average number of female workers in all workshops together.

166. X = Percentage of male workers in C.
   Y = Percentage of male workers in E.

167. X = Number of trained workers in D.
   Y = Number of trained workers in A.

168. X = Total number of male workers in A and E together
   Y = Total number of female workers in B, C and D together.

DIRECTIONS (Qs. 169-178) : *There are three quantities provided in the questions. You have to find out the values of quantities and compare them according to the given questions.*

Give answer :
- (a) Quantity – I > Quantity – II > Quantity – III
- (b) Quantity – I = Quantity – II > Quantity – III
- (c) Quantity – I < Quantity – II > Quantity – III
- (d) Quantity – I < Quantity – II < Quantity – III
- (e) Relationship can't be established

169. The weight of P, Q, R and S are in the ratio of 9 : 7 : 4 : 5.

     Quantity – I : Find the weight of P if total weight of P, Q and R is 225 kg.

     Quantity – II. : Find the weight of Q if total weight of Q, R and S is 180 kg.

     Quantity – III. Find the weight of S if total weight of Q, R and S is 180 kg.

170. 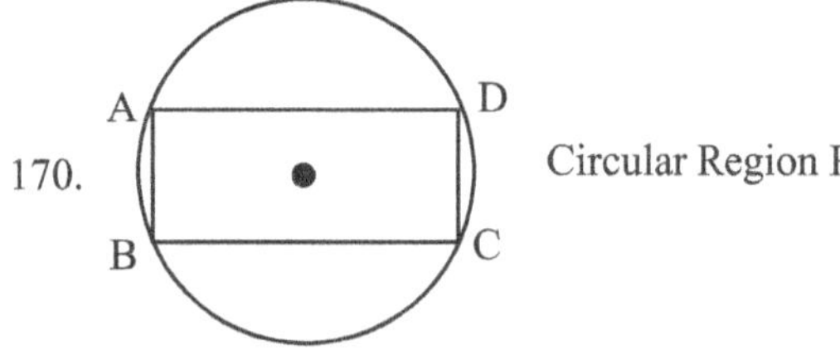

     The area of the square inscribed in the circular region P is 98 sq. cm

     Quantity – I : The area of the circular region P.

     Quantity – II : The area of the circular region P outside the square.

     Quantity – III : Perimeter of the circular region P.

171. Three friends Dipak, Sanjeet and Panas started a partnership business investing total money ₹ 22000 for 3 years. Dipak has invested ₹ 10000. Sanjeet's investment is the double of the Panas, investment. The average amount of profit earned per year is ₹ 2750.

     Quantity – I : Amount received by the Panas as the share in the total profit at the end of 3 years.

     Quantity – II : Amount received by the Sanjeet as the share in the total profit at the end of 18 months.

     Quantity – III : Amount received by the Dipak as the share in the total profit at the end of one year.

172. Two trains A and B are moving towards each other from station P and Q to reach the destination station Q and P. The two train leave their source station at 4 : 30 pm simultaneously. Distance between station P and Q is 1512.5 km and the ratio of the speed of the two trains are 5 : 6. Two trains meet at station R at 10 : 00 pm

     Quantity–I : Distance between station P and R.

     Quantity–II : Distance between station Q and R.

     Quantity–III : Distance between two trains at 7:45 pm.

173. Pravin's monthly salary is 48% more than Aman's salary and Panas's monthly salary is ₹ 10,000 less than Aman's salary. Ratio of salaries of Aman and Panas is 5 : 3.

     Quantity I : Aman's monthly Salary

     Quantity II : Average monthly Salary of Pravin and Panas

     Quantity III : Average monthly Salary of three persons.

174. There are two cylinders : The first contains 1000 ml of water, while the second contains 750 ml of alcohol. Three cups of water from the first cylinder is taken out and is mixed well in the second cylinder. Then three cups of this mixture is taken out and mixed in the first cylinder.

     Given volume of 1 cup be 251 ml.

     Quantity–I : Quantity of alcohol in cylinder–1

     Quantity–II : Quantity of water in cylinder–2

     Quantity–III : Volume of alcohol in cylinder –2

175. The ratio of the present age of Khushiram to that of Dhaniram is 3 : 4.

     Dhaniram's age after 8 years it will be $\frac{3}{2}$ times his age before 12 years.

     The ratio of the age of Dukhiram to that of Khushiram after 3 years will be 5 : 7.

     Quantity–I : Khushiram's age after 10 years.

     Quantity–II : Dhaniram's present age.

     Quantity–III : The present age of Dukhiram's mother who is 26 years older than Dukhiram.

176. A cistern has two inlet pipes A and B, one outlet pipe C. The two inlet pipes A and B can fill the cistern in 10 hours and 15 hours respectively. The pipes are opened simultaneously and it is found that due to outlet pipe, it took 2 hours excess time to fill the cistern.

     Quantity–I : Time taken to fill the cistern, when all the three pipes open simultaneously.

     Quantity–II : Time taken to empty the half filled cistern.

     Quantity–III : Time taken to fill the cistern when pipe B stop working after 2 hours.

177. Pankaj, Sanjeev and Vinod are three typists who working simultaneously, can type 228 pages in four hours. In one hour, Vinod can type as many pages more than Sanjeev as Sanjeev can type more than Pankaj. During a period of five hours, Vinod can type as many pages Pankaj can, during seven hours.

     Quantity–I : Average number of pages typed by all the three.

     Quantity–II : Average number of pages typed by Pankaj and Vinod.

     Quantity–III : Average number of pages typed by Pankaj and Sanjeev.

178. Ahmad has 15 caps of three different colours white, green and black. Difference between white caps and green caps is same as difference between green caps and black caps. Number of white caps is greater than black caps. Probability of selecting one black cap is greater than 0.2.

     Quantity–I : Probability of selecting 3 caps of exactly two of same colours.

     Quantity–II : Probability of selecting 3 colours of caps of atleast two of same colours.

     Quantity–III : Probability of selecting 3 caps of 3 different colours.

DIRECTIONS (Qs 179–188): *There are three quantities provided in the questions, you have to find out the values of the quantities and compare them according to the given codes as follows.*

@ → >
& → <
* → ≥
$ → ≤
# → = or relationship can't be established.

179. Quantity–I : $180\,p^3q^4 \div 60p^2q^{-3} \times 6\,p^6q^{-6}$; for $p > 0$; $q < 0$

Quantity–II : $36\,a^9.b^7 \times 10\,a^3.b^5 \div 24a^{-4}.b^4$ for a, b < – 1

Quantity–III : $144\,x^8y^7 \div 6x^3y^3 \div 8x^5y^4$ for $x < 0$; $y > 0$

(a) [@, $],   (b) [*, #]
(c) [&, @]   (d) [&, *]
(e) [@, #]

180. Two trains P and Q cross each other in 18 seconds when they are moving towards each other. Speed of train P is 80 km/hr and speed of train Q is 50 km/hr. Length of train P is 150 metre more than train Q.

Quantity–I : Time taken by train P to cross a platform of half of its length.

Quantity–II : Time taken by train Q to cross a platform of same length.

Quantity–III : Time taken by train P to cross a man running with speed 10 m/sec in the same direction of the train.

(a) [$, #],   (b) [&, @]
(c) [*, #]   (d) [#, &]
(e) [&, *]

181. Quantity–I : The ratio between the speed of two trains is 7 : 8. If the second train runs 400 km in 4 hours then the speed of the first train is.

Quantity–II: The speed of a train which passes a tree in 12 seconds. The length of the train is 264 m.

Quantity–III : A train of length 256 m, crosses a car in 8 seconds. The car moving towards the train with speed of 10 m/sec. The speed of the train is :

(a) [&, *],   (b) [@, *]
(c) [$, &]   (d) [$, #]
(e) [@, #]

182. Quantity–I Ram and Gopal started a business by investing ₹ 10,000 and ₹ 17,500 respectively. After 8 months, Gopal has deposit ₹2500 in the same business. Then the share of Gopal out of an annual profit of ₹ 3570.

Quantity–II : Rajat and Ali invested in a business.

Their profit ratio is 2 : 3. If Rajat invested ₹ 4000. The amount invested by Ali.

Quantity–III : John, Akbar and Shashi has started a business by investing ₹ 80,000, ₹ 50,000 and ₹ 60,000 respectively. After 6 months, Shashi withdraws ₹ 10,000 and Akbar deposited ₹ 20,000 in the same business. At the end of year, there is a profit of ₹21840.

Then, the profit share of Shashi is

(a) [$, @],   (b) [*, #]
(c) [@, @]   (d) [&, &]
(e) None of these

183. A, B, C and x are positive integers.

Quantity–I 'A' : $\dfrac{(A+x)^3 - (A-x)^3}{(x^2 + 3A^2)^2} = \dfrac{1}{8x}$, $x < -1$

Quantity–II 'B' : $\dfrac{\sqrt{B+x} - \sqrt{B-x}}{\sqrt{B-x} + \sqrt{B+x}}$ 1, $x > 1$

Quantity–III 'C' : $\dfrac{4cx(c+x)^2}{(c+x)^2 - (c-x)^2} = 1$, $x > 1$

(a) [@, &],   (b) [#, @]
(c) [$, @]   (d) [&, @]
(e) [*, #]

184. Quantity–I : $36x^9.y^7 \div 9x^5.y^2z^3 \times 7y^{-3}.z^5.xo$; $x \ge 1, y, z \le -1$

Quantity–II : $336a^3bc^{-4} \div 3a^7b^5c^{-8} \div 4a^{-4}b^{-4}.c^4$; a, b, c < 0

Quantity–III : $56p^{-3}.q^6.r^2 \times 38p^5.q^{-1}.r^8 \div 76q^3.r^7$; p, q ≤ -1 and r ≥ 0

(a) [$, *],   (b) [*, &]
(c) [*, $]   (d) [@, $]
(e) [@, &]

185. In $\triangle ACD$, $AD = AC$ and $\angle C = 2\angle E$. The distance between parallel line AB and CD is h (fig).

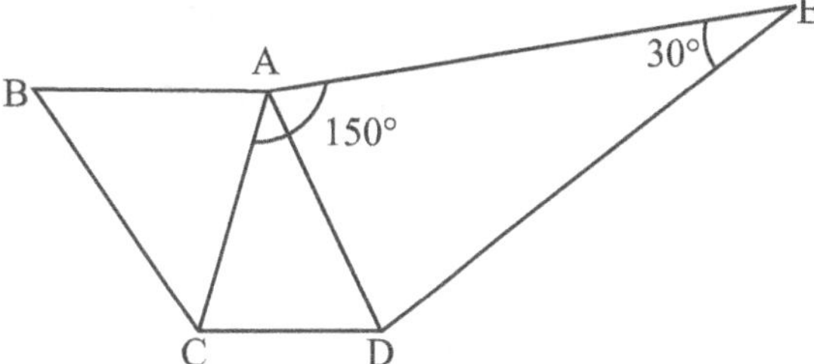

Quantity I : Area of parallelogram ABCD

Quantity II : Area of $\triangle ADE$

Quantity III : Area of $\triangle ACD$

(a) [#, @],   (b) [@, *]
(c) [#, *]   (d) [@, &]
(e) [$, @]

186. Quantity–I : $3^7 \times 4^3 \div 5^2$

Quantity–II : $\dfrac{500a^4}{b^6}$, $a \le -2$ and $-1 \le b \le 1$ but $b \ne 0$

Quantity–III : $7^3 + 6^4 \times 2^2 - 11^2$

(a) [@, $],   (b) [&, @]
(c) [@, &]   (d) [$, *]
(e) [&, #]

187. Quantity I : $360m^7n^9 \div 120m^{-2}n^3 \times 24m^{-4}n^4$, $m > 0, n < 0$

Quantity II : $240x^9y^7 \div 60x^4y^3 \div 3x^{-2}y^3$; $x < 0, y < 0$

Quantity III : $48a^8b^{12} \times 5a^3b^{-4} \div 6a^6b$; $a > 0, b < 0$.

(a) [@, &]   (b) [#, @]
(c) [$, @]   (d) [&, @]
(e) [*, #]

188. p, q, r and m are positive integers.

Quantity I : $\dfrac{(q+m)^2 - (q-m)^2}{8qm(q+m)^2} = 1$

Quantity II : $\dfrac{(r+m)^3 - (r-m)^3}{(m^2 + 3r^2)^2} = \dfrac{1}{8m}$

Quantity III : $\dfrac{\sqrt{p+m}+\sqrt{p-m}}{\sqrt{p+m}-\sqrt{p-m}} = 2$

(a) [@, &]   (b) [#, @]
(c) [$, @]   (d) [&, @]
(e) [*, #]

DIRECTIONS (189-218) : *In each of the following questions read the given statements and compare the two given quantities on its basis.*

189. Quantity I: Percentage of cement in Mortar. 1000 kg of mortar consists of 55% sand, 240 kg of lime and the rest cement.
Quantity II: Percentage of apples thrown by vendor. A vendor sells 50% of apples he had and throws away 15% of the remainder. Next day he sells 60% of the remainder and throws away the rest.
(a) Quantity I > Quantity II
(b) Quantity I < Quantity II
(c) Quantity I ≥ Quantity II
(d) Quantity I ≤ Quantity II
(e) Quantity I = Quantity II or No relation

190. Quantity I: Highest score. The average marks of a student in 8 subjects is 174. Of these, the highest marks are 4 more than the next in value. If these two subjects are eliminated, the average marks of the remaining subjects is 170.
Quantity II: Number of officers. The average monthly salary of employees, consisting of officers and workers of an organization is ₹ 3000. The average salary of an officer is ₹ 10000 while that of a worker is ₹ 2000 per month. There are a total 800 employees in the organization.
(a) Quantity I > Quantity II
(b) Quantity I < Quantity II
(c) Quantity I ≥ Quantity II
(d) Quantity I ≤ Quantity II
(e) Quantity I = Quantity II or No relation

191. Quantity I: Cost price of Sugar. If sugar is sold at 8% profit instead of 8% loss, it would have brought ₹ 12 more.
Quantity II: Cost price of a toy. A man sells a toy at a profit of 20%. If he had bought it at 20% less and sold it for ₹ 18 less he would have gained 25%.
(a) Quantity I > Quantity II
(b) Quantity I < Quantity II
(c) Quantity I ≥ Quantity II
(d) Quantity I ≤ Quantity II
(e) Quantity I = Quantity II or No relation

192. Deepak can complete a piece of work in 60 days whereas Panas and Rohit working together can complete it in 15 days. When Deepak and Rohit alternately work for a day the work gets completed in 40 days.
Quantity I: No. of days in which Panas will complete twice the work.
Quantity II: No. of days in which Rohit will complete twice the work.
(a) Quantity I > Quantity II
(b) Quantity I < Quantity II
(c) Quantity I ≥ Quantity II
(d) Quantity I ≤ Quantity II
(e) Quantity I = Quantity II or No relation

193. In the given figure, XY is the tangent to the circle, ∠XYZ = 56° and 'A' is any point on the minor arc YZ.
Quantity I : ∠YAZ
Quantity II : ∠YOZ

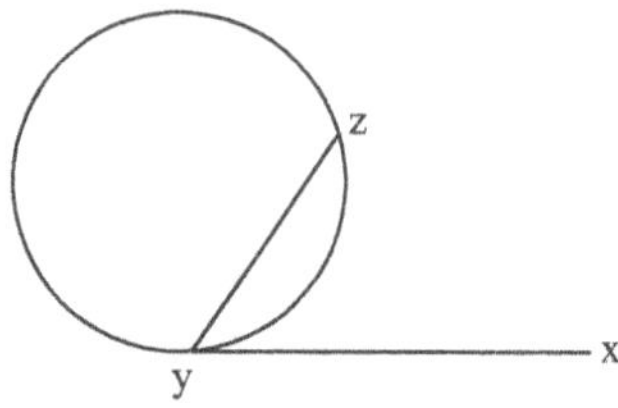

(a) Quantity I > Quantity II
(b) Quantity I < Quantity II
(c) Quantity I ≥ Quantity II
(d) Quantity I ≤ Quantity II
(e) Quantity I = Quantity II or No relation

194. Quantity I: Cost paid by an Eskimo to make an igloo with a sheet of canvas. Base radius of the tent = 9m and cost of canvas = ₹ 15/sq.m.
Quantity II: Total of A's and B's shares. An amount is to be distributed among A, B and C in the ratio 1 : 9 : 5. The difference between B's and C's shares is ₹ 3600.
(a) Quantity I > Quantity II
(b) Quantity I < Quantity II
(c) Quantity I ≥ Quantity II
(d) Quantity I ≤ Quantity II
(e) Quantity I = Quantity II or No relation

195. The difference between the time taken by two bikes to travel a distance of 700 km is 4h. 40min. The difference between their speeds is 5 km/hr.
Quantity I : Speed of faster car.
Quantity II : Speed of slower car.
(a) Quantity I > Quantity II
(b) Quantity I < Quantity II
(c) Quantity I ≥ Quantity II
(d) Quantity I ≤ Quantity II
(e) Quantity I = Quantity II or No relation

196. Quantity I: Rate of flow of the river. A motor boat can travel at 10 km/hr in still water. It travelled 91 km downstream in a river and then returned, taking altogether 20 hrs.
Quantity II: Speed of boat in still water. A boat covers a certain distance downstream in 1 hr. while it comes back in 1.5 h. The speed of stream is 3km/hr.
(a) Quantity I > Quantity II
(b) Quantity I < Quantity II
(c) Quantity I ≥ Quantity II
(d) Quantity I ≤ Quantity II
(e) Quantity I = Quantity II or No relation

197. There are two flasks: The first flask contains 500 ml. of Liquid A while the second contains 500 ml. of Liquid B. Three cups of Liquid A from the first flask is taken out and is mixed well in the second flask.
Quantity I: Proportion of Liquid B in first flask.
Quantity II: Proportion of Liquid A in second flask.
(a) Quantity I > Quantity II
(b) Quantity I < Quantity II
(c) Quantity I ≥ Quantity II
(d) Quantity I ≤ Quantity II
(e) Quantity I = Quantity II or No relation

198. Quantity I: Present age of Krishna. Krishna's age is 4 times that of Rajesh. 5 years back, it was 7 times.
Quantity II: Present age of Panas. Fifteen years hence, Panas will be four times as old as he was fifteen years ago.
(a) Quantity I > Quantity II
(b) Quantity I < Quantity II
(c) Quantity I ≥ Quantity II
(d) Quantity I ≤ Quantity II
(e) Quantity I = Quantity II or No relation

199. The ratio of the present age of Rashmi to that of Golu is 3:11.
Golu is 12 years younger than Janak. Janak's age after 7 years will be 85 years.
Quantity I: The present age of Rashmi's father, who is 25 years older than Rashmi.
Quantity II: Janak's present age
(a) Quantity I > Quantity II
(b) Quantity I < Quantity II
(c) Quantity I ≥ Quantity II
(d) Quantity I ≤ Quantity II
(e) Quantity I = Quantity II or relation cannot be established

200. Mr. Nirmal bought two shirts which together cost him ₹ 440. He sold one of the shirt at a loss of 20% and the other one at a gain of 20%. The selling price of both shirts is same.
Quantity I : CP of one of the shirt sold at a loss of 20%.
Quantity II : S.P. of one of the shirt sold at a profit of 20%
(a) Quantity I > Quantity II
(b) Quantity I < Quantity II
(c) Quantity I ≥ Quantity II
(d) Quantity I ≤ Quantity II
(e) Quantity I = Quantity II or relation cannot be established

201. Rajeev, Harish and Shetty are three typists, who working simultaneously, can type 171 pages in three hours. In one hour, Shetty can type as many pages more than Harish as Harish can type more than Rajeev. During a period of 5 hours shetty can type as many pages as Rajeev can type during seven hours.
Quantity I: Number of pages typed by Rajeev
Quantity II: Number of pages types by Harish
(a) Quantity I > Quantity II
(b) Quantity I < Quantity II
(c) Quantity I ≥ Quantity II
(d) Quantity I ≤ Quantity II
(e) Quantity I = Quantity II or relation cannot be established

202. The length of a rectangle wall is $\frac{5}{4}$ times of its height. The area of the wall is 1620m^2.
Quantity I: Height of the wall
Quantity II: Length of the wall
(a) Quantity I > Quantity II
(b) Quantity I < Quantity II
(c) Quantity I ≥ Quantity II
(d) Quantity I ≤ Quantity II
(e) Quantity I = Quantity II or relation cannot be established

203. Quantity I: $2x^2 - x - 10 = 0$
Quantity II: $8y^2 - 42y + 55 = 0$
(a) Quantity I > Quantity II
(b) Quantity I < Quantity II
(c) Quantity I ≥ Quantity II
(d) Quantity I ≤ Quantity II
(e) Quantity I = Quantity II or relation cannot be established

204. Quantity I: $8x^2 - 2x - 3 = 0$
Quantity II: $2x^2 + 7x + 3 = 0$
(a) Quantity I > Quantity II
(b) Quantity I < Quantity II
(c) Quantity I ≥ Quantity II
(d) Quantity I ≤ Quantity II
(e) Quantity I = Quantity II or relation cannot be established

205. A Tank has an inlet pipe and outlet pipe. The inlet pipe fills the tank completely in 1 hour 20 minutes when the outlet pipe is plugged. The outlet pipe empties the tank completely in 6 hours when the inlet pipe is plugged.
Quantity I: Inlet Pipe Efficiency
Quantity II: Outlet Pipe Efficiency
(a) Quantity I > Quantity II
(b) Quantity I < Quantity II
(c) Quantity I ≥ Quantity II
(d) Quantity I ≤ Quantity II
(e) Quantity I = Quantity II or relation cannot be established

206. Out of 15 applicants for a job, there are 7 women and 8 men. It is desired to select 2 persons for the job.
Quantity I: Probability of selecting no woman
Quantity II: Probability of selecting at least one woman
(a) Quantity I > Quantity II
(b) Quantity I < Quantity II
(c) Quantity I ≥ Quantity II
(d) Quantity I ≤ Quantity II
(e) Quantity I = Quantity II or relation cannot be established

207. A bag contains 7 White 3 Black 2 Pink and 4 Green balls. If four balls are picked at random,
Quantity I: Probability that at least one ball is Green
Quantity II: Probability that all balls are White.
(a) Quantity I > Quantity II
(b) Quantity I < Quantity II
(c) Quantity I ≥ Quantity II
(d) Quantity I ≤ Quantity II
(e) Quantity I = Quantity II or relation cannot be established

208 Two pipes P and Q can fill a tank in 12 hours and 18 hours respectively. The pipes are opened simultaneously and it is found that due to leakage in the bottom of the tank it took 48 minutes excess time to fill the cistern.
Quantity I: Due to leakage, time taken to fill the tank.

Quantity II: Time taken to empty the $\frac{1}{9}$th portion filled tank.

(a) Quantity I > Quantity II
(b) Quantity I < Quantity II
(c) Quantity II ≥ Quantity I
(d) Quantity II ≤ Quantity I
(e) Quantity I = Quantity II or relation cannot be established

209. Quantity I: The age of teacher, if the average age of 26 students is 24. When teacher's age is included the average increases by 1.
Quantity II: The age of teacher, if the average age of 25 students is 30. When teacher's age is included the average increases by 0.5.

(a) Quantity I > Quantity II
(b) Quantity I < Quantity II
(c) Quantity II ≥ Quantity I
(d) Quantity II ≤ Quantity I
(e) Quantity I = Quantity II or relation cannot be established

210. Quantity I: Profit Percentage, if some eggs were bought at 6 eggs for ₹5 and sold at 5 eggs for ₹6.
Quantity II: Profit Percentage, if 100 gift are bought at the rate of ₹350 and sold at the rate of ₹350 and sold at the rate of ₹48 per dozen.
(a) Quantity I > Quantity II
(b) Quantity I < Quantity II
(c) Quantity II ≥ Quantity I
(d) Quantity II ≤ Quantity I
(e) Quantity I = Quantity II or relation cannot be established

211. Quantity I: On selling 17 Caps at ₹ 720, there is a loss equal to the cost price of 5 Caps.
The cost price of a Cap is:
Quantity II: A man buys a cycle for ₹ 1350 and sells it at a loss of 12%. The selling price is:
(a) Quantity I > Quantity II
(b) Quantity I < Quantity II
(c) Quantity II ≥ Quantity I
(d) Quantity II ≤ Quantity I
(e) Quantity I = Quantity II or relation cannot be established

212. Quantity I: Ali and Ram together can do a piece of work in 4 days. If Ram alone can do the same work in 6 days, then Ali alone can do the same work in?
Quantity II: Ram can do a piece of work in 4 hours, Ali and Pavan together can do it in 3 hours, while Ram and Pavan together can do it in 2 hours. How long will Ali alone take to do it?
(a) Quantity I > Quantity II
(b) Quantity I < Quantity II
(c) Quantity II ≥ Quantity I
(d) Quantity II ≤ Quantity I
(e) Quantity I = Quantity II or relation cannot be established

213. Quantity I: Sanjeet on tour, travels first 360 km at 90 km/hr and the next 240 km at 80 km/hr.
The average speed of the tour is:
Quantity II: A went from P to Q with the speed of 60km/hr. and returned back with the speed of 90km/hr. Find the average speed.
(a) Quantity I > Quantity II
(b) Quantity I < Quantity II
(c) Quantity II ≥ Quantity I
(d) Quantity II ≤ Quantity I
(e) Quantity I = Quantity II or relation cannot be established

214. Quantity I: The ratio between the speeds of two trains is 5:6, If the second train runs 300 km in 3 hours, then the speed of the first train is:

Quantity II: Find the speed of a train which passes a tree in 14 seconds. The length of the train is 308m.
(a) Quantity I > Quantity II
(b) Quantity I < Quantity II
(c) Quantity II ≥ Quantity I
(d) Quantity II ≤ Quantity I
(e) Quantity I = Quantity II or relation cannot be established

215. Quantity I: P and Q started a business by investing ₹ 40000 and ₹ 70000 respectively.
Find the share of Q out of an annual profit of ₹ 3520.
Quantity II: A and B invested in a business. Their profit ratio is 2 : 3. If A invested ₹ 4000. Find the amount invested by B?
(a) Quantity I > Quantity II
(b) Quantity I < Quantity II
(c) Quantity II ≥ Quantity I
(d) Quantity II ≤ Quantity I
(e) Quantity I = Quantity II or relation cannot be established

216. Quantity I: The age of Ganesh is twelve times that of her daughter Rashi. If the age of Rashi is 3 years, what is the age of Ganesh?
Quantity II: The ratio between the present ages of John and Maya is 2:3. 4 years ago the ratio between their ages was 5:8. What will be John's age after 7 years?
(a) Quantity I > Quantity II
(b) Quantity I < Quantity II
(c) Quantity II ≥ Quantity I
(d) Quantity II ≤ Quantity I
(e) Quantity I = Quantity II or relation cannot be established

217. Quantity I: The difference between SI and CI compounded annually on a certain sum of money for 2 years at 4% per annum is ₹ 3.2.
Find the principal.
Quantity II: A sum fetched a total simple interest of ₹ 800 at the rate of 8% per annum in 5 years. What is the sum?
(a) Quantity I > Quantity II
(b) Quantity I ≥ Quantity II
(c) Quantity II > Quantity I
(d) Quantity II ≥ Quantity I
(e) Quantity I = Quantity II or relation cannot be established

218. There are 6 Brown balls, 3 Blue balls & 4 black balls in a bag. Four balls are chosen at random.
Quantity I: The probability of their being 2 Brown and 2 Blue ball.
Quantity II: The probability of their being 2 Brown, 1 Blue & 1 Black ball.
(a) Quantity I > Quantity II
(b) Quantity I ≥ Quantity II
(c) Quantity II > Quantity I
(d) Quantity II ≥ Quantity I
(e) Quantity I = Quantity II or relation cannot be established

HINTS & SOLUTIONS

1. (b) Let speed of first train be x km/h and speed of second train be $x \times \dfrac{150}{100}$ km/h

   $X = x \times \dfrac{5}{18} \times 20 = \dfrac{50}{9} x = 5.55x$

   $Y = \dfrac{3x}{2} \times \dfrac{5}{18} \times 15 = \dfrac{225}{36} x = \dfrac{25x}{4} = 6.25x$

   Hence, $X < Y$

2. (b) $X = \dfrac{50}{10} = 5$ m/s

   $Y = \dfrac{200 - 40}{30} = \dfrac{160}{30} = 5.33$ m/s

   Hence, $X < Y$

3. (e) Here, nothing is given about speed or length of second train.

   Hence, can't be established relation between X and Y

4. (a) Let lengths of trains be 4x and 5x respectively.

   $X = \dfrac{4x}{20} = \dfrac{x}{5}$

   $Y = \dfrac{5x}{30} \times \dfrac{x}{6}$

   Hence, $X > Y$

5. (c) $X = 9 \times \dfrac{5}{18} \times 60 = 150$ m

   $Y = 60 \times \dfrac{5}{18} \times 18 - 150 = 150$ m

   Hence, $X = Y$

6. (c) $X = 1500 \times \dfrac{60}{120} = 750$

   $Y = 1000 \times \dfrac{90}{120} = 750$

   Hence, $X = Y$

7. (b) Let marked prices of T.V and mobile be 3x and 4x respectively.

   $X = 3x \times \dfrac{70}{120} = 1.75x$

   $Y = 4x \times \dfrac{75}{100} \times \dfrac{80}{100} = 2.40x$

   Hence, $X < Y$

8. (b) $X = 12000 - 12000 \times \dfrac{100}{120} = 2000$

   $Y = 12000 \times \dfrac{100}{80} - 12000 = 3000$

   Hence, $X < Y$

9. (c) Selling price $= 15000 - 2500 = 12500$

   Cost price $= 12500 \times \dfrac{4}{5} = 10000$

   $X = 12500 - 10000 = 2500$
   $Y = 15000 - 12500 = 2500$
   Hence, $X = Y$

10. (a) $X = 2500 - 2500 \times \dfrac{70}{100} \times \dfrac{90}{100} = 925$

   $Y = 2500 - 2500 \times \dfrac{80}{100} \times \dfrac{80}{100} = 900$

   Hence, $X > Y$

Sol. (11-15) :

Items	C.P.	S.P.	M.P.	Notes
T.V.	$3000 \times \dfrac{100}{10}$ $= 30000$	$30000 \times \dfrac{110}{10}$ $= 33000$	$33000 \times \dfrac{100}{80}$ $= 41250$	Amount of profit on T.V is Rs. 3000. T.V is sold at 10% profit after a discount of 20%.
Mobile	$30000 \times \dfrac{120}{100}$ $= 36000$	$36000 \times \dfrac{75}{100}$ $= 27000$	$27000 \times \dfrac{100}{50}$ $= 54000$	Cost price of mobile is 20% more than cost price of T.V. Mobile is sold at 25% loss after 50% discount.
Laptop	$36000 \times \dfrac{100}{60}$ $= 60000$	$\dfrac{33000 \times 2}{}$ $= 66000$	$60000 \times \dfrac{100}{60}$ $= 100000$	Cost price of mobile is 40% less than cost price of laptop. Selling price of Laptop is 2 items of that of T.V and cost price of laptop is 40% less than its marked price.
Mixer	$5400 \times \dfrac{100}{120}$ $= 4500$	$\dfrac{27000}{5}$ $= 5400$	$5400 \times \dfrac{100}{80}$ $= 6750$	Selling price of mobile is 5 times of that of mixer which is sold at 20% profit after 20% discount.
A.C	$60000 \times \dfrac{100}{150}$ $= 40000$	$30000 \times \dfrac{200}{100}$ $= 60000$	$60000 \times \dfrac{100}{50}$ $= 120000$	Selling price of A.C. is 100% more than cost price of T. V. Selling price of A.C. is 50% more than its cost price and selling price of A.C. is 50% less than its marked price.

11. (b) $X = 30000 + 60000 = 90000$
         $Y = 120000$
         Hence, $X < Y$

12. (a) $X = 36000$
         $Y = 6750$
         Hence, $X > Y$

13. (a) $X = 30000 + 40000 = 70000$
         $Y = 60000$
         Hence, $X > Y$

14. (b) $X = \dfrac{\begin{array}{l}(33000 + 27000 + 66000 + 5400 + 60000)\\ -(30000 + 36000 + 60000 + 4500 + 40000)\end{array}}{5}$

$$= \frac{20900}{5} = 4180$$

$$Y = \frac{\begin{array}{l}(41250 + 54000 + 100000 + 6750 + 120000)\\ -(33000 + 27000 + 66000 + 5400 + 60000)\end{array}}{5}$$

$$= \frac{322000 - 191400}{5} = 26120$$

Hence, $X < Y$

15. (b) $X = 100000$
         $Y = 33000 + 27000 + 60000 = 120000$
         Hence, $X < Y$

Sol. (16-20) :

Train	Speed	Time	Distance	Note
A	60 km/h	10 hrs	$400 \times \dfrac{120}{80} = 600$ km	Train A starts at 7 AM and reaches its destination at 5 PM same day. Train A covers 20% more distance than B.
B	$\dfrac{500}{5} = 100$ km/h	$\dfrac{25}{5} = 5$ hrs	$400 \times \dfrac{100}{80} = 500$ km	Train C covers 400 km more than B. Time taken by B is 20% of time taken by D.
C	$\dfrac{900}{15} = 60$ km/h	$10 + 5 = 15$ hrs	$400 \times \dfrac{180}{80} = 900$ km	Train C covers 50% more distance than train A. Train C covers 400 km more than B. Time taken by train C is total time taken by A and B together.
D	$60 \times \dfrac{150}{100} = 90$ km/h	$\dfrac{2250}{90} = 25$ hrs	$1500 \times \dfrac{150}{100} = 2250$	Train D covers 50% more distance than total distance covered by A and C together. Speed of train D is 50% more than A.
E	$\dfrac{600}{12} = 50$ km/h	$10 + 2 = 12$ hrs	600 km	Train A runs 2 hrs less than E for same distance.

16. (c) $X = 10 + 15 = 25$ hrs
         $Y = 25$ hrs
         Hence, $X = Y$

17. (a) $X = 100$ km/h
         $Y = 90$ km/h
         Hence, $X > Y$

18. (a) $X = 500 + 2250 = 2750$ km
         $Y = 600 + 900 + 600 = 2100$ km
         Hence, $X > Y$

19. (a) $X = \dfrac{600 + 500 + 900 + 2250 + 600}{10 + 5 + 15 + 25 + 12} = \dfrac{4850}{67}$
         ≈ 72 km/h
         $Y = 60$ km/h
         Hence, $X > Y$

20. (a) $X = \dfrac{600 + 500 + 900 + 2250 + 600}{5} = \dfrac{4850}{5}$
         $= 970$ km
         $Y = 600$ km
         Hence, $X > Y$

21. (a) Ratio of efficiency
         $A : B : C = 80 \times \dfrac{120}{100} : 80 : 100 = 96 : 80 : 100$
         $= 24 : 20 : 25$
         $X = \dfrac{25 \times 69}{24} = \dfrac{1725}{24} = 71\dfrac{21}{24}$ days
         $Y = \dfrac{25 \times 69}{25} = 69$ days
         Hence, $X > Y$

22. (b) (5 Men + 9 Boys) 12 = (9 Men + 5 Boys) 15
         60 Men + 108 Boys = 135 Men + 75 Boys
         75 Men = 33 Boys
         $\therefore$ Men : Boy = 33 : 75 = 11 : 25
         $X = 30 \times 11 = 330$ units
         $Y = 90 \times 25 = 2250$ units
         Hence, $X < Y$

23. (b) Work completed by A in 1 day $= \dfrac{1}{25}$
         Work completed by B in 1 day $= \dfrac{1}{25} \times \dfrac{100}{80} = \dfrac{1}{20}$

Work completed by C in 1 day $= \dfrac{1}{10} - \dfrac{1}{25} - \dfrac{1}{20} = \dfrac{1}{100}$

$X = 20, Y = 100$

Hence, $X < Y$

24. (b) Share of A $= 2500 \times \left(1 - \dfrac{17}{25}\right) = 800$

Share of C $= 2500\left(1 - \dfrac{11}{25}\right) = 1400 = Y$

Share of B $= 2500 - (800 + 1400) = 300 = X$

Hence, $X < Y$

25. (c) Work of $(A + B) : C = 3 : 1$

Work of $(A + C) : B = 3 : 1$

Work completed by C $= 1/4$

Work completed by B $= 1/4$

Work completed by A $= 1 - (1/4 + 1/4) = 1/2$

Hence, $X = Y$

Sol. (26-30) :

Persons	Salary	Saving	Expenditure	Notes
A	$9000 \times \dfrac{100}{50} = 18000$	$\dfrac{15000 \times 3}{5} = 9000$	$18000 - 9000 = 9000$	Respective ratio of savings of A and E is $3 : 5$. Expenditure of A is 50% of his salary.
B	$18000 \times \dfrac{100}{120} = 15000$	$15000 \times \dfrac{25}{100} = 3750$	$15000 - 3750 = 11250$	Salary of A is 20% more than that of B B saves 25% of his salary.
C	$9000 + 22500 = 31500$	$31500 \times \dfrac{1}{3} = 10500$	$31500 - 10500 = 21000$	Salary of C is equal to total expenditure of A and E together Saving of C is 50% of his expenditure
D	$24000 \times \dfrac{3}{2} = 36000$	$36000 - 24000 = 12000$	24000	Expenditure of D is 24000. D saves one third of his salary.
E	$15000 \times \dfrac{100}{40} = 37500$	$12000 \times \dfrac{125}{100} = 15000$	$37500 - 15000 = 22500$	E saves 25% more than D. Expenditure of E is 60% of his salary.

26. (c) $X = 37500 - 36000 = 1500$

$Y = 24000 - 22500 = 1500$

Hence, $X = Y$

27. (b) $X = 9000$

$Y = 3750 + 10500 = 14250$

Hence, $X < Y$

28. (b) $X = 15000$

$Y = \dfrac{18000 + 15000 + 31500 + 36000 + 37500}{5}$

$= \dfrac{138000}{5} = 27600$

Hence, $X < Y$

29. (a) $X = \dfrac{18000 + 37500}{2} = \dfrac{55500}{2} = 27750$

$Y = 3750 + 10500 + 12000 = 26250$

Hence, $X > Y$

30. (a) $X = \dfrac{9000 + 11250 + 21000 + 24000 + 22500}{5}$

$= \dfrac{87750}{5} = 17550$

$Y = \dfrac{9000 + 15000}{2} = 12000$

Hence, $X > Y$

Sol. (31-35) :

Schools	No. of Students	No. of boys	No. of girls	Notes
A	$768 + 960 = 1728$	$640 \times \dfrac{120}{100} = 768$	$768 \times \dfrac{100}{80} = 960$	Number of boys in school A is 20% more than that of boys in school B. Number of boys in school A is 20% less than that of girls in same school.
B	$640 + 1250 = 1890$	$800 \times \dfrac{80}{100} = 640$	$1000 \times \dfrac{125}{100} = 1250$	Difference between number of boys in B and D is 160. Number of boys in school B is 20% less than that of D. Number of girls in school B is 25% more than that of girls in D.
C	$800 \times \dfrac{100}{40} = 2000$	800	$2000 - 800 = 1200$	Number of boys in school C is equal to number of girls in school E. Number of girls in school C is 60% of total no of students in this school. Number of students in school C is 50% more than that of E.

D	$800 + 1000 = 1800$	$160 \times \dfrac{100}{20} = 800$	$800 \times \dfrac{5}{4}$ $= 1000$	Difference between number of boys in school B and D is 160. Number of boys in school B is 20% less than that of D. Respective ratio of number of boys and that of girls in school D is 4 : 5.
E	$800 \times \dfrac{100}{50} = 1600$	$1600 - 800 = 800$	$1000 \times \dfrac{100}{125}$ $= 800$	Number of girls in school D is 25% more than that of E. Number of boys in school E is 50% of total no. of students in this school.

31. (c) $X = 2000 - 1800 = 200$
$Y = 1800 - 1600 = 200$
Hence, $X = Y$

32. (a) $X = \dfrac{1728 + 2000}{2} = \dfrac{3728}{2} = 1864$

$Y = \dfrac{1890 + 1800}{2} = 1845$

Hence, $X > Y$

33. (a) $X = 800 + 800 + 800 = 2400$
$Y = 960 + 1250 = 2210$
Hence, $X > Y$

34. (c) $X = 800$
$Y = 800$
Hence, $X = Y$

35. (b) $X = \dfrac{1728 + 1890 + 2000 + 1800 + 1600}{5}$

$= \dfrac{9018}{5} = 1804$

$Y = 1890$

Hence, $X < Y$

Sol. (36-40) :

Companies	Total no. of workers	No. of trained workers	No. of untrained workers	Notes
A	$2000 \times \dfrac{100}{50}$ $= 4000$	$4000 - 2400 = 1600$	$4000 \times \dfrac{60}{100}$ $= 2400$	Number of workers in D is 50% less than that of A. Number of untrained workers in A is 60% of total number of workers in this company.
B	$640 + 800 = 1440$	$800 \times \dfrac{4}{5} = 640$	$640 \times \dfrac{100}{80}$ ssss $= 1250$	Respective ratio of trained workers in B, C and D is 4 : 7 : 5. Number of trained workers in B is 20% less than number of untrained workers in this company.
C	$1120 \times \dfrac{100}{50}$ $= 2240$	$800 \times \dfrac{7}{5} = 1120$	$2240 - 1120$ $= 1120$	Respective ratio of trained workers in B, C and D is 4 : 7 : 5. Number of untrained workers in C is 50% of total number of workers in this company.
D	$400 \times \dfrac{100}{60 - 40}$ $= 2000$	$2000 \times \dfrac{40}{100}$ $= 800$	$2000 - 800$ $= 1200$	Difference between number of trained and untrained workers in D is 400. Number of trained workers in company D is 40% of total number of workers in this company.
E	$4000 \times \dfrac{100}{80}$ $= 5000$	$1120 \times \dfrac{100}{80}$ $= 1400$	$5000 - 1400$ $= 3600$	Number of girls in school D is 25% more than that of E. Number of boys in school E is 50% of total no. of students in this school.

36. (c) $X = 800$
$Y = 800$
Hence, $X = Y$

37. (a) $X = \dfrac{1600 + 640 + 1120 + 800 + 3600}{5}$

$= \dfrac{7760}{5} = 1552$

$Y = \dfrac{2400 + 800 + 1120 + 1200 + 1400}{5}$

$= \dfrac{6920}{5} = 1384$

Hence, $X > Y$

38. (b) $X = 3600 - 1400 = 2200$
$Y = 2240$
Hence, $X < Y$

39. (a) $X = 5000 - 4000 = 1000$
$Y = 2240 - 1440 = 800$
Hence, $X > Y$

40. (e) No information is given about number of males or number of females

Hence, can't be determined.

41. (b) According to the question

$$\frac{1}{X} + \frac{3}{2X} - \frac{1}{30} = \frac{1}{15}$$

$$\frac{5}{2X} = \frac{1}{10}$$

X = 25 hrs

∴ X = 25, Y = 30

Hence, X < Y

42. (c) Efficiency ratio

$$A : B : C = 1.5 : 1 : 2.5 \times \frac{60}{100} = 3 : 2 : 3$$

Hence, X = Y

43. (c) Time of A, B and C together = 30 days

Time for A + B together = 40 days ($\frac{1}{4}$ work in 10 days)

Time for C = $\frac{40 \times 30}{10} = 120$ days

Time for B = 60 days

Time for A = $\frac{40 \times 60}{20} = 120$ days

Hence, X = Y

44. (b) Let age of Meera and her mother be 3x years and 8x years respectively.\

8 years hence age of mother

= 8x + 8 years

8 years hence age of Meera's brother $= \frac{8x + 8}{2}$

= 4x + 4 years

8 years hence age of Meera = 3x + 8

According to the question

4x + 4 − 6 = 3x + 8

∴ x = 10 years

X = 3 × 10 + 3 × 10 + 6 = 66 years

Y = 8 × 10 = 80 years

Hence, X < Y

45. (e) Let age of person be x years

Age of his wife = x − 6 years

Age of son $= \frac{x}{5}$

Age of daughter $= \frac{x - 6}{4}$

Hence, cant be determined.

46. (a) Let the two cars meet after x hours

Then speed of car A

$= \frac{500}{x + 15}$ km/hr

and speed of car B $= \frac{500}{x + 25}$ km/hr

Ratio of speed of car A and B $= \frac{x + 25}{x + 15}$

= (x + 25) : (x + 15)

Hence, X > Y

47. (b) Let capital of A be x

Capital of B $= x \times \frac{150}{100} = 1.5\ x$

Capital of C $= (x + 1.5x) \times \frac{60}{100}$

$= 2.5x \times \frac{60}{100} = 1.5x$

Profit ratio of A : B : C = x × 12 : 1.5x × 8 : 1.5x × 4

= 12x : 12x : 6x = 2 : 2 : 1

X = 2 − 2 = 0

Y = 2 − 1 = 1

Hence, X < Y

48. (b) Profit share of A : B

$= (150000 \times 4 + 150000 \times \frac{75}{100} \times 8) :$

$(120000 \times 4 + 120000 \times \frac{125}{100} \times 8)$

= 600000 + 900000 : 480000 + 1200000

= 1500000 : 1680000 = 25 : 28

Hence, X < Y

49. (a) Work completed by A in 1 day $= \frac{1}{50}$

Work completed by B in 1 day

$= \frac{1}{50} \times \frac{125}{100} = \frac{1}{40}$

Time of B = 40 days

Work completed by C in 1 day

$= \frac{1}{10} - \left(\frac{1}{50} + \frac{1}{40}\right) = \frac{1}{10} - \frac{9}{200} = \frac{11}{200}$

X = 40 days

$Y = \frac{200}{11}$ days

Hence, X > Y

50. (b) Work completed by C $= 1 - \frac{7}{15} = \frac{8}{15}$

Work completed by B $= \frac{11}{15} - \frac{8}{15} = \frac{3}{15}$

Work completed by A $= 1 - \frac{11}{15} = \frac{4}{15}$

$X = \frac{4}{15}$, $Y = \frac{8}{15}$

Hence, X < Y

51. (b) Speed of boat in still water : Speed of current = 2 : 1

Speed of person in upstream $= \frac{50}{10} = 5$ km/h

Speed of boat = 10 km/h

Speed of current = 5 km/h

$$X = \frac{40}{10+5} = \frac{40}{15} = \frac{8}{3} \text{ hrs}$$

$$Y = \frac{30}{10-5} = 6 \text{ hrs}$$

Hence, X < Y

52. (b) B can complete the whole work in Y days

Work completed by B in 1 day $= \dfrac{1}{Y}$

Work completed by A in 1 day $= \dfrac{1}{Y} \times \dfrac{125}{100} = \dfrac{5}{4Y}$

According to question

$$\frac{5}{4Y} = \frac{1}{50} - \frac{1}{60} \quad \Rightarrow \quad \frac{5}{4Y} = \frac{1}{300}$$

$$Y = \frac{300 \times 5}{4} = 375$$

One day work of C $= \dfrac{1}{50} - \left(\dfrac{1}{375} + \dfrac{5}{1500} \right) = \dfrac{7}{500}$

$$X = \frac{500}{7} \text{ days}$$

Y = 375 days

Hence, X < Y

53. (c) $X = (\text{L.C.M of } 6, 5, 10, 9, 15)^2 = (90)^2 = 8100$

$Y = (\text{L.C.M of } 30, 15, 18, 15)^2 = (90)^2 = 8100$

Hence, X = Y

54. (e) Here length or speeds of trains are not given hence, can't be determined.

55. (a) $X = 60 \times \dfrac{5}{18} \times 25 - 150 = \dfrac{1250}{3} - 150 = \dfrac{800}{3}$ m

$Y = 45 \times \dfrac{5}{18} \times 20 = 250$ m

Hence, X > Y

56. (c) $X = 15000 \times \dfrac{120}{100} \times \dfrac{100}{90} = 20000$

Y = 20000

Hence, X = Y

57. (c) $X = \dfrac{360}{18} = 20$

Number of sides of regular polygon = Y

Then $\dfrac{X(X-3)}{2} = 170$

$Y^2 - 3Y = 340$

$\Rightarrow \quad Y^2 - 3Y - 340 = 0$

$\Rightarrow \quad X^2 - 20Y + 17Y - 340 = 0$

$\Rightarrow \quad Y(Y - 20) + 17(Y - 20) = 0$

$\Rightarrow \quad (Y + 17)(Y - 20) = 0$

$\therefore \quad Y = -17, 20$

Hence, Y = 20

X = Y

58. (c) Let length and breadth of rectangle be 3x and 4x respectively.

$3x \times 4x = 1200$ given

$12x^2 = 1200$

$\Rightarrow \quad x^2 = 100$

$\therefore \quad x = 10$

Area of square = 1200 + 25 = 1225

Side of square $= \sqrt{1225} = 35$

$X = 2(3 \times 10 + 4 \times 10) = 140$

$Y = 4 \times 35 = 140$

Hence, X = Y

59. (b) Length of first train is X m

$$\frac{X+200}{15} = \frac{X+400}{25}$$

$25X + 5000 = 15X + 6000$

$\Rightarrow \quad 10X = 1000$

$\therefore \quad X = 100$

X = 100 m

$Y = 36 \times \dfrac{5}{18} \times 20 = 200$ m

Hence, X < Y

60. (c) Cost price of fan is X

$$X \times \frac{150}{100} \times \frac{70}{100} - X = 50$$

$$\frac{105}{100} X - X = 50$$

$$\frac{5X}{100} = 50$$

$\therefore X = 1000$

$$Y = \frac{1100 \times 100}{110} = 1000$$

Hence, X = Y

61. (a) $X = \pi \times \left(\dfrac{20}{2} \right)^2 = 100\pi = 100 \times \dfrac{22}{7}$

$Y = (12)^2 = 144$

Hence, X > Y

62. (a) Let two cars meet after t hours

Then speed of first cars $= \dfrac{1000}{t+36}$ km/h

and speed of second cars $= \dfrac{1000}{t+64}$ km/hr

Respective ratio of speed of first cars to second cars

$$= \frac{t+60}{t+36} = (t+60) : (t+36)$$

Hence, X > Y

63. (a) Capital of A = 75000

Capital of B $= 75000 \times \dfrac{100}{75} = 100000$

Respective ratio of share of $(A + B) : C$

$$= \frac{19}{30} : \frac{11}{30} = 19 : 11$$

$A : B = 75000 \times 12 : 100000 \times 10 = 9 : 10$

$A : B : C = 19 \times \frac{9}{19} : 19 \times \frac{10}{19} : 11 = 9 : 10 : 11$

Hence, $X > Y$

Sol. (64-68):

	No. of Students	No. of Boys	No. of Girls
A	$9360 \times \frac{20}{39} = 4800$	$4800 \times \frac{5}{12} = 2000$	2800
B	$6000 \times \frac{80}{100}$ $= 4800$	$4800 \times \frac{9}{16} = 2700$	2100
C	4560	1760	2800
D	$4800 \times \frac{4}{5} = 3840$	$2700 \times \frac{100}{90} = 3000$	840
E	$4800 \times 5 \times \frac{25}{100}$ $= 6000$	3600	$6000 \times \frac{40}{100}$ $= 2400$

64. (c) $X = 4800$
$Y = 4800$
Hence, $X = Y$

65. (b) $X = 1760$
$Y = 2400$
Hence, $X < Y$

66. (a) $X = \dfrac{2000 + 2700 + 1760 + 3000 + 3600}{5}$

$= \dfrac{13060}{5} = 2612$

$Y = 4800 - 2612 = 2188$
Hence, $X > Y$

67. (a) $X = \dfrac{2000 + 1760 + 3600}{3} = \dfrac{7360}{3} = 2453$

$Y = \dfrac{2100 + 840}{2} = 1470$

Hence, $X > Y$

68. (b) $X = 4800 - 4560 = 240$
$Y = 6000 - 4800 = 1200$
Hence, $X < Y$

Sol. (69-73):

Train	Speed	Time	Distance
A	60 km/h	20 hrs	$720 \times \frac{5}{3} = 1200$ km
B	80 km/h	21 hrs	$720 \times \frac{7}{3} = 1680$ km
C	$90 \times \frac{80}{100} = 72$ km/h	10 hrs	720 km
D	$60 \times \frac{150}{100} = 90$ km/h	$20 \times \frac{10}{120}$ $= \frac{50}{3}$ hrs	$90 \times \frac{50}{3}$ $= 1500$ km
E	$\frac{6}{5} \times 60 = 72$ km/h	20 hrs	72×20 $= 1440$

69. (b) $X = 20$ hrs
$Y = 21$ hrs
Hence, $X < Y$

70. (c) $X = 72$ km/h
$Y = 72$ km/h
Hence, $X = Y$

71. (b) $X = \dfrac{1}{3}(1200 + 720 + 1400)$

$= \dfrac{3320}{3} = 1106\dfrac{2}{3}$ km

$Y = \dfrac{1680 + 1500}{2} = \dfrac{3180}{2} = 1590 km$

Hence, $X < Yt$

72. (b) $X = 1200 + 720 = 1920$
$Y = 1680 + 1500 = 3180$
Hence, $X < Y$

73. (a) $X = 72$
$Y = 20 + 21 + 10 + 20$
$= 71$
Hence, $X > Y$

Sol. (74-78):

	C.P.	S.P.	M.P.	Profit	Discount
T.V.	$36000 \times \frac{100}{120} = 30000$	36000	$24000 \times \frac{100}{40} = 60000$	6000	24000
A.C.	$50000 \times \frac{100}{120} = \frac{125000}{3}$	$30000 \times \frac{100}{60} = 50000$	$50000 \times \frac{100}{80} = 62500$	$\frac{25000}{3}$	12500

COOLER	$15000 \times \dfrac{100}{110} = \dfrac{150000}{11}$	$30000 \times \dfrac{50}{100} = 15000$	$15000 \times \dfrac{100}{80} = 18750$	$\dfrac{15000}{11}$	3750
LAPTOP	$75000 \times \dfrac{100}{120} = 62500$	$50000 \times \dfrac{150}{100} = 75000$	$75000 \times \dfrac{100}{70} = \dfrac{750000}{7}$	12500	$\dfrac{225000}{7}$
MOBILE	$31250 \times \dfrac{100}{150} = \dfrac{62500}{3}$	$\dfrac{62500}{2} = 31250$	$31250 \times \dfrac{100}{75} = \dfrac{125000}{3}$	$\dfrac{31250}{3}$	$\dfrac{31250}{3}$

74. (b) $X = \left(\dfrac{125000}{3} + \dfrac{62500}{3} \right) \div 2 = 31250$

$Y = 62500$

Hence, $X < Y$

75. (b) $X = \dfrac{6000 + \dfrac{25000}{3} + \dfrac{15000}{11} + 12500 + \dfrac{31250}{3}}{5}$

$= \dfrac{38613.6}{5}$

$Y = \dfrac{24000 + 12500 + 3750 + \dfrac{22500}{7} + \dfrac{31250}{3}}{5}$

$= \dfrac{53790.94}{5}$

Hence, $X < Y$

76. (a) $X = \dfrac{150000}{11}$

$= 13636.36$

$Y = 12500$

Hence, $X > Y$

77. (e) $X = \dfrac{31250}{3}$

$Y = \dfrac{31250}{3}$

Hence, $X = Y$

78. (a) $X = \dfrac{750000}{7}$

$Y = 62500$

Hence, $X > Y$

Sol. (79-83):

Persons	Salary	Saving	Expenditure	Note
A	$16000 \times \dfrac{100}{25} = 64000$	$10000 \times \dfrac{8}{5} = 16000$	$64000 - 16000 = 48000$	Respective ratio of savings of A and E is 8 : 5 A saves 25% of his salary.
B	$32000 \times \dfrac{100}{80} = 40000$	$40000 \times \dfrac{40}{100} = 16000$	$40000 - 16000 = 24000$	Salary of D is 20% less than that of B Savings of B is 40% of his salary.
C	$\left(\dfrac{64000 + 40000 + 32000 + 50000}{ } \right) \dfrac{80}{400}$ $= \dfrac{186000}{5} = 37200$	$37200 - 32000 = 5200$	$40000 \times \dfrac{80}{100} = 32000$	Expenditure of C is 80% of the expenditure of E salary of C is 20% less than the average salary of all others.
D	$64000 \times \dfrac{50}{100} = 32000$	$32000 \times \dfrac{20}{100} = 6400$	$32000 - 6400 = 25600$	Salary of D is 50% less than that of A. Saving of D is 20% of his salary.
E	$10000 \times \dfrac{100}{20} = 50000$	10000	$10000 \times \dfrac{80}{20} = 40000$	Savings of E is 10000. E spends 80% of his salary.

79. (b) $X = 40000$

$Y = 48000$

Hence, $X < Y$

80. (a) $X = \dfrac{64000 + 40000 + 37200 + 32000 + 50000}{5}$

$= \dfrac{223200}{5} = 44640$

$Y = 32000$

Hence, $X > Y$

81. (a) $X = 48000 + 24000 + 32000 + 25600 + 40000 = 169600$

$Y = 64000 + 32000 + 50000 = 146000$

Hence, $X > Y$

82. (b) $X = 16000$

$Y = 5200$

Hence, $X < Y$

83. (b) $X = 16000 + 16000 + 5200 + 6400 + 10000 = 44600$

$Y = 64000$

Hence, $X < Y$

Sol. (84-88):

Persons	Income	Expenditure	Saving	Notes
A	$60000 \times \dfrac{125}{100} = 75000$	$45000 \times \dfrac{80}{100} = 36000$	$75000 - 36000 = 39000$	Income of A is 25% more than that of C and his expenditure is 20% less than C.
B	$75000 \times \dfrac{4}{3} = 100000$	$100000 \times \dfrac{5}{8} = 62500$	$100000 - 62500 = 37500$	Respective ratio of income of A and that of B is 3:4. Respective ratio of expenditure and saving of B is 5:3
C	$45000 \times \dfrac{100}{75} = 60000$	$18000 \times \dfrac{100}{40} = 45000$	$60000 - 45000 = 15000$	C spends 18000 on transport. C saves 25% of his income and his transport expenditure is 40% of his total expenditure.
D	$100000 \times \dfrac{100}{80} = 125000$	$125000 - 37500 = 87500$	$125000 \times \dfrac{30}{100} = 37500$	Income of B is 20% less than D who saves 30% of his income.
E	$37500 + 37500 = 75000$	$75000 - 45000 = 30000$	$75000 \times \dfrac{60}{100} = 45000$	Income of E is equal to total saving of B and D together and E saves 60% of his income.

84. (a) X = Different between expenditure of A and that of E
 = 36000 − 30000 = 6000
 Y = Different between saving of B and that of D
 = 37500 − 37500 = 0
 Hence, X > Y

85. (b) X = Average salary of A, C and E

$$= \frac{75000 + 60000 + 75000}{3} = \frac{210000}{3} = 70000$$

 Y = Average salary of B and D

$$= \frac{100000 + 125000}{2} = 112500$$

 Hence, X < Y

86. (a) X = Percentage of expenditure of C

$$= \frac{45000}{60000} \times 100 = 75\%$$

 Y = Percentage of expenditure of A

$$= \frac{36000}{75000} \times 100 = 48\%$$

 Hence, X > Y

87. (a) Total expenditure of all persons together
 = 36000 + 62500 + 45000 + 87500 + 30000
 = 261000
 X = Average expenditure of all person together

$$= \frac{261000}{5} = 52200$$

 Total saving of all persons together
 = 39000 + 37500 + 15000 + 37500 + 45000
 = 174000
 Y = Average saving of all persons

$$= \frac{174000}{5} = 34800$$

 Hence, X > Y

88. (a) Total income of all persons together
 = 75000 + 100000 + 60000 + 125000 + 75000
 = 435000
 X = Average income of all person together

$$= \frac{435000}{5} = 87000$$

 Y = Income of C = 60000
 Hence, X > Y

Sol. (89– 93):

Electronic goods	Number of produced items	Number of defective	Number of unsold pieces	Notes
T.V	$\dfrac{9000 \times 100}{90} \times \dfrac{100}{20}$ $= 50000$	$\dfrac{50000 \times 10}{100} = 5000$	9000	Number of unsold T.V is 9000. 10% of Total number of T.V are defective and 20% of remaining are unsold.
A.C	$\dfrac{50000 \times 75}{100} = 37500$	0	$\dfrac{37500 \times 10}{100} = 3750$	Number of produced A.C is 25% less than number of produced T.V. 10% of total number of produced A.C remain unsold.

Laptop	$\dfrac{50000 \times 120}{100} = 60000$	$\dfrac{50000 \times 150}{100} = 7500$	$\dfrac{9000 \times 50}{100} = 4500$	Number of produced Laptops is 20% more than T.V. Number of defective Laptops is 50% more than that of T.V. Number of unsold Laptops is 50% of that of T.V.
P.C.	$\dfrac{50000 \times 5}{8} = 31250$	0	0	There is no defective or unsold P.C. Respective ratio of number of produced T.V, P.C. and Music system is $8 : 5 : 10$.
Music system	$\dfrac{50000 \times 10}{8} = 62500$	$\dfrac{6250 \times 3}{2} = 9375$	$\dfrac{62500 \times 10}{100} = 6250$	Respective ratio of number of produced T.V, P.C and Music system is $8 : 5 : 10$. 10% of total number of Music system remain unsold. Respective ratio of defective music system and unsold Music system is $3 : 2$.

89. (b) Total number of defective piece of all items together

$$= 5000 + 0 + 7500 + 0 + 9375 = 21875$$

X = Average number of defective pieces of all item

together $= \dfrac{21875}{5} = 4375$

Total number of unsold pieces of all items together

$$= 9000 + 3750 + 4500 + 6250 = 23500$$

Y = Average number of unsold pieces of all items

together $= \dfrac{23500}{5} = 4700$

Hence, X < Y

90. (b) X = Total number of sold T.V $= 50000 - (5000 + 9000)$
$$= 36000$$

Y = Total number of sold Music system
$$= 62500 - (9375 + 6250) = 62500 - 15625 = 46875$$

Hence, X < Y

91. (b) X = Total number of A.C produced by company = 37500

Y = Total number of Music system produced by company = 62500

Hence, X < Y

92. (b) X = Total number of defective items
$$= 5000 + 7500 + 9375 = 21875$$

Y = Average number of items

$$= \dfrac{50000 + 37500 + 60000 + 31250 + 62500}{5}$$

$$= \dfrac{241250}{5} = 48250$$

Hence, X < Y

93. (a) X = Total number of unsold T.V and A.C
$$= 9000 + 3750 = 12750$$

Y = Total number of unsold Laptop and Music system
$$= 4500 + 6250 = 10750$$

Hence, X > Y

Sol. (94–98):

Trains	Speed	Time	Distance	Notes
A	$\dfrac{630}{15} = 42$ km/h	$\dfrac{10 \times 3}{2} = 15$ hrs	$\dfrac{90 \times 21}{21 - 18} = 630$ km	Respective ratio of time taken by A and D is $3 : 2$. Difference between distance covered by trains A and D is 90 Km
B	$\dfrac{31.5 \times 120}{100} = 37.8$ km/h	$\dfrac{15 \times 100}{150} = 10$ hrs	$37.8 \times 10 = 378$ Km	Speed of train B is 20% more than that of E. Time taken by train A is 50% more than that of B.
C	$\dfrac{420}{12} = 35$ Km/h	12 hrs	$\dfrac{378 \times 100}{90} = 420$ Km	Train C starts at 5 A.M and reaches its destination at 5 P.M same day. Train B covers 10% less distance than train C.
D	$\dfrac{540}{10} = 54$ Km/h	$\dfrac{12 \times 100}{120} = 10$ hrs	$\dfrac{90 \times 18}{3} = 540$ Km	Respective ratio of speed of train A and D is $7 : 9$. Time taken by train C is 20% more than that of D. Difference between distance covered by A and D is 90 Km Speed of train D is 20% more than that of C.

E	$\dfrac{42 \times 75}{100}$ $= 31.5$ Km/h	$\dfrac{(15+10)\,40}{100} = 10$ hrs	$31.5 \times 10 = 315$ Km	Time taken by train E is 40% of total time taken by A and B together. Speed of train E is 25% less than that of A.

94. (a) X = Total time taken by all trains together
  $= 15 + 10 + 12 + 10 + 10 = 57$ hrs
  Y = Speed of train A = 42 Km/h
  Hence, X > Y

95. (a) Total distance covered by all trains together
  $= 630 + 378 + 420 + 540 + 315 = 2283$ Km
  Total time taken by all trains together
  $= 15 + 10 + 12 + 10 + 10 = 57$ hrs
  X = Average speed of all trains together
  $= \dfrac{2283}{57} = 40.05$ Km/h

  Y = Total time taken by A, B and E together
  $= 15 + 10 + 10 = 35$ hrs.
  Hence, X > Y

96. (a) Total distance covered by all trains together
  $= 630 + 378 + 420 + 540 + 315 = 2283$ Km

  X = Average distance covered by all trains together
  $= \dfrac{2283}{5} = 456.6$ Km

  Y = Distance covered by train C = 420 Km
  Hence, X > Y

97. (b) X = Length of train C $= \dfrac{35 \times 5}{18} \times 27 = 262.5$ m

  Y = Length of train E $= \dfrac{31.5 \times 5}{18} \times 36 = 315$ m
  Hence, X < Y

98. (c) X = Time taken by train B
  $= 10$ hrs
  Y = Time taken by train D
  $= 10$ hrs
  Hence, X = Y.

Sol. (99–103):

Runners	Distance	Speed	Time	Notes
A	1000 m	$\dfrac{1000}{100} = 10$ m/s	$\dfrac{200 - 100}{}$ $= 100$ sec.	A beats C by 20 m in the race of 200 m.
B	1000 m	$\dfrac{20}{5} = 4$ m/s	$\dfrac{1000}{4} = 250$ sec.	C wins by 5 sec. and B is 20 m behind him when they are running in 100 m race
C	1000 m	$\dfrac{1000}{200} = 5$ m/s	$250 - 50 = 200$ sec.	C wins by 5 sec. and B is 20 m behind him when they are running in 100 m race
D	1000 m	$\dfrac{4 \times 125}{100} = 5$ m/s	$\dfrac{1000}{5} = 200$ sec.	D is 25% more as fast runner as B.
E	1000 m	$\dfrac{1000}{270} = \dfrac{100}{27}$ m/s	$250 + 20 = 270$ sec.	B beats E by 10 sec. in a race of 500 m

99. (b) X = Time taken by A for 5 Km race
  $= 100 \times 5 = 500$ sec.
  Y = Time taken by D for 4 Km
  $= 200 \times 4 = 800$ sec.
  Hence, X < Y

100. (b) Total distance covered by all runners in 1 Km race
  $= 1 \times 5 = 5$ Km
  Total time taken by all runners for complete the race
  $= 100 + 250 + 200 + 200 + 270$
  $= 1020$ sec.
  X = Average speed of all runner for 1 Km race
  $= \dfrac{5000}{1020} = \dfrac{250}{51} = 4.9$ m/s

  Y = Speed of C = 5 m/s
  Hence, X < Y.

101. (b) X = distance covered by D in 10 min
  $= 5 \times 10 \times 60 = 3000$ m
  Y = Distance covered by E in 15 min
  $= \dfrac{100}{27} \times 15 \times 60 = 3333.3$ m
  Hence, X < Y

102. (a) Difference between speeds of A and E $= 10 - \dfrac{100}{27}$
  $= 10 - 3.70 = 6.30$ m/s
  Y = Difference between speeds of B and D
  $= 5 - 4 = 1$ m/s
  Hence, X > Y

103. (a) X = Speed of B = 4 m/s
  Y = Speed of E = 3.7 m/s
  Hence, X > Y.

Sol. (104–108):

Schools	Number of students	No. of boys	No. of girls	Notes
A	$6000 \times \dfrac{4}{5} = 4800$	$4000 \times \dfrac{75}{100} = 3000$	$4800 - 3000 = 1800$	Respective ratio of number of students in schools A, D and E is 4 : 5 : 8. Number of boys in school A is 25% less than C.
B	$3600 + 2560 = 6160$	$3000 \times \dfrac{120}{100} = 3600$	$3200 \times \dfrac{80}{100} = 2560$	Number of boys in school B is 20% more than that of A. Number of girls in school B is 20% less than that of C.
C	$9600 \times \dfrac{75}{100} = 7200$	$7200 \times \dfrac{125}{100+125}$ $= 7200 \times \dfrac{5}{9} = 4000$	$7200 - 4000 = 3200$	Number of students in school C is 25% less than number of students in school E. Number of boys in school C is 25% more than that of girls.
D	$600 \times \dfrac{100}{55-45} = 6000$	$6000 \times \dfrac{55}{100} = 3300$	$6000 - 3300 = 2700$	Difference between number of boys and that of girls in school D is 600. Number of boys in school D is 45% less than total number of students in this school.
E	$6000 \times \dfrac{8}{5} = 9600$	$9600 \times \dfrac{150}{100+150}$ $= 9600 \times \dfrac{3}{5} = 5760$	$9600 - 5760 = 3840$	Respective ratio of number of students in school A, D and E is 4 : 5 : 8. Number of boys in school E is 50% more than that of girls in this school.

104. (a) Total number of boys in all schools together
$= 3000 + 3600 + 4000 + 3300 + 5760 = 19660$
X = Average number of boys in all schools
$= \dfrac{19660}{5} = 3932$

Total number of girls in all schools together
$= 1800 + 2560 + 3200 + 2700 + 3840 = 14100$
Y = Average number of girls in all schools
$= \dfrac{14100}{5} = 2820$
Hence, X > Y

105. (e) No information is given about passed girls and passed boys in school B.
Hence, can't be determined.

106. (b) Total number of students in school C = 7200
Total passed students in school C
$= 4000 \times \dfrac{50}{100} + 3200 \times \dfrac{40}{100}$
$= 2000 + 1280 = 3280$
X = Total number of failed students in school C
$= 7200 - 3280 = 3920$

Total number of students in school E = 9600
Total number of passed students in school E
$= 5760 \times \dfrac{40}{100} + 3840 \times \dfrac{70}{100}$
$= 2304 + 2688 = 4992$
Y = Total number of failed students in school E
$= 9600 - 4992$
$= 4608$
Hence, X < Y

107. (b) X = Total number of boys in schools A and D together
$= 3000 + 3300 = 6300$
Y = Total number of girls in school B and E together
$= 2560 + 3840 = 6400$
Hence, X < Y

108. (b) X = Percentage of boys in school C
$= \dfrac{4000}{7200} \times 100 = 55\dfrac{5}{9}\%$
Y = Percentage of boys in school A
$= \dfrac{3000}{4800} \times 100 = 62\dfrac{1}{2}\%$
Hence, X < Y

Sol. (109–113)

Trains	Speed	Time	Distance	Notes
A	$\dfrac{576}{9} = 64$ km/h	$12 \times \dfrac{3}{4} = 9$ hrs	$480 \times \dfrac{120}{100} = 576$ km	Train A covers 20% more distance than train D. Respective ratio of time taken by train A and that of train D is 3 : 4.

B	$10 \times \dfrac{8}{9-8} = 80$ km/h	$\dfrac{720}{80} = 9$ hrs	$480 \times \dfrac{150}{100} = 720$ km	Difference between speed of train B and that of train C is 10 km/h. Respective ratio of speeds of trains D, B and C is 4 : 8 : 9. Train B covers 50% more distance than train D.
C	$80 \times \dfrac{9}{8} = 90$ km/h	$\dfrac{1080}{90} = 12$ hrs	$864 \times \dfrac{5}{4} = 1080$ km	Respective ratio of speeds of trains D, B and C is 4 : 8 : 9. Respective ratio of distance covered by train C and that of E is 5 : 4.
D	$80 \times \dfrac{4}{8} = 40$ km/h	$10 \times \dfrac{120}{100} = 12$ hrs	$12 \times 40 = 480$ km	Train D takes 20% more time than train E. Respective ratio of speeds of trains D, B and C is 4 : 8 : 9.
E	$\dfrac{4}{5} \times 90 = 72$ km/h	10 hrs	$576 \times \dfrac{150}{100} = 864$ km	Train E starts at 10 AM and reaches its destination at 8 PM same day. Distance covered by train E is 50% more than that of A.

109. (b) Total distance covered by all trains together
$= 576 + 720 + 1080 + 480 + 864 = 3720$

Total time taken by all trains
$= 9 + 9 + 12 + 12 + 10 = 52$ hrs

X = Average speed of all trains together

$= \dfrac{3720}{52} = 71.5$ km/h

Y = Speed of train E = 72 km/h

Hence, X < Y.

110. (a) X = Distance covered by train C = 1080 km

Total distance covered by all trains together = 3720

Y = Average distance covered by all trains together

$= \dfrac{3720}{5} = 744$ km

Hence, X > Y

111. (e) Here no information is given about lengths of these trains. Hence, can't be determined.

112. (a) X = Length of train A = $64 \times \dfrac{5}{18} \times 18 = 320$ m

Y = Length of train E = $72 \times \dfrac{5}{18} \times 12 = 240$ m

Hence, X > Y

113. (b) Speed of train B = 80 km/h

Distance = 800 km

X = Time taken by train B for 800 km = $\dfrac{800}{80} = 10$ hrs

Speed of train A = 64 km/h

Distance = 1000 km

Y = Time taken by train A for 1000 km = $\dfrac{1000}{64}$
$= 15.6$ hrs

Hence, X < Y

Sol. (114–118):

Persons	Income	Expenditure	Saving	Notes
A	$90000 \times \dfrac{100}{125}$ $= 72000$	$72000 - 18000 = 54000$	$54000 \times \dfrac{1}{3} = 18000$	Income of E is 25% more than that of A. Respective ratio of expenditure of B and saving of A is 3 : 1.
B	$54000 + 36000$ $= 90000$	$18000 \times 3 = 54000$	$54000 \times \dfrac{100}{150} = 36000$	Expenditure of B is three times of saving of E. Expenditure of B is 50% more than his saving.
C	$72000 \times \dfrac{100}{120}$ $= 60000$	$60000 - 27000 = 33000$	$22500 \times \dfrac{120}{100} = 27000$	Income of A is 20% more than that of C. C saves 20% more than D.
D	$67500 + 22500$ $= 90000$	$54000 \times \dfrac{5}{4} = 67500$	$18000 \times \dfrac{125}{100} = 22500$	Respective ratio of expenditure of B and D is 4 : 5 D saves 25% more than E.
E	$72000 \times \dfrac{125}{100}$ $= 90000$	$90000 \times \dfrac{80}{100} = 72000$	$90000 - 72000$ $= 18000$	Income of E is 25% more than that of A. Difference between income of A and that of E is 18000. E spends 80% of his income.

114. (b) X = Income of C = 60000

Y = Income of E = 90000

Hence, $X < Y$

115. (a) Total saving of all persons together

$= 18000 + 36000 + 27000 + 22500 + 18000$

$= 121500$

Total expenditure of all persons together

$= 54000 + 54000 + 33000 + 67500 + 72000$

$= 280500$

X = Difference between average expenditure and average saving of all persons together

$$= \frac{280500 - 121500}{5} = \frac{159000}{5}$$

$= 31800$

Y = Average saving of all persons together

$$= \frac{121500}{5} = 24300$$

Hence, $X > Y$

116. (b) X = Difference between income of B and that of E

$= 90000 - 90000 = 0$

Y = Difference between income of C and that of A

$= 72000 - 60000 = 12000$

Hence, $X < Y$

117. (b) X = Percentage of expenditure of B

$$= \frac{54000}{90000} \times 100 = 60\%$$

Y = Percentage of expenditure of D

$$= \frac{67500}{90000} \times 100$$

$= 75\%$

Hence, $X < Y$

118. (b) X = Income of A, B and E together

$= 72000 + 90000 + 90000 = 252000$

Y = Total expenditure of all persons together

$= 280500$

Hence, $X < Y$

Sol. (119–123):

Items	Cost Price	Selling Price	Marked Price	Notes
T.V.	$18000 \times \dfrac{100}{75} = 24000$	$24000 \times \dfrac{150}{100} = 36000$	$24000 \times \dfrac{5}{2}$ $= 60000$	Cost price of Music system is 25% less than that of T.V. Respective ratio of cost price and marked price of T.V. is 2 : 5
Laptop	$72000 \times \dfrac{100}{150} = 48000$	$96000 \times \dfrac{75}{100} = 72000$	$48000 \times 2 = 96000$	Marked price of Laptop is two times of cost of A.C. A laptop is sold at 50% profit after a discount of 25%.
A.C.	$248000 \times \dfrac{100}{50}$ $= 48000$	$48000 \times \dfrac{120}{100} = 57600$	$57600 \times 2 - 48000$ $= 115200 - 48000$ $= 67200$	Cost price of T.V. is 50% less than that of A.C. A.C. is sold at 20% profit. Selling price of A.C. is equal to average of its cost price and market price.
P.C.	$24000 \times \dfrac{120}{100} = 28800$	$28800 \times \dfrac{125}{100} = 36000$	$96000 \times \dfrac{50}{100}$ $= 48000$	Cost price of P.C. is 20% more than that of T.V. Market price of P.C. is 50% less than marked price of laptop. P.C. is sold at 25% profit.
Music system	$3600 \times \dfrac{100}{20} = 18000$	$18000 + 3600 = 21600$	$21600 \times \dfrac{100}{90}$ $= 24000$	Amount of profit on Music system is Rs. 3600. Music system is sold at 20% profit after a discount of 10%.

119. (b) Total selling price of all items together

$= 36000 + 72000 + 57600 + 36000 + 21600$

$= 223200$

Total cost price of all items together

$= 24000 + 48000 + 48000 + 28800 + 18000$

$= 166800$

Total marked price of all items together

$= 60000 + 96000 + 67200 + 48000 + 24000$

$= 295200$

X = Average profit amount of all items together

$$= \frac{223200 - 166800}{5}$$

$$= \frac{56400}{5} = 11280$$

Y = Average discount amount of all items together

$$= \frac{295200 - 223200}{5}$$

$$= \frac{72000}{5} = 14400$$

Hence, $X < Y$

120. (c) X = Difference between marked price and cost price of A.C.

$\quad$ = 67200 – 48000

$\quad$ = 19200

Y = Difference between marked price and cost price of P.C.

$\quad$ = 48000 – 28800 = 19200

Hence, X = Y

121. (b) X = Average cost price of A.C., T.V. and Music system

$$= \frac{24000 + 48000 + 18000}{3} = \frac{90000}{3}$$

$\quad$ = 30000

Y = Average marked price of P.C. and Laptop

$$= \frac{96000 + 48000}{2} = 72000$$

Hence, X < Y

122. (a) X = Profit on T.V.

$\quad$ = 36000 – 24000 = 12000

Y = Discount on music system

$\quad$ = 24000 – 21600 = 2400

Hence, X > Y

123. (b) X = Cost price of Laptop

$\quad$ = 48000

Y = Marked price of T.V.

$\quad$ = 60000

Hence, X < Y

Sol. (124–128):

Work shops	Number of workers	Number of male workers	Number of female workers	Notes
A	$6000 \times \dfrac{150}{100} = 9000$	$9000 \times \dfrac{125}{100 + 125}$ $= 5000$	$9000 - 5000 = 4000$	Number of workers in workshop A is 50% more than that of D. Number of male workers in A is 25% more than number of female workers in this workshop.
B	$11250 \times \dfrac{80}{100} = 9000$	$9000 - 6000$ $= 3000$	$9000 \times \dfrac{100}{150} = 6000$	Number of workers in workshop B is 20% less than that of workers in C. Number of workers in workshops B is 50% more than number of female workers in this workshop.
C	$9000 \times \dfrac{125}{100} = 11250$	$11250 \times \dfrac{4}{9}$ $= 5000$	$11250 - 5000 = 6250$	Number of workers in C is 25% more than number of workers in A. Respective ratio of number of male workers and female workers in C is 4 : 5.
D	$1200 \times \dfrac{100}{60 - 40} = 6000$	$6000 \times \dfrac{60}{100}$ $= 3600$	$6000 - 3600 = 2400$	Difference between number of male workers and that of female workers in D is 1200. 60% workers are male in D.
E	$5000 + 5000 = 10000$	5000	$6000 \times \dfrac{100}{120} = 5000$	Number of male workers in E is equal to that of A. Number of female workers in B is 20% more than number of female worker in E.

124. (b) X = Average number of male workers in all workshops together.

$$= \frac{5000 + 3000 + 5000 + 3600 + 5000}{5}$$

$$= \frac{21600}{5} = 4320$$

Y = Average number of female workers in all workshops together.

$$= \frac{4000 + 6000 + 6250 + 2400 + 5000}{5}$$

$$= \frac{23650}{5} = 4730$$

Hence, X < Y

125. (b) X = Difference between number of male workers in A and E

$\quad$ = 5000 – 5000 = 0

Y = Difference between number of workers in B and D

$\quad$ = 9000 – 6000

$\quad$ = 3000

Hence, X < Y

126. (a) X = Percentage of male workers in C

$$= \frac{5000}{11250} \times 100 = 44.4\%$$

Y = Percentage of female workers in D

$$= \frac{2400}{6000} \times 100 = 40\%$$

Hence, X > Y

127. (b) X = Total number of untrained male workers in C

$$= 5000 \times \frac{50}{100} = 2500$$

Y = Total number of trained female workers in C

$$= 11250 \times \frac{60}{100} - 2500 = 6750 - 2500 = 4250$$

Hence, $X < Y$

128. (b) X = Total number of workers in A and E together

$$= 9000 + 10000$$
$$= 19000$$

Y = Total number of workers in B, C and D together

$$= 9000 + 11250 + 6000$$
$$= 26250$$

Hence, $X < Y$.

Sol. (129–133):

Companies	Total number of cars	Air-conditioned cars	General cars	Notes
A	$48000 \times \dfrac{5}{8}$ $= 30000$	$30000 \times \dfrac{60}{100}$ $= 18000$	$30000 - 18000$ $= 12000$	Respective ratio of number of cars produced by C, A and E is 8 : 5 : 9. 60% of total number of cars produced by A are air-conditioned.
B	$48000 \times \dfrac{125}{100}$ $= 60000$	$60000 \times \dfrac{5}{12}$ $= 25000$	$60000 \times \dfrac{7}{12}$ $= 35000$	Number of cars produced by company B is 25% more than that of C. Respective ratio of number of air-conditioned cars and general cars produced by company B is 5 : 7.
C	$6000 \times \dfrac{8}{9-8}$ $= 48000$	$48000 \times \dfrac{1}{2} = 24000$	$48000 \times \dfrac{1}{2}$ $= 24000$	Company C produced 6000 less cars than E. Respective ratio of number of cars produced by C, A and E is 8 : 5 : 9. Company C produced equal number of air-conditioned and general cars.
D	$54000 \times \dfrac{100}{90}$ $= 60000$	$18000 \times \dfrac{100}{50}$ $= 36000$	$60000 - 36000$ $= 24000$	Number of cars produced by company E is 10% less than number of cars produced by D. Number of air-conditioned cars produced by company A is 50% less than that of D.
E	$48000 \times \dfrac{9}{8}$ $= 54000$	$54000 \times \dfrac{80}{100+80}$ $= 24000$	$54000 - 24000$ $= 30000$	Respective ratio of number of cars produced by companies C, A and E is 8 : 5 : 9. Number of air-conditioned cars produced by company E is 20% less than number of general cars produced by this company.

129. (a) X = Total number of air-conditioned cars produced by all companies together

$$= 18000 + 25000 + 24000 + 36000 + 24000$$
$$= 127000$$

Y = Total number of general cars produced by all companies together

$$= 12000 + 35000 + 24000 + 24000 + 30000$$
$$= 125000$$

Hence, $X > Y$

130. (a) X = Difference between total number of cars produced by A and E

$$= 54000 - 30000$$
$$= 24000$$

Y = Difference between total number of cars produced by B and D

$$= 60000 - 60000$$
$$= 0$$

Hence, $X > Y$

131. (b) X = Average number of cars produced by A, C and E

$$= \frac{30000 + 48000 + 54000}{3} = \frac{132000}{3}$$
$$= 44000$$

Y = Average number of cars produced by B and D

$$= \frac{60000 + 60000}{2}$$
$$= 60000$$

Hence, $X < Y$

132. (b) X = Number of general cars produced by B

$$= 35000$$

Y = Number of air-conditioned cars produced by D

$$= 36000$$

Hence, $X < Y$

133. (b) X = Number of cars produced by A

$$= 30000$$

Y = Number of cars produced by B $= 60000$

Hence, $X < Y$

Sol. (134–138):

Students	Hindi	English	Math	Notes
Full Marks	$500 \times \dfrac{2}{5} = 200$	$500 \times \dfrac{1}{5} = 100$	$500 \times \dfrac{2}{5} = 200$	Full marks of exam is 500 and respective ratio of full marks of Hindi, English and Math is 2 : 1 : 2
A	$100 \times \dfrac{125}{100} = 125$	$45 \times \dfrac{120}{100} = 54$	$500 \times \dfrac{60}{100} - (125 + 54)$ $= 300 - 179 = 121$	A obtained 60% marks in all subjects together. A obtained 20% more marks than B in English and 25% more marks than B in Hindi.
B	$200 \times \dfrac{50}{100} = 100$	$100 \times \dfrac{45}{100} = 45$	$500 \times \dfrac{60}{100} \times \dfrac{125}{100} \times \dfrac{80}{100}$ $= 300 - 145 = 155$	B obtained 50% and 45% marks in Hindi and English respectively. B obtained 20% less marks than E who obtained 25% more marks than A in all subjects together.
C	$300 \times \dfrac{7}{20} = 105$	$300 \times \dfrac{5}{20} = 75$	$300 - (105 + 75) = 120$	Total marks obtained by A is equal to that of C. Respective ratio of marks obtained by C in Hindi, English and Math is 7 : 5 : 8.
D	$300 \times \dfrac{5}{4} - (90 + 140)$ $= 375 - 230 = 145$	$75 \times \dfrac{120}{100} = 90$	$175 \times \dfrac{80}{100} = 140$	Respective ratio of total marks obtained by C and that of D is 4 : 5. D obtained 20% more marks than E in English and 20% less marks than E in Math.
E	$300 \times \dfrac{125}{100} \times \dfrac{5}{15} =$ 125	$300 \times \dfrac{125}{100} \times \dfrac{3}{15}$ $= 75$	$375 - (125 + 75) = 175$	E obtained 25% more marks than A in all subjects together. Respective ratio of marks obtained by E in Hindi English and Math is 5 : 3 : 7.

134. (b) X = Percentage of marks obtained by B in Hindi

$= \dfrac{100}{200} \times 100 = 50\%$

Y = Percentage of marks obtained by E in Math

$= \dfrac{175}{200} \times 100 = 87.5\%$

Hence, X < Y

135. (b) Total marks obtained by all students in English

$= 54 + 45 + 75 + 90 + 75$

$= 339$

X = Average percentage of marks obtained by all students in English

$= \dfrac{339}{5 \times 100} \times 100 = 67.8\%$

Total marks obtained by all students in Hindi

$= 125 + 100 + 105 + 145 + 125$

$= 600$

Y = Average percentage of marks obtained by all students in Hindi

$= \dfrac{600}{5 \times 200} \times 100 = 60\%$

Hence, X < Y

136. (b) X = Total marks obtained by A in all subjects together

$= 125 + 54 + 121 = 300$

Y = Total marks obtained by D in all subjects together

$= 145 + 90 + 140 = 375$

Hence, X < Y

137. (b) Total marks obtained by B in all subjects together

$= 100 + 45 + 155$

$= 300$

Total marks obtained by C in all subjects together

$= 105 + 75 + 120$

$= 300$

X = Difference between total marks obtained by B and C in all subjects together

$= 300 - 300 = 0$

Total marks obtained by A in all subjects together

$= 125 + 54 + 121$

$= 300$

Total marks obtained by E in all subjects together

$= 125 + 75 + 175$

$= 375$

Y = Different between total marks obtained by A and E in all subjects together

$= 375 - 300 = 75$

Hence, X < Y

138. (a) X = Total marks obtained by all students together in Math

$= 121 + 155 + 120 + 140 + 175$

$= 711$

Y = Total marks obtained by all students together in Hindi

$= 125 + 100 + 105 + 145 + 125$

$= 600$

Hence, X > Y

Sol. (139-143):

Workshops	No. of workers	No. of male workers	No. of female workers	Notes
A	$\dfrac{10800 \times 100}{150} = 7200$	$\dfrac{7200 \times 80}{100+80} = 3200$	$7200 - 3200 = 4000$	Number of workers in workshop B is 50% more than that of A. Number of male workers is 20% less than that of female workers in A.
B	$\dfrac{3600 \times (100+50)}{50}$ $= 10800$	$\dfrac{10800 \times 50}{100+50} = 3600$	$10800 - 3600 = 7200$	Difference between number of male workers and that of female workers in B is 3600. Number of male workers is 50% less than that of female workers in B
C	$\dfrac{10800 \times 2}{3} = 7200$	$\dfrac{3600 \times 125}{100} = 4500$	$7200 - 4500 = 2700$	Respective ratio of number of workers in B and C is 3 : 2 Number of male workers in C is 25% more than number of male workers in B
D	$\dfrac{8000 \times 125}{100} = 10000$	$10000 - 5000$ $= 5000$	$\dfrac{4000 \times 100}{80} = 5000$	Number of workers in D is 25% more than that of E
E	$\dfrac{7200 \times 10}{9} = 8000$	$\dfrac{8000 \times 3}{5} = 4800$	$8000 - 4800 = 3200$	Number of female workers in A is 20% less than number of female workers in E. Respective ratio of number of workers in A and E is 9 : 10 Respective ratio of number of male workers and that of female workers in E is 3 : 2

139. (c)　X = Number of workers in workshop C = 7200

　　　　Y = Number of workers in workshop A = 7200

　　　　Hence, X = Y

140. (b)　Total number of male workers in all workshops together

　　　　= 3200 + 3600 + 4500 + 5000 + 4800 = 21100

　　　　X = Average number of male workers in all workshops

　　　　$= \dfrac{21100}{5} = 4220$

　　　　Total number of female workers in all workshops together

　　　　= 4000 + 7200 + 2700 + 5000 + 3200

　　　　= 22100

　　　　Y = Average number of female workers in all workshops

　　　　$= \dfrac{22100}{5} = 4420$

　　　　Hence, X < Y

141. (e)　X = Total number of trained workers in B

　　　　Y = Total number of trained workers in D

　　　　Here, no information is given about number of trained workers in these workshops

　　　　Hence, can't be determined.

142. (a)　X = Total number of workers in B and E together

　　　　= 10800 + 8000 = 18800

　　　　Y = Total number of male workers in A, C and D together

　　　　$= 3200 + 4500 + 5000 \Rightarrow 12700$

　　　　Hence, X > Y

143. (e)　X = Percentage of trained workers in A

　　　　Y = Percentage of trained workers in D

　　　　Here, no information is given about number of trained workers in D

　　　　Hence, can't be determined.

Sol. (144–148):

144. (c)　Highest two digits number which is completely divisible by 5, 9, 18, 45

　　　　= L.C.M of 5, 9, 18, 45 = 90

　　　　X = $(90)^2 = 8100$

　　　　least number which is completely divisible by 2, 9, 18, 30

　　　　= L.C.M of 2, 9, 18, 30 = 90

　　　　Y = $(90)^2 = 8100$

　　　　Hence, X = Y

145. (a)　Speed of boat in downstream $= \dfrac{50}{2} = 25$ Km/h

　　　　Speed of boat in upstream $= \dfrac{54}{4} = 13.5$ Km/h

　　　　X = Speed of boat in still water

　　　　$= \dfrac{25+13.5}{2} = \dfrac{38.5}{2} = 19.25$ Km/h

　　　　Speed of swimmer in upstream $= \dfrac{30}{2} = 15$ Km/h

　　　　Speed of swimmer in downstream $= \dfrac{64}{4} = 16$ Km/h

Y = Speed of swimmer in still water

$$= \frac{15+16}{2} = 15.5 \ \text{Km/h}$$

Hence, X > Y

146. (c) Marked price of Fan = 1800,
Discount = 20%
Profit = 20%

X = Cost price of Fan = $\dfrac{1800 \times 80}{120} = 1200$

Y = Cost price of Fan which is sold for 1800 at 50% Profit

$$= \frac{1800 \times 100}{150} = 1200$$

Hence, X = Y

147. (c) X = length of train = $(60-6)\dfrac{5}{18} \times 15 = 225$ m

Y = length of platform

$$= 60 \times \frac{5}{18} \times 27 - 225$$

$$= 225 \ \text{m}$$

Hence, X = Y

148. (b) X = $P\left(1+\dfrac{20}{100}\right)^2 - P = 0.44\,P$

Y = $P\left(1+\dfrac{10}{100}\right)^4 - P = 0.4641\,P$

Hence, X < Y

Sol. (149-153):

Persons	Salary	Expenditure	Saving	Notes
A	$36000 \times \dfrac{3}{3-2}$ $= 36000 \times \dfrac{3}{1}$ $= 108000$	$108000 - 36000 = 72000$	36000	Saving of A is 36000. Transport expenditure of A is 20% of his salary and 30% of his expenditure $\therefore$ Respective ratio of salary of A to expenditure of A = 3 : 2
B	$108000 \times \dfrac{100}{150}$ $= 72000$	$72000 - 14400$ $= 108000 \times \dfrac{2}{3}$	$72000 \times \dfrac{20}{100}$ $= 57600$	Salary of A is 50% more than that of B. = 14400 B saves 20% of his salary.
C	57600×2 $= 115200$	$\left(\dfrac{72000+57600}{4} + \dfrac{45000+28000}{4}\right) \times \dfrac{125}{100}$ $= \dfrac{202600}{4} \times \dfrac{125}{100}$ $= 63312.5$	$115200 - 63312.5$ $= 51887.5$	Salary of C is two times of the expenditure of B. Expenditure of C is 25% more than average expenditure of four other persons..
D	$45000 + 30000$ $= 75000$	$72000 \times \dfrac{5}{8} = 45000$	$45000 \times \dfrac{2}{3}$ $= 30000$	Respective ratio of food expenditure, transport expenditure and education expenditure of D is 4 : 5 : 3. Respective ratio of expenditure of D and that of A is 5 : 8. Expenditure of D is 50% more than his saving.
E	$28000 + 18000$ $= 46000$	$18000 \times \dfrac{14}{9} = 28000$	$144000 \times \dfrac{125}{100}$ $= 14400 \times \dfrac{5}{4}$ $= 18000$	E saves 25% more amount than B. Respective ratio of expenditure and saving of E is 14 : 9.

149. (b) Total expenditure of all persons together

$$= 72000 + 57600 + 63312.5 + 45000 + 28000$$

$$= 265912.5$$

X = Average expenditure of all persons together

$$= \frac{265912.5}{5} = 53182.5$$

Y = Expenditure of C = 63312.5
Hence, X < Y

150. (a) X = Difference between expenditure and saving of B
$$= 57600 - 14400 = 43200$$

Y = Difference between expenditure and saving of D
$$= 45000 - 30000 = 15000$$
Hence, X > Y

151. (b) X = Percentage of expenditure of C

$$= \frac{63312.5}{115200} \times 100 = 54.95\%$$

Y = Percentage of expenditure of A

$$= \frac{72000}{108000} \times 100 = 66.66\%$$

Hence, $X < Y$

152. (a) X = Transport expenditure of D = $45000 \times \frac{5}{12}$

$$= \frac{225000}{12} = 18750$$

Y = Transport expenditure of E = 20% of 28000

$$= 28000 \times \frac{20}{100} = 5600$$

Hence, $X > Y$

153. (a) X = 50% of income of C and income of D together

$$= 50\% \text{ of } (115200 + 75000) = 95100$$

Y = 75% of total expenditure of A and E together

$$= 75\% \text{ of } (72000 + 28000) = 100000 \times \frac{75}{100}$$

$$= 75000$$

Hence, $X > Y$

Sol. 154-158

Schools	Number of students	Number of boys	Number of girls	Notes
A	$10800 \times \dfrac{5}{9}$ $= 6000$	$6000 \times \dfrac{5}{12}$ $= 2500$	$6000 \times \dfrac{7}{12}$ $= 3500$	Respective ratio of the number of boys and that of girls in school A is 5 : 7.
B	$9000 \times \dfrac{80}{100} = 7200$	$7200 \times \dfrac{9}{16} = 4050$	$7200 - 4050$ $= 3150$	Number of students in school B is 20% less than the number of students in school E. Respective ratio of number of boys and that of girls in school B is 9 : 7
C	$6000 \times \dfrac{4}{5} = 4800$	$4800 - 3500 = 1300$	3500	Respective ratio of number of students in schools A and C is 5 : 4. Number of girls in school C is equal to number of girls in school A.
D	$7200 \times \dfrac{5}{4} = 9000$	$4050 \times \dfrac{100}{90} = 4500$	$9000 - 4500$ $= 4500$	Respective ratio of number of students in schools B and D is 4 : 5. Number of boys in school B is 10% less than number of boys in school D.
E	$7200 \times 5 \times \dfrac{25}{100}$ $= 9000$	$9000 - 3600 = 5400$	$9000 \times \dfrac{40}{100}$ $= 3600$	Average number of students in schools A, B, C, D and E is 7200. Total number of students in schools E is 25% of total number of students in all schools together. Number of girls is 40% of total number of students in school E.

154. (c) X = Number of students in school D

$\qquad = 9000$

$\qquad Y$ = Number of students in school E

$\qquad = 9000$

Hence, $X = Y$

155. (b) X = Number of boys in school C

$\qquad = 1300$

$\qquad Y$ = Number of girls in school E

$\qquad = 3600$

Hence, $X < Y$

156. (b) Total number of boys in all schools together

$\qquad = 2500 + 4050 + 1300 + 4500 + 5400$

$\qquad = 17750$

$\qquad X$ = Average number of boys in all schools together

$$= \frac{17750}{5} = 3550$$

Total number of girls in all schools together

$\qquad = 3500 + 3150 + 3500 + 4500 + 3600$

$\qquad = 18250$

Y = Average number of girls in all schools together

$$= \frac{16250}{5} = 3650$$

Hence, $X < Y$

157. (b) Total number of boys in schools A, C and E together

$\qquad = 2500 + 1300 + 5400$

$\qquad = 9200$

X = Average number of boys in schools A, C and E

$$= \frac{9200}{3} = 3066.6$$

Total number of girls in schools B and D together

$\qquad = 3150 + 4500$

$\qquad = 7650$

Y = Average number of girls in schools B and D

$$= \frac{7650}{2}$$

$$= 3825$$

Hence, X < Y

Sol. 159-163

Items	Cost price	Selling price	Marked price	Notes
Bookshelf	$\frac{250000}{9} \times \frac{50}{100}$ $= \frac{125000}{9}$	$\frac{125000}{9} \times \frac{120}{100}$ $= \frac{50000}{3}$	$\frac{50000}{3} \times \frac{100}{80}$ $= \frac{62500}{3}$	Cost price of Bookshelf is 50% less than that of TV. Profit on Bookshelf is 20%. Discount on Bookshelf is 20%
TV	$\frac{200000}{9} \times \frac{125}{100}$ $= \frac{250000}{9}$	$\frac{50000}{3} \times \frac{4}{2}$ $= \frac{100000}{3}$	$\frac{100000}{3} \times \frac{100}{90}$ $= \frac{1000000}{27}$	Cost price of T.V is 25% more than that of P.C. Selling price of Bookshelf, TV and PC are in the respective ratio 2 : 4 : 5. Discount on TV is 10%
PC	$40000 \times \frac{5}{9}$ $= \frac{200000}{9}$	$\frac{50000}{3} \times \frac{5}{2}$ $= \frac{125000}{3}$	$\frac{125000}{3} \times \frac{100}{75}$ $= \frac{500000}{9}$	Respective ratio of cost price of PC and that of Laptop is 5 : 9. Discount on PC is 25%
Laptop	$70000 \times \frac{100}{175}$ $= 40000$	$70000 \times \frac{80}{100}$ $= 56000$	70000	Marked price of Laptop is 70000. It is sold at 20% discount. Marked price of Laptop is 75% more than its cost price.
AC	$\frac{224000}{3} \times \frac{100}{120}$ $= \frac{560000}{9}$	$56000 \times \frac{100}{75}$ $= \frac{224000}{3}$	$\frac{280000}{3}$	Selling price of Laptop is 25% less than that of AC. AC is sold at 20% profit. Respective ratio of cost price and marked price of AC is 2 : 3.

159. (a) X = Cost price of Laptop = 40000

Y = Average cost price of all things

$$= \frac{\frac{125000}{9} + \frac{250000}{9} + \frac{200000}{9} + 40000 + \frac{560000}{9}}{5}$$

$$= \frac{1495000}{5 \times 9} = \frac{299000}{9} = 33222.2$$

Hence, X > Y

160. (a) X = Average selling price of all times

$$= \frac{\frac{50000}{3} + \frac{100000}{3} + \frac{125000}{3} + 56000 + \frac{224000}{3}}{5}$$

$$= \frac{667000}{3 \times 5} = \frac{133400}{3} = \frac{400200}{9}$$

Y = Total profit accrued on all things

$$= \frac{667000}{3} - \frac{1495000}{9}$$

$$= \frac{2001000 - 1495000}{9}$$

$$= \frac{506000}{9}$$

Hence, X > Y

158. (b) X = Difference between number of students in schools A and C = 6000 – 4800

$$= 1200$$

Y = Difference between number of students in schools E and B = 9000 – 7200 = 1800

Hence, X < Y

161. (b) X = Marked price of Bookshelf = $\frac{62500}{3}$

Y = Selling price of PC = $\frac{125000}{3}$

Hence, X < Y

162. (b) X = Profit amount on AC

$$= \frac{224000}{3} - \frac{560000}{9}$$

$$= \frac{112000}{9} = 12444.4$$

Y = Profit amount of Laptop = 56000 – 40000 = 16000

Hence, X < Y

163. (a) X = Average Profit = $\frac{506000}{9 \times 5} = 11244.44$

Total discount

$$= \frac{62500}{3} + \frac{1000000}{27} + \frac{500000}{9} + 70000 + \frac{280000}{3}$$

$$- \frac{667000}{3}$$

$$= \frac{562500 + 1000000 + 1500000 + 1890000 + 2520000 - 6003000}{27}$$

$$= \frac{7472500 - 6003000}{27} = \frac{1469500}{27}$$

Y = Average discount

$$= \frac{1469500}{27 \times 5} = 10885.18$$

$\therefore \quad X > Y$

Sol. (164–168)

Workshops	Number of workers	Number of male workers	Number of female workers	Notes
A	$3000 \times \dfrac{5}{2} = 7500$	$7500 - 3000 = 4500$	3000	Number of female workers in workshop A is 3000. Respective ratio of number of male workers and that of female workers in workshop A is 3 : 2
B	$7500 \times \dfrac{6}{5} = 9000$	4500	$9000 - 4500 = 4500$	Respective ratio of number of workers in workshops B, A and C is 6 : 5 : 4 Number of male workers in B is equal to that of male workers in workshop A.
C	$7500 \times \dfrac{4}{5} = 6000$	$5000 \times \dfrac{60}{100} = 3000$	$6000 - 3000 = 3000$	Total number of workers in workshop C is 20% more than that of workers in workshop E. Respective ratio of number of workers in workshops B, A and C is 6 : 5 : 4. Number of male workers in C is 60% of total number of workers in E
D	$7500 \times \dfrac{100}{150} = 5000$	$3000 \times \dfrac{100}{75} = 4000$	$5000 - 4000 = 1000$	Number of workers in workshop A is 50% more than that of workers in workshop D. Number of female workers in C is 25% less than that of male workers in D.
E	$6000 \times \dfrac{100}{120} = 5000$	$5000 - 3750 = 1250$	$3000 \times \dfrac{125}{100} = 3750$	Number of workers in workshop C is 20% more than that of workers in workshop E. Number of female workers in E is 25% more than number of female workers in workshop A.

164. (c) X = Number of male workers in A = 4500

Y = Number of female workers is B = 4500

Hence, $X = Y$

165. (a) Total number of male workers in all workshops together

$= 4500 + 4500 + 3000 + 4000 + 1250 = 17250$

X = Average number of male workers in all workshops together

$$= \frac{17250}{5}$$

$= 3450$

Total number of female workers in all workshops together

$= 3000 + 4500 + 3000 + 1000 + 3750 = 15250$

Y = Average number of female workers in all workshops together

$$= \frac{15250}{5}$$

$= 3050$

Hence, $X > Y$

166. (a) X = Percentage of male workers in C

$$= \frac{3000}{6000} \times 100 = 50\%$$

Y = Percentage of male workers in E

$$= \frac{1250}{5000} \times 100 = 25\%$$

Hence, $X > Y$

167. (e) X = Number of trained workers in D

No information is given about trained workers in D

Y = Number of trained workers in A

$$= 4500 \times \frac{40}{100} + 3000 \times \frac{45}{100}$$

$= 1800 + 1350 = 3150$

Hence, can't be determined

168. (b) X = Total number of male workers is A and E together

$= 4500 + 1250 = 5750$

Y = Total number of female workers in B, C and D together $= 4500 + 3000 + 1000 = 8500$

Hence, $X < Y$

169. (a) Let the weight of P, Q, R and S are 9x, 7x, 4x and 5x respectively.

Quantity – I : Total weight of P, Q and R = 225 kg

$9x + 7x + 4x = 225$

$20x = 225$

$x = 11.25$

∴ Weight of P = 9x = 101.25 kg

Quantity – II : Total weight of Q, R and S = 180 kg.

$7x + 4x + 5x = 180$

$16x = 180$

$x = 11.25$

∴ Weight of Q = 7x = 78.75 kg.

Quantity III :

Weight of S = 5x

$= 5 \times 11.25 = 56.25$ kg

Hence, Quantity – I > Quantity – II > Quantity – III

170. (a) From the question,

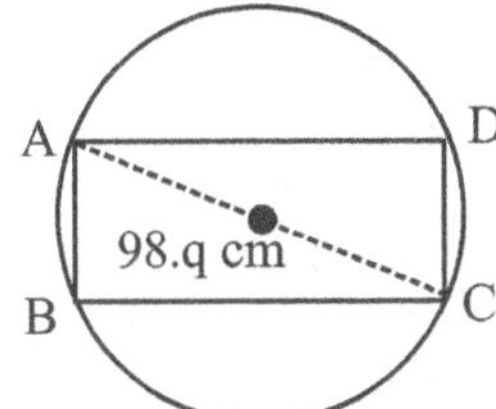

Area of the square = 98 sq. cm

∴ Side of the square = AB = AC

$= \sqrt{98} = 7\sqrt{2}$ cm

In $\triangle ABC$, $AC = \sqrt{(AB)^2 + (BC)^2}$

From the question,

$AC = \sqrt{(7\sqrt{2})^2 + (7\sqrt{2})^2}$

$= \sqrt{196} = 14$

Diameter of the circle AC = 14 cm

Quantity – I : Area of the circular region P

$= \pi \left(\dfrac{14}{2}\right)^2 = 154$ sq. cm

Quantity – II : Area of the circular region P outside the square ABCD

$= 154 - 98 = 56$ sq. cm

Quantity – III : Perimeter of the circular region P

$= \pi (14) = 44$ cm

So, Quantity – I > Quantity – II > Quantity – III.

171. (b) From question Dipak's investment = ₹1000

Let Panas's investment is ₹ x

Sanjeet's investment is ₹ 2x

Then, $10000 + 2x + x = 22{,}000$

$3x = 12000$

$x = 4000$

∴ Panas's investment = ₹ 4000

Sanjeet's investment = ₹ 8000

and Dipak's investment = ₹ 10000

Ratio of investment = 4000 : 8000 : 10000 = 2 : 4 : 5.

Quantity – I : Profit received by Panas in 3 years

$= \dfrac{2}{(2+4+5)} \times 2750 \times 3 = $ ₹ 1500

Quantity II : Profit received by Snajeet in 18 months.

$= \dfrac{4}{(2+4+5)} \times 2750 \times 1.5 = $ ₹ 1500

Quantity III : Profit received by Dipak in 1 year

$= \dfrac{5}{(2+4+5)} \times 2700 = $ ₹ 1250.

∴ Quantity I = Quantity II > Quantity III

172. (c)

Train A→   ←Train B

Station P   Station R   Station Q

←———— 1512.5 km ————→

Let the speed of train A and train B is 5x and 6x respectively.

Time taken by train A to reach station R = Time taken by train B to reach station R

$= 10:00 - 4:30$

$= 5$ hours 30 minutes.

$= 5.5$ hours

From question,

$(5x + 6x) \times 5.5 = 1512.5$

$11x \times 5.5 = 1512.5$

$\Rightarrow x = 25$

Speed of train A = 5 × 25 = 125 km/hr

Speed of train B = 6 × 25 = 150 km/hr

Quantity – I : Distance between station P and R

$= 125 \times 5.5 = 687.5$ km

Quantity – II : Distance between station Q and R

$= 150 \times 5.5 = 825$ km

Quantity – III: Relative speed of two trains

$= 125 + 150 = 275$ km/hr

Distance covered in 3 hours 15 minutes.

$= 275 \times 3.25 = 893.75$ km

∴ Distance between two trains $= 1512.5 - 893.75$

$= 618.75$ km

Hence, Quantity I < Quantity II > Quantity III

173. (c) Let Aman's monthly salary is ₹ x

Then, Panas's monthly salary is ₹ (x – 10,000)

and Pravin's monthly salary is $\left(x + x \times \dfrac{48}{100}\right) = 1.48\,x$

From question,

Ratio of salaries of Aman and Panas = 5 : 3

So, $\dfrac{x}{x - 10{,}000} = \dfrac{5}{3}$

$5x - 3x = 50{,}000$

$x = 25{,}000$

Aman's monthly salary = ₹ 25,000

Panas's monthly salary = ₹ 15,000
and Pravin's monthly salary = 1.48 × 25000 = ₹ 37,000
Quantity – I : Aman's salary = 25000
Quantity – II : Average salary of Pravin and Panas

$$= \frac{37000 + 15000}{2} = ₹ \, 26,000$$

Quantity – III : Average salary of all the three

$$= \frac{15000 + 25000 + 37000}{3}$$

$$= ₹ \, 25,667$$

Hence, Quantity – I < Quantity – II > Quantity – III

174. (b) Let volume of one cup be x ml.

Steps	Cylinder - 1		Cylinder - 2	
	Water	Alcohol	Water	Alcohol
1st step	$1000 - 3x$	0	$3x$	750
2nd step	$1000 - 3x + \dfrac{3x \times 3x}{(750 + 3x)}$ $= \dfrac{750\,(1000 + x)}{(750 + 3x)}$	$\dfrac{750 \times 3x}{(750 + 3x)}$ $= \dfrac{2250x}{(750 + 3x)}$	$3x - \dfrac{3x \times 3x}{(750 + 3x)}$ $= \dfrac{2250x}{(750 + 3x)}$	$750 - \dfrac{750x \times 3x}{(750 + 3x)}$ $= \dfrac{562500}{(750 + 3x)}$

Quantity–I : Alcohol in cylinder – 1

$$= \frac{2250x}{(750 + 3x)}$$

Quantity–II : Water in cylinder–2

$$= \frac{2250x}{(750 + 3x)}$$

Quantity–III : Alcohol in cylinder–2

$$= \frac{562500}{(750 + 3x)}$$

For x = 251
Quantity–I = Quantity II > Quantity–III.

175. (d) Let Dhaniram's present age is x years than, from question

$$(x + 8) = \frac{3}{2}\,(x - 12)$$

$$2x + 16 = 3x - 36$$

$$x = 52 \text{ years}$$

Again, $\dfrac{\text{Khushiram's age}}{52} = \dfrac{3}{4}$

∴   Khushiram's Age = $\dfrac{3}{4} \times 52$ = 39 years

Again,

$$\frac{\text{Dhakhiram's age} + 3}{\text{Khushiram's age} + 3} = \frac{5}{7}$$

$$\frac{\text{Dhakhiram's age} + 3}{39 + 3} = \frac{5}{7}$$

Dukhiram's Age + 3 = $\dfrac{5}{7}$ (42) = 30 years

∴ Dukhiram's Age = 27 years.

Quantity–I : Khushiram's Age after 10 years
      = 39 + 10 = 49 years.
Quantity–II : Dhaniram's Present Age = 52 years
Quantity–III : Dukhiram's mother Age = 27 + 26
      = 53 years.
Hence, Quantity I < Quantity II < Quantity III.

176. (d) Quantity–I : Portion of cistern filled by inlet A and B in 1 hour

$$= \frac{1}{10} + \frac{1}{15} = \frac{5}{30} = \frac{1}{6}$$

Time taken to fill the cistern by inlet pipes A and B = 6 hours.
∴ Time taken to fill the cistern when all the three pipes open simultaneously = 6 + 2 = 8 hours.
Quantity II : Time taken to empty the full cistern

$$= \frac{1}{\dfrac{1}{6} - \dfrac{1}{8}} = \frac{1}{\dfrac{4 - 3}{24}} = 24 \text{ hours}$$

∴ Time taken to empty the half filled cistern = 12 hours
Quantity–III : Portion of cistern filled in 2 hours, when all the three pipes open simultaneously

$$= \frac{2}{8} = \frac{1}{4} \text{ cistern}$$

Portion of cistern that are empty = $1 - \dfrac{1}{4} = \dfrac{3}{4}$ cistern.

Portion of cistern filled by pipe A and C in one hour

$$= \frac{1}{10} - \frac{1}{24} = \frac{7}{120}$$

Time required to fill $\dfrac{3}{2}$ cistern

$$= \frac{120}{7} \times \frac{3}{4} = 12.86 \text{ hours.}$$

Hence, Quantity–I < Quantity–II < Quantity–III

177. (b) Let Pankaj, Sanjeev and Vinod can type x, y and z pages respectively in 1 hour.

Then, they together can type $4(x + y + z)$ pages in 4 hour

$\therefore \quad 4(x + y + z) = 228$

$x + y + z = 57$ ...(i)

Also $z - y = y - x$

$\Rightarrow \quad 2y = x + z$ ...(ii)

From equation (i) and (ii), we have

$3y = 27$

$y = 19$ pages

From equation (ii), $x + z = 38$

$5x + 5z = 190$ ...(iii)

Again from question,

$5z = 7x$

So, $5x + 7x = 190$

$x \approx 16$ and $z \approx 22$

Quantity–I : Average number of pages typed by all the three

$$= \frac{16 + 19 + 22}{3} = 19$$

Quantity–II : Average number of pages typed by Pankaj and Vinod

$$= \frac{16 + 22}{2} = 19$$

Quantity–III : Average number of pages typed by Pankaj and Sanjeev

$$= \frac{16 + 19}{2}$$

$$= 17.55 \approx 15.$$

Hence, Quantity I = Quantity II > Quantity III

178. (c) Let number of white, green and black caps be x, y and z respectively.

According to the question,

$x - y = y - z$

$\Rightarrow \quad 2y = x + z$

and $x + y + z = 15$

$3y = 15$

$\Rightarrow \quad y = 5$

Now, $\dfrac{z}{x + y + z} > 0.2$

$\dfrac{z}{3y} > 0.2$

$z > 0.6\, y$

$5z > 3\, y$

As $x > z$, so, only possible values of x, y and z are x – 6, y = 5 and z = 4.

Quantity I : Probability of selecting 3 caps of exactly two of same colours

$$= \frac{{}^{6}C_2 \times {}^{9}C_1 + {}^{10}C_1 \times {}^{5}C_2 + {}^{4}C_2 \times {}^{11}C_1}{{}^{15}C_3}$$

$$= \frac{\dfrac{6 \times 5 \times 9}{2} + \dfrac{10 \times 5 \times 4}{2} + \dfrac{4 \times 3 \times 11}{2}}{\dfrac{15 \times 14 \times 13}{3 \times 2}} = \frac{43}{65}$$

Quantity II : Probability of selecting 3 caps of atleast two of same colours.

= Probability of selecting 2 caps of exactly same colour and 1 cap of different colour + Probability of selecting all the 3 caps of same colour.

$$= \frac{43}{65} + \frac{{}^{6}C_3 + {}^{5}C_3 + {}^{4}C_3}{{}^{15}C_3}$$

$$= \frac{43}{65} + \frac{34}{455} = \frac{335}{455} = \frac{67}{91}$$

Quantity–III : Probability of selecting 3 caps of three different colour.

$$= \frac{{}^{6}C_1 \times {}^{5}C_1 \times {}^{4}C_1}{{}^{15}C_3} = \frac{6 \times 5 \times 4}{\dfrac{15 \times 14 \times 13}{3 \times 2}} = \frac{24}{91}.$$

Hence, Quantity – I < Quantity – II > Quantity – III

179. (c) Quantity I : $\dfrac{180}{60} \times 6 \times p^{(3+6-2)} \times q^{(4+3-6)}$

$= 18\, p^7.q$

For $p > 0$ and $q < 0$,

$18\, p^7.q < 0$

Quantity–II : $\dfrac{36 \times 10}{24} \times a^{(9+3+4)} \times b^{(7+5-4)}$

$= 15\, a^{16}\, b^8$

For, $a, b < -1$, $15\, a^{16}\, b^8 > 15$

Quantity–III

$$\frac{144}{6 \times 8} x^{(8-3-5)} \times y^{(7-3-4)} = 3$$

$\therefore$ Quantity I < Quantity II > Quantity–III.

Hence, correct option is (c).

180. (b) Let length of train Q is x metre

Then, length of train P is $(150 + x)$ metre.

Relative speed of two trains $= (80 + 50) = 130$ km/hr

From question,

$x + (x + 150) = 130 \times \dfrac{5}{18} \times 18$

$2x + 150 = 650$

$\Rightarrow \quad x = 250$ m.

$\therefore$ Length of train P $= 250 + 150 = 400$ m.

Length of train Q = 250 m.

Quantity–I : Time taken by train P to cross a platform of 200 m

$$= \frac{(400 + 200) \times 18}{80 \times 5} = 27 \text{ sec.}$$

Quantity–II : Time taken by train Q to cross a platform of 250 m

$$= \frac{(250+250)\times 18}{50\times 5} = 36 \text{ sec.}$$

Quantity–III : relative speed of train P

$$= \frac{80\times 5}{18} - 10 = \frac{110}{9} \text{ m/sec.}$$

Time taken to cross that man

$$= \frac{400}{110}\times 9 = 37.73 \text{ sec.}$$

∴　Quantity I < Quantity II > Quantity III.
Hence, correct option is (b).

181. (e)　Quantity I : The speed of second train $= \dfrac{400}{4}$

$= 100$ km/hr

ATQ, $\dfrac{\text{Speed of first train}}{100} = \dfrac{7}{8}$

∴ Speed of first train $= \dfrac{7\times 100}{8} = 87.5$ km/hr

Quantity II : Speed of the train $= \dfrac{264}{12} = 22$ m/sec

$= \dfrac{22\times 18}{5} = 72.2$ km/hr

Quantity III : let the speed of the train is x m/sec.
Then, relative speed of the train = (x + 10) m/sec.
ATQ,

$x + 10 = \dfrac{256}{8}$

$x + 10 = 32$

$x = 22$ m/sec

$= 22\times\dfrac{18}{5} = 79.2$ km/hr.

∴　Quantity–I > Quantity–II = Quantity—III.
Hence, correct option is (e).

182. (d)　Quantity–I : Ram's investment $= ₹ 10,000$ for 12 months
Gopal's investment $= ₹ 17,500$ for 8 months
and ₹ 20,000 for 4 months
Ratio of investment
　$= (10,000 \times 12) : (17,500 \times 8 + 20,000 \times 4) = 6 : 11$
Yearly profit $= ₹ 3570$

Shares of Gopal $= \dfrac{11}{(6+11)}\times 3570 = \dfrac{11}{17}\times 3570$

$= ₹ 2310.$

Quantity–II : We know that profit ratio is same as investment ratio

So, $\dfrac{\text{Rajat's investment}}{\text{Ali's investment}} = \dfrac{2}{3}$

$\dfrac{4000}{\text{Ali's investment}} = \dfrac{2}{3}$

∴ Ali's investment $= \dfrac{4000\times 3}{2} = ₹ 6,000$

Quantity–III :
John's investment　$= ₹ 80,000$ for 12 months
Akbar's investment $= ₹ 50,000$ for 6 months and
　　　　　　　　₹ 70,000 for 6 months
Shashi's investment $= ₹ 60,000$ for 6 months and
　　　　　　　　₹ 50,000 for 6 months
Ratio of investment
$= (80,000 \times 12) : (50,000 \times 6 + 70,000 \times 6)$
　　　　　　　　　　$: (60000 \times 6 + 50000 \times 6)$
$= 16 : 12 : 11$
Profit share of Shashi

$= \dfrac{11}{(16+12+11)}\times 21840$

$= \dfrac{11}{39}\times 21840 = ₹ 6160$

∴　Quantity–I < Quantity–II < Quantity–III
Hence, correct option is (d).

183. (b)　Quantity–I : $\dfrac{(A+x)^3 - (A-x)^3}{(x^2+3A^2)^2} = \dfrac{1}{8x}$

$$\frac{A^3+x^3+3A^2x+3Ax^2 - A^3+x^3+3A^2x-3Ax^2}{(x^2+3A^2)^2}$$

$= \dfrac{1}{8x}$

$\dfrac{2x(x^2+3A^2)}{(x^2+3A^2)^2} = \dfrac{1}{8x}$

$16x^2 = x^2 + 3A^2$

$A = \pm\sqrt{5}.x$

Quantity–II :

$$\frac{\sqrt{B+x}-\sqrt{B-x}}{\sqrt{B-x}+\sqrt{B+x}}\times\frac{\sqrt{B+x}-\sqrt{B-x}}{\sqrt{B+x}-\sqrt{B-x}}\text{o} = 1$$

$$\frac{(\sqrt{B+x}-\sqrt{B-x})^2}{2x} = 1$$

$2\left(B-\sqrt{B^2-x^2}\right) = 2x$

$(B-x) = \sqrt{B^2-x^2}$

$(B-x)^2 = B^2 - x^2$

$x\,(x-B) = 0$

∴　$B = x$

Quantity–III :
　$4cx\,(c+x)^2 = (c+x)^2 - (c-x)^2$
　$4cx\,(c+x)^2 = 4cx$
　$(c+x) = \pm 1$
⇒　$c = \pm 1 - x$

∴　Quantity II > Quantity III and relation can not establish between

Quantity–I and Quantity–II or Quantity–III.
Hence, correct option is (B).

184. (c) Quantity–I :

$$\frac{36}{9} \times 7 \times x^{(9-5+1)} \times y^{(7-2-3)} \times z^{(5-3)}$$

$$= 28x^5 . y^2 . z^2$$

For y, z ≥ -1 and x ≥ 1, 28 $x^5 y^2 . z^2 \geq 28$

Quantity–II :

$$\frac{336}{3\times 4} \times a^{(3-7+4)} \times b^{(1-5+4)} \times c^{(-4+8-4)} = 28$$

Quantity–III :

$$\frac{56\times 38}{76} \times p^{(-3+5)} \times q^{(6-1-3)} \times r^{(2+8-7)} = 28\, p^2 q^2 r^3$$

For p, q ≤ -1 and r ≥ 1

$$= 28\, p^2 q^2 r^3 \geq 28$$

$\therefore$ Quantity–I $\geq$ Quantity–II $\leq$ Quantity–III
Hence, correct option is (c).

185. (a) Let side AD = AC = x

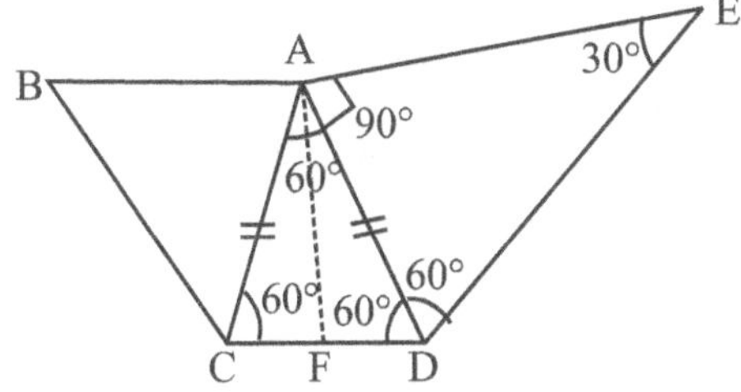

And $\angle C = 2. \angle E$ (Given)

$\therefore \angle C = 2 \times 30° = 60°$

As, AC = AD

Then, $\angle ACD = \angle ADC = 60°$

$\therefore \angle CAD = 180° - 60° - 60° = 60°$

ΔACD is equilateral triangle.

Hence,

AD = CD = AC = x.

Again,

$\angle CAE = 150°$

$\angle CAD + \angle DAE = 150°$

$\angle DAE = 150° - 60° = 90°$

$\therefore \Delta DAE$ is right triangle.

In ΔACF,

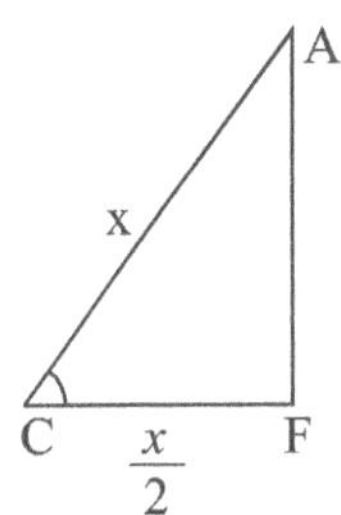

$(AC)^2 = (AF)^2 + (CF)^2$

$$x^2 = (h)^2 + \left(\frac{x}{2}\right)^2$$

$$\frac{3}{4}x^2 = h^2$$

$$x^2 = \frac{4}{3}h^2$$

$$\Rightarrow x = \frac{2}{\sqrt{3}}h$$

Quantity I : Area of parallelogram ABCD = AF × CD

$$= h \times \frac{2}{\sqrt{3}}h = \frac{2h^2}{\sqrt{3}} \text{ cm}^2$$

Quantity II : In ΔDAE

$$\tan 60° = \frac{AE}{AD} \Rightarrow \sqrt{3} = \frac{AE}{x}$$

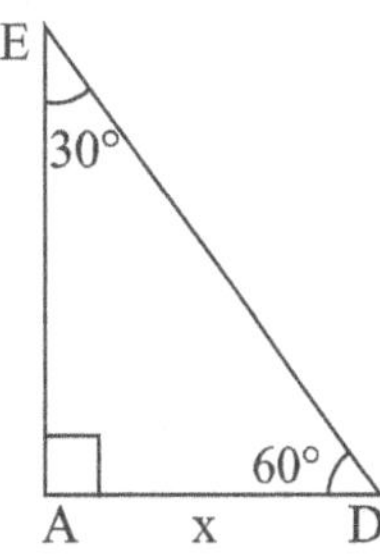

$AE = \sqrt{3}x$

Area of $\Delta DAE = \frac{1}{2} \times AD \times AE$

$$= \frac{1}{2} \times x \times \sqrt{3}x$$

$$= \frac{\sqrt{3}}{2}.x^2 = \frac{\sqrt{3}}{2} \times \frac{4}{3}h^2 = \frac{2}{\sqrt{3}}h^2 \text{ cm}^2$$

Quantity III : Area of ΔACD,

$$= \frac{\sqrt{3}}{4}(CD)^2$$

$$= \frac{\sqrt{3}}{4}.x^2 = \frac{\sqrt{3}}{4} \times \frac{4}{3}h^2$$

$$= \frac{h^2}{\sqrt{3}} \text{ cm}^2$$

$\therefore$ Quantity I = Quantity II > Quantity III.
Hence, correct option is (a).

186. (b) Quantity–I : $3^7 \times 4^3 \div 5^2 = 2187 \times 64 \div 25$

$$= 2187 \times 2.56 = 5598.72$$

Quantity–II : $\dfrac{500a^4}{b^6}$

for a ≤ -2, $a^4 \geq 16$

and, for $-1 \leq b \leq 1$, $b^6 \leq 1$

Hence, $\dfrac{500a^4}{b^6} \geq 500 \times 16 \geq 8000$

Quantity –III :

$7^3 + 6^4 \times 2^2 - 11^2$

$= 343 + 1296 \times 4 + 121$

$= 343 + 5184 + 121 = 5648$

∴   Quantity I < Quantity II > Quantity III

Hence, correct option is (b).

187. (b)   Quantity I : $\dfrac{360}{120} \times 24 . m^{7+2-4} . n^{9-3+4} = 72\, m^5 n^{10}$

If $m > 0$ and $n < 0$, $72\, m^5 n^{10} > 0$

∴ Quantity –I > 0

Quantity II : $\dfrac{240}{60 \times 3} x^{9-4+2} . y^{7-3-3} = \dfrac{4}{3} x^7 y$

If $x, y < 0$, then, $\dfrac{4}{3} x^7 y > 0$

∴ Quantity II > 0

Quantity III : $\dfrac{48 \times 5}{6} a^{8+3-6} . b^{12-4-1} = 40 a^5 . b^7$

If $a > 0$, $b < 0$, then $40\, a^5 b^7 < 0$

∴ Quantity III < 0

Hence, Quantity I, Quantity II > Quantity III,

But relation can not be establish between Quantity I and Quantity II.

So, correct option is (b).

188. (d)   Quantity I :

$$\dfrac{(q+m)^2 - (q-m)^2}{8qm(q+m)^2} = 1$$

$$\dfrac{q^2 + m^2 + 2qm - q^2 - m^2 + 2qm}{8qm(q+m)^2} = 1$$

$$\dfrac{4qm}{8qm(q+m)^2} = 1 \Rightarrow (q+m)^2 = \dfrac{1}{2}$$

$$q = \dfrac{1}{\sqrt{2}} - m$$

Quantity II :

$$\dfrac{(r+m)^3 - (r-m)^3}{(m^2 + 3r^2)^2} = \dfrac{1}{8m}$$

$$\dfrac{r^3 + m^3 + 3r^2 m + 3rm^2 - r^3 + m^3 + 3r^2 m - 3m^2 r}{(m^2 + 3r^2)^2}$$

$$= \dfrac{1}{8m}$$

$$\dfrac{2m^3 + 6r^2 m}{(m^2 + 3r^2)^2} = \dfrac{1}{8m}$$

$$\Rightarrow \dfrac{2m(m^2 + 3r^2)}{(m^2 + 3r^2)^2} = \dfrac{1}{8m}$$

$$\dfrac{2m}{(m^2 + 3r^2)} = \dfrac{1}{8m}$$

$16m^2 = m^2 + 3r^2$

$r = \sqrt{5}\ m$

Quantity III :

$$\dfrac{\sqrt{p+m} + \sqrt{p-m}}{\sqrt{p+m} - \sqrt{p-m}} = 2$$

$$\sqrt{p+m} + \sqrt{p-m} = 2\left(\sqrt{p+m} - \sqrt{p-m}\right)$$

$$3\left(\sqrt{p-m}\right) = \sqrt{p+m}$$

$9\,(p-m) = p + m$

$8\,p = 10\,m$

$p = 1.25\ m$

∴ Quantity I < Quantity II > Quantity III.

Hence, correct option is (d).

189. (b)   Quantity I: Amount of cement

$$= 1000 - 240 - \dfrac{55}{100} \times 1000$$

$$= 1000 - 790 = 210\ \text{kg.}$$

Percentage of cement

$$= \dfrac{210}{1000} \times 100 = 21\%$$

Quantity II: % of apples thrown on day 1

$= 15\%$ of $50\% = 7.5\%$

% of apples thrown on day 2

$= 40\%$ of $42.5\% = 17\%$

Total % of apples thrown

$= (7.5 + 17)\% = 24.5\%$

Quantity I < Quantity II.

190. (a)   Quantity I: Let highest marks be x,

Then the next in value is $x - 4$

$x + (x - 4) = 8 \times 174 - 6 \times 170$

$\qquad = 1392 - 1020 = 372$

$$\Rightarrow \ x = \dfrac{376}{2} = 188$$

Quantity II:

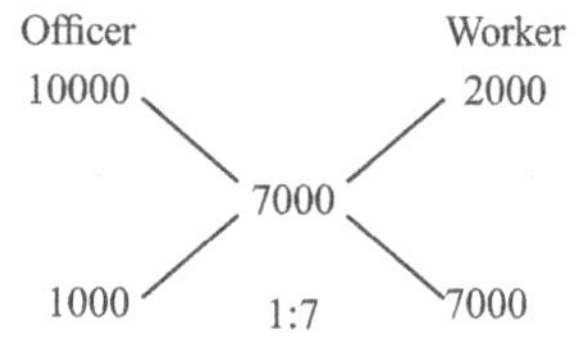

No. of officers $= \dfrac{1}{8} \times 800 = 100$

Quantity I > Quantity II.

191.   **(b)**   Quantity I:

$$\dfrac{108x}{100} - \dfrac{92x}{100} = 12$$

$$\Rightarrow \ \dfrac{16x}{100} = 12$$

$$\Rightarrow \ x = 75$$

Quantity II:

$$\left(\frac{120}{100}x - 18\right) - \frac{80}{100}x = \frac{25}{100} - \frac{80}{100}x$$

$$\Rightarrow \quad \frac{40x}{100} - \frac{20x}{100} = 18$$

Quantity II > Quantity I

192. (e) Let total units of work be 60 units.
Then units done by Deepak in one day = 1 unit
For 40 days, Deepak and Rohit work alternately.
Work done by Deepak in 20 days
= 20 × 1 = 20 units and Rohit does 40 units in 20 days.
i.e. Rohit does 2 units/day.
Panas and Rohit do all the units in 15 days.
Which means Rohit does 15 x 2 = 30 units and Panas
does remaining 30 units.
Hence, Panas does 2 units/day.
Efficiency of Panas & Rohit is same.
Hence, Quantity I = Quantity II

193. (a)

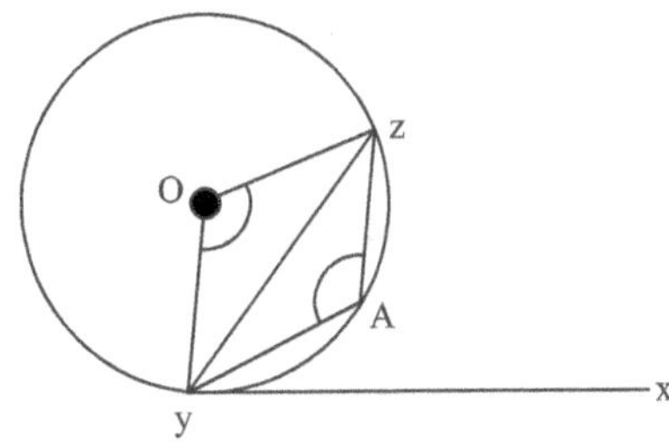

Quantity II : Let 'O' be the centre of circle
$\angle OYZ = \angle OYX - \angle XYZ$
$\qquad = 90° - 56° = 34°$
and $\angle OYZ = \angle OZY = 34°$
$\angle YOZ = 180 - 34° - 34° = 112°$

Quantity I : $\angle YAZ = \dfrac{1}{2}$ reflex $\angle YOZ$

$$= \frac{1}{2}(360° - 112°)$$

$$= \frac{1}{2} \times 248° = 124°$$

Quantity I > Quantity II

194. (b) Quantity I: Area of canvas required

$$= 2\pi r^2 = 2 \times \frac{22}{7} \times 9 \times 9$$

$$= 509.14 \text{ sq.m.}$$

Cost of the canvas = 509.14 × 15 = ₹7637.1
Quantity II: Let shares of A, B and C be x, 9x and 5x
Then, 9x – 5x = 3600
$\Rightarrow \quad x = 900$
Total of A's and B's shares = x + 9x = 10x = ₹ 9000
Quantity I < Quantity II

195. (a) $\dfrac{700}{x-5} - \dfrac{700}{x} = \dfrac{14}{3}$

$$\Rightarrow \quad x = 50 \times 3 \left(\frac{x - x + 5}{x(x-5)}\right) = 1$$

$\Rightarrow \quad x^2 - 5x - 750 = 0$
$\Rightarrow \quad (x - 30)(x + 25) = 0$
$\Rightarrow \quad x = 30$
Speed of faster car = 30 km/hr
Speed of slower car = 30 – 5 = 25 km/hr
Quantity I > Quantity II

196. (b) Quantity I : Let the rate of flow of the river is x km/hr

So, $\dfrac{91}{10-x} + \dfrac{91}{10+x} = 20$

$\Rightarrow \quad x = 3$
$\Rightarrow \quad$ Rate of flow of river = 3 km/hr.
Quantity II:
Let the speed of boat in still water is y km/hr

$$\frac{D}{y+3} = 1, \quad \dots \text{(i)} \qquad \frac{D}{y-3} = 1.5 \qquad \dots \text{(ii)}$$

Solving (i) and (ii)

$$\frac{y-3}{y+3} = \frac{2}{3}$$

$\Rightarrow \quad y = 15$
$\Rightarrow \quad$ Speed of boat in still water = 15 km/hr
Quantity II > Quantity I

197. (e) Let volume of 1 cup be x ml.

	Flask 1			Flask 2	
	Liquid A	Liquid B		Liquid A	Liquid B
1st Step	$500 - 3x$	0		$3x$	500
2nd step	$500 - 3x + \dfrac{3x \times 3x}{(500+3x)}$	$\dfrac{500 \times 3x}{(500+3x)} = \dfrac{1500x}{500+3x}$	$3x - \dfrac{3x \times 3x}{(500+3x)} = \dfrac{1500x+9x-9x}{500+3x} = \dfrac{1500x}{500+3x}$		$500 - \dfrac{500 \times 3x}{(500+3x)}$

Quantity I = Quantity II

198. (a) Quantity I: Let present age of Rajesh be x, then
Krishna's present age is 4x
$\qquad 4x - 5 = 7(x - 5)$

$\Rightarrow \quad 30 = 3x$
$\Rightarrow \quad x = 10$
Present age of Krishna = 4x = 40 years

Quantity 2:

$$x + 15 = 4(x - 15)$$
$$\Rightarrow 3x = 75$$
$$\Rightarrow x = 25.$$ Hence, present age of Paras = 25 years.

Quantity I > Quantity II

199. (b) $11x = 85 - 7 - 12$

$x = 6$

Present age of Rashmi = 18 years

Present age of Rashmi's father

$= 18 + 25 = 43$ years

Janak's present age = 78 years

Quantity I < Quantity II

200. (a) Let the C.P. of two shirts are x & y respectively.

Then, $80/100 * x = 120/100 * y$

$$x = \frac{3}{2}y$$

$x + y = 440$

$y = 176; x = 264$

S.P. of the shirt sold at 20% profit of

$$= 176 \times \frac{120}{100} = 211.2.$$

Hence, quantity 1 > quantity II.

201. (b) Let Rajeev, Harish and Shetty can type x, y, and z pages respectively in 1 h.

Therefore, they together can type 3 (x + y + z) pages in 3h

$\therefore \quad 3 (x + y + z) = 171$

$\Rightarrow \quad x + y + z = 57$ ...(i)

Also, $z - y = y - x$

i.e., $2y = x + z$ ...(ii)

$5z = 7x$ ...(iii)

From Eqs. (i) and (ii), we get $3y = 57 \Rightarrow y = 19$

and $x + z = 38$.

$\therefore \quad x = 16$ and $z = 22$

Hence, Quantity I < Quantity II

202 (b) Let length = 5x

Height = 4x

Area of the wall = $5x * 4x = 20x^2 = 1620$

Length = 45m & Height = 36m

Hence, Quantity I < Quantity II.

203. (d) Quantity I : $2x^2 - x - 10 = 0$

$2x^2 - 5x + 4x - 10 = 0$

$(2x - 5)(x + 2) = 0$

$$x = -2 \text{ and } \frac{5}{2}$$

Quantity II : $8y^2 - 42y + 55 = 0$

$8y^2 - 22y - 20y + 55 = 0$

$(4y - 11)(2y - 5) = 0$

$$y = \frac{5}{2}, \frac{11}{4}$$

Quantity I ≤ Quantity II

204. (c) $8x^2 - 2x - 3 = 0$

$8x^2 - 6x + 4x - 3 = 0$

$(2x + 1)(4x - 3) = 0$

$$x = -\frac{1}{2}, \frac{3}{4}$$

Quantity-II:

$2y^2 + 7y + 3 = 0$

$2y^2 + y + 6y + 3 = 0$

$(2y + 1)(y + 3) = 0$

$$y = -3, \frac{-1}{2}$$

Quantity I ≥ Quantity II

205. (a) Inlet Pipe Efficiency = $100/(8/6) = 75\%$

Outlet Pipe Efficiency = $100/(6) = 16.66\%$

Quantity I > Quantity II

206. (c) Quantity I : Number of ways of selecting two applicants out of 15 applicants

$= 15C_2 = 105$

Number of ways of selecting two Men

$= 8C_2 = 28$

Probability of selecting no woman $= \dfrac{28}{105}$

Probability of selecting at least one woman

$$= 1 - \frac{28}{105} = \frac{77}{105}$$

Hence, Quantity I < Quantity II.

207. (a) I.   Total Balls = 16

Number of ways of selecting 4 balls out of 16 balls

$= 16c_4.$

Number of ways of selecting 4 balls, such that no ball is green = $12c_4$.

Probability that no ball is green

$$= \frac{12c_4}{16c_4} = \frac{99}{364}$$

Probability that atleast One ball is green

$$= 1 - \frac{99}{364} = \frac{265}{364}$$

II. Number of ways of selecting 4 white balls out of 7 white balls = $7c_4$.

Probability that all balls are White

$$= \frac{7c_4}{16c_4} = \frac{1}{52}$$

Quantity I > Quantity II

208. (e) Work done by the two pipes in 1 hour

$$= \left(\frac{1}{12}\right) + \left(\frac{1}{18}\right) = \left(\frac{15}{108}\right).$$

Time taken by these pipes to fill the tank

$$= \frac{108}{15} = 7 \text{ hours } 12 \text{ min.}$$

Due to leakage, time taken to fill the tank
  = 7 hours 12 min + 48 min = 8 hours

Work done by two pipes and leak in 1 hour = $\dfrac{1}{8}$

Work done by the leak in 1 hour

$= \dfrac{15}{108} - \dfrac{1}{8} = \dfrac{1}{72}$.

Leak will empty the $\left(\dfrac{1}{9}\right)^{th}$ filled tank in $\dfrac{72}{9} = 8$ hours.

Quantity I = Quantity II

209. (a) I : 24 + (27 × 1) = 24 + 27 = 51 yrs.
II : 30 + (26 × 0.5) = 30 + 13 = 43 yrs.
Quantity I > Quantity II

210. (a) I : No. of eggs bought is LCM of 6 and 5 which is 30

CP of 30 eggs = $\dfrac{5}{6} \times 30 = ₹\,25$

SP of 30 eggs = $\dfrac{6}{5} \times 30 = ₹\,36$

Profit = 36 – 25 = 11

Profit % = $\dfrac{11}{25} \times 100 = 44\%$

II : CP of 1 gift = $\dfrac{350}{100} = 3.50$

SP of 1 gift = $\dfrac{48}{12} = 4$.

Profit = 4 – 3.5 = 0.5.

Profit % = $\left(\dfrac{0.5}{3.5}\right) \times 100 = 14\dfrac{2}{7}\%$

Quantity I > Quantity II

211. (b) I. C.P. of 12 Caps = S.P. of 17 Caps = ₹ 720.

CP of 1 Cap = $\dfrac{720}{12} = ₹\,60$.

II. SP = 88% of 1350

$= \dfrac{88}{100} \times 1350 = ₹\,1188$.

Quantity I < Quantity II

212. (a) I. Ali alone can do the work

$= \dfrac{1}{4} - \dfrac{1}{6} = \dfrac{2}{24}$

$\Rightarrow$ 12 days

II. Ram's 1 hr work $= \dfrac{1}{4}$.

(Ali + Pavan's) 1 hr work = $\dfrac{1}{3}$

(Ram + Pavan's) 1 hr work = $\dfrac{1}{2}$.

Together 1 hr work

$= \dfrac{1}{4} + \dfrac{1}{3} = \dfrac{7}{12}$.

Ali's work = $\dfrac{7}{12} - \dfrac{1}{2} = \dfrac{1}{12}$

12 hours
Quantity I > Quantity II

213. (c) I. Total time taken

$= \left(\dfrac{360}{90} + \dfrac{240}{80}\right) = 7$ hrs

Then avg speed

$= \dfrac{360 + 240}{7} = \dfrac{600}{7} = 85.7$ km/hr

II. $\dfrac{(2 \times 60 \times 90)}{150} = 72$ km/hr.

Quantity I > Quantity II

214. (a) I. Let the speed of two trains be 5x and 6x.

Speed of second train = $\dfrac{300}{3} = 100$ km/hr

Now, 6x = 100
$\Rightarrow$ x = 16.67
Then speed of first train = 6 x 16.67
                = 100 km/hr
II. Length of the train = 308m
Time taken to pass the tree = 14 seconds.

Speed of the train = $\dfrac{308}{14}$ m/sec = 22 m/sec

$= 22 \times \dfrac{18}{5}$ km/hr = 79.2 km/hr.

Quantity I > Quantity II

215. (b) I. Ratio = 4:7

Share of Q = $\dfrac{7}{11} \times 3520$

$= ₹\,2240$

II. 4000/y = 2/3
y = ₹ 6000.

Quantity I < Quantity II

216. (a) I. Ratio
Ganesh : Rashi = 12:1
Age of Rashi = 3 years

$\therefore$ $\dfrac{12}{1} = \dfrac{?}{3}$

? = 12 x 3 = 36 years.

II. $\dfrac{(5x + 4)}{(8x + 4)} = \dfrac{2}{3}$

15x + 12 = 16x + 8
x = 4
John's age 4 yrs ago = 5 × 4 = 20

Then John's age after 7 yrs is $20 + 4 + 7$
$= 31$ years.

Quantity I > Quantity II

217. (e) I. $SI - CI = \dfrac{Pr^2}{(100)^2}$

$\dfrac{P \times 4^2}{(100)^2} = 3.2$

$\dfrac{16P}{(100 \times 100)} = 3.2$

$P = ₹\ 2000.$

II. $SI = \dfrac{Pnr}{100}$

$800 = P \times 8 \times \dfrac{5}{100}$

$P = 800 \times \dfrac{100}{40} = ₹\ 2000.$

Quantity I = Quantity II

218. (c) I. $\dfrac{6_{C_2} \times 3_{C_2}}{13_{C_4}} = \dfrac{45}{715}$

$= \dfrac{9}{143}$

II. $\dfrac{6_{C_2} \times 3_{C_1} \times 4_{C_1}}{13_{C_4}} = \dfrac{180}{715}$

$= \dfrac{36}{43}$

Quantity II > Quantity I